Data Governance, DevSecOps, and Advancements in Modern Software

Bahaa Eddine Elbaghazaoui
National School of Applied Sciences (ENSA) Beni Mellal, Sultan Moulay Slimane University, Morocco

Mohamed Amnai
Faculty of Sciences, Ibn Tofail University, Kenitra, Morocco

Noreddine Gherabi
National School of Applied Sciences (ENSA) Khouribga, Sultan Moulay Slimane University, Morocco

IGI Global
Scientific Publishing
Publishing Tomorrow's Research Today

Vice President of Editorial	Melissa Wagner
Managing Editor of Acquisitions	Mikaela Felty
Managing Editor of Book Development	Jocelynn Hessler
Production Manager	Mike Brehm
Cover Design	Phillip Shickler

Published in the United States of America by
IGI Global Scientific Publishing
701 East Chocolate Avenue
Hershey, PA, 17033, USA
Tel: 717-533-8845
Fax: 717-533-7115
Website: https://www.igi-global.com E-mail: cust@igi-global.com

Library of Congress Cataloging-in-Publication Data

LCCN: 2024058321 (CIP Data Pending)
ISBN13: 9798337303659
EISBN13: 9798337303673

British Cataloguing in Publication Data
A Cataloguing in Publication record for this book is available from the British Library.

Table of Contents

Detailed Table of Contents

The rapid growth of software development and deployment has brought both opportunities and challenges, with organizations facing fast-changing market demands, increasing security risks, and stricter regulations. This chapter examines how Data Governance and DevSecOps provide critical solutions to these issues by addressing risks, ensuring security and compliance, and fostering innovation. Data governance establishes structured frameworks for managing, securing, and leveraging data across hybrid and multi-cloud environments, while DevSecOps integrates security throughout the software development lifecycle to mitigate vulnerabilities and enhance reliability. Through an exploration of the latest trends, including governance as code, cross-functional collaboration, continuous monitoring, and automation, this chapter offers actionable insights for researchers, practitioners, and decision-makers aiming to build secure, compliant, and efficient software ecosystems.

In today's fast-paced technological landscape, organizations face the dual challenge of delivering innovative software quickly while ensuring robust data governance, security, and compliance. This chapter examines the critical intersections between data governance, DevSecOps, and agile methodologies, offering a unified framework to balance agility and compliance effectively. By integrating practices like iterative governance and shift-left security into agile workflows, organizations can address risks associated with speed-focused development while maintaining operational efficiency and reliability. Through core principles, practical strategies, and emerging trends, this chapter provides actionable insights for managing the complexities of modern software development environments. It concludes with future directions and recommendations to guide organizations in adapting to evolving demands and implementing secure, scalable, and compliant workflows.

In the fast-paced world of software development, integrating security into the DevOps pipeline is essential for achieving Continuous Protection. This chapter provides a comprehensive overview of DevSecOps, an approach that unifies security with development and operations to create secure, reliable, and scalable software systems. The chapter begins by examining the challenges of traditional security in DevOps and introduces key principles of DevSecOps, such as early vulnerability detection, security automation, and fostering a security-first culture. Practical insights into implementing security tools, managing risks, and enhancing collaboration among cross-functional teams are provided. Readers will gain an understanding of how DevSecOps can be leveraged to ensure software remains secure without compromising on agility and innovation.

the chapter discusses is zero trust and AI in cybersecurity. Thus, improving DevSecOps strategies will help organizations reduce risks, comply with regulatory requirements, and reign in threats that exploit the advancing technologies.

With the movement of IT assets to the cloud, strong security and resilience are more important than ever. This paper discusses DevOps and SecOps integration, or DevSecOps, to increase security while enabling fast deployments. Encouraging collaboration between development, operations, and security teams, organizations can find and fix vulnerabilities early in the software lifecycle. The paper highlights the main idea of embedding automated security checks throughout the CI/CD pipeline using 24/7 monitoring, real-time threat detection, and agile incident response. This can be taken further with AI and ML integration through automating processes, offering predictive analytics, and mitigating vulnerabilities before exploitation. This framework helps to speed up threat mitigation and enhances reliability and agility in security responses. DevSecOps enables organizations to innovate safely while protecting digital assets amid evolving threats.

Cloud-native technologies have transformed the landscape of system design and deployment, establishing innovative frameworks for creating robust and resilient systems. This chapter explores the critical role of containers and Kubernetes in developing robust cloud-native systems that can withstand failures, scale dynamically, and recover seamlessly. Containers, with their portability, lightweight architecture, and modularity, enhance operational resilience by ensuring consistency across diverse environments, enabling isolation, and supporting rapid recovery and scaling. Kubernetes amplifies this resilience with features like automated deployment, self-healing capabilities, dynamic scaling, and multi-zone deployments. Additionally, the chapter highlights the challenges of managing stateful applications in a containerized ecosystem and proposes mitigation strategies, including Kubernetes StatefulSets and dynamic volume provisioning. Advanced topics such as Chaos Engineering, GitOps, and service meshes are explored to underline their role in fostering operational resilience.

Microservices architecture has revolutionized software development by enabling scalability, resilience, and agility. However, its distributed and decentralized nature introduces unique security challenges. This paper explores the implications of adopting microservices, emphasizing the expanded attack surface, inter-service communication vulnerabilities, and distributed data management risks. Key areas covered include robust authentication mechanisms (OAuth 2.0, JWT), secure inter-service communication via mutual TLS, and the role of service meshes like Istio in enhancing security. Emerging trends, such as the integration of AI/ML for anomaly detection and blockchain for transaction integrity, are discussed alongside future developments in API security standards. By addressing vulnerabilities and implementing proactive security measures, this paper aims to guide organizations in achieving a secure and efficient microservices environment.

While edge computing has revolutionized where we process data, a shift away from the traditional cloud-based model results in an entirely new set of security challenges. Constant verification is a key feature of Zero Trust, but this approach is not optimal in decentralized edge settings, especially given the high latency demands of edge environments. In this chapter, we introduce real-time access control and monitoring as a solution for edge-embedded applications as it is quite dynamic. In comparison to static models, the real-time access control identifies and dynamically adapt according to user behaviour, location of the device and status of networks, thereby enabling edge devices to take actions independently to the threats. We examine innovations—low-latency detection, behavioral analytics, and dynamic policies—that drive edge security, through examples in IoT, healthcare, and smart cities. New developments like predictive access models and quantum-safe encryption are raising the bar for adaptive, resilient edge protection.

The Cypher query language, widely used in Neo4j for graph data management, is optimized for Online Transaction Processing (OLTP) but lacks robust support for Online Analytical Processing (OLAP) operations. This limitation arises due to its high-level abstractions, which are not designed to handle complex analytical workloads efficiently. This chapter explores an approach to extend the Cypher syntax and implement query rewriting using Neo4j's low-level API to facilitate seamless OLAP operations. By enabling direct interaction with the underlying graph engine, the proposed extensions empower developers to define and execute sophisticated analytical tasks while maintaining the expressive simplicity of Cypher. The paper outlines the architectural modifications, illustrates query rewriting techniques, and demonstrates the benefits of this hybrid approach through practical use cases.

IoT systems have provided humans with incredible benefits. However, its features related to analyzing collected data and automatically executing established guidelines restrict them from comprehending the intent of these data, retrieving human intention, or understanding behaviors. The Internet of Behaviors

Preface

AN OVERVIEW OF THE SUBJECT MATTER

In an era where data has become the lifeblood of modern enterprises, ensuring its governance, security, and efficient utilization has become paramount. Organizations across industries are grappling with increasing volumes of data, evolving security threats, and the need for agility in software development and deployment.

Data has transformed from being a mere operational asset to a critical strategic resource. As businesses collect and process vast amounts of information, the ability to manage this data effectively defines their success. However, with the increasing sophistication of cyber threats, regulatory requirements, and the dynamic nature of software development, organizations face significant challenges in maintaining data security, compliance, and efficiency. The demand for solutions that can integrate governance, security, and agility has never been more pressing.

This book brings together three essential disciplines: **Data Governance, DevSecOps, and Modern Architectures** to provide a holistic perspective on how organizations can secure, manage, and optimize their data ecosystems. These three pillars are deeply interconnected. Data governance ensures data integrity, consistency, and compliance, laying the foundation for reliable business intelligence and decision-making. DevSecOps introduces security as an integral component of software development, ensuring that applications and data are protected throughout the lifecycle. Meanwhile, modern architectures provide the technological backbone, enabling scalability, flexibility, and performance optimization in a cloud-native and microservices-driven landscape.

By integrating these themes, the book presents a comprehensive exploration of strategies, methodologies, and cutting-edge technologies that drive resilience, security, and compliance in modern software and data management. The synergy between these disciplines creates a robust framework for organizations aiming to balance innovation with security, speed with compliance, and operational efficiency with regulatory adherence.

Each chapter delves into specific challenges, offering pragmatic solutions supported by real-world case studies, industry best practices, and emerging trends. Readers will gain insights into how data governance frameworks can enhance decision-making, how security can be embedded seamlessly into development workflows, and how modern architectures can enable high-performance, scalable, and secure applications.

Through this interdisciplinary approach, the book aims to bridge the knowledge gap between governance, security, and engineering teams, fostering collaboration and alignment in achieving enterprise-wide resilience. The ultimate goal is to equip businesses, practitioners, and researchers with actionable knowledge to navigate the complex digital ecosystem, ensuring that data remains not just a valuable asset but a securely managed and efficiently utilized resource for driving innovation and success.

WHERE THIS TOPIC FITS IN THE WORLD TODAY

The digital transformation of businesses, accelerated by cloud computing, artificial intelligence, and big data analytics, has introduced both opportunities and challenges. Organizations are now dealing with exponential data growth, expanding security threats, and increasingly stringent regulatory landscapes. Data governance has become an indispensable requirement, ensuring data quality, integrity, and compliance with global regulations such as GDPR, CCPA, and HIPAA. The need for structured governance policies has never been more pressing as enterprises struggle to balance data accessibility with privacy and regulatory mandates.

Meanwhile, the rise of DevSecOps reflects a fundamental shift in software development. Traditional security practices, which once acted as bottlenecks, are now evolving into seamless, automated security integrations within CI/CD pipelines. DevSecOps promotes a culture where security is built into the software development lifecycle from the outset, rather than being an afterthought. This approach mitigates risks associated with software vulnerabilities and strengthens overall cybersecurity postures in an era where cyber threats are more sophisticated and frequent than ever.

At the same time, modern architectures, including microservices, Kubernetes, serverless computing, and edge computing, are redefining how applications are built and deployed. These innovations provide organizations with the scalability and agility needed to remain competitive. However, they also introduce new challenges in security, observability, and compliance, making the integration of governance and security principles within these architectures a necessity rather than an option.

In this evolving landscape, organizations must navigate the intricate interplay between these domains to ensure robust security, regulatory compliance, and operational efficiency. The convergence of data governance, DevSecOps, and modern architectures is not just a theoretical concept but a practical necessity for organizations aiming to build resilient, high-performing, and secure digital infrastructures.

This book serves as a comprehensive guide, offering practical insights, real-world case studies, and emerging trends to equip practitioners, researchers, and policymakers with the necessary knowledge to thrive in this dynamic environment. Whether it's ensuring regulatory compliance in data governance, implementing security automation in DevSecOps, or designing scalable and resilient modern architectures, this book provides actionable strategies to help organizations stay ahead in an increasingly complex digital world.

TARGET AUDIENCE

This book is intended for a diverse audience, spanning multiple roles and industries that intersect with data governance, security, and modern software architectures. Each group will find valuable insights tailored to their specific needs and challenges:

- ***Data Governance Professionals**: Those responsible for ensuring data quality, compliance, and regulatory adherence. This book provides them with a strategic view of how governance can be seamlessly integrated with security practices and modern software architectures.*
- ***Security Experts & DevSecOps Engineers**: Professionals focused on embedding security into software development and deployment pipelines. They will gain insights into security automation, proactive threat detection, and how DevSecOps can reinforce data governance frameworks.*
- ***Software Architects & Developers**: Individuals seeking to understand how modern architectures influence security, scalability, and efficiency. The book explores best practices for building resilient software systems that prioritize data integrity and security.*
- ***IT Managers & Executives**: Decision-makers responsible for implementing secure and governed data ecosystems within their organizations. They will find strategic guidance on balancing agility, security, and compliance in a rapidly evolving digital landscape.*
- ***Cloud and Infrastructure Specialists**: Professionals working with cloud-native technologies, microservices, and Kubernetes who need to integrate security and data governance within highly scalable infrastructures.*
- ***Compliance Officers & Risk Managers:**Those responsible for ensuring that organizational data handling aligns with industry regulations and legal mandates. The book provides a roadmap for integrating compliance into development and operational workflows.*
- ***Academics & Researchers**: Scholars exploring advancements in data security, AI-driven governance, and resilient system architectures. The book serves as a valuable resource for understanding the intersection of data governance, security, and modern architectures.*

By addressing both theoretical foundations and practical applications, this book is an invaluable resource for anyone involved in the domains of data governance, security, and software architecture.

DESCRIPTION OF EACH CHAPTER

Part 1: Data Governance

1. Data Governance, Key Insights, Strategic Challenges, and Future Imperatives

This chapter provides an in-depth analysis of data governance strategies, focusing on foundational principles, regulatory compliance, and the impact of emerging technologies. It explores key challenges such as regulatory fragmentation, cross-border data flows, and ethical AI governance. Additionally, it discusses future imperatives, including the role of automation and AI-driven governance models in enhancing data stewardship.

2. Ensuring Data Quality and Integrity in Modern Enterprises

Examining the critical role of data quality in decision-making, this chapter presents best practices for establishing data quality frameworks. It details methodologies such as data profiling, cleansing, validation, and master data management. The chapter also introduces tools and technologies that enable organizations to maintain high standards of accuracy, consistency, and completeness across enterprise datasets.

3. Metadata Management and Its Role in Data Governance

Metadata serves as the backbone of effective data governance, facilitating data discovery, lineage tracking, and regulatory compliance. This chapter explores various metadata management models, including business, technical, and operational metadata. It provides insights into implementing metadata repositories, automated cataloging, and AI-driven metadata enrichment strategies.

4. Data Lineage – Tracing Data Across Systems

Understanding how data moves across systems is crucial for compliance, security, and transparency. This chapter introduces techniques for tracking and visualizing data lineage using graph-based models and automated tracing tools. It discusses practical applications in regulatory reporting, impact analysis, and anomaly detection within complex data ecosystems.

5. Data Governance in Education: Enhancing Predictions and Decision-Making for Performance Monitoring

A case study-driven exploration of how data governance frameworks can enhance predictive analytics and performance monitoring in the education sector. The chapter covers strategies for ensuring data privacy, integrating diverse data sources, and leveraging AI-driven insights to optimize student outcomes and institutional decision-making.

Part 2: DevSecOps

6. Modern Software Challenges: Innovations in Data Governance and DevSecOps

This chapter explores the intersection of data governance and DevSecOps, detailing how organizations can implement agile security frameworks while maintaining compliance. Topics include regulatory-driven DevOps, infrastructure as code (IaC) security, and the role of policy-as-code in modern software development.

7. Agility Meets Compliance: The Convergence of Data Governance and DevSecOps

A deep dive into how enterprises can integrate compliance-driven data governance into their DevSecOps workflows without compromising agility. It includes practical case studies on balancing rapid software delivery with security controls, risk assessment methodologies, and continuous compliance monitoring.

8. Embedding Security into DevOps: Achieving Continuous Protection and Harmonized Software Development Practices

This chapter outlines best practices for embedding security within DevOps, ensuring security considerations are proactive rather than reactive. It covers secure coding practices, automated vulnerability scanning, shift-left security, and security-as-code implementation.

9. Integrating Security in Cloud-Native Development: A DevSecOps Approach to Resilient Software Systems

A comprehensive guide to implementing security in cloud-native environments. Topics include container security, securing CI/CD pipelines, Kubernetes security policies, and zero-trust principles in cloud-native applications.

10. Integrating Security in DataOps: A Framework for Securing Data Pipelines in Real-Time Analytics

As data analytics shift towards real-time processing, securing data pipelines becomes critical. This chapter presents a structured approach to integrating security within DataOps, including threat modeling for data flows, encryption strategies, and automated compliance enforcement.

11. Safeguarding Sensitive Data in the DevSecOps Pipelines: Strategies, Tools, and Best Practices

An exploration of techniques for protecting sensitive data in software development pipelines. The chapter covers secret management, data masking, homomorphic encryption, and compliance-driven data security policies.

12. The Role of Artificial Intelligence in Bridging DevOps and SecOps for Cloud Infrastructure

AI-driven security is revolutionizing DevSecOps by enabling intelligent threat detection, automated response mechanisms, and adaptive security policies. This chapter highlights the integration of AI-powered analytics in cloud security monitoring, incident detection, and automated remediation strategies.

Part 3: Modern Architectures

13. Building Resilient Systems: The Role of Containers and Kubernetes

A comprehensive guide to leveraging containers and Kubernetes for building scalable, resilient applications. The chapter explores advanced Kubernetes patterns, service mesh implementations, and resilience engineering techniques.

14. The Security Implications of Microservices in Modern Software Development

Microservices architecture introduces security challenges such as API vulnerabilities, service-to-service authentication, and distributed data security. This chapter outlines best practices for securing microservices, including service mesh integration, mutual TLS, and API security gateways.

15. Adaptive Security at the Edge with Real-Time Access Control and Monitoring Beyond Zero Trust

Edge computing expands the attack surface, requiring adaptive security measures. This chapter introduces real-time access control models, AI-driven anomaly detection, and policy enforcement mechanisms tailored for distributed environments.

16. Enhancing Cypher for OLAP: Extending Syntax and Optimizing Query Execution

A technical deep dive into extending Cypher query language for OLAP workloads. Topics include query optimization techniques, performance tuning strategies, and extending Cypher for analytical processing in graph databases.

17. Exploring the Internet of Behaviors Capabilities: A Comprehensive Survey

An analysis of the Internet of Behaviors (IoB) and its potential to transform data-driven decision-making. This chapter explores behavioral data collection, predictive analytics, and ethical considerations surrounding IoB applications.

18. Navigating the Internet of Behaviors (IoB) Potential Across Domains

Building on the previous chapter, this section examines real-world IoB applications across industries such as healthcare, retail, and smart cities. It also discusses regulatory and privacy challenges related to behavioral analytics.

19. Generative AI Ethical Dimensions, Data Privacy Challenges, and Future Prospects

As generative AI advances, ethical and privacy concerns become increasingly relevant. This chapter examines the impact of AI-generated content on data security, misinformation risks, and potential regulatory frameworks for responsible AI governance.

CONCLUSION: IMPACT AND CONTRIBUTION TO THE FIELD

This book provides a unique blend of theoretical insights and practical strategies, offering a well-rounded understanding of data governance, DevSecOps, and modern architectures. By bringing together thought leaders and industry experts, we aim to equip readers with the knowledge to implement secure, compliant, and efficient data ecosystems. The cross-disciplinary approach ensures that readers not only understand the foundations of each field but also gain practical insights into how these domains intersect to create more robust and agile organizations. We hope this book serves as a valuable resource for professionals, academics, and decision-makers seeking to navigate the complex landscape of modern data-driven enterprises. As technology continues to evolve, staying informed about best practices and emerging trends will be crucial in fostering innovation while maintaining security and compliance. By embracing these principles, organizations can build resilient and future-proof systems that drive sustainable growth and success in an increasingly data-centric world.

Chapter 1
Data Governance, Key Insights, Strategic Challenges, and Future Imperatives

Soukaina Nai
https://orcid.org/0009-0002-4819-2198
Faculty of Sciences, University Ibn Tofail, Kenitra, Morocco

Amal Rifai
https://orcid.org/0000-0003-2793-3102
Regional Center for the Professions of Education and Training, Morocco

Abdelalim Sadiq
https://orcid.org/0000-0003-1478-8807
Faculty of Sciences, University Ibn Tofail, Kenitra, Morocco

ABSTRACT

This article discusses the importance of data governance in managing data availability, integrity, usability, and security within organizations. Without a governance framework, businesses risk fragmented and vulnerable data systems. Effective data governance improves data quality, security, regulatory compliance (e.g., GDPR, HIPAA, CCPA), decision-making, and operational efficiency. Key principles include data ownership, stewardship, quality maintenance, security, privacy safeguards, compliance, and lifecycle management. It also highlights challenges such as cultural resistance, data silos, platform complexity, and technology barriers. The article suggests best practices for implementation, such as clear role definitions, leveraging technology, starting pilot projects, and ongoing monitoring. Prioritizing data governance allows organizations to transform data into a strategic asset.

1. INTRODUCTION

In today's landscape of digital transformation, data has become an invaluable asset for organizations across diverse sectors (Kraus & al., 2021). As businesses increasingly depend on data to inform decisions, improve operational efficiency, and establish competitive advantages, the necessity for effective data

DOI: 10.4018/979-8-3373-0365-9.ch001

governance has reached critical levels (Benfeldt & al., 2020). Data governance refers to the structured framework and processes established to manage data availability, integrity, usability, and security within an organization (Al-Badi & al., 2018). This governance framework ensures that data is not only accurate and reliable but is also utilized appropriately to unlock its full potential (Hassani & al., 2023).

Without a solid data governance framework in place, organizations face significant risks, including fragmented data systems, compliance challenges, and increased vulnerability to security breaches (Janssen & al., 2020). The intricacies of modern data environments require organizations to clearly define roles, responsibilities, and processes to manage their data effectively (Martinez & al., 2021).

This article explores the core principles of data governance, emphasizing its importance in today's data-driven world. It will address the key principles that underpin effective governance, the challenges organizations encounter during implementation, and best practices for developing and enhancing governance frameworks. By prioritizing data governance, organizations can protect sensitive information, comply with regulatory requirements, and cultivate a culture of transparency and trust. This strategic approach to data governance not only safeguards data but also transforms it into a key asset that facilitates informed decision-making and fosters sustainable growth. Ultimately, as data continues to evolve in complexity and volume, a robust governance framework will be essential for organizations aiming to thrive in an increasingly competitive environment.

2. DATA GOVERNANCE

Data governance is a strategic and comprehensive framework designed to ensure data within an organization is managed with precision, security, and efficiency (Dal Maso, 2019). This framework involves establishing policies, roles, standards, and metrics that govern how data is accessed, processed, used, and protected across departments (Sargiotis, 2024). The structured approach provided by data governance is essential for making data accessible, accurate, and compliant with internal standards and external regulations. Notably, these regulations include the General Data Protection Regulation (GDPR), which is a set of rules governing the protection of personal data in the European Union, and the California Consumer Privacy Act (CCPA), which provides privacy rights and consumer protection for residents of California, USA. These regulations are key in ensuring data is handled responsibly and legally (Voss, 2019). By implementing clear, organization-wide guidelines for data handling, organizations can maximize the value of their data assets while mitigating potential risks like data breaches, inconsistencies, and privacy violations (Ayereby, 2018).

The impact of an effective data governance framework is substantial, especially for organizations dealing with sensitive or personal data, as it helps them avoid costly fines and legal issues stemming from non-compliance (Zhang & al., 2022). Beyond compliance, data governance strengthens accountability by assigning stewardship responsibilities, ensuring employees understand their roles in managing and safeguarding data. With roles and responsibilities clearly defined, organizations can foster a culture of accountability, where data integrity and security become top priorities (Lindkvist & Llewellyn, 2003).

In addition to risk management, a robust data governance framework directly enhances decision-making capabilities (Mao & al., 2022). High-quality data improves business intelligence, enabling leaders to make more informed, data-driven decisions. This accurate data flow across the organization also supports operational efficiency, allowing teams to leverage reliable data for strategic planning and customer insights. Furthermore, as data governance reinforces secure and responsible data use, it builds organizational trust in data-driven processes, fostering confidence at all levels (VanOoijen & al., 2019).

Ultimately, data governance is about managing data as a valuable strategic asset that supports both the immediate operational needs and the long-term goals of the organization. Through these structured practices, organizations can ensure data is both protected and used to its full potential, aligning data management with broader business objectives for sustainable growth and competitive advantage (Grover, & al., 2018). In this context, Figure 1 is an illustration showcasing the data governance framework, highlighting its key components.

3. IMPORTANCE OF DATA GOVERNANCE

In today's data-driven environment, organizations generate massive amounts of data daily, ranging from customer information to operational metrics. Without an effective data governance framework, this data can quickly become fragmented and unstructured, leading to inefficiencies and reduced data reliability (Abraham & al., 2019) . Disorganized data not only limits its value for insights and decision-making but also increases exposure to security risks. Unstructured data environments are more vulnerable to breaches and compliance violations, posing significant legal and reputational risks (Hikmawati & al., 2021).

Figure 1. Importance of Data Governance

Data governance provides the structure needed to ensure data integrity, security, and accessibility, enabling organizations to harness data effectively while minimizing potential risks as shown in figure 1. In this context, Table 1 summarizes the importance of data governance in modern organizations.

Table 1. Key Aspects Highlighting the Importance of Data Governance

Aspect	Description
Data Quality	- Ensures accuracy and reliability of data, vital for decision-making (Fan & al., 2007). - High-quality data enables valuable insights and informed judgments. - Regular audits and data cleansing practices maintain quality. - Enhances trust among employees and stakeholders. - Promotes operational efficiency, regulatory compliance, and a data-driven culture (Verma & al., 2023).
Security & Compliance	- Safeguards sensitive data while adhering to regulations like GDPR, HIPAA (Health Insurance Portability and Accountability Act), and CCPA (Mulgund & al., 2021). - Reduces risks of data breaches and legal penalties. - Builds customer trust through responsible data handling. - Fosters accountability and ensures ethical, transparent data practices.
Improved Decision-Making	- Access to accurate, secure data enhances strategic decision-making (Grover & al., 2018). - Facilitates trend analysis, outcome forecasting, and opportunity identification. - Stakeholder trust is reinforced, promoting cross-departmental collaboration. - Empowers well-informed decisions, improving performance and competitive advantage.
Operational Efficiency	- Streamlined data management boosts accessibility across departments. - Minimizes data silos, reducing time spent on data retrieval (Kenyon & al., 2023). - Standardized processes improve consistency, accuracy, and workflow. - Supports productivity and agile responses, enhancing overall effectiveness.

4. KEY PRINCIPLES OF DATA GOVERNANCE

Understanding the key principles of data governance is essential for organizations looking to effectively manage their data assets. These principles provide a framework that ensures data is handled consistently, securely, and in alignment with organizational goals. By establishing clear roles, responsibilities, and processes, organizations can foster a culture of accountability and transparency around data usage. Additionally, these principles emphasize the importance of data quality, compliance, and security, enabling organizations to mitigate risks while maximizing the value of their data (Brous & al., 2016). Embracing these core tenets lays the groundwork for robust data governance that supports informed decision-making and operational efficiency. In this context, figure 2 shown the most key principles of Data Governance are:

Figure 2. Key of Data Governance

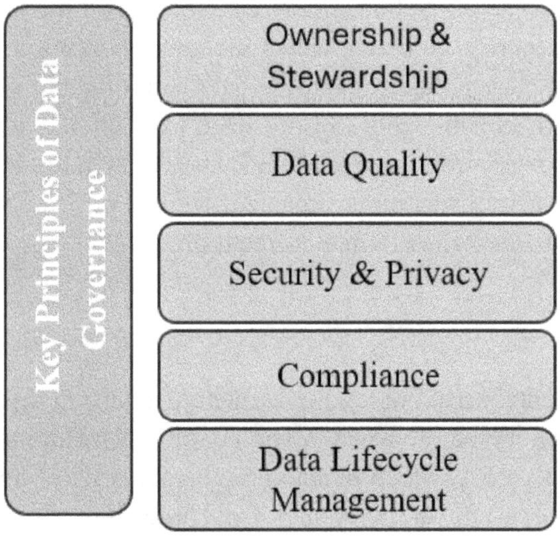

4.1. Ownership & Stewardship

Clear ownership of data is vital for effective data governance, often designated to a role known as a data steward. This individual is responsible for managing the data lifecycle, ensuring its accuracy, integrity, and security from creation to deletion (Piasecki & Cheah, 2022). By assigning data ownership, organizations establish accountability, making it easier to enforce data management policies and standards. Data stewards serve as the point of contact for any issues related to data quality or compliance, facilitating collaboration across departments. This structure not only enhances data governance but also empowers organizations to leverage their data assets more effectively, fostering informed decision-making and operational efficiency.

4.2. Data Quality

Data quality is crucial for effective data governance, necessitating the implementation of processes and tools that ensure the accuracy, completeness, and consistency of data. Organizations should establish regular data validation procedures, including audits and cleansing routines, to identify and rectify errors or discrepancies (Truong & al., 2017). Utilizing automated tools can streamline these processes, making it easier to maintain high data quality standards. Furthermore, creating clear guidelines for data entry and management promotes uniformity across departments. By prioritizing data quality, organizations can enhance decision-making, improve operational efficiency, and foster trust among stakeholders, ultimately maximizing the value derived from their data assets.

4.3. Security & Privacy

Security and privacy are critical components of effective data governance, requiring robust safeguards to protect data from breaches and unauthorized access (Hilliman, 2013). Organizations should implement a multi-layered security approach, which includes encryption, access controls, and regular security audits. Establishing clear policies regarding data handling and user permissions helps ensure that sensitive information is accessible only to authorized personnel. Additionally, organizations must stay compliant with relevant regulations, such as GDPR and HIPAA, to safeguard personal information. By prioritizing security and privacy measures, organizations can mitigate risks, protect their reputation, and maintain stakeholder trust in their data management practices.

4.4. Compliance

Compliance is a fundamental aspect of data governance, requiring organizations to align their data practices with legal and regulatory requirements (Manoharan, 2024). This includes adhering to regulations such as GDPR, HIPAA, and CCPA, which dictate how personal data should be collected, processed, and stored. Organizations must establish clear policies and procedures to ensure compliance, conducting regular audits to identify potential gaps. Training employees on data protection and privacy laws is also essential to foster a culture of compliance. By prioritizing adherence to legal standards, organizations can avoid significant penalties, enhance their reputation, and build trust with customers and stakeholders.

4.5. Data Lifecycle Management:

Data Lifecycle Management (DLM) is essential for effective data governance, encompassing the comprehensive management of data from its creation through to its usage, storage, and eventual deletion (Ige & al., 2024). Implementing a DLM strategy ensures that data is accurately captured and stored in a manner that meets organizational and regulatory requirements. During the usage phase, organizations must monitor data access and integrity to support decision-making. Proper storage solutions are crucial for maintaining data security and accessibility. Finally, establishing clear policies for data deletion ensures that obsolete or unnecessary information is removed responsibly, thereby optimizing storage resources and minimizing compliance risks. By effectively managing the data lifecycle, organizations can maximize the value of their data assets while mitigating potential risks.

5. CHALLENGES IN IMPLEMENTING DATA GOVERNANCE

Implementing a data governance framework is essential for organizations aiming to harness the full potential of their data, yet it comes with a variety of challenges that can impede progress. Understanding these challenges is crucial for successfully establishing a robust data governance strategy. In this context, Table 2 outlines the various challenges in implementing data governance.

Table 2. Key Challenges in Implementing Data Governance

Challenge	Description
Cultural Resistance	Cultural Resistance is a significant barrier to effective data governance, as employees may be skeptical of new processes or hesitant to embrace change (Seiner, 2014). This resistance often stems from a fear of the unknown, concerns about increased workloads, or a lack of understanding of the benefits of data governance initiatives. Employees who are accustomed to established workflows may view new practices as disruptive, leading to pushback and non-compliance. To overcome this challenge, organizations must prioritize change management by clearly communicating the benefits of data governance, providing adequate training, and fostering a culture of collaboration that encourages employee buy-in and support (Pansara, 2023).
Data Silos	Data Silos refer to isolated pockets of data within departments that are not easily shared or accessible across the organization (Patel, 2019). Each department may maintain its own datasets, leading to fragmentation and inconsistency in information. This lack of integration hinders collaboration and prevents teams from gaining a comprehensive view of organizational data. As a result, decision-making can become inefficient and based on incomplete information. Data silos not only complicate data management but also impede the ability to leverage insights across the organization (Valleru & al., 2023). Breaking down these silos is essential for fostering a culture of data sharing and enhancing overall operational efficiency.
Complexity	Managing data across multiple platforms, departments, and geographical locations introduces significant complexity for organizations (Yebenes & Zorrilla, 2019). Each department may utilize different systems, tools, and formats, making it challenging to achieve a unified view of the data. Furthermore, geographical disparities can lead to variations in data regulations, compliance requirements, and cultural contexts, complicating data management processes (Micheli & al., 2020). This complexity can hinder effective communication and collaboration among teams, resulting in inefficiencies and potential data inconsistencies. To address these challenges, organizations must implement integrated data management solutions that streamline processes and ensure consistent data governance across the entire organization.
Technology Barriers	Selecting the Right Tools for data governance is a significant challenge, particularly in large organizations with diverse needs (Othman & al., 2011). The wide array of available technologies can overwhelm decision-makers, making it difficult to identify solutions that align with specific governance objectives. Additionally, integrating new tools with existing systems may pose compatibility issues, complicating implementation (Yudatama & al., 2017). Resistance from employees who are accustomed to legacy systems can further hinder adoption. Organizations must carefully assess their requirements and evaluate various options, ensuring that selected tools facilitate data quality, security, and compliance while promoting user adoption and streamlined workflows across departments.

6. BEST PRACTICES FOR IMPLEMENTING DATA GOVERNANCE

Implementing a successful data governance framework requires careful planning and execution. In this context figure 3 shown some best practices to guide organizations in establishing effective data governance:

Figure 3. Best Practices for Implementing Data Governance

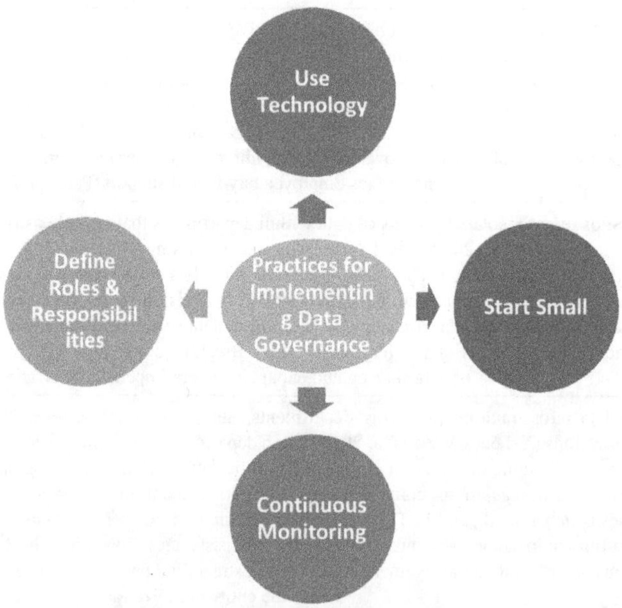

6.1. Define Clear Roles & Responsibilities

Defining clear roles is essential for effective data governance. Assigning specific responsibilities, such as data stewards and data governance teams, is key to establishing accountability and ensuring structured management of data (Brous & al., 2016). Data stewards are tasked with maintaining data quality, overseeing data integrity, ensuring compliance with internal policies and external regulations, and acting as intermediaries between technical teams (e.g., IT and data engineers) and business units (e.g., marketing, finance). They ensure that data is accurate, consistent, and accessible to the right stakeholders.

Data governance teams, on the other hand, are responsible for the development, implementation, and enforcement of data governance policies. They ensure that these policies align with the organization's strategic goals and that data management practices are standardized across departments. Governance teams also monitor compliance with data standards, enforce data access controls, and address any data-related issues that arise.

By clearly defining and separating these roles, organizations can enhance collaboration between technical and business teams, streamline decision-making, and improve communication. This structured approach leads to more effective data management, reduces risks associated with poor data governance, and ultimately contributes to better overall governance outcomes, ensuring that data serves as a strategic asset across the organization (Abraham & al., 2019).

6.2. Use Technology

Leveraging technology is essential for enhancing data governance efficiency and effectiveness (Karo & al., 2024). Tools like metadata management systems and data catalogs automate many governance tasks, reducing manual work and enhancing data management. Metadata management systems, such as Alation or Collibra, help organizations track data assets, monitor data lineage (from origin to usage), and ensure compliance with data standards by capturing detailed metadata about data sources, formats, and usage. Data catalogs, like Informatica or Google Cloud Data Catalog, provide a centralized platform for discovering, accessing, and understanding data across the organization (Khodijah & al., 2023). By organizing data with clear metadata tags, these catalogs make it easier for users to find and understand the data they need, fostering a data-driven culture.

These tools also promote collaboration by offering a unified platform for sharing data and insights. For example, Collibra enables teams to annotate and share data context, ensuring transparency. Automation of governance tasks improves data quality, ensures consistency, and supports compliance with regulations like GDPR and CCPA. By reducing the risk of human error and aligning data with internal standards, organizations can maximize the value of their data assets and make more informed decisions across all levels of the business.

6.3. Start Small:

Starting small with a pilot project is a strategic and practical approach to implementing data governance (Berndtsson & al., 2020). For example, a global retail company might begin by testing data governance in its marketing department. This department generates a significant amount of customer data, which needs to be accurate, secure, and compliant with data privacy regulations like GDPR.

During the pilot, the company implements data governance tools like Collibra for metadata management and Informatica for data cataloging. These tools help ensure that data is properly classified, monitored for compliance, and accessible to authorized users. The marketing team, along with data stewards, focuses on maintaining data quality by tracking data lineage—identifying where customer data originates, how it flows through systems, and where it is used. The pilot also tests governance processes, such as setting up data access controls and ensuring data stewardship responsibilities are clearly defined. For instance, data stewards within the marketing department are responsible for ensuring customer data meets quality standards, is kept secure, and is used properly within campaigns.

Throughout the pilot phase, the company monitors challenges, such as discrepancies in data quality or delays in reporting. These issues are addressed in real-time, and adjustments are made to improve data management practices. Success in this pilot demonstrates the value of governance tools, encouraging buy-in from other departments (Sharp & al., 2022). Based on the lessons learned, the company can expand the governance practices to other departments, such as finance and operations, ensuring smoother implementation and a more effective, organization-wide data governance strategy.

6.4. Continuous Monitoring:

Continuous monitoring is essential for maintaining the effectiveness of data governance policies. For example, a healthcare organization may implement regular assessments of its data governance practices to ensure compliance with healthcare regulations like HIPAA (Health Insurance Portability and Accountability Act) and to improve the quality of patient data (Pansara, 2023). The organization establishes Key Performance Indicators (KPIs) such as the percentage of patient records with complete data fields, the speed of incident response for potential data breaches, and the number of unauthorized access attempts. By tracking these metrics, the organization can measure the effectiveness of its data governance in maintaining data quality, security, and accessibility.

During one assessment, the monitoring reveals that a significant number of patient records are incomplete due to inconsistent data entry practices. The organization also discovers that certain departments are not fully adhering to established access controls, increasing the risk of unauthorized data access. Additionally, feedback from data stewards indicates that users find it difficult to access data due to unclear permissions. As a result, the organization adjusts its data entry guidelines, implements additional training for staff, and refines its data access policies. By continuously assessing and adjusting governance practices, the organization ensures its data governance remains aligned with evolving regulations, business needs, and security requirements, fostering a culture of accountability and continuous improvement.

6.5. Practical Approaches to Establishing Robust Data Governance Frameworks in Complex Data Environments

In complex data environments, such as those found in large organizations or industries with strict regulatory requirements, establishing a robust data governance framework requires careful planning and the integration of several core principles. Below are practical steps to build a strong data governance framework using key elements like defining clear roles, leveraging technology, starting small with pilot projects, and ensuring continuous monitoring. Table 3 summarizing the practical approaches to establishing robust data governance frameworks in complex data environments.

Table 3. Real-World Examples Of Establishing Data Governance In Complex Data Environments

Approach	Description	Example
1.Defining Clear Roles	Assign specific roles to ensure accountability and effective management of data. Key roles include data stewards (responsible for data quality and compliance) and data governance teams (responsible for policies and oversight).	In a healthcare organization, data stewards are responsible for managing patient data, ensuring it complies with HIPAA regulations, while the governance team oversees the overall data governance strategy and enforces policies across departments.
2.Leverage Technology	Implement tools like metadata management systems, data catalogs, and data quality platforms to automate and streamline governance tasks, such as data lineage tracking, classification, and access control.	A manufacturing company might use Collibra for metadata management to track data lineage and ensure that data from suppliers is accurately monitored. They can also deploy Google Cloud Data Catalog to make supply chain data discoverable and accessible for teams across the organization.
3.Start Small with Pilot Projects	Begin with a pilot project in a single department or data domain to test governance processes and tools before scaling. This allows for refinement based on lessons learned and stakeholder feedback.	A global retail company could start by testing data governance in its marketing department. By using metadata tools and setting access controls, they can identify challenges (e.g., data access issues) and make improvements before expanding governance practices to other departments like sales or finance.
4.Continuous Monitoring and Feedback	Establish regular assessments using KPIs to track data quality, security, and compliance. Continuously gather feedback from stakeholders to address emerging risks and ensure governance practices evolve with changing business needs and regulations.	A financial services firm monitors KPIs such as data accuracy and compliance with GDPR and SOX. If discrepancies in data quality are found, tools like Informatica's Data Quality can automatically flag issues. Feedback from data users allows the organization to adjust its policies and tools to address emerging issues such as unauthorized access or misalignment with regulatory standards.

7. CONCLUSION

Data governance is a critical aspect of modern business strategy, essential for effective data management and risk mitigation. As organizations navigate increasingly complex data environments, establishing robust governance frameworks becomes crucial for enhancing data quality and ensuring compliance with evolving regulatory standards. By defining clear guidelines and accountability, businesses can safeguard sensitive information and foster a culture of transparency and trust among stakeholders. Moreover, a proactive approach to data governance not only protects against data misuse but also enhances customer loyalty by demonstrating a commitment to ethical data handling. As the value of data continues to rise, prioritizing data governance will empower organizations to leverage their data assets strategically, driving informed decision-making and sustaining a competitive advantage in an ever-evolving, data-driven landscape. Investing in data governance is not just a regulatory requirement; it is a strategic imperative that enables organizations to thrive in today's information-centric world.

REFERENCES

Abraham, R., Schneider, J., & Vom Brocke, J. (2019). Data governance: A conceptual framework, structured review, and research agenda. *International Journal of Information Management*, *49*, 424–438. DOI: 10.1016/j.ijinfomgt.2019.07.008

Abraham, R., Schneider, J., & Vom Brocke, J. (2019). Data governance: A conceptual framework, structured review, and research agenda. *International Journal of Information Management*, *49*, 424–438. DOI: 10.1016/j.ijinfomgt.2019.07.008

Abraham, R., Schneider, J., & Vom Brocke, J. (2019). Data governance: A conceptual framework, structured review, and research agenda. *International Journal of Information Management*, *49*, 424–438. DOI: 10.1016/j.ijinfomgt.2019.07.008

Al-Badi, A., Tarhini, A., & Khan, A. I. (2018). Exploring big data governance frameworks. *Procedia Computer Science*, *141*, 271–277. DOI: 10.1016/j.procs.2018.10.181

Benfeldt, O., Persson, J. S., & Madsen, S. (2020). Data governance as a collective action problem. *Information Systems Frontiers*, *22*(2), 299–313. DOI: 10.1007/s10796-019-09923-z

Berndtsson, M., Ericsson, A., & Svahn, T. (2020). Scaling up data-driven pilot projects. *AI Magazine*, *41*(3), 94–102. DOI: 10.1609/aimag.v41i3.5307

Brous, P., Herder, P., & Janssen, M. (2016). Governing asset management data infrastructures. *Procedia Computer Science*, *95*, 303–310. DOI: 10.1016/j.procs.2016.09.339

Brous, P., Janssen, M., & Vilminko-Heikkinen, R. (2016). Coordinating decision-making in data management activities: a systematic review of data governance principles. In Electronic Government: 15th IFIP WG 8.5 International Conference, EGOV 2016, Guimarães, Portugal, September 5-8, 2016 [Springer International Publishing.]. *Proceedings*, *15*, 115–125.

Dal Maso, A. (2019). The evolution of Data Governance: a tool for an improved and enhanced decision-making process.

Fan, W., Geerts, F., & Jia, X. (2007). Improving data quality: Consistency and accuracy. ACM.0

Grover, V., Chiang, R. H., Liang, T. P., & Zhang, D. (2018). Creating strategic business value from big data analytics: A research framework. *Journal of Management Information Systems*, *35*(2), 388–423. DOI: 10.1080/07421222.2018.1451951

Grover, V., Chiang, R. H., Liang, T. P., & Zhang, D. (2018). Creating strategic business value from big data analytics: A research framework. *Journal of Management Information Systems*, *35*(2), 388–423. DOI: 10.1080/07421222.2018.1451951

Hassani, H., & MacFeely, S. (2023). Driving excellence in official statistics: Unleashing the potential of comprehensive digital data Governance. *Big Data and Cognitive Computing*, *7*(3), 134. DOI: 10.3390/bdcc7030134

Hikmawati, S., Santosa, P. I., & Hidayah, I. (2021). Improving Data Quality and Data Governance Using Master Data Management: A Review. [International Journal of Information Technology and Electrical Engineering]. *IJITEE*, *5*(3), 90–95. DOI: 10.22146/ijitee.66307

Hilliman, C. A. (2013). Data Privacy, Security, and Compliane through Data Governance. N. Bhansali, Data Governance: Creating Value from Information Assets, 125-148.

Ige, A. B., Chukwurah, N., Idemudia, C., & Adebayo, V. I. (2024). Managing Data Lifecycle Effectively: Best Practices for Data Retention and Archival Processes. International Journal of Engineering Research and Development e-ISSN, 453-461.

Janssen, M., Brous, P., Estevez, E., Barbosa, L. S., & Janowski, T. (2020). Data governance: Organizing data for trustworthy Artificial Intelligence. *Government Information Quarterly*, *37*(3), 101493. DOI: 10.1016/j.giq.2020.101493

Karo, M. B., Miller, B. P., & Al-Kamari, O. A. (2024). Leveraging data utilization and predictive analytics: Driving innovation and enhancing decision making through ethical governance. [ITEE]. *International Transactions on Education Technology*, *2*(2), 152–162.

Kenyon, G. N., Goldsmith, M., Neureuther, B. D., & Zhou, D. (2018). Improving the return on investment in ports: Opportunities in data management. *Maritime Economics & Logistics*, *20*(4), 514–530. DOI: 10.1057/s41278-017-0078-4

Khodijah Kadarsah, D. R. A., Govindaraju, R., & Prihartono, B. (2023). Leveraging Data Management Capabilities for Innovation Capabilities: The Moderating Role of Cross-Functional Integration. *Journal of ICT Research & Applications*, *17*(3), 385–411. DOI: 10.5614/itbj.ict.res.appl.2023.17.3.7

Kraus, S., Jones, P., Kailer, N., Weinmann, A., Chaparro-Banegas, N., & Roig-Tierno, N. (2021). Digital transformation: An overview of the current state of the art of research. *SAGE Open*, *11*(3), 21582440211047576. DOI: 10.1177/21582440211047576

Lindkvist, L., & Llewellyn, S. (2003). Accountability, responsibility and organization. *Scandinavian Journal of Management*, *19*(2), 251–273. DOI: 10.1016/S0956-5221(02)00027-1

Manoharan, G. (2024). Data governance frameworks for AI implementation in banking: Ensuring compliance and trust. [IJARET]. *INTERNATIONAL JOURNAL OF ADVANCED RESEARCH IN ENGINEERING AND TECHNOLOGY*, *15*(3), 101–109.

Mao, Z., Wu, J., Qiao, Y., & Yao, H. (2022). Government data governance framework based on a data middle platform. *Aslib Journal of Information Management*, *74*(2), 289–310. DOI: 10.1108/AJIM-03-2021-0068

Martinez, I., Viles, E., & Olaizola, I. G. (2021). Data science methodologies: Current challenges and future approaches. *Big Data Research*, *24*, 100183. DOI: 10.1016/j.bdr.2020.100183

Micheli, M., Ponti, M., Craglia, M., & Berti Suman, A. (2020). Emerging models of data governance in the age of datafication. *Big Data & Society*, *7*(2), 2053951720948087. DOI: 10.1177/2053951720948087

Mulgund, P., Mulgund, B. P., Sharman, R., & Singh, R. (2021). The implications of the California Consumer Privacy Act (CCPA) on healthcare organizations: Lessons learned from early compliance experiences. *Health Policy and Technology*, *10*(3), 100543. DOI: 10.1016/j.hlpt.2021.100543

Othman, M., Chan, T., Foo, E., & Timbrell, G. (2011). Barriers to information technology governance adoption: a preliminary empirical investigation. In Knowledge Management and Innovation-A Business Competitive Edge Perspective: Proceedings of the 15th International Business Information Management Association Conference (pp. 1771-1787). International Business Information Management Association.

Pansara, R. (2023). Unraveling the Complexities of Data Governance with Strategies, Challenges, and Future Directions. *Transactions on Latest Trends in IoT*, *6*(6), 46–56.

Pansara, R. (2023). Unraveling the Complexities of Data Governance with Strategies, Challenges, and Future Directions. *Transactions on Latest Trends in IoT*, *6*(6), 46–56.

Patel, J. (2019). Bridging data silos using big data integration. International Journal of Database Management Systems, 11(3), 01-06.

Piasecki, J., & Cheah, P. Y. (2022). Ownership of individual-level health data, data sharing, and data governance. *BMC Medical Ethics*, *23*(1), 104. DOI: 10.1186/s12910-022-00848-y PMID: 36309719

Sargiotis, D. (2024). Data Governance Policies and Standards: Development and Implementation. In *Data Governance: A Guide* (pp. 247–277). Springer Nature Switzerland. DOI: 10.1007/978-3-031-67268-2_7

Seiner, R. S. (2014). *Non-invasive data governance: The path of least resistance and greatest success.* Technics Publications.

Sharp, D., Anwar, M., Goodwin, S., Raven, R., Bartram, L., & Kamruzzaman, L. (2022). A participatory approach for empowering community engagement in data governance: The Monash Net Zero Precinct. *Data & Policy*, *4*, e5. DOI: 10.1017/dap.2021.33

Truong, T., George, R., & Davidson, J. (2017). Establishing an effective data governance system. *Pharmaceutical Technology*, *41*(11), 42–45.

Valleru, V., & Alapati, N. K. K. (2022). Breaking Down Data Silos: Innovations in Cloud Data Integration. Advances in Computer Sciences, 5(1).

van Ooijen, C., Ubaldi, B., & Welby, B. (2019). A data-driven public sector: Enabling the strategic use of data for productive, inclusive and trustworthy governance.

Verma, P., Kumar, V., Mittal, A., Rathore, B., Jha, A., & Rahman, M. S. (2023). The role of 3S in big data quality: A perspective on operational performance indicators using an integrated approach. *The TQM Journal*, *35*(1), 153–182. DOI: 10.1108/TQM-02-2021-0062

Voss, W. G. (2019). Cross-border data flows, the GDPR, and data governance. Wash. Int'l LJ, 29, 485.
Ayereby, M. P. M. (2018). Overcoming data breaches and human factors in minimizing threats to cybersecurity ecosystems (Doctoral dissertation, Walden University).

Yebenes, J., & Zorrilla, M. (2019). Towards a data governance framework for third generation platforms. *Procedia Computer Science*, *151*, 614–621. DOI: 10.1016/j.procs.2019.04.082

Yudatama, U., Nazief, B. A., & Hidayanto, A. N. (2017, September). Benefits and barriers as a critical success factor in the implementation of IT governance: Literature review. In 2017 International Conference on ICT For Smart Society (ICISS) (pp. 1-6). IEEE.

Zhang, Q., Sun, X., & Zhang, M. (2022). Data matters: A strategic action framework for data governance. *Information & Management*, *59*(4), 103642. DOI: 10.1016/j.im.2022.103642

Chapter 2
Ensuring Data Quality and Integrity in Modern Enterprises

Rajesh Vayyala
https://orcid.org/0009-0001-0227-0675
PRA Group Inc., USA

ABSTRACT

Businesses are increasingly reliant on data to drive their decisions; consequently, it is imperative that the data they acquire be accurate and complete. Inappropriate data management could lead to problems with security, inefficiency, and noncompliance with legal norms. The function of data governance systems, security measures, and technology developments in preserving high-quality data is investigated in this chapter. DevSecOps guarantees data integrity and dependability and protects against illegal access by including security in software development. Modern technologies include blockchain, artificial intelligence, and machine learning that enable data tracking and trustworthiness also abound. This chapter addresses data fragmentation, cybersecurity issues, and complicated regulations, stressing the need for proactive government and automated integrity checks. By combining innovative technologies, security-driven software systems, and robust governance requirements, companies may achieve data integrity, compliance, and resilience in an always-shifting digital environment.

INTRODUCTION

Modern companies cannot function without consistent, high-quality data; they depend more on data-driven decisions than ever. Assurances of data consistency, reliability, and integrity become even more crucial to businesses as they compile enormous amounts of both organized and unstructured data. Excellent data helps enterprises to stimulate creativity, simplify processes, and enhance consumer experiences. Incorrect insights, legal noncompliance, and security issues might reduce companies' bottom-line handling of bad-quality data. Apart from basic data management techniques, the complicated data integrity problem requires sophisticated software solutions containing built-in security aspects and robust governance frameworks.

Reliable data requires data governance. Within an organization, data governance is its set of policies and practices for data gathering, storage, processing, and distribution (Janssen et al., 2020). Data is only valuable and pristine if good government is absent. This ensures that errors, hacks, or system

DOI: 10.4018/979-8-3373-0365-9.ch002

failures will not produce any variances. Moreover, data governance systems are needed for businesses operating in complex legal environments, like the General Data Protection Regulation (GDPR) and the California Consumer Privacy Act (CCPA) (Farhad, 2024). Governance solutions guarantee compliance and support a data-responsibility culture by verifying that staff members from throughout the company follow set data management rules.

As DevSecOps (a method involving security in software development) emerges, data governance must be able to incorporate security elements. Given that traditional security solutions are not protective of data, Chittala (2024) argues that companies incur the risk of data leaks. DevSecOps instead employs automated validation, continuous compliance audits, and real-time monitoring to integrate security from the start. Following these rules helps strengthen data integrity by protecting against corruption, unauthorized access, and manipulation. Version control and immutable logging help DevSecOps systems (which also feature data traceability and preservation of data provenance) allow businesses to detect and fix issues quickly. Including security in agile development, cycles help companies improve data resilience and reduce insider attack and data breach risk.

New software advances force businesses to reconsider their programs on data integrity and quality. Modern automated data cleansing, predictive analytics, and anomaly detection rely on ML and artificial intelligence. These rapid corrections for differences discovered by these devices produce more precision (Jacobs et al., 2023). Claims Hossain et al. (2024), blockchain technology offers a further innovative way to ensure data integrity using an immutable distributed ledger. As computers move to the brink and the cloud, new possibilities and risks for companies also appear. To eliminate variances in far-off systems, robust data validation methods must be followed, and scalability must be allowed.

This chapter investigates current companies' intricate approaches to ensuring data quality and integrity concerning the interrelated character of data governance, security, and software development. It covers topics including the theoretical underpinnings of data quality, DevSecOps's protection of data integrity, and governance system purposes. We then discuss the challenges businesses have in trying to keep onto premium data in a continuously evolving technological world. We then discuss inventive tools meant to increase data accuracy and lifespan. This chapter investigates further data management best practices, ways businesses may improve their digital ecosystems with new ideas, and how to mix industry standards with scholarly research.

UNDERSTANDING DATA QUALITY AND INTEGRITY

The requirement of ensuring data quality and integrity has grown dramatically as businesses rely more and more on big data sets for innovation, regulatory compliance, decision-making, and other essential chores. Poor data management might result in inefficiencies, financial losses, and damage to the reputation of a business, even if data is used to promote strategic goals, simplify processes, and improve customer experiences. Although the phrases are frequently used synonymously, data integrity and quality represent different ideas with different technological needs. As said by Wang et al. (2024), data must be accurate, complete, consistent, dependable, current, authentic, and so valuable. Unlike Duggineni (2023), data integrity is focused on avoiding corruption, unauthorized alterations, and inadvertent loss, preserving data correctness and dependability throughout time. A coin's two sides are integrity and complementarity of data. Strong integrity policies are needed to prevent corruption, breaches, or unauthorized changes that can undermine data accuracy and consistency, preserving high-quality data. Whether the data is secure depends on faulty datasets resulting from uneven data governance policies or inadequate data entering methods. Companies that want to create dependable data ecosystems, use security-driven DevSecOps techniques and create strong data governance systems must have a strong knowledge of these two ideas.

Defining Data Quality

The degree to which businesses may use information is called "data quality." Excellent data allows companies to maintain operational efficiency, remain compliant with industry standards, and make wise judgments. Numerous variables characterize data utility and trustworthiness.

Accuracy: This assesses how faithfully real-world items and events are represented in the data. Smooth operations, accurate analysis, and wise judgments depend on consistent data. For example, erroneous ERP data might lead to misleading financial reporting and perhaps official fines. Data reliability depends on strong validation procedures and real-time error detection.

Completeness: This confirms that the required data elements are readily available. Missing or partial data might result in less-than-ideal company results and useless research. For instance, according to Rane et al. (2023), if the client profiles in a CRM system lack sufficient information, this can result in poor personalization and reduced customer satisfaction.

Consistency: This ensures the homogeneity of the data utilized in all systems and databases. Governance gaps or inadequate integration might causc data conflicts wherein many systems record the same information differently (Mahmudnia et al., 2022). For instance, logistical problems in order fulfillment might follow from one system failing to update a customer's address.

Reliability: This relates to the data's dependability and trustworthiness. Significant reasons for erroneous data are uneven data input techniques or system faults, which can undermine business intelligence reports and trust in predictive analytics models. Strong data governance ideas and automated integrity testing are essential for reliability.

Timeliness: This shows whether data is available when needed. Decisions in industries like banking and healthcare, where real-time data is vital, are especially susceptible to disruptions in data updates (Boppiniti, 2021). For a supply chain system, for example, outdated stock data might cause a shortage or excess goods.

Validity: This confirms that the data complies with particular standards. Invalid input, such as numerical values outside the allowed range or a wrong email format, might result in processing mistakes and security hazards (Saffady, 2020). Rule-based validation and automatic corrective processes help to reduce this risk.

Defining Data Integrity

Data integrity is the discipline of guaranteeing that data is unaffected, consistent, and accurate. Unlike data quality, which mainly emphasizes the value of data, data integrity protects data against corruption, illegal alterations, and unintended deletions. The two most common types are logical and physical data integrity, which handles various facets of data security (Mushtaq et al., 2022).

i. **Logical Integrity:** Logical integrity (Vagadia & Vagadia, 2020) verifies that every link and dependency between data in a system is legitimate and enforced. Rule-based structured data systems, such as relational databases, depend critically on consistent, dependable data.

Entity Integrity: Every entry inside the database will have some additional unique identification linked with a primary key. Maintaining entity integrity is essential to prevent duplicate or orphaned objects from generating data retrieval and reporting problems.

Referential Integrity: In this sense, one can be sure that the relationships among all the database tables will be maintained. Referential integrity guarantees that connections stay valid when a foreign key in one table refers to a primary key in another. Should a customer record be deleted without removing connected orders, orphaned order data in an e-commerce system might cause reporting problems.

Domain Integrity: This ensures rule compliance by limiting data type and value and verifying the inputs. Date-containing database columns should reject non-date values to stop erroneous data entry.

User-defined integrity: This guarantees data accuracy through tailored corporate policies. To eliminate erroneous financial computations, an economic system can, for instance, mandate that all transactions always have a positive amount.

ii. **Physical Integrity:**Vagadia and Vagadia (2020) claim that data must be physically protected to prevent unauthorized access, modification, and hacking.

Hardware and Software Failures: Data corruption caused by disc failure, machine malfunction, or software defect might result in permanent data loss. Using fault-tolerant storage systems and backup strategies might help reduce these risks.

Human Errors: Erroneous settings, altered data, or inadvertent removals are potential sources of data destruction. Role-based access controls (RBAC) and audit logs help avoid and track these mistakes.

Cybersecurity Threats: Insiders, ransomware, and data breaches can compromise data integrity. Real-time monitoring, access control techniques, and encryption help companies protect against deliberate manipulation.

Key Differences and Interdependencies Between Data Quality and Integrity

Data integrity and quality seem at first unrelated, yet they are very complimentary. Quality will always suffer from poor data integrity, so inefficient data quality control will make integrity measures useless. For example, duplicate or orphaned items might cause data completeness and correctness issues without referential integrity. On the other hand, while integrity standards are insufficient, data quality checks verifying correctness and consistency are essential to guarantee meaningful data. Among the newly developing technologies helping to close the integrity and quality gap are data governance systems, DevSecOps approaches, and blockchain-based immutable records (Chintale, 2023). Businesses must defend their data from corruption and unauthorized changes by integrating strong governance, automated validation, and security-driven DevSecOps pipelines.

Figure 1. Differences Between Data Integrity and Quality

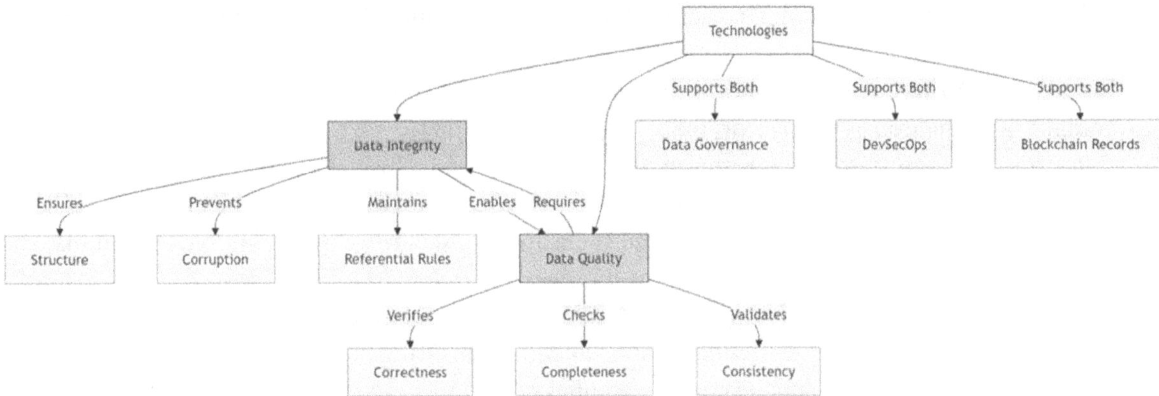

By maintaining accurate, complete, trustworthy, and safe data, businesses can create dependable data ecosystems that support decision-making, regulatory compliance, and resilience in a digital world.

DATA GOVERNANCE FRAMEWORKS AND THEIR ROLE IN ENSURING DATA QUALITY

Data is vital for today's digital economy companies to remain legally compliant, improve user experiences, and lead strategic decisions. Still, data value depends on security, dependability, and quality of data. Organizations must utilize a methodical approach to data management to stop mistakes in data, inconsistencies, and security flaws resulting in financial and reputation losses. In this sense, data governance structures are critical. Data governance, which defines roles, norms, standards, and duties within an organization or other body, ensures good data management. Janssen et al. (2020) put forth requirements for data ownership, responsibility, and quality management in addition to guarantees of compliance with legal and industry standards. DevSecOps guarantees that security is a part of development and operational operations via effective data governance, improving data quality. Strong data governance systems help with compliance, wise decisions based on reliable data, and prevention of security breaches.

Principles of Data Governance

The cornerstone of data governance is providing reliable, safe, and valuable company data. These recommendations could help companies define their responsibilities, improve governance systems, and guarantee compliance.

1. **Ownership and Accountability:** Data governance offers clear roles and responsibilities regarding data management. Many companies have their chief data officer or governance council, ensuring every department follows the same data management policies. Those in charge of keeping accurate records, such as data stewards, also have an inherent stake in the result.

2. **Consistency and Standardization:** By defining shared data definitions, structures, and formats, companies may maintain consistent systems. Hosen et al. (2024) discovered that standardizing analytics and reporting helps remove discrepancies, enabling companies to depend on one trustworthy source.
3. **Regulatory Adherence and Compliance:** Companies must ensure that their governance policies comply with the ever-growing corpus of data protection laws, such as GDPR, HIPAA, and ISO standards. Ignoring rules might result in heavy penalties and a loss of customer confidence.
4. **Data Privacy and Security:** Effective governance is based on eradicating unethical practices, illegal access, and data breaches. Organizations must ensure data security via encryption, audit trails, and role-based access limits (RBAC).
5. **Data Integrity and Quality:**Hassani and MacFeely (2023) claim that governance systems provide guidelines for data cleaning, enrichment, and validation, ensuring data accuracy, completeness, and consistency. Recording techniques and referential constraints are data integrity solutions used to block unwanted modifications.

According to Hassani and MacFeely (2023), governance systems offer directions for data cleansing, enrichment, and validation, guaranteeing data correctness, completeness, and consistency. Recording methods and referential restrictions are data integrity solutions that support blocking undesirable updates.

Frameworks and Standards in Data Governance

Several data governance methods and guidelines enable businesses to manage their data effectively. These models can be applied to fit the specific requirements of an industry to a company's governance rules.

DAMA-DMBOK (DATA MANAGEMENT BODY OF KNOWLEDGE)

The Data Management Association (DAMA) created DMBOK as a complete source of data management best practices. It covers numerous government domains, including data security, metadata management, and architecture (DAMA International, 2017). Companies usually contact DMBOK when they need to develop governance policies or implement data stewardship guidelines.

Control Objectives for Information and Related Technologies (COBIT): Created by the Information Systems Audit and Control Association (ISACA) with an eye on IT control, compliance, and risk management, Bagja et al. (2024) believe COBIT offers a methodical approach to data security, business continuity, and regulatory compliance. According to COBIT, data governance could support business objectives by combining IT operations with those targets.

Data Quality Standard (ISO 8000): Globally, ISO 8000 ensures data reliability and correctness. The criteria for accurate, complete, and consistent data are discussed together with recommended practices for data validation and interoperability (Zhang et al., 2021). By improving data accuracy and streamlining compliance processes, ISO 8000 might primarily benefit businesses.

General Data Protection Regulation (GDPR): The General Data Protection Regulation (GDPR) imposes strict guidelines on privacy, consent management, and security in Europe (Bakare et al., 2024). Data subjects' rights, breach notification obligations, and impact assessments are among the aspects of government this enforces. Ignoring GDPR when handling consumer data might lead to fines and damage to a company's reputation.

Health Insurance Portability and Accountability Act (HIPAA): American legislators enacted HIPAA to safeguard individuals' medical record-related right to privacy. Healthcare companies must set policies for audit logging, data security, and access control (Choice & Williams, 2022). Following HIPAA rules helps ensure that patient information is safe and secure, therefore helping to reduce data breaches.

Figure 2. Data Governance Frameworks and Standards

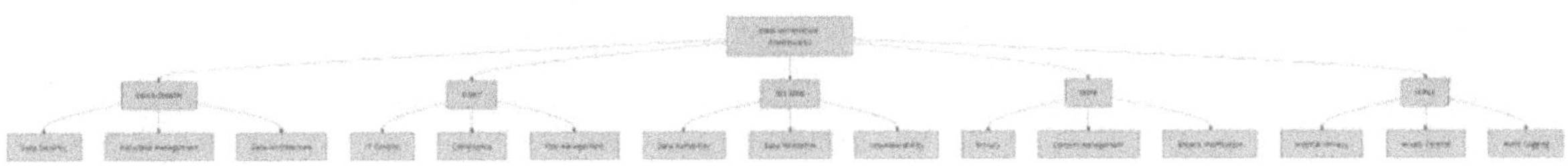

These rules can help companies develop effective governance structures, enhancing data security, compliance, and quality in many sectors.

Data Stewardship and Best Practices for Data Management

Data stewardship, which ensures that data is accurate and up to code, is among the most crucial components of government. Working with governance teams, data stewards guarantee correct data cleansing, validation, and monitoring.

Dealing with data requires one to keep in mind:

Defining Data Ownership: Data stewardship and departmental duties will be precisely defined.

Data Quality Monitoring: Automated data profiling and data validation help one to find inconsistencies.

Metadata Management: Guaranturing data provenance and traceability with methodical metadata organization.

Data Access Control: Tightly implementing least privilege access policies will assist in lowering any security leaks.

Regular Audits and Reviews: By way of their results, regular governance studies help to ensure regulatory compliance.

Applying these best practices helps businesses to reduce operating hazards while maintaining accurate data and regulatory compliance.

How Data Governance Supports DevSecOps

Thus, with DevSecOps methods, data governance is crucial for the security and quality assurance of the software development life cycle (SDLC). By adding security measures into development operations, Leshchenko et al. (2024) say DevSecOps focuses on protecting production systems against vulnerabilities.

Governance-driven DevSecOps guarantees:

1. **Automated Check on Data Quality**: Policies driving continuous supply pipelines and ongoing integration must incorporate automated validation and anomaly detection.
2. **Safe Methodologies for Data Management**: Developers encrypt data and regulate access using security systems established by the government.
3. **Pipelines for Regulatory Compliance in DevOps**: DevSecOps cannot obey GDPR, HIPAA, and ISO8000 rules without governance systems.
4. **Incident Response and Documentation**: DevSecOps is designed to manage two things in line with governance standards: audits and forensic data change monitoring.

Data governance ideas included in DevSecOps might help businesses prevent security breaches, leaks, and regulatory violations. This helps them maintain outstanding data quality throughout the program's implementation.

This section explains why contemporary businesses if they are to ensure compliance, security, and data quality, require data governance solutions. Companies using standardized governance models like DAMA-DMBOK, COBIT, ISO8000, GDPR, and HIPAA should effectively manage data ownership, validity, and security demands. Moreover, as it integrates security and quality assurance into software development, DevSecOps depends much on governance. Strong data ecosystems produced by data stewardship, automated validation, and rules-driven by compliance assist businesses in removing security concerns and enhancing decision-making. As cloud computing and quick digital transformation develop, data governance becomes crucial to protect software environments from security concerns, maintain data integrity, and ensure quality.

THE ROLE OF DevSecOps IN DATA INTEGRITY AND SECURITY

Data security and integrity become vital as more businesses use cloud computing, big data analytics, and AI-guided decision-making. Data breaches, corruption, and unauthorized access were widespread as security was sometimes given second attention in past software development methods. DevSecOps (Development, Security, and Operations) is the foundation of modern software systems to ensure data integrity and security. DevSecOps depends on automation and continuous data protection, compliance, and integrity procedures (Sandu, 2021) by including security ideas into the development lifeline. Ahmad et al. (2022) claim that current data governance systems embed security regulations into development processes to lower security risks and human mistakes, which is why this approach fits these models. DevSecOps helps companies keep safe, high-quality, and tamper-resistant data environments through automation, anomaly detection driven by artificial intelligence, and constant validation processes.

Overview of DevSecOps in Modern Software Development

Aimed initially at automating development and operational procedures to speed up software delivery, DevOps is a subset of DevSecOps. Companies faced growing cybersecurity risks and regulatory issues, so incorporating security into DevOps processes became necessary. DevOps is expanding and includes security controls, risk assessments, and compliance checks in software development pipelines (Sandu, 2021). "Shift-Left Security," a feature of DevSecOps, integrates data integrity and security measures into software development early in the software development life cycle (SDLC). Fixing vulnerabilities was expensive and labor-intensive due to the late timing of security checks. From strategy to design, coding, testing, and deployment, every phase of the DevSecOps lifecycle incorporates security.

A key component of DevSecOps is automating security and data integrity tests, running constantly and free from human involvement. Tools ranging from automated compliance testing, static code analysis, vulnerability scanners, and artificial intelligence-driven threat identification make rapid risk assessment and remedial action possible. DevSecOps guarantees data integrity by using security-by-design ideas throughout the program's lifetime.

Integrating Data Quality Measures in DevSecOps Pipelines

The ability of DevSecOps to automate and enforce data quality criteria through development is one of its primary advantages. CI/CD pipelines may be configured to continually monitor and validate data to guarantee it is correct, consistent, and intact using DevSecOps.

CI/CD PIPELINES AND AUTOMATED DATA VALIDATION

CI/CD pipelines are the foundation of present DevOps systems. Automating daily tasks, including building, testing, and deployment, speeds up the software development process and lowers the possibility of human error. These methods allow CI/CD systems to include data quality measures:

- **Automated Data Validation Tests:** Thanks to these, all databases and apps will constantly use correct, current data.
- **Schema Enforcement Tools:** Strict data structure standards help us stop processing inconsistent or troublesome data.
- **Data Lineage Tracking:** Recording changes to datasets at every stage guarantees their auditable and tracking back capability.

Data quality checking into CI/CD can help businesses safeguard manufacturing systems against data corruption, unauthorized alterations, and regulatory breaches.

AI-Driven Anomaly Detection and Integrity Checks

Modern DevSecOps tools improve data integrity monitoring by leveraging artificial intelligence and machine learning models. AI-powered systematic anomaly detection allows one to do the following:

Point out unusual trends in data that could point to security lapses, illegal modifications, or corruption.
Foretell any risks to data integrity using past trends and patterns.
Automatically apply checks and balances, including the capacity to rectify erroneous data or stop illegal activity (Chen et al., 2020).

DevSecOps solutions driven by artificial intelligence help financial institutions rapidly identify fraudulent transactions and fight money laundering (Zhang & Chen, 2024). Using artificial intelligence to enforce data integrity aggressively helps companies prevent risks from escalating.

Threats to Data Integrity and DevSecOps Strategies for Mitigation

Whether DevSecOps has advanced or not, insider threats, ransomware, misconfigurations, and outside vulnerabilities can still jeopardize corporate data. These threats compromise data security, authenticity, and trustworthiness, affecting financial losses and official fines.

1. **Insider Threats:** Any employee, contractor, or business partner with access to systems essential for the organization's functioning is called "insider danger." Data integrity issues may surface whether workers intentionally or accidentally modify or remove data.

Mitigation Strategy:

Apply Zero Trust Architecture grounded on least privilege access control (Rose et al., 2020).
Using behavioral analytics might help find suspicious user behaviors.
Add multi-factor authentication (MFA) and employ user roles-dependent access constraints.

2. **Ransomware Attacks**: Ransomware encrypts important files; until a ransom is paid, their decryption cannot occur. Attackers frequently target backup systems to impede recovery.

Mitigation Strategy:

Make sure backups are immutable, as ransomware cannot change them.
Use AI-driven threat detection to find early-stage ransomware outbreaks.
Install endpoint detection and response (EDR) technologies to stifle harmful activity.

3. **Misconfigurations:** Inappropriate settings might compromise data security or expose private information in a database or cloud environment.

Mitigation Strategy:

- Infrastructure as code (IaC) solutions provide automated configurable security enforcement.
- Use security compliance models to drive frequent configuration audits.

4. **Third-Party Risks**: Companies use outside vendors for APIs, cloud storage, and other external services. Third-party integrations' inadequate security mechanisms might threaten data integrity.

Mitigation Strategy:

- Review any contracts and security audits generated by outside third parties to be sure they adhere to guidelines.
- Put up safe API gates with degrees of data validation.

Figure 3. Data Integrity Threats and DevSecOps Mitigations

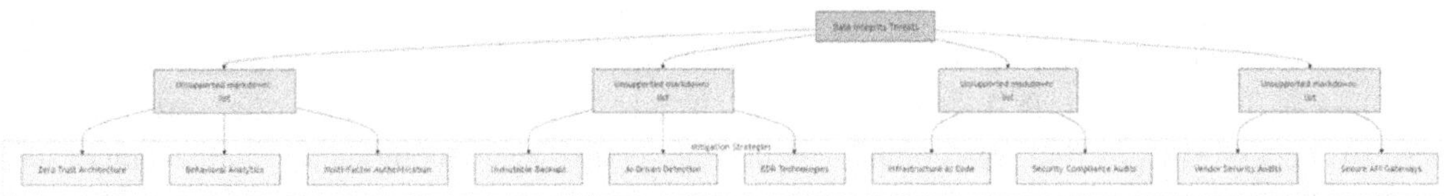

Using mitigation techniques from DevSecOps will enable businesses to safeguard compliance, data integrity, and availability in challenging digital contexts.

Case Studies of DevSecOps Enhancing Data Integrity

Case Study 1: Financial Industry – Real-Time Fraud Prevention and Compliance

The frequency of fraudulent transactions and data anomalies in real-time financial operations increasingly jeopardized an important investment bank. The bank answered by strengthening its continuous integration and delivery pipelines under DevSecOps-led automated fraud protection and anomaly detection. Artificial intelligence systems examined past transaction records and identified suspicious trends meant to halt fraudulent behavior. Using AI-driven threat intelligence and real-time data validation, the bank guaranteed compliance with AML criteria and cut illicit transactions by 70%. By raising consumer confidence and regulatory transparency, the deployment established that DevSecOps successfully controlled the integrity of financial data.

Case Study 2: Healthcare – Protecting Patient Data and HIPAA Compliance

For a prominent healthcare provider, verifying the adherence to the security, compliance, and HIPAA rules among millions of electronic health data was challenging. The supplier automated integrity monitoring, RBAC, and encryption by including DevSecOps security measures in their software development cycle. One of the extra security steps used to prevent illegal users from deleting or changing patient medical information is immutable audit recording. Protecting patient privacy and stopping data tampering helps to lower the possibility of compliance violations. With this solution, DevSecOps proved its capacity to protect compliance-driven companies' most sensitive healthcare data.

Case Study 3: Cloud Computing – Securing Multi-Tenant Environments

Privacy, integrity, and data authenticity are issues for a cloud service, keeping data for several tenants. Automating DevSecOps makes continuous security monitoring, risk assessments powered by artificial intelligence, and data validation via microservices possible. Zero-trust authentication and policy-based access limits let the vendor guarantee data segregation, security, and compliance for every tenant and lower the risk of data leakage. Consumers trusted the security of the cloud more. Hence, the likelihood of data leaks affecting numerous renters simultaneously was lowered.

By adding rules to guarantee data integrity and security in product life, DevSecOps has transformed software development. Automated validation systems, artificial intelligence anomaly detection, and continuous integration/delivery pipelines let companies actively control risks and maintain data quality on scale. Verifiable data from the banking, cloud, and healthcare sectors supports the theory that DevSecOps can successfully guard private company data, stop regulatory noncompliance, and terminate data breaches. Companies experiencing digital transformation must ensure the trustworthiness, dependability, and security of contemporary software systems using the data integrity approaches made possible by DevSecOps.

ADVANCEMENTS IN MODERN SOFTWARE FOR DATA QUALITY AND INTEGRITY

Software technology development has significantly changed how businesses guarantee the dependability and quality of their data. Modern companies rely on intelligent systems to control the growing diversity, velocity, volume, and accuracy of data in distant environments. Technologies, including artificial intelligence, machine learning, blockchain, data operations, automation, cloud, and edge computing, are driving progress in these fields. These technologies improve data validation, anomaly detection, lineage tracking, and security; data governance, compliance, and cybersecurity also benefit.

AI and Machine Learning for Data Quality Assurance

Intelligent automation made possible by artificial intelligence and machine learning has transformed data profiling, cleaning, and validation (Vijayalakshmi & Jayasudha, 2024). Typical rule-based data cleansing techniques generally fail to be applied to enterprise-scale systems as they depend on human interaction. Conversely, artificial intelligence (AI) systems rapidly find and fix discrepancies using pattern recognition and anomaly detection. Predictive modeling is one of the main applications of ML in data quality assurance, as it forecasts likely data anomalies before they influence business operations (2024). ML systems may, for example, examine previous data patterns to forecast future deviations and offer pre-made fixes. Natural Language Processing (NLP) makes systematic extraction, classification, and assessment of unstructured text data across many datasets feasible using various sources, considerably enhancing data quality. Besides lowering duplication and redundancy and enhancing accuracy, data reconciliation systems driven by artificial intelligence search data from several sources to identify differences. AI-driven data cleaning solutions included in DevSecOps pipelines help companies guarantee data quality and validation throughout the software development lifecycle.

AI-driven data quality assurance has certain shortcomings, even if it offers many benefits. One such weakness is the need to continually maximize and track models since training data bias is needed (Ejjami & Boussalham, 2024). Not every business can also afford the vast computing capability needed by artificial intelligence systems. This is especially true for businesses struggling with limits in their old infrastructure.

Blockchain for Data Integrity and Traceability

Modern businesses depend critically on blockchain technology to guarantee data veracity, immutability, and traceability. Operating on a decentralized ledger system, blockchain makes data unchangeable and verifiable throughout scattered networks. This is not the case in conventional databases based on centralized control. Digital signatures and cryptographic data hashings (Habib et al., 2022) are the essential traits of blockchain technology that provide data tamper-proofness. Every data transaction forms the unchangeable chain by being recorded as a cryptographically linked block to the next block. Data fraud and unapproved access are less likely, as once captured, data cannot be changed or removed without network authorization. Blockchain technology is invaluable in sectors like healthcare, supply chain management, and finance, according to Dutta et al. (2020) and Hastig and Sodhi (2020). These sectors need a high degree of data integrity and traceability. Thanks to blockchain technology's permanent, verifiable transaction records, the banking sector could at last bid farewell to human error and fraud. Healthcare companies may guarantee GDPR and HIPAA compliance using blockchain technology, safely distributing patient data to authorized parties.

However, blockchain technology raises questions regarding scalability and energy use. Traditional blockchain networks, like Ethereum and Bitcoin, are known to be resource-intensive (Auhl et al., 2022) as the processing capability required for consensus techniques, including Proof of Work (PoW), is what defines them. Companies looking for energy-efficient solutions to these problems are turning to hybrid blockchain technology and Proof of Stake (PoS). Using these techniques, scalability is improved without compromising security.

DataOps and the Role of Automation

DevSecOps offers ongoing data quality, security, and compliance by cooperatively integrating DevSecOps concepts with data governance and automation. This process aims to increase data flow throughout a company. Data pipeline automation, monitoring, and real-time quality control all fit here. As Munappy (2021) rightly notes, continuous data validation is a fundamental component of DataOps. Automated testing systems help to avoid data corruption; schema drifts, and inconsistencies that affect business operations. DataOps employs version control systems to monitor, evaluate, and allow dataset updates before publication, lowering the likelihood of unauthorized changes or data breaches. Manchana (2024) claims that automated DataOps processes improve data lineage monitoring, which might enable companies to maintain track of data transitions, dependencies, and system migration between systems. This is vital for compliance efforts as authorities need companies to be transparent and responsible with the data they acquire and apply. Financial firms might provide real-time compliance reports by automating data operations, enabling them to remain compliant with industry standards such as Basel III and GDPR.

Figure 4. DataOps and Automation Flow

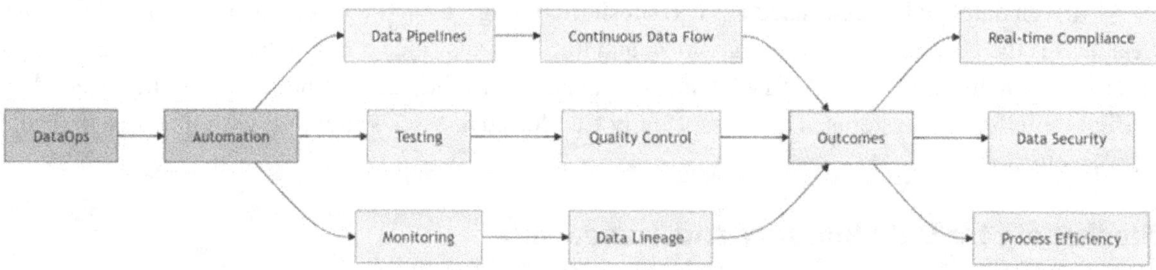

Adopting DataOps requires a significant mental and cultural change to embrace data-centric DevSecOps integration, which, despite its benefits, requires a comprehensive organizational transformation. Companies must address issues with the interoperability between old and new technologies to guarantee flawless data flow and automation even more.

Cloud and Edge Computing Challenges for Data Quality

The decentralized character of data storage and processing brought about by the development of cloud and edge computing has made data quality and integrity maintenance increasingly difficult. Real-time data governance is vital in cloud systems with enormous data volumes to avoid data corruption, inconsistencies, and unauthorized access. Data fragmentation, which results from businesses storing data on numerous sites, formats, and cloud providers, is a significant problem with cloud computing (Katari & Ankam, 2022). Data duplication, disparities, and silos resulting from this disconnected system might impede regulatory compliance and decision-making by itself. Using native cloud-based data quality systems will help companies overcome these obstacles. These systems use schema enforcement, automatic data synchronization, and cross-cloud integrity checks.

Edge computing is the close-to-source data processing comprising IoT devices and sensors. This method introduces even more complexity to data integrity issues brought on by device constraints, network interruptions, and latency. Kong (2022) estimated that edge devices distributed and heterogeneous systems are more likely to cause data loss, duplication, and unauthorized alterations than centralized cloud deployments. Artificial intelligence-powered edge analytics might evaluate data quality before cloud migration, addressing specific problems. Maintaining data integrity in scenarios combining numerous clouds and edge computing depends on cloud security driven by DevSecOps. Automated access control, encryption, continuous compliance monitoring, and against unauthorized access and breaches help businesses protect sensitive data maintained on various platforms.

Figure 5. Cloud and Edge Computing Data Challenges

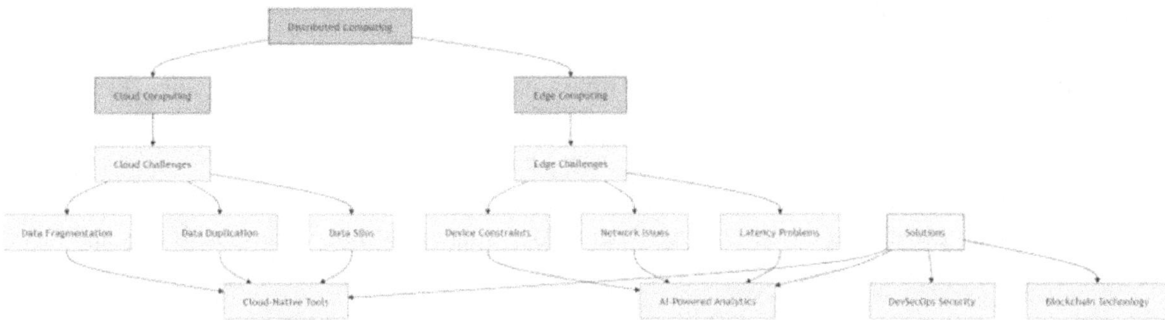

Modern businesses must employ innovations in data operations (DataOps), cloud computing, data quality and integrity, artificial intelligence (AI), and blockchain technology to keep up with this part's constantly changing digital environment. Artificial intelligence-driven data profiling and anomaly detection increase real-time validation; blockchain technology assures the immutability and traceability of transactional data. Although cloud-native security solutions lower risks, DataOps supports compliance and continuous automation in distributed computing environments. Some problems, including cloud and edge computing security, data operations interoperability, blockchain scalability, and AI model bias, may be solved using DevSecOps and legal compliance. Data security and integrity are of enormous value for many companies in this digital transformation era, even when current software ecosystems aim to allow operational success and innovation.

CHALLENGES AND RISKS IN ENSURING DATA QUALITY AND INTEGRITY

Modern companies' lifeblood is data, which lets them stay competitive, improve consumer experiences, and drive decisions. The many operational, security-related, and technological factors surrounding data quality and integrity provide ongoing difficulty. Among the main difficulties are human mistakes, poor government, cybersecurity issues, data fragmentation and silos, and complicated rules on regulatory compliance. Dealing with these risks and guaranteeing consistent data security, dependability, and correctness calls for integration of data governance, DevSecOps guidelines, and technology developments. This will decrease vulnerabilities.

Data Silos and Fragmentation

Data silos (internal data repositories unconnected, inconsistent, or inaccessible) represent a significant threat to data integrity and quality (Tadi, 2020). Data duplication and discrepancies emerge when businesses grow from many departments using multiple systems and platforms to handle their data. A global company's storage of consumer, financial, and operational data across several cloud providers and on-site databases constitutes a fragmented data environment. Insufficient definition of data synchronization and interchange compromises data dependability and usefulness. There are differences. When companies combine, it gets much more complex since they occasionally have to include antiquated systems with various architecture and formats.

Some consequences of data silos are as follows:

Inconsistent decision-making: Different divisions use contradictory data, making it difficult for corporate leaders to make wise judgments.

Poor data governance: Information not shared across several systems becomes challenging to guarantee it is secure, compliant, and satisfies quality standards.

Increased operational costs: Duplicate data processing and storage delays activities and raises the cost of IT infrastructure.

Figure 6. Data Silos and Their Impact

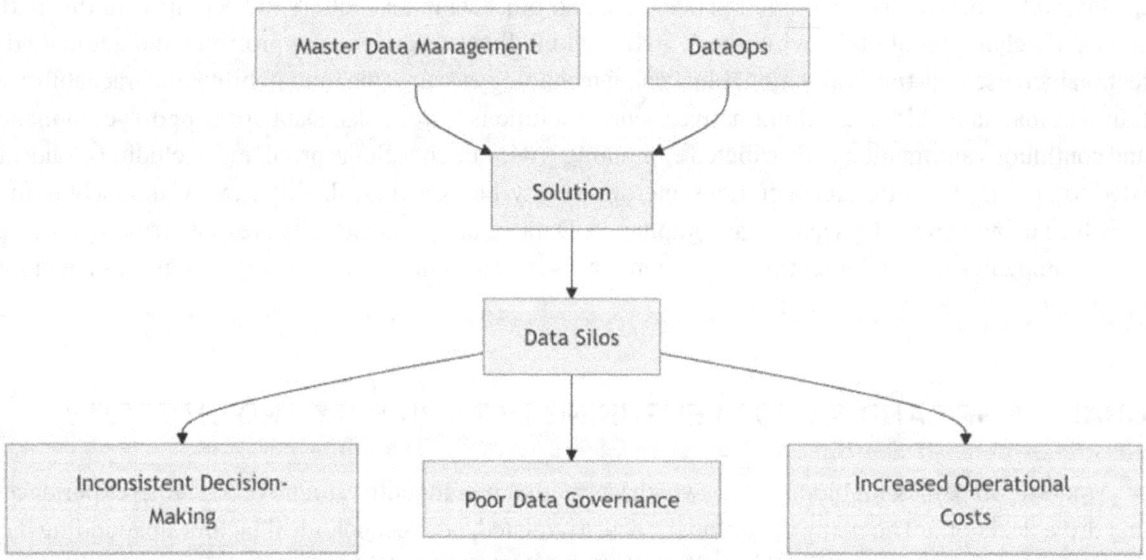

By aggregating and standardizing their most important data assets, Master Data Management (MDM) technologies help companies minimize data silos. DataOps approaches provide continuous data integration, validation, and governance to help further ensure that data is consistent and available for all business functions.

Human Errors and Governance Gaps

Human error is a leading cause of data quality problems in companies that depend on hand-entry data, have unclear policies and lack sufficient documentation. Human error in data collecting, processing, and administration implies that incomplete, false, or misleading data still exists even with artificial intelligence-driven validation and automation.

Common human mistakes endangering data integrity consist of the following:

- **Inaccurate data entry:** Lack of appropriate training, supervision, or system complexity could cause employees to enter incorrect data.
- **Failure to follow governance policies:** Unauthorised changes and damaged data result from conflicting data validation, documentation, and version control standards.
- **Mismanagement of data access:** Compliance and security are compromised when insufficient protections exist to stop unauthorized people from accessing private data.

Organizations have governance gaps due to the lack of well-defined policies, responsibility systems, and enforcement tools to guarantee data accuracy. Companies employ data governance systems such as DAMA-DMBOK and COBIT extensively, although effective standard implementation and compliance monitoring is not always guaranteed (Wibisono et al., 2021). Without data stewards and governance teams, companies fight with data consistency, responsibility, and traceability.

Companies should build thorough data governance systems, including these components, in order to handle these problems:

- **Role-based access controls (RBAC):** Limiting data modification rights to authorized staff helps stop deliberate or inadvertent changes.
- **Automated data validation and audit trails:** Monitoring all data changes could help to establish accountability and traceability in case of a mistake.
- **Ongoing employee training:** Staff involvement in regular training courses clarifies data governance best practices and lowers the possibility of human error.

Figure 7. Human Errors and Governance Solutions

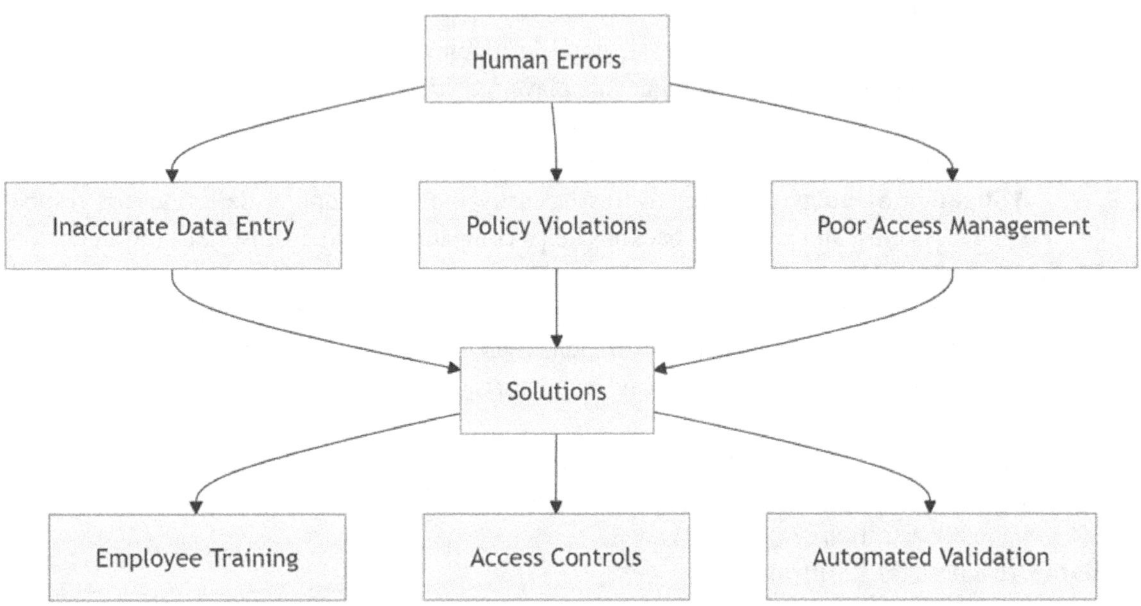

Cybersecurity Threats Impacting Data Integrity

Cyberattacks represent one of the main hazards to protecting company data in the contemporary corporate environment. External assaults, malicious insider activity, ransomware, and poor configuration may all severely compromise business data availability, reliability, and correctness.

The following are major cyber threats possibly compromising data dependability:

Figure 8. Cybersecurity Threats and Mitigations

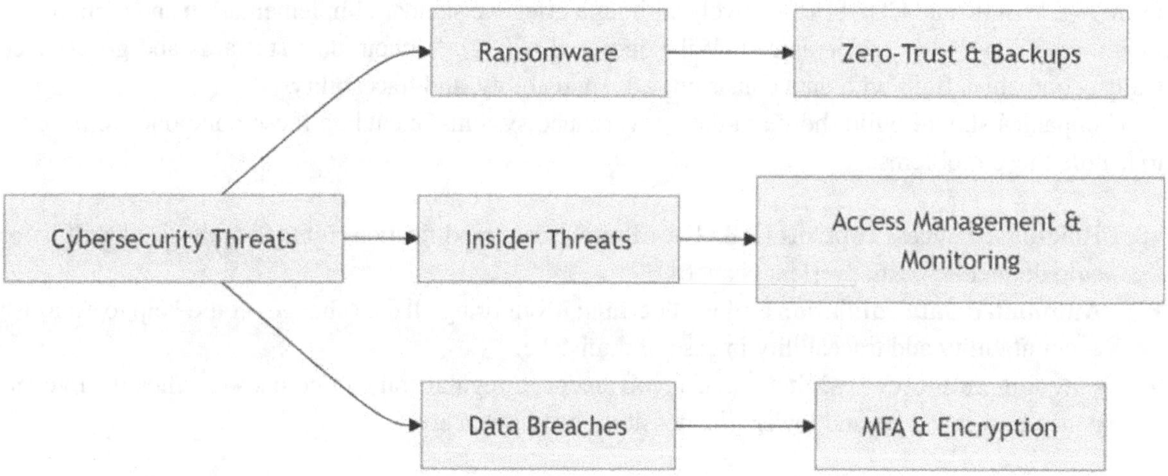

1. **Ransomware Attacks**
    - o Ransomware can encrypt business data; decryption will cost money. Recovering encrypted data might prove difficult should hostile players corrupt or change them.
    - o Ransomware attacks have compromised hospital information, government systems, and financial transactions. Hence, these industries are easy targets.
    - o **Mitigation Strategy:** Using zero-trust security models, endpoint detection and response (EDR) systems, and perpetual backups helps companies guard against ransomware threats.
2. **Malicious Insider Threats**
    - o Those with more wide access permissions run the risk of either purposefully or unintentionally altering or deleting vital information. Banking and vital infrastructure businesses are particularly susceptible to fraud and regulatory violations resulting from apparently little modifications.
    - o **Mitigation Strategy:** Malicious activities may be stopped by combining real-time behavioral monitoring, privileged access management (PAM), and artificial intelligence-powered anomaly detection.
3. **Data Breaches and Exfiltration**
    - o By taking advantage of weaknesses in cloud storage, APIs, and outside connectors, cybercriminals can steal or alter business data.

- o **Mitigation Strategy:** Using multi-factor authentication (MFA), API security standards, and end-to-end encryption can help companies improve their security protocols.

Regulatory and Compliance Complexity

Expanding their activities abroad regarding security, privacy, and accuracy of consumer data forces businesses to negotiate a complex web of laws. Strong governance policies inside companies help businesses avoid legal consequences resulting from strict data protection obligations imposed by laws such as GDPR (European Union), CCPA (California), HIPAA (United States), and India's Data Protection Bill.

Significant obstacles to compliance include:

- **Cross-border data transfers:** Data localization rules indicate that some kinds of data (including financial records or medical information) cannot leave particular locations. Companies must be careful when following these limits.
- **Industry-specific mandates**: Data governance policies that are globally applicable would not help sectors like healthcare, banking, and telecommunications, which are subject to numerous levels of control.
- **Real-time compliance reporting**: The demand of regulators for constant audits, breach reports, and openness forces companies to track and reveal all data operations in real time (Varshney & Singh, 2021).

Figure 9. Regulatory Compliance Challenges and Solutions

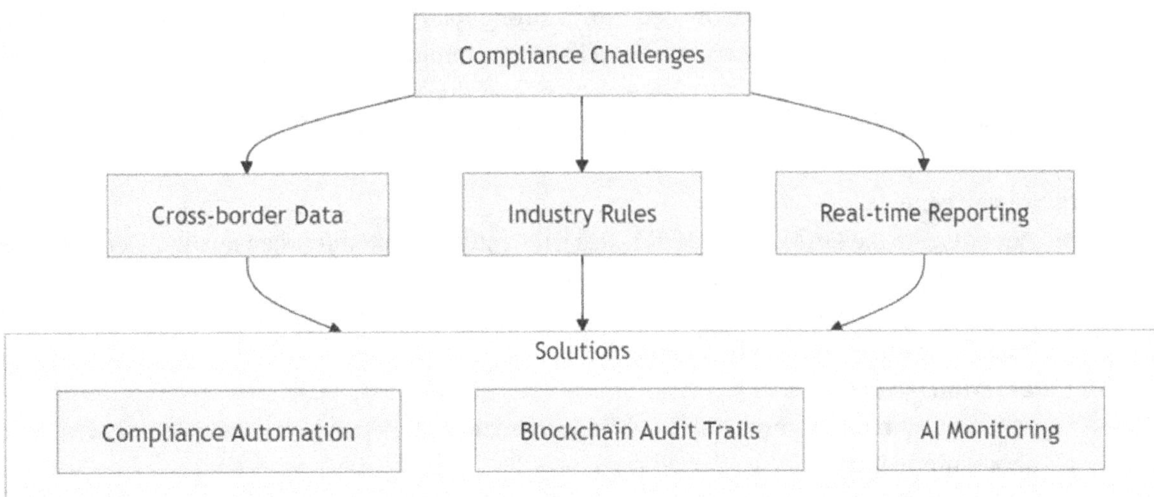

To handle these issues and guarantee that data governance rules match legal frameworks, companies are including compliance automation solutions in their DevSecOps systems. Blockchain audit trails and AI-powered compliance monitoring, as well as each other, improve data traceability, responsibility, and regulatory adherence.

As this section has shown, the difficult task of guaranteeing the quality and integrity of data in contemporary businesses consists of various moving elements. This group includes personal hazards and those presented by laws, security, and technology development. Cybersecurity suffers; human mistake threatens data dependability; governance gaps compromise data security; strict regulations compromise compliance; and data silos limit integration and consistency. Strong DevSecOps practices, automated validation systems, and robust data governance mechanisms can help businesses reduce their vulnerability to these risks. Among the numerous approaches businesses might use to raise their capacity for maintaining their data ecosystem are artificial intelligence anomaly detection, blockchain traceability, zero-trust security, and regulatory compliance automation. Companies that genuinely want to protect data integrity in the digital era have to give security-centric development, proactive governance, and continuous compliance monitoring first importance. The increasing data complexity is causing this.

BEST PRACTICES AND STRATEGIES FOR ENSURING DATA QUALITY AND INTEGRITY

Modern companies cannot afford to sacrifice operational performance, security, compliance, or decision-making, as data assurance affects all these aspects. Bad data quality might lead to erroneous evaluations, lost reputations, fines for laws, and financial losses. Companies who wish to surpass these obstacles must have inventive technologies, data-conscious cultures, security-oriented DevOps techniques, and strong governance mechanisms.

Practical Implementation of Strong Data Governance Models

Maintaining data integrity and quality requires a strong data governance architecture. "Data governance" refers to the policies, practices, tools, and systems implemented to ensure data dependability and security.

Key Components of a Strong Data Governance Model

1. **Data Stewardship**
    - o According to the DAMA-DMBOK (2023), data stewards monitor data quality, fix discrepancies, and ensure every department follows governance values.
    - o They work with compliance officials, IT departments, and business executives to align data practices with corporate goals and policies.
2. **Metadata Management**
    - o Data validation, categorization, and lineage tracing all depend on metadata - that is, data about information.
    - o Good metadata management helps identify, standardize, and contextualize data appropriately, lowering system discrepancies (Patel et al., 2023).
3. **Data Lineage Tracking**
    - o Data lineage enables one to track the development of data and notice its interactions with other systems.
    - o Improved data traceability helps auditing, validation, and anomaly identification to be more straightforward (Erl et al., 2022).

Figure 10. Data Governance Model Components

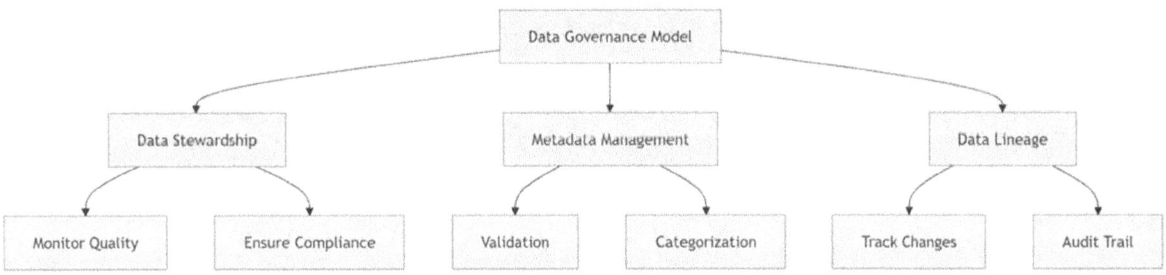

A data governance plan must contain specific elements to ensure the ongoing integrity of data: automatic monitoring of compliance, access restrictions depending on responsibility, and real-time validation processes.

Leveraging DevSecOps for Secure Data Pipelines

Data management systems integrating Development, Security, and Operations into their operations improve security, data integrity, and quality control. These systems, including DevSecOps, provide security and compliance throughout the data lifetime, from collecting to processing and storage.

Core Strategies in DevSecOps for Data Quality and Integrity

1. **Continuous Monitoring and Validation**
    - o Real-time automated monitoring systems can track data anomalies, disparities, and illegal modifications.
    - o AI powered data validation engines may automatically find mistakes and make repairs, according to Quazi et al. (2022), producing more accurate data.
2. **Real-time Logging and Auditing**
    - o Unchanged audit logs allow one to track and confirm all data transactions and changes.
    - o To prevent these problems from worsening, logs of data breaches, attempts at unauthorized access, and compliance violations must be maintained.
3. **Infrastructure as Code (IaC) for Secure Data Pipelines**
    - o In many settings, IaC streamlines building a reliable, consistent, safe data infrastructure (Aziz et al., 2023).
    - o Agrawal (2024) claims that security settings and lowering the danger of human mistakes guarantee compliance with industry standards.

Figure 11. DevSecOps Strategies for Data Quality

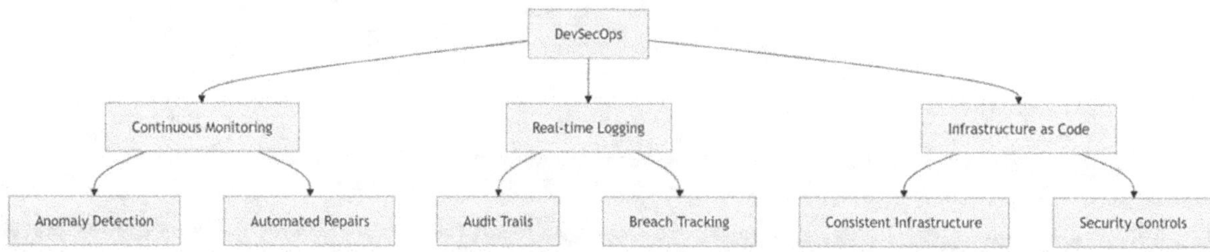

By incorporating DevSecOps ideas into data governance, companies may achieve proactive security, perform real-time data assessments, and create strong data pipelines. As a result, data assets are more secure, and people have more trust in them.

Adopting Emerging Technologies

New approaches to improving data security, dependability, and quality transform data management. Developments in artificial intelligence (AI), blockchain technology, and automated anomaly detection enable these approaches.

1. Artificial Intelligence (AI) and Machine Learning for Data Quality

   AI-powered data cleansing and matching finds inconsistent, absent, or repeated data.

   Machine learning techniques uncover data anomalies, helping lower the likelihood of making flawed conclusions.

   Artificial intelligence guarantees that material is current and thorough via automatic data enrichment (Özcan et al., 2021).
2. Blockchain for Data Integrity and Traceability

   Blockchain technology allows data not to be changed or deleted without permission to be done so.

   Safe data transfers and audit tracks made possible by its distributed and unchangeable ledger allow for

   A few of the sectors fast embracing blockchain technology for its open and verifiable data integrity include fintech, healthcare, and supply chain management.
3. Predictive Analytics and Automated Anomaly Detection

   Using artificial intelligence algorithms and past data trends, predictive analytics projects possible hazards to data quality.

   Real-time data pipeline monitoring by automatic anomaly detection systems immediately starts remedial action should a problem be found.

Figure 12. Emerging Technologies in Data Management

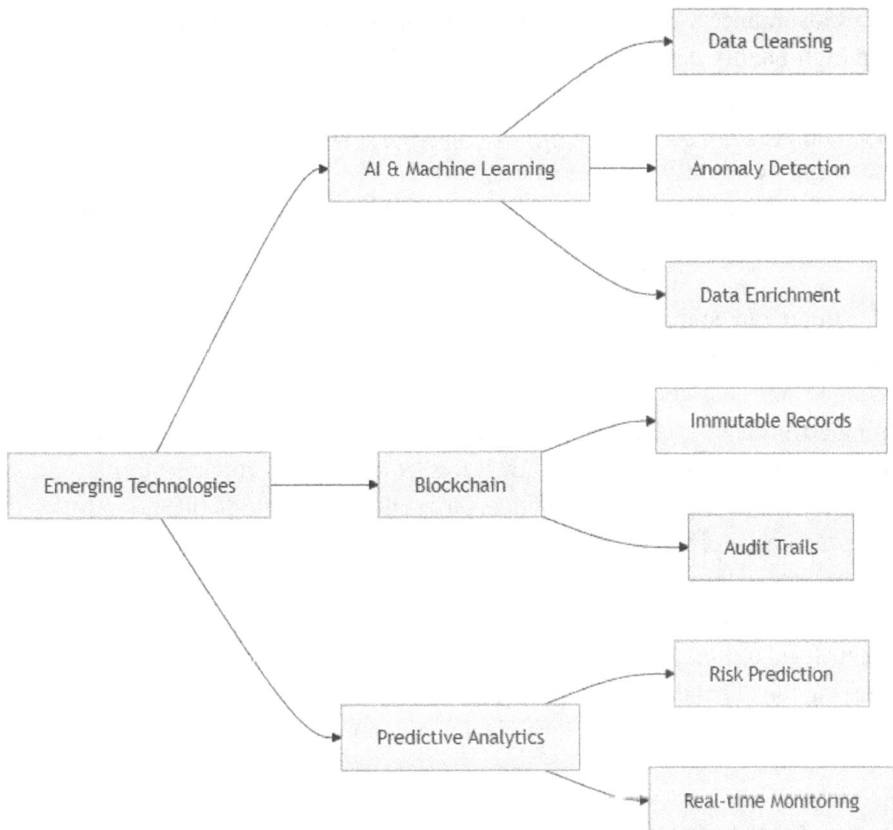

These new technologies enable self-healing data ecosystems, significantly improving data security and quality while lowering the need for human interaction. Therefore, they help meet businesses' always-shifting needs.

Organizational Culture and Data Quality Awareness

In the long run, neither technology nor governance systems will be sufficient to guarantee data quality. Raising responsibility, knowledge, and best practices requires an organizational-wide concentration on data-driven decision-making.

Key Strategies for Fostering a Data-Driven Culture

1. **Employee Training and Awareness Programs**
   - A company's training program should address best practices, cybersecurity issues, and data governance concepts.
   - Great ways to improve data handling abilities are by working on simulated phishing attacks, real-life case studies, and data validation drills.
2. **Executive Leadership and Buy-in**

- o Corporate executives must drive data governance projects to guarantee that data quality takes the front stage in strategic decision-making.
- o Data Governance Committees and Chief Data Officers (CDOs) would help companies to keep high-quality data ecosystems (Mahanti & Mahanti, 2021).

3. **Incentives for Data Quality Compliance**
   - o Based on their success, teams whose members regularly uphold the security and integrity of data might be rewarded by their companies.
   - o Motivating proactive data management is much enhanced by acknowledging and recognizing data stewardship efforts.

Companies can guarantee that data is legally compliant, accurate, and current through a data-aware culture of ongoing development.

A multi-pronged approach combining new technology, cultural changes, security-driven DevSecOps initiatives, strong governance systems, and other actions guarantees data quality and integrity. Data stewardship, metadata management, and lineage tracking let companies create a strong foundation for data asset management. Even as artificial intelligence, blockchain, and automatic anomaly detection improve data quality, constant monitoring, recording, and auditing guarantees safe and clear data pipelines. Once a data-driven corporate culture is developed, all aspects of the business also start to be more conscious, compliant, and accountable. Organizations must create proactive and adaptable data governance policies to fulfill their legal obligations, keep up with technological advancements, and reach their business goals. Guaranteeing the dependability, security, and safety of their data assets helps companies, in turn, strengthen digital innovation, operational efficiency, and competitive advantage.

CONCLUSION AND FUTURE DIRECTIONS

Modern companies require a thorough plan, including governance, security, and technology, to solve the fundamental problems with data integrity and quality. Companies that follow the rules keep ahead of the competition, make wise decisions, and have strong systems guaranteeing accuracy, consistency, and data security. Effective data asset management is made possible by defining the required criteria, practices, and obligations for ensuring individual responsibility. If their governance systems are poorly defined, companies face the danger of ineffective operations, regulatory fines, and insufficient data quality. DAMA-DMBOK, ISO standards, and regulatory compliance procedures are among the governance systems supporting data dependability and lifetime value.

Modern software systems have dramatically improved data security and integrity thanks primarily to DevSecOps tools and practices. Including security and validation procedures into pipelines of continuous integration and deployment helps businesses proactively identify and fix data quality problems. Thanks to artificial intelligence, automatic data validation, real-time monitoring, and anomaly detection, data integrity has been considerably improved, and the danger of cyberattacks, human mistakes, and system failures has been lowered. Data management in tech-driven, fast-paced enterprises depends much on DevSecOps as it facilitates security integration from the beginning. Well-run data ecosystems using security-driven development strategies guarantee ongoing data integrity and quality maintenance.

Among other new forms of automation, machine learning, and blockchain are altering the landscape of data integrity. Big datasets are now significantly more reliable and trustworthy thanks to AI-provided data profiling and anomaly identification, which dramatically reduce the incidence of mistakes and inconsistencies. Fresh methods of validating data traceability and immutability introduced by blockchain technology make illicit modifications more challenging to go undetectable. Automating chores guarantees data consistency and real-time updates, advancing data management using machine learning techniques and data operations. Especially in large-scale and distributed systems, these developments provide feasible solutions for specific long-standing issues with data governance.

These advances have not made ensuring data integrity across complex business networks simpler. Data fragmentation challenges companies because they cannot merge different data sources regularly. Another problem raised by the exponential growth of data is scalability, which can make traditional data governance solutions challenging in the context of more complex data ecosystems. Data privacy laws, related guidelines, and standards continually evolve, complicating further problems. Growing their digital footprints will force companies to reconcile compliance, data accessibility, and security using increasingly creative and adaptable governance solutions.

Many will rely on the degree of upcoming research and technology development to allow our conquering of these challenges. Data integrity management may be scaled and automated with artificial intelligence-based governance systems. Quantum computing's new security paradigms might improve data encryption and integrity validation, avoiding new threats. As technologies like the edge and the cloud keep evolving, more complicated methods for protecting data integrity in dispersed systems will be required. When businesses start basing decisions on data, interdisciplinary teams of data scientists, security specialists, and regulatory body representatives will be valuable.

Apart from technological solutions and robust security measures, good governance that can suit the continually changing digital environment will characterize the data integrity of contemporary companies. Merging DevSecOps with governance systems would improve security even more since they are increasingly important in guaranteeing data integrity and traceability. Companies wishing their data to be constantly accurate and complete should follow industry standards, support a data-aware culture, and commit money to solutions that address these issues. If companies want to optimize their data assets, reduce risks, and maintain confidence in this digital world, they must follow appropriate data management techniques and always be innovative.

REFERENCES

Agrawal, R. (2024). The Role of Infrastructure as Code in Disaster Recovery and Business Continuity. *Journal*, 14(11). http://www. ijmra. us

Ahmad, K., Maabreh, M., Ghaly, M., Khan, K., Qadir, J., & Al-Fuqaha, A. (2022). Developing future human-centered smart cities: Critical analysis of smart city security, Data management, and Ethical challenges. *Computer Science Review*, 43, 100452. DOI: 10.1016/j.cosrev.2021.100452

Auhl, Z., Chilamkurti, N., Alhadad, R., & Heyne, W. (2022). A Comparative study of consensus mechanisms in blockchain for IoT networks. *Electronics (Basel)*, 11(17), 2694. DOI: 10.3390/electronics11172694

Aziz, W. A., Eleraky, M. W., & Soliman, J. N. (2023). Using Cloud Infrastructure as a Code IaC to Set Up Web Applications. *International Journal of Simulation--Systems, Science & Technology, 24*(3).

Bagja, A., Amri, Z., Imtihan, K., Rodi, M., & Rusniatun, S. Y. (2024). Enhancing Public Sector IT Governance through COBIT 2019: A Case Study on Service Continuity and Data Management in the Central Lombok. *Journal of Information Systems and Informatics*, 6(4), 2761–2776.

Bakare, S. S., Adeniyi, A. O., Akpuokwe, C. U., & Eneh, N. E.,. (2024). Data privacy laws and compliance: A comparative review of the EU GDPR and USA regulations. *Computer Science & IT Research Journal*, 5(3), 528–543. DOI: 10.51594/csitrj.v5i3.859

Boppiniti, S. T. (2021). Real-time data analytics with ai: Leveraging stream processing for dynamic decision support. *International Journal of Management Education for Sustainable Development*, 4(4).

Chintale, P. (2023). *DevOps Design Pattern: Implementing DevOps best practices for secure and reliable CI/CD pipeline (English Edition)*. Bpb Publications.

Chittala, S. (2024). Securing DevOps Pipelines: Automating Security in DevSecOps Frameworks. [JRTCSE]. *Journal of Recent Trends in Computer Science and Engineering*, 12(5), 31–44. DOI: 10.70589/JRTCSE.2024.5.5

Choi, Y. B., & Williams, C. E. (2022). A HIPAA security and privacy compliance audit and risk assessment mitigation approach. In *Research Anthology on Securing Medical Systems and Records* (pp. 706–725). IGI Global. DOI: 10.4018/978-1-6684-6311-6.ch032

DAMA International. (2017). *DAMA-DMBOK: Data management body of knowledge*. Technics Publications, LLC.

Duggineni, S. (2023). Impact of controls on data integrity and information systems. *Science and Technology*, 13(2), 29–35.

Dutta, P., Choi, T. M., Somani, S., & Butala, R. (2020). Blockchain technology in supply chain operations: Applications, challenges and research opportunities. *Transportation research part e: Logistics and transportation review, 142*, 102067.

Ejjami, R., & Boussalham, K. (2024). Industry 5.0 in Manufacturing: Enhancing Resilience and Responsibility through AI-Driven Predictive Maintenance, Quality Control, and Supply Chain Optimization. *International Journal For Multidisciplinary Research, 6*(4).

Farhad, M. A. (2024). Consumer data protection laws and their impact on business models in the tech industry. *Telecommunications Policy*, 48(9), 102836. DOI: 10.1016/j.telpol.2024.102836

Habib, G., Sharma, S., Ibrahim, S., Ahmad, I., Qureshi, S., & Ishfaq, M. (2022). Blockchain technology: Benefits, challenges, applications, and integration of blockchain technology with cloud computing. *Future Internet*, 14(11), 341. DOI: 10.3390/fi14110341

Hassani, H., & MacFeely, S. (2023). Driving excellence in official statistics: Unleashing the potential of comprehensive digital data Governance. *Big Data and Cognitive Computing*, 7(3), 134. DOI: 10.3390/bdcc7030134

Hastig, G. M., & Sodhi, M. S. (2020). Blockchain for supply chain traceability: Business requirements and critical success factors. *Production and Operations Management*, 29(4), 935–954. DOI: 10.1111/poms.13147

Hosen, M. S., Islam, R., Naeem, Z., Folorunso, E. O., Chu, T. S., Al Mamun, M. A., & Orunbon, N. O. (2024). Data-driven decision making: Advanced database systems for business intelligence. *Nanotechnology Perceptions*, 20(3), 687–704.

Hossain, M. I., Steigner, T., Hussain, M. I., & Akther, A. (2024). Enhancing data integrity and traceability in industry cyber physical systems (ICPS) through Blockchain technology: A comprehensive approach. *arXiv preprint arXiv:2405.04837*.

Jacobs, P. G., Herrero, P., Facchinetti, A., Vehi, J., Kovatchev, B., Breton, M. D., Cinar, A., Nikita, K. S., Doyle, F. J., Bondia, J., Battelino, T., Castle, J. R., Zarkogianni, K., Narayan, R., & Mosquera-Lopez, C. (2023). Artificial intelligence and machine learning for improving glycemic control in diabetes: Best practices, pitfalls, and opportunities. *IEEE Reviews in Biomedical Engineering*, 17, 19–41. DOI: 10.1109/RBME.2023.3331297 PMID: 37943654

Janssen, M., Brous, P., Estevez, E., Barbosa, L. S., & Janowski, T. (2020). Data governance: Organizing data for trustworthy Artificial Intelligence. *Government Information Quarterly*, 37(3), 101493. DOI: 10.1016/j.giq.2020.101493

Katari, A., & Ankam, M. (2022). Data Governance in Multi-Cloud Environments for Financial Services: Challenges and Solutions. [IJMCER]. *Educational Research*, 4(1), 339–353.

Kong, L., Tan, J., Huang, J., Chen, G., Wang, S., Jin, X., Zeng, P., Khan, M., & Das, S. K. (2022). Edge-computing-driven internet of things: A survey. *ACM Computing Surveys*, 55(8), 1–41. DOI: 10.1145/3555308

Leshchenko, B., Snisar, B., Stupak, A., & Osadchyi, V. (2024). Integrating DevSecOps into the software development lifecycle: A comprehensive model for securing containerized and cloud-native environments. *CPITS II 2024-Cybersecurity Providing in Information and Telecommunication Systems*, (3826), 153-161.

Mahanti, R., & Mahanti, R. (2021). Strategy and Data Governance. *Data Governance Success: Growing and Sustaining Data Governance*, 67-98.

Mahmudnia, D., Arashpour, M., & Yang, R. (2022). Blockchain in construction management: Applications, advantages and limitations. *Automation in Construction*, 140, 104379. DOI: 10.1016/j.autcon.2022.104379

Manchana, R. (2024). *DataOps: Bridging the Gap Between Legacy and Modern Systems for Seamless Data Orchestration* (Vol. 3, No. 2, pp. 2-10). SRC/JAICC-137. DOI: doi. org/ (3) E137 J Arti Inte & Cloud Comp.DOI: 10.47363/JAICC/2024

Munappy, A. R. (2021). *Data management and Data Pipelines: An empirical investigation in the embedded systems domain*. Chalmers Tekniska Hogskola.

Mushtaq, M. S., Mushtaq, M. Y., Iqbal, M. W., & Hussain, S. A. (2022). Security, integrity, and privacy of cloud computing and big data. In *Security and privacy trends in cloud computing and big data* (pp. 19–51). CRC Press. DOI: 10.1201/9781003107286-2

Noman, A. H. M., Mustaquim, S. M., Molla, S., & Siddique, I. M. (2024). Enhancing Operations Quality Improvement through Advanced Data Analytics. *Journal of Computer Science Engineering and Software Testing*, 10(1), 1–14. DOI: 10.46610/JOCSES.2024.v10i01.001

Özcan, F., Lei, C., Quamar, A., & Efthymiou, V. (2021, June). Semantic enrichment of data for AI applications. In *Proceedings of the Fifth Workshop on Data Management for End-To-End Machine Learning* (pp. 1-7).

Quazi, S., Saha, R. P., & Singh, M. K. (2022). Applications of artificial intelligence in healthcare. *Journal of Experimental Biology and Agricultural Sciences*, 10(1), 211–226. DOI: 10.18006/2022.10(1).211.226

Rane, N., Choudhary, S., & Rane, J. (2023). Hyper-personalization for enhancing customer loyalty and satisfaction in Customer Relationship Management (CRM) systems. *Available atSSRN* 4641044. DOI: 10.2139/ssrn.4641044

Saffady, W. (2020). *Managing information risks: threats, vulnerabilities, and responses*. Rowman & Littlefield Publishers.

Sandu, A. K. (2021). DevSecOps: Integrating Security into the DevOps Lifecycle for Enhanced Resilience. *Technology & Management Review*, 6, 1–19.

Tadi, V. (2020). Optimizing Data Governance: Enhancing Quality through AI-Integrated Master Data Management Across Industries. *North American Journal of Engineering Research*, 1(3).

Vagadia, B., & Vagadia, B. (2020). Data integrity, control and tokenization. *Digital Disruption: Implications and opportunities for Economies, Society, Policy Makers and Business Leaders*, 107-176.

Vijayalakshmi, A., & Jayasudha, M. (2024). *Artificial Intelligence And Data Analytics*. Academic Guru Publishing House.

Wang, J., Liu, Y., Li, P., Lin, Z., Sindakis, S., & Aggarwal, S. (2024). Overview ofdata quality: Examining the dimensions, antecedents, and impacts of data quality. *Journal of the Knowledge Economy*, 15(1), 1159–1178. DOI: 10.1007/s13132-022-01096-6

Wibisono, N., Soetomo, M. A., Ipung, H. P., Bawono, M. W. A., & Budiarto, E. (2021, October). Data Integration Readiness Analysis in Merged Telecommunication Company. In *2021 International Conference on Informatics, Multimedia, Cyber and Information System (ICIMCIS* (pp. 317-322). IEEE. DOI: 10.1109/ICIMCIS53775.2021.9699131

Zhang, L., Jeong, D., & Lee, S. (2021). Data quality management in the internet of things. *Sensors (Basel)*, 21(17), 5834. DOI: 10.3390/s21175834 PMID: 34502723

Zhang, W., & Chen, L. (2024). Real-Time Transaction Monitoring Using AI: Detecting Suspicious Activities and Money Laundering in Banking. *Asian American Research Letters Journal, 1*(3).

Chapter 3
Metadata Management and Its Role in Data Governance

Rajesh Vayyala
https://orcid.org/0009-0001-0227-0675
PRA Group Inc., USA

ABSTRACT

Modern data governance would lack a necessary layer of structure and clarity for the large and always-shifting digital information environment without metadata management. Translating as "data about data," the term "metadata" has many uses in many different fields, including healthcare, banking, and e-commerce, where it encourages creativity by improving operational efficiency and compliance. Including procedural, structural, descriptive, and administrative information helps to provide informed decisions, traceability, and interoperability. Including it in contemporary software systems helps to trace data lineage and provide real-time analytics, thereby enhancing data storage, access, and consumption. Metadata is essential for DevSecOps as it helps to match security and compliance with ongoing development cycles. Data mesh and data fabric are two frameworks displaying metadata-driven decentralization that improve analytics and collaboration. Businesses that want to succeed in the digital age and satisfy legal and technological criteria have to be masters in metadata management.

INTRODUCTION TO METADATA MANAGEMENT

The exponential growth of digital data has made metadata management a critical component of modern information governance. Metadata, commonly known as "data about data," enables us to make sense of and do something valuable with the massive amounts of daily data. Metadata management solutions are vital for modern software systems because they incorporate data governance, operational efficiency, and security. In this first chapter, we will look at the primary goals of metadata management and the many strategies that can be used to achieve them. We will also see if it is compatible with other frameworks like DevSecOps, modern software development, and data legislation.

DOI: 10.4018/979-8-3373-0365-9.ch003

Definition and Importance of Metadata

Metadata serves as a descriptive layer to improve the interpretability and usefulness of unprocessed data. Details on its source, structure, shape, and intended application help one appreciate and place data in perspective. For instance, the metadata of a database allows one to specify the name, data type, and related limitations of a column. Metadata helps consumers to get insightful information by grouping and making searchable once disorganized data components (Haynes, 2018). Metadata offers a foundation for good data management as a rudder in an otherwise unintelligible sea of information. For reasons other than only organization convenience, metadata is essential. Compliance with regulatory rules, data quality, and traceability must all be guaranteed. Caliskan et al. (2023) claim that by ensuring that data is reliable and available, metadata supports decision-making in sectors including banking, e-commerce, and healthcare, therefore supporting System-to-system communication, which metadata facilitates is the foundation of effective cross-domain and cross-platform collaboration. Metadata management has become a key component in operational efficiency, innovation, and competitive advantage as companies depend increasingly on data-driven insights.

Historical Overview of Metadata Evolution

From its essential function of information classification, metadata has developed into a vital component of contemporary data governance. Metadata was already used when library science began grouping volumes using catalog cards. With the development of metadata systems, including Machine-Readable Cataloguing (MARC), digital indexing became possible for libraries in the twentieth century. Metadata was essential for data structuring and management even during the height of relational database popularity in the 1970s. Developed during the dot-com explosion of the 1990s, metadata standards such as XML and Dublin Core significantly improved the search capability of the web. Big data, artificial intelligence, and cloud computing of the 2000s mainly depend on metadata to provide compliance, security, and automation. Metadata is becoming increasingly important in data protection rules like GDPR, DevSecOps, and artificial intelligence-driven analytics as it guarantees organized, trackable, interactive data ecosystems. Given the continually growing complexity of data, metadata is constantly changing to support governance, efficiency, and innovation.

Types of Metadata

Every data management and governance ecosystem element depends on metadata, a complex and multifarious tool. They include the following:

Structural metadata: In computing, data format and structure refers to the blueprints for items, including database structures, table linkages, and document layouts (Miller, 2022). It facilitates the uniform and regular data layout that helps systems process and grasp information. Relational databases provide efficient data integration and querying by linking between tables containing structural information.

Descriptive metadata: The main emphasis is on the data's material; thus, titles, keywords, summaries, and annotations are included. This data type also benefits discovery and retrieval (Pinoli, 2019). For example, digital libraries provide descriptive information, letting users search for books, papers, or multimedia depending on particular keywords or subjects. This function shows how important descriptive information is for raising usability and accessibility.

Administrative metadata: This controls all aspects of data management's technical and operational elements. It includes essential responsibility, security, and compliance elements (access rights, use logs, and file permissions) (Haynes, 2018). By tracking who saw and changed files, the administrative metadata in cloud storage systems can, for instance, support audits and regulatory compliance.

Process Metadata: This new category spans information on data transformations, processes, and their lineage. Knowing when and how data changes is vital for auditing, debugging, and preserving pipeline integrity (Pinoli, 2019). This is especially important in DevSecOps pipelines and automated systems. For instance, the process metadata records of ETL operations make them auditable since they document data changes.

Metadata's Role in Modern Software Systems

With the inclusion of metadata, modern software systems have entirely changed data storage, access, and usage. Features such as data lineage tracing, search optimization, and real-time analytics depend on metadata. Karanumurthy et al. (2023) claim that metadata helps understand system needs and consumption patterns in cloud computing settings, enabling dynamic resource allocation. Significant data ecosystems also depend on metadata management technologies such as Apache Atlas and Collibra to arrange and control datasets so that data scientists and analysts can access trustworthy information. The rise of artificial intelligence and machine learning has underlined the already incredible value of metadata. Training and validation of artificial intelligence models in annotated datasets depend on the background given by metadata (Pachouly et al., 2022). For instance, metadata, such as images categorized as "dog" or "cat," could affect the model's prediction accuracy. Moreover, metadata preserves their parameters, settings, and decision-making practices, making AI models more understandable (Li et al., 2023). This is consistent with the current trend towards explainable artificial intelligence, whose aim is to assign algorithms responsibility for the results they generate.

By applying DevSecOps ideas, we have attracted attention to the value of metadata in contemporary software systems. Using metadata included in the development process, organizations might automate security policy execution, real-time system performance monitoring, and compliance checks. Modern software engineering is incomplete without metadata-driven automation, which increases agility, lowers risks, and calls for less human involvement.

Metadata Management and Broader Themes

The Growing relevance of information in AI-driven decisions raises specific ethical questions about fairness, openness, and responsible use. Metadata affects how artificial intelligence systems categorize, evaluate, and prioritize data, so it is essential to maintain justice and responsibility together. Inaccurate, incomplete, or biased datasets might result in biased metadata that can cause discrimination in employment, lending, or healthcare. Ethical metadata governance is necessary for responsible artificial intelligence use to ensure data inclusion, authenticity, and provenance. Companies should evaluate their metadata sources and apply bias detection methods to stop aggravating social inequalities. Transparency is essential, as consumers should be able to grasp how metadata affects outcomes generated by artificial intelligence.

GDPR and other regulatory systems require companies to defend automated decisions and promote moral metadata use. Explainability elements in metadata systems driven by artificial intelligence will enable human control and intervention as needed. Managing data to avoid prejudice and ethical issues will help guarantee that artificial intelligence continues to be a tool for innovation, justice, and responsible decision-making.

Metadata management is intimately associated with data governance, development security operations, and software development. Using metadata, one can design and enforce data accessibility, privacy, and quality policies, thus supporting data governance. The General Data Protection Regulation (GDPR) and the California Consumer Privacy Act (CCPA) are just two laws companies could follow with excellent metadata management. By defining roles and duties, metadata promotes trust and simplifies data governance. DevSecOps depends mostly on metadata since it closes the gap between operations, security, and development. Including metadata in DevSecOps processes helps organizations reach CI/CD with strong security and compliance protections. Teams can utilize metadata to automate vulnerability assessments, limit software dependencies, and provide audit trails, among other risk-control responsibilities. Since it conforms with DevSecOps approaches, metadata management is necessary to create better and more cooperative software development processes.

Due to developments in contemporary software, metadata has grown increasingly valuable from a strategic perspective. Two novel concepts termed *"Data Fabric and Data Mesh"* employ metadata to build scalable, creative, decentralized systems targeted at specific industries, according to Goedegebuure et al. (2024). These techniques show appropriate regard for metadata, which is necessary for self-service analytics, cross-functional collaboration, and real-time decision-making. Metadata management may help companies negotiate the digital transformation maze by providing a coherent framework for grouping technology developments with main objectives.

CORE CONCEPTS IN DATA GOVERNANCE

Data governance is now more important than ever since it could present opportunities and challenges for a business's strategy. Data governance makes practical data asset management possible, meeting legal and organizational requirements for accessibility, security, and accuracy. It promotes data management responsibility at the nexus of compliance, technology, and strategy. Here, we investigate the fundamental ideas, ideas, and links between data governance and metadata management, providing a window into how different sectors meet their goals using metadata-driven governance.

Overview of Data Governance

Data governance mechanisms inside companies help to guarantee data security. Among these systems are guidelines, policies, laws, and rules of behavior. An organization's data should be considered a strategic advantage capable of helping it reach objectives, a fundamental concept of data governance. Zahid et al. (2023) claim that data governance is essential for the security and management of data at every step of its lifetime, including creation, storage, usage, and archiving. Good data governance is based on transparency, accountability, and data protection. Clearing who is liable for what in terms of data management is essential as part of making everyone responsible. Documenting data processes helps one see data gathering, processing, and application. Transparency will follow. At the core of stewardship is assigning people or groups to track compliance, safety, and data integrity; this highlights the organization's dedication to moral data handling even more.

Data governance seeks more than only compliance assurance and risk control. Businesses strive to increase the accuracy of their data, weed out unnecessary information, and enable sophisticated analytics (Wang et al., 2018) to maximize its value of it. A strong basis for decision-making by an efficient data governance framework promotes creativity. Within modern software, which depends on data moving across linked systems and applications, solid governance produces trustworthy and consistent data regardless of complexity or volume.

Key Pillars of Data Governance

Data governance's four pillars are security, compliance, accessibility, and quality. These pillars should be applied to manage data in a beneficial and safe way while also following all relevant legal and ethical criteria.

Data quality: This is the foundation of data governance since high-quality data makes exact analysis, informed decisions, and efficient operations possible. Data quality spans timeliness, consistency, completeness, and accuracy (Mahanti, 2019). The need for robust data governance systems is underlined by the fact that poor data quality can lead to operational inefficiencies, financial losses, and damage to reputation.

Security: Given today's always-rising cyber risks and data breaches, this is an even more crucial pillar. Data governance ensures the protection of private data by including policies such as encryption, access restrictions, and monitoring (Pansara, 2022). Both technical and procedural security measures, such as policies and training programs, help promote a culture of responsibility and continuous awareness.

Compliance: This is vital to data governance since regulatory systems are becoming more complex. Many legislations prioritize protecting personal data, including GDPR and the California Consumer Privacy Act. Governance systems help companies negotiate these constraints and fulfill their ethical and legal obligations by specifying data collection, storage, and distribution policies.

Accessibility: This assures that authorized persons can access your data. Data governance systems set metadata management mechanisms in place to enable data access. Consequently, users will locate, grasp, and use information more quickly. This accessibility also encourages creative innovation across departments.

How Metadata Management Enables Effective Data Governance

Since metadata management offers the tools and structures required for proper data governance, it is vital to manage the complexity of today's data ecosystems. As a descriptive layer tying raw data with valuable insights, metadata offers context, organization, and traceability. Data governance seeks to offer reliable, safe, and readily available data, which fits very well with the responsibilities of this post.

One great advantage of data governance is the ability of metadata management to raise data quality. Because metadata precisely identifies data properties like format, usage, and provenance, companies can find and correct mistakes or discrepancies. Automating data quality checks enabled by metadata-driven systems helps to lower the possibility of errors and ensures that the data is current (Bhaskaran, 2020). Fine-grained monitoring and access restrictions made possible by meta-data management help to further enhance data security. By assigning rights and obligations for users using metadata, you can guarantee that only authorized staff members may access confidential data. Systems can log who accessed and altered what data using metadata. These audit trails can help you whether your needs call for proof of regulatory compliance, analysis of events, or identification of any questionable behavior.

For regulatory compliance, metadata management provides a methodical approach to following the sources of data. Using metadata to monitor the data lifetime (from creation to present), companies may show their accountability and respect for standards. This competence is crucial in medically and financially controlled fields, where non-compliance might result in severe fines. Another advantage of metadata management is increasing accessibility, the fourth data governance criterion. As central repositories, metadata catalogs let users locate and retrieve critical datasets. These catalogs may have images, summaries, and comments to help consumers grasp and apply the material. More effective teams made possible by improved data accessibility help to speed up decision-making and encourage innovation.

Metadata-Driven Governance in Industry

Industries all around have realized the transforming potential of metadata-driven government. For example, metadata management is vital in the healthcare sector to ensure EHR integrity and safety. By providing thorough descriptions of patient data, which supports interoperability among healthcare providers, metadata allows for seamless care coordination. Furthermore, systems controlled by metadata enable companies to follow legislation like HIPAA, which calls for strict data security practices (Nookala, 2021). Likewise, The financial services sector depends on metadata-driven governance to manage complex regulatory environments and increase operational efficiency. Financial companies can monitor transactions, identify risks, and provide reports compliant with legal standards using metadata (2022). Metadata-driven systems enable advanced analytics (such as credit risk assessment and fraud detection) by providing reliable, ordered datasets.

Retail companies should prioritize metadata management to maximize supply chain effectiveness and offer improved consumer experiences. Gregorczuk (2022) notes that stores employ data for customer behavior research, inventory tracking, and delivery monitoring. Retailers enable faster reaction to market changes and delivery of tailored services, enhancing consumer loyalty by including metadata into their data governance systems. The spread of new technologies like the Internet of Things (IoT) and artificial intelligence (AI) have accentuated the relevance of metadata-driven governance in many fields. Artificial intelligence models rely on the amount of data IoT devices give to ensure that training sets are relevant and of high quality. This metadata can help to clarify user behavior and system performance (Deekshith, 2021). These advances underline the need for robust metadata management systems to manage the volume and complexity of modern data ecosystems.

CASE STUDIES THAT DEMONSTRATE THE ROLE OF METADATA IN GOVERNANCE

As seen by the experiences of well-known companies like ING Group and Pfizer, good data governance depends on metadata. Better metadata management can solve complex data problems, increase operational effectiveness, and guarantee research integrity and regulatory compliance.

Case Study 1: ING Group

Meeting regulatory criteria presents challenges for ING Group, especially about BCBS 239. This criterion demands efficient data governance and risk data aggregation. Their data was scattered and lacked a consistent perspective, which made it challenging to produce accurate reports and implement good risk management. In response to these issues, ING developed a data governance project anchored on a shared metadata repository. They established unambiguous data ownership, described data lineage, and tracked data quality metrics using this repository. From creation to consumption, ING could track data at every level of its lifecycle using metadata, guaranteeing data integrity. This work produced significant results. The results were improved data quality, regulatory compliance, and openness for ING's data assets. Agg aggressively addressing data quality issues using a metadata-driven strategy improved their decision-making capacity and reduced operational risks.

Case Study 2: Pfizer's

Pfizer is one of the big pharmaceutical companies that has embraced metadata management to improve research and development efficiency and data security.

Clinical trials, laboratory research, and outside databases provide the massive amounts of data that Pfizer's R&D operations produce. Drug research and regulatory filings mainly depend on these data. Hence, their quality and dependability must be closely watched and guaranteed. Using a metadata management system, Pfizer—a pharmaceutical company—organized and categorized its trial data. Data validation techniques, experimental methodologies, and data provenance recorded in metadata would help researchers to guarantee that their results could be duplicated, follow the data's source, and point up possible biases or mistakes. Pfizer's R&D processes were much enhanced by this emphasis on metadata management. They achieved this by guaranteeing the accuracy of data sent to regulatory authorities, lowering the likelihood of mistakes in clinical trials, and accelerating the drug discovery process. The secret to both situations of effective data governance (which paid off handsomely for data-intensive, highly regulated businesses) is deliberate metadata management.

THE INTERPLAY BETWEEN METADATA MANAGEMENT AND DevSecOps

A pillar of the dynamic and often shifting field of modern software development is DevSecOps, that is, the junction of development, security, and operations. This guarantees systems that are scalable, quick, and safe. DevSecOps has brought about a fresh perspective on security in software development. This has maintained strict security policies while yet allowing constant delivery. This section looks into the need for metadata management to enhance DevSecOps processes and offer a compliant, quick, and safe development methodology.

Introduction to DevSecOps

By combining the Dev and Ops teams, DevSecOps is a better form of the original DevOps method meant to boost software agility and responsiveness. According to DevSecOps' guiding ideas, security should not be an afterthought or distinct activity but pervade every software development lifecycle (SDLC) phase. From idea to development, testing, implementation, and maintenance, all phases are vulnerable to the security emphasis of the strategy. DevSecOps, according to Ugwueze and Chukwunweike (2024), is founded on the following ideas: automation, continuous integration (CI), continuous delivery (CD), and security testing ingrained throughout the development process. Automated security systems covering vulnerability scanning, encryption, identity management, and compliance checks help prevent human error and guarantee the consistent application of security measures throughout life (Khair, 2018). As cloud-native architectures and microservices are adopted increasingly by businesses, a strong security framework capable of both proactive and reactive vulnerability detection and mitigation is highly sought after.

Metadata as a Tool for Secure Development and Operational Practices

Metadata management is primarily important for the DevSecOps security objectives. Fundamentally, metadata explains data, systems, and processes; it provides raw data meaning and structure, augmenting its value. In the framework of DevSecOps, metadata is used in addition to the codebase and configurations to monitor and regulate software system security properties. According to Joseph (2023), metadata lets one better understand software assets and infrastructure, offering additional insight into security vulnerabilities and guarantees of compliance. In safe development and operating processes, metadata finds multiple applications. Tracking data provenance, for instance, helps to clarify the flow of private data between systems and the locations of possible vulnerability. By cataloging the data kinds, storage sites, and users accessing them, metadata enables teams to apply security controls such as encryption or access restrictions. When metadata contains data on the configurations of different components, teams can more effectively guarantee compliance with security best practices and laws (Alkhard, 2024).

Another key role metadata performs in DevSecOps is its ability to increase openness and responsibility. Working independently in pipelines with several phases and complexity is not unusual for developers and security teams. When metadata is included in the pipeline, teams get a bird's-eye perspective of the processes and can better discover security concerns early on. Metadata documenting code changes, build settings, and system dependencies helps one find security problems in the architecture of an application considerably.

Role of Metadata in Automated Security and Compliance Checks

DevSecOps depends critically on the application of automated processes. Automating chores such as vulnerability discovery, patch management, and compliance assessment helps companies ensure their security policies are followed everywhere. According to Fawzy et al. (2024), metadata is essential for the CI/CD pipeline's automated security and compliance checks. Automated security scans are common elements of DevSecOps pipelines carried out with every code change and build. Metadata allows one to tag and classify code components, facilitating the application of the pertinent security mechanisms. Using metadata, we may evaluate the codebase for vulnerabilities, including the most critical system components and the smallest libraries. Automated systems may undertake real-time security evaluations using metadata that details the libraries or dependencies being used and their known vulnerabilities, claims Ponta et al. (2020). Teams are thus more suited to identify and resolve weaknesses early on in the development process.

Figure 1. Metadata-Driven DevSecOps: Automated Security and Compliance Workflow

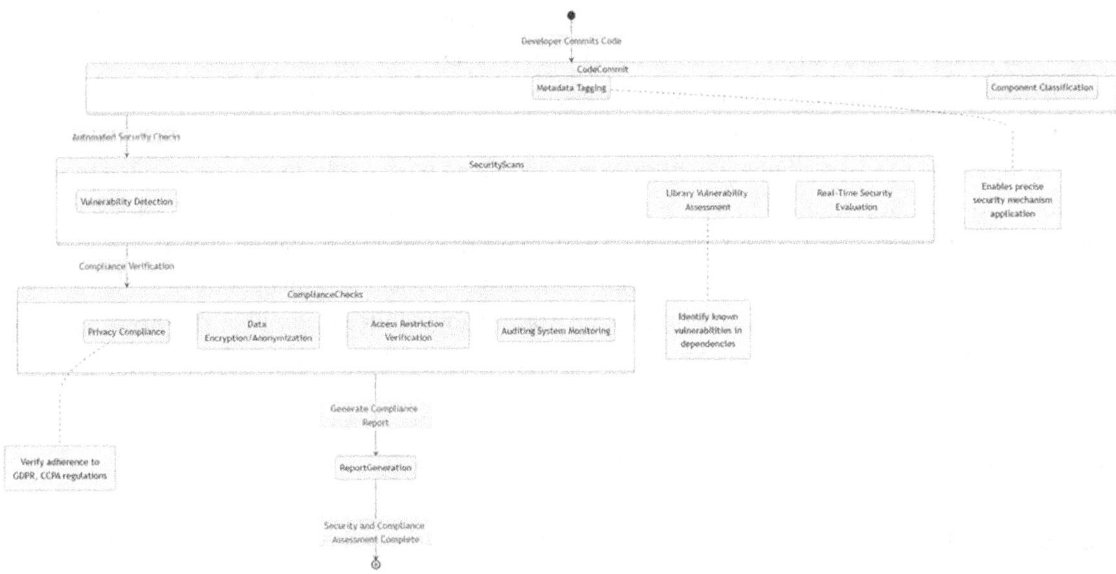

Metadata might be helpful in areas such as compliance when automating DevSecOps processes. Businesses realize daily how crucial data privacy laws such as the California Consumer Privacy Act (CCPA) and the General Data Protection Regulation (GDPR) are for their adherence. By including metadata related to compliance in their development and execution processes, teams may automate compliance testing. Metadata can show whether anonymizing or encrypting security measures are present or absent, proving adherence to legal criteria for processing personal data. Metadata also helps monitor if auditing systems are running and whether access restrictions for sensitive data are suitable (Pasquier et al., 2018). This information allows compliance solutions to create real-time reports for security teams to examine non-compliance concerns.

ADVANCEMENTS IN METADATA MANAGEMENT FOR MODERN SOFTWARE

From a data governance side issue, metadata management has developed into a necessary component of modern software system security, access, and integrity. Using distributed data models, cloud-native architectures, and artificial intelligence/machine learning has complicated organizational IT systems and calls for new tools and technologies for metadata management. We will discuss how metadata tools have evolved, how artificial intelligence and machine learning have changed metadata management, why cloud-native solutions are so popular, why it is so difficult to interface with current data architectures, and what opportunities and challenges companies face to scale metadata management for modern enterprises.

Evolution of Metadata Tools and Technologies

Like software and IT, metadata management systems have seen explosive technical advancement. With a lack of automation and interactivity, the solutions for handling historical data primarily consisted of stationary cataloging and storage options. These older methods, meant for managing quite simple data structures, find their complexity too much in today's software systems. According to Paik et al. (2019), data governance models fundamentally changed metadata management. These approaches allow meta-data to be included in more full data management systems. These systems had sophisticated capabilities, including data profiling, quality checks, and automatic classification, transcending simple data lineage and dictionary chores. Understanding and controlling data flow depends on metadata management, especially in big data and distributed computing environments where solutions have evolved to manage increasingly complicated datasets in response to the rising demand to control data quantities.

Older, more rigid systems are being replaced with more flexible and modular metadata management systems that can interact with numerous kinds of data. Modern metadata management systems such as Apache Atlas, Collibra, and Alation may ingest data from various sources, combine various stakeholders' viewpoints, and facilitate data sharing among numerous applications. This shift lets companies handle their data resources better and fits the decentralized data ownership and management trend.

Traditional Metadata Governance Strategies

Before AI and automation, organizations used traditional metadata governance strategies to manage data quality, security, and compliance. These strategies focused on manual processes, standardized policies, and organizational roles to ensure metadata was used effectively.

Metadata Cataloging and Documentation: Companies have developed metadata catalogs to track their data assets, including descriptions, owners, and access permissions. Using the data in these databases, teams might work together and better understand one another.

Standardization and Policies: Companies applied industry standards such as ISO 11179, the Metadata Registry Standard to offer uniform metadata management. Policy created norms for data naming, access, and classification. Then, the metadata was arranged so that any system could interpret it.

Data Stewardship and Governance Committees: Data stewards for a corporation are staff members whose responsibility is to guarantee consistent and correct metadata. Comprising C-suite business and IT leaders, governance committees watched adherence to HIPAA and GDPR. These groups focused on policymaking around metadata.

Manual Audits and Compliance Checks: Organisations routinely conducted metadata audits to check for data security, correctness, and regulatory compliance, as automation was not widely used then. Manually recorded metadata updates helped trace data lineage and stop illegal changes.

Role-Based Access Control (RBAC): Only individuals with specific user roles could access metadata. While pay stubs for employees might not be exposed to financial experts, sales data could. This ensured that only permitted users could access critical data, preventing unwanted access.

These more labor-intensive methods helped us develop our contemporary view of metadata governance. Although artificial intelligence has automated many jobs, appropriate metadata management still depends on following fundamental ideas such as security, stewardship, and standardization.

Use of AI/ML in Metadata Management for Pattern Detection and Decision-Making

Companies' rising adoption of artificial intelligence (AI) and machine learning (ML) technology has created fresh prospects for automating metadata discovery, classification, and analysis. Combining AI and ML helps metadata management systems identify anomalies, hidden patterns, and correlations vital for decision-making, hence transcending their simple data cataloging capability.

Though pattern identification and predictive analysis are two domains where they truly shine, metadata can gain from AI/ML techniques in various ways. Geo, 2022. For example, machine learning models may scan metadata for data usage patterns to assist companies predict when they might need more data in the future or discover security concerns like hacking. These models may thus also automatically classify data and assign it to suitable categories or compliance regimes by automatically spotting trends in metadata, hence removing the requirement for user involvement. Metadata management would be inadequate without artificial intelligence and machine learning to support data lineage tracking (Nishat & Azmat, 2021). Improving the accuracy and quality of lineage mapping, artificial intelligence and machine learning data flow across several systems and finding connections between data sources, processing systems, and destinations. This becomes important when handling complex, large setups where human monitoring is challenging. According to Stier et al. (2024), companies can accomplish real-time lineage tracking using AI-enhanced metadata management systems. This helps them to quickly assess the effects of system or data modifications, assess the downstream effects of data manipulations, and preserve data integrity.

Figure 2. AI/ML in Metadata Management

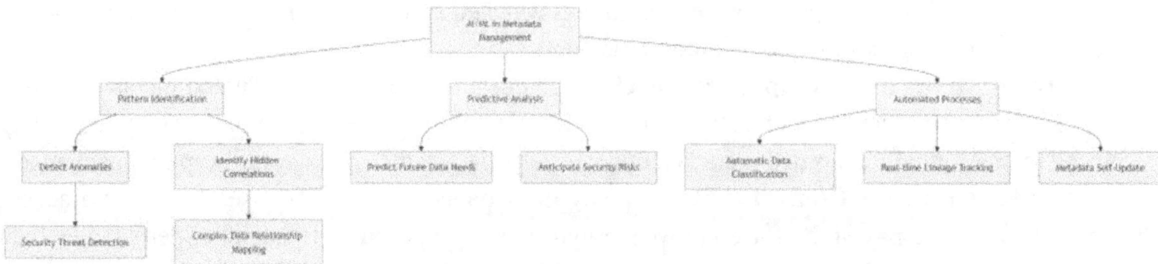

Artificial intelligence can also enable automatic metadata curation. Metadata curation, which involves collecting, arranging, and editing metadata, used to be a labor-intensive, clumsy human process. Using AI integration, automating this process helps metadata systems self-update in response to changes in data usage patterns, data structures, or corporate goals.

Cloud-Native Metadata Management Solutions

As cloud computing has evolved, data management has seen a sea change. The expenses and challenges of growing conventional on-site metadata management systems were too significant for companies who wanted to be fast on their feet. Moving to these systems has resulted in cloud-based approaches for metadata management development. These are excellent matches as they are scalable, reasonably priced, and competent in real-time, managing enormous volumes of data. Using native cloud-based metadata management systems offers several primary benefits. Its seamless interaction with other cloud services is one of the advantages. Among others, it runs with AWS, Azure, and Google Cloud. Moving metadata management to these platforms helps companies to manage better data assets dispersed over several cloud or on-site systems and receive worldwide access to their data.

Furthermore, cloud-native systems utilize the scalability and adaptability of the cloud to manage variations in workload (Kanchepu, 2023). Companies that need tools to evaluate and handle demand data would gain especially from cloud-native solutions. Usually dealing with vast datasets, metadata management is especially relevant in data lakes or big data environments. Furthermore, cloud-native metadata tools simplify orchestration and automation, unlike more traditional systems (Laszewski et al., 2018). Among the tools that increase output and reduce human effort in cloud-native metadata management systems are automated data discovery, auto-scaling, and real-time data lineage monitoring.

Two cloud firms, Google and Amazon Web Services (AWS), approach metadata differently. Organizations implementing cloud-based data governance strategies and technologies like AWS Glue and Google Cloud's Data Catalogue, designed to connect with the greater cloud services ecosystem, may effectively manage metadata.

Integration across Data Warehouses, Data Lakes, and Data Mesh with Metadata Management

Contemporary data architectures could incorporate metadata management to effectively govern and organize data across several processing and storage tiers. Effective metadata management ensures that data within data lakes, warehouses, and mesh architectures remains discoverable, accessible, and compliant. The utilization of extensive data processing and storage technologies is increasing significantly.

1. **Data Lakes**: Data lakes, whether structured, semi-structured, or unstructured, serve as a practical repository for preserving data in its original format (Thomas & Praseetha, 2020). The large volume and diversity of data in data lakes impede metadata management. Without context, data may be challenging to identify, secure, or employ; organizations risk amassing it without an adequate metadata framework. Properly documented and classified data lakes, facilitated by effective metadata management, allow organizations to implement governance rules and security standards across all datasets. This is particularly crucial in managing intricate situations and data privacy requirements.
2. **Data Warehouses**: In contrast, data warehouses are structured databases facilitating analytics and business intelligence (Shiyal, 2021). In these contexts, metadata management is advantageous as it ensures accurate arrangement, indexing, and data formatting, facilitating straightforward analysis. Dependable insights from Business Intelligence systems, which are becoming increasingly vital due to the intricacies of data analytics, require metadata tools. These tools provide historical monitoring, quality assessments, and data profiling, among other activities.
3. **Data Mesh**: Data mesh is more prevalent as organizations enhance the amount and complexity of their data management systems globally. As Dibouliya and Jotwani (2023) articulated, data meshes promote domain-oriented decentralized data ownership, delegating the responsibility for data management to other teams or business units. In this setting, metadata management is crucial to ensure data assets comply with security and governance standards. It facilitates the integration and information sharing among various teams. Companies may maintain consistent data quality, access restrictions in place, and regulatory compliance by effective metadata management inside a data mesh framework even with a distributed architecture.

Opportunities and Challenges in Extended Metadata Management for Modern Companies

Although this technology benefits modern companies, implementing metadata management techniques across big companies and sophisticated systems presents specific difficulties. One main challenge is the vast volume of produced metadata. Managing metadata for large-scale data collection is challenging with cloud computing and the IoT (Awotunde et al., 2020). Businesses must control their data by utilizing artificial intelligence-powered automated systems. Since hand processes are not fit for handling the volume, metadata has to be sorted, organized, and protected in real-time.

The second challenge is getting organisational goals, data governance, and metadata management systems and activities to cooperate. Machado et al. (2022) claim that using sophisticated data architectures such as data lakes and meshes aggravates information management challenges across many systems. Organizations are looking for a standard metadata management solution so that policies are regularly enforced on all platforms.

Even with these difficulties, companies that enhance their metadata systems have a lot of promise. One of the main chances is to improve their decision-making. Using all-encompassing metadata management solutions may lead to improved analytics, data discovery, and data quality, among other things. By enhancing data accessibility and security with metadata management systems, companies may better negotiate the always-shifting regulatory terrain, lower risks, and release new opportunities.

THE ROLE OF METADATA IN COMPLIANCE AND REGULATIONS

Metadata is essential for data governance and regulatory compliance. Assuring compliance with key compliance systems such as the General Data Protection Regulation (GDPR), Health Insurance Portability and Accountability Act (HIPAA), and the California Consumer Privacy Act (CCPA) depends on metadata. Governments all across are examining closely how businesses manage private and sensitive data. Metadata is a rich mine of data for compliance management as it specifies the data it marks, facilitating monitoring, auditing, and reporting. This study explores the increasing regulatory difficulties businesses face, how metadata is applied for audits and data lineage monitoring, and how it could help reach regulatory compliance.

Importance of Metadata in Achieving Regulatory Compliance

Stringent regulations govern data collection, storage, and management practices as outlined in GDPR, HIPAA, and CCPA frameworks. These rules advocate for transparency, accountability, and data security to uphold individuals' privacy rights. Adhering to these compliance criteria fundamentally relies on metadata (data elucidating other data) by offering context, traceability, and accountability for data management throughout its lifecycle.

1. **GDPR Compliance**: Adherence to the General Data Protection Regulation (GDPR) (Labadie & Legner, 2023) necessitates the documenting of data categories, processing objectives, and the legal basis for processing requirements. Organizations can efficiently oversee this data through the utilization of metadata. Consent for data processing, data subject access requests (DSARs), and data retention schedules are three essential elements of compliance with the General Data Protection Regulation (GDPR); metadata facilitates the documentation of each. Metadata can facilitate the right to erasure by indicating personal data locations stored in distributed systems, allowing for prompt deletion when necessary.
2. **HIPAA Compliance**: According to Tovino (2022), HIPAA delineates regulations for the healthcare industry to protect patient PHI. Monitoring access to protected health information (PHI) relies on metadata to ensure only authorized individuals can see or modify confidential data. HIPAA mandates the ability to maintain audit trails that document the access, modification, or transfer of data, thereby protecting health information's confidentiality, integrity, and availability. Metadata fulfills this criterion. If organizations meticulously keep metadata records, they can demonstrate compliance with regulations during inquiries and audits.
3. **CCPA Compliance**: The CCPA (Bonta, 2022) ensures that Californians possess the right to be informed about the data collected, processed, and disseminated regarding them. Metadata furnishes the framework necessary to uphold these anticipations for transparency and accessibility. Companies

can react to data subject access requests (DSARs) while maintaining data-sharing policy records and efficiently identifying and tracing data sets associated with specific individuals through metadata. Identifying data sources that facilitate anonymizing or eliminating personal information, thereby ensuring compliance with the CCPA's right to deletion, is achievable through metadata.

Role of Metadata in Audits, Data Lineage Tracking, and Reporting

Data audits, lineage tracing, and reporting, crucial for showing regulatory compliance, predominantly depend on metadata.

1. **Audits**: Regulatory audits are essential for ensuring compliance; metadata facilitates audits by offering a comprehensive overview of data activity (Sargiotis, 2024). Numerous compliance standards mandate metadata to record the times and individuals involved in data access, modification, or destruction. This data monitors an audit. Preserving this data for prolonged durations and ensuring its accessibility during audits demonstrates the organization's adherence to standards. Metadata management systems can automatically generate and maintain audit logs, enhancing accuracy and alleviating administrative burdens.
2. **Data Lineage Tracking**: Data lineage refers to data tracking through various systems, processes, and transformations inside an organization. Data lineage management is essential for regulatory compliance since it enables the demonstration of data flows, origins, and processing alterations (Syed, 2020). Businesses could find metadata helpful for tracking processing activity, including data conversions, guaranteeing GDPR compliance. Companies could monitor data genealogy using metadata to show compliance with rules requiring data traceability. This helps to hold data management practices public and responsible.
3. **Reporting**: Producing comprehensive and accurate reports required by regulatory agencies greatly depends on metadata. According to Borgogno and Colangelo (2019), regulatory systems routinely demand thorough data processing, sharing, and security coverage. Crucial compliance criteria that companies might quickly generate reports on utilizing metadata include data retention periods, legal justifications for processing, and forms of personally identifiable information acquired. These reports must be regularly assessed and updated if new data management systems or procedures developed inside the company come to light. One significant advantage is having real-time data insights, which guarantees the creation of compliant, standard reports using automated metadata management systems.

Emerging Regulatory Challenges and How Metadata Management Can Help

The ever-changing regulatory environments make compliance increasingly difficult for businesses. Among the latest developments adding complexity to metadata management include the increasing use of artificial intelligence and machine learning in data processing, data sovereignty rules, and worldwide data flows.

1. **Data Sovereignty**: Data sovereignty regulations compel enterprises to store and oversee consumer data within designated countries (Voss, 2019). Metadata management will significantly impact if organisations guarantee their metadata meets local data residency requirements. Metadata manage-

ment solutions assist businesses by identifying data storage locations and verifying the legality of cross-border data flows.

2. **Cross-Border Data Transfers**: Numerous multinational corporations encounter challenges in regulating cross-border data transfers while adhering to regulations such as GDPR (Voss, 2019). Metadata facilitates the oversight of data transmission to ensure compliance with international standards and frameworks, such as the EU-U.S. Privacy Shield.
3. **AI and ML in Data Processing**: Cheong (2024) contends that the increasing integration of artificial intelligence and machine learning into data processing activities gives rise to new legal challenges around algorithmic transparency and accountability. Metadata monitors the data utilized for training algorithms, ensures the documentation of data provenance, and enables audits of AI evaluations for fairness and compliance, thereby aiding in resolving these issues.

Risks of Metadata Mismanagement

Effective metadata management, compliance, and data security rely on one another. Improper information management can lead to various hazards, including regulatory non-compliance, privacy violations, and metadata sprawl.

Metadata Sprawl: Companies with "metadata sprawl", that is, too much unstructured or duplicate metadata dispersed over numerous platforms, may find themselves in Inefficiencies, distorted thinking, and difficulties with data retrieval follow from this. Without a centralized metadata approach, companies find data integrity and quality challenging. Crawl makes compliance evaluations and judgments more challenging and can generate obsolete or incorrect data.

Privacy Concerns and Regulatory Non-Compliance: Careless metadata handling might reveal private business or personal data, therefore violating data protection laws, including GDPR and CCPA. Unauthorized users might possibly get access to metadata like access logs, customer profiles, and document histories, raising security questions. Ignorance of metadata changes can also result in inadequate audit trails, which would cause noncompliance fines.

Security Vulnerabilities: Insufficient metadata management makes systems open for assault. Important information like data ownership, processing history, and sources usually find a place in metadata. Should this data be compromised, hackers might use it to alter records, build phishing scams, or pilfer critical data. If companies neglect to encrypt data or apply stringent access limits, they run the danger of financial losses and data breaches.

Poor Data Usability and Decision-Making: Incorrect or inconsistent data might mislead business intelligence systems and produce erroneous findings. False information used in bad strategic decisions can compromise the company's credibility and bottom line. Duplication of information and inconsistent governance standards impede operations.

Companies may reduce their sensitivity to these threats by implementing security controls, explicit metadata rules, and frequent metadata system audits to guarantee compliance, security, and dependability.

METADATA MANAGEMENT TOOLS AND TECHNOLOGIES

Metadata management solutions are essential for a firm to achieve scalable and effective data governance systems. Utilizing these tools, a firm may oversee its data assets and manage metadata throughout its processes. As enterprises produce increasing amounts of data across many platforms and complicate information retention, the significance of metadata management solutions is escalating. What are the most essential aspects of open-source or commercial tools, and how has using these tools in real-world scenarios influenced data governance? This section will evaluate the latest options for metadata management.

Overview of Modern Metadata Management Tools

Metadata management has progressed over the last decade and currently provides diverse solutions suitable for contemporary data environments. Apache Atlas, Collibra, and Alation are this domain's most frequently utilized technologies.

1. **Apache Atlas**: According to Jahnke and Otto (2023), Apache Atlas is an open-source information management and governance platform. Its goal is to provide a consistent framework for tracking data lineage, metadata, and data governance across several business systems. Access restrictions, material arrangement and classification, and source tracking are all under the user's control. Apache Atlas' compatibility with Hadoop frameworks and other projects makes it an excellent choice for significant data ecosystems. Stringent lineage tracking, for example, is critical to data governance transparency and compliance.
2. **Collibra**: Collibra is a limited solution for managing metadata; it is a full-featured data governance system. Sargiotis (2024) claims that organization, classification, and control enable companies to handle their data on several platforms. Collibra offers data cataloguing, policy enforcement, and data quality management among its capabilities. Customers could gain from the Data Governance Center when creating data standards, monitoring data quality, and following legal frameworks like GDPR. Companies seeking efficient governance fit for their present IT infrastructure might choose Collibra.
3. **Alation**: Alation offers a commercial system (a shared data library) to enable companies to control their data better. Based on Subramaniam et al. (2021), this tool helps teams to find, comprehend, and control the present data assets. Alation's simpler architecture and AI-enhanced search tools help users find relevant information. Its compatibility with technologies such as Tableau, Snowflake, and Databricks makes it a perfect choice for companies adopting cloud-native or data warehouse architectures. Alation enhances data use and governance norms by aggregating metadata management with machine learning recommendations.

Comparison of Open-Source vs. Commercial Solutions

When selecting metadata management systems, businesses should consider the advantages and disadvantages of both open-source and commercial systems. This choice involves possibilities, technical proficiency, financial restrictions, and other elements.

1. **Open-Source Solutions:** Open-source solutions such as Apache Atlas are an excellent alternative for firms who value system customization or have limited money due to their low cost and flexibility. According to Tall and Zou (2023), Apache Atlas excels in data lineage, metadata classification, and governance. Because it is open-source, businesses may customize its features to meet their needs and integrate it into their existing infrastructure. Technical knowledge may be required for open-source system setup, modification, and continuous maintenance (Eghbal, 2020). Despite being free, they provide difficulty for organizations without dedicated IT workers owing to a lack of qualified help. The cost-benefit analysis demonstrates that open-source solutions are the best alternative for technically proficient but financially challenged SMEs.
2. **Commercial Solutions:** Commercial solutions such as Alation and Collibra give consumers enhanced features, tailored assistance, and better refinement. Designed for business environments, these technologies offer, among other things, seamless interaction with other systems, AI-generated insights, and thorough data governance, among other things. Their simplicity of installation and ongoing customer assistance match companies that prioritize efficiency and compliance. Smaller companies, meanwhile, might be turned off by their high cost. Larger companies, on the other hand, typically justify the cost as these solutions offer scalability and continuous support (qualities essential for handling complicated data environments).

Key Features to Look for in Metadata Management Tools for Modern Software

When deciding on metadata management solutions for contemporary software systems, companies should prioritize features in line with data governance goals. Data processes are sure to follow all rules, be secure, and be quick. Choosing a metadata management system depends critically on the following elements:

1. **Data Lineage**: Data lineage is essential to follow the evolution of data changes, their source, and their path to get there. Good metadata tools follow data from its source to its destination, guaranteeing accuracy and consistency in data processing. Strong lineage tracking improves traceability (Singh et al., 2018) and exposes data management, helping companies with compliance audits. Making data management more open helps to satisfy GDPR and other regulatory requirements.
2. **Data Cataloging:** A thorough data catalog simplifies data asset availability and administration. As Hong (2023) points out, automated cataloging methods save data analysts and scientists time and effort. Metadata tools in a structured repository help increase data usability, facilitating more informed decision-making and greater departmental cooperation.
3. **Data Quality Management:** Good government depends on accurate, comprehensive, and current data. Metadata management systems' data quality features help guarantee that errors or inconsistencies have no impact on decision-making. With their data-driven insights, automated data quality checks enable companies to become more trustworthy and efficient, claims Bammidi et al. (2024).
4. **Security and Access Controls:** Protecting private data in compliance with HIPAA and GDPR calls for strong security and access control policies. Organizations may set access policies and track user behavior using technologies like role-based access controls (RBAC) and thorough audit logs. Mpamugo and Ansa (2024) say these are essential for preventing unauthorized access and data breaches.

5. **Collaboration and Integration:** Mostly aiming to facilitate team communication and enable integration with other platforms like cloud and business intelligence tools, and metadata management solutions. Two excellent examples of tools that enable users to collaborate on data governance initiatives that fit well with more extensive analytics frameworks are Alation and Collibra. Nookala (2022) claims that this skill enhances user engagement with information and facilitates decision-making in numerous functional areas using which one might simplify their activities.
6. **Scalability:** As companies expand, metadata rules get increasingly complicated. Given the rising data volume from many different sources, a scalable metadata management system is vital. While open-source solutions like Apache Atlas provide technical knowledge, adaptability, and flexibility to businesses, commercial solutions like Collibra are designed for massive systems.

FUTURE TRENDS IN METADATA MANAGEMENT AND DATA GOVERNANCE

While new technologies can revolutionize how companies collect, manage, and use data, the metadata management and data governance fields are quickly changing. The quick advancement of digital transformation and the broad use of modern technologies such as cloud computing, the Internet of Things (IoT), and edge computing are making metadata more relevant. Due to several developments, including blockchain capability, edge computing, Internet of Things (IoT) real-time information management, and the effects of quantum computing, metadata management will change in the coming years. Companies should monitor these developments to observe how the scene develops and help them make future data governance plans.

The Role of Blockchain for Immutable Metadata Tracking

Many have focused on blockchain records' immutability, openness, and security. Applying blockchain technology to metadata management can help to improve data integrity and traceability practically (Paik et al., 2019). Blockchain's distributed ledger technology keeps metadata decentrally, preventing alteration or manipulation once recorded. Blockchain technology lets companies better track data flow across systems by capturing every modification and data point on an unchangeable ledger. This immutability is fundamental for supply chain management, banking, and healthcare sectors to ensure data integrity and openness. Blockchain technology guarantees the immutability and veracity of metadata by building an audit trail capable of withstanding governmental inspection.

Furthermore, as blockchain is distributed, many authorities might concurrently be in charge of maintaining metadata (Demichev et al., 2021). This is especially beneficial in businesses with intricate stakeholder networks, as trust cannot be developed without a shared, permanent data record. As blockchain technology grows progressively linked with metadata management systems, a more reliable and open data governance structure will be accessible.

Advances in Real-Time Metadata Management for IoT and Edge Computing

Managing real-time data becomes more crucial as edge computing and the IoT get traction. Real-time decision-making calls for fast interpretation as IoT devices generate so much data. Faster responses and reduced delay are made possible by edge computing, that is, local data processing instead of centralized cloud computing. Heynes (2018) argues that for real-time data processing and tracking, metadata management systems must help to facilitate this paradigm shift. Changes made to data at the edge during manufacturing and processing call for real-time metadata changes. For instance, sensors linked to the Internet of Things (IoT) may track manufacturing equipment performance continually. Real-time metadata monitoring helps companies better understand how data flows through the system and guarantees that metadata is current as blockchain technology develops and is increasingly linked with metadata management systems.

Real-time metadata management is a difficult chore given the incredible speed and volume of data produced by Internet of Things devices. Standard metadata management solutions cannot meet the processing needs of real-time data. More complicated metadata tracking is becoming feasible thanks to machine learning and automation developments; this new technology can automatically identify and classify data as it is generated, therefore addressing these issues. This real-time tracking allows companies to base their judgments on up-to-minute data.

Potential Disruptions from Quantum Computing on Metadata Systems

Although still in its early years, quantum computing can potentially transform several facets of the IT sector, including metadata management. Unlike conventional computers, Quantum computers process data using the rules of quantum physics (Nofer et al., 2023). Still, in its early years, quantum computing is predicted to fundamentally change data governance in the following years. With their lightning-fast processing rates relative to conventional systems, quantum computers can transform metadata handling. Powerful quantum computers capable of handling and analyzing vast information libraries in real time will transform data lineage tracking and compliance monitoring in hitherto unthinkable ways. Furthermore, quantum computing helps to make metadata management systems far more secure. Using quantum encryption techniques (which offer increased security), metadata should be shielded from malicious actors. The capacity of quantum computers to offer more solid encryption solutions may soon be needed to keep sensitive data safe as the complexity of assaults keeps increasing.

Ranga et al. (2024) say that present encryption approaches and metadata frameworks need to be re-evaluated given the possibilities given by quantum computing pose fresh issues for metadata management systems from extensive usage of quantum computing. The unique qualities of quantum technologies (such as quantum entanglement and superposition) may compel companies to rethink their data governance policies and even change their data storage and processing methods.

CONCLUSION AND WAY FORWARD

Modern data governance is mainly based on metadata management, guaranteeing compliance, security, data quality, and accessibility. Companies depend on and produce enormous volumes of data, so powerful metadata systems are even more crucial for managing, enhancing, and regulating this data. By using metadata, which offers a bird' s-eye view of data access, usage, and history, companies may better monitor their data assets, enhancing governance.

Data governance will fail horribly if data is not securely kept, easily accessed, and correct. Businesses depend on thorough data records produced by metadata management to achieve regulatory compliance, auditability, and risk management. Especially crucial are metadata systems in highly regulated sectors like banking and healthcare, which must follow rules like GDPR and HIPAA. Metadata simplifies compliance reporting, audits, and risk reduction by tracking data transfer, ancestry, and access.

Metadata depends on the interaction between software development, DevSecOps, and governance structures. Thanks to metadata, DevSecOps can fit the always-shifting software development environment that values speed and security. Data incorporated into the development pipeline makes security risk monitoring, compliance mandate enforcement, and process optimization from development to deployment feasible. Consequently, security and governance are now fundamental elements of the software development lifecycle as they help to lower risk and raise performance.

Given its weight, metadata will only become increasingly important in the digital world. As more and more businesses apply creative technologies such as blockchain, artificial intelligence, and machine learning, data complexity and volume are expected to rise. Metadata management systems must get increasingly advanced to manage data flows in real-time, connect with cloud-native settings, and grow to satisfy contemporary companies' needs. Blockchain technology offers prominent and reliable data since its unchangeable metadata monitoring. The development of quantum computing would provide unheard-of processing capability and data complexity, which might call for new metadata systems to control.

In conclusion, technical demands and metadata management will also impact software development, data security, and governance. As the digital era develops, companies must continue investing in all-encompassing metadata management solutions if they are to effectively address all data concerns, present and future. This will allow companies to simultaneously satisfy legal requirements and support operational excellence, security, and innovation. Since it impacts business operations, metadata management follows a complex and dynamic path.

REFERENCES

Alkhard, A. (2024). Enhancing asset management through integrated facilities data, digital asset management, and metadata strategies. *Construction Economics and Building, 24*(3), 76-94. https://search.informit.org/doi/10.3316/informit.T2024081300001000356599362

Awotunde, J. B., Ogundokun, R. O., & Misra, S. (2021). Cloud and IoMT-based big data analytics system during COVID-19 pandemic. In *Efficient Data Handling for Massive Internet of Medical Things: Healthcare Data Analytics* (pp. 181–201). Springer International Publishing. DOI: 10.1007/978-3-030-66633-0_8

Bammidi, T. R., Gutta, L. M., Kotagiri, A., & Samayamantri, L. S., & krishna Vaddy, R. (2024). The Crucial Role of Data Quality in Automated Decision-Making Systems. *International Journal of Management Education for Sustainable Development*, 7(7), 1–22.

Bhaskaran, S. V. (2020). Integrating Data Quality Services (DQS) in Big Data Ecosystems: Challenges, Best Practices, and Opportunities for Decision-Making. *Journal of Applied Big Data Analytics, Decision-Making, and Predictive Modelling Systems*, 4(11), 1–12. http://polarpublications.com/index.php/JABADP/article/view/4

Bonta, R. (2022). California consumer privacy act (CCPA). *Retrieved from State of California Department of Justice:*https://oag. ca. *gov/privacy/ccpa*. Accessed January 22, 2025.

Borgogno, O., & Colangelo, G. (2019). Data sharing and interoperability: Fostering innovation and competition through APIs. *Computer Law & Security Report*, 35(5), 105314. DOI: 10.1016/j.clsr.2019.03.008

Caliskan, A., Dangwal, S., & Dandekar, T. (2023). Metadata integrity in bioinformatics: Bridging the gap between data and knowledge. *Computational and Structural Biotechnology Journal*, 21, 4895–4913. Advance online publication. DOI: 10.1016/j.csbj.2023.10.006 PMID: 37860229

Cheong, B. C. (2024). Transparency and accountability in AI systems: Safeguarding wellbeing in the age of algorithmic decision-making. *Frontiers in Human Dynamics*, 6, 1421273. DOI: 10.3389/fhumd.2024.1421273

Deekshith, A. (2021). Data engineering for AI: Optimizing data quality and accessibility for machine learning models. *International Journal of Management Education for Sustainable Development*, 4(4), 1–33.

Demichev, A., Kryukov, A., & Prikhod'ko, N. (2021). Business process engineering for data storing and processing in a collaborative distributed environment based on provenance metadata, smart contracts and blockchain technology. *Journal of Grid Computing*, 19(1), 3. DOI: 10.1007/s10723-021-09544-4

Dibouliya, A., & Jotwani, D. V. (2023). Review on Data Mesh Architecture and its Impact. *Journal of Harbin Engineering University*, 44(7), 2353–2363.

Eghbal, N. (2020). *Working in public: the making and maintenance of open source software*. Stripe Press.

Fawzy, A., Tahir, A., Galster, M., & Liang, P. (2024). Data Management Challenges in Agile Software Projects: A Systematic Literature Review. *arXiv preprint arXiv:2402.00462*.

Goedegebuure, A., Kumara, I., Driessen, S., Van Den Heuvel, W. J., Monsieur, G., Tamburri, D. A., & Nucci, D. D. (2024). Data mesh: A systematic gray literature review. *ACM Computing Surveys*, 57(1), 1–36. DOI: 10.1145/3687301

Gregorczuk, H. (2022). Retail analytics: Smart-stores saving bricks-and-mortar retail or a privacy problem? *Law. Technology and Humans*, 4(1), 63–78. DOI: 10.5204/lthj.2088

Haynes, D. (2018). *Metadata for Information Management and Retrieval: Understanding metadata and its use*. Facet Publishing. DOI: 10.29085/9781783302161

Hong, J. H. (2023). Harnessing AI-Driven Data Cataloging Techniques for Enhanced Discoverability and Usability in Big Data Ecosystems. *Journal of Computational Innovation*, 3(1).

Jahnke, N., & Otto, B. (2023). Data catalogs in the enterprise: Applications and integration. *Datenbank-Spektrum: Zeitschrift fur Datenbanktechnologie: Organ der Fachgruppe Datenbanken der Gesellschaft fur Informatik e.V*, 23(2), 89–96. DOI: 10.1007/s13222-023-00445-2

Joseph, A. (2023). A Holistic Framework for Unifying Data Security and Management in Modern Enterprises. *International Journal of Social and Business Sciences*, 17(10), 602–609.

Kanchepu, N. (2023). Cloud-Native Architectures: Design Principles and Best Practices for Scalable Applications. *International Journal of Sustainable Development Through AI. ML and IoT*, 2(2), 1–21.

Khair, M. A. (2018). Security-Centric Software Development: Integrating Secure Coding Practices into the Software Development Lifecycle. *Technology & Management Review*, 3(1), 12–26.

Labadie, C., & Legner, C. (2023). Building data management capabilities to address data protection regulations: Learnings from EU-GDPR. *Journal of Information Technology*, 38(1), 16–44. DOI: 10.1177/02683962221141456

Laszewski, T., Arora, K., Farr, E., & Zonooz, P. (2018). *Cloud Native Architectures: Design high-availability and cost-effective applications for the cloud*. Packt Publishing Ltd.

Li, Z., Kant, H., Hai, R., Katsifodimos, A., Brambilla, M., & Bozzon, A. (2023). Metadata representations for queryable repositories of machine learning models. *IEEE Access : Practical Innovations, Open Solutions*, 11, 125616–125630. DOI: 10.1109/ACCESS.2023.3330647

Machado, I. A., Costa, C., & Santos, M. Y. (2022). Data mesh: Concepts and principles of a paradigm shift in data architectures. *Procedia Computer Science*, 196, 263–271. DOI: 10.1016/j.procs.2021.12.013

Mahanti, R. (2019). *Data quality: dimensions, measurement, strategy, management, and governance*. Quality Press.

Miller, S. J. (2022). *Metadata for digital collections*. American Library Association.

Mpamugo, E., & Ansa, G. (2024). Enhancing Network Security in Mobile Applications with Role-Based Access Control. *Journal of Information Systems and Informatics*, 6(3), 1872–1899. DOI: 10.51519/journalisi.v6i3.863

Nishat, A., & Azmat, H. (2021). Enhancing Data Governance through AI-Driven Data Lineage Tracking and Impact Analysis in Complex Data Ecosystems. *Artificial Intelligence Horizons*, 1(1), 1–9.

Nofer, M., Bauer, K., Hinz, O., van der Aalst, W., & Weinhardt, C. (2023). Quantum Computing. *Business & Information Systems Engineering*, 65(4), 361–367. DOI: 10.1007/s12599-023-00823-w

Nookala, G. (2022). Metadata-Driven Data Models for Self-Service BI Platforms. *Journal of Big Data and Smart Systems*, 3(1).

Pachouly, J., Ahirrao, S., Kotecha, K., Selvachandran, G., & Abraham, A. (2022). A systematic literature review on software defect prediction using artificial intelligence: Datasets, Data Validation Methods, Approaches, and Tools. *Engineering Applications of Artificial Intelligence*, 111, 104773. DOI: 10.1016/j.engappai.2022.104773

Paik, H. Y., Xu, X., Bandara, H. D., Lee, S. U., & Lo, S. K. (2019). Analysis of data management in blockchain-based systems: From architecture to governance. *IEEE Access : Practical Innovations, Open Solutions*, 7, 186091–186107. DOI: 10.1109/ACCESS.2019.2961404

Pansara, R. R. (2022). Cybersecurity Measures in Master Data Management: Safeguarding Sensitive Information. *International Numeric Journal of Machine Learning and Robots*, 6(6), 1–12.

Pasquier, T., Singh, J., Powles, J., Eyers, D., Seltzer, M., & Bacon, J. (2018). Data provenance to audit compliance with privacy policy in the Internet of Things. *Personal and Ubiquitous Computing*, 22(2), 333–344. DOI: 10.1007/s00779-017-1067-4

Pinoli, P., Ceri, S., Martinenghi, D., & Nanni, L. (2019). Metadata management for scientific databases. *Information Systems*, 81, 1–20. DOI: 10.1016/j.is.2018.10.002

Ponta, S. E., Plate, H., & Sabetta, A. (2020). Detection, assessment and mitigation of vulnerabilities in open source dependencies. *Empirical Software Engineering*, 25(5), 3175–3215. DOI: 10.1007/s10664-020-09830-x

Ranga, D., Rana, A., Prajapat, S., Kumar, P., Kumar, K., & Vasilakos, A. V. (2024). Quantum Machine Learning: Exploring the Role of Data Encoding Techniques, Challenges, and Future Directions. *Mathematics*, 12(21), 3318. DOI: 10.3390/math12213318

Sargiotis, D. (2024). Data Governance Tools and Technologies: Navigating the Options. In *Data Governance: A Guide* (pp. 305–325). Springer Nature Switzerland. DOI: 10.1007/978-3-031-67268-2_9

Shiyal, B. (2021). Modern data warehouses and data lakehouses. In *Beginning Azure Synapse Analytics: Transition from Data Warehouse to Data Lakehouse* (pp. 21–48). Apress. DOI: 10.1007/978-1-4842-7061-5_2

Singh, J., Cobbe, J., & Norval, C. (2018). Decision provenance: Harnessing data flow for accountable systems. *IEEE Access : Practical Innovations, Open Solutions*, 7, 6562–6574. DOI: 10.1109/ACCESS.2018.2887201

Stier, S. P., Kreisbeck, C., Ihssen, H., Popp, M. A., Hauch, J., Malek, K., Reynaud, M., Goumans, T. P. M., Carlsson, J., Todorov, I., Gold, L., Räder, A., Wenzel, W., Bandesha, S. T., Jacques, P., Garcia-Moreno, F., Arcelus, O., Friederich, P., Clark, S., & Kozdras, M. (2024). Materials Acceleration Platforms (MAPs): Accelerating Materials Research and Development to Meet Urgent Societal Challenges. *Advanced Materials*, 36(45), 2407791. DOI: 10.1002/adma.202407791 PMID: 39239995

Subramaniam, P., Ma, Y., Li, C., Mohanty, I., & Fernandez, R. C. (2021). Comprehensive and comprehensible data catalogs: The what, who, where, when, why, and how of metadata management. *arXiv preprint arXiv:2103.07532*.

Syed, S. (2020). Data Lineage Strategies-A Modernized View. *Educational Administration: Theory and Practice*.

Tall, A. M., & Zou, C. C. (2023). A framework for attribute-based access control in processing big data with multiple sensitivities. *Applied Sciences (Basel, Switzerland)*, 13(2), 1183. DOI: 10.3390/app13021183

Thomas, K., & Praseetha, N. (2020). Data Lake: A Centralized Repository. *Int. Res. J. Eng. Technol*, 7, 2978–2981.

Tovino, S. A. (2022). Health Privacy, Security, and Information Management. In *Laws of Medicine: Core Legal Aspects for the Healthcare Professional* (pp. 223–238). Springer International Publishing. DOI: 10.1007/978-3-031-08162-0_13

Ugwueze, V. U., & Chukwunweike, J. N. (2024). Continuous integration and deployment strategies for streamlined DevOps in software engineering and application delivery. *Int J Comput Appl Technol Res*, 14(1), 1–24.

Voss, W. G. (2019). Cross-border data flows, the GDPR, and data governance. *Wash. Int'l LJ*, 29, 485.

Zahid, R., Altaf, A., Ahmad, T., Iqbal, F., Vera, Y. A. M., Flores, M. A. L., & Ashraf, I. (2023). Secure data management life cycle for government big-data ecosystem: Design and development perspective. *Systems*, 11(8), 380. DOI: 10.3390/systems11080380

Chapter 4
Data Lineage:
Tracing Data Across Systems

Rajesh Vayyala
https://orcid.org/0009-0001-0227-0675
PRA Group Inc., USA

ABSTRACT

Modern digital ecosystems may be open, compliant, and safe only by following data back to its source. This chapter covers the background, relevance, and function of data lineage in data governance and DevSecOps completely. Emphasizing the requirement of metadata management, policy-driven lineage systems for maintaining data integrity, and automated tracking, Thanks to the growth of cloud-native architectures and artificial intelligence-driven analytics, companies realize more and more the requirement of real-time lineage tracking in risk management and regulatory compliance. Investigated alongside challenges like regulatory complexity, scalability problems, and a lack of interoperability are innovations, including blockchain-based tracking and AI-enhanced lineage. This chapter explains that good data lineage is more of a benefit than a need. Establishing trust is crucial and provides companies with tools to negotiate the complex data ecosystems of today confidently.

INTRODUCTION

From storage to transformation and ultimately to its intended use, tracking data from its inception through its lifetime is known as "data lineage." Understanding data lifecycles calls for this thorough mapping as current, dynamic, networked software systems are growingly complicated. Data lineage is all about openness and auditability, qualities necessary for data lifecycle visibility and traceability. Included here are updates to calculations, aggregations, and migrations. This competence defines the dependability of data-driven systems, error detection, and validation of outputs, as well as other aspects. One cannot stress the value of data lineage in contemporary software systems. More complex data flows (such as the transfer from on-site to cloud or hybrid-based infrastructures) result from fast technological advancement. Data provenance in former IT environments was often handled using simple tracking systems or handwritten notes depending on central databases and batch processing. Many companies use automated, real-time data lineage as cloud-native agile systems provide constant integration and delivery

DOI: 10.4018/979-8-3373-0365-9.ch004

pipelines. New technologies are advancing sectors, including risk management, regulatory compliance, and granular data acquisition.

Data lineage has consequences well beyond simple error detection. Data quality monitoring and maintenance is, therefore, a fundamental part of data governance so that stakeholders may rely on the data when making important decisions based on it. In the field of DevSecOps, for example, where including data lineage into the software development lifecycle helps to find vulnerabilities as data passes between systems, data pipelines might be better guarded. Preemptive actions are especially crucial today as data breaches and compliance problems could cause significant financial losses and damage to reputation. Companies are spending more and more on artificial intelligence and sophisticated analytics. Thus, they need to know data transformation. This will provide dependability and simplicity of interpretation for models created from converted data. These days, the software also depends much on data lineage. Conventional information technology solutions offer a more simple and predictable data flow. These days, distributed software systems usually run on various platforms and cloud environments. Positive as well as negative results follow from this evolution. The dynamic character of cloud resources, the increasing complexity of data flows, and the cohabitation of current platforms with older systems provide new obstacles for automated lineage tracking. Still, the advantages considerably exceed the disadvantages. Accurate documentation of every modification improves operational efficiency, regulatory compliance, monitoring and issue-resolution timelines, and automated data lineage support for data-driven decision-making.

Together, metadata management and data lineage have shown the always-shifting nature of data quality. Combining technical specifics with business context helps companies understand how data affects downstream operations and find mistakes early on. The book depends on data lineage and governance; these ideas provide stability, openness, and adaptability to changing technologies. This book applies this method to investigate how the strategic demands of contemporary corporate environments have shaped data management systems.

Data lineage might be a strategic benefit rather than only a technical instrument. Businesses' back-to-its-source monitoring enhances quality, assists with compliance, and fosters a transparent and accountable culture. Businesses need strong data lineage rules to negotiate the complicated hybrid cloud market and the always-shifting software ecosystem. This chapter will present data lineage and its applications in efficient data governance, software development, and supporting DevSecOps approaches. We expect data to be dependable and readily available in our digital environment.

THE ROLE OF DATA GOVERNANCE IN DATA LINEAGE

Today, data governance is more important than ever to ensure organizations employ trustworthy, high-quality, safe data. Organizations need data lineage to stay compliant, maintain high-quality data, and make wise decisions. Data is tracked as it changes and flows. This section critically analyses data governance in data lineage using GDPR compliance, DAMA DMBOK, and FAIR. Data quality, metadata integration, policy-driven lineage, and system-to-system trust maintenance are covered extensively. Examples demonstrate how this may enhance governance, which is crucial for software system effectiveness, safety, and data lineage.

Data Governance Frameworks: Establishing the Foundation

Data governance is the system of checks and balances to guarantee data's correct and efficient use to reach corporate goals. By delineating standards and best practices for data quality, metadata management, and regulatory compliance, data management systems -like DAMA DMBOK (Data Management Body of Knowledge) - offer a complete strategy (Gupta & Soni, 2020). To guarantee that data is equally exploitable by humans and machines, the FAIR (Findability, Accessibility, Interoperability, and Reusability) values provide rules for open and effective data management (Inau et al., 2023). Like the EU's General Data Protection Regulation (GDPR), regulatory systems likewise impose significant pressure on data governance guidelines. If a corporation maintains thorough records of processing operations, limits data access, and tracks data transfers, it may be confident it is in GDPR compliance. Regulatory pressure is driving more and more the adoption of data lineage approaches. Companies today have to show their dedication to safe and moral data handling by offering an auditable record of data sources.

Data Quality and Metadata Management in Lineage Tracking

Properly managing metadata, which is information about data, is an integral part of data history. Using raw data with context, structure, and meaning, metadata management helps companies understand the systems handling data changes. Inmon and Linstedt argue that creating effective lineage maps that show data flow (2015) relies on having trustworthy data. Data quality systems, like DAMA DMBOK, focus mainly on regularly cleaning, checking, and tracking data. By combining data tracking with quality standards, businesses can identify and fix problems faster. A sound history system helps track where mistakes or inconsistencies in panel data come from, whether it involves data entry, conversion, or storage. By ensuring they follow the rules and regulations, businesses can improve their management systems by using methods to maintain data quality and handle information. This will help their info gain trust.

Figure 1. Data Quality and Metadata Management Flow

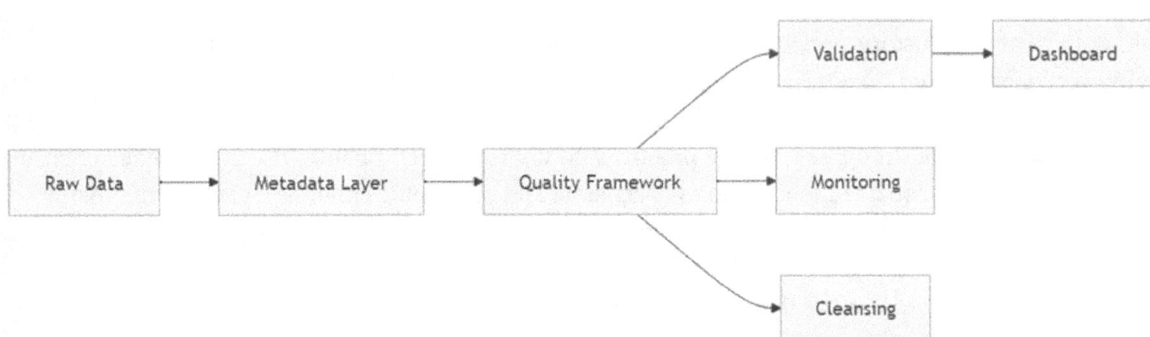

Policy-Driven Lineage: Ensuring Security, Compliance, and Accuracy

Policy-driven lineage helps data processing processes follow data governance rules (Zeydan & Mangues-Bafalluy, 2022). Rules for data integration, access restrictions, and security measures can enhance how we handle data lineage. All changes, transfers, and groupings must follow specific rules to ensure the data stays accurate and secure. Imagine a company that handles personal information for its clients. Policy-based lineage system standards allow for secure data exchanges that follow set rules. Access limits are constantly applied throughout the data process, and any rule-breaking is quickly identified. These technologies create a clear record that can be used for checks by regulators and internal reviews. Including control criteria in lineage tracking systems helps companies protect themselves against data breaches and non-compliance. Having this level of control is essential because, in a DevSecOps setting, any security or quality problem can lead to serious issues. Standards allow for quick setup and continuous merging. A sound lineage system helps track where mistakes or inconsistencies in panel data come from, whether it involves data entry, conversion, or storage. By ensuring they follow the rules and regulations, businesses can improve their management systems by using methods to maintain data quality and handle information. This will help their info gain trust.

Figure 2. Policy-Driven Lineage Flow

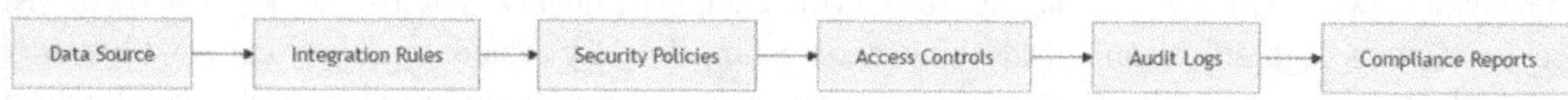

Maintaining Trust in Data Flow Across Systems

Organizations that use analytics and automatic decision-making should prioritize data trust above all else. Building and maintaining trust relies on understanding where data comes from and how it moves, which is what data history provides. Being completely open and able to verify data at all stages will help everyone involved, like business leaders and data experts, trust that the data is reliable. Radoslav (2024) explains that companies keep trust in data flows by merging automatic lineage tracking with human supervision in strong governance practices. Many finance companies use data lineage to ensure that the data in risk models or legal reports is accurate and complete. Think of a global bank that wants to understand how data moves from one reporting system to another. This highlights the valuable benefits of automatic data tracking technology. In this sense, businesses may find and fix human data entry mistakes in their records before they affect legal reporting (Gartner, 2020). These steps make the data more accurate and increase trust in the systems that support essential business activities.

Figure 3. Data Trust and Flow

Examples of Data Lineage Improving Governance

Several companies have demonstrated that data history can enhance their data control systems. The healthcare business is a good example because HIPAA and other privacy laws have strict rules for tracking patient data. A well-known healthcare company added a detailed data tracking system to its electronic health record (EHR) system. The practitioner kept track of patient information using the lineage system from the initial visit to evaluation, treatment, and billing. During government checks, the company showed it followed the rules, which helped improve data accuracy and reduce mistakes in patient records.

One area is banking services. Regulators regularly check financial institutions to ensure everything works well, so the data used for critical financial models must be accurate and reliable. An investment bank follows data flow from its trade systems to its risk management screens using automatic data lineage methods. As a result, the bank could quickly evaluate how shifts in the market or new regulations would impact it. Analyzers can watch for unusual activity in real-time and promptly fix issues, making it easier to make choices and follow the rules.

Big companies in software development and DevSecOps, like IBM, have included data history as part of their data control standards. By working with information management systems, IBM's Manta Data Lineage system helps users understand how data moves between cloud and on-site systems. This integration makes audits and ongoing tracking possible, improving data control security and compliance (IBM, nd.). Organizations need clear policies for data transfers to ensure their software systems are modern, safe, and efficient for growth. Until then, they will not have enough confidence in their facts.

Data Governance as a Cornerstone of Secure and Efficient Software Systems

Data control is essential to any sound software system, not just a separate topic. When strong rules are set for managing data, each piece of information is carefully checked, confirmed, and managed according to industry standards and legal requirements. This increases the reliability and importance of the company's data while reducing the chances of data leaks and compliance problems.

Companies today need to take charge of managing data in our fast-moving, tech-savvy world. Better tracking of data origins and careful handling of data details, along with the DAMA DMBOK and FAIR models, can help companies build a culture that values data. This combination helps speed creation because analytics, artificial intelligence, and machine learning programs depend on reliable and quality data. Data control is increasingly important to ensure that data is handled responsibly, reliably, and transparently, especially as digital changes happen quickly. Modern software systems rely on data control, made possible by clear data history. This helps companies work better, meet their rules, and make more intelligent choices. Businesses can become stronger and more flexible in today's digital world by promoting a culture of regularly looking at, assessing, and improving data.

Figure 4. Data Governance Framework and Impacts

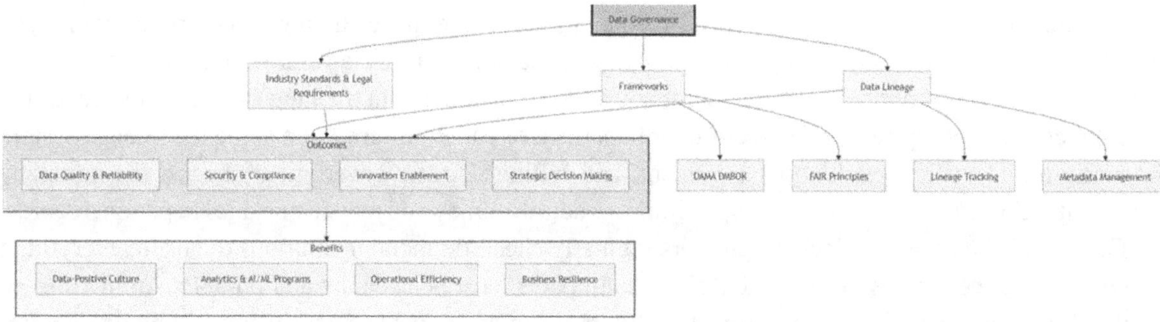

DevSecOps and Data Lineage: The Security Perspective

A new approach called "DevSecOps" has emerged in response to the quick changes in software development methods. DevSecOps is like having a security guard with construction workers while they build a house instead of checking for security after the house is finished. It includes security measures throughout the software development process, ensuring everyone is responsible for security. This approach uses security best practices to enhance every stage of the software development process. For companies that view data as necessary, following rules, ensuring data quality, and keeping it safe rely on data history. This means closely tracking data from its creation to its use. Adding data history to DevSecOps processes boosts public trust and enhances the security of software systems. This part focuses on data tracking and security in DevSecOps. It looks at how safe software development processes can include tracking data origin and monitoring security weaknesses. It also explains ways to reduce risks such as shadow IT, data theft, and insider threats. Two new ways to protect private data are version control and AI-based oddity identification.

Figure 5. DevSecOps and Data Lineage Security Framework

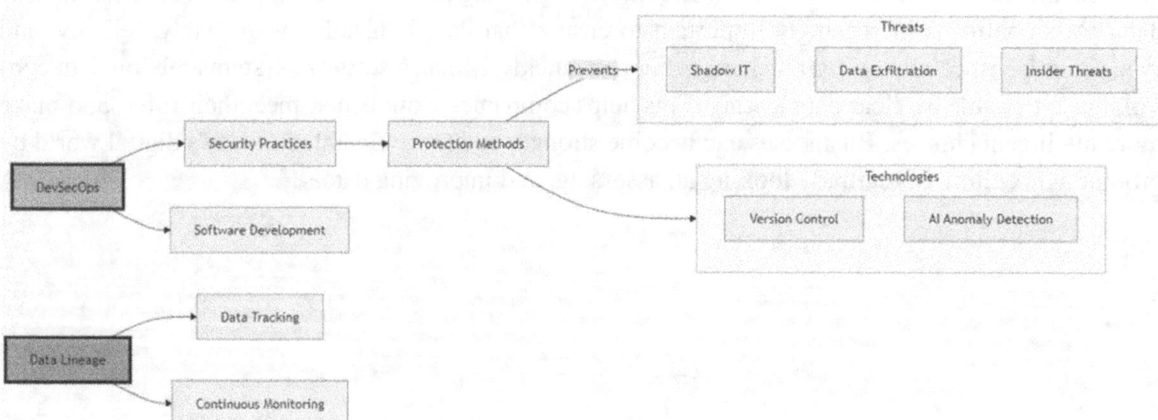

DATA LINEAGE INTO DevSecOps

Yadav et al. (2021) argue that security should be essential to growth, not just an extra consideration. DevSecOps emphasizes this. Many apps need to track where data comes from, how it changes, and where it ends up. This is known as data lineage. Every move and change needs to follow the rules for control and security. Security teams can use data history to show how data flows. By including data lineage in DevSecOps design, companies may build a system that tracks and audits all changes made to data throughout its lifetime. When included in the SDLC, data tracing guarantees that operations staff, security teams, and developers view data processing similarly (Sayles, 2024). When a security issue is found, we need to track the data from where it comes from and through all its changes. This helps us quickly identify the problem's cause and take action to fix it. In a live report, lineage tracking can help determine if the data mismatch is due to the ETL processing, how data is presented, or how data is collected. Teams that understand these points might improve the problem from the ground up, reducing future risks.

Automating Lineage Tracking as Part of a Secure SDLC

Automating data lineage tracking is a new way to advance modern DevSecOps practices through automation. Praveen (2024) argues that human methods for tracking data have weaknesses in accuracy, scalability, and the use of advanced data processes. Automated lineage tracking systems make it easier to safely integrate software development by continuously recording data changes and information as they happen (Davoudian & Liu, 2020). CI/CD pipelines, or continuous integration and delivery, can help software systems proliferate. Automated systems record every change in data flows without requiring any human involvement. Modern data management systems have APIs that automatically update lineage maps with details collected from data flows. This helps emphasize important information. This technology will reduce human errors and help find vulnerabilities faster. Integration of automated lineage tracking within a safe SDLC allows companies to evaluate data flow constantly. Any change from the norm will be noticeable everywhere.

Continuous Monitoring of Data Flow for Security Vulnerabilities

Staying alert is essential for DevSecOps and effective data tracking. Nookala (2024) says that moving data between on-site, cloud, and mixed systems can increase the chance of security problems. These flaws could come from mistakes during setup, illegal access to data, or issues with how data is translated. Continuous tracking tools track data in real time, helping to detect problems or security breaches as they occur. Automated data tracking and regular checking add an extra layer of security. The lineage system regularly updates the data flow map to identify and assess any changes, whether they are valid or not. Second, sensors use this past data to create standard behavior patterns in how data moves. Data showing odd patterns of access or unexpected changes is one example of not following the usual standards. Security teams are notified if any unusual activity is detected. This preventive approach helps identify potential risks before they become serious security problems.

Figure 6. Continuous Data Flow Monitoring System

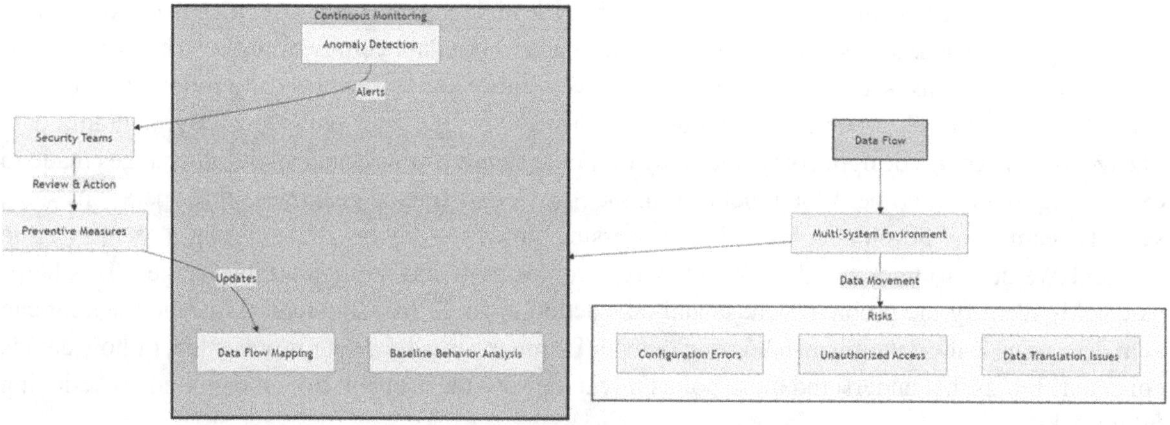

Threats in Data Movement and Transformation

Moving and changing data can have risks. Information can be captured or altered through different platforms (James & Rabbi, 2023). An insider threat occurs when authorized individuals secretly change or steal essential data by abusing their entry permissions. This poses a serious risk. The rise of shadow IT, where employees use unapproved tools and apps to manage data, is another outcome of today's quick software development. If these new technologies are allowed to go around current security systems, it could increase the risk of data breaches. Knowing the origin of data is essential to protect against these risks. Forensic proof can be gathered using lineage systems, which record data changes permanently. This helps to find data breaches or unauthorized modifications. Think about a situation where vital customer information is either not available or has been altered. Looking at the events will help figure out if the change happened because of an accepted process or due to someone inside the organization. Ancestral tracking helps to find out exactly how data left the company. This allows for a quick and accurate response to any data leaks.

Insider Threats, Data Exfiltration, and Shadow IT Risks

One challenging aspect of data security is managing hidden threats. Employees or agents who have legal approval might accidentally or deliberately harm data security (Duggineni, 2023). Data lineage systems record every change and entry point, keeping a complete audit trail to help reduce these hazards. This record helps with investigations after something goes wrong and stops dangerous behavior, making it more likely that people will get caught. It serves two primary purposes. Identifying where data was taken can help understand why it happened and reveal if any unauthorized devices or hidden systems were used. Another issue is using unofficial software or systems, often called "shadow IT." Upadhyay and Sampalli (2020) say that data from official systems usually has stricter security rules than data from private places. Automated data lineage tracking helps find untracked data flows by highlighting the differences between absolute and recorded data paths. Businesses can help prevent data leaks and avoid breaking the rules by using or shutting down platforms based on their visibility.

DevSecOps Practices and Tools for Secure Data Lineage

To use DevSecOps, it's essential to use tools and methods that help create safe and effective development processes. Using one of the available options to track data history in a DevSecOps pipeline will help ensure data is secure throughout the process. One example of this growth is using artificial intelligence to help with family tree research. Alzaabi and Mehmood (2024) say these systems can automatically find security problems by spotting odd data trends, like strange changes or unexpected access. This knowledge helps security staff take action before minor issues become more significant. Data security relies heavily on solutions driven by artificial intelligence and version control systems. Lekkala (2024) notes that version control, usually known for saving source code, is also used more for managing data. Version control systems help with compliance and security checks because they record every change made to data and when it occurred. Version control logs help recover data safely and identify who made unauthorized changes. This method keeps private data safe and consistent over time like undoing a lousy code update in a software delivery process.

According to González-Granadillo et al. (2021), SIEM systems are helpful tools for DevSecOps. These systems use automatic tracking to create dashboards that display the status of data flow protection and health, along with real-time alerts. SIEM systems can identify trends that indicate security events by mixing data from different sources, like data history systems, and using specific rules to connect the information. Using SIEM and automatic lineage tracking will create a solid security system that watches for weaknesses in data and technology in real time.

Figure 7. DevSecOps Tools and Practices for Data Security

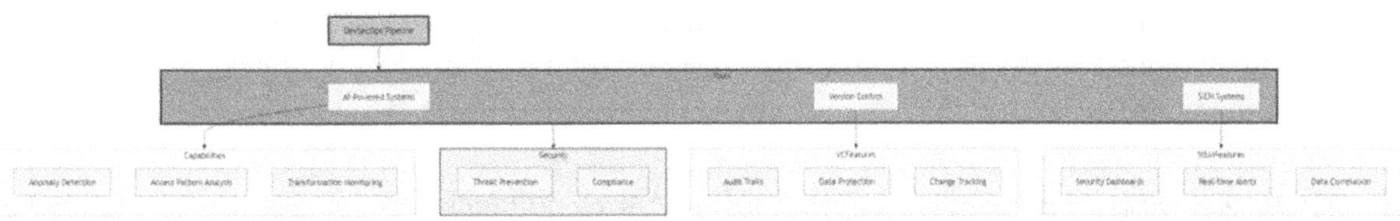

DATA LINEAGE IN MODERN SOFTWARE ARCHITECTURES

Modern software systems depend on data history, tracking data from its source to its final use, including all its changes, moves, and storage. It's hard to keep track of data changes when working with large amounts of data, AI, event-driven systems, live data, APIs, cloud services, mixed environments, and decentralized apps in a fast-changing technology world. This section discusses microservices, how data is transferred using APIs, cloud and mixed systems, event-driven designs, and how to track data in big data and AI systems. This part says that keeping data well keeps it high quality, consistent, and trustworthy, even when changes happen. It uses the top techniques and studies to do this.

Microservices and API-Driven Data Flow

Microservices have changed how we design and run programs. Modern software systems usually consist of more minor, individual services that talk to each other using APIs (Blinowski et al., 2022). Getting rid of fixed power helps groups build and manage more open and independent systems. Microservices are distributed, making it difficult to trace the data source and its movement. Khanyi et al. (2024) say that in an API-driven setup, different services handle data, with each one possibly using its own business rules or changes. For example, one microservice can handle user logins while another manages transaction data. These services rely on RESTful APIs or messaging systems, so we must carefully handle data flow. The main issue is gathering history information whenever an API is called, or a service is contacted. Microservices systems have complex and asynchronous interactions, which makes it difficult for regular tracking tools to monitor them effectively. These methods started with big, straightforward systems with clear routes for data travel.

To solve these problems, systems have been developed for automatically tracking data origins and connections, along with API links and service networks. These systems track where data comes from, how it changes, and where it goes by gathering information from API calls and replies. Debugging and security checks require easy access to data, and these automatic tools supply that. This also makes the work easier for coders.

Challenges of Tracking Data Lineage in Decentralized Architectures

Microservices-based decentralized systems, notwithstanding, help to build no central point of truth. Finding the source of data can be challenging when it is spread across many services, databases, and recording systems. Key problems include:

- **Data Fragmentation:** In decentralized systems, each service usually has its separate database for managing data. Different types of data and sources need to be joined to trace ancestry.
- **Asynchronous Processing:** Microservices usually run tasks in a way that does not need to be done simultaneously. Data flows are not straight lines, so it is hard to pinpoint precisely where data changes.
- **Heterogeneous Technologies:** Modern software uses different technologies, such as relational databases, NoSQL systems, and message queues. Using many other data systems and processing tools makes standardizing and collecting information harder.

More companies are using shared lineage systems, which gather data from different sources in one place, to overcome these challenges. These systems can use proven standards like OpenLineage to ensure that lineage data remains unchanged. Using these factors makes it easier to understand how data moves, especially in systems that are spread out.

Cloud-Native Environments and Hybrid Systems

Cloud-native options are transforming the data lineage setting even more. Many companies use their own systems and public cloud services like AWS, Azure, and GCP. The growth and speed of cloud systems make it hard to control and view data. Tools that can work with different cloud companies and older on-site systems are essential for managing data tracking in mixed systems. This combination needs constant monitoring and adherence to rules to happen. Companies must keep a careful record of data exchanges, no matter where data is processed or stored, due to restrictions from the General Data Protection Regulation (GDPR). According to Vaño et al. (2023), cloud applications often use container management systems like Kubernetes. These methods allow programs to adjust their size based on need. Regular updates in these areas ensure that data history shows changes in the system, such as new or removed instances. Automatic lineage systems are designed for the unique conditions of the cloud. They track changing factors by linking to cloud APIs and tracking tools. These great tools allow keeping track of data on AWS, Azure, GCP, and systems by regularly updating history maps.

Figure 8. Cloud-Native and Hybrid System Architecture

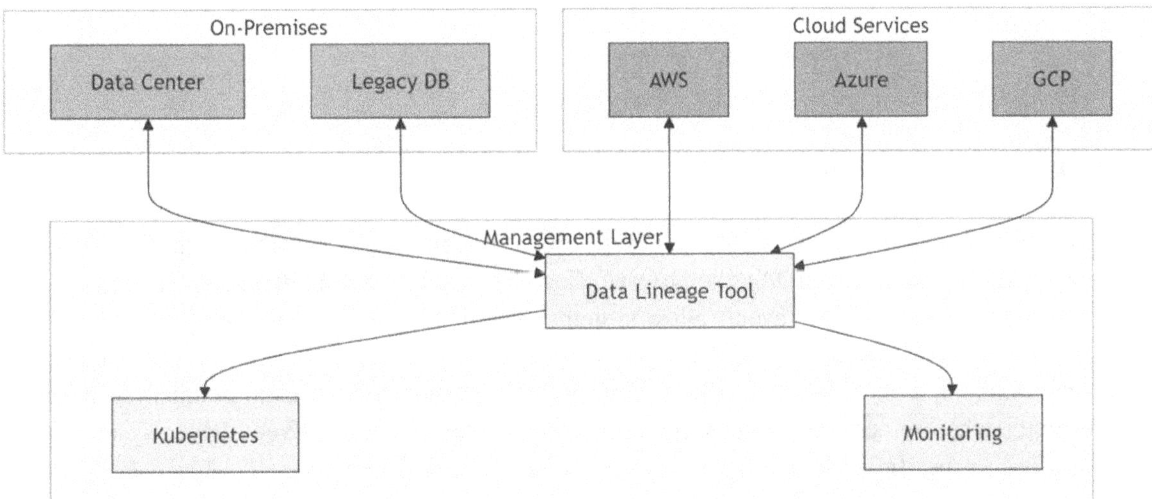

Big Data and AI Integration

The subsequent significant development in data genealogy uses big data, artificial intelligence, and machine learning. In today's data-driven world, it is common to process, change, and analyze large amounts of data to reach results. For AI and ML models to work well, the data needs to be reliable and able to be repeated. Data history means following the path of data and tracking how it changes. This helps ensure the data is copied correctly and can help find any biases. The complex changes in data needed for artificial intelligence and machine learning will make it hard to keep track of the origin of data during feature engineering, model training, and evaluation (Goshisht, 2024). To spot bias in AI models, we need a method to track any new biases during the data preprocessing steps. Data history is a vital audit trail to ensure the accuracy of the data utilized in model training.

Another essential factor to consider is whether results can be repeated. The importance of reliable results is growing in both academic and business settings. Automated lineage tracking in AI/ML processes records each step, from collecting and cleaning data to producing model results. This helps ensure that experiments can be repeated and verified (Maxwell, 2024). Tools like MLflow are adding features to track data flow throughout managing models to make AI systems more open and responsible.

Figure 9. Big Data and AI Integration Workflow

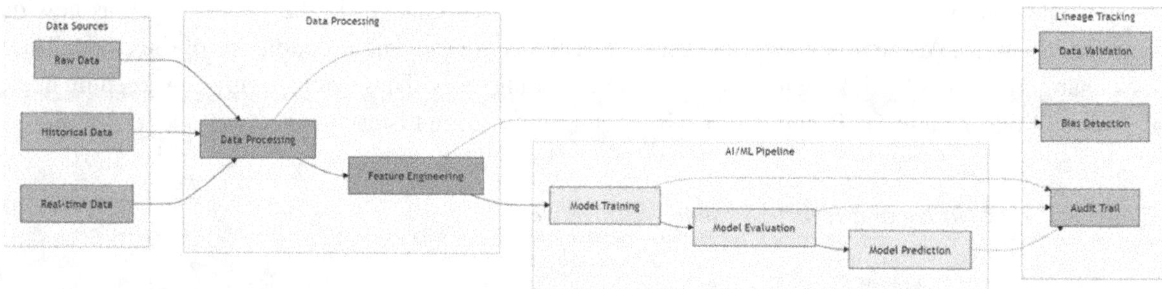

Event-Driven Architecture and Streaming Data

Modern distributed systems now focus on event-driven design (EDA) and flowing data as key ideas. In Event-Driven Architecture (EDA), the program flow is shaped by events like human actions, sensor data, or system messages. These events allow systems to respond quickly to changing situations while remaining flexible and efficient by activating services that are not closely linked. Event-driven design is like an intelligent, alert system that notifies your phone when you receive a text or email. Your phone only responds when something happens, not constantly looking for texts. Event-driven systems work by responding to specific events.

Figure 10. Even Processing Flow

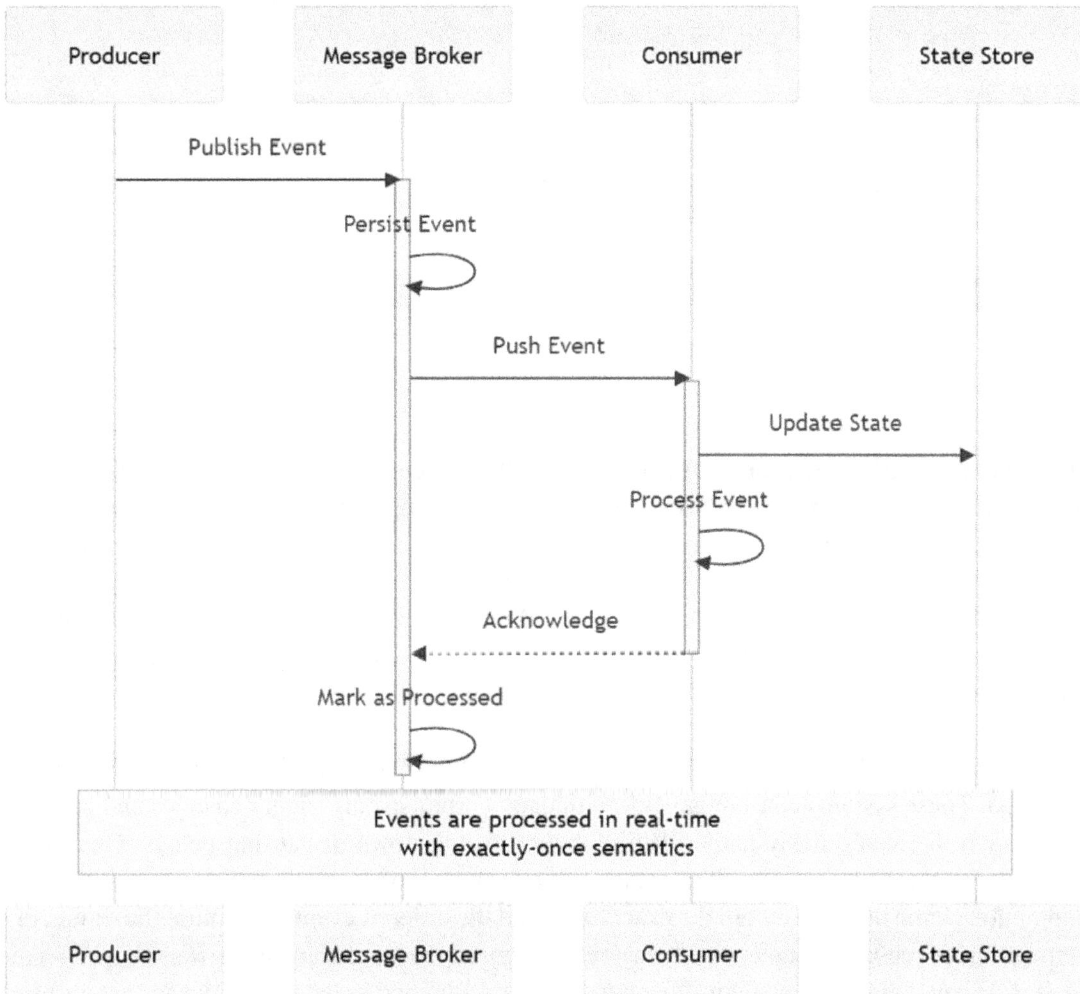

Streaming data improves EDA by providing continuous information that can be processed and analyzed instantly. Streaming allows data to be processed as soon as it comes, rather than collecting and handling it at set times. This method is beneficial when we need quick answers or fast insights, like spotting scams, watching IoT sensors, or doing real-time analysis. Watching streaming data is similar to watching a live video instead of getting a whole movie. Data comes in quickly, and the system processes it immediately, like how social media updates with new posts without needing to refresh the page.

Figure 11. Event Driven Architecture and Streaming Data Flow

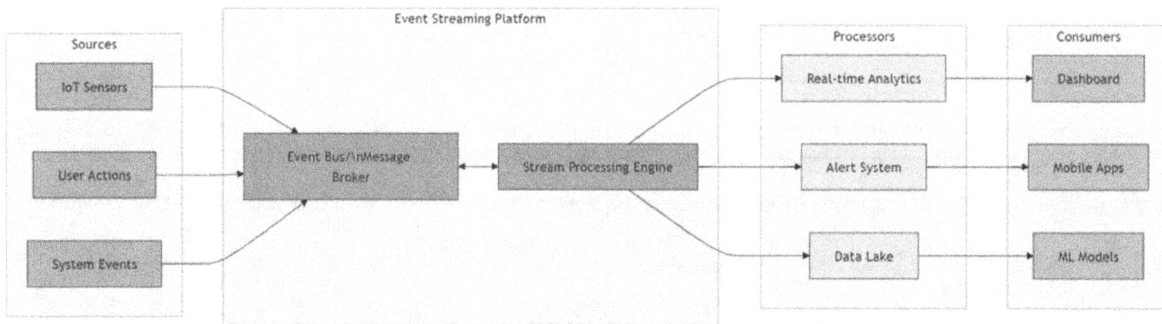

With live data, EDA creates robust systems that handle challenging, real-time situations. For example, a financial trade tool may examine live data from several exchanges simultaneously and react to market events using EDA. A smart city can use these trends to manage traffic, adjust power use, and quickly respond to environmental changes.

Modern tools and frameworks like Apache Kafka, Amazon Kinesis, and Azure Event Hubs have made it easier to implement these systems. They provide reliable systems for handling events and processing streams, ensuring low delay for real-time tasks and allowing for reliability, resistance to errors, and the ability to grow.

Real-time tools such as Apache Kafka and Apache Flink make tracking data history much more complicated. These systems constantly work with data; certain events trigger changes and actions. We need a system that can quickly gather data without slowing down or causing delays when handling live streaming data. Streaming services manage large amounts of events in real-time. In this situation, tracking information needs to record the exact times and the order of events to capture the timing of data movement. This time-based context is necessary to diagnose the system and understand how data moves through it. When a real-time analytics display shows a difference in data, the lineage system needs to quickly find out what caused it or what steps led to this finding.

Lightweight agents gather information from event streams in near real-time to allow lineage tracking coupled with streaming data systems. Their practical form lets the streaming system work smoothly. Modern tools connect events from different services using distributed tracking methods, making it easy to see how data moves, even when events happen quickly.

How Real-Time Processing Impacts Lineage Tracking

Real-time processing requires data tracking tools that can keep pace. Because ideas and reactions to unusual situations depend on timing, it's essential to have continuous and quick tracking of their origins. New data's fast and changing nature means regular batch processing methods can't keep up. Modern techniques for detecting and recording data changes in real-time allow a real-time lineage tracking system to be effective. AI anomaly detection is a part of these systems that helps identify and record problems with data flow. If an event-driven system suddenly experiences more mistakes or odd changes in data, the lineage system can trigger alarms to prompt further investigation. This ability is essential for ensuring that decisions based on data are backed by trustworthy information and that the system stays in good shape.

Real-time tracking of lineage will have different impacts. Systems need to handle large amounts of data that come in quickly quickly. The first factors for this are spread computing and horizontally scalable storage systems. Make sure that the history and basic data flow are always aligned. If there is a gap between the two, it could raise questions about the accuracy of the genealogy system. Thus, one of the most pressing problems in contemporary software architecture study is building scalable, low-latency lineage tracking systems.

TECHNIQUES AND TOOLS FOR IMPLEMENTING DATA LINEAGE

Modern data management relies on data lineage systems that help companies track data from its beginning to its final use, including all the changes it goes through. This method helps build trust in data decisions and supports following regulations and improving data quality. To track data flow, businesses need to use different tools and techniques. This field includes methods for managing and tagging information, monitoring data movement (both active and passive), linking SQL with ETL processes and data stores, and using advanced techniques like graphs and AI-enhanced tracking. Many commercial and open-source tools are available to help with this, such as OpenLineage, Marquez, Collibra, Informatica, and Alation. This discussion focuses on studies and best practices in the field and looks more closely at these techniques and tools.

Metadata Management and Tagging Strategies

Raw data-holding assets greatly benefit from metadata, "data about data." This extra information provides essential context. For data lineage systems, managing information is vital because it helps keep track of where data comes from, how it changes, and where it is stored. Mitchell et al. (2022) posit that in bloodline tracking, the accuracy and reliability of the data affect how trustworthy it is. Using tagging methods, which include details about control, sensitivity, type of data, and business area, we can improve data assets further with metadata. One way to use tags is to make a common language that connects technical data with how it is understood in business. Communication between the technology team and business users will get better. Companies could use a combination of automatic tagging and person tagging, depending on their needs. To make metadata instantly, He and Fang (2024) explain that computer systems can check databases, logs, and ETL scripts. Data guardians must review and improve the data to ensure it is relevant and accurate. Additionally, information should be created according to the FAIR principles (Findability, Accessibility, Interoperability, and Reusability) to help track data origins and encourage data sharing between systems.

Active vs. Passive Lineage Tracking

Wagner and Klein (2020) claim that active lineage monitoring requires gathering lineage data while data is processed in real time. In this method, every data transformation and transfer is noted and kept throughout the process. This approach is helpful in dynamic contexts, including streaming applications and microservices systems, as changes happen often and must be gathered in real-time. Active tracking systems quickly create a data flow map by recording every API call, update, and movement. Large e-commerce companies like Amazon use active lineage tracking to track customer data in real time across different platforms. When a client makes an order, the details, like things, shipping address, and payment information, are closely monitored as they move from the ordering system to the systems that handle fulfillment, shipping, and bills. Finding and fixing data quality problems ensures that orders are processed correctly and customers are happy.

On the other hand, passive lineage tracking is compiling metadata following the events. Looking at logs, transaction records, or snapshots of historical data operations helps one find data lineage in a passive system (Pushkin, 2020). Though it is easier to design and usually has less overhead in performance-sensitive applications, passive tracking may overlook the fine-grained information that results from real-time activities. Passive systems are often employed in forensic investigation and troubleshooting as they offer a plausible retrospection view. Although active tracking might affect performance, it is becoming increasingly common as modern apps need constant monitoring and instant access. In finance, a bank like JP Morgan Chase might use inactive lineage tracking to track where the data for regulatory reports comes from and how it changes. After an event, the bank looks at logs, audit trails, and information from different systems to understand the data's path instead of watching the data move in real-time. This ensures auditability and transparency by giving a historical record of how essential risk measures were calculated, helping them meet rules like Basel III.

ETL Pipelines and Data Warehouses: SQL-Based Tracking

Essential to data warehouses, data lineage inside ETL (Extract, Transform, Load) pipelines must be guaranteed to preserve data quality and compliance (Moses et al., 2022). Many firms rely on SQL-based monitoring techniques to compile ancestral data for data warehouses such as Snowflake, Databricks, and Google Big Query. By including lineage metadata in SQL queries and transformation scripts, systems may record every data element's source, transformation, and destination, allowing SQL-based tracking. Users could find lineage information by examining query logs and data transformation records in Snowflake, a well-known cloud data warehouse. Connecting various data bits allows one to follow the data from raw intake tables to converted, analytics-ready sets (Snowflake Inc., 2020). Databricks and Google Big Query have built-in capabilities for monitoring genealogy using SQL searches and job data. Both systems also provide partner connections that simplify this operation. Using the suitability and structure included in SQL databases, these SQL-based approaches consistently and in a queryable way surpass the competitors.

Graph-based approaches and AI-augmented lineage

In remote and decentralized systems, graph-based data history methods are a helpful way to understand complex data processes. In graph-based lineage systems, data is represented as points (nodes), and the changes or connections between them are shown as lines (edges). This approach makes it easier to understand how data moves and changes. Lineage mapping uses Neo4j, a leading graph database, to preserve complex connections between data items (Bratanic, 2024). Research by Ho et al. (2023), Pazho et al. (2023), and Ekle and Eberle (2024) shows that using graph-based models makes it easier to find correlations and anomalies, which speeds up data processing. Another use of graph-based methods is found in Apache Atlas. The open-source metadata management and control tool Atlas might be used to watch data as it moves between several systems and undergoes changes (Yang et al., 2024). Atlas also offers significant data lineage potential. Graph-based solutions help systems that deal with connected and complex data by allowing users to look into specific changes and study the family tree of data in real time.

Graph-based history helps a pharmaceutical business like Johnson & Johnson understand the various connections between the systems they use in drug research. Looking at data flows as a graph lets us see how changes in one dataset affect other studies. This keeps the info the same and helps follow legal rules.

AI-powered lineage tracking uses traditional methods for tracking family lines and machine learning to spot unusual cases and predict issues before they happen. AI systems that use past data can detect errors or security issues by analyzing expected data trends and looking for any changes or differences. Himeur et al. (2021) highlight two advantages of using artificial intelligence for tracking family histories: First, extremes are easy to see. Secondly, it provides better predictions that can help avoid potential problems. In complex situations like AI and machine learning systems, small mistakes in data translation can impact the success of later models. This skill is essential.

For instance, Citigroup uses artificial intelligence-augmented lineage in the finance sector to automatically find and record data flows throughout its big IT area. AI programs simplify data management by identifying links in data usage and information. This cuts down the work people must do to keep data records correct.

Open-source and Commercial Data Lineage Tools

Many free and paid online tools will significantly assist with data history projects. Two popular open-source projects for family tree study are Marquez and OpenLineage. They offer flexible and expandable structures. The OpenLineage standard allows interoperability and consistent tracking in many situations by storing and sharing lineage information over different systems (Parciak et al., 2023). Marquez's simple user interface and API make it easy for companies to track the origins of their data flows, setting a new standard. Some good data governance tools one can buy include Informatica, Collibra, and Alation. They have impressive features for tracking data history. Consider Collibra, for example. Its strong image comes from its skill in combining business and technical data to create detailed lineage maps. These maps help projects focused on maintaining data quality and meeting regulations. Enhanced enterprise-grade lineage tracking made possible by interaction with Informatica's more complete data management and integration systems helps to watch data flows constantly and support audits. Alation's improved lineage display and search tools assist expert users and business partners understand and use data lineage information.

These professional systems have many features, can grow with businesses, and offer support services, which is why many big companies use them. A company's goals, level of technical experience, and budget will decide whether a paid or free software option is the best fit for them.

CHALLENGES AND LIMITATIONS IN DATA LINEAGE

In today's data management and control, understanding data history is essential. This means tracking data from where it starts to where it ends up, including all the changes it goes through. Creating and maintaining reliable data tracking systems has some challenges and limitations. Some challenges include issues with speed and scale, problems working with different systems, the need to follow complicated rules, the chance of human errors, and a lack of data skills within companies. This section looks closely at these limitations using business experience and research to help explain the challenges of creating reliable data history systems.

Scalability and Performance Overheads

Data lineage is a significant challenge when trying to grow without losing speed. The systems that collect lineage information must manage metadata because the amount of data is increasing rapidly due to cloud apps and big data. In monolithic systems, capturing lineage was simple because the data flow was limited and steady. Lineage systems can't handle complex current setups like distributed databases, microservices, and event-driven processes.

Since changes are recorded immediately in active lineage tracking, processing pipelines may be overloaded (Fu & Soman, 2021). For example, the information created by every SQL query, API call, or contact with a microservice needs to be stored and managed. This ongoing lineage data collection may cause speed problems, particularly in high-velocity settings. Praveen (2024) found that using exact family trees requires more computer power, which can slow down data processing. Real-time data and how quickly an organization can respond can affect each other. Companies that collect data occasionally or use sampling instead of constant recording often meet the need for accurate source information and manage any possible performance issues.

Also, poor distribution or optimization can hurt the storage and search speed of the lineage library during development. Adding lineage systems makes it much harder to scale in cloud-native designs, especially when horizontal growth is essential. We must use complex search methods and shared storage options to help the lineage store grow along with the data systems. Without these changes, keeping the data history accurate wouldn't be helpful due to lower system speed and running costs.

Interoperability Issues in Heterogeneous Environments

One choice among numerous for data keeping is standard relational databases. Other options include data lakes, on-site tools, and current NoSQL data stores. Many businesses today use different cloud services, such as Google Cloud Platform, Microsoft Azure, and Amazon Web Services (AWS). Data history systems have a hard time working well with different platforms. Systems often use multiple logging tools, custom data forms, and data-changing languages. Real-time streaming systems like Apache Kafka or Apache Flink can get other data from what an ETL tool provides from its history information. Using standardized protocols and interfaces is the only way to remove these differences and provide a clear view of where data comes from, from beginning to end. OpenLineage and similar open standards aim to fix compatibility issues but are not widely accepted.

Data history is a significant challenge when trying to grow without losing speed. Scalability without losing speed is limited mainly by data lineage. Ancestral systems must collect, merge, and organize data from different sources to work well in various situations. It's hard to standardize this method because there are challenges in organizing different data models, dealing with varying naming rules, and fixing issues from similar metadata descriptions. If true compatibility can't be achieved, the usefulness of the lineage system for tracking, debugging, and compliance will decrease. This could lead to partial or scattered lineage views (Parker et al., 2020). The need for special links or software to track the history between old systems and new platforms makes the system more complicated and requires additional upkeep. Businesses that ignore effective connectivity solutions risk building closed systems without the complete perspective needed for good data management.

Human Error and Organizational Gaps in Data Literacy

The success of data lineage relies not only on technology but also on people and the company culture. Many companies do not have enough understanding of complex data lineage systems. Staff members with low data skills are more likely to make mistakes in settings, paperwork, and understanding data connections. Data lineage is complex, and mistakes people make are critical in it. Incomplete or incorrect lineage records can be caused by errors in tagging by people, lack of suitable paperwork, and poorly set up tracking systems. Alkhatib and Gaede (2024) state that people still need to check and improve the information the system collects. When data skills are limited, there is a higher chance of misunderstanding or not entirely using the data. This reduces the benefits of using lineage information for safety and control.

Different departments in a company could make these problems worse. If other teams work separately and don't understand data governance ideas, it can lead to inconsistent data tracking across the company. Making wise choices and finishing thorough compliance audits becomes more complicated when poor cooperation results in split lineage views. To get the best use out of data lineage, it's essential to promote understanding of data and teamwork between different departments Durango et al. (2024). Companies should invest in training and change management programs so that all employees know what data lineage is and how it can be used.

FUTURE TRENDS IN DATA LINEAGE AND GOVERNANCE

The rapid increase in data amount, variety, and speed in today's data systems makes having good data tracking and management systems more critical than ever. New data management solutions are needed to enhance transparency, security, and speed since data plays a crucial role in companies' strategic decisions. Changing the data lineage and governance game will be achieved by combining AIOps and observability, applying AI to manage data lineage, blockchain immutable tracking, and zero-trust data governance models. This section examines upcoming changes and how they could transform data management using industry standards and existing research.

AI-Driven Automated Data Lineage

Another way AI is changing data management is through data history. Using artificial intelligence, data lineage systems with machine learning can continuously learn, understand, and change data through complex data processes. These systems can track data flows in real time, allowing them to evaluate large amounts of log data, ETL scripts, and API contacts. According to Côté et al. (2024), hidden technological debt emerging from human error-prone lineage tracking is a significant problem with current data systems. Artificial intelligence (AI) can help pay off debt by providing quick and accurate insights into data. This can reduce costs and minimize human errors.

One clear advantage of using artificial intelligence in genetics is its ability to identify unusual patterns. These systems look for mistakes, security problems, or rule violations by examining standard data flow patterns and notifying users when there are differences. AI technologies can quickly notify data managers about unexpected data types or working amounts, helping fix problems rapidly. In areas like healthcare and finance, having accurate data is crucial. Predicting results is helpful because it allows data processes to be more consistent and better managed.

AI technology ensures that lineage maps remain correct by learning and adjusting to new data types. We need automatic systems that adapt to changing data without losing quality or needing human help. This is very important when businesses use more flexible and adaptable IT options.

Blockchain for Immutable Lineage Tracking

Blockchain technology keeps a permanent record of data, which leads to new and impressive improvements in how we manage information. Blockchain technology keeps a permanent record of all data exchanges and changes. Adding lineage content to a blockchain ensures that companies can't alter or remove data lineage information unless everyone in the network agrees. It is beneficial because its unchanging nature highlights the importance of keeping records and following rules at different levels, such as financial reports and regulatory checks. Blockchain history systems are prominent because any changes to the data are recorded in a shared ledger that all approved users can see. This method reduces the chances of illegal changes and data loss. Think about a supply chain. Blockchain technology helps keep track of raw materials from when they are bought to when they reach their destination. This ensures that the information is correct and that everyone involved acts responsibly.

Using blockchain technology in data tracking systems has some unique challenges. Many blockchain systems face issues with speed and delays, making it hard to handle the large amounts of data seen in today's designs. Thinking about immutability helps us understand the extra computing power and energy needed to maintain a blockchain network. Despite these challenges, research on permissioned blockchain systems and more potent consensus methods make this technology more suitable for business use.

Integration with Observability and AIOps

A key new feature coming soon to observability systems and AIOps is better data path integration. In data control, "observability" means checking a system's internal state by looking at what it produces. It involves regularly watching data processes, changes, and how well the system works. Combining lineage tracking with observability tools helps understand and manage a company's data processes, data flow, and any issues. AIOps systems use big data and machine learning to automate IT processes. AIOps works with data lineage systems to quickly find and fix problems by connecting system performance issues with specific events in the data's history. An observability tool can automatically use lineage data to identify the process causing a mistake if error rates increase in a data processing chain. The method works faster and is more reliable because everything is organized well.

Data history, AIOps, and observability all help enhance continuous development. By regularly checking lineage data against performance standards, businesses can simplify data processes, identify recurring problems, and fix security gaps. This link improves data systems' ability to adapt to changing needs and tasks while maintaining safety and efficiency, following DevOps principles.

Zero Trust Data Governance Models

The zero trust security model requires checking every request for entry carefully. This method suggests one cannot trust anyone, whether from inside or outside, without thinking carefully. In data governance, zero trust models ensure that data is always checked for compliance and security, no matter where it is used or how the system works. This way is essential for systems that are spread out or use a mix of different platforms because data is increasingly moving across borders and between various systems. To use a zero-trust data control approach, one must set strict access limits, keep checking who is accessing the data, and monitor data movement in real-time. Data lineage, which tracks changes to data, and access behavior are significant for this method. By connecting each data move to a verified and allowed action, companies can reduce the risk of insider threats and data breaches. Trust in data systems relies on regular checks, especially for private or controlled data.

Additionally, strong encryption tools are used in zero-trust models, and access to data is restricted based on identification throughout its lifespan. Using permanent history records, zero-trust governance, and blockchain technologies ensures security from the time data is received until it is used. Besides meeting legal rules like GDPR and CCPA, these models help create a responsible and secure atmosphere within the company.

The Convergence of Trends and Their Impact on Future Data Governance

How these new trends work together will shape the future of data tracking and management. AI technology for automatic data tracking and blockchain ensures that data records cannot be changed. So, they are ideal for handling complex, live data streams. Zero trust models will strengthen security by regularly checking all access and changes. At the same time, observability and AIOps will help with quick problem-solving and ongoing tracking. These patterns will lead to essential changes in how companies handle their data and overall governance plans. The FAIR principles highlight the importance of making data available and easy to access. AI, blockchain, and zero-trust methods can help make this easier (Jacobsen et al., 2020).

These improvements should make it much easier to track and manage lineage manually. Businesses can reduce costs and human errors by streamlining data tracking and linking it with security systems and ongoing monitoring. This will help the teams responsible for managing data and IT processes focus on long-term projects rather than quick fixes.

CONCLUSION AND KEY TAKEAWAYS

This chapter has shown that having good data tracking is more helpful for today's business than just being necessary. Data lineage, which tracks the journey of data from its source to its final destination, leads to three main benefits: better efficiency in operations, greater openness, and meeting legal requirements. Combining data tracking with strong information management and control systems creates a solid base for trustworthy, high-quality data that aids in wise decision-making. We have repeatedly emphasized the need for automatic real-time data tracking monitoring during our talk. It's essential to have accurate history information while keeping things fast in constantly changing environments, like those using apps, cloud-based systems, and AI analytics. Automated lineage monitoring helps companies quickly identify and resolve issues by reducing human mistakes and boosting trust in their data systems.

Remember that two new technologies, artificial intelligence and blockchain, will soon change how we watch and handle data. Blockchain technology ensures that historical data remains unchanged, making it reliable and easy to check. Using artificial intelligence (AI), lineage tracking can spot problems and predict issues before they worsen. This helps with proactive government actions and ongoing improvement. Adding data tracking to DevSecOps processes makes them even more critical. Linking lineage monitoring with a secure software development process improves oversight, speeds up problem-solving, and ensures that all data changes meet strong security standards. Zero-trust models rely heavily on this connection, requiring ongoing checks to ensure data access and safety.

Companies that include data history in their data governance rules could improve their information management and gain a competitive advantage. Good lineage tracking is essential for a complete data management system. It helps meet legal requirements, improves data quality, and boosts decision-making, leading to better business outcomes.

REFERENCES

Alkhatib, R., & Gaede, K. I. (2024). Data management in biobanking: Strategies, challenges, and future directions. *Biotech*, 13(3), 34. DOI: 10.3390/biotech13030034 PMID: 39311336

Alzaabi, F. R., & Mehmood, A. (2024). A review of recent advances, challenges, and opportunities in malicious insider threat detection using machine learning methods. *IEEE Access : Practical Innovations, Open Solutions*, 12, 30907–30927. DOI: 10.1109/ACCESS.2024.3369906

Bhaskaran, S. V. (2020). Integrating Data Quality Services (DQS) in Big Data Ecosystems: Challenges, Best Practices, and Opportunities for Decision-Making. *Journal of Applied Big Data Analytics, Decision-Making, and Predictive Modelling Systems*, 4(11), 1–12.

Blinowski, G., Ojdowska, A., & Przybyłek, A. (2022). Monolithic vs. microservice architecture: A performance and scalability evaluation. *IEEE Access : Practical Innovations, Open Solutions*, 10, 20357–20374. DOI: 10.1109/ACCESS.2022.3152803

Bratanic, T. (2024). *Graph Algorithms for Data Science: With Examples in Neo4j*. Simon and Schuster.

Côté, P. O., Nikanjam, A., Bouchoucha, R., Basta, I., Abidi, M., & Khomh, F. (2024). Quality issues in machine learning software systems. *Empirical Software Engineering*, 29(6), 149. DOI: 10.1007/s10664-024-10536-7

Davoudian, A., & Liu, M. (2020). Big data systems: A software engineering perspective. *ACM Computing Surveys*, 53(5), 1–39. DOI: 10.1145/3408314

Duggineni, S. (2023). Impact of controls on data integrity and information systems. *Science and Technology*, 13(2), 29–35.

Durango, I., Gallud, J. A., & Penichet, V. M. (2024). Human-Data Interaction Framework: A Comprehensive Model for a Future Driven by Data and Humans. *arXiv preprint arXiv:2407.21010.*

Ekle, O. A., & Eberle, W. (2024). Anomaly Detection in Dynamic Graphs: A Comprehensive Survey. *ACM Transactions on Knowledge Discovery from Data*, 18(8), 1–44. DOI: 10.1145/3669906

Faraj, O., Megias, D., & Garcia-Alfaro, J. (2024). Security Approaches for Data Provenance in the Internet of Things: A Systematic Literature Review. *arXiv preprint arXiv:2407.03466.*

Fu, Y., & Soman, C. (2021, June). Real-time data infrastructure at uber. In *Proceedings of the 2021 International Conference on Management of Data* (pp. 2503-2516). DOI: 10.1145/3448016.3457552

George, A. S., George, A. H., & Baskar, T. (2023). Digitally immune systems: Building robust defences in the age of cyber threats. *Partners Universal International Innovation Journal*, 1(4), 155–172.

González-Granadillo, G., González-Zarzosa, S., & Diaz, R. (2021). Security information and event management (SIEM): Analysis, trends, and usage in critical infrastructures. *Sensors (Basel)*, 21(14), 4759. DOI: 10.3390/s21144759 PMID: 34300500

Goshisht, M. K. (2024). Machine learning and deep learning in synthetic biology: Key architectures, applications, and challenges. *ACS Omega*, 9(9), 9921–9945. DOI: 10.1021/acsomega.3c05913 PMID: 38463314

Guitton, F., Oehmichen, A., Bossé, É., & Guo, Y. (2024). Honest Computing: Achieving demonstrable data lineage and provenance for driving data and process-sensitive policies. *Data & Policy*, 6, e84. DOI: 10.1017/dap.2024.68

Gupta, R., & Soni, S. (2020). Developing Effective Big Data Strategies and Governance Frameworks: Principles, Tools, Challenges and Best Practices. *International Journal of Responsible Artificial Intelligence*, 10(8), 10–19.

He, Z., & Fang, W. (2024). Research data management in institutional repositories: An architectural approach using data lakehouses. *Digital Library Perspectives*.

Himeur, Y., Ghanem, K., Alsalemi, A., Bensaali, F., & Amira, A. (2021). Artificial intelligence based anomaly detection of energy consumption in buildings: A review, current trends and new perspectives. *Applied Energy*, 287, 116601. DOI: 10.1016/j.apenergy.2021.116601

Ho, T. K. K., Karami, A., & Armanfard, N. (2023). Graph-based time-series anomaly detection: A survey. *arXiv preprint arXiv:2302.00058*. IBM (nd.). IBM Manta Data Lineage. Retrieved from https://www.ibm.com/products/manta-data-lineage Accessed January 15, 2025.

Inau, E. T., Sack, J., Waltemath, D., & Zeleke, A. A. (2023). Initiatives, concepts, and implementation practices of the findable, accessible, interoperable, and reusable data principles in health data stewardship: Scoping review. *Journal of Medical Internet Research*, 25, e45013. DOI: 10.2196/45013 PMID: 37639292

Jacobsen, A., de Miranda Azevedo, R., Juty, N., Batista, D., Coles, S., Cornet, R., Courtot, M., Crosas, M., Dumontier, M., Evelo, C. T., Goble, C., Guizzardi, G., Hansen, K. K., Hasnain, A., Hettne, K., Heringa, J., Hooft, R. W. W., Imming, M., Jeffery, K. G., & Schultes, E. (2020). FAIR principles: Interpretations and implementation considerations. *Data Intelligence*, 2(1-2), 10–29. DOI: 10.1162/dint_r_00024

James, E., & Rabbi, F. (2023). Fortifying the IoT landscape: Strategies to counter security risks in connected systems. *Tensorgate Journal of Sustainable Technology and Infrastructure for Developing Countries*, 6(1), 32–46.

Khanyi, M. B., Xaba, S. N., Mlotshwa, N. A., Thango, B., & Matshaka, L. (2024). A Roadmap to Systematic Review: Evaluating the Role of Data Networks and Application Programming Interfaces in Enhancing Operational Efficiency in Small and Medium Enterprises. *Sustainability (Basel)*, 16(23), 10192. DOI: 10.3390/su162310192

Kumar, Y., Marchena, J., Awlla, A. H., Li, J. J., & Abdalla, H. B. (2024). The AI-Powered Evolution of Big Data. *Applied Sciences (Basel, Switzerland)*, 14(22), 10176. DOI: 10.3390/app142210176

Lekkala, C. (2024). Implementing Efficient Data Versioning and Lineage Tracking in Data Lakes. *Available atSSRN* 4907973.

Maxwell, R. (2024). Automation in the Era of ML and AI. In *Azure Arc Systems Management: Governance and Administration of Multi-cloud and Hybrid IT Estates* (pp. 217–250). Apress. DOI: 10.1007/978-1-4842-9480-2_9

Mitchell, S. N., Lahiff, A., Cummings, N., Hollocombe, J., Boskamp, B., Field, R., Reddyhoff, D., Zarebski, K., Wilson, A., Viola, B., Burke, M., Archibald, B., Bessell, P., Blackwell, R., Boden, L. A., Brett, A., Brett, S., Dundas, R., Enright, J., & Reeve, R. (2022). FAIR data pipeline: Provenance-driven data management for traceable scientific workflows. *Philosophical Transactions. Series A, Mathematical, Physical, and Engineering Sciences*, 380(2233), 20210300. DOI: 10.1098/rsta.2021.0300 PMID: 35965468

Moses, B., Gavish, L., & Vorwerck, M. (2022). *Data quality fundamentals*. O'Reilly Media, Inc.

Nookala, G. (2024). Adaptive Data Governance Frameworks for Data-Driven Digital Transformations. *Journal of Computational Innovation*, 4(1).

Ohrimenco, S., Borta, G., & Cernei, V. (2024). The digital world has a long shadow. In *The Elgar Companion to Information Economics* (pp. 481–504). Edward Elgar Publishing. DOI: 10.4337/9781802203967.00035

Parciak, M., Suhr, M., Schmidt, C., Bönisch, C., Löhnhardt, B., Kesztyüs, D., & Kesztyüs, T. (2023). FAIRness through automation: Development of an automated medical data integration infrastructure for FAIR health data in a maximum care university hospital. *BMC Medical Informatics and Decision Making*, 23(1), 94. DOI: 10.1186/s12911-023-02195-3 PMID: 37189148

Parker, A., Spoonhower, D., Mace, J., Sigelman, B., & Isaacs, R. (2020). *Distributed tracing in practice: Instrumenting, analyzing, and debugging microservices*. O'Reilly Media.

Pazho, A. D., Noghre, G. A., Purkayastha, A. A., Vempati, J., Martin, O., & Tabkhi, H. (2023). A survey of graph-based deep learning for anomaly detection in distributed systems. *IEEE Transactions on Knowledge and Data Engineering*, 36(1), 1–20. DOI: 10.1109/TKDE.2023.3282898 PMID: 36506788

Praveen, R. V. S. (2024). *Data Engineering Concepts: From Basics To Advance Techniques*. Addition Publishing House.

Praveen, R. V. S. (2024). *Data Engineering for Modern Applications*. Addition Publishing House.

Pushkin, E. (2020). Theoretical Model and Practical Considerations for Data Lineage Reconstruction. *arXiv preprint arXiv:2001.11506*.

Radoslav, L. (2024). Enhancing Data Governance through AI-Driven Data Lineage Tracking and Impact Analysis in Complex Data Ecosystems. *Journal of Big Data and Smart Systems*, 5(1).

Sayles, J. (2024). Aligning AI Governance, AI Development Lifecycle, and Systems Development Lifecycle Processes. In *Principles of AI Governance and Model Risk Management: Master the Techniques for Ethical and Transparent AI Systems* (pp. 383–408). Apress. DOI: 10.1007/979-8-8688-0983-5_21

Upadhyay, D., & Sampalli, S. (2020). SCADA (Supervisory Control and Data Acquisition) systems: Vulnerability assessment and security recommendations. *Computers & Security*, 89, 101666. DOI: 10.1016/j.cose.2019.101666

Vaño, R., Lacalle, I., Sowiński, P., S-Julián, R., & Palau, C. E. (2023). Cloud-native workload orchestration at the edge: A deployment review and future directions. *Sensors (Basel)*, 23(4), 2215. DOI: 10.3390/s23042215 PMID: 36850813

Vemulapalli, G. (2023). Optimizing Analytics: Integrating Data Warehouses and Lakes for Accelerated Workflows. *International Scientific Journal for Research*, 5(5), 1–27.

Wagner, D. E., & Klein, A. M. (2020). Lineage tracing meets single-cell omics: Opportunities and challenges. *Nature Reviews. Genetics*, 21(7), 410–427. DOI: 10.1038/s41576-020-0223-2 PMID: 32235876

Yadav, B., Choudhary, G., Shandilya, S. K., & Dragoni, N. (2021). AI Empowered DevSecOps Security for Next Generation Development. In *Frontiers in Software Engineering: First International Conference, ICFSE 2021, Innopolis, Russia, June 17–18, 2021, Revised Selected Papers 1* (pp. 32-46). Springer International Publishing. DOI: 10.1007/978-3-030-93135-3_3

Yang, W., Fu, R., Amin, M. B., & Kang, B. (2024). Impact and influence of modern AI in metadata management. *arXiv preprint arXiv:2501.16605.*

Zeydan, E., & Mangues-Bafalluy, J. (2022). Recent advances in data engineering for networking. *IEEE Access : Practical Innovations, Open Solutions*, 10, 34449–34496. DOI: 10.1109/ACCESS.2022.3162863

Chapter 5
Data Governance in Education:
Enhancing Predictions and Decision-Making for Performance Monitoring

Soukaina Nai
https://orcid.org/0009-0002-4819-2198
Faculty of Sciences, University Ibn Tofail, Morocco

Amal Rifai
https://orcid.org/0000-0003-2793-3102
Regional Center for the Professions of Education and Training, Morocco

Abdelalim Sadiq
https://orcid.org/0000-0003-1478-8807
Faculty of Sciences, University Ibn Tofail, Morocco

ABSTRACT

Data governance is crucial for enhancing the effectiveness of performance monitoring and evaluation (M&E) in education. This article emphasizes the role of robust data governance frameworks in ensuring data quality, consistency, and accessibility, which are vital for informed decision-making. Well-governed data enables improved predictions, real-time assessments, and targeted interventions that boost student outcomes and institutional performance. By setting clear policies for data collection, management, and analysis, data governance supports accurate tracking of educational progress, identifies areas for improvement, and optimizes resource allocation. It also ensures accountability, transparency, and compliance with privacy regulations, fostering trust among stakeholders. The article highlights challenges faced by educational institutions, such as limited resources, data fragmentation, and resistance to change. Ultimately, effective data governance is essential for improving predictions, decision-making, and continuous improvement in educational outcomes.

DOI: 10.4018/979-8-3373-0365-9.ch005

1. INTRODUCTION

In educational systems, data plays a pivotal role in driving improvements in student performance, resource allocation, and institutional effectiveness (Khalid & Hidayatullah, 2024). As education increasingly focuses on data-driven decision-making, having access to accurate and reliable data is essential for understanding academic trends, tracking progress, and guiding educational strategies. However, to fully harness the power of data, it is necessary to establish a strong data governance framework that ensures the integrity, security, and consistency of the data being used (Khatri & Brown, 2010).

Data governance encompasses the set of policies, procedures, and standards that govern how data is collected, stored, managed, and analyzed. In educational institutions, robust data governance ensures that decision-makers can rely on high-quality, accessible data to monitor performance, assess outcomes, and make informed choices (Agasisti & Bowers, 2017). By setting clear guidelines for how data is handled and shared, data governance supports performance monitoring and evaluation (M&E) processes, helping to identify areas for improvement and design effective interventions (Nai & al., 2022).

Despite its importance, many educational systems face significant obstacles in implementing effective data governance (Blau & Presser, 2013). These challenges include limited financial resources, fragmented data systems, and institutional resistance to adopting new practices. This article delves into how data governance can enhance decision-making in education, focusing on its role in improving predictions and strengthening performance monitoring and evaluation. By addressing these challenges, schools and universities can create a data-driven environment that fosters continuous improvement and better outcomes for students and educators alike (Munagandla & al., 2024).

2. LITERATURE REVIEW OF STUDIES ON DATA GOVERNANCE

The importance of data governance in the educational sector has been increasingly recognized in recent studies, with many reports highlighting its substantial benefits as well as the challenges that institutions face in its implementation. According to Gartner (Morgan & al., 2022), institutions with strong data governance frameworks see a 30-50% improvement in data accuracy, which is crucial for effective decision-making. Accurate data enables educational leaders to identify trends, make informed choices, and improve operational efficiency. When data is accurate, it not only supports better administrative decisions but also directly impacts student performance by providing clearer insights into learning needs and opportunities for improvement.

In terms of data security and privacy, (Sargiotis, 2024) found that strong data governance practices reduce 40% of data breaches in educational institutions. Data governance ensures compliance with critical privacy regulations such as FERPA and GDPR, which protect sensitive student information. These frameworks help institutions avoid potential data breaches and maintain trust with students, parents, and regulators by safeguarding personal and academic data.

Furthermore, (Herridge, 2024) reports that 65% of universities with data governance frameworks have higher levels of faculty trust in grading and assessment practices. This increased trust stems from the transparency and accountability fostered by data governance policies, which ensure that grading practices are fair, consistent, and based on reliable data. The clarity and consistency provided by governance frameworks also promote better decision-making within institutions.

Author in (Chui & al., 2023) highlights the impact of data governance on student outcomes, reporting a 15-20% improvement in retention and graduation rates in schools with robust data governance practices. Data-driven interventions, based on accurate and consistent data, help identify at-risk students and provide targeted support. Additionally, data governance enables more effective curriculum design by facilitating longitudinal data analysis, allowing educators to make data-informed adjustments to improve student success.

Despite these benefits, (Sweeney, 2021) point out that educational institutions often face significant challenges in implementing data governance, including fragmented data systems and resistance to change among faculty. These challenges hinder the integration of data across platforms, such as Learning Management Systems (LMS) and Student Information Systems (SIS), making it difficult for institutions to fully leverage the potential of data governance.

3. IMPORTANCE OF DATA GOVERNANCE IN EDUCATION

Data governance is a set of principles, policies, and practices that provide a structured framework for managing data within an organization (Abraham & al., 2019). It encompasses all aspects of data management, from ensuring data quality to managing data access and protection, thereby facilitating the effective use of data as a strategic asset (Koltay, 2016). Data governance is increasingly essential as organizations generate and rely on massive volumes of data, making it critical to ensure that this data is accurate, accessible, and secure (Eryurek & al., 2021).

Data governance, as shown in Figure 1, serves as the foundational structure for overseeing data availability, integrity, usability, and security. It is designed to ensure that data remains accessible and reliable for users across the organization, while also meeting regulatory requirements and protecting against unauthorized access. By establishing clear roles, responsibilities, and processes around data, governance frameworks prevent misuse, loss, or compromise of data assets. In particular, data governance defines who is accountable for various aspects of data, setting up mechanisms for data stewardship and quality control.

Figure 1. Importance of Data Governance

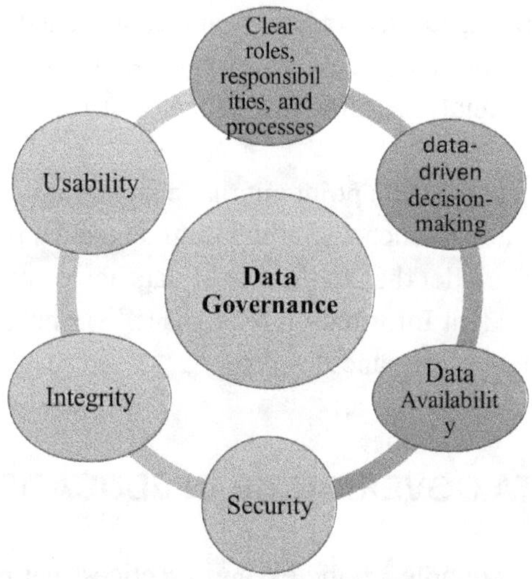

The importance of data governance in education cannot be overstated. As educational institutions increasingly rely on data to inform decisions, improve student outcomes, and allocate resources efficiently, having a robust data governance structure ensures that data is used responsibly and effectively (Elugbaju & al., 2024). It enhances data accuracy, minimizes errors, and enables institutions to make data-driven decisions that can lead to improved educational strategies and policies (figure 1). Furthermore, data governance supports transparency and accountability, fostering trust among stakeholders by ensuring that data is handled securely and ethically. It also ensures compliance with regulations like FERPA (Family Educational Rights and Privacy Act) and GDPR (General Data Protection Regulation), protecting student privacy and data security. Ultimately, data governance in education helps institutions build a solid foundation for evidence-based decision-making, ensuring that data serves its intended purpose of enhancing learning and institutional performance (Schildkamp & al., 2012). Key components of data governance in education include data quality management, data security and privacy, data policies and standards, data stewardship, data accessibility, data integration, and stakeholder engagement (Figure 2). Table 1 provides an overview of the key components of data governance within educational systems, focusing on their importance in supporting better decision-making, collaboration, and improving educational outcomes (Sargiotis, 2024).

Figure 2. Key components of data governance in education

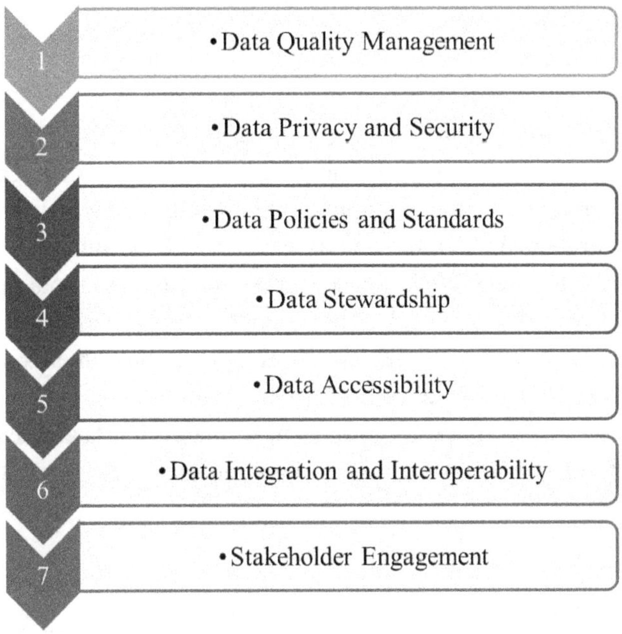

The following table summarizes the key components of data governance and their specific applications within educational settings. Each component plays a critical role in ensuring that data is accurately managed, securely protected, and accessible to the appropriate stakeholders. By outlining how data quality, privacy, security, accessibility, and integration are handled, the table provides a concise overview of how educational institutions can establish robust data governance frameworks to enhance decision-making, improve educational outcomes, and ensure regulatory compliance.

Table 1. Applications Of Each Key Data Governance Component In Educational Settings

Key Component	Application in Education
Data Quality Management	Ensures accurate, complete, and reliable data for decision-making, supporting curriculum improvements and student services.
Data Privacy and Security	Protects sensitive data from breaches and unauthorized access, ensuring compliance with laws like FERPA and GDPR.
Data Policies and Standards	Establishes consistent data management practices, standardizes formats, and ensures legal compliance across the institution.
Data Stewardship	Assigns responsibility for managing data integrity, privacy, and compliance, creating best practices for ethical data use.
Data Accessibility	Balances access to necessary data for educators and administrators while protecting sensitive information.
Data Integration and Interoperability	Ensures seamless data exchange between systems to create a comprehensive view of student progress and institutional performance.
Stakeholder Engagement	Involves all relevant parties in data governance development to ensure transparency, meet needs, and foster trust in data usage.

4. ROLE OF DATA GOVERNANCE IN PERFORMANCE MONITORING AND EVALUATION

4.1 Regular Assessments

Data governance is essential in ensuring that regular assessments in education are accurate, secure, and meaningful. By establishing clear policies and procedures for data management, it ensures that assessment data is reliable, timely, and properly protected. Strong data governance frameworks improve data quality, enabling accurate insights into student performance, while also ensuring compliance with privacy regulations like FERPA and GDPR. These frameworks also promote transparency and accountability in grading and assessment practices. Furthermore, data governance facilitates efficient feedback loops and longitudinal analysis, which can lead to continuous improvements in teaching methods, curriculum design, and student support. The following table highlights the key roles and benefits of data governance in regular assessments, backed by relevant statistics and examples. Table 2 condenses the key points, statistics, and insights from the full explanation on the role of data governance in regular assessments within education.

Table 2. Role of Data Governance in Regular Assessments

Benefit	Statistics
Ensuring Accuracy and Reliability of Assessment Data	- Data Quality Control: Strong data governance improves data accuracy by 30-50% (Makitalo, 2023). - Data Validation: Ensures correct data entry, minimizing errors in assessments.
Enhancing Data Security and Privacy	- Compliance with Regulations: Data governance helps reduce data breaches by 40% (Olaniyi & al., 2023). - Access Control: Defines authorized access to assessment data, ensuring privacy and security.
Facilitating Timely and Effective Feedback	- Timeliness of Data: Institutions with data governance reported 30% faster turnaround times for assessments and feedback (Gadde, 2020). - Actionable Insights: Quick data analysis for targeted feedback and interventions.
Improving Accountability and Transparency	- Consistency in Assessments: Ensures fair grading and assessment practices, leading to 65% of institutions reporting higher faculty trust (Shi & al., 2022). - Improved Accountability: Tracks and audits assessment results, ensuring transparency in grading and performance.
Support for Longitudinal Data Analysis	- Tracking Long-Term Progress: Longitudinal data analysis helps track student progress, improving the effectiveness of curriculum adjustments. - Curriculum Evaluation: 15-20% improvement in student outcomes based on effective curriculum changes (Wilson & al., 2024).
Case Study: University Data Governance for Assessments	- Improved Assessment Accuracy: Improved accuracy by 35% through data validation. - Faster Feedback: Provided feedback 50% faster due to better data management. – Increased Student Satisfaction: 15% higher satisfaction regarding grading fairness.

4.2 Iterative Improvements

Data governance plays a crucial role in driving iterative improvements within the education sector. By ensuring the accuracy, security, and accessibility of data, it enables educational institutions to make data-driven decisions that continuously refine teaching practices, student support systems, and administrative processes. With strong data governance, schools and universities can monitor student performance, identify trends, and implement timely interventions to improve outcomes. It also ensures compliance with regulations, such as FERPA and GDPR, while reducing the risk of data breaches. Through consistent feedback loops and data analysis, educational institutions can adapt their curricula, improve operational efficiency, and enhance overall student success. Table 3 highlights the key roles, statistics, and case studies showcasing the impact of data governance on iterative improvements in education.

Table 3. Role of Data Governance in Iterative Improvements

Benefit	Statistics
Data Security and Compliance	- Data governance reduces 40% of data breaches in educational institutions. - Ensures compliance with privacy regulations like FERPA and GDPR, protecting sensitive student data (Liu & al., 2020).
Transparency and Accountability	- 65% of universities with data governance frameworks report higher faculty trust in grading and assessment practices. - Promotes transparency and accountability, leading to fairer evaluations and data-driven decisions (Revesai, 2024).
Improved Student Outcomes	- Schools with robust data governance report a 15-20% improvement in student outcomes, particularly retention and graduation rates. - Data-driven interventions support at-risk students and foster academic achievement (Purcarea, 2023)
Curriculum and Program Improvement	- Longitudinal analysis enabled by data governance leads to more effective curriculum design. - Improves student outcomes by tracking progress and making data-informed adjustments Purcarea, 2023)

This table groups the benefits of data governance into key categories; data security, transparency, student outcomes, and curriculum improvement, while highlighting the relevant studies and findings.

5. THE IMPACT OF DATA GOVERNANCE ON DECISION-MAKING IN EDUCATION SYSTEMS

Data governance has a significant and multifaceted impact on decision-making in education systems. It ensures the availability of high-quality, accessible, and reliable data, which leads to improved educational outcomes (Hillman, 2023). Effective data governance enhances decision-making by promoting data consistency, transparency, and accuracy. By setting clear policies for data collection, management, and analysis, it enables informed decisions and supports strategic interventions. Reliable data also helps track progress, identify areas for improvement, and optimize resources. In sum, strong data governance frameworks empower educational institutions to make data-driven decisions, driving continuous improvement and better student outcomes. Several key ways in which effective data governance influences decision-making include:

1. **Improved Data Quality**: Data governance ensures that the data used for decision-making is accurate, consistent, and reliable (Koltay, 2016). By establishing standards for data collection, validation, and maintenance, educational leaders can trust the data they rely on, which leads to more informed and effective decisions.

2. **Enhanced Accountability and Transparency**: With clear data governance policies, educational institutions can track how decisions are made and who is responsible for them. This fosters transparency, ensuring that all stakeholders—teachers, administrators, policymakers, and parents—can see the rationale behind decisions, leading to greater trust and accountability (Kayyali, 2024).
3. **Timely and Relevant Insights**: Data governance structures ensure that the right data is collected and accessible when needed. This allows decision-makers to react quickly to emerging trends, such as changes in student performance or resource needs, leading to more responsive and adaptive decision-making (Su & al., 2020).
4. **Support for Long-Term Planning**: Effective data governance allows education systems to collect and analyze longitudinal data, which is essential for making strategic, long-term decisions about curriculum development, resource allocation, and policy implementation. This results in more sustainable, data-driven educational strategies (Anand & Honeycutt, 2020).

6. IMPLEMENTING DATA GOVERNANCE IN EDUCATION

6.1 Challenges in Implementing Data Governance in Education

Implementing data governance in education presents several challenges (Astuti & al., 2024). Limited resources, both financial and human, often hinder the establishment of comprehensive data governance frameworks. Many educational institutions also face fragmented data systems, where data is dispersed across various departments, making integration and consistency difficult. Additionally, there is often resistance to change from staff who may be unfamiliar with new data management processes or perceive them as burdensome (Starr, 2011). Ensuring compliance with privacy regulations, while maintaining transparency and security, also poses a challenge. Overcoming these obstacles requires strong leadership, training, and investment in technology to create an effective data governance structure. Table 4 recapping the challenges in implementing data governance in education systems:

Table 4. Challenges In Implementing Data Governance In Education Systems

Challenge	Explanation
Lack of Resources and Expertise	Educational institutions often lack the necessary resources and skilled personnel to implement and manage data governance frameworks. Without proper training and staff, it becomes difficult to maintain consistent data management and ensure adherence to governance policies.
Data Privacy and Security Concerns	Protecting student data is a critical issue, especially when complying with laws like FERPA and GDPR. Ensuring data security while allowing for its accessibility can create tensions, and institutions may struggle with securing systems against cyber threats while following legal requirements.
Data Silos and Fragmentation	Data is often scattered across different departments or platforms, creating silos. This fragmentation prevents the integration of data and makes it difficult to form a comprehensive, institution-wide data governance strategy, hindering effective decision-making.
Resistance to Change	Many educators and staff members may resist adopting new data management systems due to concerns about complexity, increased workload, or skepticism about the benefits of data governance. Overcoming this resistance requires strong leadership and a cultural shift toward data-driven practices.
Evolving Technology and Standards	Rapid advancements in educational technology create challenges for maintaining data governance. As new tools and platforms are introduced, institutions must update their data governance frameworks to ensure compatibility, compliance, and effective management.

The implementation of data governance in education systems requires a strategic approach that addresses key challenges such as resource limitations, data fragmentation, and resistance to change. Successful implementation involves clear planning and the allocation of necessary resources, including technology, training, and skilled personnel. Additionally, fostering a supportive culture around data use is crucial, where educators, administrators, and stakeholders embrace data-driven decision-making and adhere to governance policies. By promoting data literacy and encouraging collaboration across departments, educational institutions can overcome obstacles and create an environment that values data governance, ensuring long-term success and continuous improvement in educational outcomes.

6.2 Solutions for Implementing Data Governance in Education

Table 5 outlines proposed solutions to common challenges encountered when implementing data governance in educational systems. These challenges include a lack of resources and expertise, data privacy and security concerns, data silos, resistance to change, and the rapid evolution of technology and standards. For each challenge, targeted solutions are presented to help educational institutions overcome barriers and establish effective data governance frameworks. By addressing these issues, institutions can improve data management practices, enhance data security, foster greater collaboration, and ensure compliance with regulations, ultimately supporting better decision-making and educational outcomes.

Table 5. Solutions for Implementing Data Governance In Education Systems

Challenges	Proposed Solutions
Lack of Resources and Expertise	- Invest in training programs to upskill existing staff in data governance and security. - Partner with external experts or consulting firms for guidance. - Leverage open-source tools and cloud-based solutions to reduce costs.
Data Privacy and Security Concerns	- Implement comprehensive data security policies (encryption, multi-factor authentication). - Ensure compliance with data protection laws like FERPA and GDPR. - Conduct regular staff training on data handling and security practices.
Data Silos and Fragmentation	- Implement a centralized data management system to enable interoperability across platforms. - Standardize data formats and create a unified data repository. - Promote data integration through clear governance policies.
Resistance to Change	- Engage stakeholders early to explain the benefits of data governance. - Provide training and continuous support to ease the transition. - Create a feedback loop to address concerns and foster buy-in from all involved parties.
Evolving Technology and Standards	- Establish a flexible data governance framework that can adapt to technological changes. - Regularly review and update governance practices. - Collaborate with other institutions and industry groups to stay ahead of trends.

7. CONCLUSION

Effective data governance in educational systems is essential for optimizing performance monitoring and evaluation. By ensuring high-quality, consistent, and accessible data, it enables educational institutions to make informed decisions that enhance student outcomes and institutional performance. A strong data governance framework supports the accurate tracking of educational progress, highlights areas for improvement, and ensures the efficient use of resources. While challenges such as limited resources and resistance to change exist, data governance fosters accountability, transparency, and compliance with privacy regulations, building trust among stakeholders. Ultimately, effective data governance strengthens decision-making and drives continuous improvements in educational outcomes, ensuring a more responsive and effective learning environment.

REFERENCES

Abraham, R., Schneider, J., & Vom Brocke, J. (2019). Data governance: A conceptual framework, structured review, and research agenda. *International Journal of Information Management, 49*, 424–438. DOI: 10.1016/j.ijinfomgt.2019.07.008

Agasisti, T., & Bowers, A. J. (2017). Data analytics and decision making in education: towards the educational data scientist as a key actor in schools and higher education institutions. In *Handbook of contemporary education economics* (pp. 184–210). Edward Elgar Publishing. DOI: 10.4337/9781785369070.00014

Anand, P., & Honeycutt, T. C. (2020). Long-term outcomes for transition-age youth with mental health conditions who receive postsecondary education support. *Journal of Disability Policy Studies, 30*(4), 223–232. DOI: 10.1177/1044207319848069

Astuti, H. M., Wibowo, R. P., & Herdiyanti, A. (2024). Towards the National Higher Education Database in Indonesia: Challenges to Data Governance Implementation from The Perspective of a Public University. *Procedia Computer Science, 234*, 1322–1331. DOI: 10.1016/j.procs.2024.03.130

Blau, I., & Presser, O. (2013). e-L eadership of school principals: Increasing school effectiveness by a school data management system. *British Journal of Educational Technology, 44*(6), 1000–1011. DOI: 10.1111/bjet.12088

Chui, M., Issler, M., Roberts, R., & Yee, L. (2023). Technology trends outlook 2023.

Elugbaju, W. K., Okeke, N. I., & Alabi, O. A. (2024). Conceptual framework for enhancing decision-making in higher education through data-driven governance. Global Journal of Advanced Research and Reviews, 2(02), 016-030.

Eryurek, E., Gilad, U., Lakshmanan, V., Kibunguchy-Grant, A., & Ashdown, J. (2021). *Data governance: The definitive guide*. O'Reilly Media, Inc.

Gadde, H. (2020). AI-Enhanced Data Warehousing: Optimizing ETL Processes for Real-Time Analytics. *Revista de Inteligencia Artificial en Medicina, 11*(1), 300–327.

Herridge, C. (2024). The Patterns and Structures of Information Technology Departments in Higher Education.

Hillman, V. (2023). Bringing in the technological, ethical, educational and social-structural for a new education data governance. *Learning, Media and Technology, 48*(1), 122–137. DOI: 10.1080/17439884.2022.2052313

Kayyali, M. (2024). Quality Enhancement Frameworks in Higher Education. In *Quality Assurance and Accreditation in Higher Education: Issues, Models, and Best Practices* (pp. 61–141). Springer Nature Switzerland. DOI: 10.1007/978-3-031-66623-0_2

Khalid, M., & Hidayatullah, R. (2024). THE ROLE OF EDUCATIONAL ADMINISTRATION IN ENHANCING LEARNING QUALITY: A LITERATURE REVIEW. *Sindoro: Cendikia Pendidikan, 7*(4), 21–30.

Khatri, V., & Brown, C. V. (2010). Designing data governance. *Communications of the ACM, 53*(1), 148–152. DOI: 10.1145/1629175.1629210

Koltay, T. (2016). Data governance, data literacy and the management of data quality. *IFLA Journal, 42*(4), 303–312. DOI: 10.1177/0340035216672238

Koltay, T. (2016). Data governance, data literacy and the management of data quality. *IFLA Journal, 42*(4), 303–312. DOI: 10.1177/0340035216672238

Liu, C. W., Huang, P., & Lucas, H. C.Jr. (2020). Centralized IT decision making and cybersecurity breaches: Evidence from US higher education institutions. *Journal of Management Information Systems, 37*(3), 758–787. DOI: 10.1080/07421222.2020.1790190

Makitalo, K. (2023). Using custom data quality maturity tool for improving data quality in an organization.

Morgan, G., Yanckello, R., Thayer, T. L., Sheehan, T., Farrell, G., Mahmood, S., ... & MacDonald, N. (2022). Top technology trends in higher education for 2022.

Munagandla, V. B., Dandyala, S. S. V., & Vadde, B. C. (2024). Improving Educational Outcomes Through Data-Driven Decision-Making. *International Journal of Advanced Engineering Technologies and Innovations, 1*(3), 698–718.

Nai, S., Rifai, A., Sadiq, A., & Bakrim, M. H. (2022, May). Preliminary Study Of A Smart Computer System For Scholar Support. In 2022 IEEE 9th International Conference on Sciences of Electronics, Technologies of Information and Telecommunications (SETIT) (pp. 249-253). IEEE. DOI: 10.1109/SETIT54465.2022.9875526

Olaniyi, O. O., Olaoye, O. O., & Okunleye, O. J. (2023). Effects of Information Governance (IG) on profitability in the Nigerian banking sector. Asian Journal of Economics. *Business and Accounting, 23*(18), 22–35.

Purcarea, I. M. (2023). The importance of disruptive technologies in e-commerce for higher education. *Journal of Information Systems & Operations Management, 17*(1), 186–199.

Revesai, Z. (2024). Ethical Implications of AI-Driven Education Systems on Digital Rights: A Comparative Analysis. The Fountain. *Journal of Interdisciplinary Studies, 8*(1), 126–152.

Sargiotis, D. (2024). Overview and Importance of Data Governance. In *Data Governance: A Guide* (pp. 1–85). Springer Nature Switzerland. DOI: 10.1007/978-3-031-67268-2_1

Sargiotis, D. (2024). Key Principles of Data Governance: Building a Strong Foundation. In *Data Governance: A Guide* (pp. 137–163). Springer Nature Switzerland. DOI: 10.1007/978-3-031-67268-2_3

Schildkamp, K., Lai, M. K., & Earl, L. (Eds.). (2012). Data-based decision making in education: Challenges and opportunities.

Shi, Y., Peng, F., & Sun, F. (2022). A blended learning model based on smart learning environment to improve college students' information literacy. *IEEE Access : Practical Innovations, Open Solutions, 10*, 89485–89498. DOI: 10.1109/ACCESS.2022.3201105

Starr, K. (2011). Principals and the politics of resistance to change. *Educational Management Administration & Leadership*, *39*(6), 646–660. DOI: 10.1177/1741143211416390

Su, X., Chen, M., Yur-Austin, J., & Liu, Y. (2020). Restructuring degree roadmaps to improve timely graduation in higher education. *International Journal of Educational Management*, *34*(2), 432–449. DOI: 10.1108/IJEM-07-2019-0257

Sweeney, T. J. (2021). Leadership for the counseling profession. In *Professional counseling excellence through leadership and advocacy* (pp. 3–21). Routledge. DOI: 10.4324/9781003049050-2

Wilson, E., Roche, T., Goode, E., & McKenzie, J. W. (2024). Creating the conditions for student success through curriculum reform: The impact of an active learning, immersive block model. *Higher Education*, •••, 1–21. DOI: 10.1007/s10734-024-01283-1

Chapter 6
Modern Software Challenges: Innovations in Data Governance and DevSecOps

Busra Ozdenizci Kose
https://orcid.org/0000-0002-8414-5252
Gebze Technical University, Turkey

ABSTRACT

The rapid growth of software development and deployment has brought both opportunities and challenges, with organizations facing fast-changing market demands, increasing security risks, and stricter regulations. This chapter examines how Data Governance and DevSecOps provide critical solutions to these issues by addressing risks, ensuring security and compliance, and fostering innovation. Data governance establishes structured frameworks for managing, securing, and leveraging data across hybrid and multi-cloud environments, while DevSecOps integrates security throughout the software development lifecycle to mitigate vulnerabilities and enhance reliability. Through an exploration of the latest trends, including governance as code, cross-functional collaboration, continuous monitoring, and automation, this chapter offers actionable insights for researchers, practitioners, and decision-makers aiming to build secure, compliant, and efficient software ecosystems.

INTRODUCTION

Software development and deployment have grown rapidly, bringing both great opportunities and new challenges. Organizations rely more than ever on software to achieve their goals, but they face issues like fast-changing market needs, increasing security risks, and stricter regulations. These challenges require smart solutions to ensure software remains reliable, scalable, and compliant, while keeping up with the competition.

Some of the biggest challenges today include managing the huge amounts of data being created, dealing with cybersecurity threats, and connecting different systems in complex environments (Djenna et al., 2021; Sarker et al., 2020). As shown in Figure 1, the global cloud infrastructure market size accounted for USD 262.68 billion in 2024 and is projected to reach approximately USD 837.97 billion by 2034, reflecting a compound annual growth rate (CAGR) of 12.3% during this period (Precedence Research, 2024). In North America alone, the cloud infrastructure market reached USD 98.24 billion

DOI: 10.4018/979-8-3373-0365-9.ch006

in 2023, showcasing significant investment in cloud technologies. These figures highlight the growing reliance on cloud services across industries and underscore the need for strong data governance and security frameworks to manage the complexities and risks of cloud-based infrastructures.

Figure 1. Cloud Infrastructure Market Size

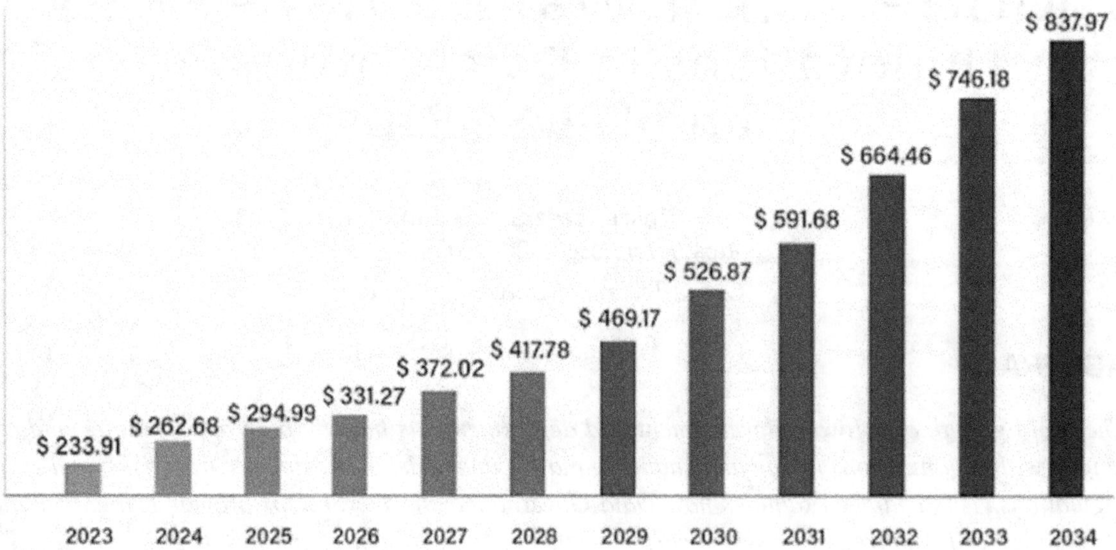

(Source: Precedence Research, 2024)

The rise of cloud computing, big data, and Artificial Intelligence (AI) has made it even more important to manage and protect data effectively (Chen et al., 2021; Sandhu, 2021a). At the same time, the push for faster and more automated software development has shown weaknesses in traditional security practices, leading to the need for new methods that include security throughout the development process. The complexity of modern software systems, combined with increasing regulatory demands like GDPR and CCPA, underscores the importance of adopting innovative approaches to ensure compliance and operational efficiency.

Data governance and DevSecOps have become key solutions to these issues (Gade, 2023; Janssen et al., 2020; Rajapakse et al., 2022; Sandhu, 2021b). Data governance is a framework that ensures data is systematically managed, secured, and utilized to support business objectives while meeting legal and ethical standards. It involves establishing clear roles, policies, and processes to govern data assets, enabling organizations to maintain data quality, mitigate risks, and unlock actionable insights (Nookala, 2024; Benfeldt et al., 2020). As organizations grapple with the complexities of hybrid and multi-cloud environments, data governance offers a structured approach to managing data sprawl, ensuring consistent practices across diverse platforms, and addressing the growing demands for data privacy and security.

DevSecOps, on the other hand, represents a paradigm shift in how software is developed and secured. By embedding security practices throughout the entire software development lifecycle, it ensures that vulnerabilities are identified and addressed early, reducing the cost and impact of potential breaches (Akbar et al., 2022; Rajapakse et al., 2022). DevSecOps extends the collaborative ethos of DevOps, bringing developers, security teams, and operations closer together. It emphasizes automation, leveraging tools such as automated security testing, container scanning, and continuous monitoring to maintain the pace of agile development without compromising security. This integrated approach creates a culture where security is seen not as an afterthought but as an integral component of innovation and reliability.

This chapter explores how data governance and DevSecOps can address modern software challenges by examining their roles in managing risks, ensuring compliance, and fostering innovation. It highlights the latest trends and innovations in these fields, provides a detailed discussion on the synergies between these two domains, and includes case studies to illustrate real-world applications. By delving into the practical and theoretical aspects, this chapter will provide valuable insights for researchers, practitioners, and decision-makers striving to build secure and efficient software ecosystems.

DATA GOVERNANCE: CHALLENGES AND INNOVATIONS

Data governance refers to the framework and set of practices that ensure data is managed effectively and responsibly throughout its lifecycle. It defines roles, policies, standards, and procedures to ensure data quality, security, and usability (Prasad, 2024; Kumara et al., 2023; Deekshith, 2021; Benfeldt et al., 2020). At its core, data governance is guided by several key principles. These include accountability, which assigns clear ownership of data assets; transparency, ensuring visibility into data practices; and compliance, maintaining adherence to relevant regulations and standards. Other principles such as data quality, security, and value focus on ensuring that data is accurate, protected, and strategically leveraged to meet organizational goals.

In a data-driven economy, organizations depend on reliable and accurate data to make informed decisions, improve operational efficiency, and maintain regulatory compliance (Mahanti & Mahanti, 2021; Janssen et al., 2020; Micheli et al., 2020). Effective data governance not only helps mitigate risks but also builds trust among stakeholders by ensuring data privacy and transparency. The integration of cloud environments, big data, and hybrid ecosystems has made data governance essential for managing data sprawl and maintaining consistency across platforms. Organizations must align their practices with strategic goals while addressing the challenges of distributed data systems.

Beyond its foundational role, data governance serves as a strategic enabler. It empowers teams by providing clear accountability frameworks, allowing them to use data effectively while minimizing risks. The rise of AI and machine learning further amplifies the need for high-quality, structured data governance. These technologies thrive on accurate datasets to provide actionable insights, making governance a cornerstone of innovation.

Industries such as healthcare, finance, and retail showcase the practical importance of data governance. In healthcare, effective governance facilitates secure sharing of patient data for research, driving advancements in personalized medicine. In finance, it ensures compliance with anti-money laundering regulations while enabling sophisticated fraud detection through analytics. Retailers rely on governance to unify customer data, fostering personalized marketing and enhancing customer experiences.

As organizations expand their reliance on cloud services and hybrid ecosystems, the scope of data governance continues to evolve. Modern frameworks now include real-time monitoring, automated compliance checks, and robust metadata management systems. These advancements ensure that data remains a strategic asset, enabling organizations to adapt and innovate in an increasingly complex digital landscape.

Modern Challenges in Data Governance

Organizations today face increasingly complex challenges in implementing effective data governance frameworks (Figure 2). These challenges arise from the rapid expansion of data ecosystems, evolving regulatory landscapes, and growing demands for real-time and secure data usage (Prasad, 2024; Nookala, 2024; Gade, 2023; Chakravorty, 2020).

Figure 2. Challenges in Data Governance

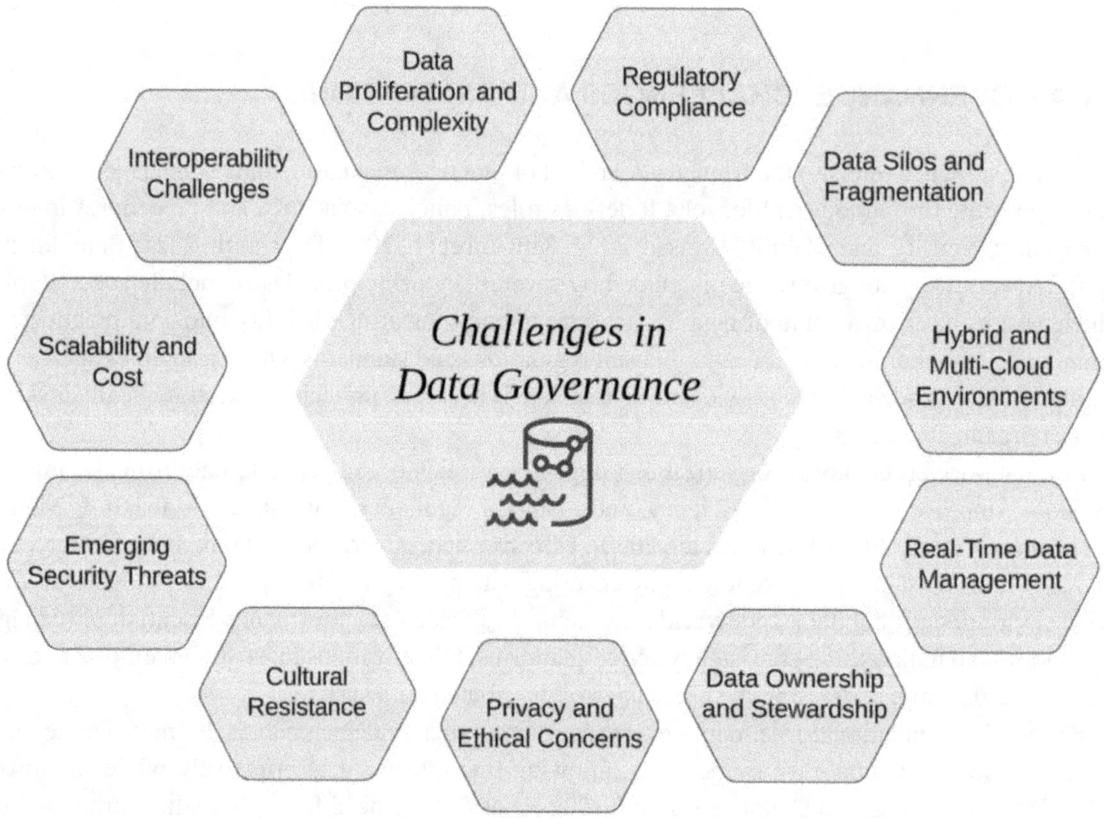

Data Proliferation and Complexity: The exponential growth in data generated by IoT devices, social media, business systems, and other sources has created significant challenges. For example, an energy company managing data from millions of smart meters must deal with real-time updates and ensure that the data is accurate and reliable for billing and energy optimization. Organizations must manage diverse data formats, including structured, semi-structured, and unstructured data, which require advanced tools for cataloging, organizing, and governing. This rapid proliferation often overwhelms traditional governance systems, making it difficult to maintain accuracy and consistency.

Regulatory Compliance: The growing number of data protection laws, such as GDPR, CCPA, and HIPAA, adds layers of complexity to governance practices. For instance, a multinational retailer must comply with GDPR for its European customers while adhering to CCPA regulations for its U.S.-based clients. Navigating these overlapping and sometimes conflicting regulatory requirements is a major challenge. Non-compliance can lead to financial penalties, reputational damage, and operational disruptions, highlighting the importance of robust compliance mechanisms.

Data Silos and Fragmentation: In many organizations, data resides in isolated systems across departments or platforms. For example, a healthcare provider may have patient records stored in separate systems for billing, medical history, and diagnostics, making it difficult to create a unified view of a patient's data. This fragmentation hinders the development of a unified governance strategy, leading to inefficiencies and challenges in ensuring data quality, consistency, and security. Addressing silos requires significant effort in integration and standardization.

Privacy and Ethical Concerns: The widespread adoption of AI and advanced analytics brings ethical challenges, particularly regarding privacy and bias. For example, a recruitment platform using AI to screen candidates could unintentionally prioritize certain demographics if the training data is biased. Improper data handling or algorithmic decisions based on biased data can harm individuals and lead to legal and public relations issues. Organizations must establish clear guidelines for ethical data use to avoid these pitfalls.

Hybrid and Multi-Cloud Environments: The shift to hybrid and multi-cloud architectures has transformed data management practices. Organizations now handle data spread across on-premises systems and various cloud providers, each with its governance and security requirements. For example, a financial institution managing customer transactions across AWS, Azure, and its private cloud must ensure consistent governance policies across all platforms. Maintaining consistent governance across these environments is critical but highly complex.

Real-Time Data Management: With the demand for real-time decision-making, traditional governance frameworks often struggle to validate, monitor, and assure the quality of live data streams. For example, an e-commerce company must analyze customer behavior in real time to provide personalized recommendations, requiring a governance framework that ensures the accuracy and security of the data while maintaining speed. This limitation can hinder organizations' ability to act quickly and accurately in dynamic markets.

Data Ownership and Stewardship: Clear ownership and accountability for data assets are often lacking in large organizations. For example, in a global manufacturing company, unclear data stewardship can lead to inconsistencies in inventory records, affecting supply chain efficiency. This creates gaps in enforcing governance policies and leads to confusion over responsibilities, particularly in cross-departmental initiatives.

Cultural Resistance: Employees and departments may resist data governance efforts, viewing them as overly bureaucratic or restrictive. For instance, a marketing team may push back against governance policies requiring stricter controls over customer data, fearing that it will slow down their campaigns. Overcoming this resistance requires leadership commitment, effective communication, and training to emphasize the benefits of governance initiatives.

Emerging Security Threats: Cybersecurity risks, including ransomware, phishing, and insider threats, are becoming more sophisticated. For example, a ransomware attack on a hospital's patient data system could disrupt critical care services and compromise sensitive data. Data governance must balance accessibility and security, ensuring sensitive data is protected while remaining available for legitimate use.

Scalability and Cost: As organizations grow, scaling data governance frameworks becomes a challenge. For example, a fast-growing tech startup may struggle to allocate resources for implementing robust governance tools while prioritizing rapid product development. The associated costs—tools, processes, and training—can strain budgets, particularly for smaller businesses. Demonstrating the long-term value of governance initiatives is critical to gaining organizational buy-in.

Interoperability Challenges: With data flowing across multiple systems, platforms, and formats, achieving seamless interoperability is essential. For example, a logistics company using different systems for fleet management and warehouse operations must integrate these systems to ensure accurate and timely data sharing. Standardized governance practices must address these challenges to ensure data can move efficiently and securely without compromising its integrity.

Innovations in Data Governance

Innovations in data governance have transformed how organizations manage and secure their data, enabling them to address the complexities of modern data ecosystems (Balan et al., 2023; Kumar et al., 2023; Dulam et al., 2022; Zhang et al., 2022; Migeon & Bobbert, 2022; Eryurek et al., 2021; Serrano & Zorrilla, 2021; Janssen et al., 2020).

AI and Machine Learning are at the forefront of these advancements, automating tasks such as data classification, anomaly detection, and metadata tagging. For instance, a financial institution can use AI-driven tools to identify sensitive customer information across its systems, ensuring compliance with GDPR and CCPA while reducing manual labor. AI also enables real-time monitoring of data quality, allowing organizations to detect inconsistencies and address them before they affect decision-making.

Blockchain technology is another breakthrough, providing a transparent and tamper-proof ledger for tracking data lineage and ensuring accuracy. This innovation is particularly valuable in industries like pharmaceuticals, where tracking clinical trial data is crucial for compliance and maintaining integrity throughout its lifecycle. Similarly, **Self-Service Data Governance** platforms have empowered business users to govern data responsibly without relying heavily on IT departments. Tools like Tableau and Alation allow users to access curated datasets, apply governance policies, and ensure compliance via user-friendly dashboards. For example, a marketing team can analyze customer data while adhering to privacy regulations, streamlining operations and improving accountability.

Real-Time Data Governance has also gained traction, enabling organizations to manage data as it is generated. Event-driven architectures allow e-commerce platforms to monitor customer interactions in real time, ensuring sensitive payment data complies with PCI DSS standards and minimizing risks associated with delayed validation. Meanwhile, integrating **Zero-Trust Security Models** into data governance frameworks ensures that every user and device accessing data is continuously verified. This approach is particularly effective for healthcare providers, where securing patient data across cloud and on-premises systems is critical to preventing unauthorized access and mitigating insider threats.

Cloud-native governance tools further enhance data management by centralizing control across hybrid and multi-cloud environments. Platforms like Google Cloud's Data Catalog provide metadata management solutions, allowing global retailers and other businesses with distributed data landscapes to maintain consistent governance policies. The concept of **Governance as Code** is also gaining momentum, embedding governance policies directly into development pipelines for automated enforcement. For example, tools like HashiCorp Sentinel help DevOps teams enforce data access policies during application deployment, ensuring compliance without manual intervention.

Other significant innovations include **data mesh architecture**, which decentralizes data ownership while maintaining centralized governance. An e-commerce company, for instance, might assign responsibility for product data to the merchandising team and customer data to the sales team, while a governance team ensures adherence to company-wide standards. **Privacy-enhancing technologies** such as differential privacy and homomorphic encryption also enable organizations to analyze sensitive information without compromising confidentiality. A healthcare organization, for example, can share anonymized patient data for research purposes while maintaining compliance with privacy regulations.

Finally, **Metadata-Driven Automation** has become a cornerstone of modern data governance, simplifying data discovery, classification, and policy enforcement. Media companies, for instance, use metadata to classify and tag their content libraries, ensuring copyright and usage rights are managed consistently. Automated metadata systems enhance visibility and streamline governance processes, enabling faster cataloging and improved policy enforcement. These innovations collectively empower organizations to navigate the complexities of data governance while driving efficiency, security, and compliance.

DEVSECOPS: CHALLENGES AND INNOVATIONS

The transition from DevOps to DevSecOps reflects a critical shift in software development, where security becomes an integral part of the process rather than an afterthought. DevOps was introduced to break down silos between development and operations teams, enabling faster delivery through practices like continuous integration and continuous delivery (CI/CD) (Khan et al., 2022; Battina, 2021; Mishra & Otaiwi, 2020; Al-Saqqa et al., 2020). While these practices improved efficiency, they often left security as a separate concern, leading to vulnerabilities in production environments that could undermine the benefits of rapid deployment.

The increasing complexity of software systems and the growing sophistication of cyberattacks exposed the limitations of traditional security methods. Conducting audits or testing only at the end of the development cycle was no longer sufficient in a fast-paced DevOps environment. This gap led to the rise of DevSecOps, which embeds security into every phase of the development lifecycle, ensuring it is treated as a shared responsibility among all teams. DevSecOps aligns security with the speed and agility of modern development practices, making it an essential evolution (Ozdenizci Kose, 2024; Akbar et al., 2022; Sandu, 2021b; Sánchez-Gordón & Colomo-Palacios, 2020).

Key to DevSecOps is the practice of addressing security concerns early in the development process, often referred to as shift-left security (Prates & Pereira, 2025; Reddy et al., 2021; Zaydi & Nassereddine, 2020). This approach integrates security measures into coding and design, reducing the likelihood of vulnerabilities and cutting down on the costs associated with fixing issues after deployment. Automation also plays a vital role, enabling security tests, vulnerability scans, and compliance checks to be seamlessly integrated into CI/CD pipelines. This ensures that security checks are both efficient and effective, keeping pace with rapid development cycles.

Collaboration is another foundational element of DevSecOps. By bringing developers, operations teams, and security professionals together, organizations create a unified approach to secure software delivery. Continuous monitoring adds another layer of protection, allowing for real-time detection of threats and immediate feedback to development teams. This proactive stance ensures that risks are identified and addressed quickly, minimizing the chances of vulnerabilities being exploited.

The benefits of adopting DevSecOps are substantial. Organizations can enhance their security posture, accelerate time-to-market, and reduce costs by addressing vulnerabilities early. Automated compliance checks help ensure adherence to regulatory requirements, which is especially valuable in industries with strict security standards. Ultimately, DevSecOps represents a significant improvement over traditional methods by embedding security into every step of the process, enabling organizations to deliver secure, reliable, and compliant software in today's demanding digital landscape.

Challenges in DevSecOps Adoption

Adopting DevSecOps is not without its challenges. While the framework offers significant advantages in terms of security and agility, many organizations struggle with cultural, technical, and operational barriers (Zhao et al., 2024; Anjaria & Kulkarni, 2022; Chinamanagonda, 2021; Sánchez-Gordón & Colomo-Palacios, 2020). These challenges often arise from the need to balance speed with security and integrate new practices into established workflows.

Cultural Resistance: In many organizations, development and security teams operate in silos with different priorities. Developers are often under pressure to deliver features quickly, leading them to perceive security practices as a hindrance to progress. For example, a development team may push back against integrating automated vulnerability scans into the CI/CD pipeline because it adds a few extra minutes to deployment time. Overcoming this resistance requires a cultural shift where security is viewed as a shared responsibility. Leadership must foster collaboration by incorporating security objectives into development goals and incentivizing cross-functional teamwork.

Skill Gaps: DevSecOps requires both developers and security professionals to broaden their expertise. Developers need to understand secure coding practices, such as preventing SQL injection and cross-site scripting, while security teams must familiarize themselves with agile workflows and modern tools like Jenkins or GitLab CI. For instance, a team working on cloud-native applications may struggle to secure Kubernetes deployments due to limited knowledge of container security best practices. Addressing this challenge often involves providing training, hiring specialists, or leveraging external consultants to fill the gaps.

Balancing Speed and Security: Maintaining the agility of DevOps while embedding robust security measures is a complex balancing act. For example, a fintech company racing to release a new mobile app may be tempted to bypass comprehensive penetration testing to meet a tight launch deadline. Such compromises can lead to vulnerabilities that undermine the application's security. Organizations must carefully select and configure tools that automate security checks, such as static application security testing (SAST) and dynamic application security testing (DAST), to minimize delays without sacrificing security.

Integration Complexity: Many organizations rely on legacy systems that were not designed with modern security practices in mind. Integrating DevSecOps into these environments can be challenging and expensive. For instance, an enterprise with an outdated ERP system may need to retrofit security tools, such as vulnerability scanners, which can require extensive customization. Hybrid and multi-cloud environments add another layer of complexity, as organizations must ensure consistent security policies across diverse platforms. Standardizing workflows and adopting tools designed for hybrid environments, like Terraform for infrastructure as code, can help address these challenges.

Measuring Effectiveness: Traditional security metrics, such as the number of vulnerabilities found during audits, do not fully capture the proactive and continuous nature of DevSecOps. Organizations may struggle to define meaningful metrics that reflect the impact of their efforts. For example, tracking the average time to remediate vulnerabilities or the percentage of automated security tests passed during each build can provide better insights. Developing these metrics requires collaboration across teams to align on what constitutes success in a DevSecOps framework.

Innovations in DevSecOps

DevSecOps has introduced a wave of innovations aimed at embedding security seamlessly into software development and deployment processes. These advancements leverage automation, AI, and modern practices to enhance security without compromising the agility of development teams (Zhao et al., 2024; Chittala, 2024; Sadovykh & Ivanov, 2024; Bernardino et al., 2024; Sharma 2024; Zaydi & Nassereddine, 2020; Sánchez-Gordón & Colomo-Palacios, 2020).

One key innovation in DevSecOps is the use of **Automated Security Testing Tools**. These tools, such as SAST and DAST, integrate directly into CI/CD pipelines. For instance, tools like SonarQube or OWASP ZAP can identify vulnerabilities during the coding and testing phases, allowing developers to address issues early. This automation ensures that security checks do not slow down development cycles while maintaining robust protection.

AI-Driven Threat Detection is another transformative innovation. AI and machine learning algorithms analyze vast amounts of data to identify patterns that may indicate security risks. For example, AI can detect unusual access patterns that might suggest insider threats or compromised accounts. This proactive approach enables organizations to mitigate risks before they escalate.

Shift-Left Security Practices have redefined how organizations approach secure software development. By embedding security measures in the earliest stages of the development lifecycle, organizations can reduce vulnerabilities and minimize costs. For example, tools like Snyk enable developers to scan dependencies for known vulnerabilities as they write code, ensuring secure foundations for applications.

The use of **Secure Coding Frameworks and Real-Time Feedback Systems** has empowered developers to take ownership of security. Tools like CodeQL provide immediate feedback on code vulnerabilities, guiding developers toward secure coding practices. This shift not only improves the security posture of applications but also enhances developers' skill sets over time.

Container and Cloud Security Solutions have also advanced significantly in DevSecOps. Tools like Aqua Security and Twistlock provide runtime protection for containerized applications, ensuring that containerized environments remain secure during deployment. These solutions are critical in hybrid and multi-cloud environments where applications are distributed across diverse infrastructures.

Another important innovation is the concept of **Policy as Code**, where security policies are defined and enforced programmatically. Using tools like HashiCorp Sentinel, organizations can embed compliance checks into infrastructure-as-code (IaC) workflows, ensuring consistent enforcement of security policies across environments.

The integration of **Real-Time Monitoring and Analytics** tools has enhanced visibility into system security. Platforms like Splunk and Datadog enable teams to monitor live application traffic and detect anomalies. These insights allow for immediate responses to potential security incidents, reducing downtime and mitigating risks.

By adopting these innovations, organizations can achieve a secure, agile, and efficient DevSecOps framework. These advancements empower teams to address security proactively, enabling them to deliver reliable and compliant software in an increasingly complex digital landscape.

SYNERGIES BETWEEN DATA GOVERNANCE AND DEVSECOPS

Data governance and DevSecOps are distinct frameworks, yet they complement each other in securing modern digital operations. Data governance ensures the accuracy, security, and compliance of data throughout its lifecycle, while DevSecOps embeds security into every stage of software development to protect applications and infrastructure. Together, these frameworks address critical aspects of digital security, with data governance safeguarding the data itself and DevSecOps securing the systems that manage and utilize that data.

Integrating data protection and secure development practices creates a unified approach to security and compliance. This alignment not only strengthens the organization's overall security posture but also improves operational efficiency by reducing redundancies and ensuring that both data and systems work seamlessly together. By combining the strengths of data governance and DevSecOps, organizations can build resilient and trustworthy digital ecosystems capable of adapting to evolving challenges.

Governance as Code

Governance as code represents a transformative approach to embedding governance policies directly into DevSecOps pipelines. By defining governance rules programmatically, organizations can automate policy enforcement and ensure consistent application of standards across their software development and deployment processes. This integration eliminates the need for manual intervention, reducing errors and improving efficiency.

One of the key benefits of governance as code is automation. Policies such as data encryption, user access controls, and compliance checks can be codified and integrated into CI/CD pipelines. For instance, automated scripts can enforce encryption of sensitive data before it is deployed to production environments, ensuring that no unprotected data leaves the pipeline. Similarly, access control policies can restrict unauthorized users from accessing critical systems, reducing security risks.

Another advantage is consistency. By embedding governance policies as code, organizations ensure that the same standards are applied uniformly across all environments, from development to production. This reduces variability and ensures that compliance requirements are met consistently, regardless of the complexity of the system.

Scalability is also a major benefit. As organizations grow and their infrastructure expands, governance as code allows them to apply policies seamlessly across multiple teams, projects, and environments. For example, in a hybrid cloud environment, governance policies can automatically adapt to different platforms, ensuring consistent data security and compliance across on-premises and cloud-based systems.

In practice, tools like HashiCorp Sentinel or OPA (Open Policy Agent) are often used to implement governance as code. These tools allow organizations to embed rules directly into their infrastructure-as-code workflows, ensuring that every deployment adheres to predefined governance standards. For instance, a DevSecOps pipeline can include checks to verify that all deployed resources comply with data encryption requirements and access restrictions.

By integrating governance as code into DevSecOps pipelines, organizations can create a streamlined, scalable, and secure framework that ensures compliance and mitigates risks throughout the software lifecycle. This approach not only enhances security but also aligns governance with the agility and speed of modern development practices.

Shared Challenges and Collaborative Solutions

Despite their distinct focuses, data governance and DevSecOps share several challenges that require collaborative solutions to overcome. Both frameworks face obstacles such as cultural resistance, integration complexity, and the need to balance agility with security and compliance. Addressing these shared challenges necessitates a unified approach that leverages the strengths of both frameworks.

One common challenge is cultural resistance. Teams often operate in silos, with developers prioritizing speed and functionality, while governance and security teams focus on compliance and risk management. This misalignment can lead to conflicts and delays. Encouraging cross-functional collaboration is key to breaking down these silos. For example, regular joint training sessions and shared performance metrics can foster a culture where security and governance are seen as enablers rather than barriers.

Integration complexity is another shared challenge. Both data governance and DevSecOps require seamless integration of tools and workflows into existing environments, which can be particularly difficult in hybrid or multi-cloud systems. By adopting common standards and interoperable tools, organizations can simplify these integrations. For instance, integrating real-time monitoring tools that flag both governance and security issues ensures that teams can address potential risks proactively and collaboratively.

Balancing agility with compliance also poses significant difficulties. Data governance frameworks ensure compliance with regulations like GDPR or HIPAA, while DevSecOps emphasizes speed and agility in software delivery. Automation provides a collaborative solution to this challenge. Automating compliance checks and security tests within CI/CD pipelines ensures that agility is maintained without compromising on governance standards.

Collaborative solutions can also enhance risk management. A DevSecOps pipeline that includes automated vulnerability scans can be configured to identify potential data governance issues, such as unauthorized access or unencrypted sensitive data. This integration ensures that both governance and security goals are met simultaneously, reducing redundancies and enhancing overall system resilience.

By addressing these shared challenges through collaboration and innovation, organizations can unlock the full potential of data governance and DevSecOps. This unified approach not only ensures robust security and compliance but also drives operational efficiency, enabling organizations to adapt to the complexities of modern digital ecosystems.

Table 1 provides a detailed comparison of the roles, challenges, and innovations in data governance and DevSecOps, highlighting their complementary nature and shared goals. This comparison highlights how data governance and DevSecOps tackle unique challenges while offering opportunities for synergy. For example, governance as code—embedding governance policies directly into DevSecOps pipelines—serves as a bridge between the two, enabling automation, scalability, and consistent compliance. Collaborative solutions like shared workflows and cross-functional training programs further strengthen their integration, ensuring both data and systems are protected effectively.

Real-World Applications

The integration of data governance and DevSecOps has demonstrated tangible benefits across various industries, enabling organizations to address complex challenges while enhancing security and compliance. These real-world applications illustrate how the combined frameworks strengthen digital ecosystems and drive operational efficiency.

In the **finance** industry, compliance and security are paramount due to strict regulatory standards. For example, a leading global bank implemented a metadata-driven data governance framework to ensure adherence to GDPR and PCI DSS. At the same time, its DevSecOps pipelines automated vulnerability testing and enforced encryption policies during deployment. This approach not only protected sensitive customer data but also ensured the rapid delivery of secure banking applications.

The **healthcare** sector faces unique challenges related to protecting sensitive patient information and meeting stringent data privacy laws like HIPAA. A large healthcare provider addressed these challenges by combining robust data governance practices with DevSecOps. Automated compliance checks were embedded in DevSecOps workflows to secure electronic health record (EHR) systems while maintaining the flexibility to adapt to evolving regulations. This integration enhanced patient trust and streamlined operations.

In **e-commerce**, companies handle vast amounts of customer data while managing complex supply chains and financial transactions. One major e-commerce platform integrated data governance with DevSecOps to address these demands. Real-time monitoring tools in DevSecOps pipelines detected security threats and unauthorized data access, while automated compliance checks ensured that payment systems adhered to PCI DSS requirements. These measures improved customer trust and enhanced the platform's operational efficiency.

Table 1. Analysis of Data Governance and DevSecOps

Aspect	Data Governance	DevSecOps
Objective	Manages and protects data assets to ensure quality, security, and compliance throughout their lifecycle.	Embeds security into every phase of software development to safeguard applications and systems.
Scope	Primarily focuses on data—its collection, storage, usage, and compliance.	Primarily focuses on software, infrastructure, and their interaction with data.
Challenges	Managing data silos, proliferation, and compliance across hybrid environments.	Balancing speed with security, addressing skill gaps, and integrating security into workflows.
Key Innovations	AI for anomaly detection, blockchain for data lineage, and metadata-driven automation.	Automated testing, AI-driven threat detection, and shift-left practices in CI/CD pipelines.
Team Involvement	Involves data stewards, analysts, compliance officers, and business users.	Involves developers, operations, and security teams working collaboratively.
Cultural Barriers	Resistance to new data policies; lack of understanding of governance benefits among non-technical staff.	Perception of security as a bottleneck; conflicts between development and security priorities.
Integration Complexity	Ensuring consistent governance policies across distributed, hybrid, and multi-cloud environments.	Integrating security tools into CI/CD workflows and legacy systems while maintaining agility.
Regulatory Focus	Ensures compliance with data-centric regulations like GDPR, HIPAA, and CCPA.	Aligns with standards like PCI DSS, ISO 27001, and industry-specific security requirements.
Security Role	Focuses on data security, privacy, and ethical data use.	Focuses on protecting software and infrastructure from threats and vulnerabilities.

continued on following page

Table 1. Continued

Aspect	Data Governance	DevSecOps
Automation Role	Relies on tools for real-time monitoring, compliance checks, and data tagging.	Uses automated vulnerability scans, security testing, and continuous monitoring in CI/CD.
Example Use Case	A bank uses metadata-driven automation to ensure data accuracy and lineage for regulatory audits.	A fintech company integrates SAST and DAST tools to secure applications during development.
Outcome	Builds trust, ensures compliance, and unlocks the strategic value of data.	Enhances security posture, reduces risks, and ensures secure and rapid software delivery.

From these examples, several lessons and best practices emerge. Firstly, fostering collaboration between governance, development, and security teams is essential to success. Shared training programs and unified objectives help align team efforts. Secondly, automation is critical for scalability and consistency. By embedding compliance and security checks into DevSecOps pipelines, organizations can ensure that governance policies are uniformly applied. Finally, proactive integration of data governance and DevSecOps enables organizations to adapt to new challenges and maintain resilience in dynamic environments.

By leveraging the strengths of both frameworks, these industries have demonstrated how data governance and DevSecOps can work together to create secure, compliant, and efficient digital ecosystems. These examples provide a roadmap for other organizations seeking to enhance their security and governance practices while achieving operational excellence.

Best Practices for Integrating Data Governance and DevSecOps

Successfully integrating data governance and DevSecOps requires a strategic approach that aligns their practices and overcomes common challenges. By adopting best practices, organizations can enhance collaboration, ensure consistent compliance, and build a robust security framework.

One key practice is fostering cross-functional collaboration. Data governance teams, developers, operations, and security professionals must work together to align their objectives and workflows. Establishing regular communication channels, such as joint planning meetings or shared performance metrics, helps break down silos and promotes a unified approach. For instance, creating cross-functional teams to handle compliance and security issues in CI/CD pipelines ensures that governance policies are seamlessly embedded into software workflows.

Investing in training and education is another critical step. Both developers and security professionals need to expand their skill sets to understand each other's domains. Developers should be trained in secure coding practices and compliance requirements, while security teams must become familiar with agile development and CI/CD pipelines. Providing regular training sessions and certifications can bridge these knowledge gaps and foster a culture of shared responsibility.

Leveraging automation is essential for scalability and consistency. Automating compliance checks, vulnerability scans, and governance enforcement within DevSecOps pipelines ensures that policies are applied uniformly without hindering development speed. Tools like automated security testing frameworks or governance-as-code solutions can streamline these processes. For example, integrating SAST tools alongside metadata-driven governance frameworks reduces manual intervention while maintaining high security and compliance standards.

A proactive approach to continuous monitoring further strengthens the integration of data governance and DevSecOps. Real-time monitoring tools that detect security threats and governance violations enable organizations to address issues before they escalate. Combining DevSecOps pipelines with real-time governance systems ensures that data security and compliance are maintained throughout the software lifecycle.

Finally, organizations must adopt adaptive frameworks that evolve with changing regulations, technologies, and threats. Regularly reviewing and updating governance policies, security practices, and automation tools ensures that the integration remains effective over time. Building flexibility into governance and DevSecOps strategies allows organizations to adapt to new challenges and maintain a competitive edge.

By following these best practices, organizations can create a unified framework that leverages the strengths of both data governance and DevSecOps. This alignment not only enhances security and compliance but also fosters innovation and operational efficiency, ensuring resilience in an ever-evolving digital landscape.

CONCLUSIONS AND FUTURE TRENDS

This chapter explored the integration of data governance and DevSecOps, highlighting their distinct yet complementary roles in modern digital ecosystems. Data governance ensures that data remains accurate, secure, and compliant, while DevSecOps focuses on embedding security into every stage of software development to protect applications and systems. Through detailed analysis, case studies, and best practices, we demonstrated how these frameworks, when aligned, address shared challenges, enhance operational efficiency, and strengthen overall security. By fostering collaboration, leveraging automation, and embedding governance as code, organizations can achieve a comprehensive approach to managing and securing both data and systems effectively.

Looking ahead, the integration of data governance and DevSecOps will be influenced by several key trends:

- Increased Use of AI and Machine Learning: AI and ML will enhance both frameworks through predictive analytics and real-time anomaly detection. These technologies will automate security testing and governance processes, identifying risks and compliance issues proactively.
- Expansion of Zero-Trust Architectures: Organizations will increasingly adopt zero-trust models, ensuring continuous verification of users, devices, and applications accessing data. This will strengthen security and align governance and security practices.
- Wider Adoption of Policy as Code: Embedding sophisticated governance and compliance rules directly into CI/CD pipelines will become more prevalent. This approach will enhance automation, scalability, and consistency across development and deployment environments.
- Emphasis on Data Ethics and Privacy: As big data and AI adoption grow, organizations will prioritize ethical data usage and privacy compliance to align with global standards such as GDPR and CCPA.
- Addressing Edge Computing and IoT Challenges: The proliferation of edge computing and IoT devices will require adaptive governance and security frameworks that can manage distributed and dynamic data ecosystems.

- Integration of Collaborative Platforms and Tools: Organizations will leverage unified platforms to streamline data governance and DevSecOps workflows, fostering cross-functional collaboration and addressing challenges holistically.

These trends will shape the future of data governance and DevSecOps, enabling organizations to build secure, compliant, and efficient systems in an increasingly complex and dynamic digital landscape.

REFERENCES

Akbar, M. A., Smolander, K., Mahmood, S., & Alsanad, A. (2022). Toward successful DevSecOps in software development organizations: A decision-making framework. *Information and Software Technology*, 147, 106894. DOI: 10.1016/j.infsof.2022.106894

Al-Saqqa, S., Sawalha, S., & AbdelNabi, H. (2020). Agile software development: Methodologies and trends. *International Journal of Interactive Mobile Technologies*, 14(11).

Anjaria, D., & Kulkarni, M. (2022). Effective DevSecOps Implementation: A Systematic Literature Review. *Cardiometry*, (24), 410–417.

Atlassian. (2024). DevSecOps tools. Retrieved from https://www.atlassian.com/devops/devops-tools/devsecops-tools

Balan, A., Alboaie, S., Kourtit, K., & Nijkamp, P. (2023). Blockchain systems for smart cities and regions: an illustration of self-sovereign data governance. Knowledge Management for Regional Policymaking, 163-190.

Battina, D. S. (2021). The Challenges and Mitigation Strategies of Using DevOps during Software Development. International Journal of Creative Research Thoughts (IJCRT), ISSN, 2320-2882.

Benfeldt, O., Persson, J. S., & Madsen, S. (2020). Data governance as a collective action problem. *Information Systems Frontiers*, 22(2), 299–313. DOI: 10.1007/s10796-019-09923-z

Bernardino, N. A., Sequeira, B., Piza, E., Henriques, F., Neves, F., & Reis, C. I. (2024, June). Enhancing DevSecOps: Three Custom Tools for Continuous Security. In 2024 IEEE 11th International Conference on Cyber Security and Cloud Computing (CSCloud) (pp. 53-58). IEEE.

Chakravorty, R. (2020). Common challenges of data governance. *Journal of Securities Operations & Custody*, 13(1), 23–43. DOI: 10.69554/GAKU4007

Chen, J., Ramanathan, L., & Alazab, M. (2021). Holistic big data integrated artificial intelligent modeling to improve privacy and security in data management of smart cities. *Microprocessors and Microsystems*, 81, 103722. DOI: 10.1016/j.micpro.2020.103722

Chinamanagonda, S. (2021). DevSecOps: Integrating Security in DevOps Pipelines-Security becoming an integral part of DevOps practices. Innovative Computer Sciences Journal, 7(1).

Chittala, S. (2024). Securing DevOps Pipelines: Automating Security in DevSecOps Frameworks. [JRTCSE]. *Journal of Recent Trends in Computer Science and Engineering*, 12(5), 31–44. DOI: 10.70589/JRTCSE.2024.5.5

Deekshith, A. (2021). Data engineering for AI: Optimizing data quality and accessibility for machine learning models. *International Journal of Management Education for Sustainable Development*, 4(4), 1–33.

Djenna, A., Harous, S., & Saidouni, D. E. (2021). Internet of things meet internet of threats: New concern cyber security issues of critical cyber infrastructure. *Applied Sciences (Basel, Switzerland)*, 11(10), 4580. DOI: 10.3390/app11104580

Dulam, N., Gade, K. R., & Gosukonda, V. (2022). Data Mesh and Data Governance: Finding the Balance. *Journal of AI-Assisted Scientific Discovery*, 2(2), 226–250.

Eryurek, E., Gilad, U., Lakshmanan, V., Kibunguchy-Grant, A., & Ashdown, J. (2021). *Data governance: The definitive guide*. O'Reilly Media, Inc.

Gade, K. R. (2023). Data Governance in the Cloud: Challenges and Opportunities. MZ Computing Journal, 4(1).

Janssen, M., Brous, P., Estevez, E., Barbosa, L. S., & Janowski, T. (2020). Data governance: Organizing data for trustworthy Artificial Intelligence. *Government Information Quarterly*, 37(3), 101493. DOI: 10.1016/j.giq.2020.101493

Khan, M. S., Khan, A. W., Khan, F., Khan, M. A., & Whangbo, T. K. (2022). Critical challenges to adopt DevOps culture in software organizations: A systematic review. *IEEE Access : Practical Innovations, Open Solutions*, 10, 14339–14349. DOI: 10.1109/ACCESS.2022.3145970

Kumar, A., Mishra, A., & Kumar, S. (2023). Data Democratization, Governance, and Security. In *Architecting a Modern Data Warehouse for Large Enterprises: Build Multi-cloud Modern Distributed Data Warehouses with Azure and AWS* (pp. 255–305). Apress.

Kumara, I., Kayes, A. S. M., Mundt, P., & Schneider, R. (2023). Data governance. In *Data Science for Entrepreneurship: Principles and Methods for Data Engineering, Analytics, Entrepreneurship, and the Society* (pp. 37–62). Springer International Publishing. DOI: 10.1007/978-3-031-19554-9_3

Mahanti, R., & Mahanti, R. (2021). Introduction to Data, Data Governance, and Data Management. Data Governance and Data Management: Contextualizing Data Governance Drivers, Technologies, and Tools, 1-3.

Micheli, M., Ponti, M., Craglia, M., & Berti Suman, A. (2020). Emerging models of data governance in the age of datafication. *Big Data & Society*, 7(2), 2053951720948087. DOI: 10.1177/2053951720948087

Migeon, J. H., & Bobbert, Y. (2022, July). Leveraging zero trust security strategy to facilitate compliance to data protection regulations. In *Science and Information Conference* (pp. 847-863). Cham: Springer International Publishing. DOI: 10.1007/978-3-031-10467-1_52

Mishra, A., & Otaiwi, Z. (2020). DevOps and software quality: A systematic mapping. *Computer Science Review*, 38, 100308. DOI: 10.1016/j.cosrev.2020.100308

Nookala, G. (2024). Adaptive Data Governance Frameworks for Data-Driven Digital Transformations. *Journal of Computational Innovation*, 4(1).

Ozdenizci Kose, B. (2024). Mobilizing DevOps: Exploration of DevOps adoption in mobile software development. *Kybernetes*. Advance online publication. DOI: 10.1108/K-04-2024-0989

Prasad, A. N. (2024). Establishing a Data Governance Framework. In *Introduction to Data Governance for Machine Learning Systems: Fundamental Principles, Critical Practices, and Future Trends* (pp. 49–108). Apress. DOI: 10.1007/979-8-8688-1023-7_2

Prates, L., & Pereira, R. (2025). DevSecOps practices and tools. *International Journal of Information Security*, 24(1), 1–25. DOI: 10.1007/s10207-024-00914-z

Precedence Research. (2024). Cloud infrastructure market size and forecast 2024 to 2034. Retrieved from https://www.precedenceresearch.com/cloud-infrastructure-market

Rajapakse, R. N., Zahedi, M., Babar, M. A., & Shen, H. (2022). Challenges and solutions when adopting DevSecOps: A systematic review. *Information and Software Technology*, 141, 106700. DOI: 10.1016/j.infsof.2021.106700

Reddy, A. K., Alluri, V. R. R., Thota, S., Ravi, C. S., & Bonam, V. S. M. (2021). DevSecOps: Integrating Security into the DevOps Pipeline for Cloud-Native Applications. *Journal of Artificial Intelligence Research and Applications*, 1(2), 89–114.

Sadovykh, A., & Ivanov, V. (2024). Enhancing DevSecOps with continuous security requirements analysis and testing. *Computer*, 16(7), 1687–1702.

Sánchez-Gordón, M., & Colomo-Palacios, R. (2020, June). Security as culture: a systematic literature review of DevSecOps. In *Proceedings of the IEEE/ACM 42nd international conference on software engineering workshops* (pp. 266-269). DOI: 10.1145/3387940.3392233

Sandhu, A. K. (2021a). Big data with cloud computing: Discussions and challenges. *Big Data Mining and Analytics*, 5(1), 32–40. DOI: 10.26599/BDMA.2021.9020016

Sandu, A. K. (2021b). DevSecOps: Integrating Security into the DevOps Lifecycle for Enhanced Resilience. *Technology & Management Review*, 6, 1–19.

Sarker, I. H., Kayes, A. S. M., Badsha, S., Alqahtani, H., Watters, P., & Ng, A. (2020). Cybersecurity data science: An overview from machine learning perspective. *Journal of Big Data*, 7(1), 1–29. DOI: 10.1186/s40537-020-00318-5

Serrano, J. Y., & Zorrilla, M. (2021). A data governance framework for industry 4.0. *Revista IEEE América Latina*, 19(12), 2130–2138. DOI: 10.1109/TLA.2021.9480156

Sharma, P. (2024). DevSecOps Integration-Security in the Software Delivery Pipeline: Exploring the integration of security practices into the software delivery pipeline to ensure secure software development practices. *Australian Journal of Machine Learning Research & Applications*, 4(1), 46–54.

Zaydi, M., & Nassereddine, B. (2020). DevSecOps practices for an agile and secure it service management. *Journal of Management Information and Decision Sciences*, 23(2), 1–16.

Zhang, Q., Sun, X., & Zhang, M. (2022). Data matters: A strategic action framework for data governance. *Information & Management*, 59(4), 103642. DOI: 10.1016/j.im.2022.103642

Zhao, X., Clear, T., & Lal, R. (2024). Identifying the primary dimensions of DevSecOps: A multi-vocal literature review. *Journal of Systems and Software*, 214, 112063. DOI: 10.1016/j.jss.2024.112063

Chapter 7
Agility Meets Compliance: The Convergence of Data Governance and DevSecOps

Busra Ozdenizci Kose
https://orcid.org/0000-0002-8414-5252
Gebze Technical University, Turkey

ABSTRACT

In today's fast-paced technological landscape, organizations face the dual challenge of delivering innovative software quickly while ensuring robust data governance, security, and compliance. This chapter examines the critical intersections between data governance, DevSecOps, and agile methodologies, offering a unified framework to balance agility and compliance effectively. By integrating practices like iterative governance and shift-left security into agile workflows, organizations can address risks associated with speed-focused development while maintaining operational efficiency and reliability. Through core principles, practical strategies, and emerging trends, this chapter provides actionable insights for managing the complexities of modern software development environments. It concludes with future directions and recommendations to guide organizations in adapting to evolving demands and implementing secure, scalable, and compliant workflows.

INTRODUCTION

In today's rapidly changing technology world, organizations are under constant pressure to deliver secure and high-quality software quickly. Customers expect smooth experiences and innovative features, while businesses must compete by reducing the time it takes to launch new products. At the same time, organizations must follow strict regulations and ensure their processes are efficient, flexible, and reliable. Balancing these demands can be difficult, as the need for speed and flexibility often conflicts with the structured processes required for governance, security, and compliance.

Delivering software quickly without compromising security or data quality requires organizations to rethink their methods. This is not just a technical challenge; it also involves changing the way teams work, collaborate, and use resources (Popoolaet al., 2024; Tatineni, 2024a; Srivastav et al., 2023). For example, teams often focus on speed to meet deadlines, which can lead to shortcuts in important areas

DOI: 10.4018/979-8-3373-0365-9.ch007

like documentation, testing, and compliance. These shortcuts can create risks such as data breaches, operational failures, and damage to the organization's reputation.

Modern software development often relies on agile methods, which focus on delivering results in short, frequent cycles and adapting to changes. These practices help teams work faster and adjust to new requirements, but they can sometimes overlook critical areas like data governance and security (Block et al., 2023; Duzha et al., 2023; Hassani & MacFeely, 2023). These areas are essential for long-term success but are often pushed aside in the rush to deliver quickly.

One key challenge is the trade-off between speed and thoroughness. Agile workflows prioritize quick delivery, which can make it hard to include detailed governance and security checks. This can lead to missed steps, such as ensuring data is properly tracked, complying with regulations, or fixing security issues. Ignoring these steps can increase the risk of non-compliance, data breaches, or customer trust issues.

Traditional governance and security practices, on the other hand, are often too rigid for agile workflows. These methods usually require detailed planning and heavy documentation, which may not fit well with agile's flexible and fast-paced approach. This mismatch can cause delays, confusion, or missed opportunities to align governance and security with development processes.

The growing use of distributed systems, cloud platforms, and global development teams adds even more complexity. Organizations must use a variety of tools and platforms while ensuring consistent governance and security across all stages of development. Without proper integration, this can lead to inefficiencies, isolated data, and higher risks, especially in environments that require quick and informed decisions.

Modern software development must find a balance between speed, scalability, and compliance. Agile practices can meet the need for faster delivery, but they must be carefully aligned with governance and security to avoid problems. Organizations that successfully combine these elements can achieve faster delivery while maintaining secure and reliable systems. This ensures long-term success in a highly competitive and regulated world (Tatineni, 2024b; Khan et al., 2024; Duzha et al., 2023).

This chapter explores the critical intersections between data governance, DevSecOps, and agile methodologies. It offers a unified framework for integrating these domains, enabling organizations to balance agility and compliance effectively. By examining core principles, practical strategies, and emerging trends, the chapter provides actionable insights to address the complexities of today's software environments. It focuses on key aspects such as data governance in agile workflows, embedding security within development cycles, and aligning these practices through a cohesive framework. Finally, future directions and recommendations are presented to guide organizations in navigating the evolving technological landscape and implementing these integrations in their own workflows.

DATA GOVERNANCE IN AGILE ENVIRONMENTS

Data Governance serves as a critical framework for organizations to manage data as a strategic resource. It encompasses policies, processes, and tools that ensure data is handled effectively, securely, and in compliance with regulations (Nookala, 2024; Eryurek et al, 2021). As highlighted in Figure 1, by integrating people, processes, and technology, data governance establishes clear accountability and promotes consistent practices across the organization. The following components highlight the key principles of a successful data governance framework (Prasad, 2024; Zhang et al., 2022; Deekshith, 2021; Janssen et al., 2020; Benfeldt et al., 2020):

Figure 1. The Principles and Foundations of Data Governance

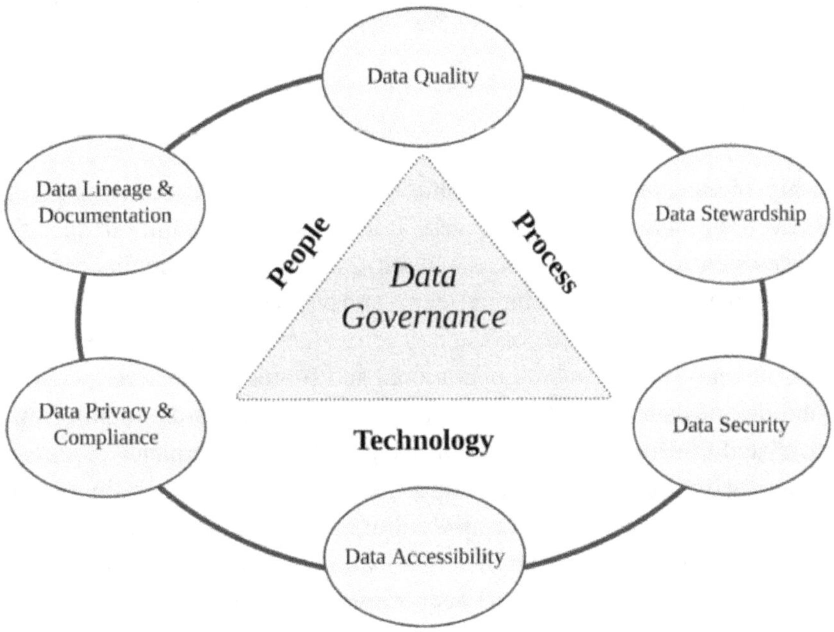

Data Quality

Data quality is the foundation of effective data governance, ensuring that data is accurate, consistent, complete, and reliable throughout its lifecycle. High-quality data enables organizations to make well-informed decisions, streamline operations, and comply with regulatory requirements. Conversely, poor data quality can lead to costly errors, inefficiencies, and damage to an organization's reputation, undermining trust and strategic goals.

To achieve and maintain data quality, organizations must implement a combination of processes and technologies. Validation is a critical step that ensures data accuracy at the point of entry or during processing, reducing the risk of incorrect information entering systems. Data cleansing detects and corrects inaccuracies, duplicates, and inconsistencies within datasets, improving their overall usability. Additionally, standardization enforces predefined formats and structures, making data easier to integrate, analyze, and share across systems and teams.

Advanced tools such as automated quality checks and data quality dashboards play a vital role in monitoring and improving data quality in real-time. These tools allow organizations to identify and address issues proactively, minimizing disruptions to operations. Regular audits and feedback loops further strengthen data quality by providing continuous evaluation and improvement, ensuring that the data remains fit for its intended purpose over time.

Organizations that prioritize data quality improve their operational efficiency and also enhance their ability to innovate, respond to market changes, and meet customer needs. By embedding data quality processes into their governance frameworks, they create a solid foundation for sustainable growth and long-term success.

Data Stewardship

Data stewardship, in other words data ownership, plays a vital role in ensuring that data is managed responsibly and effectively throughout its lifecycle. It assigns accountability to specific individuals or teams, known as data stewards, who oversee the quality, security, and compliance of data assets. Data stewards act as intermediaries between technical teams and business units, ensuring that data governance policies are implemented seamlessly and consistently across the organization. They bridge gaps between stakeholders to ensure that data meets both operational and strategic objectives.

Key responsibilities of data stewards include defining data standards, monitoring data usage, resolving conflicts related to data handling, and ensuring that data governance practices are adhered to at all times. They are also responsible for maintaining the integrity and usability of data, ensuring that it can be trusted as a reliable asset. By fostering a culture of accountability, data stewardship enhances collaboration and also builds confidence in the organization's ability to manage data responsibly. This approach supports compliance with regulatory requirements, minimizes data risks, and maximizes the value of data for decision-making and innovation.

Data Security

Data security is a critical principle of data governance, focusing on protecting data from unauthorized access, breaches, corruption, and loss. In a world of escalating cyber threats and evolving attack methods, safeguarding sensitive information is essential for maintaining trust, preserving reputation, and ensuring business continuity. Organizations must adopt proactive and comprehensive security measures to mitigate risks and secure their data assets.

Effective data security involves implementing robust safeguards such as encryption, access controls, and incident response plans. Encryption ensures that data is protected both during storage and transmission, while access controls limit access to authorized individuals based on their roles and responsibilities. Incident response plans enable organizations to detect, respond to, and recover from security breaches swiftly, minimizing damage and downtime. Real-time monitoring systems help identify vulnerabilities, while regular security audits and penetration testing ensure that defenses remain up to date. Additionally, organizations should establish clear data protection policies and provide ongoing training to employees to create a security-conscious culture. By integrating these measures into data governance frameworks, organizations can protect their data assets, meet compliance standards, and foster trust among customers, partners, and stakeholders.

Data Accessibility

Data accessibility ensures that authorized users can access the data they need, when they need it, while safeguarding the privacy and security of sensitive information. This principle promotes collaboration, fosters innovation, and supports data-driven decision-making by removing unnecessary barriers to data usage. When implemented effectively, accessibility empowers teams to extract maximum value from data while maintaining governance standards.

Organizations ensure accessibility by building efficient systems for data storage and retrieval, defining clear access permissions, and using secure sharing protocols. Self-service platforms, such as data portals and dashboards, have become increasingly popular, allowing users to independently access relevant data without relying on IT departments. This autonomy increases efficiency while still ensuring that governance policies are followed. To strike the right balance between accessibility and security, organizations implement robust authentication measures, regularly review access permissions, and monitor data usage patterns to prevent misuse. By enabling secure and seamless access to data, organizations create an environment where teams can work more effectively, make better decisions, and drive continuous improvement.

Data Privacy and Compliance

Data privacy and compliance are essential aspects of modern data governance, focusing on protecting personal and sensitive information while adhering to legal and ethical standards. Key regulations such as the General Data Protection Regulation (GDPR) in the European Union, the California Consumer Privacy Act (CCPA) in the United States, and the Health Insurance Portability and Accountability Act (HIPAA) for healthcare data mandate stringent controls over how data is collected, stored, processed, and shared. These laws aim to safeguard privacy, promote responsible data use, and build trust between organizations and their stakeholders.

To ensure compliance with these regulations, organizations establish robust privacy policies and procedures. These include restricting access to sensitive information on a need-to-know basis, implementing anonymization or pseudonymization techniques to protect personal data, and using secure methods for data transfer and storage. Regular audits and real-time monitoring tools play a vital role in identifying privacy risks and ensuring that organizations meet regulatory requirements.

Employee training programs further strengthen privacy practices by educating staff on their responsibilities and the importance of compliance. These initiatives reduce the likelihood of accidental data breaches and non-compliance while fostering a culture of accountability. By prioritizing privacy and compliance, organizations minimize legal and financial risks, and also enhance customer trust, loyalty, and overall reputation in an increasingly data-driven world.

Data Lineage and Documentation

Understanding the journey and context of data is crucial for effective data governance. This involves documenting information about data sources, transformations, and usage patterns to ensure transparency, accountability, and trust within the organization. Clear and consistent documentation allows teams to trace the relationships between datasets, promoting better collaboration and alignment across departments.

Data lineage management enables organizations to track the flow of data throughout its lifecycle, from its origin to its current state. This capability helps teams quickly identify errors, understand their root causes, and assess the downstream impact of any changes. For example, by mapping how data moves through systems and is processed, teams can address inconsistencies promptly and ensure compliance with regulatory requirements.

The use of automated tools to visualize and track data lineage significantly reduces manual effort and increases accuracy. These tools provide comprehensive insights into data flows, enabling organizations to manage their data ecosystems more effectively. By prioritizing data lineage and documentation, organizations enhance their ability to make informed decisions, maintain compliance, and foster trust in their data assets.

The Foundations of Data Governance: People, Process, and Technology

The success of data governance depends on three essential foundations: people, process, and technology. These elements work together to ensure data is managed effectively, securely, and in alignment with organizational objectives. Each foundation contributes uniquely to building a robust and sustainable data governance framework.

People are the cornerstone of data governance, as they bring expertise, accountability, and collaboration to ensure its successful implementation. This includes data stewards who oversee the quality, security, and compliance of data assets, governance committees that establish policies and resolve conflicts, and IT teams who provide technical expertise to support governance solutions. Equally important are the employees who interact with data in their daily roles, as their understanding of governance principles directly impacts compliance and effectiveness. By fostering a culture of accountability and collaboration, supported by regular training and clear communication, organizations can ensure that data governance practices are consistently applied and aligned with both operational and strategic objectives.

Processes form the structured framework within which data governance operates, guiding how data is collected, stored, accessed, shared, and deleted. These processes ensure consistency and reliability, reducing risks associated with errors, inefficiencies, and non-compliance. They include workflows for data quality management, access control, compliance monitoring, and incident response. For example, well-defined processes ensure that data is validated and standardized before use, while compliance workflows help organizations adhere to regulatory standards like GDPR and HIPAA. Regular reviews and updates to governance processes ensure they remain adaptable to evolving business needs and regulatory environments, embedding governance into the organization's operational fabric.

Technology acts as the enabler of modern data governance, providing the tools and platforms necessary to automate and scale governance activities. Advanced solutions for data quality monitoring, metadata management, access control, and compliance tracking streamline governance practices, reducing manual effort and minimizing errors. For example, tools that monitor data quality in real-time can identify and resolve inconsistencies immediately, while metadata management systems provide visibility into data lineage and flow. Emerging technologies like artificial intelligence and machine learning further enhance these capabilities by predicting data issues, automating compliance checks, and detecting anomalies. By leveraging these technologies, organizations can ensure efficient, secure, and scalable data governance practices that support long-term success.

Integrating Data Governance into Agile Environments

Integrating data governance into agile environments is a strategic challenge that requires balancing the need for speed and flexibility with the structured demands of governance. Agile methodologies prioritize iterative development, rapid feedback, and cross-functional collaboration, while data governance focuses on ensuring data quality, compliance, and security (Balan et al., 2023; Dulam, 2022 Mahanti

& Mahanti, 2021; Chakravorty, 2020). Successfully merging these approaches allows organizations to maintain the accuracy and trustworthiness of their data without compromising the agility needed for modern workflows.

To achieve this balance, governance practices must be seamlessly embedded into agile workflows. This begins by aligning **Governance Checkpoints** with key agile ceremonies such as sprint planning, daily stand-ups, and retrospectives. For example, sprint planning provides an opportunity for teams to assess data quality requirements and compliance considerations for upcoming tasks. Meanwhile, retrospectives allow teams to reflect on governance outcomes, identify areas for improvement, and refine their processes based on feedback.

Collaboration is central to this integration. Cross-functional teams that include data stewards, security experts, and compliance officers ensure governance expertise is available in real time. These specialists provide ongoing guidance on data standards, security protocols, and regulatory requirements, reducing delays and minimizing the risk of rework. By fostering close collaboration between governance stakeholders and agile practitioners, organizations can align their efforts and maintain momentum in development cycles.

Automation further streamlines the integration of data governance into agile environments. Automated tools for data validation, quality checks, and compliance monitoring reduce the manual effort associated with traditional governance tasks. For instance, tools that track data lineage offer transparency into data flows and transformations, enabling agile teams to address issues proactively without disrupting development. Real-time dashboards also provide actionable insights into data quality and usage, empowering teams to make informed decisions at every stage of the development process.

In addition to automation, **Lean Governance** practices offer a pragmatic approach to balancing agility and control. By focusing on critical tasks such as ensuring data accuracy and safeguarding sensitive information, lean governance minimizes unnecessary overhead for agile teams. **Iterative Governance,** which aligns naturally with agile's incremental development model, allows organizations to implement policies step by step. This gradual approach supports short-term goals while building a strong foundation for long-term compliance and data integrity.

Open Communication and **Shared Understanding** are vital for ensuring successful integration. Governance experts must work closely with developers, product owners, and other team members to clarify requirements and integrate governance into daily activities. Collaboration platforms, wikis, and other shared tools facilitate knowledge sharing and ensure alignment. Establishing **Governance Champions** within agile teams further strengthens this integration by providing dedicated advocates for governance practices who can bridge gaps between stakeholders.

When governance is effectively integrated into agile environments, the benefits are significant. Teams can make faster, more reliable decisions using accurate and compliant data, reducing risks associated with non-compliance or security breaches. This integration also fosters a culture of accountability and trust, enabling organizations to scale agile practices while maintaining robust governance standards.

Ultimately, by embedding governance into agile workflows, leveraging automation, and promoting collaboration, organizations can create an environment where agility and governance complement each other. This balanced approach supports innovation, ensures compliance, and drives sustainable success in an increasingly data-driven world.

Tools and Technologies for Agile Data Governance

Effective integration of data governance into agile environments relies heavily on the right tools and technologies. These solutions enable organizations to automate governance tasks, monitor data quality, and maintain compliance without disrupting the fast-paced nature of agile workflows. By leveraging advanced tools, teams can ensure that governance practices align seamlessly with development cycles, supporting iterative development and real-time decision-making.

The adoption of these technologies allows agile teams to streamline complex governance activities, reduce manual effort, and focus on innovation. From data quality and metadata management to compliance monitoring and security enforcement, the right tools bridge the gap between governance requirements and agile workflows (Prasad, 2024; Nookala, 2024; Gade, 2023; Kumara et al., 2023; Deekshith, 2021; Micheli et al., 2020). Table 1 presents some popular tools and technologies for agile data governance, highlighting their capabilities and use cases.

Table 1. Popular Tools and Technologies for Agile Data Governance

Tool/Technology	Category	Capabilities	Use Cases
Talend Data Quality	Data Quality	Automates data validation, cleansing, and standardization	Ensures accurate and reliable data for agile teams
Informatica Data Quality	Data Quality	Monitors and enhances data quality using machine learning	Identifies and resolves data inconsistencies in real time
Collibra	Data Lineage and Documentation	Tracks data lineage, maintains metadata, and enhances data transparency	Provides agile teams with insights into data origin and transformation
Alation	Data Lineage and Documentation	Offers collaborative data cataloging and lineage tracking	Helps teams document and understand data usage effectively
BigID	Data Compliance	Automates regulatory compliance checks and identifies sensitive data	Ensures adherence to GDPR, HIPAA, and other regulations in agile workflows
OneTrust	Data Compliance	Manages data privacy, risk assessments, and regulatory requirements	Flags potential violations during development cycles
Tableau	Real-Time Dashboards	Visualizes data quality, usage, and governance metrics	Provides agile teams with actionable insights for data-driven decisions
Jira	Collaboration Platform	Facilitates collaboration between governance experts and agile teams	Tracks governance tasks and integrates with agile development workflows
Okta	Data Security and Access Control	Implements role-based access controls to secure sensitive data	Restricts data access to authorized users while supporting agile operations
Azure Active Directory	Data Security and Access Control	Provides secure identity and access management	Ensures data security while enabling agile teams to work efficiently

By incorporating these tools and technologies, organizations can simplify data governance in agile environments, enabling teams to maintain compliance and data quality while operating at speed. These solutions empower teams to integrate governance seamlessly into their workflows, ensuring both agility and accountability.

EMBEDDING SECURITY IN AGILE SOFTWARE DEVELOPMENT

In today's fast-paced software development environment, embedding security into agile workflows is both a necessity and a challenge. Agile methodologies prioritize speed, flexibility, and collaboration, which often clash with the structured and slower processes of traditional security practices. As organizations work to maintain rapid delivery cycles while addressing evolving security threats, the DevOps approach emerged as a solution to streamline development and operations workflows.

From DevOps to DevSecOps

DevOps integrates development and operations teams, breaking down silos to enhance collaboration, automate workflows, and enable continuous delivery through CI/CD pipelines as described in Table 2. By doing so, DevOps accelerates software delivery and improves reliability (Ozdenizci Kose, 2024; Reddy et al., 2021). However, in the rush to meet speed and efficiency goals, security considerations were often overlooked or deferred, creating vulnerabilities that posed significant risks to organizations.

To address these gaps, DevSecOps evolved as an extension of DevOps, embedding security as a foundational element of the Software Development Lifecycle (SDLC). This approach integrates security into every stage of development rather than treating it as an afterthought. By emphasizing automation, collaboration, and iterative processes, DevSecOps aligns seamlessly with agile principles, enabling organizations to deliver secure, compliant, and high-quality software without compromising agility (Rajapakse et al., 2022; Sandu, 2021b; Sánchez-Gordón & Colomo-Palacios, 2020).

Introduction to DevSecOps and Agile Alignment

DevSecOps bridges the gap between security and agility by ensuring that security practices are an integral part of agile workflows. Agile emphasizes iterative development, frequent feedback, and responsiveness to change, which can sometimes deprioritize comprehensive security practices. DevSecOps addresses this challenge by fostering a culture of shared responsibility, where security is owned collectively by development, operations, and security teams (Kaledio & Lucas, 2024; Akbar et al., 2022).

Unlike traditional security models that rely on end-stage testing, DevSecOps emphasizes proactive and continuous security. Vulnerabilities are identified and mitigated early in the development process, reducing the likelihood of costly fixes later. By automating repetitive security tasks, teams maintain their focus on delivering features while ensuring robust security protocols. This approach complements demand of agile for speed, flexibility, and collaboration.

Table 2. Comparison of DevOps and DevSecOps

Aspect	DevOps	DevSecOps
Focus	Integration of development and operations	Integration of development, operations, and security
Primary Goal	Speed and efficiency in software delivery	Secure, compliant, and efficient software delivery
Security Approach	Often addressed late in the SDLC; Reactive	Embedded throughout the SDLC; Proactive

continued on following page

Table 2. Continued

Aspect	DevOps	DevSecOps
Automation	Focuses on automating development and deployment tasks	Extends automation to include security testing and monitoring
Responsibility	Developers and operations teams share responsibility	Shared responsibility, including security teams
Key Practices	Continuous integration and delivery (CI/CD)	CI/CD with continuous security checks and shift-left practices
Challenges Addressed	Operational inefficiencies, silos between teams	Security vulnerabilities, compliance gaps

Table 3 highlights the key aspects of DevSecOps in agile workflows, illustrating their benefits and potential challenges to ensure seamless integration. These aspects form the foundation of secure and efficient software delivery within agile environments (Zhao et al., 2024; Anjaria, 2022; Chinamanagonda, 2021; Mishra & Otaiwi, 2020; Al-Saqqa et al., 2020; Zaydi & Nassereddine, 2020):

- Continuous Security: DevSecOps mirrors agile's iterative cycles by embedding continuous security checks throughout the SDLC. Vulnerabilities are identified and addressed early, during each sprint or iteration, rather than accumulating until the final stages of development. This reduces the risk of security bottlenecks and ensures compliance from the outset.
- Automation: Automation is central to DevSecOps, enabling tasks such as vulnerability scanning, compliance monitoring, and code analysis to be performed without slowing down development. Automated tools like Static Application Security Testing (SAST) and Dynamic Application Security Testing (DAST) integrate seamlessly into CI/CD pipelines, providing real-time feedback to developers and maintaining the momentum of agile workflows.
- Collaboration and Shared Responsibility: DevSecOps fosters a culture of collaboration by involving security teams in agile processes from the beginning. Cross-functional teams that include developers, product owners, and security experts ensure that security is woven into the fabric of every development activity. This shared responsibility shifts security from being a separate function to an integral part of agile workflows.

Table 3 summarizes these key aspects, emphasizing their benefits and outlining the challenges that must be overcome for successful integration. While these key aspects demonstrate how DevSecOps aligns with agile methodologies, organizations must address several challenges to fully integrate security without compromising agility.

Table 3. Key Aspects of DevSecOps in Agile Workflows

Aspect	Description	Benefits	Challenges
Continuous Security	Incorporating security checks throughout the development lifecycle, mirroring agile's iterative cycles	Early identification of vulnerabilities, reducing costs and risks of late-stage fixes	Maintaining thoroughness without slowing down rapid delivery cycles
Automation	Leveraging tools like SAST and DAST for automated testing and compliance monitoring	Increases efficiency, reduces manual effort, and ensures consistency across workflows	Ensuring compatibility of tools with CI/CD pipelines and agile frameworks.
Shift-Left Security	Conducting security testing during early stages, such as code reviews or builds	Prevents security issues from escalating; integrates seamlessly with agile's focus on early feedback	Requires cultural change and training to shift responsibility to developers
Collaboration	Promoting shared responsibility for security among developers, operations, and security teams	Breaks down silos, fostering teamwork and shared accountability for secure software delivery	Overcoming resistance to change and ensuring alignment across cross-functional teams
Dynamic Threat Response	Real-time monitoring and adaptive responses to evolving cyber threats during and after deployment	Enhances resilience and mitigates potential damage quickly	Keeping up with a constantly evolving threat landscape while maintaining agile speeds

While DevSecOps offers a robust framework for embedding security into agile workflows, it is not without its challenges. These hurdles must be addressed to ensure a seamless and effective integration of security practices into the fast-paced nature of agile development cycles:

- Speed vs. Thoroughness: Agile's rapid delivery cycles often prioritize feature development and time-to-market, which can lead to shortcuts in security reviews. Teams may focus on immediate deliverables, potentially neglecting comprehensive vulnerability assessments, leaving systems exposed to threats.
- Tool Compatibility: Security tools must seamlessly integrate with agile frameworks and CI/CD pipelines to avoid bottlenecks. However, many legacy security tools lack the flexibility to align with modern, iterative workflows, causing inefficiencies and delays in development processes.
- Knowledge Gaps: Agile teams are primarily composed of developers and product managers who may lack specialized security expertise. Without adequate training or involvement of security professionals, critical vulnerabilities may go undetected or unresolved, increasing the risk of breaches.
- Dynamic Threat Landscape: The constantly evolving nature of cyber threats presents a significant challenge. Agile teams must adapt quickly to emerging vulnerabilities. However, staying ahead of new risks while maintaining development speed requires advanced tools, continuous monitoring, and proactive planning.
- Cultural Shifts: Integrating security into agile workflows requires a shift in mindset. Teams need to embrace shared responsibility for security, which can be difficult in environments where security is traditionally siloed. Overcoming resistance to change and fostering collaboration between developers, security experts, and operations teams is essential but may take time.
- Resource Constraints: Smaller teams or organizations with limited budgets may struggle to adopt comprehensive DevSecOps practices. Procuring modern tools, training staff, and dedicating resources to continuous security monitoring can pose significant financial and logistical challenges.

- Balancing Innovation and Compliance: Agile workflows thrive on innovation and experimentation, but ensuring compliance with regulatory standards like GDPR, HIPAA, or PCI DSS within an agile framework can create additional complexity. Striking a balance between regulatory adherence and maintaining flexibility is often a delicate task.

Key Practices for Proactive Security

To ensure robust security without hindering agility, organizations can adopt the following best practices (Prates, 2025; Chittal, 2024; Sadovykh & Ivanov, 2024; Bernardino et al., 2024; Sharma, 2024). These approaches enable teams to integrate security seamlessly into agile workflows, enhancing both efficiency and resilience.

- Shift-Left Security: Shift-left security involves conducting security testing early in the SDLC. By addressing vulnerabilities during activities like code reviews or build stages, teams can prevent issues from escalating later in the process. This proactive approach reduces both costs and risks associated with late-stage fixes. Shift-left security aligns well with agile's iterative nature, as it allows teams to embed security within their regular development cycles without introducing significant delays.
- Automated Testing: Automated tools are central to DevSecOps. These tools enable continuous security testing, eliminating the need for manual intervention. By integrating with CI/CD pipelines, automated testing provides developers with real-time feedback on vulnerabilities, ensuring issues are promptly addressed before deployment. Automation not only saves time but also ensures consistency, which makes it a critical component of security in fast-paced agile environments.
- Continuous Monitoring: Real-time monitoring solutions play a vital role in detecting and mitigating security threats during and after deployment. These tools provide visibility into application behavior, enabling teams to respond quickly to potential vulnerabilities or breaches. Continuous monitoring ensures that live applications remain secure and resilient against evolving threats, offering an additional layer of protection that complements pre-deployment security measures.
- Security Training: Educating agile teams on secure coding practices and threat awareness fosters a security-first mindset. Training programs empower developers to identify and address vulnerabilities during the development process, reducing the likelihood of introducing flaws inadvertently. Additionally, ongoing education keeps teams updated on emerging threats and best practices, ensuring they can adapt to the dynamic security landscape.
- Security Champions: Designating team members as security champions bridges the gap between development and security functions. These individuals advocate for security best practices within agile teams and serve as a point of contact for resolving issues. By promoting shared responsibility, security champions ensure that security considerations are integrated consistently across all stages of development, fostering a culture of accountability.

DevSecOps transforms how organizations approach security in agile environments, embedding it as a continuous, collaborative, and automated process. By overcoming challenges such as speed vs. thoroughness and knowledge gaps, teams can deliver secure, compliant, and reliable software without compromising agility. Through practices like shift-left security, automated testing, and continuous monitoring, organizations can create workflows that are both resilient and efficient. Ultimately, DevSecOps strengthens security and also enhances the overall quality and trustworthiness of agile software development.

Real-World Examples of Security Integration

Netflix is a prime example of how DevSecOps can enhance security in agile environments (Miglani, 2023; Dhaduk, 2022). Operating in a fast-paced, high-demand industry, Netflix faced challenges in maintaining security across its microservices architecture while adhering to rapid software delivery cycles. To address this, the company implemented automated security tools, including static code analysis and vulnerability scanning, directly into its CI/CD pipelines. Additionally, Netflix leveraged tools like Chaos Monkey for Security (ChAP) to test system resilience against security failures. By embedding these automated tools into their workflows, Netflix ensured early detection and resolution of vulnerabilities, enabling them to maintain both speed and robust security. Their innovative approach showcases how automation and iterative security checks can protect large-scale systems without disrupting agile development.

Similarly, Capital One, a leading financial services provider, faced the dual challenges of maintaining regulatory compliance and integrating security into its agile cloud-first strategy (Qualys, 2024; MachOne Digital, 2024). To achieve this, Capital One adopted a shift-left security approach, incorporating security testing at early development stages using tools like SAST and DAST. Automated compliance checks were added to their CI/CD pipelines to ensure adherence to regulations such as PCI DSS. This proactive integration of security measures allowed Capital One to achieve regulatory compliance without delaying product delivery timelines, reinforcing customer trust and operational efficiency. These examples illustrate how embedding security practices into agile workflows through DevSecOps can enhance both agility and security in real-world settings.

BRIDGING DATA GOVERNANCE, SECURITY, AND AGILITY

The integration of data governance, security, and agility is a cornerstone for modern software development (Figure 2). While each domain addresses distinct organizational needs -ensuring compliance, protecting assets, and accelerating delivery- bridging these elements enables organizations to deliver secure, compliant, and high-quality solutions without compromising speed or innovation.

Figure 2. The Triad of Modern Software Development

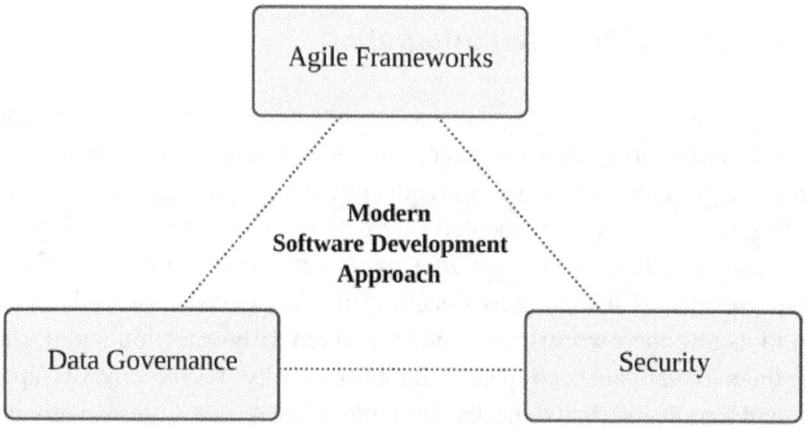

Modern software development demands seamless collaboration between governance, security, and agile practices. Data governance provides the foundation for ensuring data quality, lineage, and compliance with regulations. Security ensures that applications and data are protected from unauthorized access or breaches, maintaining customer trust and operational continuity. Agility focuses on delivering software quickly and adapting to changing market demands. However, these domains often operate in silos, leading to inefficiencies, miscommunication, and missed opportunities.

A unified framework that aligns data governance, security, and agility transforms these interdependent practices into a cohesive system. By integrating these domains, organizations can address challenges such as inconsistent compliance practices, unaddressed vulnerabilities, and delays caused by misaligned workflows. This integration ensures scalable, secure, and adaptive software development practices that meet both organizational and market demands.

Key Elements of the Unified Framework

Integrating data governance, security, and agility into a unified framework requires a deliberate and structured approach. Each domain must complement the others to create a cohesive system that supports rapid delivery, robust security, and regulatory compliance. The following elements are essential to achieving this integration:

Automated Governance and Compliance: Automation is the backbone of modern data governance. By automating critical tasks like data quality checks, compliance monitoring, and metadata management, organizations can ensure that governance practices scale seamlessly with agile workflows. Automated tools reduce manual overhead and provide real-time insights into data quality, lineage, and compliance status. For instance, tools like Collibra and Alation enable automated metadata management and data lineage tracking, ensuring transparency and accountability. Similarly, compliance automation tools like BigID and OneTrust help organizations stay aligned with regulatory requirements such as GDPR and HIPAA without disrupting agile processes. These solutions ensure that governance is consistent, efficient, and adaptable to fast-changing environments. Table 4 presents examples of data governance tools and technologies for integration.

Table 4. Examples of Data Governance Tools and Technologies for Integration

Tool	Key Features	Examples of Use	Relevance to Unified Framework
Collibra	Metadata management, data lineage tracking, and compliance monitoring	Tracks data flow for GDPR compliance, ensuring transparency and accountability across systems	Ensures governance tasks like compliance and lineage are automated and scalable
Alation	Data cataloging, collaborative data discovery, and stewardship workflows	Helps teams organize and share data assets efficiently, improving data quality and accessibility	Enhances data transparency and simplifies governance across distributed teams
BigID	Automated privacy and security compliance, sensitive data discovery	Identifies sensitive information (e.g., personal data) and ensures adherence to privacy regulations	Helps integrate privacy-focused governance with agile workflows
OneTrust	Privacy management, consent tracking, and regulatory compliance	Facilitates compliance with GDPR, CCPA, and other global data protection regulations	Streamlines compliance processes to reduce manual overhead in governance tasks

Integrated Security Workflows: Security must be embedded into every stage of the to prevent vulnerabilities from being overlooked. DevSecOps practices, such as shift-left security and continuous monitoring, integrate security directly into agile workflows. By addressing security early in development, organizations can mitigate risks proactively and avoid costly rework later. For example, tools like SAST and DAST provide real-time feedback to developers, identifying vulnerabilities as they arise. Continuous monitoring solutions, such as Splunk and Datadog, enable real-time threat detection and response, ensuring that live applications remain secure. These practices align security efforts with the speed and flexibility demanded by agile methodologies. Table 5 presents examples of security tools and technologies for integration.

Table 5. Examples of Security Tools and Technologies for Integration

Tool	Key Features	Examples of Use	Relevance to Unified Framework
SonarQube	Static code analysis for identifying security vulnerabilities and code quality issues	Detects security flaws during development stages, integrated into CI/CD pipelines	Embeds proactive security checks directly into agile development processes
Veracode	Dynamic Application Security Testing (DAST) and vulnerability scanning for web applications	Performs real-time vulnerability testing for applications during and after development	Enables continuous security testing aligned with iterative agile cycles
Splunk	Real-time security monitoring, log analysis, and incident response	Provides visibility into potential security breaches and helps teams respond to threats proactively	Supports continuous monitoring to ensure live application security
Datadog	Infrastructure monitoring, application performance monitoring and threat detection	Monitors live applications to identify anomalies and potential security issues in real time	Enhances visibility into operational security while maintaining agile speeds

Agile-Friendly Governance Practices: Traditional governance practices can feel rigid and counterproductive in agile environments. To address this, organizations must adopt lean governance principles, focusing on "just enough governance" to meet compliance and quality requirements without overburdening agile teams. This approach minimizes bureaucracy while maintaining the integrity and trustworthiness of data. For instance, governance tasks such as reviewing data policies or tracking lineage can be embedded into agile ceremonies like sprint reviews or retrospectives. This ensures that governance aligns with agile workflows without creating bottlenecks. Iterative governance allows organizations to refine policies incrementally, adapting them to evolving business needs and regulatory changes.

Collaborative Platforms: Effective integration of data governance, security, and agility depends on seamless collaboration between cross-functional teams. Collaborative platforms like Jira, Confluence, and GitLab provide a unified workspace for developers, security experts, and governance stakeholders to communicate, track progress, and share accountability. These platforms enable transparency and alignment by offering shared dashboards, task-tracking features, and knowledge repositories. For example, teams can use Jira to assign governance or security tasks during sprint planning, ensuring that these considerations are embedded into the development process. By fostering open communication and shared responsibility, collaborative platforms help break down silos and improve operational efficiency. Table 6 presents examples of collaboration tools and technologies for integration.

Table 6. Examples of Collaboration Tools and Technologies for Integration

Platform	Key Features	Benefits	Relevance to Unified Framework
Jira	Task and project management, sprint planning, customizable workflows	Facilitates agile workflow management and accountability among team members	Assigns and tracks governance and security tasks within agile workflows
Confluence	Knowledge sharing, team collaboration, and document management	Centralized repository for governance policies, security guidelines, and team documentation	Acts as a single source of truth for cross-functional teams
GitLab	CI/CD pipelines, version control, and security integration	Enables integration of DevSecOps practices with development processes	Combines development, security, and operations workflows in one platform
Slack	Real-time communication, integrations with other tools	Encourages quick decision-making and fosters open communication across teams	Bridges silos between developers, security experts, and governance teams
Microsoft Teams	Video calls, file sharing, and team collaboration	Combines real-time collaboration with file-sharing capabilities, enhancing teamwork	Useful for discussing and aligning on governance and security strategies
Trello	Visual task boards, checklists, and progress tracking	Simplifies task assignment and tracking for smaller teams or focused projects	Supports lightweight governance or security initiatives within agile teams

The key elements of a unified framework -automated governance, integrated security workflows, agile-friendly governance practices, and collaborative platforms- work together to align data governance, security, and agility. By adopting these practices, organizations can create an environment where speed, compliance, and innovation coexist seamlessly. This integrated approach supports operational efficiency and also ensures that software solutions remain secure, scalable, and compliant in an increasingly dynamic and regulated market.

Benefits of a Unified Approach to Modern Software Development

The integration of data governance, security, and agility into a unified framework offers transformative advantages for modern software development. By harmonizing these domains, organizations can achieve greater efficiency, resilience, and adaptability while ensuring compliance and security. The key benefits include:

- Improved Compliance and Risk Management: A unified approach ensures that compliance with regulations such as GDPR, HIPAA, and CCPA is seamlessly integrated into development workflows. Automated tools for data governance and security reduce the risk of non-compliance by continuously monitoring data usage, privacy standards, and security protocols. This proactive approach minimizes the likelihood of penalties, data breaches, and reputational damage.
- Enhanced Security: Embedding security practices into agile workflows strengthens the organization's ability to prevent, detect, and respond to threats. Continuous monitoring, shift-left security, and automated vulnerability testing address risks early in the development cycle, reducing exposure to potential breaches. This results in a secure and resilient application environment that fosters trust with customers and stakeholders.
- Faster Delivery Cycles: By integrating governance and security directly into agile workflows, a unified approach eliminates bottlenecks caused by last-minute compliance reviews or security checks. Automated processes and collaboration platforms enable teams to work more efficiently, delivering high-quality software on time. This streamlined approach ensures speed without compromising quality or compliance.
- Increased Collaboration and Shared Accountability: Cross-functional teams that include developers, security experts, and governance officers work together more effectively under a unified framework. Tools like Jira, Confluence, and GitLab facilitate transparency and shared accountability, breaking down silos and fostering a culture of collaboration. This alignment reduces miscommunication and ensures that governance, security, and agility objectives are met concurrently.
- Scalability and Adaptability: A unified approach is inherently flexible, allowing organizations to adapt to evolving market demands, regulatory changes, and emerging threats. Iterative governance practices and agile methodologies enable teams to refine policies and workflows incrementally, ensuring that the organization remains resilient in a dynamic environment.
- Cost and Resource Optimization: Automation reduces the manual effort required for governance and security tasks, freeing up resources for innovation and development. Early detection of vulnerabilities lowers the costs associated with late-stage fixes or post-deployment breaches. This efficiency translates into tangible savings while maintaining high standards for compliance and security.
- Enhanced Decision-Making: Real-time insights provided by governance and security tools empower teams to make informed decisions based on reliable, high-quality data. Data lineage tracking, compliance dashboards, and security monitoring ensure that decision-makers have a comprehensive view of risks, opportunities, and operational health.

STRATEGIES FOR INTEGRATING GOVERNANCE, SECURITY, AND AGILITY

This section highlights practical guidelines and strategies designed to help researchers and practitioners effectively integrate data governance, security, and agility into modern software development workflows. By following these approaches, organizations can ensure compliance, security, and operational efficiency while maintaining the flexibility and speed required by agile methodologies.

Embedding Governance into Agile Workflows

One effective strategy is aligning governance tasks with agile ceremonies such as sprint planning, daily stand-ups, and retrospectives. This approach ensures that activities like compliance checks and data quality validation occur regularly and naturally within development cycles. For instance, during sprint planning, teams can allocate tasks related to tracking data lineage or updating governance policies. Tools like Jira enable teams to monitor governance-related tasks, while platforms like Confluence serve as centralized repositories for documentation and policies. By integrating governance into existing workflows, organizations minimize disruptions and maintain consistent oversight.

Shift-Left Security

Shift-left security focuses on addressing vulnerabilities early in the software development lifecycle, during stages like code reviews and builds. This proactive approach reduces the likelihood of costly and time-consuming fixes later in the process. Tools such as SonarQube and Veracode automate vulnerability detection, providing real-time feedback to developers. By embedding security into the development phase, organizations can ensure their applications are robust and secure without slowing down delivery.

Integrating Security into CI/CD Pipelines

Embedding security into CI/CD pipelines ensures that every stage of the software lifecycle incorporates thorough security checks. Platforms like GitLab and Azure DevOps allow automated testing tools to scan code for vulnerabilities before deployment. This continuous integration of security ensures that software remains compliant and resilient against emerging threats, aligning perfectly with agile's iterative approach.

Continuous Monitoring for Threat Detection

Real-time monitoring solutions are critical for maintaining application security post-deployment. Tools like Splunk and Datadog enable teams to detect and respond to potential threats in real time. These platforms provide visibility into system performance and security anomalies, allowing organizations to address issues proactively. Continuous monitoring complements agile workflows by ensuring live systems remain secure without compromising operational speed.

Cross-Functional Collaboration

Fostering collaboration between governance, security, and development teams is essential for effective integration. Cross-functional teams, supported by platforms like Slack and Microsoft Teams, can align on priorities and share responsibilities. This approach promotes transparency and accountability, ensuring that all team members are actively engaged in achieving compliance, security, and agility goals. Real-time communication tools streamline decision-making and help teams address challenges collaboratively.

Iterative Governance Practices

Iterative governance aligns naturally with the incremental nature of agile methodologies. Instead of enforcing rigid, comprehensive policies upfront, organizations can implement "just enough" governance incrementally, refining policies over time based on feedback and evolving needs. Tools like Jira and Trello facilitate tracking governance tasks alongside development activities, while platforms like Collibra automate compliance monitoring, ensuring alignment with regulations like GDPR and HIPAA.

Automating Compliance Monitoring

Automation reduces the manual workload associated with maintaining compliance and governance. Tools like BigID and OneTrust streamline tasks such as data discovery, privacy management, and consent tracking. By automating these processes, organizations ensure that compliance is continuously maintained without diverting resources from agile workflows.

Building a Security-First Culture

Equipping teams with the knowledge and mindset to prioritize security is critical for long-term success. Regular training sessions on secure coding practices and regulatory requirements empower teams to identify and mitigate potential risks. Designating security champions within agile teams ensures that security considerations are consistently addressed throughout development.

CONCLUSIONS AND FUTURE TRENDS

This chapter explored the integration of data governance, security, and agility within modern software development, emphasizing their interdependencies and presenting actionable strategies to unify these domains. By embedding governance tasks into agile workflows, adopting DevSecOps principles, and leveraging tools like automated compliance monitors and continuous security checks, organizations can deliver secure, compliant, and high-quality software efficiently. The unified framework supports collaboration, enhances adaptability, and ensures regulatory adherence while maintaining development speed.

Such an approach is particularly valuable for highly regulated sectors like finance, healthcare, and energy, where compliance, security, and agility are critical for navigating evolving regulations, safeguarding sensitive data, and responding quickly to market demands. Moreover, industries like e-commerce, telecommunications, and manufacturing benefit from enhanced operational efficiency and secure innovation, enabling them to remain competitive in dynamic environments.

Looking forward, emerging technologies and evolving challenges open up numerous research opportunities for advancing this integration further:

- AI-Powered Governance: Investigating the use of machine learning models for anomaly detection, predictive compliance checks, and automated data quality monitoring.
- Blockchain for Security and Lineage: Exploring blockchain's potential for transparent, tamper-proof data lineage tracking and automated regulatory compliance through smart contracts.
- Governance in Edge Computing: Developing lightweight, decentralized governance and security models tailored to edge environments where data is processed closer to its source.
- Cross-Disciplinary Collaboration Models: Studying frameworks that enhance cooperation between governance, security, and agile teams, incorporating behavioral and organizational science.
- Risk Assessment in Agile Workflows: Creating dynamic, real-time risk assessment tools that integrate with CI/CD pipelines to balance speed and thoroughness.

These directions will help researchers and practitioners address the challenges of modern software development, ensuring that organizations remain resilient, innovative, and secure in an ever-changing technological landscape.

REFERENCES

Akbar, M. A., Smolander, K., Mahmood, S., & Alsanad, A. (2022). Toward successful DevSecOps in software development organizations: A decision-making framework. *Information and Software Technology*, 147, 106894. DOI: 10.1016/j.infsof.2022.106894

Al-Saqqa, S., Sawalha, S., & AbdelNabi, H. (2020). Agile software development: Methodologies and trends. *International Journal of Interactive Mobile Technologies*, 14(11).

Anjaria, D., & Kulkarni, M. (2022). Effective DevSecOps Implementation: A Systematic Literature Review. *Cardiometry*, (24), 410–417.

Balan, A., Alboaie, S., Kourtit, K., & Nijkamp, P. (2023). Blockchain systems for smart cities and regions: an illustration of self-sovereign data governance. Knowledge Management for Regional Policymaking, 163-190

Battina, D. S. (2021). The Challenges and Mitigation Strategies of Using DevOps during Software Development. International Journal of Creative Research Thoughts (IJCRT), ISSN, 2320-2882.

Benfeldt, O., Persson, J. S., & Madsen, S. (2020). Data governance as a collective action problem. *Information Systems Frontiers*, 22(2), 299–313. DOI: 10.1007/s10796-019-09923-z

Bernardino, N. A., Sequeira, B., Piza, E., Henriques, F., Neves, F., & Reis, C. I. (2024, June). Enhancing DevSecOps: Three Custom Tools for Continuous Security. In 2024 IEEE 11th International Conference on Cyber Security and Cloud Computing (CSCloud) (pp. 53-58). IEEE.

Block, S. (2023). How to Adapt and Implement a Large-Scale Agile Framework in Your Organization. In *Large-Scale Agile Frameworks: Agile Frameworks, Agile Infrastructure and Pragmatic Solutions for Digital Transformation* (pp. 65–168). Springer Berlin Heidelberg. DOI: 10.1007/978-3-662-67782-7_4

Chakravorty, R. (2020). Common challenges of data governance. *Journal of Securities Operations & Custody*, 13(1), 23–43. DOI: 10.69554/GAKU4007

Chinamanagonda, S. (2021). DevSecOps: Integrating Security in DevOps Pipelines-Security becoming an integral part of DevOps practices. Innovative Computer Sciences Journal, 7(1).

Chittala, S. (2024). Securing DevOps Pipelines: Automating Security in DevSecOps Frameworks. [JRTCSE]. *Journal of Recent Trends in Computer Science and Engineering*, 12(5), 31–44. DOI: 10.70589/JRTCSE.2024.5.5

Deekshith, A. (2021). Data engineering for AI: Optimizing data quality and accessibility for machine learning models. *International Journal of Management Education for Sustainable Development*, 4(4), 1–33.

Dhaduk, H. (2022). How Netflix Became A Master of DevOps? An Exclusive Case Study. Retrieved from https://www.simform.com/blog/netflix-devops-case-study/

Dulam, N., Gade, K. R., & Gosukonda, V. (2022). Data Mesh and Data Governance: Finding the Balance. *Journal of AI-Assisted Scientific Discovery*, 2(2), 226–250.

Duzha, A., Alexakis, E., Kyriazis, D., Sahi, L. F., & Kandi, M. A. (2023, August). From Data Governance by design to Data Governance as a Service: A transformative human-centric data governance framework. In *Proceedings of the 2023 7th International Conference on Cloud and Big Data Computing*(pp. 10-20). DOI: 10.1145/3616131.3616145

Eryurek, E., Gilad, U., Lakshmanan, V., Kibunguchy-Grant, A., & Ashdown, J. (2021). *Data governance: The definitive guide*. O'Reilly Media, Inc.

Gade, K. R. (2023). Data Governance in the Cloud: Challenges and Opportunities. MZ Computing Journal, 4(1).

Haidabrus, B., Grabis, J., Psarov, O., & Druzhinin, E. (2023). Agile Framework as a Key to Information Management Systems Delivery. In *Design, Simulation, Manufacturing: The Innovation Exchange* (pp. 113–120). Springer Nature Switzerland. DOI: 10.1007/978-3-031-32767-4_11

Hassani, H., & MacFeely, S. (2023). Driving excellence in official statistics: Unleashing the potential of comprehensive digital data Governance. *Big Data and Cognitive Computing*, 7(3), 134. DOI: 10.3390/bdcc7030134

Janssen, M., Brous, P., Estevez, E., Barbosa, L. S., & Janowski, T. (2020). Data governance: Organizing data for trustworthy Artificial Intelligence. *Government Information Quarterly*, 37(3), 101493. DOI: 10.1016/j.giq.2020.101493

Kaledio, P., & Lucas, D. (2024). Agile DevOps Practices: Implement agile and DevOps methodologies to streamline development, testing, and deployment processes.

Khan, H. U., Ali, F., & Nazir, S. (2024). Systematic analysis of software development in cloud computing perceptions. *Journal of Software (Malden, MA)*, 36(2), e2485. DOI: 10.1002/smr.2485

Khan, M. S., Khan, A. W., Khan, F., Khan, M. A., & Whangbo, T. K. (2022). Critical challenges to adopt DevOps culture in software organizations: A systematic review. *IEEE Access : Practical Innovations, Open Solutions*, 10, 14339–14349. DOI: 10.1109/ACCESS.2022.3145970

Kumar, A., Mishra, A., & Kumar, S. (2023). Data Democratization, Governance, and Security. In *Architecting a Modern Data Warehouse for Large Enterprises: Build Multi-cloud Modern Distributed Data Warehouses with Azure and AWS* (pp. 255–305). Apress.

Kumara, I., Kayes, A. S. M., Mundt, P., & Schneider, R. (2023). Data governance. In *Data Science for Entrepreneurship: Principles and Methods for Data Engineering, Analytics, Entrepreneurship, and the Society* (pp. 37–62). Springer International Publishing. DOI: 10.1007/978-3-031-19554-9_3

MachOne Digital. (2024). DevSecOps tools and techniques: A guide to optimizing your development pipeline. Retrieved from https://www.machonedigital.com/blog/devsecops-tools-and-techniques-a-guide-to-optimizing-your-development-pipeline

Mahanti, R., & Mahanti, R. (2021). Introduction to Data, Data Governance, and Data Management. Data Governance and Data Management: Contextualizing Data Governance Drivers, Technologies, and Tools, 1-3

Micheli, M., Ponti, M., Craglia, M., & Berti Suman, A. (2020). Emerging models of data governance in the age of datafication. *Big Data & Society*, 7(2), 2053951720948087. DOI: 10.1177/2053951720948087

Migeon, J. H., & Bobbert, Y. (2022, July). Leveraging zero trust security strategy to facilitate compliance to data protection regulations. In *Science and Information Conference* (pp. 847-863). Cham: Springer International Publishing. DOI: 10.1007/978-3-031-10467-1_52

Miglani, R. (2023). DevSecOps at Netflix: Digital Security. Retrieved from https://blog.nashtechglobal.com/netflix/

Mishra, A., & Otaiwi, Z. (2020). DevOps and software quality: A systematic mapping. *Computer Science Review*, 38, 100308. DOI: 10.1016/j.cosrev.2020.100308

Nookala, G. (2024). Adaptive Data Governance Frameworks for Data-Driven Digital Transformations. *Journal of Computational Innovation*, 4(1).

Ozdenizci Kose, B. (2024). Mobilizing DevOps: Exploration of DevOps adoption in mobile software development. *Kybernetes*. Advance online publication. DOI: 10.1108/K-04-2024-0989

Popoola, O. A., Adama, H. E., Okeke, C. D., & Akinoso, A. E. (2024). Conceptualizing agile development in digital transformations: Theoretical foundations and practical applications. *Engineering Science & Technology Journal*, 5(4), 1524–1541. DOI: 10.51594/estj.v5i4.1080

Prasad, A. N. (2024). Establishing a Data Governance Framework. In *Introduction to Data Governance for Machine Learning Systems: Fundamental Principles, Critical Practices, and Future Trends* (pp. 49–108). Apress. DOI: 10.1007/979-8-8688-1023-7_2

Prates, L., & Pereira, R. (2025). DevSecOps practices and tools. *International Journal of Information Security*, 24(1), 1–25. DOI: 10.1007/s10207-024-00914-z

Qualys (2024). Capital One: Building security into DevOps. Retrieved from https://www.qualys.com/customers/success-stories/capital-one-building-security-devops/

Rajapakse, R. N., Zahedi, M., Babar, M. A., & Shen, H. (2022). Challenges and solutions when adopting DevSecOps: A systematic review. *Information and Software Technology*, 141, 106700. DOI: 10.1016/j.infsof.2021.106700

Reddy, A. K., Alluri, V. R. R., Thota, S., Ravi, C. S., & Bonam, V. S. M. (2021). DevSecOps: Integrating Security into the DevOps Pipeline for Cloud-Native Applications. *Journal of Artificial Intelligence Research and Applications*, 1(2), 89–114.

Sadovykh, A., & Ivanov, V. (2024). Enhancing DevSecOps with continuous security requirements analysis and testing. *Computer*, 16(7), 1687–1702.

Sánchez-Gordón, M., & Colomo-Palacios, R. (2020, June). Security as culture: a systematic literature review of DevSecOps. In *Proceedings of the IEEE/ACM 42nd international conference on software engineering workshops*(pp. 266-269). DOI: 10.1145/3387940.3392233

Sandu, A. K. (2021b). DevSecOps: Integrating Security into the DevOps Lifecycle for Enhanced Resilience. *Technology & Management Review*, 6, 1–19.

Sharma, P. (2024). DevSecOps Integration-Security in the Software Delivery Pipeline: Exploring the integration of security practices into the software delivery pipeline to ensure secure software development practices. *Australian Journal of Machine Learning Research & Applications*, 4(1), 46–54.

Srivastav, S., Allam, K., & Mustyala, A. (2023). Software Automation Enhancement through the Implementation of DevOps. *International Journal of Research Publication and Reviews*, 4(6), 2050–2054. DOI: 10.55248/gengpi.4.623.45947

Tatineni, S. (2024a). Applying DevOps Practices for Quality and Reliability Improvement in Cloud-Based Systems. *DevOps-An Open Access Journal*, 3(1), 25–31.

Tatineni, S. (2024b). Compliance and Audit Challenges in DevOps: A Security Perspective. *DevOps-An Open Access Journal*, 3(2), 53–60.

Zaydi, M., & Nassereddine, B. (2020). DevSecOps practices for an agile and secure it service management. *Journal of Management Information and Decision Sciences*, 23(2), 1–16.

Zhang, Q., Sun, X., & Zhang, M. (2022). Data matters: A strategic action framework for data governance. *Information & Management*, 59(4), 103642. DOI: 10.1016/j.im.2022.103642

Zhao, X., Clear, T., & Lal, R. (2024). Identifying the primary dimensions of DevSecOps: A multi-vocal literature review. *Journal of Systems and Software*, 214, 112063. DOI: 10.1016/j.jss.2024.112063

Chapter 8
Embedding Security into DevOps:
Achieving Continuous Protection and Harmonized Software Development Practices

Bahaa Eddine Elbaghazaoui
https://orcid.org/0000-0002-3206-5162
National School of Applied Sciences, Sultan Moulay Slimane University, Beni Mellal, Morocco

Rabha Allaoui
National School of Applied Sciences, Sultan Moulay Slimane University, Beni Mellal, Morocco

ABSTRACT

In the fast-paced world of software development, integrating security into the DevOps pipeline is essential for achieving Continuous Protection. This chapter provides a comprehensive overview of DevSecOps, an approach that unifies security with development and operations to create secure, reliable, and scalable software systems. The chapter begins by examining the challenges of traditional security in DevOps and introduces key principles of DevSecOps, such as early vulnerability detection, security automation, and fostering a security-first culture. Practical insights into implementing security tools, managing risks, and enhancing collaboration among cross-functional teams are provided. Readers will gain an understanding of how DevSecOps can be leveraged to ensure software remains secure without compromising on agility and innovation.

1. INTRODUCTION: THE NEED FOR INTEGRATED SECURITY IN DevOps

In today's ever-evolving software development landscape, the traditional boundaries that once defined the roles of development, operations, and security are proving increasingly unsustainable. For decades, development teams concentrated primarily on building and enhancing the functionality of applications, while operations teams were tasked with ensuring reliable deployment and maintaining the underlying infrastructure. Security teams, on the other hand, were often brought into the process only at the final

DOI: 10.4018/979-8-3373-0365-9.ch008

stages to assess vulnerabilities and mitigate risks. This siloed approach, though common in the past, has consistently led to significant inefficiencies. These inefficiencies include bottlenecks in workflows, delays in project releases, and, most critically, overlooked or inadequately addressed security risks. In such scenarios, vulnerabilities were often discovered too late to allow for effective remediation, leaving systems exposed to potential threats (Rajapakse et al., 2022).

Modern software development practices, however, operate under vastly different conditions and expectations. Today's delivery pipelines are characterized by the need for rapid iteration, seamless continuous deployment, and the ability to scale dynamically in response to shifting demands. At the same time, the sophistication and frequency of cyber threats have reached unprecedented levels. Malicious actors now exploit vulnerabilities at every stage of the software lifecycle, targeting weaknesses in code, infrastructure, and even supply chains. High-profile incidents such as data breaches, ransomware attacks, and supply chain compromises have underscored the critical need for a more proactive and integrated approach to security. Without such measures, organizations risk not only financial losses but also reputational damage and operational disruption (Gupta, 2022).

To effectively confront these multifaceted challenges, organizations are increasingly adopting DevSecOps—a transformative methodology that integrates security directly into the DevOps framework. Unlike traditional security practices that treated security as a separate, reactive process, DevSecOps emphasizes the seamless embedding of security as a fundamental and continuous aspect of the software development lifecycle. The methodology is grounded in the principle of "shifting left," which involves addressing security considerations as early as possible during the development process. This proactive approach ensures that vulnerabilities are detected and mitigated before they escalate, significantly reducing both risks and costs (Sandu, 2021).

This chapter explores the core principles and practical applications of DevSecOps, providing insights into how organizations can successfully navigate and overcome the limitations of traditional security frameworks. By embedding security into every stage of the DevOps pipeline, teams can achieve a state of Continuous Protection. This state not only removes security as a potential bottleneck but also positions it as a driving force for innovation. DevSecOps represents a convergence of cultural change, process reengineering, and the strategic adoption of advanced tools. Together, these elements enable teams to accelerate software delivery while enhancing security, creating a foundation for both agility and resilience in the face of evolving cybersecurity threats (Sandu, 2021).

The chapter further emphasizes the critical importance of integrating security measures into the DevOps lifecycle to ensure Continuous Protection. It begins by examining the inherent limitations of traditional security approaches, which are often reactive and disjointed. DevSecOps is introduced as a comprehensive and holistic solution designed to secure software development within agile and dynamic environments. Key concepts, such as shifting security left, automating vulnerability detection processes, and fostering a collaborative culture of shared responsibility, are discussed in detail.

In addition, this chapter provides actionable guidance on implementing DevSecOps principles effectively. Real-world case studies are included to illustrate successful applications of DevSecOps, offering readers practical examples of how these principles can be applied in different organizational contexts. The chapter also recommends a suite of tools that can facilitate the adoption of DevSecOps, enabling teams to automate key security processes and integrate them seamlessly into their existing workflows. By embracing DevSecOps, organizations can not only address the complex cybersecurity challenges of the modern era but also maintain the speed and innovation required by contemporary software development practices. In this way, DevSecOps serves as a vital enabler of both security and progress, ensuring that organizations can thrive in an increasingly digital and interconnected world.

2. THE LIMITATIONS OF TRADITIONAL SECURITY IN AGILE DEVELOPMENT

In traditional software development, security is typically treated as a separate phase, often carried out towards the end of the development lifecycle. This "reactive" approach focuses on identifying and mitigating vulnerabilities after the software has been built, leading to significant inefficiencies and risks. In the context of agile development and DevOps, where the emphasis is on continuous integration and delivery, such practices fall short. This section delves into the challenges posed by traditional security models and why they are incompatible with modern development workflows.

1. Reactive vs. Proactive Security

Traditional security methods often involve manual reviews, penetration testing, or audits performed just before deployment. While these techniques are valuable, their reactive nature introduces several challenges:

- **Delayed Vulnerability Discovery**: For example, if a security flaw in a web application's authentication module is identified during the final stages of deployment, resolving it may require significant code changes. This delays the release and increases development costs.
- **Cost of Fixes**: Studies such as those by the National Institute of Standards and Technology (NIST) have shown that fixing a vulnerability in production is exponentially more expensive than addressing it during the coding or design phase (Hahn & Layne-Farrar, 2006).
- **Example**: Consider an e-commerce platform that discovers a SQL injection vulnerability in its payment processing system during a pre-deployment security audit. Fixing this flaw would involve halting deployment, rewriting critical code, and retesting the entire system, leading to delays and financial losses.

A proactive security approach in DevSecOps shifts these activities to earlier stages, such as integrating Static Application Security Testing (SAST) tools directly into the development pipeline. These tools scan the code for vulnerabilities as it is being written, enabling developers to address issues immediately.

2. The Rise of Zero-Day Vulnerabilities

Zero-day vulnerabilities are security flaws that are unknown to the developers or vendors at the time of exploitation. Traditional security practices struggle to address such threats effectively for several reasons:

- **Slow Response Times**: Traditional methods often lack mechanisms to detect and respond to zero-day exploits quickly. In fast-paced environments, this can leave systems exposed for extended periods.

- **Limited Flexibility**: Once deployed, software built under traditional models often requires significant downtime to implement patches or updates, which may not be feasible in modern agile workflows.
- **Example**: In 2017, the WannaCry ransomware attack exploited a zero-day vulnerability in Windows systems (Algarni, 2021). Organizations relying on traditional security practices struggled to patch systems promptly, resulting in widespread disruption.

In contrast, DevSecOps practices prioritize continuous monitoring and automated vulnerability detection, allowing teams to identify and address zero-day vulnerabilities in real time. Tools like Intrusion Detection Systems (IDS) and Web Application Firewalls (WAF) integrated into the CI/CD pipeline provide an additional layer of defense.

3. Security as a Bottleneck

In traditional workflows (Yarlagadda, 2018), security is often treated as an isolated process, separate from development and operations. This siloed approach leads to inefficiencies and delays:

- **Time-Consuming Manual Processes**: Security assessments and approvals can become a bottleneck, slowing down agile development cycles.
- **Lack of Alignment with Agile Practices**: Security teams may not be aligned with the iterative nature of agile sprints, resulting in miscommunication and delays.
- **Example**: Imagine a software development team preparing to release an update to a mobile application. The update is delayed for weeks because the security team requires additional time to perform manual penetration testing. Meanwhile, competitors release similar features, giving them a market advantage.

DevSecOps addresses this issue by integrating security directly into the development pipeline, automating many tasks that previously caused delays. For example:

- Tools like SonarQube and Checkmarx automatically scan code for vulnerabilities during development, providing immediate feedback to developers (Rajapakse et al., 2022).
- Continuous integration tools such as Jenkins can be configured to halt builds if security checks fail, ensuring that vulnerabilities are addressed without delaying subsequent processes (Paul, Soundarapandiyan, & Krishnamoorthy, 2021).

3. DevSecOps: PRINCIPLES AND CORE CONCEPTS

DevSecOps represents a paradigm shift in how organizations approach security, embedding it as a shared responsibility across all stages of the DevOps lifecycle. Unlike traditional models where security is a separate phase or team, DevSecOps integrates security practices directly into the workflows of development and operations (Chittala, 2024). This section elaborates on the core principles of DevSecOps, explaining how they enable continuous protection without compromising speed or agility.

1. Shift Left: Moving Security to the Earliest Stages of Development

The "shift left" principle emphasizes incorporating security practices at the beginning of the software development lifecycle (SDLC) rather than waiting until deployment. This proactive approach ensures that vulnerabilities are identified and addressed early when they are less costly and disruptive (Bender et al., 2021).

- **Early Threat Modeling**: Teams analyze potential attack vectors during the design phase, enabling the development of secure architectures from the outset.
- **Secure Coding Practices**: Training developers to follow security best practices, such as input validation and avoiding common pitfalls like hardcoded credentials, significantly reduces vulnerabilities.
- **Example**: A banking application undergoing threat modeling during the design phase might identify risks in its API authentication mechanism. Addressing these risks early can prevent exploits such as token hijacking (Kumar & Goyal, 2020).

By shifting security left, organizations not only reduce costs but also build a foundation for secure software development (Sermpezis, 2024).

2. Automation First: Using Automated Tools for Vulnerability Detection and Remediation

Automation is a cornerstone of DevSecOps, enabling teams to maintain the speed of DevOps while ensuring robust security. Automated tools perform tasks such as code scanning, vulnerability assessment, and compliance checks, minimizing human error and accelerating workflows (Rajapakse et al., 2022).

- **Static Application Security Testing (SAST)**: Tools like SonarQube scan source code for vulnerabilities during development, providing immediate feedback to developers.
- **Dynamic Application Security Testing (DAST)**: Tools like OWASP ZAP simulate real-world attacks on running applications to identify runtime vulnerabilities (Rajapakse et al., 2022).
- **Infrastructure as Code (IaC) Security**: Tools like Checkov and Terraform Validator ensure cloud and container configurations are secure before deployment.
- **Example**: An e-commerce platform integrates SAST tools into its CI/CD pipeline. With every code commit, the platform's security scanner detects vulnerabilities such as SQL injection risks, allowing developers to address them before the build proceeds.

By automating these processes, DevSecOps ensures continuous protection without introducing delays (Fu, Pasuksmit, & Tantithamthavorn, 2024).

3. Collaboration and Shared Responsibility: Breaking Silos Between Teams

In traditional models, security is often the sole responsibility of a dedicated team, leading to communication gaps and inefficiencies. DevSecOps breaks these silos by fostering collaboration and shared responsibility between development, operations, and security teams (Algarni, 2021).

- **Cross-Functional Training**: Developers are trained to understand basic security principles, while security professionals learn the nuances of development workflows.
- **Integrated Workflows**: Tools like Jira and GitLab facilitate collaboration by allowing all teams to track and address security issues in real time.
- **Blameless Postmortems**: After security incidents, teams conduct reviews without assigning blame, focusing instead on identifying root causes and improving processes.
- **Example**: A SaaS company organizes regular "security hackathons," where developers and security teams collaborate to identify and resolve vulnerabilities in the application. This builds trust and enhances the team's collective expertise (Gupta, 2022).

By promoting shared ownership, DevSecOps creates a culture where security is everyone's responsibility (Sandu, 2021).

4. Continuous Monitoring and Feedback Loops: Ensuring Security Measures Evolve

Applications and their operating environments are constantly evolving, making continuous monitoring critical for maintaining security. DevSecOps implements feedback loops to detect new vulnerabilities, assess risks, and adapt security measures accordingly (Srivastava, n.d.).

- **Real-Time Monitoring**: Tools like Splunk and ELK Stack provide visibility into system activity, enabling quick detection of suspicious behavior.
- **Incident Response Automation**: Security Orchestration and Automation (SOAR) tools streamline response efforts by automating workflows (de Vicente Mohino et al., 2019).
- **Metrics and Dashboards**: Continuous feedback helps teams track the effectiveness of security measures and identify areas for improvement.
- **Example**: A healthcare application uses real-time monitoring to detect unusual login patterns that indicate potential credential stuffing attacks. Automated incident response tools block malicious IPs and alert the security team immediately (Paul, Soundarapandiyan, & Krishnamoorthy, 2021).

Continuous monitoring ensures that security remains adaptive, addressing both known and emerging threats (Chinamanagonda, 2021).

4. AUTOMATING SECURITY FOR CONTINUOUS PROTECTION

Automation forms the backbone of DevSecOps, allowing organizations to implement robust security practices while maintaining the speed and agility of DevOps. By embedding automated security checks and tools into development workflows, teams can detect and address vulnerabilities in real-time. Below, we explore the key areas where automation enhances security in the DevOps lifecycle.

1. Continuous Integration/Continuous Deployment (CI/CD) Pipeline Security

Embedding security checks into the CI/CD pipeline ensures that every stage of the development and deployment process is fortified against vulnerabilities (Chittala, 2024). This approach integrates security tools and tests directly into the pipeline, enabling early and frequent detection of issues.

- **Automated Build Scans**: Tools like Snyk, Trivy, and Checkmarx scan code and dependencies during builds, identifying vulnerabilities in real time.
- **Security Gates**: Configuring security thresholds that halt the pipeline if critical vulnerabilities are detected, preventing unsafe code from being deployed.
- **Compliance Checks**: Automating policy enforcement for industry standards such as GDPR, HIPAA, or PCI-DSS.
- **Example**: A financial services company incorporates automated compliance checks into its CI/CD pipeline. Each build is scanned for regulatory violations, and the pipeline is halted if issues are identified, ensuring secure and compliant releases.

2. Dynamic Application Security Testing (DAST)

Dynamic Application Security Testing (DAST) focuses on detecting runtime vulnerabilities by simulating real-world attack scenarios against a running application (Rajapakse et al., 2022). This complements static code analysis by identifying vulnerabilities that only appear during execution.

- **Automated Runtime Scans**: Tools like OWASP ZAP and Burp Suite test web applications for vulnerabilities such as cross-site scripting (XSS), SQL injection, and authentication flaws.
- **Continuous Testing**: Integrating DAST tools into the CI/CD pipeline ensures that applications are tested for runtime vulnerabilities at every release.
- **Example**: An e-commerce platform uses OWASP ZAP to scan its staging environment during deployment. The tool identifies an XSS vulnerability in a shopping cart feature, which is resolved before the application goes live.

3. Infrastructure as Code (IaC) Security

Infrastructure as Code (IaC) allows teams to define and manage infrastructure through code, offering significant benefits in scalability and consistency (Reddy et al., 2021). However, misconfigurations in IaC files can expose applications to security risks. Automated tools help secure IaC configurations before they are applied.

- **Template Scanning**: Tools like Checkov, Terraform Validator, and AWS Config scan IaC templates for security misconfigurations, such as overly permissive access controls or unencrypted storage.
- **Policy Enforcement**: Automating the enforcement of security policies ensures that all infrastructure adheres to best practices.
- **Example**: A cloud-based SaaS company uses Checkov to scan its Terraform templates. The tool flags a misconfigured S3 bucket that allows public access, which is corrected before deployment.

4. Container Scanning

With the rise of containerized environments, ensuring the security of container images has become essential (Heijstek, 2023). Containers often rely on prebuilt images, which may contain vulnerabilities. Automated scanning tools help secure containerized environments by detecting risks in images and configurations.

- **Image Scanning**: Tools like Clair, Aqua Security, and Anchore analyze container images for known vulnerabilities in their base layers and dependencies.
- **Runtime Security**: Tools like Falco monitor container behavior in real-time to detect suspicious activities.
- **Registry Integration**: Scanning tools integrated into container registries (e.g., Docker Hub) ensure only secure images are deployed.
- **Example**: A DevOps team uses Aqua Security to scan its Kubernetes-based application (Algarni, 2021). The scan identifies vulnerabilities in the base image of a containerized microservice, prompting the team to update the image before deploying it to production.

5. IMPLEMENTING DevSecOps: TOOLS AND FRAMEWORKS

DevSecOps relies heavily on the use of tools and frameworks to seamlessly integrate security into the development and operations lifecycle. These tools enable teams to identify vulnerabilities, enforce compliance, and automate incident response, all while maintaining the speed and agility of DevOps. This section explores key categories of tools and frameworks that support DevSecOps initiatives.

1. Static and Dynamic Security Testing Tools

Static and Dynamic Application Security Testing (SAST and DAST) tools are foundational to DevSecOps. They help detect vulnerabilities in both the code and the running application, providing comprehensive security coverage.

- **Static Application Security Testing (SAST)**: These tools analyze source code, binaries, or bytecode for vulnerabilities during the development phase.
- **Examples**:
- **SonarQube**: Identifies issues like SQL injection, cross-site scripting (XSS), and code quality problems in multiple programming languages.
- **Veracode**: Provides static analysis with detailed vulnerability remediation guidance.
- **Dynamic Application Security Testing (DAST)**: These tools identify vulnerabilities in a running application by simulating real-world attack scenarios.
- **Examples**:
- **Snyk**: Combines SAST and DAST capabilities, focusing on open-source dependency vulnerabilities.
- **Burp Suite**: Widely used for penetration testing and runtime vulnerability detection.
- **Example Use Case**: A development team integrates SonarQube into their CI/CD pipeline to perform SAST scans on each code commit. Additionally, they use Snyk to scan third-party libraries for vulnerabilities (Rajapakse et al., 2022).

2. Security Orchestration and Automation (SOAR)

Security Orchestration, Automation, and Response (SOAR) tools streamline incident response by automating workflows, reducing manual intervention, and ensuring consistent responses to security events.

- **Key Features**:
- Automated playbooks for incident handling.
- Centralized dashboards for real-time monitoring and reporting.
- Integration with other security tools for seamless communication.
- **Examples**:
- **Splunk Phantom**: Automates security tasks like threat detection, investigation, and remediation.
- **Demisto (by Palo Alto Networks)**: Offers playbook-driven incident response with machine learning insights.
- **Example Use Case**: A financial services organization uses Splunk Phantom to automate responses to phishing emails, including extracting malicious attachments and scanning them for malware (de Vicente Mohino et al., 2019).

3. Open-Source Tools for DevSecOps

Open-source tools provide cost-effective solutions for organizations adopting DevSecOps, offering flexibility and community support for customization and enhancements.

- **Examples**:
- **OWASP ZAP**: A powerful DAST tool for scanning web applications, capable of detecting vulnerabilities like XSS and SQL injection.
- **Trivy**: A vulnerability scanner for container images, Kubernetes configurations, and IaC templates.
- **Clair**: Focuses on static vulnerability analysis for container images.
- **Benefits**:
- Reduced costs compared to proprietary tools.
- Community-driven updates ensure tools remain relevant to emerging threats.
- Flexibility for integration and customization.
- **Example Use Case**: A DevOps team uses Trivy to scan container images during build processes in a Kubernetes-based deployment. The tool identifies outdated dependencies, prompting developers to update the container base images (Heijstek, 2023).

4. Custom Frameworks

While commercial and open-source tools provide significant value, some organizations require tailored security solutions that address unique needs or integrate with existing workflows.

- **Building Custom Frameworks**:
- Integrate open-source and proprietary tools into a unified platform.
- Automate security policies and workflows using scripting languages (e.g., Python or Shell scripts).
- Leverage APIs for tool integration and customization.

- **Examples**:
- A custom CI/CD pipeline built with Jenkins that integrates SAST tools (e.g., SonarQube) and container scanning tools (e.g., Clair) to enforce security policies.
- Custom dashboards for tracking KPIs such as vulnerability trends and compliance status.
- **Example Use Case**: A healthcare company builds a custom security framework to enforce HIPAA compliance, combining automated SAST scans with DAST tools and custom scripts to generate compliance reports automatically (Reddy et al., 2021).

6. THE FUTURE OF DevSecOps: TRENDS AND INNOVATIONS

The As the landscape of software development evolves, so too does the field of security. DevSecOps continues to mature, integrating advanced technologies and methodologies to address emerging threats and challenges. This section explores the key trends and innovations shaping the future of DevSecOps, emphasizing how they will transform the way organizations secure their software systems.

1. Artificial Intelligence (AI) and Machine Learning (ML) in Security

AI and ML are revolutionizing security practices by enabling predictive analytics, anomaly detection, and automated responses.

- **Threat Prediction**: AI models analyze historical data to identify patterns that indicate potential threats, allowing teams to proactively address vulnerabilities before they are exploited.
- **Behavioral Anomaly Detection**: ML algorithms monitor user and system behaviors to detect deviations that might indicate a security breach, such as unusual login locations or abnormal data access patterns.
- **Automation of Security Responses**: AI tools can automatically isolate compromised systems, block malicious IPs, or apply patches based on predefined criteria.

Examples:

- **Darktrace**: An AI-driven platform that monitors network traffic and detects insider threats or advanced persistent threats (APTs).
- **CrowdStrike Falcon**: Combines ML algorithms with real-time telemetry to identify and mitigate endpoint threats.

Future Impact: As AI-powered tools improve, they will enable more proactive and autonomous security measures, reducing reliance on manual intervention and minimizing response times (Fu, Pasuksmit, & Tantithamthavorn, 2024).

2. Zero-Trust Architectures

The zero-trust model assumes that every user, device, and application interaction could potentially be malicious, requiring strict verification and access controls.

- **Principles of Zero Trust**:
  - **Never Trust, Always Verify**: Continuous authentication and authorization for every interaction, even within the network perimeter.
  - **Least Privilege Access**: Ensuring users and applications have only the access necessary to perform their tasks.
  - **Micro-Segmentation**: Dividing networks into smaller segments to contain potential breaches.

Examples:

- **Google BeyondCorp**: A zero-trust framework that provides secure access to applications and services without relying on traditional VPNs.
- **Okta**: Implements zero-trust identity management with adaptive multi-factor authentication (MFA).

Future Impact: As organizations adopt more distributed and remote work models, zero-trust architectures will become a cornerstone of DevSecOps strategies, ensuring secure interactions across all environments (Sermpezis, 2024).

3. Policy as Code (PaC)

PaC involves defining and enforcing security policies programmatically, integrating them directly into automated workflows.

- **Benefits**:
  - **Consistency**: Policies are codified, eliminating variability in enforcement.
  - **Automation**: Policies are automatically applied during build and deployment processes, reducing manual errors.
  - **Version Control**: Policies can be stored in version control systems like Git, enabling tracking and rollback of changes.

Examples:

- **Open Policy Agent (OPA)**: A PaC tool that allows organizations to enforce fine-grained security policies across applications, infrastructure, and CI/CD pipelines.
- **HashiCorp Sentinel**: Enables policy definition and enforcement for Terraform, Vault, and other HashiCorp tools.

Future Impact: PaC will standardize and streamline security policy enforcement across diverse platforms, reducing compliance risks and ensuring scalability (de Vicente Mohino et al., 2019).

4. Cloud-Native Security

As organizations increasingly adopt cloud-native architectures, including serverless computing, microservices, and multi-cloud deployments, securing these environments presents unique challenges.

- **Key Challenges**:
    - o **Dynamic and Ephemeral Environments**: Cloud resources are often created and destroyed rapidly, requiring real-time security monitoring.
    - o **Shared Responsibility Models**: Organizations must secure their applications while cloud providers handle infrastructure security.
    - o **Complexity of Multi-Cloud**: Managing consistent security across multiple cloud platforms adds operational complexity.

Innovations in Cloud-Native Security:

- **Workload Identity Management**: Tools like SPIFFE and SPIRE provide secure service identities for workloads.
- **Serverless Security Tools**: Platforms like Protego and Palo Alto Prisma Cloud monitor and secure serverless applications.
- **Cloud Security Posture Management (CSPM)**: Tools like Palo Alto Prisma Cloud and Aqua Security ensure compliance and secure configurations across cloud environments.

Future Impact: Cloud-native security solutions will evolve to address the dynamic nature of modern architectures, ensuring that security keeps pace with the agility of cloud deployments (Reddy et al., 2021).

7. CONCLUSION

DevSecOps represents a pivotal shift in software development, integrating security as a shared responsibility throughout the DevOps lifecycle. By embedding security early—through principles like shifting left, automation, and continuous monitoring—organizations can proactively address vulnerabilities, ensuring robust protection without slowing down delivery. Automation plays a critical role, streamlining processes such as CI/CD pipeline security, dynamic application testing, and container scanning, while tools like SonarQube, OWASP ZAP, and Terraform Validator enhance efficiency and consistency.

Emerging trends like AI-powered tools, zero-trust architectures, and policy as code demonstrate the adaptability of DevSecOps to evolving technologies and threats. Beyond tools and practices, DevSecOps fosters a cultural transformation, breaking down silos between teams and promoting collaboration. This unified approach not only strengthens security but also enables organizations to innovate and deliver at speed, making DevSecOps a vital strategy for thriving in today's dynamic digital landscape.

REFERENCES

Algarni, S. (2021). *"Cybersecurity attacks: Analysis of "wannacry" attack and proposing methods for reducing or preventing such attacks in future." ICT Systems and Sustainability: Proceedings of ICT4SD 2020* (Vol. 1). Springer Singapore.

Bender, B. J., Gahbauer, S., Luttens, A., Lyu, J., Webb, C. M., Stein, R. M., Fink, E. A., Balius, T. E., Carlsson, J., Irwin, J. J., & Shoichet, B. K. (2021). A practical guide to large-scale docking. *Nature Protocols*, 16(10), 4799–4832. DOI: 10.1038/s41596-021-00597-z PMID: 34561691

Chinamanagonda, S. (2021). DevSecOps: Integrating Security in DevOps Pipelines-Security becoming an integral part of DevOps practices. *Innovative Computer Sciences Journal*, 7, 1.

Chittala, S. (2024). Securing DevOps Pipelines: Automating Security in DevSecOps Frameworks. [JRTCSE]. *JOURNAL OF RECENT TRENDS IN COMPUTER SCIENCE AND ENGINEERING*, 12(5), 31–44. DOI: 10.70589/JRTCSE.2024.5.5

de Vicente Mohino, J., Bermejo Higuera, J., Bermejo Higuera, J. R., & Sicilia Montalvo, J. A. (2019). The application of a new secure software development life cycle (S-SDLC) with agile methodologies. *Electronics (Basel)*, 8(11), 1218.

Fu, M., Pasuksmit, J., & Tantithamthavorn, C. "AI for DevSecOps: A Landscape and Future Opportunities." *arXiv preprint arXiv:2404.04839* (2024).

Gupta, A. (2022). An Integrated Framework for DevSecOps Adoption. arXiv preprint arXiv:2207.04093.

Hahn, R. W., & Layne-Farrar, A. (2006). The law and economics of software security. *SSRN*, 30, 283. DOI: 10.2139/ssrn.897725

Heijstek, A. (2023). Bridging Theory and Practice: Insights into Practical Implementations of Security Practices in Secure DevOps and CI/CD Environments (Doctoral dissertation, Ph. D. thesis, Universiteit van Amsterdam).

Kumar, R., & Goyal, R. (2020). Modeling continuous security: A conceptual model for automated DevSecOps using open-source software over cloud (ADOC). *Computers & Security*, 97, 101967. DOI: 10.1016/j.cose.2020.101967

Paul, D., Soundarapandiyan, R., & Krishnamoorthy, G. (2021). Security-First Approaches to CI/CD in Cloud-Computing Platforms: Enhancing DevSecOps Practices. *Australian Journal of Machine Learning Research & Applications*, 1(1), 184–225.

Rajapakse, R. N., Zahedi, M., Babar, M. A., & Shen, H. (2022). Challenges and solutions when adopting DevSecOps: A systematic review. *Information and Software Technology*, 141, 106700. DOI: 10.1016/j.infsof.2021.106700

Reddy, A. K.. (2021). DevSecOps: Integrating Security into the DevOps Pipeline for Cloud-Native Applications. *Journal of Artificial Intelligence Research and Applications*, 1(2), 89–114.

Sandu, A. K. (2021). DevSecOps: Integrating Security into the DevOps Lifecycle for Enhanced Resilience. *Technology & Management Review*, 6, 1–19.

Sermpezis, E., Karapiperis, D., & Tjortjis, C. (2024, July). Integration of Security in the DevOps Methodology. In 2024 15th International Conference on Information, Intelligence, Systems & Applications (IISA) (pp. 1-6). IEEE.

Virmani, M. (2015, May). Understanding DevOps & bridging the gap from continuous integration to continuous delivery. In Fifth international conference on the innovative computing technology (intech 2015) (pp. 78-82). IEEE.

Chapter 9
Integrating Security in Cloud-Native Development:
A DevSecOps Approach to Resilient Software Systems

Pravin Pandey
https://orcid.org/0009-0008-0016-6947
Tiffany & Co, USA

Advait Patel
https://orcid.org/0009-0001-2693-2346
Broadcom, USA

ABSTRACT

Cloud-native technologies, such as microservices, containers, and serverless computing, have evolved over the years to become staples in software development, but at the same time, they present several new security risks. DevSecOps has been discussed briefly in this chapter, as well as the practices needed to secure cloud-native applications, focusing on prevention, compliance checks, and sustained monitoring. It explores the automation aspects of CI/CD pipelines, Kubernetes clusters, serverless workloads firewalls, and security policy enforcement through IaC. The chapter also considers novel practices such as Aqua Security, Snyk, and Prisma Cloud familiarization and growing trends in AI-assisted security automation and modern-day standardization. Embedding security through the software development life cycle can help organizations adopt security while attaining the requisite level of security moats while retaining the flexibility necessary in today's cloud environment.

INTRODUCTION TO INTEGRATING SECURITY IN CLOUD-NATIVE DEVELOPMENT

Cloud-native architecture is a transformational concept in modern software application development, deployment, and management. Kubernetes is mainly used in these architectures to foster scalability, flexibility, and high availability by deploying microservices and running containers. An application based on cloud-native architecture is a microservice loaded into containers and deployed independently

DOI: 10.4018/979-8-3373-0365-9.ch009

(Singh & Peddoju, 2017). These containers could be managed across distributed systems to deliver the capability of scalability, which will enable organizations to address changing requirements. Moreover, serverless computing takes an extra level of abstraction, which means that developers do not need to think about the physical resources needed for their application in any way.

Cloud-native technologies have given organizations significant advantages, but new challenges in cybersecurity have accompanied those advantages. Due to the short-lived nature of workloads, the fluctuating nature, and the distributed nature of the services, traditional security measures are insufficient (Theodoropoulos et al., 2023). In the past, security was seen primarily as a protective shield at the edges of an application or a network. However, the cloud-native environment is no longer a controlled perimeter. Applications cannot be considered tightly coupled with simple architectural designs or static underpinnings of the application; workloads can come and go in seconds.

Most well-known safety mechanisms used in traditional computing infrastructures, including firewalls, technical rules, and checklists for weaknesses, do not consider cloud-native traits characterized by their dispersed, ever-changing nature (Alquwayzani et al., 2024). For example, a complex of containerized applications is tightly interconnected and depends on shared resources. This leads to additional exposures, which make it challenging to implement secure business rules across the organization. The other relevant threats to the environments include misconfigurations in the Infrastructure as Code (IaC) templates, exposed secrets, and insecure APIs.

Moreover, the high rate of utilizing DevOps approaches may increase the rate of challenges and dangers that endanger security mechanisms since, in such applications, speed is a key factor for utilizing services and applications. Continuous integration and deployment mean new applications are released faster, and organizations cannot cope with the changes (Shahin et al., 2017). This lag creates opportunities for breaches, accentuating the effects of the failure to be proactive and/or inadequacies in the concept of integration in security.

Cloud-native security is different from traditional security and should be conceptualized differently (See Table 1 for detailed comparison). It includes integrating security into the software development life cycle, using automated tools to identify threats, and using policies adaptable to the environment. In the DevSecOps approach, security solutions become integrated into the development operations responsibilities of the development, operations, and security teams. It is advised to 'proactively integrate security' to protect the innovative, however complicated, space of cloud-native applications.

Table 1. Key Differences Between Traditional Security and Cloud-Native Security

Aspect	Traditional Security	Cloud-Native Security
Infrastructure	Static, centralized systems such as on-premises servers.	Dynamic, distributed environments like microservices.
Architecture	Monolithic, single-tiered applications.	Decentralized, containerized, and serverless architectures.
Scalability	Limited scalability due to fixed infrastructure.	Highly scalable with auto-scaling and ephemeral workloads.
Deployment Cycle	Security checks often conducted late in the development cycle.	Security integrated into CI/CD pipelines for rapid iteration.
Threat Landscape	Predictable and easier to define.	Complex and evolves rapidly with distributed systems.

continued on following page

Table 1. Continued

Aspect	Traditional Security	Cloud-Native Security
Automation	Minimal automation, manual processes dominate.	High reliance on automation for threat detection and response.
Compliance	Focused on meeting static regulatory requirements.	Continuous compliance tracking with real-time updates.
Monitoring	Periodic monitoring with limited scope.	Continuous monitoring across dynamic, multi-cloud environments.
Tools	Firewalls, antivirus, and intrusion detection systems (IDS).	Tools like CSPM, IaC scanners, and runtime protection.

UNDERSTANDING DevSecOps

DevSecOps Principles and Cultural Shifts

DevSecOps is an extension of the DevOps practice with a key focus on security distributed across the SDLC. DevSecOps, in contrast with traditional approaches where security became a separate phase or even a team, is integrated at the beginning of the DevOps process. This paradigm shift means that security cannot be an add-on extra in the evolving new paradigms of software development; instead, it needs to form part and parcel of every process in this line of development.

At its core, DevSecOps is built on the following key principles:

Shift Left Philosophy: This principle aims to elevate security issues in the SDLC. Gaining vulnerabilities during the development and testing phases allows organizations to tackle problems likely in production, significantly minimizing risks and costs (Magowan, 2020).

Automation and Continuous Integration: DevSecOps uses automation to enforce such security tools in the CI/CD systems. Security testing, for example, automated testing, vulnerability scans, and compliance checks, ensures that security is built throughout the processes while development progresses without being slowed by security processes (Vemula, 2024).

Collaboration and Shared Responsibility: One of the most significant cultural changes in DevSecOps is the degradation of siloed structures that separate development, operations, and security departments (Smith, 2020). Security shifts from an isolated activity where a product owner relies on security experts to an activity where all stakeholders can participate actively in creating a secure product.

Resilience and Continuous Improvement: DevSecOps dictates conditions for coping with breaches and enhancing security readiness. Updating security policies and evolving new tools and threat models guarantee the organization's protection (these core components are summarized in Figure 1 below).

Figure 1. DevSecOps Framework

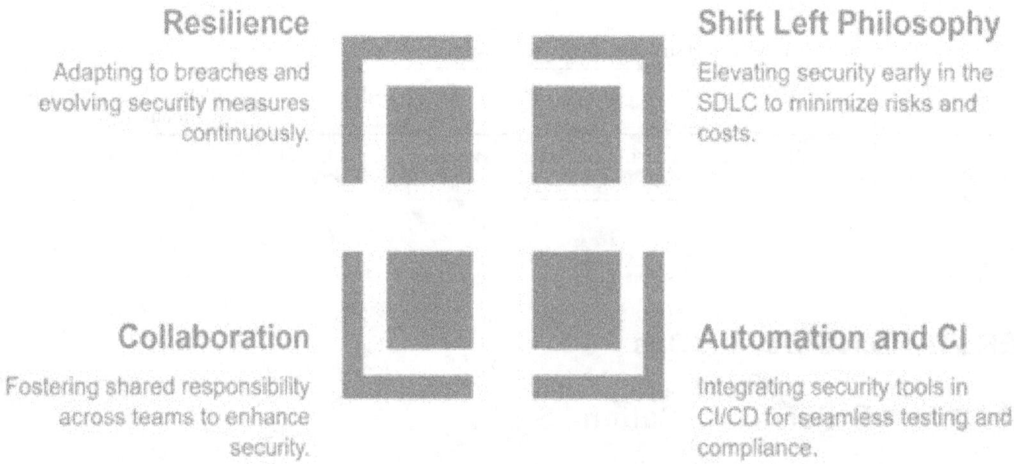

This new culture means security must become integrated as one of the core values in organizational systems. This also means that developers are provided with the tools and knowledge to write secure code, operation teams ought to have security measurements provided to them, and security staff should work as facilitators rather than restrictors.

Benefits of Integrating Security Early at the SDLC

Integrating security early in the SDLC offers numerous advantages, both in terms of operational efficiency and overall security posture:

Reduced Costs and Faster Remediation: Securing the vulnerabilities that might occur during the development phase is way cheaper and easier than doing it at the production stage. Early warnings avoid expensive incidents, business disruption, and loss of brand image.

Improved Collaboration and Efficiency: Incorporation of security means that developers, operations, and security teams sit together and work with a common goal. It also reduces gorilla business and complexities that make the delivery of secured software harder.

Proactive Risk Management: Integrating security from early work enables organizations to prevent risks from arising within their systems (Heusser, 2024). Integrated into CI/CD pipelines, security tools act immediately on code commits to prevent certain vulnerability types from ever-increasing the attack surface.

Enhanced Compliance and Governance: Across many industries, security needs to be integrated early, specifically for compliance needs and where compliance is mandatory. Accounting identities and auditing features guarantee conformity to security measures and policies.

Improved Security Posture: In this context, security assurance results from security testing and assessment at each SDLC phase. Challenges like injection, misconfiguration, insecure dependencies, and code vulnerabilities are controlled before exploitation.

Accelerated Development Cycles: Contrary to popular belief, security hinders development; incorporating security into the development process can speed it up (Security Compass, 2024). The numerous automated means employed for security lessen the testing time spent manually checking the reviews or the later patch releases.

Building Trust with Stakeholders: Secure applications help build trust with the customers, partners, and regulatory bodies. A proactive security approach means a willingness to safeguard critical information, making customers believe in the company.

Implementation of DevSecOps

To implement DevSecOps effectively, organizations must invest in the right tools, practices, and mindset:

Security Education and Training: An emphasis should be placed on training developers in security issues and providing them with tools for detecting security weaknesses. Security teams should embrace a security support development model.

Automation Tools: CI/CD must include static and dynamic application security testing and dependency management tools. These tools seek to detect vulnerabilities and offer reports with solutions to identified problems.

Policy as Code: Security regulations ought to be established and automatically implemented. This removes the chance of human error and guarantees consistency.

Continuous Monitoring: Protection does not stop once the asset is used. Real-time applications, APIs, and infrastructure monitoring guarantee that threats are identified immediately and acted on in real time.

THREATS AND CHALLENGES OF CLOUD-NATIVE ENVIRONMENT

Cloud-native technologies have become a new approach to building applications that have dramatically changed how software solutions are developed and deployed. However, this shift also brought new security threats and challenges related to cloud-native environments and new uses. The complexity of these systems has continued to grow, along with the broad utilization of microservices, containers, and serverless computing, which has substantially enlarged the attack vectors. Therefore, for organizations to effectively secure these environments, the most common threats should be known, misconfigurations should be solved, and compliance should not be an issue.

Key Attack Vectors in Cloud-Native Environments

Cloud-native applications run in distributed and constantly evolving environments where opportunities for attackers appear. Key attack vectors include:

Container Vulnerabilities

Docker containers are the foundation of microservices and are not automatically secure. Finding unpatched software or insecure dependencies in the container images is relatively easy and frequent (Shu et al., 2017). Malicious users can use these vulnerabilities to gain unauthorized access and higher privileges and inject code. Moreover, containers use a single kernel host, so the system is open to kernel attacks.

Insecure APIs

APIs are used for inter-service communication and external systems; they are essential to microservice architectures. However, if implemented insecurely, APIs can access protected data, enable unauthorized utilization, and sometimes launch distributed denial-of-service (DDoS) attacks (Rodriguez, 2021). Most API vulnerabilities result from poor or improper authentication, lack of or flawed rate limiting, and flawed input data validation (A summary of these attacks are shown in Figure 3).

Supply Chain Attacks

Third-party libraries, open-source components, and container images are standard in the modern distributed application ecosystem, and their use has played the role of extensive supply chain attacks. The external dependencies are attacked to introduce the malware injected into cloud-native apps. These attacks are mainly challenging to identify as developers trust the implant components.

Lateral Movement and Privilege Escalation

After blending into a cloud-native architecture, an attacker can use improper security settings to escalate their position inside the network (Mehmood et al., 2023). This can involve access to one or several containers, adjacent structures, microservices, or other architecture cloud resources. The lack of these barriers and poor compartmentalization greatly enhance this risk.

Data Breaches and Exposed Secrets

Applications developed from scratch with consideration for cloud adoption are filled with secrets like API keys, credentials, and encryption keys. If such secrets are leaked due to bad management or poor storage, the attacker will easily compromise the sensitive assets and information.

Figure 2. An Overview of Cloud-Native Security Threats

The Impact of Misconfigurations

System misconfigurations are among cloud-native ecosystems' most frequent and severe security issues. Because of the difficulties of managing distributed systems and the velocity of operations in DevOps, misconfigurations that open the system to attack occur frequently (these impacts are summarized in Figure).

Misconfigured Containers and Orchestrators

Although powerful, container orchestrators like Kubernetes are complicated and need careful setup. Problems in these architectures include liberal network policies, weak default configurations, and open control planes (Doidge, 2024). For example, an intended malicious configuration, such as a misconfigured Kubernetes dashboard or open Etcd server, gives attackers complete control over the cluster.

Weak Identity and Access Management (IAM)

Unauthorized access to cloud resources may result from IAM misconfigurations, such as comprehensive permissions or unprotected access keys. Lack of proper implementation of role-based access control (RBAC) also contributes to the likelihood of privilege escalation (Khan, 2024).

Insecure Network Configurations

Cloud-native environments are extraordinary because they are based on dynamic networks that likely lead to the misconfiguration of firewalls, opened ports, or unprotected channels. This makes it easier for attackers to eavesdrop on traffic, launch Distributed Denial of Service (DDoS) attack applications, and exploit services exposed by the lack of intermediary servers.

Ineffective Logging and Monitoring

The absence of proper logging and monitoring makes it extremely difficult to identify threats in cloud-native infrastructure (Palo Alto Networks, n.d.). Misconfigured or incomplete logging solutions become significant issues for organizations that cannot address threats in real time.

Infrastructure as Code (IaC) Risks that are Easily Overlooked

Cloud infrastructure provisioning can be automated with IaC templates (Sandobalin et al., 2017). However, developers can become victims of such templates, and a standard error or vulnerability disseminates an insecure environment throughout the system. For instance, a single mistake in designing a security group embodied in IaC can open multiple cloud resources to external attacks.

Figure 3. Impact of System Misconfigurations in Cloud-Native Environment

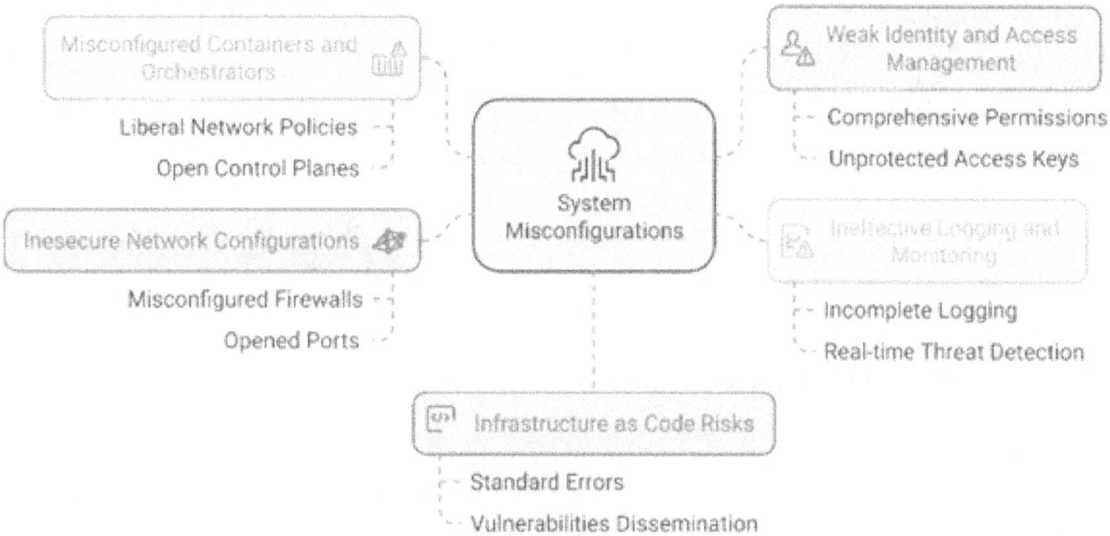

Compliance Gaps in Cloud-Native Environments

The increasing dependence of organizational operations on cloud services also means that they have to deal with compliance and standards. Meeting these compliance obligations in cloud-native environments poses several challenges:

Dynamic and Ephemeral Resources

Microservices are usually stateless and short-lived, and the workloads themselves are highly dynamic, which poses challenges when it comes to compliance (Lloyd et al., 2018). It challenges traditional compliance monitoring tools and methodologies, which are not adequately suited for monitoring transient resources.

Lack of Visibility

Cloud-native applications are designed to be distributed across various servers; hence, there is limited visibility in infrastructure and workloads. The lack of comprehensive information about system activities poses a challenge when organizations seek to confirm compliance with the stipulated security standards.

Data Residency and Privacy Concerns

Building applications that reside on the cloud is typical, primarily when the application is distributed across different geographic locations; this creates a challenge in handling data sovereignty and localization (Chen, 2024). An organization has to guarantee that personal information is protected and managed according to the country's legislation, such as GDPR or HIPAA.

Inconsistent Policy Enforcement

Maintaining a consistent security and compliance posture across hybrid and multi-cloud environments is challenging. Measures implemented by cloud service providers are different, and they may not have similar capabilities, so the policies may not be evenly enforced.

Audit and Reporting Challenges

Auditing cloud-native environments and creating compliance reports becomes challenging because these environments produce massive amounts of data. Moreover, the lack of a normalized guideline for keeping records and progress reports to show compliance makes it even harder.

PRACTICUM IN DevSecOps IN CLOUD-NATIVE APPLICATIONS

A closer look at what it takes to adopt DevSecOps for cloud-native solutions practically involves a structured approach where security is incorporated conversationally in the development and operation processes. This approach aims to automate security, protect independent services such as Kubernetes and serverless functions, and adopt security policies through Infrastructure as Code. Each of these practices, taken together, aims to embed security in the software development lifecycle (SDLC) instead of considering it an afterthought.

Automating Security Using CI/CD Pipelines

Modern DevOps approaches rely heavily on Continuous Integration and Continuous Deployment (CI/CD) pipelines, facilitating quick software development and deployment. These pipelines are expanded to incorporate security automation in DevSecOps, making CI/CD pipelines essential for preserving a secure application lifetime.

Integrating Automated Security Testing

Security tests incorporated into the Continuous Integration /Continuous Delivery pipeline guarantee that more troubles are detected and fixed during the Security Development Life Cycle. They include Static Application Security Testing (SAST) and Dynamic Application Security Testing (DAST), which can be employed to scan the code for security flaws and scrutinize applications in operation for possible malicious activity (Schmitt, 2022). Likewise, Software Composition Analysis (SCA) tools assist in identifying insecure dependencies and older libraries at the time of build.

Vulnerability Scanning

Many applications designed for containerized deployments, characteristic of cloud-native structures, utilize preconstructed container images. During the pipeline's build process, these images can be scanned using automated vulnerability scanners, such as Aqua Security or Trivy. To this end, an organization can address issues before implementation or use in production, minimizing the chances of introducing new vulnerabilities .

Figure 4. Vulnerability Scanning in Cloud-native Development

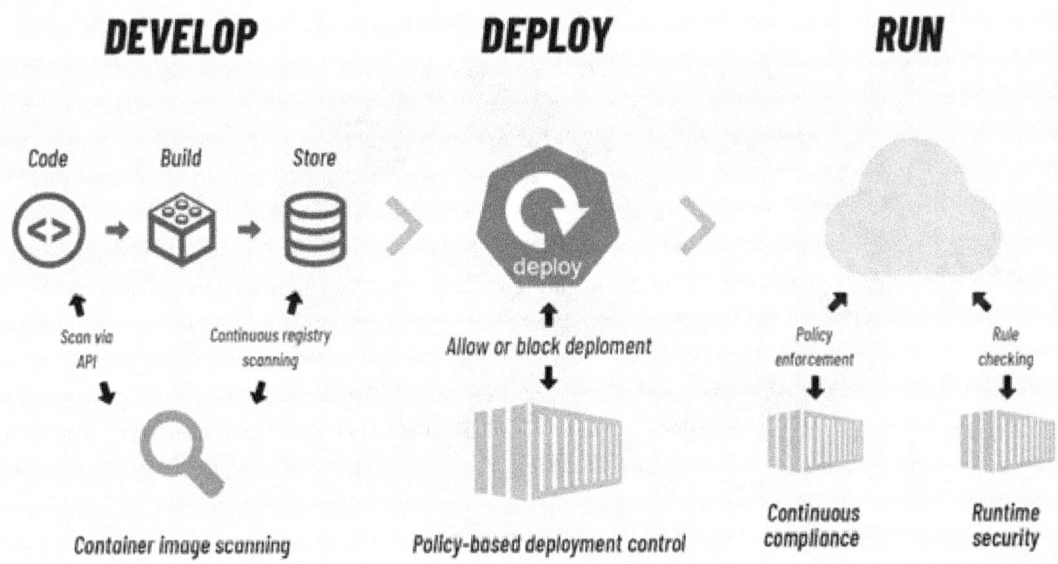

Figure 4 above illustrates the protection of containerized applications at the DevOps phases of development, deployment, and running while focusing on the software supply chain. In the development stage, the code is created, compiled, and built into containers, then stored in a registry with an API-based code scan and continuous registry scan for vulnerability. The deployment stage deploys the strategy for approving or denying the deployment of containers to ensure only compliant ones get to production (SparkFabrik, 2022). Continuous compliance checks and runtime security are performed during the run stage so that threats are noticeable and addressed. These practices span container images security issues such as image vulnerability, unauthorized deployment, and runtime issues while embracing such best practices as scanning, enforcing, and monitoring security vulnerabilities at runtime on containerized applications.

Shift-Left Security

As presented in Figure 3 below, the shift left principle is based on developing security from the beginning of development. Buried in automated security sweeps like code checks for compliance and pre-commit hooks, the developer is presented with a message or notification of a security problem (McNamara, 2021). These sweeps help reduce the time and costs of remediating vulnerabilities later in the cycle. As early in the CI/CD pipeline as feasible, shift left testing incorporates testing best practices.

Figure 5. The Shift-Left Approach

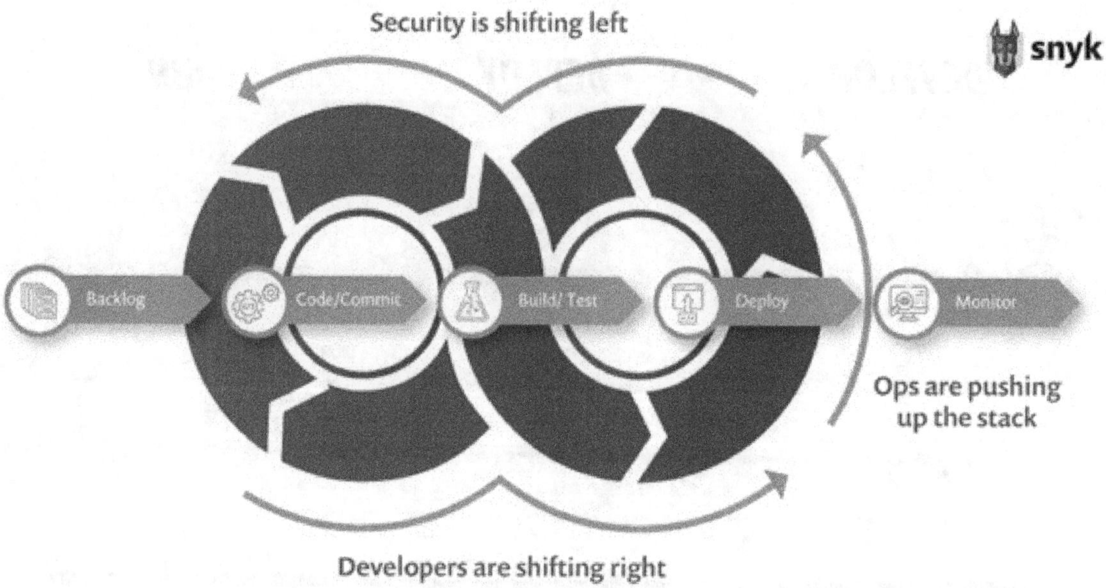

This image illustrates the integration of security into the DevOps lifecycle, emphasizing two key shifts: "security is shifting left" and "ops are pushing up the stack." Moving security left literally means using security from the backlog through coding, committing, build/test. At the same time, operations are adopted higher within the stack and embrace more control and duty regarding safety aspects in the end stages of deployment in addition to runtime (Smith, 2020). The approach adopted in implementing this concept ensures that there is integration of security as a life cycle that creates more application security since it involves collaboration between developers and operational teams.

Continuous Monitoring and Alerts

Continuous integration and delivery pipelines integrated with monitoring tools present actual information regarding application security. Real-time monitoring allows changes to code, infrastructure, or configurations to be made and scanned for security implications. Notification that comes along with these tools means that threats that have been identified can be quickly addressed to promote proactive security.

Securing Kubernetes, Containers, and Serverless Workloads

Cloud-native applications can be created mainly on spaces like Kubernetes, containers, and serverless functions. The acquisition of these components is equally crucial to the security of the whole system.

Kubernetes Security

Kubernetes, as a container orchestration platform, introduces several security considerations:

Namespace Isolation: By differentiating workloads through namespaces, applications find it difficult to access other applications they should not. This segmentation reduces the blast radius on a platform if a specific platform is breached.

Pod Security Policies: Kubernetes enables administrators within an organization to implement and enforce security policies granularity at the pod level; a pod cannot run a container with root privileges or access host information.

RBAC and Authentication: It defines users' and services' reach and confines them to their necessary privileges, a Role-Based Access Control (RBAC) (Gajbhiye et al., 2024). To further strengthen Kubernetes' security, support is needed to implement and enable more robust authentication systems like OpenID Connect (OIDC); refer to Figure 3 below.

Figure 6. RBAC Overview

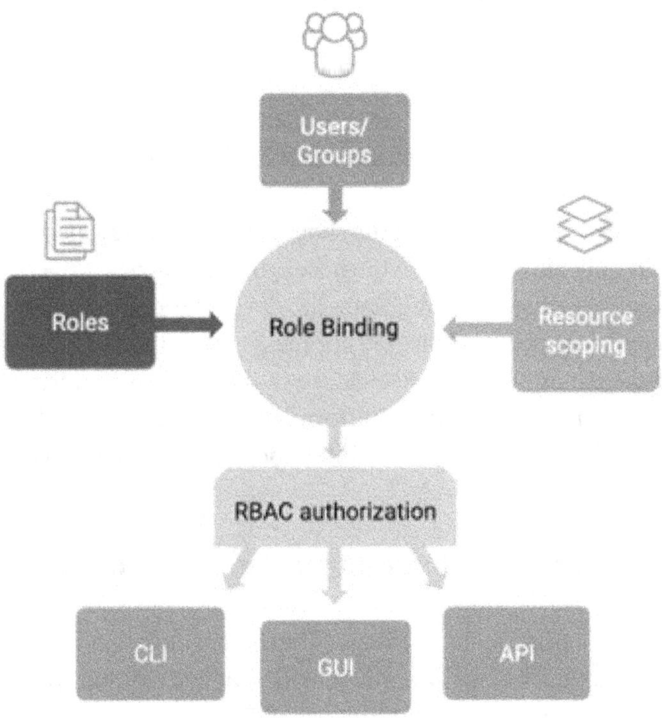

As presented in the Figure above, role binding is the process by which the user administrator assigns roles using the lightweight directory access protocol (LDAP) to users and groups that are scoped to particular resources using RBAC. Once a role binding has been established using the Confluent CLI confluent IAM rbac role-binding create command, users cannot circumvent it and access resources by going to an API or Confluent Control Center (Confluent, 2025). Client administrators can avoid explicitly granting each user access to every component by binding roles to groups.

Control Plane Protection: In a production cluster, the control plane, which is responsible for managing the cluster activities, should have its communication restricted by network restrictions, encrypted, and operate under limited administrative privileges.

Container Security

Containers are lightweight and efficient, but their security depends on careful management:

Securing Container Images: Credible sources of container images must be used, and images must be updated frequently, reducing vulnerability. Some image signing and scanning tools can be used to authenticate the image (Amazon Web Services, 2023).

Runtime Security: After a container is launched, it must constantly be supervised for any signs of unhealthy behavior, such as accessing the wrong network or running a process that should not be run. Contemporary security instruments like Falco can quickly identify and counter these threats in runtime.

Immutable Infrastructure: According to the principles of containers, any change must induce the generation of a new layer rather than alter the existing container (Kodekloud, 2023). This limits recurrent threats, which can be eliminated by taking necessary measures in advance.

Serverless Security

Although they encapsulate the underlying infrastructure, serverless systems are not impervious to security threats:

Minimizing Permissions: Serverless functions should run with as few permissions as possible. IAM roles and policies should only allow access to the necessary resources.

Securing Event Sources: As the name suggests, the developer does not initiate serverless functions but is invoked by third-party services such as APIs or message queues. This prevents malicious triggers, and authenticating and validating such sources addresses their volatile nature.

Function-Level Monitoring: Application performance monitoring tools specially designed for serverless computing include AWS Lambda runtime monitoring, which assists in detecting issues and weaknesses in serverless computing.

Security Policy Enforcement via Infrastructure as Code (IaC)

Infrastructure as Code is a methodology widely adopted for cloud-native solutions, as it guarantees infrastructure definition as code. Thus, IaC improves work productivity and is easily scalable, but security measures may be compromised if they are not followed diligently.

Codifying Security Policies

Security policies can be written in code when embedded in IaC templates. For example, rules like encrypting storage buckets or excluding public access to some resources can be embedded into services like Terraform and AWS CloudFormation. This way, policies are not arbitrary across environments; instead, they are standardized.

Automated Compliance Checks

Open Policy Agent (OPA) and Checkov can be used to validate IaC templates against set security standards (Almeida, 2024). Before being used in an organization or system that must ensure regulatory compliance, these tools check for security misuse, such as open security groups or missing much-needed logging configurations.

For instance in Amazon Web Service cloud, open policy agent (OPA) is used alongside Terraform to automate security and compliance checks refer to Figure 2 below:

Figure 7. Using Terraform and Open Policy Agent Workflow

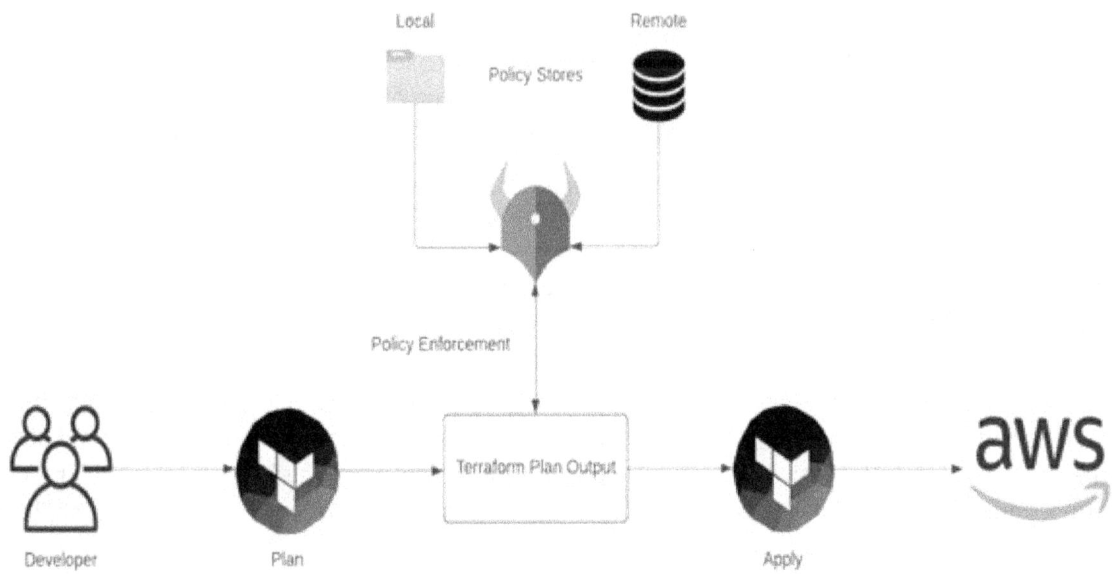

From the figure, the developer and the creation of the Terraform Code itself initiate the process's initial phase. We are unable to assess our OPA policies in the absence of Terraform code. Once the appropriate infrastructure setup has been put into place, we use terraform plan *-out tfplan* to create a Terraform plan output. We may see the modifications Terraform plans to make and develop an execution plan with Terraform Plan. OPA will then examine resource additions, modifications, and deletions and match the intended changes to the authorized activities specified in custom policy documents (Hagen, 2023). It is possible to store policy papers locally or remotely, such as in a database. The review is deemed effective if the planned modifications adhere to the guidelines specified in the policies.

Version Control and Auditing

The key concept of compartmentalizing IaC templates by storing them in version control systems, for example, Git, is flexibility coupled with a strong audit trail that can track changes (Honig, n.d.). This transparency allows calculating when and where specific misconfigurations were created, making it easier to fix them.

Continuous Enforcement

IaC says that security is not a one-time event that happens when the architectures and resources are pushed out. The available enforcement instruments, such as drift detection systems, are constantly assessed to see if the resources put into deployment change form to contradict templates present at launch. For instance, if the access control of a specific resource is adjusted manually, these instruments can provide alerts to the managers or even roll back the alteration to ensure that correct settings are used.

CI / CD Integration

IaC templates should be implemented exclusively to make security checks an intrinsic CI/CD pipeline component. As with any provisioning operation, resource templates are thoroughly scanned for misconfigurations, compliance issues, and best security practices. Such integration helps avoid cases of human error risk within the given process.

TOOLS AND TECHNOLOGIES FOR SECURING CLOUD-NATIVE ENVIRONMENTS

Protecting cloud-native applications is possible only with the help of robust strategies, proven practices, and powerful instruments. Of all the available tools, Aqua Security, Snyk, and Prisma Cloud have the most extensive lists of features purported to address multiple fronts of Cloud-native security. These tools help organizations identify risks before they are exploited, manage compliance, and protect application systems and structures at the different phases of the SDLC.

Aqua Security

Aqua Security provides security for containers, Kubernetes, application platforms, and serverless functions. It provides the least amount of container security, runtime protection, and cloud security posture management.

Key Features

Container Image Scanning: Aqua Security delivers deep container image analysis to detect security weaknesses, incorrect configurations, or registered credentials. It is built into CI/CD processes to detect and remove insecure images before they are used within the chain.

Runtime Protection: Aqua safeguards containers during runtime by paying particular attention to observing different behaviors, such as file access or network connections that do not conform to standard patterns. Policies can lock or ban some deemed weird activities in real-time (Aqua, n.d.).

Kubernetes Security: The platform also consists of security functions designed natively for Kubernetes, including workload protection, configuration checks, and cluster behavior analytics. It aids in managing conformance with hold benchmarks such as the Kubernetes CIS benchmark.

Cloud Security Posture Management (CSPM): Another benefit is Aqua's ability to secure cloud resources beyond the traditional endpoint, review cloud resource configurations, and assist in fixing misconfigurations that can lead to breaches.

Benefits

Comprehensive Visibility: Aqua provides detailed information on the containers and Kubernetes activity, giving the teams a better picture of their security situation.

Proactive Threat Detection: Aqua uses vulnerability scanning and runtime monitoring to detect threats and prevent them before they become prominent (Mohanan, 2023).

Compliance and Governance: GDPR, PCI DSS, and HIPAA are among the compliance frameworks that the tool assists in facilitating organizational compliance.

Use Cases

- Broadly, a workload application can run on a workload platform in a multi-cloud or hybrid environment.
- Protecting KT for Pro clusters.
- Automation can perform compliance checks during the development process.

Snyk

Snyk is on the developer security platform to help teams and developers identify the proper steps and measures to secure their code, open source libraries, containers, and infrastructure such as Code (IaC). Being tightly integrated with developer tools and processes, Snyk is the tool of choice for DevSecOps.

Key Features

Open-Source Vulnerability Scanning: The Snyk project scans open-source libraries and dependencies for known vulnerabilities, explains them in detail, and offers remedial services (Synk, 2024).

Container Security: The platform can scan for vulnerabilities and outdated or misconfigured packages in container images in Docker.

Infrastructure as Code (IaC) Security: Snyk takes instances of Infrastructure as Code (IaC), including Terraform and AWS CloudFormation, to detect security issues in the templates and secure the infrastructure.

Continuous Monitoring: Using Snyk, a project can be continually scanned for emerging vulnerabilities, and apps remain protected upon deployment.

Benefits

Developer Integration: Snyk connects with key development platforms such as GitHub, GitLab, and Bitbucket, as well as with CI/CD processes. This integration allows developers to quickly focus on mistakes inherent to running these processes (Atlassian, 2024).

Actionable Insights: The tool offers straightforward suggestions, such as possible enhancements and patches that indicate where a developer needs to fix a problem.

Rapid Response: Continuous scanning helps Snyk take action on vulnerabilities as soon as possible and minimizes the prospect of exploitation.

Use Cases

- Protection of apps that have a rich usage of open-source libraries.
- Incorporating security into IaC practices to achieve secure Cloud implementations.
- Using containerization to detect application vulnerabilities in production systems.

Prisma Cloud

Prisma Cloud by Palo Alto Networks is a cloud-native security platform that enables visibility, compliance, and protection in the multi- and hybrid cloud. It covers container, serverless, and cloud security postures and translates to a comprehensive CSPM solution for cloud-native protection.

Key Features

Cloud Security Posture Management (CSPM): Prisma Cloud corrects cloud misconfiguration and provides run-time protection with compliance with standards like NIST, PCI DSS, and SOC 2 (Palo Alto, n.d.).

Container and Kubernetes Security: It offers security solutions for containers in development, deployment, and runtime, shields Kubernetes clusters, and enables them to scan, protect, and enforce policy.

Serverless Security: Prisma Cloud protects serverless functions by understanding how they run, their privileges, and their relationships to other components to guarantee that they run safely.

Identity and Access Management (IAM) Security: The tool evaluates IAM configurations for excessively promoting roles and policies to ensure that cloud resources are not exposed to unwelcome users or applications.

Benefits

Unified Security Platform: Prisma Cloud aims to provide a single solution to address multiple security needs, eliminating the need for multiple tools and systems.

Scalability: This is vital if an enterprise operates across many cloud forums to accommodate large-scale implementations.

Threat Intelligence: Based on Palo Alto Networks threat intelligence, Prisma Cloud adds enhanced detection and prevention functionality.

Use Cases

- Achieving compliance in multi-cloud settings.
- Securing serverless systems against runtime hazards.
- Getting insights on complex cloud-native architectures.

Comparative Analysis

While Aqua Security, Snyk, and Prisma Cloud offer overlapping capabilities, each tool has unique strengths that cater to specific use cases.

Table 2. Comparison Between Different Security Tools

Feature	Aqua Security	Synk	Prisma Cloud
Primary Focus	Container and Kubernetes	Developer-centric security	Comprehensive cloud-native
CI/CD Integration	Strong	Excellent	Moderate
CSPM	Yes	Limited	Strong
IaC Security	Moderate	Strong	Moderate
Serverless Protection	Moderate	Limited	Strong
Compliance and Governance	Strong	Moderate	Strong

CASE STUDIES AND USE CASES

Many organizations have improved the security of their cloud-native applications by implementing DevSecOps methods. Here are some actual cases that show how businesses have effectively included security in their development procedures.

ScienceLogic Cloud Native and DevSecOps Transformation

ScienceLogic is an IT operations management solution provider that wanted to update its deployment life cycle to embrace cloud natively and DevSecOps principles. ScienceLogic partnered with Oteemo, a technology consulting firm, to transition wholly to cloud-native architecture focusing on automation and security (Oteemo, 2024). This change brought on the evolution of a strong set of automation tools and processes to facilitate the deployment of their SL1 platform in 40 minutes at most, sometimes days or weeks before. This approach meant that while applications were being rolled out much faster, they all had to comply with security best practices.

DevSecOps Implementation in Telos Corporation

Telos Corporation, focusing on providing cybersecurity solutions, attempted to update its deployment lifecycle with modern DevOps and cloud-native frameworks. To this end, Telos collaborated with Oteemo to start its security transformation program that focused on bringing security into the SDLC (Telo, 2024). This drive was to increase the automation of security scans and checks within the CI/CD pipeline, integrate DevSecOps by engaging the development and security teams, and move to the cloud services that allow for scalability and expansion. Therefore, Telos saw a more stable and flexible setting for improvement that could adapt immediately to newer risks and requirements within a field.

Digital Transformation of Cognizant's DevSecOps

One of the largest multinational technology companies, Cognizant, employed automation to help it digitize hundreds of applications used by its employees, for example, by embracing cloud-native applications. This migration was conducted as part of the DevSecOps initiative to achieve end-to-end security integration into the development process (Team, 2024). Security was made a part of CI/CD and the DevSecOps culture, which led to significant cost savings and enhanced the security of their application. This change enabled the company to deliver secure applications for their clients and employees.

Deepfactor's Approach to Cloud-Native Application Security

Security firm Deepfactor has developed an application security testing tool explicitly built with microservices and Kubernetes in mind. Their solution watches running applications and delivers complete security details to the developers in the integrated development environment (Deepfactor, 2023). Besides system and regression testing, Deepfactor campaigns apply security testing to capture high-severity risks and vulnerabilities before production. This approach brings the benefits of centralized application security testing for DevSecOps by extending a single, organic platform into current CI/CD pipelines to improve security for cloud-native applications.

Akto's Cloud-Native Security

Akto, which is a cloud-native application protection company, underlined the matter of security involvement in DevSecOps practices. It also references actual events and uses current examples and scenarios where cloud-native apps have been secured through DevSecOps (Akto, 2023). Some issues covered are system complexity observed in microservices architecture, compliance as organizations adapt to new development environments, and the security aspect incurred trying to catch up with modern development's fast pace. Through adopting such technologies and superb cooperation in their development process, the organizations above have boosted the security of their products while simultaneously adopting the Agile principles that enable quick adaptation to change.

FUTURE TRENDS AND RECOMMENDATIONS

The cloud-native security domain is relatively new. This is because most of these solutions are still in development, yet cloud services are continually growing in complexity. AI integration for security automation and the formation of new standards and frameworks are becoming the focal points of secure cloud-native application development.

AI in the Security Automation

Artificial intelligence has been playing an essential role as a key to modern approaches to security. Solutions built using artificial intelligence allow for improved identification, prevention, and counter-action of threats in cloud-native environments due to the nature of these architectures.

Threat Detection and Response

AI uses ML to create models that can determine anomalies in the traffic on the network, users, and the applications they use. While the rules constrain rule-based systems, AI continues to adapt as it factors in new data; therefore, it can detect zero-day vulnerabilities and APTs (IBM, n.d.). Companies like Darktrace and CrowdStrike are already live with their AI to deliver threat intelligence in real-time.

Predictive Analytics

AI-based predictive models take the historical security data and the existing threats and risks an organization faces and use these data to make predictions about future threats and risks. Such strategies allow organizations to look for vulnerabilities before they can be capitalized on, minimizing the time wasted and the risks involved.

Automated Remediation

AI is integrated into solving security concerns, where it can detect and correct problems. For instance, it can isolate compromised containers, reduce excessive permissions to the root of excessive permissions, or recreate mismanaged resources. These capabilities allow for ongoing security while not disrupting the DevOps life cycle.

Natural Language Processing for Security Insights

AI-based NLP solutions can discover many threats from academic papers, threat databases, and forums. In doing so, security teams obtain tangible intelligence about strengthening protection systems against these threats. In the long run, while AI becomes more innovative, its incorporation into DevSec-Ops will improve so that security automation meets the needs of cloud-native applications (Obaloluwa Ogundairo & broklyn, 2024).

Emerging Standards and Frameworks for Cloud-Native Security

Cohesion is necessary for deploying rigid measures throughout various companies and fields to prevent security threats. Cloud-native applications have raised new concerns, encouraging the development of new emerging standards and frameworks.

Cloud Native Computing Foundation (CNCF) Initiatives

Organizations managing Kubernetes and other cloud-native projects, such as the Cloud Native Computing Foundation (CNCF), have created standards such as Kubernetes Security Posture Management (KSPM). These guides offer guidelines for protecting Kubernetes clusters, including RBAC, network policies, and auditing (Chauhan & Shiaeles, 2023).

The NIST Guidelines,

The latest guidance from NIST has focused on providing approaches specific to cloud-native settings. The NIST CSF and the Secure Software Development Framework (SSDF) focus on security becoming an integral part of the software development process, which fits well with DevSecOps.

OWASP for Containers – Open Web Application Security Project

Container and Kubernetes security was a relatively new domain that OWASP recently incorporated. The OWASP Kubernetes Security Cheat Sheet has good practice guidance for the Kubernetes container workload with key focuses on configuration and runtime security.

Compliance Standards for Cloud Native Applications

Professional associations like the Cloud Security Alliance (CSA) have created standards like Cloud Controls Matrix that can be used to meet the GDPR, CCPA, and HIPAA requirements, among others (Chauhan & Shiaeles, 2023).

RECOMMENDATIONS FOR ORGANIZATIONS

To stay ahead in securing cloud-native applications, organizations should:

Adopt AI-Powered Tools: Apply advanced AI and ML technologies for real-time threat detection analytics and automated mitigation.

Embrace Emerging Standards: Integrate with CNCF KSPM, NIST SSDF, CSA CCM, and other industry leaders to optimize security practices and conform to best practices.

Foster a Security-First Culture: Integrating security into every phase of the system development life cycle and educational initiative for the development and security professionals.

Automate Wherever Possible: Engineering processes must incorporate security automation into development and deployment pipelines at IaC and runtime levels.

If implemented, these trends and recommendations would transform security as future organizations seek to establish a secure cloud-native application environment amidst emerging challenges.

CONCLUSION

Protecting cloud-native applications has emerged as a significant concern protecting applications in today's dynamic and distributed environment. Integrating DevSecOps principles into the development lifecycle makes designing and constructing secure, resilient systems possible. Achieving security at the software development phase enables organizations to have a secure software system by dealing with threats at their source. Also, it conforms to various benchmarks that the organization wants to address or meet to become less vulnerable to cyber threats. New-generation applications built on containerization, microservices, and serverless need different approaches to security. The examples discussed, as well as state-of-the-art instruments and means, show that automation and constant monitoring with the help of proactive detection mechanisms are critical for protecting such systems. Information communication technologies (ICT) such as AI can identify and respond to threats in real-time, hence keeping up with security without hammering on slowness. Implementing new standards and frameworks also helps manage organizational practice in terms of standard practices and regulations, and it opens the door to building a sustainable security practice. With collaboration culture and security responsibility in mind, organizations can safely and effectively leverage cloud-native environments. The future of secure software development in this dynamic digital environment depends on adopting DevSecOps, utilizing automation, and staying ahead of risks via creativity and adaptation. Besides, today's cloud-native security domain experiences fast development because of rising cloud services complexity. Security automation advances through artificial intelligence to detect threats better and perform predictive analytics and automated remediation. Together, real-time detection and response towards zero-day vulnerabilities and APTs are performed by AI-powered solutions from Darktrace and CrowdStrike. Learning models based on past trends help forecast upcoming danger situations, and NLP technology enabled by AI transforms voluminous data from different threat sources into practical security analysis. Cloud-native application security and resilience will experience increased strength through the ongoing AI innovations that merge with DevSecOps.

REFERENCES

Akto. (2023). *Cloud Native Security | Cloud Native Application Protection - Akto*. Akto.io. https://www.akto.io/devsecops/securing-cloud-native-applications-in-devsecops

Almeida, H. (2024). *IaC Security and Compliance Tools*. BoldLink. https://boldlink.io/2022/06/07/iac-security-and-compliance-tools/

Alquwayzani, A., Aldossri, R., & Frikha, M. (2024). Prominent Security Vulnerabilities in Cloud Computing. *International Journal of Advanced Computer Science and Applications*, 15(2). Advance online publication. DOI: 10.14569/IJACSA.2024.0150281

Amazon Web Services. (2023, July 24). *Building better container images | Amazon Web Services*. Amazon Web Services. https://aws.amazon.com/blogs/containers/building-better-container-images/

Aqua. (n.d.). *Aqua Cloud Native Security, Container Security & Serverless Security*. Aqua. https://www.aquasec.com/

Atlassian. (2024). *Bitbucket Snyk Integration to Enable DevSecOps | Atlassian*. Atlassian. https://www.atlassian.com/devops/security-tutorials/jira-snyk-devsecops

Chauhan, M., & Shiaeles, S. (2023). An Analysis of Cloud Security Frameworks, Problems and Proposed Solutions. *Network (Bristol, England)*, 3(3), 422–450. https://www.mdpi.com/2673-8732/3/3/18

Chen, M. (2024, May 2). *What Is Data Sovereignty?* Oracle.com; Oracle. https://www.oracle.com/ke/cloud/sovereign-cloud/data-sovereignty/

Confluent. (2025). Use role-based access control (RBAC) for authorization in Confluent Platform | Confluent Documentation. Confluent.io. https://docs.confluent.io/platform/current/security/authorization/rbac/overview.html

Deepfactor. (2023, March 22). *Use Case: Cloud Native Application Security*. Deepfactor. https://www.deepfactor.io/cloud-native-application-security/

Doidge, F. (2024). *Best practices to beat container misconfiguration*. ComputerWeekly.com. https://www.computerweekly.com/feature/Best-practices-to-beat-container-misconfiguration

Gajbhiye, B., Goel, O., & Pandian, G. (2024). Managing Vulnerabilities in Containerized and Kubernetes Environments. *Journal of Quantum Science and Technology.*, 1(2), 59–71. DOI: 10.36676/jqst.v1.i2.16

Hagen, H. (2023, March 17). *Open Policy Agent for AWS and Terraform*. Tecracer.com. https://www.tecracer.com/blog/2023/03/open-policy-agent-for-aws-and-terraform.html

Heusser, M. (2024). *CI/CD pipeline security: Know the risks and best practices*. IT Operations; TechTarget. https://www.techtarget.com/searchitoperations/tip/9-ways-to-infuse-security-in-your-CI-CD-pipeline

Honig, J. (n.d.). *What is Version Control & Why Is It Important?* Start.docuware.com. https://start.docuware.com/blog/document-management/what-is-version-control-why-is-it-important

IBM. (n.d.). *The power of AI: Security*. IBM. https://www.ibm.com/thought-leadership/institute-business-value/en-us/report/ai-security-automation

Khan, M. (2024, August 30). *The Importance of Enforcing Proper Role-Based Access Control (RBAC) in Web Security*. Medium. https://medium.com/@mustafa_kamal/the-importance-of-enforcing-proper-role-based-access-control-rbac-in-web-security-7375415f0503

Kodekloud. (2023, May 16). *What Are Docker Image Layers and How Do They Work?* DevOps Blog. https://kodekloud.com/blog/docker-image-layers/

Lloyd, W., Ramesh, S., Chinthalapati, S., Ly, L., & Pallickara, S. (2018). Serverless Computing: An Investigation of Factors Influencing Microservice Performance. *2018 IEEE International Conference on Cloud Engineering (IC2E)*. DOI: 10.1109/IC2E.2018.00039

Magowan, K. (2020, November 30). *Shift Left Testing: What, Why & How To Shift Left*. BMC Blogs. https://www.bmc.com/blogs/what-is-shift-left-shift-left-testing-explained/

McNamara, R. (2021, August 31). *Implementing Shift Left Security Effectively*. Snyk. https://snyk.io/articles/shift-left-security/

Mehmood, M., Amin, R., Muslam, M. M. A., Xie, J., & Aldabbas, H. (2023). Privilege Escalation Attack Detection and Mitigation in Cloud using Machine Learning. *IEEE Access : Practical Innovations, Open Solutions*, 11, 1–1. DOI: 10.1109/ACCESS.2023.3273895

Mohanan, R. (2023, April 11). *Aqua Security vs. XebiaLabs: What Tool Is Right For You?* Spiceworks Inc; Spiceworks. https://www.spiceworks.com/tech/devops/articles/aquasecurity-vs-xebialabs/

Obaloluwa Ogundairo, & broklyn, peter. (2024). Natural Language Processing for Cybersecurity Incident Analysis. *Journal of Cyber Security*. https://www.researchgate.net/publication/382917950_Natural_Language_Processing_for_Cybersecurity_Incident_Analysis

Oteemo. (2024, October 23). *ScienceLogic's Transformation into a Cloud Native and DevOps organization | Oteemo*. Oteemo. https://oteemo.com/case-study/sciencelogic-cloud-native-and-devsecops-transformation/

Palo Alto. (n.d.). *Cloud Security Posture Management | CSPM*. Palo Alto Networks. https://www.paloaltonetworks.com/prisma/cloud/cloud-security-posture-management

Palo Alto Networks. (n.d.). *What Is Insufficient Logging and Visibility?* Palo Alto Networks. https://www.paloaltonetworks.com/cyberpedia/insufficient-logging-visibility-cicd-sec10

Rodriguez, W. (2021). *API Security Best Practices | Blog | Fluid Attacks*. Fluidattacks.com. https://fluidattacks.com/blog/api-security-best-practices/

Sandobalin, J., Insfran, E., & Abrahão, S. (2017). *An Infrastructure Modelling Tool for Cloud Provisioning*. DOI: 10.1109/SCC.2017.52

Schmitt, J. (2022, April 15). *SAST vs DAST: what they are and when to use them*. CircleCI. https://circleci.com/blog/sast-vs-dast-when-to-use-them/

Security Compass. (2024, February 16). *Speed and Security: Recent Innovations in Secure Design and Development*. Security Compass. https://www.securitycompass.com/whitepapers/delivering-both-speed-and-security-through-secure-design-and-development-practices/

Shahin, M., Ali Babar, M., & Zhu, L. (2017). Continuous Integration, Delivery and Deployment: A Systematic Review on Approaches, Tools, Challenges and Practices. *IEEE Access : Practical Innovations, Open Solutions*, 5, 3909–3943. DOI: 10.1109/ACCESS.2017.2685629

Shu, R., Gu, X., & Enck, W. (2017). A Study of Security Vulnerabilities on Docker Hub. *Proceedings of the Seventh ACM on Conference on Data and Application Security and Privacy*, 15–25. DOI: 10.1145/3029806.3029832

Singh, V., & Peddoju, S. K. (2017). Container-based microservice architecture for cloud applications. *2017 International Conference on Computing, Communication and Automation (ICCCA)*. DOI: 10.1109/CCAA.2017.8229914

Smith, J. (2020, March 19). *DevSecOps Culture*. Snyk. https://snyk.io/articles/devsecops/culture/

Smith, J. (2020, October 19). Infrastructure as Code in a DevSecOps World. Snyk. https://snyk.io/articles/infrastructure-as-code-iac/

SparkFabrik . (2022). Container Security: what it is and how to implement it. Sparkfabrik.com. https://doi.org/DOI: 1031595/1712911637336/module_29821031595_gallery-masonry

Synk. (2024). *Fix your vulnerabilities | Snyk User Docs*. Snyk.io. https://docs.snyk.io/scan-with-snyk/snyk-open-source/manage-vulnerabilities/fix-your-vulnerabilities

Team, C. I. (2024, September 16). *A DevSecOps transformation story*. Www.cognizant.com. https://www.cognizant.com/us/en/insights/insights-blog/devsecops-digital-transformation

Telo. (2024, June 24). *Telos Announces Latest Version of its Next-Generation Cyber Risk Management Platform - Telos Corporation*. Telos Corporation. https://www.telos.com/press-release/telos-announces-latest-version-of-its-next-generation-cyber-risk-management-platform/

Theodoropoulos, T., Rosa, L., Benzaid, C., Gray, P., Marin, E., Makris, A., Cordeiro, L., Diego, F., Sorokin, P., Girolamo, M. D., Barone, P., Taleb, T., & Tserpes, K. (2023). Security in Cloud-Native Services: A Survey. *Journal of Cybersecurity and Privacy*, 3(4), 758–793. DOI: 10.3390/jcp3040034

Vemula, S. R. (2024). Automating Security Testing: Strategies for Vulnerability Scanning, Penetration Testing, and Compliance Checks. *International Research Journal of Engineering Science Technology and Innovation, 11*(7), 560–568. https://www.researchgate.net/publication/382737843_Automating_Security_Testing_Strategies_for_Vulnerability_Scanning_Penetration_Testing_and_Compliance_Checks

KEY TERMS AND DEFINITIONS

Continuous Monitoring: An ongoing and active process of monitoring and reviewing program performance, security, and legal compliance status in real time to identify emerging threats as soon as possible.

Infrastructure as Code (IaC): A technique of providing and operating infrastructure (like servers and networks) using code that makes it automated, consistent, or versioned.

Cloud Security Posture Management (CSPM): A collection of processes and best practices that enable the constant observation of the cloud environments for signs of threats and compliance nonconformity.

Serverless Security: Best practices for the security of serverless architectures referred to as Lambda; security aspects related to functions, API Gateway, and concerns such as injection attacks or privilege escalation.

Shift-Left Security: A strategy of integrating security into the design phase of the software development lifecycle, particularly during the coding phase.

Misconfigurations: Vulnerabilities in IT infrastructures result from mistakes or less-than-ideal system configuration settings, like excessively lax access limits.

Secure Software Development Framework (SSDF): A collection of requirements and recommendations for implementing security at any stage of software development to eliminate risks and strengthen the software.

Natural Language Processing (NLP): A subfield of AI that enables machines to understand the content of human language, its production, and its interpretation.

Chapter 10
Integrating Security in DataOps: A Framework for Securing Data Pipelines in Real-time Analytics

Khalil Soussane
https://orcid.org/0009-0002-8892-3581
Faculty of Sciences, Ibn Tofail University, Kenitra, Morocco

Bahaa Eddine Elbaghazaoui
https://orcid.org/0000-0002-3206-5162
National School of Applied Sciences, Sultan Moulay Slimane University, Beni Mellal, Morocco

Mohamed Amnai
Faculty of Sciences, Ibn Tofail University, Kenitra, Morocco

ABSTRACT

DataOps is crucial for managing complex data pipelines and driving efficient data analytics, but it introduces significant security challenges as data flows through ingestion, transformation, storage, and distribution stages. Each phase exposes unique vulnerabilities that threaten data integrity, confidentiality, and compliance. This chapter outlines a structured framework for embedding security into DataOps workflows, focusing on methods like encryption, access control, and real-time monitoring to safeguard data without disrupting operations. Leveraging advanced tools, including Security Orchestration, Automation, and Response (SOAR) platforms and cloud-native security solutions, we demonstrate how to automate threat detection and response for scalable data environments. Case studies from industries such as healthcare and finance illustrate successful implementation, offering practical insights and lessons learned. This framework equips data and security professionals to build secure, resilient pipelines, fostering trust and agility in data ecosystems.

DOI: 10.4018/979-8-3373-0365-9.ch010

1-INTRODUCTION

DataOps approach to managing complex data pipelines and ensuring efficient data analytics in today's data-driven world. However, as organizations increasingly rely on DataOps practices, they face significant security challenges across various stages of the data lifecycle - ingestion, transformation, storage, and distribution.

This chapter addresses these pressing concerns by presenting a comprehensive framework for integrating security directly into DataOps workflows. We focus on practical methods such as encryption, access control, and real-time monitoring to safeguard data integrity, confidentiality, and compliance while maintaining operational efficiency.

Our proposed framework draws inspiration from the latest security technologies, including Security Orchestration, Automation, and Response (SOAR) platforms and cloud-native security tools. These solutions automate threat detection and response processes, enabling scalable and resilient data environments.

Through case studies from sectors such as healthcare and finance, we demonstrate successful applications of these security practices, providing concrete examples and lessons learned 3. Our goal is to guide data and security professionals in building more secure, resilient data pipelines, ultimately paving the way for trusted, agile data ecosystems.

This chapter contributes to the evolving discourse on DataOps and security by bridging the gap between data management practices and cybersecurity best practices. By exploring the intersection of DataOps principles and security requirements, we aim to equip organizations with the knowledge and tools necessary to mitigate risks associated with data-intensive operations while realizing the full potential of DataOps for business value extraction.

2-BACKGROUND AND RELATED WORK

The integration of security into DataOps has become a critical area of focus as organizations increasingly rely on complex data pipelines to support real-time analytics. DataOps combines agile methodologies with data engineering practices to streamline the development, deployment, and management of data workflows. However, with the growing complexity of these workflows, security risks such as unauthorized access, data breaches, and compliance violations have become significant concerns. Existing literature has explored various aspects of DataOps, such as its benefits for operational efficiency and collaboration, but often overlooks the specific security challenges it introduces. This section provides an overview of the evolution of DataOps, outlines the key security challenges it faces, and highlights the related work that addresses the need for integrating security into these data pipelines.

1. DataOps: A Catalyst for Modern Data Management

DataOps has emerged as a transformative approach to data management, combining principles from Agile, DevOps, and Lean manufacturing to streamline the development and operation of data pipelines. By promoting collaboration between data engineers, analysts, and operations teams, DataOps enhances the speed, quality, and reliability of data processing. However, as the complexity and volume of data grow, so do the associated security risks. Gartner projects that by 2026, 50% of organizations will adopt

DataOps practices to support their data analytics needs. Yet, only a fraction of these implementations prioritize security as a core component, leaving critical vulnerabilities unaddressed.

2. Security Challenges in DataOps Workflows

Traditional data security measures often fall short in dynamic DataOps environments, where data flows across diverse platforms, including on-premises, cloud, and hybrid systems. Each stage—data ingestion, transformation, storage, and distribution—introduces specific risks, such as unauthorized access, data breaches, and regulatory non-compliance. Moreover, the rapid iteration cycles and continuous integration/deployment (CI/CD) pipelines characteristic of DataOps further complicate security enforcement, as manual interventions are impractical at scale. Security vulnerabilities in DataOps workflows have been documented in recent research, which identifies issues such as access control failures, data breaches, and the risk of data manipulation during transformation processes (Munappy et al., 2020)(Chavan, 2020).

3. Evolving Security Paradigms: From DevSecOps to DataSecOps

The integration of security into software development and IT operations—popularized as DevSecOps has set a precedent for embedding security into DataOps. However, DataOps presents unique challenges due to its focus on data rather than code. Recent advancements in **DataSecOps** aim to fill this gap, emphasizing automated security controls tailored for data-centric workflows. Key innovations include real-time anomaly detection, end-to-end encryption, and automated incident response, which align security with the velocity and scale of DataOps pipelines (Demchenko, 2020).

4. Technological Innovations: SOAR and Cloud-Native Security

Security Orchestration, Automation, and Response (SOAR) platforms have become instrumental in modern data security strategies. These platforms enable organizations to automate threat detection, investigation, and response, significantly reducing response times and minimizing human error. Similarly, cloud-native security tools—integrated within platforms like AWS, Azure, and Google Cloud—offer scalable, built-in capabilities such as serverless security, identity management, and data loss prevention (DLP). Organizations are increasingly turning to these innovations to safeguard their data operations (Reddy et al., 2021).

5. Case Studies in High-Risk Industries

The healthcare and finance sectors, which handle sensitive and regulated data, have been at the forefront of integrating security in DataOps. For example, healthcare organizations leverage SOAR solutions to secure patient data in compliance with HIPAA, while financial institutions employ real-time fraud detection systems to protect transactional data. These case studies highlight not only the efficacy of integrated security frameworks but also the challenges of maintaining compliance and operational agility (Bahaa et al., 2023).

6. Current Gaps and Opportunities

Despite these advancements, a significant gap remains in comprehensive, standardized frameworks for securing DataOps workflows. Existing studies often focus on specific technologies or isolated use cases without providing holistic solutions applicable across industries. This chapter aims to bridge that gap by proposing a unified framework for integrating security into DataOps, emphasizing practicality and scalability (Demchenko, 2020) (Bell et al., 2017).

The integration of security within DataOps workflows is crucial for safeguarding data throughout its lifecycle. While advancements like DataSecOps and modern security tools offer promising solutions, there remain gaps in providing comprehensive and standardized frameworks. The related work reveals that the rapid pace of DataOps often outpaces traditional security methods, but emerging technologies and practices, such as real-time threat detection and automated response, are closing this gap. A unified approach to security in DataOps can provide the resilience and trust needed to protect sensitive data while supporting the agility required for modern data analytics.

3-THE DataOps SECURITY FRAMEWORK

DataOps, while enhancing the agility and efficiency of data pipelines, requires a robust security framework to address the vulnerabilities present at every stage of the pipeline. Integrating security directly into the DataOps workflows ensures data privacy, integrity, and compliance without sacrificing operational speed. This section outlines a comprehensive security framework that integrates key practices across the stages of data operations, focusing on encryption, access control, real-time monitoring, and automated threat detection. In this context, Figure 1 shows the key components of the DataOps Security Framework, highlighting essential measures to ensure security and compliance across the data pipeline.

Figure 1. The DataOps Security Framework

1. **Data Ingestion and Collection**

The first stage of any data pipeline, data ingestion, is highly prone to external threats, such as unauthorized access or data interception. In this phase, it is crucial to implement strong encryption protocols like Transport Layer Security (TLS) to safeguard data as it travels across networks. Additionally, the use of tokenization or encryption at the source ensures that sensitive data is protected before it enters the pipeline (Polimeno et al., 2024)(Bhat, 2021).

Key Security Measures for Data Ingestion:

- TLS/SSL encryption for secure data transfer.
- Source-based encryption of sensitive data using encryption algorithms like AES (Advanced Encryption Standard).
- Authentication and authorization protocols, such as OAuth2 or OpenID Connect, to control access to data sources.

2. **Data Transformation and Processing**

Data transformation, involving the cleaning, manipulation, and reshaping of raw data, is another critical phase where security must be enforced. This is where most data breaches could occur if proper security measures are not in place. A combination of role-based access control (RBAC) and policy-driven security ensures that only authorized users and systems can access or modify sensitive data during processing (Babu et al., 2021).

Key Security Measures for Data Transformation:

- RBAC to ensure that users only have access to data needed for their roles.
- Data masking to obfuscate sensitive information during transformation processes.
- Logging and auditing to track data processing activities for compliance and forensic analysis.

3. **Data Storage and Retention**

Data storage presents significant risks, as data is often stored for long periods, making it vulnerable to both internal and external threats. Data at rest must be encrypted using strong encryption algorithms such as AES-256. Additionally, organizations should implement data retention policies to ensure that obsolete or unnecessary data is securely deleted or anonymized (Bell et al., 2017).

Key Security Measures for Data Storage:

- Encryption at rest using AES-256 or similar encryption algorithms.
- Data retention policies that enforce data deletion after a set period or based on data classification.
- Access control lists (ACLs) and fine-grained permissions to limit access to sensitive stored data.

4. **Data Distribution and Sharing**

The distribution of data, either for real-time analytics or sharing across systems, introduces security challenges related to unauthorized data access, data leakage, and compliance violations. In this phase, data encryption should continue to be enforced, and access control mechanisms should be strictly applied. Additionally, the use of secure API gateways can ensure that data requests are authenticated and authorized before processing (Ametepe et al., 2021).

Key Security Measures for Data Distribution:

- End-to-end encryption during data transfer to ensure data integrity and confidentiality.
- API security by utilizing OAuth2, API keys, and web application firewalls (WAFs) to protect data sharing.
- Continuous monitoring of data access patterns to detect anomalies or potential breaches.

5. **Real-Time Monitoring and Threat Detection**

Real-time monitoring is essential to detect any malicious activity or anomalies that could indicate a security breach. A comprehensive monitoring system should collect logs from all stages of the pipeline, enabling the detection of unusual access patterns, unauthorized data manipulation, or unexpected data flows. Automated tools like Security Orchestration, Automation, and Response (SOAR) platforms can play a key role in identifying and responding to threats in real-time (Atwal, 2020).

Key Security Measures for Real-Time Monitoring:

- Log aggregation using tools like ELK (Elasticsearch, Logstash, Kibana) or Splunk to gather and analyze logs from all stages.
- Threat detection systems that leverage machine learning algorithms to identify anomalies in real-time.
- SOAR platforms to automate incident response, reducing the time to react to potential breaches.

6. **Automation and Security Orchestration**

To manage the growing complexity of data operations and security challenges, organizations should leverage automation to reduce human intervention and enhance response times. Automated security measures, such as automated encryption and tokenization, alongside orchestration tools, ensure that security policies are consistently applied across all stages of the pipeline (Reddy et al., 2021).

Key Security Measures for Automation:

- Security as Code: Incorporating security policies directly into the CI/CD pipeline to ensure consistent enforcement across all environments.
- Automated threat response via orchestration tools that trigger actions based on predefined security rules.
- Cloud-native security tools that provide seamless integration with existing cloud platforms to enforce security policies automatically.

The DataOps Security Framework aims to address the security challenges introduced by real-time analytics and complex data pipelines. By incorporating encryption, access control, real-time monitoring, and automated threat detection into DataOps workflows, organizations can safeguard data integrity and confidentiality without compromising operational efficiency. Through the adoption of the latest security technologies and best practices, this framework provides a path toward building secure, resilient data ecosystems that are adaptable to the evolving threat landscape.

4-TECHNOLOGIES AND TOOLS FOR SECURITY IN DataOps

Integrating security into DataOps requires leveraging a wide range of modern technologies and tools that can secure data pipelines while maintaining operational agility. These technologies span across data encryption, access control, real-time monitoring, and threat detection. Below, we discuss the key tools and technologies for each stage of the DataOps pipeline and their role in ensuring a secure and compliant data environment.

1. Data Encryption and Tokenization

Data encryption is one of the most critical aspects of securing data at rest and in transit within DataOps workflows. Encryption ensures that sensitive data remains protected from unauthorized access during processing and storage. Tools such as HashiCorp Vault, AWS KMS (Key Management Service), and Azure Key Vault enable secure key management and encryption at scale, providing automated encryption mechanisms to secure data across cloud environments without compromising pipeline performance (Thusoo & Sarma, 2017) (Gunnam et al., 2023).

Tokenization, another powerful security technique, replaces sensitive data with an algorithmically generated token that can be mapped back to the original data only by authorized users or systems. This method is particularly useful in industries like healthcare and finance, where privacy regulations are stringent (Gunnam et al., 2023).

2. Access Control and Identity Management

Managing access to data resources is fundamental for maintaining security in DataOps. Role-based access control (RBAC) and attribute-based access control (ABAC) are widely adopted models for managing permissions. Keycloak, Okta, and Auth0 are common identity and access management (IAM) tools that integrate with DataOps pipelines to enforce access policies based on user roles, attributes, and authentication methods (Indu et al., 2018). These tools allow for fine-grained control over who can access and modify data at different stages of the pipeline.

Furthermore, leveraging OAuth 2.0 and OpenID Connect enables secure user authentication and authorization across distributed systems, ensuring that only authenticated users and services can interact with sensitive data (Indu et al., 2018).

3. Real-Time Monitoring and Threat Detection

Real-time monitoring is essential for maintaining the security and performance of data pipelines. Tools like Prometheus, Grafana, and Elastic Stack offer powerful observability capabilities to track pipeline performance, monitor security threats, and provide real-time alerts for anomalies or suspicious activities. These tools can be integrated with SOAR (Security Orchestration, Automation, and Response) platforms such as Splunk or ServiceNow to automate threat detection and response actions.

By leveraging machine learning-based anomaly detection, these platforms can help identify potential data breaches, unauthorized access, and data integrity issues before they become critical threats. Moreover, integration with cloud-native security tools like AWS GuardDuty or Azure Security Center allows for continuous, automated threat detection in real-time (Cadet et al., 2024).

4. Security in Data Transformation and Distribution

In addition to securing data at rest, it is crucial to secure data during transformation and distribution processes. Apache Kafka and Apache Flink are popular stream processing tools that enable the transformation of data in real-time. These tools offer built-in security features, such as encryption in transit (via TLS/SSL), authentication, and access control through Kerberos or OAuth.

For data distribution, tools like MinIO and Amazon S3 can be used to securely store and share data, ensuring encrypted storage and secure access policies. Data Loss Prevention (DLP) tools such as Digital Guardian help protect sensitive data during these stages, ensuring compliance with industry regulations like GDPR, HIPAA, or CCPA (Singu, 2021).

5. Automation and DevSecOps Integration

Automating security throughout the DataOps pipeline is a key approach to reducing human error and improving response times. DevSecOps practices integrate security directly into the CI/CD pipeline, automating security checks, vulnerability assessments, and compliance validation at every stage of data management .

Tools like Aqua Security, Twistlock, and Falco provide container security for applications running in Kubernetes and Docker environments, ensuring that only secure containers are deployed. SonarQube and OWASP ZAP are valuable for static and dynamic application security testing (SAST/DAST), providing automated vulnerability scanning for code (Sharma, 2024).

6. Cloud-Native Security Tools

Many DataOps pipelines are hosted on cloud platforms, which offer a wide range of security tools that can be directly integrated into the pipeline. AWS Security Hub, Google Cloud Security Command Center, and Azure Security Center provide centralized security monitoring and threat intelligence for cloud resources. These tools also offer compliance auditing features that ensure data security aligns with industry standards.

Cloud-native tools can be particularly beneficial for scalable, multi-cloud environments, as they automate security monitoring, vulnerability management, and threat detection across distributed resources (Reddy et al., 2021).

The security of DataOps pipelines requires an integrated approach, incorporating multiple layers of protection, monitoring, and response mechanisms. By leveraging a combination of encryption, access control, real-time monitoring, and cloud-native security tools, organizations can ensure that their data pipelines remain secure and compliant while maintaining the agility and scalability needed for modern data analytics.

5-IMPLEMENTING SECURITY IN REAL-TIME DATA PIPELINES

As organizations increasingly rely on real-time data analytics for decision-making, the integrity and security of data flowing through real-time data pipelines have become paramount. These pipelines typically involve a series of steps, including data ingestion, processing, storage, and distribution. In a rapidly evolving landscape, security measures must be seamlessly integrated into these pipelines without compromising performance or throughput. This section explores strategies and best practices for securing real-time data pipelines while ensuring agility and responsiveness.

1. Data Ingestion Security

Data ingestion is the first point of entry for data into a pipeline, and securing this phase is crucial for preventing unauthorized access or tampering. Real-time data ingestion is often facilitated through tools like Apache Kafka, Apache Flink, or cloud-native solutions like AWS Kinesis. To secure the ingestion phase:

- Encryption: Data should be encrypted both in transit and at rest using strong encryption algorithms like AES-256. This ensures that data remains confidential while moving through various stages of the pipeline. Many cloud providers offer encryption options for data streams, ensuring compliance with security standards (Sharma, 2024).

- Authentication and Authorization: Implementing strict authentication protocols (e.g., OAuth, API keys, and mutual TLS) ensures that only authorized entities can access the data stream. Fine-grained access control using tools like Apache Ranger or cloud-native IAM (Identity and Access Management) services ensures that users and services have the least privilege necessary for operation (Sharma, 2024).
- Data Validation: To prevent malicious data from entering the pipeline, implementing real-time data validation checks at the ingestion phase is essential. This includes schema validation, anomaly detection, and integrity checks to ensure data authenticity (Sharma, 2024).

2. Data Transformation and Processing Security

During data transformation, data is often enriched, cleaned, or aggregated before being passed to downstream systems. Given the complexity of real-time processing, maintaining security here involves preventing data corruption, unauthorized changes, and ensuring that sensitive information is protected.

- Access Control: Fine-grained access control mechanisms, such as Role-Based Access Control (RBAC) or Attribute-Based Access Control (ABAC), should be applied to ensure that only authorized services or users can modify or process sensitive data (Gunnam et al., 2023).
- Data Masking and Tokenization: Real-time processing of sensitive data, such as personally identifiable information (PII) or financial records, should be protected through data masking or tokenization techniques. This ensures that even during processing, sensitive data remains secure and protected from unauthorized access (Gunnam et al., 2023).
- Secure APIs: As APIs often serve as the interface between data processing components, securing them with proper authentication and authorization methods (OAuth, API gateways) is crucial. Real-time API security also includes rate limiting, logging, and monitoring to detect and mitigate attacks like DDoS (Distributed Denial of Service) (Gunnam et al., 2023).

3. Data Storage Security

Real-time data is often stored in databases, object storage systems, or distributed storage solutions like **Hadoop**, **S3**, or **NoSQL** databases. Ensuring that this storage is secure is vital for maintaining data integrity and confidentiality.

- Encryption at Rest: Data should be encrypted when stored to protect it from unauthorized access. Cloud providers offer native encryption mechanisms, but it's important to also manage encryption keys properly, using key management systems (KMS) to maintain control (Rao, 2016).
- Backup and Redundancy: Real-time data often includes business-critical information that must be recoverable in the event of a failure. Implementing automated backup and replication strategies ensures that data remains available, even during a disaster recovery event (Rao, 2016).
- Access Controls and Auditing: Tightening access to data storage systems with role-based access and leveraging logging mechanisms to monitor who accesses what data and when is essential.

This creates an audit trail that can be useful for both security audits and compliance reporting (Rao, 2016).

4. Real-Time Monitoring and Threat Detection

Real-time monitoring is critical for identifying and mitigating security threats as they happen. In data pipelines, this includes monitoring for unusual activity, data breaches, and performance degradation.

- Real-Time Threat Detection Tools: Implementing Security Information and Event Management (SIEM) systems like Splunk or cloud-native security services (AWS GuardDuty, Azure Security Center) can provide near-instant detection of security anomalies. These systems are capable of analyzing large volumes of data in real-time and can alert security teams to potential threats.
- Automated Security Response: Security Orchestration, Automation, and Response (SOAR) platforms allow organizations to automate responses to detected threats, minimizing the time between detection and mitigation. For example, automatic quarantine of suspicious data or throttling of abnormal data flows can help prevent damage (Cadet et al., 2024).
- Anomaly Detection and Machine Learning: Machine learning models can be used to identify patterns in data flows and flag unusual or potentially harmful activity. These models can be trained on historical data to understand typical behavior, making it easier to spot deviations that may indicate a security incident (Cadet et al., 2024).

Integrating security into real-time data pipelines is not an afterthought but a crucial aspect of building resilient and trusted data ecosystems. By adopting a comprehensive approach that spans data ingestion, transformation, storage, and real-time monitoring, organizations can mitigate the risks associated with data breaches and data integrity issues. With the right combination of encryption, access control, monitoring, and automation, security can be embedded seamlessly into **DataOps** workflows, ensuring both operational efficiency and data protection.

6-CHALLENGES AND FUTURE DIRECTIONS IN SECURING REAL-TIME DATA PIPELINES

Securing real-time data pipelines is a complex task, requiring the integration of robust security measures at every stage of the data lifecycle. As data continues to grow in volume, velocity, and variety, the challenges associated with securing real-time data pipelines are evolving. This section explores the primary security challenges organizations face and offers a glimpse into the future directions of securing data pipelines in dynamic, real-time environments.

1. Challenges in Securing Real-Time Data Pipelines

a. Scalability and Performance Overhead

One of the biggest challenges in securing real-time data pipelines is the potential performance overhead that security measures may introduce. Encryption, authentication, and anomaly detection systems, when not properly optimized, can significantly impact the speed and responsiveness of data processing.

In high-throughput environments where data is processed in microseconds, ensuring that security measures do not introduce latency or slow down operations is critical.

- Solution Direction: Leveraging hardware acceleration (e.g., using GPUs for encryption/decryption operations) or specialized encryption algorithms designed for low-latency environments can mitigate this challenge. Additionally, optimizing security systems to run efficiently in cloud-native environments can also improve performance scalability.

b. Complexity of Multi-Cloud and Hybrid Environments

Many organizations use multi-cloud or hybrid architectures for their real-time data pipelines. These environments introduce additional security complexities, as data moves between cloud providers and on-premise infrastructure. Each cloud provider has its own set of security tools, configurations, and compliance standards, making it difficult to ensure consistent security policies across the entire pipeline (Shrivastava & Agrawal, 2024).

- Solution Direction: The adoption of cloud-agnostic security frameworks, such as using containers and Kubernetes to abstract underlying cloud infrastructures, can help manage these complexities. Additionally, unified security solutions that can span multi-cloud environments—offering centralized logging, threat detection, and access control—are vital to overcoming this challenge.

c. Data Privacy and Compliance Requirements

Data privacy laws and regulations, such as the GDPR (General Data Protection Regulation) in the EU, HIPAA (Health Insurance Portability and Accountability Act) in the U.S., and others, impose strict requirements on how data should be handled, especially when dealing with sensitive information. Complying with these regulations while maintaining real-time data processing can be difficult. For example, ensuring that personal data is not processed without proper consent or that data is adequately anonymized or encrypted can add layers of complexity to pipeline design.

- Solution Direction: Privacy-enhancing technologies (PETs) like homomorphic encryption and differential privacy could be leveraged to ensure that sensitive data can be processed in real-time while meeting regulatory requirements. Automated compliance tools that scan data pipelines for potential violations of regulatory policies can also help maintain compliance without interrupting data flow.

d. Handling Insider Threats

While external threats such as hackers are a known concern, insider threats remain one of the most significant risks in securing data pipelines. This includes both malicious actors within an organization and employees who inadvertently expose sensitive data due to negligence or lack of awareness. Managing who has access to specific parts of the data pipeline and ensuring that the access levels are appropriate are crucial tasks.

- Solution Direction: Role-based access control (RBAC) and least-privilege principles can be extended across the entire data pipeline to limit access to sensitive information. Advanced monitoring systems that can detect unusual behavior or access patterns, coupled with machine learning algorithms, can help detect and mitigate insider threats in real-time (Cadet et al., 2024).

e. Dynamic Threat Landscape

The landscape of cybersecurity threats is continually evolving, and new attack vectors are emerging as attackers develop more sophisticated methods to breach systems. Real-time data pipelines, which operate in an environment of constant data influx, are especially vulnerable to evolving threats like ransomware, DDoS attacks, and supply chain attacks.

- Solution Direction: Adopting a proactive security strategy, such as continuous security monitoring and adaptive threat detection using AI and machine learning, is essential. The use of Security Orchestration, Automation, and Response (SOAR) platforms can also help organizations quickly respond to threats as they arise, ensuring that they can adapt to the dynamic threat landscape.

2. Future Directions in Securing Real-Time Data Pipelines

a. AI-Powered Security Automation

As the complexity of securing real-time data pipelines increases, so does the need for automated security solutions. Artificial intelligence (AI) and machine learning (ML) are already being used to enhance anomaly detection and improve threat intelligence. In the future, AI will play an even more significant role in automating security tasks, such as the automatic detection of potential vulnerabilities, patching of security gaps, and responding to incidents in real time.

- Future Trend: AI-driven security systems that can autonomously monitor, detect, and respond to security events in real-time, dramatically reducing the time to mitigate risks and threats.

b. Zero Trust Architectures for Data Pipelines

Zero Trust Architecture (ZTA) is an emerging security model that operates on the principle that no entity, whether inside or outside an organization's network, should be trusted by default. In the context of real-time data pipelines, adopting Zero Trust principles would mean enforcing strict access controls and continuous verification for every interaction within the pipeline. This approach minimizes the risk of a breach spreading throughout the system.

- Future Trend: A shift toward adopting Zero Trust models across all components of data pipelines, ensuring continuous authentication and authorization for every request, transaction, or data flow.

c. Blockchain for Data Integrity and Traceability

Blockchain technology, known for its transparency and immutability, can be used in real-time data pipelines to ensure the integrity and traceability of data. By leveraging decentralized ledgers, data modifications or transformations can be tracked with high accuracy, creating an immutable audit trail. This technology can be particularly useful in industries like healthcare, finance, and supply chain management, where data integrity is paramount.

- Future Trend: The integration of blockchain into real-time data pipelines to ensure that data changes are secure, traceable, and auditable, making it virtually impossible to tamper with historical data (Hossain et al., 2024).

d. Enhanced Encryption Techniques

As data encryption remains a cornerstone of data security, the development of more efficient and effective encryption techniques will continue to be a focal point. Homomorphic encryption, which allows computations to be performed on encrypted data without the need to decrypt it first, holds significant promise for securing data in real-time pipelines without compromising performance.

- Future Trend: Widespread adoption of advanced encryption methods like homomorphic encryption and quantum-resistant encryption algorithms to secure real-time data while maintaining computational efficiency.

e. Edge Computing Security

As real-time data processing increasingly moves to the edge (e.g., IoT devices, mobile apps), securing data pipelines at the edge becomes crucial. Edge computing enables faster data processing by reducing latency, but it also introduces new security challenges due to the distributed nature of edge devices (Xiao et al., 2019).

- Future Trend: The integration of advanced security frameworks tailored for edge computing, combining local encryption, device authentication, and real-time monitoring to secure data as it is processed at the edge.

Securing real-time data pipelines presents significant challenges due to the increasing complexity and volume of data, evolving threat landscapes, and regulatory requirements. However, these challenges also drive innovation and the development of advanced security technologies. In the future, organizations can expect to see more sophisticated, automated, and AI-driven security solutions, which will not only secure data pipelines but also ensure that they remain agile, scalable, and efficient. By addressing both current and emerging security threats, organizations can build secure and resilient real-time data pipelines that support the demands of modern data-driven enterprises.

CONCLUSION

As DataOps becomes a cornerstone for managing data pipelines and enabling real-time analytics, ensuring robust security is no longer optional it's essential. This chapter introduced a comprehensive framework for embedding security practices directly into DataOps workflows, addressing vulnerabilities across all stages of the data lifecycle.

By incorporating techniques such as encryption, access control, and real-time monitoring, and leveraging advanced tools like SOAR platforms and cloud-native solutions, organizations can protect data integrity, confidentiality, and compliance without compromising efficiency. Case studies from sectors like healthcare and finance illustrate the real-world impact of these practices, showcasing their potential to create secure, resilient data pipelines.

While challenges remain, including evolving threats and the need to balance security with performance, the strategies outlined here provide a foundation for building more trustworthy and agile data ecosystems. By embracing these practices, organizations can confidently harness the power of DataOps, ensuring that their data remains secure and reliable in an ever-evolving digital world.

REFERENCES

Ametepe, W., Dukeman, J., & Walker, S. (2021). Data provenance collection and security in a distributed environment: A survey. *International Journal of Computers and Applications*, 43(1), 11–25. DOI: 10.1080/1206212X.2018.1501937

Atwal, H., & Atwal, H. (2020). DevOps for DataOps. In Practical DataOps: Delivering Agile Data Science at Scale (pp. 161-189). DOI: 10.1007/978-1-4842-5104-1_7

Babu, R. G., Srinivasan, P., Kumar, N., & Reddy, S. (2021). Multimedia security and privacy on real-time behavioral monitoring in machine learning IoT application using big data analytics. In Multimedia Technologies in the Internet of Things Environment (pp. 137–156).

Bahaa, S., Ghalwash, A. Z., & Harb, H. (2023). DataOps lifecycle with a case study in healthcare. *International Journal of Advanced Computer Science and Applications*, 14(1), 15–29. DOI: 10.14569/IJACSA.2023.0140115

Bell, L., Arnold, J., & Evans, T. (2017). *Agile application security: Enabling security in a continuous delivery pipeline*. O'Reilly Media, Inc.

Bhat, A. K. (2021). Improve real-time fraud detection with DataOps on resilient elastic platforms. *Journal of Resilient Data Platforms*, 5(2), 210–222.

Cadet, E., Ndiaye, T., Parker, S., & Leclerc, A. (2024). AI-powered threat detection in surveillance systems: A real-time data processing framework. *ResearchGate*, 21(10), 125–138.

Chavan, M. (2020). Integrating DataOps practices in signature verification systems for seamless data orchestration. *Journal of DataOps Practices*, 45(2), 102–114.

Demchenko, Y. (2020). From DevOps to DataOps: Cloud based software development and deployment. In *The International Conference on High Performance Computing and Simulation (HPCS 2020)* (pp. 321-330).

Gunnam, V., Cheemakurthi, S. K. M., & Kilaru, N. B. (2023). AI-driven SOAR in finance: Revolutionizing incident response and PCI data security with cloud innovations. *Journal of Financial Security*, 12(4), 130–142.

Hossain, M. I., Gonzalez, A. R., & Kar, N. (2024). Enhancing data integrity and traceability in industry cyber physical systems (ICPS) through blockchain technology: A comprehensive approach. arXiv Preprint, arXiv:2405.04837.

Indu, I., Anand, P. M. R., & Bhaskar, V. (2018). Identity and access management in cloud environment: Mechanisms and challenges. *Engineering Science and Technology, an International Journal*, 21(4), 574–588. DOI: 10.1016/j.jestch.2018.05.010

Munappy, A., Raj, A., Bosch, J., & Homström Olsson, H. (2020). Data pipeline management in practice: Challenges and opportunities. In Product-Focused Software Process Improvement: 21st International Conference, PROFES 2020, Turin, Italy, November 25–27, 2020 [Springer International Publishing.]. *Proceedings*, 21, 123–135.

Polimeno, A., Conte, G., Lamina, D., & Pellizzi, F. (2024). Balancing protection and quality in big data analytics pipelines. *Big Data*, 18(1), 124–137. DOI: 10.1089/big.2023.0065 PMID: 38603580

Rao, B. T. (2016). A study on data storage security issues in cloud computing. *Procedia Computer Science*, 92, 128–135. DOI: 10.1016/j.procs.2016.07.335

Reddy, A. K., Kumar, S., & Mishra, V. (2021). DevSecOps: Integrating security into the DevOps pipeline for cloud-native applications. *Journal of Artificial Intelligence Research and Applications*, 1(2), 89–114.

Sharma, P. (2024). DevSecOps integration-security in the software delivery pipeline: Exploring the integration of security practices into the software delivery pipeline to ensure secure software development practices. *Australian Journal of Machine Learning Research & Applications*, 4(1), 46–54.

Shrivastava, S., & Agrawal, Y. (2024). Multi-cloud deployments and hybrid cloud architecture. *International Journal of Cloud Systems*, 18(3), 4754–4760.

Singu, S. K. (2021). Real-time data integration: Tools, techniques, and best practices. *ESP Journal of Engineering & Technology Advancements*, 1(1), 158–172.

Thusoo, A., & Sarma, J. (2017). *Creating a data-driven enterprise with DataOps*. O'Reilly Media, Inc.

Xiao, Y., Zheng, S., & Li, H. (2019). Edge computing security: State of the art and challenges. *Proceedings of the IEEE*, 107(8), 1608–1631. DOI: 10.1109/JPROC.2019.2918437

Chapter 11
Safeguarding Sensitive Data in the DevSecOps Pipelines:
Strategies, Tools, and Best Practices for Modern Software Development

Advait Patel
https://orcid.org/0009-0001-2693-2346
Broadcom, USA

Pravin Pandey
https://orcid.org/0009-0008-0016-6947
Tiffany & Co, USA

ABSTRACT

This chapter focuses on ways, practices, and resources available to protect data in DevSecOps processes, an essential element of application development. It focuses on software security in the Software Development Life Cycle (SDLC) context, including secure code, data covering techniques like masking and encryption, and role-based access. Innovative examples of appropriate organizations like Netflix or Capital One show the necessity of performing preventive management of data breaches. Another interesting trend the chapter discusses is zero trust and AI in cybersecurity. Thus, improving DevSecOps strategies will help organizations reduce risks, comply with regulatory requirements, and reign in threats that exploit the advancing technologies.

1. INTRODUCTION

As software development continues astoundingly, securing information is now a significant concern. This means that even user data, whether personally identifiable information (PII), financial data, or proprietary information, is much more likely to be targeted thanks to the advanced cyber threats and the sheer scale and interconnected nature of today's software systems. It is noteworthy that conventional approaches to secure such data have proved ineffective, and failing to protect such data results in eradicating user confidence, apart from inviting very stiff regulatory fines, monetary losses, and reputational risks (Tariq et al., 2023). Therefore, multiple data protection measures are considered the foundation of

DOI: 10.4018/979-8-3373-0365-9.ch011

the secure software development cycle. Over time, DevSecOps has become a new paradigm that embeds IT systems' development, security, and operation into a single production line. In this manner, DevSecOps enhances security rather than mitigating risks; security becomes a middle-of-the-line development process (Sandu, 2021).

In contrast to the traditional development models, where security is often considered an add-on feature, DevSecOps implements security from the design inception of software during development, implementation, and even usage. This cultural shift allows teams to produce high-quality, fast, secure software with more assurance. However, integrating data protection with the DevSecOps cycles is incredibly complex. Data governance frameworks must integrate well with organizations with standard iterative and continuous delivery (Akbar et al., 2022). There is a lack of correct configurations, unknown flows of sensitive data, and inadequate controls the attacker can leverage. Also, general knowledge of the rules of data protection legislation such as GDPR, HIPAA, and CCPA is insufficient to guarantee compliance with the laws and the techniques used to implement them. Considering these challenges, this chapter provides practical recommendations for protecting sensitive data in DevSecOps pipelines. The objectives are fourfold:

- To describe the information often processed in contemporary software development and the consequences of reckless approaches to their processing.
- To bring awareness about how DevSecOps has been adopted to reshape the software development security environment.
- To help organizations establish a measure for adequately protecting essential data.
- To analyze new technologies and directions in DevSecOps that affect data security.

Therefore, by analyzing these aspects, the chapter aims to provide software development teams with the essential information and tools to design and establish secure, compliant, and reliable DevSecOps processes. By incorporating technology, strategy, and governance, organizations can reinforce their barriers and safeguard the appropriation of data at the SDLC stages.

2. UNDERSTANDING SENSITIVE DATA IN MODERN SOFTWARE DEVELOPMENT

Palo Alto Networks (2024) mentions that sensitive data, sometimes called sensitive personal data or sensitive personally identifiable information (SPII), could harm, discriminate against, or adversely affect the person to whom it relates if it is revealed, misused, or accessed without consent. Others, like the University of Edinburgh (2022), define sensitive data as data that, if disclosed or mismanaged, can lead to monetary loss, damage the reputations of individuals and organizations, or attract penalties under the law. With the evolution of modern software engineering, sensitive data is widely distributed across systems, applications, and environments and thus requires strict security measures for the former.

Definition and Types of Sensitive Data

Sensitive data encompasses various categories based on its nature and purpose:

Personally Identifiable Information (PII): Data that are personal to a person and thus can be used to pinpoint that individual, including name and address, phone digits, social security number, and the person's driver's license details (The Turing Way Community, 2024).

Protected Health Information (PHI): Patient records that contain details about the patient's health condition, physician-prescribed medicines, and insurance information; data that falls under the ambit of HIPAA.

Financial Data: Further, information relating to payment cards, bank accounts, and tax records is governed under standards such as the PCI DSS.

Intellectual Property (IP): Confidential business knowledge and new technological information vital to an organization because of competitors and other malicious parties (The Turing Way Community, 2024).

Authentication Credentials: These include passcodes, login information such as usernames and passwords, APIs, and encryption keys that open systems or data. These sensitive data are represented in Figure 1 below.

Figure 1. Various Types of Sensitive Data

Key Risks Associated with Mishandling Sensitive Data

Failure to secure sensitive data can lead to severe repercussions, including;

Data Breaches: Malicious computer crimes that involve hacking computer software to obtain malicious data (Guyer, 2024).

Identity Theft and Fraud: Identity theft or embezzlement fraud by using or sharing an individual's PII or finances.

Operational Disruptions: If, for example, data becomes compromised or manipulated, downtime servicing affects the regular running of the business, resulting in loss-making.

Reputational Damage: Hacked incidents give a bad impression to clients and lead to the contraction of trust in products.

Legal and Financial Penalties: Failure to observe or follow data protection laws attracts heavy penalties, fines, and suits, especially regarding ransom payments and client lawsuits (Guyer, 2024).

By integrating security into each phase of the software development lifecycle, developers and organizations may proactively reduce these risks.

Regulatory and Compliance Landscape

The increasing importance of data security has led to the establishment of stringent regulations to protect sensitive information; these regulations include;

General Data Protection Regulation (GDPR): Implemented in the European Union, GDPR requires recitals to pursue data protection in design, involve users in data processing through consent, and strictly respond to breaches.

Health Insurance Portability and Accountability Act (HIPAA): This law regulates the health care management of PHI through encryption, access management, and required risk analysis.

California Consumer Privacy Act (CCPA): This law enshrines certain rights in Californian consumers by giving them the right to access, delete, and not be sold their data.

Payment Card Industry Data Security Standard (PCI DSS): This global standardization regulation helps protect the payment card data of organizations that accept or process payments. Figure 2 summarizes the regulations.

Figure 2. Regulatory and Compliance Landscape

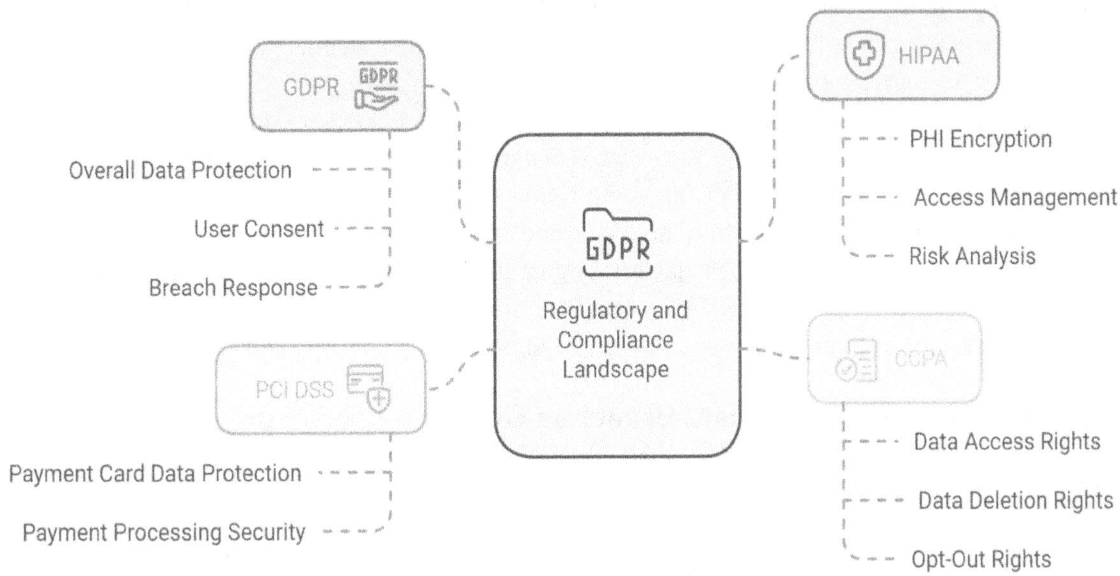

To meet such regulations, good data governance policies, sound coding best practices, and constant auditing of those technologies. Therefore, some software development teams have additional regulatory concerns about access rights and controls, encryption, and logging formats and mechanisms. The knowledge about what kind of data is sensitive and what danger such data poses forms the basis of a secure development process. When security controls are designed to comply with existing or planned regulations, organizations can secure data and gain the confidence of users and customers. The following sections of this chapter shall further unpack how the practice, approach, and tool known as DevSecOps can be used to achieve the above goals appropriately.

3. THE ROLE OF DEVSECOPS IN DATA PROTECTION

DevSecOps may be defined as continuously incorporating security within the SDLC process without disrupting the software development (Prates & Pereira, 2024). This approach aligns development with the issues that have plagued previous models of development and security, where security was viewed as an adjunct or function to be appended at the end of the development process. DevSecOps is the concept of strengthening security at every phase of software development and the operations cycle so that development and operations teams are encouraged to actively seek out and address security problems on an ongoing basis before they can be used to exploit sensitive information.

Applying security to the SDLC means implementing methods and technologies that secure data throughout the application development lifecycle. In the planning phase, threat modeling helps highlight risks in the project involving sensitive data so that they can be addressed as soon as possible. During coding, secure coding standards reduce such things as injection flaws or insecure storage. Pre-code automatically can pinpoint and correct problems before development reaches the next level or phase. During the build and test life cycle phases, CI/CD integrates dynamic application security testing (DAST) and dependency scanning to deliver real-time vulnerability findings (Bigelow, 2021). Operating security enforces runtime security policies and monitors the integrity and confidentiality of data during operation, while deployment enforces runtime security policies of an application.

The strength of this process is that this approach implies the cooperation of three crucial teams: development, security, and operations. This shared responsibility model is peace of mind, knowing that data security will not be an afterthought but will be part of every development. Software automation and integration are essential for teams, as they are secure and fast. For example, secrets management solutions for HashiCorp Vault or AWS Secret Manager will guarantee safe storage and access to credentials and encryption keys (Finch, 2024). The RBAC system controls permission to use and has limitations when considering roles, but it implements the principle of least privilege in exposing sensitive data.

Case Studies Highlighting Data Breaches Due to Weak Security in Pipelines

1. Capital One (2019)

In 2019, Capital One encountered a massive data leakage, compromising the details of more than 100 million people. The breach was initiated due to weaknesses in its cloud functioning profile, especially in the AWS settings (Khan et al., 2022). A former AWS employee used this misconfiguration to obtain credit card applications, social security numbers, and bank statements. The breach pointed out the poor security postures in the organization's DevSecOps pipeline. Namely, there are insufficiently studied access controls and weak secret management. CI/CD processes were compromised as hardcoded credentials in the organization, and overly privileged access was achieved without legitimate authorization. Run-time monitoring and identification of actual-time threats also could not be adequately performed by Capital One, which also contributed to the delay in breach discovery by the company. The consequences involved an $80 million fine from the end of U.S. regulators and a significant loss of reputation (Schroeder, 2020).

Figure 3. Attack Process of Capital One (Source: Khan et al., 2022)

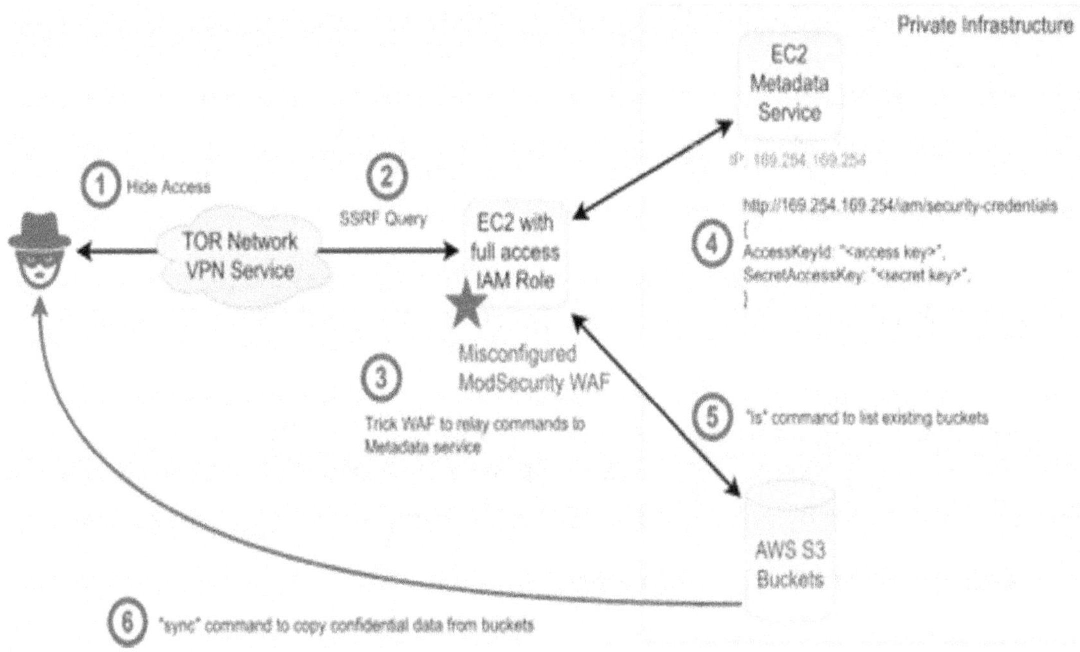

Figure 3 depicts how Capital One experienced a data breach. The first phase involves the attacker concealing his identity by accessing anonymizing services such as the TOR networks and VPN. Turning to the second class of attack, the attacker abuses the incorrect configuration of the ModSecurity Web Application Firewall (WAF) and makes it deliver unauthorized Server-Side Request Forgery (SSRF) requests. These commands target the AWS EC2 metadata service, which, unfortunately, provides Identity and Access Management (IAM) credentials with full access (Khan et al., 2022). With such credentials, the attacker retrieves the available Amazon S3 buckets and, utilizing the "sync" command, exports thousands of confidential data files from the buckets. This exploit takes advantage of WAF misconfiguration, SSRF, and lack of monitoring of cloud resources, leading to the leakage of important customer data.

2. SolarWinds (2020)

One recent cyberattack was the SolarWinds breach in 2020, which was defined by vulnerabilities in the company software supply chain. Hackers compromised SolarWinds' build servers and then inserted malware into updates of the Orion software platform, which was employed by countless administrations, including many Fortune 500 corporations and several branches of the federal government (Harvard Business Review, 2024). This attack leveraged gaps in pipeline protection, with the main areas being weak or non-existent code signing checks or scanning and the general absence of multifactor authentication in high-risk areas. Furthermore, in several instances, the actual developer accounts, which in many cases had been comprised due to more extensive exposure and subsequently contained ludicrous levels of authority, further empowered the attackers to move both laterally and omnidirectionally across the pipeline (Temple-Raston, 2021). Notably, SolarWinds failed to detect odd activity in its build environment. It introduced the need to protect every aspect of the DevSecOps lifecycle and sparked increased demand for better supply chain security.

From these examples, it is significant to discern that DevSecOps centralizes data security and makes it automated and team-involved. It decreases the chances of data compromise by introducing automation of processes, safe coding, and communication that facilitate the quick development of high-quality software. Modern software development problems, including diverse supply chains and fluctuating policies and regulations, require DevSecOps as a framework for organizations wanting to implement end-to-end safeguards for sensitive information (Domoney, 2024).

4. STRATEGIES FOR SAFEGUARDING DATA IN DEVSECOPS PIPELINES

Reducing vulnerabilities and guaranteeing the security of sensitive data require integrating strong data protection techniques into DevSecOps pipelines. Throughout the software development lifecycle, organizations can reduce risks and protect data by implementing techniques including role-based access control (RBAC), data masking, secure coding, and CI/CD pipeline security.

Implementing Secure Coding Practices

Establishing good coding practices is the cornerstone of a good DevSecOps cycle. These practices allow security to be the coding focus, preventing issues such as SQL injection, cross-site scripting (XSS), and improper data storage (Sharma et al., 2012). Generally, developers have to abide by forms that have already been established, including the OWASP Secure Coding Practices Checklist. For instance, input validation is essential to comprehensive amounts of secure code. Thus, by checking the inputs provided by the users for compliance with strict requirements, the developers can eliminate receipt of unlawful inputs (McCarvill, 2023).

Furthermore, authorized access and parameterized queries utilize prepared statements to reduce the susceptibility of an application to SQL injection, a type of attack on an application's security. Here is a code snippet in Python demonstrating secure database interaction. The codes in this chapter are italicized for differentiation.

```
import sqlite3

def get_user_data(user_id):

connection = sqlite3.connect("database.db")

cursor = connection.cursor()

query = "SELECT * FROM users WHERE id = ?"
```

```
cursor.execute(query, (user_id,))

return cursor.fetchall()
```

This code example lowers the danger of SQL injection by using parameterized queries to ensure that user inputs cannot change the database query structure.

Data Masking and Anonymization Techniques

Two techniques, data masking and anonymization, can protect sensitive data during development and testing (AWS, n.d.). They change concrete data into formats presented in a way that is still useful to the user but is in no way identifiable. For instance, an actual credit card number may be replaced with a randomly generated one that appears viable to the user but meaningless to the attackers.

Besides, real-time data masking, also known as dynamic data masking (DDM), allows the application of a security mask depending on how the user logs into the system (AWS, n.d.). In testing instances, other tools like Mockaroo or Faker can be used to introduce test datasets similar to the production one but without using the real one (Keployio, 2024).

For instance, the following is an example of data anonymization in Python with the Faker library:

```
from faker import Faker

fake = Faker()

fake_data = {

"name": fake.name(),

"email": fake.email(),

"credit_card": fake.credit_card_number()

}

print(fake_data)
```

By creating fake user data, this method ensures private data stays in the production environment.

Continuous Integration/Continuous Deployment (CI/CD) Pipeline Security

Continuous Integration/Continuous Development pipelines are essential in maintaining a seamless flow in software delivery but also present an entry point into our systems if not secured. That is why several measures must be taken to protect sensitive data in CI/CD pipelines. All the credentials, secrets, and tokens used in pipelines should be encrypted using frameworks such as HashiCorp Vault or AWS Secrets Manager. Configuration files may contain hardcoded credentials, which must be strictly prohibited. Secrets should also only be available to authorized processes and people. In addition, pipelines could and should require code signing by imposing concrete checklists on code artifacts to ensure their validity and non-tampering. Static and dynamic application security testing should be conducted as part of the pipeline to identify all vulnerabilities. Moreover, pipelines run at runtime to check for breaches and other potential issues like pipeline changes or resource consumption. Another tool can scan repositories for secrets and monitor pipeline activity for suspicious actions, including GitGuardian or Aqua Security.

Role-Based Access Control (RBAC) and Least Privilege Access

RBAC is an essential security feature that applies priority control to limit users' access rights to only those required to perform their duties effectively (Nyame & Qin, 2020). This principle limits the chances of exposing organizational data and the consequences in case of a loss of security. Similarly, RBAC in a DevSecOps pipeline is feasible at the repository, build environment and deployment server levels. For instance, programmers can archive/read/write code repositories, whereas, in deployment, permissions are only given to DevOps engineers.

Figure 4. Example of a Role-Based Access Control (RBAC) (Source: Kompaniiets, 2024)

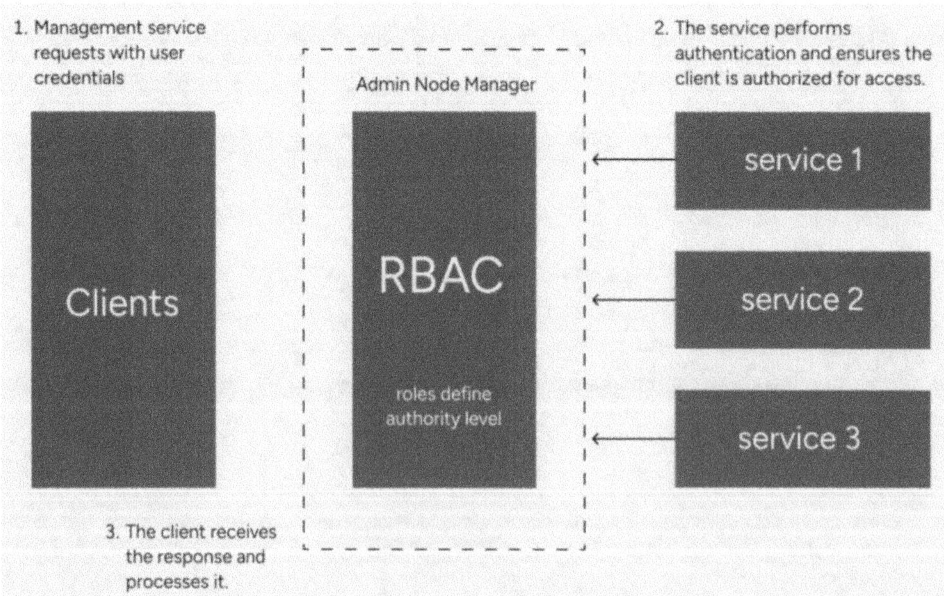

Figure 4 shows the overall flow detailing the Role-Based Access Control (RBAC) in a system. In this case, the clients make a request to a management service using their credentials. An admin node manager considers these requests in terms of roles and authority levels that have been defined under RBAC. If the client is authorized, the system will provide the feasibility of utilization for the following services: Service 1, Service 2, or Service 3 (Kompaniiets, 2024). For example, in a DevSecOps pipeline, the programmers have read/write access to the source code control. At the same time, the DevOps engineers who deal with the release are responsible for the deployments. The response is then implemented and sent back to the client for further processing. For RBAC to be most effective, roles and permissions need to be implemented very strictly, and breaches must be constantly checked for in the least amount of time possible.

For RBAC to be efficient, measures include describing rigid roles and permissions and continuously evaluating access management policies. Therefore, the access logs must be constantly monitored to detect and remove outdated and no longer relevant permissions.

An illustration of RBAC in Kubernetes, a popular platform for containerized apps, is provided below:

```
apiVersion: rbac.authorization.k8s.io/v1

kind: Role

metadata:

namespace: dev

name: developer-role

rules:

- apiGroups: ["”]

resources: ["pods”, "services”]

verbs: ["get”, "list”, "watch”]

---
```

```
apiVersion: rbac.authorization.k8s.io/v1
kind: RoleBinding
metadata:
name: bind-developer-role
namespace: dev
subjects:
- kind: User
name: developer-user
apiGroup: ""
roleRef:
kind: Role
name: developer-role
apiGroup: "rbac.authorization.k8s.io"
```

This YAML file creates a developer position connected to a particular user. Depending on their access level, the developer can access pods and services. This guarantees the developer cannot carry out unapproved tasks outside their scope.

5. TOOLS AND TECHNOLOGIES FOR SECURING DEVSECOPS PIPELINES

Specific, secure, and optimized DevSecOps tools and solutions are needed for data protection in the rapidly developing world of software creation. These tools make the pipeline more secure, visible, and robust by handling weaknesses, secrets, encryption, or ways to monitor it.

Tools for Static and Dynamic Code Analysis

Static and dynamic code analysis techniques are essential for finding vulnerabilities at various phases of the software development lifecycle.

Static Application Security Testing (SAST): Some SAST tools, like Snyk and Checkmarx, work at analyzing source code or binaries, but that does not involve the running of the application (Piskachev et al., 2023). These tools identify security issues such as SQL injection, XSS or unsecured API calls during development. SAST tools are also built in the CI/CD pipeline, where developers must solve security issues. For example, Snyk natively connects to central code repositories such as GitHub or GitLab, checks the code as part of the commit action, and offers recommendations.

Dynamic Application Security Testing (DAST): Other tools like DAST, including OWASP ZAP and Burp Suite, scan running applications to identify weaknesses (Pahuja, 2022). Unlike SAST, these tools analyze the application dynamically and provide information on real-time impending challenges such as authentication vulnerabilities or runtime configuration problems. Thus, DAST tools guarantee that applications are secure in their operation environments by mimicking real-world attacks. Implementing SAST and DAST into the DevSecOps framework provides the concept of continuously checking for vulnerabilities in code both during the writing and use processes.

Figure 5. The Architecture of OWASP ZAP and How it Works (Source: Ashwani, 2023)

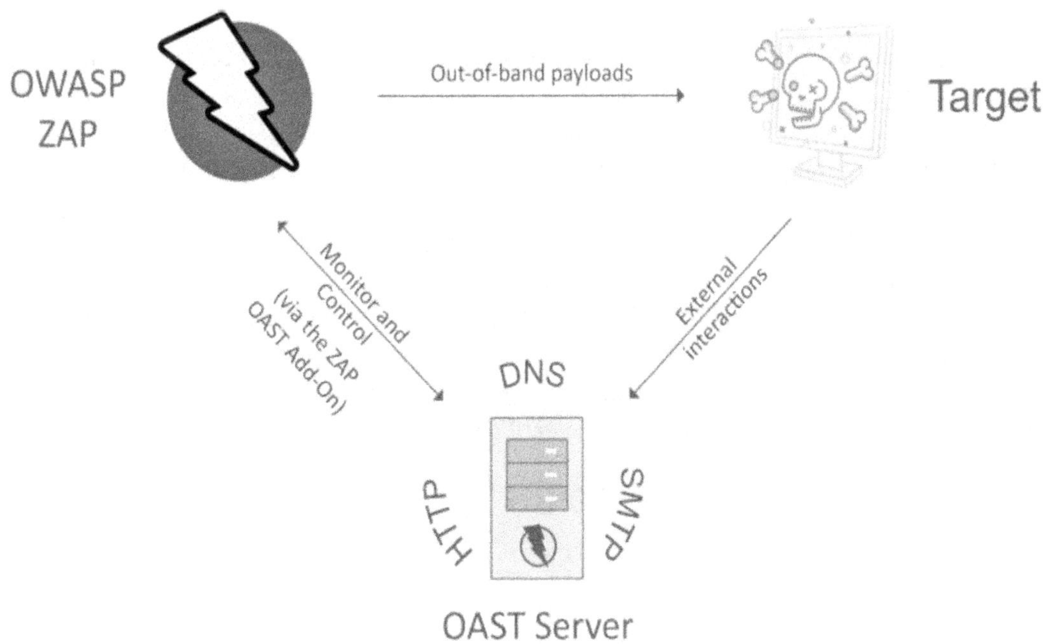

As presented in Figure 5, OWASP ZAP is an advanced web application security assessment tool that leverages an analytically crafted web proxy that captures the HTTP/HTTPS traffic of a user with the target application. For discovering endpoints, it possesses spidering and crawling capabilities; the captured traffic analysis comprises passive scanning, and to detect vulnerabilities like SQL injection and cross-site scripting, it has features of active scanning that send payloads to the application. There are special features for the test interactions, in particular the "Break" option, which permits users to intervene and change the requests (Ashwani, 2023). ZAP now offers scripting or automation and allows the addition of additional plug-in tools and authors. It provides specific vulnerability reports with suggestions for solving them, so the tool is highly customizable when it comes to finding and treating all web application security threats.

Secret Management Tools

Keys and passwords, such as API, password, and encryption keys, are vital for pipeline activities but could pose high risks if leaked. Solutions such as HashiCorp Vault, AWS Secrets Manager, and Microsoft Azure Key Vault are intended to protect and manage secrets. HashiCorp Vault offers extended capabilities such as dynamic secrets, which are temporary credentials for services and significantly reduce the prospects of getting compromised by an unauthorized individual (HashiCorp, 2024). AWS Secrets Manager self-rotates secrets and is directly linked with AWS IAM to manage users' permissions. They guarantee that secrets are never typed directly in scripts or configuration files, one of our most significant security weaknesses. These solutions further protect secrets by enforcing encryption in transit and at rest, guaranteeing that private information is safeguarded even while being transmitted. Pipelines can dynamically retrieve secrets at runtime without disclosing them in logs or environments, thanks to integration with CI/CD tools.

Data Encryption and Tokenization Tools

Data encryption and tokenization should be used when data is at rest, in motion, or being processed. VeraCrypt, Thales CipherTrust, and AWS KMS have powerful encryption capabilities to secure the data. Encryption refers to changing data to a form that cannot be read or understood without using specific decryption codes. For example, AWS KMS helps developers encrypt data with AWS standard keys or CMKs. It works seamlessly with other AWS services, such as S3 and DynamoDB, for complete chain encryption (Tahir, 2024). Tokenization, in turn, substitutes the actual values of different data fields with other values, called tokens, which have no real meaning except when used in a protected context (Lutkevich, 2023). Products like Protegrity and Micro Focus Voltage are tokenization tools that let developers work with data on the application development level without displaying the original data. For example, in credit card processing, tokenization replaces the card number with a token, minimizing exposure during the processing or storing of the card data.

Monitoring Auditing Tools for Pipeline Security

Monitoring and auditing should be necessary to ensure the visibility of the DevSecOps pipelines. Platforms such as Splunk, Elastic Stack (ELK), and Aqua Security contain detailed solutions for monitoring, tracking and countering threats.

Log Monitoring: With Splunk and ELK Stack, logs produced across the pipeline are collected and analyzed to provide security event information (Son & Kwon, 2017). These tools incorporate machine learning approaches that help identify suspicious activities, such as unauthorized attempts on the system or abnormally high activity, and prevent them before they occur.

Pipeline Auditing: Auditing should ensure that every developer adheres to corporate security policies and industrial regulations (Fastercapital, 2024). Other tools, such as Aqua Security, allow scanning for vulnerabilities involving containerized applications before images used in the pipeline are deployed. Furthermore, Freestyle, Jenkinsfile, GitFlux, WeaveWorks, and Argo CD tools of GitOps check changes in code repositories to ensure CI/CD are not compromised.

Real-Time Monitoring: Programs such as Datadog and Prometheus monitor real-time pipeline security and performance. These solutions enable teams to react quickly to breaches by creating alerts for preset security events, such as privilege escalation or illegal deployments (detailed explanations are in Table 1).

The power of these tools is not only in their effectiveness but in the fact that they are designed to work in the architecture of DevSecOps. For example, secrets management integrates with CI/CD pipelines to allow secure usage and transfer of information. The runtime monitors are used side by side with the code analysis tools because the former deals with errors after coding is done, while the latter helps to find the probable issues with the code before the actual release. These tools put an effective security-in-depth measure in place since they guard against different risks in the pipeline.

Table 1. Detailed Summary of Tools and Technologies for Securing DevSecOps Pipelines in the Market

Category	Tool	Description	Example/Usage
Static Code Analysis (SAST)	Snyk	Scans source code or binaries for vulnerabilities during development without running the application.	Integrates with GitHub/GitLab to check code at commit time and suggests fixes.
	Checkmarx	Analyzes code to find security issues such as SQL injection, XSS, and unsecured API calls.	Used in CI/CD pipeline for early detection of code vulnerabilities.
Dynamic Code Analysis (DAST)	OWASP ZAP	A dynamic analysis tool that captures HTTP/ HTTPS traffic and scans running applications for vulnerabilities.	Used to identify runtime issues like authentication flaws and XSS attacks.
	Burp Suite	Provides dynamic scanning of live applications to find security issues in real-time.	Detects vulnerabilities during actual application use, including server misconfigurations.
Secret Management	HashiCorp Vault	Manages and protects secrets such as API keys and encryption keys, supports dynamic secrets and encryption at rest.	Used to secure credentials and secrets in a DevSecOps pipeline.
	AWS Secrets Manager	Provides secret management with automated key rotation and integration with AWS IAM for secure access control.	Used for storing, rotating, and securely retrieving API keys in AWS environments.

continued on following page

Table 1. Continued

Category	Tool	Description	Example/Usage
	Microsoft Azure Key Vault	Stores secrets, certificates, and keys with built-in encryption to manage access in the Azure cloud environment.	Helps securely manage secrets in Azure-based pipelines.
Data Encryption and Tokenization	Thales CipherTrust	Manages encryption keys and data protection in hybrid cloud environments.	Encrypts data at rest and in motion, ensuring data privacy and compliance.
	VeraCrypt	Offers strong encryption for files and volumes, securing data at rest.	Used to encrypt sensitive data stored in storage during pipeline execution.
	AWS KMS	AWS Key Management Service for managing encryption keys and applying encryption to data across AWS services.	Ensures secure data storage with encryption integrated across AWS services.
	Protegrity	Provides tokenization services that replace sensitive data with tokens to reduce data exposure.	Used in PCI DSS-compliant applications to tokenize sensitive payment data.
	Micro Focus Voltage	Tokenizes sensitive data to minimize exposure, particularly in payment card processing.	Protects sensitive personal information in credit card transactions.
Monitoring and Auditing	Splunk	Collects and analyzes logs to provide insights into system behavior and security events in real-time.	Monitors logs for abnormal activity and potential security threats.
	Elastic Stack (ELK)	Collects, stores, and visualizes log data from various sources for monitoring and analyzing security events.	Used to monitor logs and identify suspicious activities across the pipeline.
	Aqua Security	Scans containerized applications and Kubernetes environments for vulnerabilities before deployment.	Audits container images and ensures compliance in cloud-native environments.
	Datadog	Monitors cloud environments, infrastructure, and applications for security, performance, and operational insights.	Provides real-time monitoring and alerting of potential security breaches.
	Prometheus	A monitoring and alerting toolkit designed for large-scale containerized environments, particularly Kubernetes.	Tracks performance and security of microservices and containerized apps.
CI/CD Pipeline Auditing	Jenkins (Jenkinsfile)	Automates CI/CD pipelines while ensuring compliance by tracking code changes and security vulnerabilities.	Used to monitor Jenkins pipeline for security vulnerabilities and policy violations.
	GitOps (Argo CD, GitFlux)	Ensures continuous delivery with GitOps, auditing every change in the code repository for security compliance.	Automatically monitors and audits Git repositories for security breaches.

6. BEST PRACTICES FOR DATA GOVERNANCE AND SECURITY

It is crucial to note that data governance and security play a pivotal role in implementing DevSecOps since protecting sensitive data is extremely important for most organizations and falls into compliance with the relevant standards (Rajapakse et al., 2022). These practices also keep data secure and support compliance with objectives and requirements that an organization sets for development processes, making stakeholders put their trust in what is being delivered to them.

One of the significant areas in integrating data governance with DevSecOps relates to the regulation of existing practices about existing standards. International standards such as ISO 27001 or the NIST Cybersecurity Framework offer frameworks of best practices for running information security to guarantee the protection, further integrities and accessibility of data (OneTrust, 2022). Thus, by incorporating these frameworks into the DevSecOps process, the field will be capable of recognizing owners and responsible parties for data and access rights. This alignment assists in maintaining sound security policies across development and operation to minimize risks of data leakages and non-compliance.

Data classification and sensitivity levels are the strong pillars of data governance. Another opinion on where to apply DevSecOps is significant for understanding the quality of the processed data. Classification means sorting data by sensitivity, including PII, financial records or IP. After the information has been classified, an organization can put in specific security measures commensurate to the risk level assigned to the data (Kranz, 2022). For example, as posting top-secret information is improper, such data must be encrypted or accessed only by the authorized person. In contrast, the information that is not restricted may have less lenient measures. Creating these classifications guarantees that all data is being processed within the firm's internal policies and the external regulatory requirements to prevent leakage or misuse of this information.

The underpinning of modern DevSecOps is automation, and its utilization in data governance and protection makes lucrative sense (Patni, 2023). Integrating security checks and policies into the CI/CD pipeline means that incidences of vulnerabilities or non-compliant configurations will be flagged and resolved before going to production. Again, code analysis, both structural and behavioral, and compliance auditing tools that scan the application for compliance with security standards can run all the time (Smith, 2022). For instance, protocols relating to encrypted messaging and banned storage can be implemented without human intervention to minimize errors in security regulation. Automation also improves productivity, enabling a team to concentrate on creativity without worrying about risk factors.

Incident response and recovery planning are crucial in handling data and security within DevSecOps (Kumar, 2024). Although breaches should not happen, incidents may occur occasionally, so structured plans are essential. These plans provide a roadmap on how to detect, avoid and control the occurrences of security breaches to preserve business operations. Incident response planning requires the identification of duties and tasks, organizing response communication procedures, and conducting exercises that involve emulating real-life events (Kirvan, 2024). Furthermore, recovery strategies guarantee that lost systems and data can be regained quickly so that downtimes and business losses will be honorable. Therefore, data accuracy and security in DevSecOps also require collaboration and management culture. Security must not be viewed as an issue hindering trialing and innovation but as a means of setting up protective measures. Thus, organizations can have a security governance structure in which security is part of processes and outcomes and share responsibility for improving software deterministic security. This shifted culture makes it possible that data governance is not an add-on issue but a core aspect of the developmental process.

7. ADAPTING TO EMERGING TECHNOLOGIES

Securing data in AI-driven and ML pipelines

With the new technologies being released in software development, DevSecOps must adapt to the updated functions of protecting vital information. Technologies like AI, ML, cloud-native solutions, and zero-trust security concepts are open possibilities but have risks. Implementing solutions for these trends is comparable with proactive actions involving security at every development stage.

Protecting the input and output data in AI and ML processes is one of the most challenging tasks in the modern DevSecOps environment. AI and ML models require some data input, and such data may contain PII data or financial records and health information. Preserving this data requires cooperation across multiple strategies (Khalid et al., 2023). Data anonymization approaches, including differential privacy, can supplement the condition whereby sensitive data cannot be connected directly to individuals, even during the data preparation for training the ML components. Besides, the pipeline must be safeguarded by encryption for stored data and in transit and access controls for user roles (Shenoy, 2024).

Also, adversarial attacks on AI models entail attacks in which malicious parties try to alter the input data, affecting the performance of the models present. Traditional methods like adversarial training, where clean models are trained on manually poisoned data, and overall secure model deployment frameworks are emerging as essential (Zhou et al., 2022). Ensuring that ML models are explainable and auditable improves their reliability and safeguarding.

Handling Sensitive Data In Cloud-Native And Containerized Environments

Managing information and data assets stored in cloud-native and containerized systems involves covering new challenges linked to distributed architectures. Several architectural patterns are characteristic of cloud-native applications, including microservices, containers, and serverless functions, which depend on APIs and shared services (Oyeniran et al., 2024). Protecting these environments entails restricting the levels of privileges that its members possess, using encryption to cover communications between services, and keeping a close eye on API abuse.

Most modern applications are containerized using tools like Docker and run on the Kubernetes platform, which has security concerns. Situations when containers are placed on the public network, or workloads are not adequately separated can compromise the system. DevSecOps teams must use container orchestration, like Kubernetes Network Policies, to get the segmentation and container runtime security tools like Aqua Security or Falco to detect suspicious activities (Pournader, 2024). Another critical step is the vulnerability scan of the container images before deploying them on production, which is another paramount measure.

Adopting Zero Trust Architecture in DevSecOps

Zero Trust Architecture (ZTA) within DevSecOps is a modern approach that transforms how organizations defend their data. Unlike perimeter-based models, Zero Trust does not assume trust within a network and operates on the principle of "never trust, always verify." This philosophy fits perfectly with modern software development pipelines' mobile and distributed nature, where resources are accessed from multiple physical locations and devices (Garey, 2024). In the Zero Trust model, every sign-in must be authenticated, authorized and continuously validated, whether within or outside the network. This is done by integrating advanced identity and access management (IAM) solutions, multi-factor authentication (MFA), and commoditization of access control methods (Gittlen, 2021). For example, developers accessing sensitive data in a storehouse must undergo strict identity verification and comply with predefined security policies.

Zero Trust also requires micro-segmentation of the network and smaller sub-networks that reduce the potential damage from a break-in. Micro-segmentation in a DevSecOps pipeline means an attacker might penetrate one component, such as a container or CI/CD process, but this cannot spread to other system parts (Maayan, 2022). Paired with continual monitoring to detect threats, this Zero Trust provides staff with the immediate sight of security hazards to act on deviations from normal in real-time.

In addition, by implementing Zero Trust in cloud-native environments, developers could deploy tools and practices that had been specifically designed for dynamic infrastructure, such as using service mesh technology like Istio to protect inter-service communications; policy-as-code frameworks are brought in to define and enforce access rules automatically Zero Trust principles are combined with DevSecOps pipelines to help protect sensitive data, reduce insider threats, and ensure compliance with strict regulatory requirements.

8. CASE STUDIES AND INDUSTRY INSIGHTS

Case Study 1: Capital One's Transformation Towards Secure DevSecOps

DevSecOps can be described well in terms of the real-life example of Capital One, one of the most significant financial companies. Seeing the desperate need for data protection, especially when dealing with highly monitored areas such as the banking sector, Capital One began adopting DevSecOps as part of its cloud transformation journey (Orban, 2018). Security has been embedded through the code development life cycle by adopting SDLC, where security by design has been adopted, automating security into products, making security more transparent and involving developers, security and operations teams (Dhaduk, 2022).

This way, Capital One deployed automated static and dynamic code analysis applications that helped eliminate possible risks at the initial development stage. Data was encrypted at rest and in motion while a strict RBAC was applied to prevent unauthorized access. One of them was that they had a secret centralization system that allowed securely storing credentials, API keys, etc.

Nevertheless, Capital One's 2019 data breach is an excellent lesson for why cybersecurity must be carried out actively, with constant monitoring and penetration testing to determine possible flawed configurations that require fixing (Khan et al., 2022). Consequently, Capital One has focused on developing the monitoring system and improving the action plan in case of incidents. This case shows that deploying appropriate security features and ensuring that all necessary configurations are done correctly is crucial.

Case Study 2: DevSecOps Practices Used by Netflix

DevSecOps has been grooming its presence in Netflix, a leading member of cloud-native emulations, and has effectively accommodated security mechanisms to control its decentralized environment. The company's DevSecOps principle is centered on automation, scalability, and resiliency. With open-source tools and custom paid services, the primary data safety in Netflix's development frameworks remains unblemished.

Among them, Netflix builds an in-house tool, Security Monkey, to identify misconfigurations and various security vulnerabilities within AWS environments (Venkatraman, 2014). Similarly, Netflix runs Chaos Engineering to challenge its security procedures and check system reliability under pressure (Pinnepu, 2023). Netflix also places importance on employee education, such that developers are security conscious, beginning with their education regarding loopholes in DevSecOps. Altogether, this proactive behavior has reduced the likelihood of such practices and improved the security of their systems (Payne, 2017). That is why, making security a part of DevSecOps, corresponding with their accelerated rate and scale of organization development, Netflix proves that DevSecOps can work at large organizations.

Lessons Learned from Data Breaches

Using successful implementation successes like Capital One and Netflix as references, it's essential to know that notorious data breaches show examples of vulnerabilities in DevSecOps pipelines. For example, the attack in 2020 with SolarWinds showed that the lack of security measures in software supply chains is a threat (Martínez & Durán, 2021). The hack involved injecting tainted code into updates for SolarWinds Orion, which were then disseminated to thousands of customers, such as large companies and governmental entities.

The breach revealed critical lessons: the need for a secure and strict supply chain, the role of code signing, which ensures program textual consistency, and the effectiveness of high access control measures to eliminate modifications from hostile individuals or groups. This experience highlighted the need to continuously implement a zero-trust model, especially as it relates to the protection of software delivery pipelines. Besides, these occurrences highlight the necessity of robust cybersecurity procedures, such as frequent patching, sophisticated threat detection, and user education.

Emerging Trends and Future Directions

DevSecOps is still early, but some main trends define it now. One realization that has taken place recently is the incorporation of AI and ML into security processes (Zhao et al., 2024). Advanced data analysis associated with AI solutions is widely utilized to identify discrepancies and forecast risks in security information processing. Another trend is related to the increasing concern to protect IaC. Since organizations increasingly depend on IaC to provision and manage cloud resources, software like Terraform and AWS CloudFormation needs security scans to validate configurations for compliance with best practices (Castro, 2024). Moreover, the implementation of Zero Trust Architecture (ZTA) is increasing steadily. Some may argue that DevSecOps is just an adoption of the "never trust, always verify" principle of ZTA, where all access requests are constantly checked to eliminate insider threats and attacker lateral movement. With increasing strictness in laws and regulations worldwide, compliance automation is on the rise. Firms are now using tools to self-check against compliance requirements to avoid penalties while achieving secure data handling.

9. CONCLUSION

Data security in DevSecOps pipelines is the primary concern when building software applications in contemporary society with great regard for innovation and security. This chapter has discussed basic concepts, approaches, and techniques for integrating security into the application development life cycle, secure programming, data obfuscation and hardening, advanced static and dynamic code analysis, secrets management, and monitoring solutions. Using security measures such as role-based access control, encryption, and, more importantly, security testing ensures the system has an elaborate defense against threats.

With organizations migrating increasingly to the cloud, cloud-native architectures, AI-driven pipelines and Zero Trust, the position of DevSecOps has been critical in securing data. Best practices were gained from cyber breaches, and the recent measures taken by popular Netflix and Capital One firms also focus on continuous security awareness and the shift towards constant technology change.

To address these challenges, organizations need to adopt information security, which operates on a model where security is everyone's concern, invest in modern tools and ensure compliance with policies regarding information protection. When implementing DevSecOps and striving to protect potentially vulnerable information, companies can better prepare and protect themselves as threats continue to evolve. It is now or never for anyone willing to protect the future of software development.

10. REFERENCES

Akbar, M. A., Smolander, K., Mahmood, S., & Alsanad, A. (2022). Toward successful DevSecOps in software development organizations: A decision-making framework. *Information and Software Technology*, 147, 106894. DOI: 10.1016/j.infsof.2022.106894

Ashwani, K. (2023, September 15). *What is OWASP ZAP and use cases of OWASP ZAP?* DevOpsSchool.com. https://www.devopsschool.com/blog/what-is-owasp-zap-and-use-cases-of-owasp-zap/

AWS. (n.d.). *What is Data Masking? - Static and Dynamic Data Masking Explained - AWS*. Amazon Web Services, Inc. https://aws.amazon.com/what-is/data-masking/

Bigelow, S. J. (2021, May 13). *CI/CD pipelines explained: Everything you need to know*. SearchSoftwareQuality. https://www.techtarget.com/searchsoftwarequality/CI-CD-pipelines-explained-Everything-you-need-to-know

Castro, H. (2024, December 9). *Integrating Infrastructure as Code (IaC) and Security into AWS DevSecOps Pipelines*. https://www.researchgate.net/publication/387270734_Integrating_Infrastructure_as_Code_IaC_and_Security_into_AWS_DevSecOps_Pipelines

Dhaduk, H. (2022, February 23). *Capital One DevOps Case Study: A Bank with the Heart of Tech Company*. Insights on Latest Technologies - Simform Blog. https://www.simform.com/blog/capital-one-devops-case-study/

Domoney, C. (2024). *7 DevSecOps tools to secure each step of the SDLC*. Search Security; TechTarget. https://www.techtarget.com/searchsecurity/tip/DevSecOps-tools-to-secure-each-step-of-the-SDLC

Fastercapital. (2024). *Pipeline Auditing: How to Check and Assess the Compliance and Conformance of Your Pipeline - FasterCapital*. FasterCapital. https://fastercapital.com/content/Pipeline-Auditing--How-to-Check-and-Assess-the-Compliance-and-Conformance-of-Your-Pipeline.html

Finch, H. (2024, February 15). *Managing Secrets in Your CI/CD Pipeline: Best Practices and Strategies*. Medium. https://medium.com/@haroldfinch01/managing-secrets-in-your-ci-cd-pipeline-best-practices-and-strategies-aef0d10e5395

Garey, L. (2024, October 3). *What Is Zero Trust Security?* Oracle.com; Oracle. https://www.oracle.com/ke/security/what-is-zero-trust/

Gittlen, S. (2021, August). *What Is Identity and Access Management? Guide to IAM*. SearchSecurity. https://www.techtarget.com/searchsecurity/definition/identity-access-management-IAM-system

Guyer, N. (2024, January 18). *Critical Considerations for Sensitive Information in a Data Breach*. Complete Discovery Source. https://cdslegal.com/insights/advisory-services/critical-considerations-for-sensitive-information-in-a-data-breach/

Harvard Business Review. (2024, January 16). *How SolarWinds Responded to the 2020 SUNBURST Cyberattack*. Harvard Business Review. https://hbr.org/podcast/2024/01/how-solarwinds-responded-to-the-2020-sunburst-cyberattack

HashiCorp. (2024). *Dynamic secrets | HashiCorp Cloud Platform | HashiCorp Developer*. Dynamic Secrets | HashiCorp Cloud Platform | HashiCorp Developer; HashiCorp. https://developer.hashicorp.com/hcp/docs/vault-secrets/dynamic-secrets

Keployio. (2024, October 11). *Mock Data: A Developer's Essential Tool for Testing and Development*. Medium. https://medium.com/@keployio/in-the-world-of-software-development-and-testing-mock-data-plays-a-crucial-role-in-simulating-e66b7b0182ca

Khalid, N., Qayyum, A., Bilal, M., Al-Fuqaha, A., & Qadir, J. (2023). Privacy-preserving artificial intelligence in healthcare: Techniques and applications. *Computers in Biology and Medicine*, 158(1), 106848. DOI: 10.1016/j.compbiomed.2023.106848 PMID: 37044052

Khan, S., Kabanov, I., Hua, Y., & Madnick, S. (2022). A Systematic Analysis of the Capital One Data Breach: Critical Lessons Learned. *ACM Transactions on Privacy and Security*, 26(1), 1–29. Advance online publication. DOI: 10.1145/3546068

Kirvan, P. (2024, October 16). *5 critical steps to creating an effective incident response plan*. SearchSecurity. https://www.techtarget.com/searchsecurity/feature/5-critical-steps-to-creating-an-effective-incident-response-plan

Kompaniiets, F. (2024, February 15). *Role-Based Access Control (RBAC) in Your CI/CD Pipeline: Best Practices for DevSecOps*. Gart. https://gartsolutions.com/role-based-access-control-rbac-in-your-ci-cd-pipeline-best-practices-for-devsecops/

Kranz, G. (2022, July). *What is Data Classification and Why is it Important?* SearchDataManagement. https://www.techtarget.com/searchdatamanagement/definition/data-classification

Kumar, V. (2024, June 9). *The Critical Role of Incident Response in DevSecOps - Practical DevSecOps*. Practical DevSecOps. https://www.practical-devsecops.com/the-critical-role-of-incident-response-in-devsecops/

Lutkevich, B. (2023, February). *What is Tokenization?* SearchSecurity. https://www.techtarget.com/searchsecurity/definition/tokenization

Maayan, G. D. (2022, November 28). *Why Microsegmentation is Critical for Securing CI/CD*. Security Boulevard. https://securityboulevard.com/2022/11/why-microsegmentation-is-critical-for-securing-ci-cd/

Martínez, J., & Durán, J. M. (2021). Software Supply Chain Attacks, a Threat to Global Cybersecurity: SolarWinds' Case Study. *International Journal of Safety and Security Engineering*, 11(5), 537–545. DOI: 10.18280/ijsse.110505

McCarvill, A. (2023, August 11). *An Introduction to the Importance of Input Validation in Preventing Security Vulnerabilities*. Bright Security. https://brightsec.com/blog/an-introduction-to-the-importance-of-input-validation-in-preventing-security-vulnerabilities/

Nyame, G., & Qin, Z. (2020). Precursors of Role-Based Access Control Design in KMS: A Conceptual Framework. *Information (Basel)*, 11(6), 334. DOI: 10.3390/info11060334

OneTrust. (2022, September 12). *ISO 27001 vs. NIST Cybersecurity Framework*. OneTrust. https://www.onetrust.com/blog/iso-27001-vs-nist-cybersecurity-framework/

Orban, S. (2018, April 6). *Capital One's Cloud Journey Through the Stages of Adoption*. AWS Enterprise Collection. https://medium.com/aws-enterprise-collection/capital-ones-cloud-journey-through-the-stages-of-adoption-bb0895d7772c

Oyeniran, O., Okechukwu, A., Adams, N., Anthony, L., & Azubuko, F. (2024). Microservices architecture in cloud-native applications: Design patterns and scalability. *Computer Science & IT Research Journal*, 5(9), 2107–2124. DOI: 10.51594/csitrj.v5i9.1554

Pahuja, A. (2022, January 4). *15 Best Dynamic Application Security Testing (DAST) Software*. Astra Security. https://www.getastra.com/blog/security-audit/top-dast-tools/

Palo Alto Networks. (2024). *What Is Sensitive Data?* Palo Alto Networks. https://www.paloaltonetworks.com/cyberpedia/sensitive-data

Patni, A. (2023, January 23). *What is DevSecOps Automation and its 5 Benefits*. Practical DevSecOps. https://www.practical-devsecops.com/devsecops-automation/

Payne, B. D. (2017, June 20). *Netflix Culture Meets Product Security*. Medium. https://medium.com/@bdpsecurity/netflix-culture-meets-product-security-599ceecd615d

Pinnepu, H. (2023, March 11). *How Netflix embraced Chaos*. Medium. https://medium.com/@haasitapinnepu/how-netflix-embraced-chaos-b1f054ab9892

Piskachev, G., Becker, M., & Bodden, E. (2023). Can the configuration of static analyses make resolving security vulnerabilities more effective? - A user study. *Empirical Software Engineering*, 28(5), 10–20. DOI: 10.1007/s10664-023-10354-3

Pournader, B. (2024, July 17). *Kubernetes and Container Security - Ben Pournader - Medium*. Medium. https://benpournader.medium.com/kubernetes-and-container-security-146b4dc7c742

Prates, L., & Pereira, R. (2024). DevSecOps practices and tools. *International Journal of Information Security*, 24(1), 11. Advance online publication. DOI: 10.1007/s10207-024-00914-z

Rajapakse, R. N., Zahedi, M., Babar, M. A., & Shen, H. (2022). Challenges and solutions when adopting DevSecOps: A systematic review. *Information and Software Technology*, 141, 10–67. DOI: 10.1016/j.infsof.2021.106700

Sandu, A. K. (2021). *DevSecOps: Integrating Security into the DevOps Lifecycle for Enhanced Resilience*. 6(1), 1–19. https://www.researchgate.net/publication/380629263_DevSecOps_Integrating_Security_into_the_DevOps_Lifecycle_for_Enhanced_Resilience

Schroeder, P. (2020, August 6). *Capital One to pay $80 million fine after data breach*. Reuters. https://www.reuters.com/article/business/capital-one-to-pay-80-million-fine-after-data-breach-idUSKCN2522D8/

Sharma, P., Johari, R., & Sarma, S. S. (2012). Integrated approach to prevent SQL injection attack and reflected cross site scripting attack. *International Journal of System Assurance Engineering and Management*, 3(4), 343–351. DOI: 10.1007/s13198-012-0125-6

Shenoy, S. (2024, February 2). *Authentication of Data Pipelines: Key Strategies to Secure and Control Your Workflow*. Learn | Hevo; Hevo Data. https://hevodata.com/learn/authentication-of-data-pipelines/

Smith, J. (2022, May 19). *Code security auditing 101*. Snyk. https://snyk.io/articles/code-security-audit/

Son, S. J., & Kwon, Y. (2017, November 1). *Performance of ELK stack and commercial system in security log analysis*. IEEE Xplore. DOI: 10.1109/MICC.2017.8311756

Tahir. (2024, December 15). *Encrypt Data with AWS Key Management Service KMS - Tahir - Medium*. Medium. https://medium.com/@tahirbalarabe2/encrypt-data-with-aws-key-management-service-kms-ccdddeb46b59

Tariq, U., Ahmed, I., Bashir, A. K., & Shaukat, K. (2023). A critical cybersecurity analysis and future research directions for the internet of things: A comprehensive review. *Sensors, 23*(8). MDPI. DOI: 10.3390/s23084117

Temple-Raston, D. (2021, April 16). *A "worst nightmare" cyberattack: the untold story of the SolarWinds hack*. NPR. https://www.npr.org/2021/04/16/985439655/a-worst-nightmare-cyberattack-the-untold-story-of-the-solarwinds-hack

The Turing Way Community. (2024). *Types of Sensitive Data - overview — The Turing Way*. The-Turing-Way.org. https://book.the-turing-way.org/project-design/sdp/types.html

University of Edinburgh. (2022, October 27). *Definition of sensitive data*. The University of Edinburgh. https://infosec.ed.ac.uk/how-to-protect/encrypting/use-cases/short-definition-of-sensitive-data

Venkatraman, A. (2014). *Netflix releases its AWS monitoring tool Security Monkey into the wild*. ComputerWeekly.com. https://www.computerweekly.com/news/2240223908/Netflix-releases-its-AWS-monitoring-tool-Security-Monkey-into-the-wild

Zhao, X., Clear, T., & Lal, R. (2024). Identifying the primary dimensions of DevSecOps: A multi-vocal literature review. *Journal of Systems and Software/the Journal of Systems and Software*, 112063–112063. DOI: 10.1016/j.jss.2024.112063

Zhou, S., Liu, C., Ye, D., Zhu, T., Zhou, W., & Yu, P. S. (2022). Adversarial Attacks and Defenses in Deep Learning: From a Perspective of Cybersecurity. *ACM Computing Surveys*, 55(8), 1–39. Advance online publication. DOI: 10.1145/3547330

KEY TERMS AND DEFINITIONS

Software Development Life Cycle (SDLC): A plan employed in software development to organize the process of writing, testing, implementing and maintaining the software. It comprises the following steps: requirements, analysis and design, implementation, testing, deployment and maintenance, hence improving the quality of software.

Role-based Access Control (RBAC): An access control model that prevents different users in an organization from accessing most parts of a system based on their responsibilities. Users are created with relevant roles to the resources they need to utilize and have preprogrammed authorities that maintain security and organization.

Chaos Engineering: A process carried out in software systems in order to assess and enhance their capability to recover from faults and failures in an environment that simulates such incidents. The objective is to look for the flaws and confirm that systems can cope with different incidents.

Machine Learning (ML): A broad field of AI that uses statistical techniques to analyse data and make predictions. An ML system learns from experience, which means that its performance is adjusted in the context of its use without coding it.

Artificial Intelligence (AI): AI can be defined as the creation of human intelligence in machines intended, for instance, for solving problems, learning, perceiving or making decisions. This application of AI has different subtopics, such as machine learning, natural language processing and robotics.

Zero Trust Architecture: An architectural model that is derived from the need to ask the question, "never trust, always verify." It presumes that threats may emanate from inside and outside the network and thus demand constant authentication and validation of all users and devices.

Dynamic Application Security Testing (DAST): DAST is a technique for testing software during and at its runtime. It involves emulating an external attacker in an attempt to find security flaws in a given running application. DAST usually searches for security vulnerabilities in Web applications that might be dangerous to an organization.

Continuous Integration and Continuous Delivery (CI/CD): Continuous Integration (CI) specifically means that developers frequently integrate changes in code into a common source code repository and then run a set of tests for those changes. Continuous Delivery (CD) then takes these changes and automates their delivery to production environments, meaning that the code is always in a state for deployment, hence shortening the release cycles.

Data Masking: A procedure that replaces actual information with simulated data that looks realistic while concealing shareholders' identities. This is used to shield data where perhaps actual data is not required or ought not to be used, such as in testing, developing and similar cases.

Anonymization: The action of withdrawing certain information from data so that the particulars cannot be easily recognized.

Micro-segmentation: Micro-segmentation is a security concept that involves segmenting a network into smaller compartments to reduce the attacker's mobility. Compared to large, broad security zones, micro-segmentation reduces the possible attack paths and improves security on the extended network.

Chapter 12
The Role of Artificial Intelligence in Bridging DevOps and SecOps for Cloud Infrastructure

Karthik Ratnam
https://orcid.org/0009-0003-3725-6165
Workday Inc., USA

ABSTRACT

With the movement of IT assets to the cloud, strong security and resilience are more important than ever. This paper discusses DevOps and SecOps integration, or DevSecOps, to increase security while enabling fast deployments. Encouraging collaboration between development, operations, and security teams, organizations can find and fix vulnerabilities early in the software lifecycle. The paper highlights the main idea of embedding automated security checks throughout the CI/CD pipeline using 24/7 monitoring, real-time threat detection, and agile incident response. This can be taken further with AI and ML integration through automating processes, offering predictive analytics, and mitigating vulnerabilities before exploitation. This framework helps to speed up threat mitigation and enhances reliability and agility in security responses. DevSecOps enables organizations to innovate safely while protecting digital assets amid evolving threats.

1. INTRODUCTION

With increasing digitization, businesses these days leverage cloud computing to innovate and scale with unparalleled speeds. Cloud infrastructure has really pushed innovation in application development and deployment because of its elasticity and cost optimization. This rapid pace of evolution also created some very serious security and operational resilience challenges. Traditional security often doesn't work for these environments that change almost each hour due to updates and new deployments. Addressing

DOI: 10.4018/979-8-3373-0365-9.ch012

these challenges requires making the integration of Development Operations and Security Operations, now coined as DevSecOps, a necessity.

This chapter focuses on the changing significance of combining Artificial Intelligence (AI) with DevOps and SecOps in building cloud infrastructure security and operational resilience. Aside from the fact that during such a period of rapid digital transformation forcing unprecedented scalability and innovation, cloud environments are increasingly plagued by complexities, challenges, and compliance requirements that grow over time. The developmental Operations integrated with Security Operations are herein referred to as DevSecOps; it is a major approach that embeds security throughout the software development lifecycle. Organizations will significantly augment their capabilities to identify threats, verify compliance, and make effective use of resources thereby creating more secure and efficient cloud operations when integrating AI with ML into the mix.

Advanced AI capabilities in DevSecOps will empower organizations to confidently tackle the complexities associated with today's cloud environments while ensuring scalable, secure, and innovative solutions. This chapter gives an in-depth overview of these key concepts and their application.

1.1 Literature Review: Theoretical Foundations and Recent Studies

The combination of DevOps, SecOps, and cloud infrastructure with Artificial Intelligence (AI) marks a significant shift in the fight against current operational challenges and security issues. Literature that examines the changing role of AI in making security operations easier, increasing automation, and being resilient in cloud contexts is essential for developing a solid theoretical background. The impact of pioneering research and contemporary developments on the transformation of cloud systems by AI-driven DevSecOps practices is crucial while considering ethical, practical, and technological dimensions.

The inclusion of security within DevOps practices, commonly referred to as DevSecOps, arose due to the identification of security vulnerabilities inherent in traditional development methodologies. Foundational principles, such as those described by Ebert et al. (2016), require the instillation of security measures throughout the SDLC process so that risks can be diminished and responses to incidents hastened. Likewise, Zhao et al. emphasize the multi-dimensionality of their 2024 exposition on key elements that foster secure and resilient systems: collaboration, automation, and continuous compliance with regulations. The two provided frameworks will aid in establishing a convergence between artificial intelligence and enhanced agility in deploying DevOps and SecOps harmonization.

Recent studies emphasize the significant change that AI and ML are bringing to the existing DevSecOps frameworks. Tools powered by AI greatly enhance the capability of detecting threats, responding to incidents, and optimizing resources. For instance, Rahman et al. (2023) point out that machine learning algorithms analyze vast amounts of data to determine anomalies and predict vulnerabilities before they can grow. These predictive analytics not only bolster an organization's security posture but also enhance its operational resilience by proactively tackling potential risks. In practical terms, AI-driven solutions slash response times, automate compliance checks, and reduce the manual workload needed to sustain systems' integrity.

Moreover, empirical research demonstrates the effectiveness of AI-driven automation in cloud-native environments. For instance, Colander's 2022 study illustrates that organizations integrating AI within DevSecOps pipelines experience tangible improvements in system availability while effectively reducing downtime and compliance deviations. Here, continuous monitoring tools rely on AI to detect threats in real time and make dynamic adjustments to changing security landscapes, particularly when operating in multi-cloud or hybrid cloud environments. This level of automation ensures that security controls remain consistent and flexible across even the most complex infrastructures.

However, alongside its advantages, AI brings about significant ethical considerations that require attention in the quest for fair and transparent AI. Previous literature on AI ethics has warned about the potential risks of biases within algorithms operating under AI, especially in threat detection systems where data inputs are insufficiently represented; this could lead to false positives or even vulnerabilities being missed. Zhao, Clear, and Lal (2024) suggest that we need to have Explainable AI (XAI) frameworks rather than just if something will work out of XAI so that the decisions made by AI are interpretable, transparent, and auditable. The debates over ethical issues such as data privacy and regulatory compliance like GDPR also remind companies how important it is to strike a balance between innovation and responsible use of AId.

Case studies further illustrate the practical challenges and benefits of employing AI in DevSecOps, especially for small and medium-sized enterprises. On one hand, small and medium-sized enterprises often face different types of challenges when implementing advanced security frameworks due to factors such as budget constraints or limited access to technical expertise. However, recent research has shown that cloud-native, AI-driven tools fill the gap by providing scalable and affordable solutions for threat detection, compliance verification, and operational resilience. Such as in the case of anomaly detection and predictive analytics capabilities; AI-enabled platforms allow SMEs to practice effective security methodologies without overhead on infrastructure. More importantly, these demonstrate how AI democratizes security capabilities regardless of organizational size.

The addition of recent research, empirical evidence, and ethical considerations makes the expanded literature review resourceful enough to expose the relationship between DevOps, SecOps, and AI. This conceptual framework will capture the disruptiveness of AI-enabled DevSecOps implementations while confronting their related challenges. Continuously changing cloud environments require this convergence to be relevant for improvements in security, operational efficiency, and resilience of contemporary IT infrastructures.

2. ENHANCING CLOUD SECURITY AND OPERATIONAL RESILIENCE WITH Dev Ops & Sec Ops

2.1 Cloud security

Cloud security comprises a set of policies, controls and procedures that work together to protect information/data in the cloud. Many businesses are already using cloud-based applications with application & data residing in the cloud. Therefore, it becomes extremely critical to deploy good security measures in place that will help businesses to protect sensitive data and maintain business continuity.

Cloud Security is one of the foremost concerns among related stakeholders. Each concern brings diverse effects on discrete assets while analyzing the security issues in Cloud Computing. In spite of various studies, we still fail to define the needs of security, resulting in a slow pace in cloud adoption. Accordingly, a fresh approach is required to facilitate end-users and service providers to better understand the domain so that they can easily address their security requirements and find their solutions.

Some of the Cloud Security building blocks are:

Data Protection:

Encryption: All data that flows in and out of the cloud including those using the approach of APIs, as well as when they are at rest, need to be protected with quality encryption technology.

Data Loss Prevention (DLP): Describes precautions to take to avoid loss of data and its main function lies in monitoring the transfer of data.

IAM (Identity and Access Management): Limit Cloud resources to approved & privileged users. The combination may involve multi factor authentication, role-based access controls and user identity verification.

Network Security: It's important to secure the cloud Infrastructure from External Threats. Such controls are Firewalls, Intrusion Detection Systems and Virtual Private Networks (VPNs)

Intrusion Detection and Response: Using continuous monitoring solutions to detect anomalies and threats in real time This comprises threat intelligence via an artificial intelligence and machine learning perspective.

Incident Response Planning: Creating and updating incident response plans for responding to security incidents in a rapid manner. This involves communication standards and response mechanisms.

Challenges in Cloud Security

Shared Responsibility Model: In the cloud, typically security is shared between the cloud vendor and their consumers. Businesses must know that they oversee securing their data and applications.

Dynamic Environments: The high-speed provisioning and deployment of resources is at crossroads with traditional security controls. The practices on security need to adjust to this constantly changing scenario.

Challenges in Multi-Cloud Strategies: As various organizations, one preferably enterprise, move to multi-cloud strategies, it may be difficult to enforce the security configurations uniformly and consistently across multiple platforms.

Cloud Security Best Practices

Security first: Embed security in the lifecycle early by requiring that security be part of application design and deployment process.

Compliance with New Security Policies: Because requirements are regularly evolving, security policies continually need to adapt, and new compliance policies must be met.

User Education and Training: Ongoing training to enable employees to recognize security threats, use best practices; compliance with security protocols.

Automation and AI: Automation tools for threat detection, incident response, compliance management reduce the dependent on manual processes, improve accuracy (reduced human errors)

Develop Clear Policies and Procedures: Establish a well-documented security policy that clearly delineates administration roles, responsibilities and processes for maintaining cloud security.

Therefore, in this era of evolutions in cloud computing, security is the success factor for any enterprise by protecting their assets and with it holding up their client faith. Leveraging these best practices and proactive security approach, enterprises can overcome the challenges around cloud environments to secure their data from evolving threats.

Security is one of the biggest obstacles that hamper the widespread adoption of cloud computing. Several business and research organization are reluctant in completely trusting cloud computing to shift digital assets to the third-party service providers. Adams and Bellucci highlight the necessity of embedding security within the continuous integration and continuous deployment (CI/CD) pipelines to ensure that security is a priority throughout the development lifecycle, not an afterthought. Jones et al.

detail these challenges, emphasizing the importance of adopting a unified security strategy that is both comprehensive and adaptable to the fluid nature of hybrid cloud infrastructures.

2.2 Operational Resilience

Operational resilience in the realm of cloud infrastructure describes how well an organization can keep its services running and critical capabilities functioning through any kinds of disaster be it from technical failures, cyber-attacks, or natural disasters. Today, many of primary workloads are on the cloud, so forming an operational resilience is important for business continuity and to reduce downtimes.

Few of the building blocks for Operational Resilience:

High Level of Redundancy and Availability: Multiple DC (data centers) or backup systems are designed in a way that there is always some redundancy to handle these failures. Such systems include load balancers and failover mechanisms.

Disaster Recovery Planning: Creating detailed disaster recovery plans that delineate processes for recovering information and returning services to operational states following a service interruption. This involves routine examination of recovery procedures to evaluate their efficacy.

Incident Management: Developing robust guidelines around how to recognize, react, and fix a problem. The process includes defining the role and responsibility, communication plans, and escalation procedures.

Monitoring and Analytics: Continuous Monitoring solutions to track the performance of your system and catch potential problems before they become big. Operations metrics and performance trends through use of analytics

Scalability: Quickly adjusts on the scale-out cloud model based on the changing needs. It means resources that automatically scale with usage patterns to meet performance needs during peak times.

Change Management: Implementing change management in the cloud which does not adversely affect the infrastructure to service continuity. This involves testing and verification of changes made.

Operational Resilience Challenges

Cloud Environments Complexity: With multi-cloud and hybrid cloud strategies, businesses can face complexity problems which make it difficult to keep a single operational resilience across all the platforms.

Third-party dependencies: Use of third-party services can always be a downside as any disruption to these means going down for the organization.

Threat landscape continues to evolve: Just like cybersecurity threats themselves, businesses also need to be ready for new strategies of resilience due to fresh vulnerabilities.

Operational Resilience Practices

Perform Risk Analysis: Continuously assess potential threats in relation to operational continuity and classify them according to frequency and impact.

Develop a Business Continuity Plan (BCP): A BCP provides strategies and monetary plans in case of emergencies, including devices for resource acquisitions and communications.

Invest in Training and Awareness: Training on the importance of operational resilience for all employees while ensuring that they know their part to stick to an operation as well as providing incident response and recovery practices.

Leverage Automation: Automate common tasks as well as recovery processes to eliminate human errors and decrease reaction times when incidents occur.

Key behaviors to foster in every team are proactivity and continuous improvement in operational practices fostering a culture of resilience.

All resilience plans to include disaster recovery and business continuity strategies should be reviewed and re-worked to reflect changes in the business environment on a regular basis.

Organizations running workloads on cloud infrastructure need to be operationally resilient to maintain their ability to support systems and services during disruptions. By following best practices, adopting cloud services, and instilling a culture of resilience in the organisation, organisations can better prepare themselves to handle these challenges, secure their properties and uphold customer confidence as they navigate an ever more volatile world.

Scalability allows these systems to adjust resources based on business needs without significant hardware investments, benefiting SMEs with fluctuating demands or rapid growth. More so, since these systems are hosted on the cloud, they can be accessed from anywhere with an internet connection, enabling real- time data sharing and effective collaboration across the organization, essential in today's globalized business environment. The application of anomaly detection in cloud resilience can help to improve system availability, reduce downtime, and improve system performance. It can also help to improve system security by detecting and preventing malicious activity. AI/ML can be used to identify patterns and anomalies in large volumes of data, monitor system performance, and detect and predict potential failures or outages. It can also be used to optimize resource utilization and dynamically adjust resource provisioning to meet changing demand. This combination of AI/ML techniques has the potential to improve the reliability and efficiency of cloud systems.

2.3 Security & Resilience with DevOps & SecOps

The convergence of DevOps & SecOPs are important to cloud workloads when we think about security & operational resiliency. By making sure that data is safe, and business can continue even when a critical system like an AWS cloud platform has been set up as a significant part of operations, to address the needs.

The formulation of a list, enumerating potential threats during the IaC process remains an unattained goal. However, it is not enough to recounting IaC threats only, it is imperative for Development (Dev), Security (Sec), and Operations (Ops) teams to synergistically collaborate from early developmental stages to conduct thorough risks' analysis, estimation, and mitigation procedures concerning IaC-related risks. Moreover, adhering to security standards and risk management framework throughout the IaC lifecycle will enhance the overall security of the deployment process. A risk management framework for IaC is essential. The extant risk management and threat modelling methodologies may necessitate tailoring to effectively protect the Software Development Lifecycle (SDLC) from IaC misuse.

The main type of security that needs to be implemented on all possible levels (from employees to engineering, and beyond) is Cloud Security. This includes data protection, identity and access management, compliance, and threat detection.

It is the ability of an organization to quickly restore critical services and return to its normal mode of operation following a disruption. This umbrella includes redundancy, disaster recovery, incident management, and continuous monitoring of basically every workload to ensure the services stay online.

DevOps: Collaboration culture and practices businesses should follow between development & operations teams. Its goal is to simplify processes, speed up deployment and enhance the overall quality of the software.

SecOps: Integration of security practices into the DevOps culture, meaning to keep security from being treated as an afterthought but in fact a priority that ties together with every DevOps aspect while application flows through development life cycle.

How can both DevOps and SecOps benefit to enhance security and resiliency within a cloud environment?

Security practices: By including security in the DevOps pipeline, businesses can automate these checks throughout the code development and deployment process. It is not just for automated testing, vulnerability scanning or compliance checks but for creating a secure development pipeline from the birth of the application stage.

Continuous Monitoring and Feedback: With the help of DevOps practices, businesses can use an open-source continuous monitoring tool which helps in gaining a real-time glimpse of security posture or operational performance. Time to Remediate allows teams to react quickly in the event of an incident, viewing system health, and identifying potential vulnerabilities before they grow into a serious issue.

Agile Incident Response: By integrating security teams into the DevOps process, SecOps extends and refines incident response capabilities. It enables the quick detection and investigation of security incidents, which in turn minimizes downtime and potential harm.

Built to Scale: How Automation Drives Resiliency

Automation tools can help to streamline security and operational resilience processes equally. With automated backups, recovery procedures, and security patches, organizations can always be prepared to regain services and compliance in a rapid fashion with minimal manual effort.

Compliance and Governance: By incorporating SecOps into DevOps businesses have continuous compliance adherence instead of occasional auditing. The approach automates most compliance checks and maintains extensive logs that organizations can use to facilitate regulatory reporting and audits.

Cultural Shift to Collaboration: Developing the culture of collaboration among development, operations, and security agencies is of utmost importance. The cultural change empowers everyone to take responsibility for their security and operational resilience, and as a result fosters more proactive risk management and innovation.

Practices to Improve Security and Operational Resilience in the Cloud

Develop a Security-First Approach: Incorporate security as part of every stage in the development process, making security something that is baked in throughout planning to release.

Training and Awareness: Provide similar awareness to teams, including regular training on latest security threats and guidance on how to use security tools and best practices.

Establish your robust change management process: Put in place run books for handling changes in the cloud that could lead to undesired disruptions or security flaws.

Schedule frequent security audits: Continually assess security practices and operational resilience strengthening measures looking for failure points, gaps or areas to improve.

Utilize Cloud Native Security Tools: Leverage indigenous security functionalities, such as encryption, identity management and monitoring tools provided by cloud service providers.

Establish a Complete Incident Response: Whole outputs fall flat if businesses never have a course for response to the incidents. It's important to have an incident response plan those details roles, responsibilities and procedures to handle security incidents and operational disruptions effectively

Modern organizations require to infuse DevOps and SecOps in the cloud security and operational resilience frameworks. The more an organization can work together, automate operations and focus attention on raising detection alerts, the better its chances of staving off a digital disaster. This non-siloed methodology not only secures cloud environments, but it also enables businesses to unabashedly innovate knowing they can handle the biggest challenges and opportunities in the cloud.

Rapid innovation and potential security oversight necessitate a profound integration of security into the development lifecycle, transforming traditional DevOps into a more robust DevSecOps framework.

Figure 1. DevSecOps Model

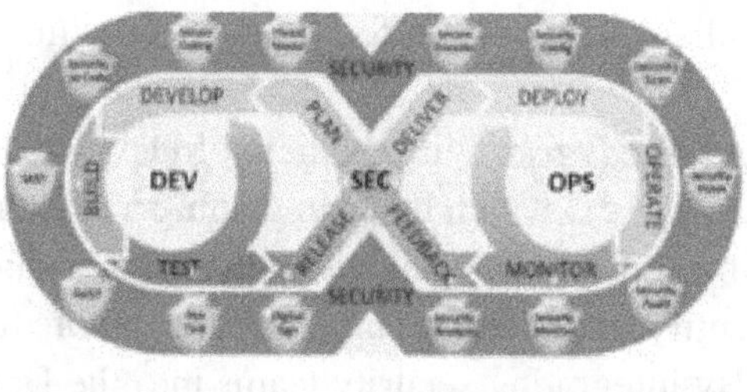

Organizations that have adopted DevOps experienced 60 times fewer failures and deploy 30 times more frequently than organizations that have not adopted DevOps. Despite the popularity, security aspects of DevOps remain a concern for organizations that want to adopt DevOps. Security as a key non-functional requirement of software development is often ignored and devalued in DevOps programs, with security seen as an inhibitor to high velocity required in DevOps implementation. Hence, the DevSecOps approach as a security-orientated expansion to DevOps, has aimed to integrate security into DevOps implementation by promoting collaboration among development, operation and security teams. Cloud systems, cloud resources, and cloud services need to be designed to counter the risks identified in the operating environment. Based on the jurisdiction, industry, and consumers the program represents, any of the various international, state, legislative, industry, and regional security requirements may apply. These specifications define security features and deployment procedures in the application or on the network and networks on which the software runs.

2.4 Practical Case Studies in AI-Driven DevSecOps

The integration of DevOps, SecOps, and Artificial Intelligence (AI) has fundamentally transformed how organizations address cloud security, operational resilience, and software delivery. While the theoretical frameworks highlight the potential benefits, real-world case studies provide practical insights into the challenges and opportunities faced by organizations of varying sizes. Practical examples illustrate how AI-driven DevSecOps solutions have improved security posture, automated compliance, and reduced operational downtime in complex cloud environments.

2.4.1 Case Study: Automating Threat Detection for Large Enterprises

A global financial services company faced significant challenges in managing security threats within their cloud-native environment. The traditional SecOps processes relied heavily on manual incident monitoring, resulting in delayed responses to critical threats. By implementing an AI-driven threat detection system integrated into their DevSecOps pipeline, the organization achieved significant improvements.

- **AI Implementation**: The system utilized machine learning algorithms to analyze real-time data streams, identify anomalies, and predict potential security breaches before they occurred.
- **Outcomes**:
  - o Threat detection time was reduced by 70%.
  - o False positives decreased by 50%, enabling SecOps teams to focus on high-priority alerts.
  - o Automated incident response workflows improved resolution times and minimized operational disruptions.

This case demonstrates how large enterprises can leverage AI to streamline threat detection, reduce manual intervention, and proactively address vulnerabilities, ensuring both security and operational resilience.

2.4.2 Case Study: Enhancing Compliance for SMEs with AI-Based Automation

Small and Medium-Sized Enterprises (SMEs) often face challenges in adopting DevSecOps frameworks due to resource constraints, limited expertise, and compliance complexities. A mid-sized e-commerce company implemented an AI-powered compliance automation tool to overcome these barriers.

- **AI Implementation**: The AI-driven system integrated with the DevOps pipeline to automate compliance checks, such as GDPR and PCI DSS requirements. It provided continuous monitoring of cloud configurations and identified misconfigurations or non-compliance issues in real-time.
- **Outcomes**:
  - o Compliance reporting time was reduced by 60%.
  - o Operational costs for manual audits decreased significantly.
  - o The system ensured ongoing adherence to regulatory standards without requiring additional staff or expertise.

This example highlights how AI tools enable SMEs to achieve continuous compliance efficiently and cost-effectively, leveling the playing field with larger organizations.

2.4.3. Case Study: AI-Driven Incident Management in Hybrid Cloud Environments

A multinational technology company operating in a hybrid cloud environment experienced frequent security incident caused by the complexity of managing multi-cloud workloads. Traditional incident response strategies struggled to keep up with the dynamic threat landscape.

- **AI Implementation**: The company deployed an AI-enabled incident management platform that combined predictive analytics and automated workflows to detect, prioritize, and respond to incidents across multiple cloud platforms.
- **Outcomes**:
  - o Incident resolution time was reduced from hours to minutes.
  - o The platform identified patterns and vulnerabilities across multi-cloud workloads, enhancing system visibility.
  - o Downtime due to security incidents decreased by 40%, ensuring higher operational resilience.

This case study demonstrates how AI-powered solutions can simplify incident management, improve response times, and reduce complexity in hybrid cloud environments.

2.4.4. Case Study: Resource Optimization Using AI in Cloud Infrastructure

A startup operating in the healthcare sector faced challenges related to resource utilization and performance optimization in their cloud infrastructure. With fluctuating workloads, maintaining operational efficiency and security was a constant concern.

- **AI Implementation**: AI-driven tools for resource optimization were integrated into the DevSecOps framework. These tools analyzed usage patterns, identified underutilized resources, and dynamically adjusted provisioning to meet demand.
- **Outcomes**:
    - Resource costs were reduced by 30% through efficient allocation.
    - Performance bottlenecks were eliminated, improving system response times during peak workloads.
    - Continuous security monitoring ensured that resource adjustments did not introduce vulnerabilities.

This case highlights how AI can optimize cloud infrastructure, reduce operational costs, and enhance both performance and security—critical for resource-sensitive industries like healthcare.

2.5 Challenges & Considerations

There are numerous challenges to consider before implementing the strategies of combining DevOps and SecOps to improve cloud security and operational resilience. The importance of appreciating such challenges cannot be underestimated when establishing resilient strategies capable of combating changing threats and operational considerations.

2.5.1 Cloud Environments Complexity

Problem: As enterprises shift to multi-cloud and hybrid cloud deployments, the corresponding expansion of complexity can fracture security policies and practices from one platform to another.
Cloud security strategy fields: An organization should build an all-encompassing cloud security strategy in this regard which ensures that the compatibility and interoperability of security tools and practices across isn't compromised.

2.5.2 Shared Responsibility Model

Problem: When it comes to cloud computing security, there is a shared responsibility between the service providers and their customers. This model can be misunderstood, and this will make it very easy for security holes to crop up.

Businesses must solve the problem of responsibility and put in place a governance structure where all teams are aware about their role in safeguarding the company's security and operational resilience.

2.5.3 Cultural Resistance

Problem: Merging DevOps and SecOps can be difficult and requires a cultural change in the work's natural flow of things, which leads to resistance from teams that work with older legacy workflows.

A leadership style should embrace a culture of working together and accountability for outcomes. Training and open communication will make the move easier for everyone, so that everyone is in this together.

2.5.4 Balancing Speed and Security

Problem: DevOps promotes agility while security measures are supposed to be as rigid as possible, so there's a significant risk for creating a new attack surface here.

Implement security by design throughout the DevOps pipeline. The process keeps its pace by automatically checking for security

2.5.5 Evolving Threat Landscape

Cyber threats are constantly changing, and organizations must have an inch over these to ensure security and resilience.

Monitoring and intelligence must be part of the security strategy on an ongoing basis. Enhancing the ability to detect and respond to emerging threats in Real Time. Organizations need to invest in advanced analytics, and machine learning techniques that can significantly improve the detection & response times of security teams.

While this combination is a clear win for improved cloud security and operationally resiliency by embedding a shared concern structure from design to operating, adopting these approaches poses various challenges along the way. Understanding these challenges beforehand, businesses can construct a solid security posture that does not constrain the agility and innovation in cloud environments. And the more organizations work on collaboration, automation and continuous improvement, the better they will adapt to the growing complexity of operating in a digital landscape.

Cloud computing is a technology that helps businesses to manage and utilize computing resources on demand. Cloud computing has been embraced by businesses & industries over the past decade. Cloud computing can offer services such as storage, compute cycles and applications over the internet in-lieu of on-premises servers or local infrastructure. Cloud service providers are entrusted with valuable customer information, and any compromise could have severe consequences, including financial losses and reputational damage. Cloud computing is one of the most powerful inventions that has grabbed the curiosity of technologists all around the world. Cloud computing has many advantages, but it also has a slew of security risks that no organization can afford to ignore. For a successful Cloud Computing adoption in a corporation, proper planning and awareness of emerging risks, threats, vulnerabilities, and potential solutions are necessary. As a result, determining the most effective solution instructions to increase cloud security has become important for all cloud operations.

3. BRIDGING DEVOPS AND SECOPS FOR CLOUD INFRASTRUCTURE AND ROLE OF ARTIFICIAL INTELLIGENCE

3.1 What is DevOps

DevOps is a set of practices aimed at improving better coordination between development (Dev) and operations (Ops) teams. The ultimate objective being to reduce the development lifecycle and deliver good quality software faster and more reliably.

Some of the elements that are common to DevOps include:

Collaboration: DevOps encourages, promotes collaborative work between development and operational staff, tearing down silos and ensuring that everyone shares the responsibility.

Automation: DevOps lays a lot of stress on automation-related processes like testing, deployment and infrastructure managing this quickens the process and reduces human error.

Continuous Integration and Continuous Deployment (CI/CD): This practice allows code changes to be delivered as new features or corrections quickly, safely, stable and delivered frequently.

Feedback and Monitoring: One of the primary principles of DevOps is to monitor applications and infrastructure continuously to collect performance data alongside user feedback so that it can be used for making fact-based decisions for betterment.

Increased Speed to Market: DevOps shortens delivery cycles which make teams more agile and flexible, allowing organizations to keep up with changing market trends and evolving user requirements better.

At its core, DevOps strives to enable newer faster mechanisms for delivering software development through process and automation, which results in better products and customer satisfaction.

DevOps is a collaborative and multidisciplinary organizational effort to automate continuous delivery of new software updates while guaranteeing their correctness and reliability. Four main dimensions of DevOps are identified: collaboration, automation, measurement and monitoring. An initial conceptual framework is developed to communicate the phenomenon to practitioners and the scientific community as well as to facilitate input for future research.

3.2 What is SecOPS

SecOps is a combination of security practices and IT operations for the protection of data, and information systems. It underscores the need for security to partner with IT operations to embed security into daily operations and workflow.

SecOps include the following:

Threat Detection and Response: SecOps covers monitoring systems for security-related incidents, investigating alert activity to respond actively to security breaches or attacks that are taking place.

Incident Management: This includes setting up and following guidelines to answer, act upon and mitigate the security incidents so that they should get resolved as soon as possible after occurring.

Continuous Monitoring: SecOps puts a premium on continuous network and system monitoring to identify irregularities, vulnerabilities, and security threat vectors early so that businesses can take proactive steps to counteract these issues.

Collaboration and Communication: SecOps encourages the work together between the security team and other areas, helping a broader perspective of what safety means in an organization.

Risk Management: The act of identifying, assessing and prioritizing risks to devise strategies to manage or control these threats as they pose a risk to the organization's assets and data.

Compliance and Governance: Security Operations is responsible for ensuring that security practices meet regulatory demands and/or are aligned with industry standards to enable organizations to stay compliant and protect their data.

SecOps blends security into operational processes to establish a position of preventative defense that enables an organization to protect against loss while maintaining business objectives.

SecOps, on the other hand is responsible for managing and protecting an organization's information and technology systems from cyber threats and vulnerabilities. This includes implementing and maintaining security policies and procedures, monitoring for and responding to security incidents, and performing risk assessments and vulnerability management. The goal is to ensure the confidentiality, integrity, and availability of the organization's sensitive data and systems. Software security can be divided into security of the software development environment (security threats in the factory) and security of the software being developed (software security testing).

3.3 Bridging DevOps & SecOps

DevOps is a software development methodology focusing on connecting, as the name suggests, the developer and operations teams. For this purpose, DevOps uses various tools to integrate and automate different processes to make the development cycle more streamlined. However, although this approach is effective in decreasing the length of the SDLC, it misses some critical functions. One of the drawbacks is the absence of well-defined security management in the different stages of the DevOps cycle. The need for security testing can often create a bottleneck in the development process of an application as it is a time-consuming process. Developers often push security testing to the end of the cycle, which can lead to security issues being more expensive and time consuming to fix if they emerge at the end of the pipeline. To address this issue, an approach to integrate security steps into the DevOps cycle emerged, known as DevSecOps.

Teams practicing DevSecOps aim to apply a shift-left mindset to integrate security tests and other practices and techniques into the earlier stages of the SDLC. This way, security aspects are integrated into the continuous processes present in the DevOps process. By integrating security processes earlier in the cycle, the frequency of application deployments can be upheld.

Cloud Infrastructure has made a massive impact in changing the way organizations Develop & Deploy Applications. With the speed of innovation picking up, DevOps and SecOps integration is now more necessary than before. An integrated approach is essential to make security an integral part of software development life cycle so that Security is not a roadblock for agility and at the same time ensuring the software remains robust with all available security measures applied.

Importance of Collaboration: As a result, businesses find DevOps and SecOps working in default silos that represent themselves as the great danger to present security issues. This combination ensures developers take responsibility for security which in turn solidifies a culture of collaboration between the two and shares insights. This partnership enables teams to focus on security at the beginning of development, instead of as an afterthought by integrating security with every design and deployment. Open communication and aligned objectives help organizations build a resilient cloud environment where innovation can grow fast with secure boundaries.

Leveraging Automation and AI: Automation is the key to bridge DevOps and SecOps, but human intelligence must be involved as a safety measure. Automation of security checks, compliance monitoring, and incident response that can take the burden off teams and automate workflows. This automation can be further improved with the implementation of AI tools, which add the ability to detect threats faster and provide predictive analytics. AI is capable of processing huge volumes of data in real-time which can be a trigger for understanding trends and abnormalities that may signify security risks. And we can not only respond faster to incidents but also better manage vulnerability further uptight in the stack, contributing to a more resilient cloud overall.

Another good practice is to continuously monitor and take feedback on the same.

Businesses in today's digital ecosystem can be successful only if they bridge DevOps and SecOps and enforce continuous monitoring practices that enable security teams to see what the relationship between development and operational environment looks like from a real-time perspective. Monitoring helps teams to collect insights on how modules interact, which informs decisions when to adapt. Feedback loops: lessons from security incidents can inform improvements in future designs, as an example of making this culture sustainable. Businesses that embrace this iterative approach to cloud governance can consistently chart their path and maintain a dynamic and secure cloud infrastructure that is in alignment with the needs of its changing business operations.

Connecting the DevOps and SecOps is not just a strategic initiative but a necessity for an organization using cloud infrastructure. These measures allow companies to strengthen their security posture, while at the same time meeting agility innovations. The integrated approach allows organizations to traverse the maze and complexity that modern cloud environments can be, making security and development part of the same strategy.

*Figure 2. DevSecOps Model - Source: https://miro.medium.com/max/1082/ 0*8zmHcgGpZnH26fcX*

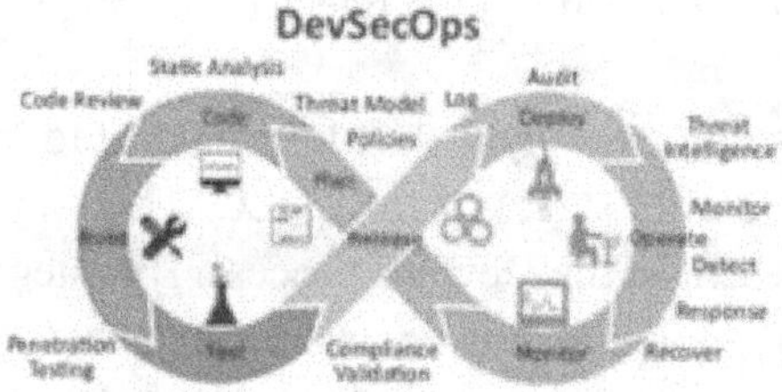

3.4 What is DevSecOps for Cloud infrastructure

Cloud-enabled DevSecOps aims to include security into the developer lifecycle process with a core focus on integrating security practices within the Development lifecycle as well to improve the overall security of applications and infrastructure in cloud environments.

Software development and operations are increasingly adopting cloud-native environments. The popularity of development practices such as DevSecOps is one of the reasons for this change. It is identified that monitoring is one essential practice in DevSecOps and currently, a wide variety of tool offerings are available on the market to address this new transformation.

Lately, organizations are adopting ways to increase the speed of development even further by composing teams with both development and operation engineers (DevOps teams) Brum et al. This rapid deployment of changes to production environments has security practices struggling to keep up with the pace. This, combined with the cloud transformation of the past decade, has led to rethinking security principles and dealing with risks.

So, here are the important things we should know regarding DevSecOps in cloud services,

Integration with Cloud-Native Security: There are measures to take as businesses go with DevSecOps and more which will include security in cloud-native applications. This includes using cloud-specific security tools and practices like identity and access management (IAM), encryption, and secure configuration management to defend assets from creation through decommissioning.

Collaboration Across Teams: DevSecOps promotes collaboration between development, operations and security teams in cloud environments. Together, the collaboration means security is built into an application's full lifecycle from design, deployment to ongoing management effectively delivering more secure applications that are compliant with regulatory requirements.

Automated Security Controls: Especially important in DevSecOps because it allows for businesses to respond promptly at scale which is why automation is a fundamental element of cloud services. Security checks such as static and dynamic application security testing (SAST/DAST) can be automated through the CI/CD pipeline, checking pull requests based on their impact on possible kinds of security vulnerabilities.

Continuous Monitoring and Threat Detection: The second significant process is that of continuous monitoring of cloud environments following the model in DevSecOps. This helps businesses to detect a security threat and to respond as soon as possible. Businesses can also take advantage of Cloud-Native monitoring and AI-driven analytics to find out security holes in their posture themselves and respond proactively to security abnormalities or breaches.

Compliance and Governance: Since cloud providers are often governed by several different regulations and compliance standards, DevSecOps makes a priority to reduce the impact of those checks through continuous compliance. Automated compliance tools can help ensure that configurations will continue to meet industry standards, thus also reducing the risk of non-compliance penalties.

Resilience and response to incident: Security incident management is operationalized into cloud operations. Incident readiness and preparation through DevSecOps helps in responding to security events, businesses should practise these processes regularly and absolutely be activated via cloud-native services for incident management and recovery.

DevSecOps immerses security much earlier in the development cycle as compared to traditional waterfall approach. Organizations can build, deploy and better manage secure applications in the cloud by weaving security into every step of the DevOps lifecycle. Not only does this reduce risk, but it also helps to create a culture of security awareness amongst teams, which is essential being that cloud environments are getting more complex every day.

3.5 Scope of AI in DevOPs & SecOps

Artificial Intelligence (AI) is sweeping across DevOps and SecOps, improving efficiency, security and decision making by both sides.

The successful implementation of AI- driven tools and technologies in DevSecOps requires a systematic method that encompasses the selection, deployment, and operationalization of AI-powered security solutions in the DevSecOps pipeline. The first step is to evaluate the specific security requirements and challenges cloud environments, identifying the areas wherein AI-based strategies can provide the maximum value in enhancing security posture and resilience. This evaluation must bear in mind the forms of threats and vulnerabilities common in cloud-based infrastructures, the existing security controls and procedures, and the desired effects from incorporating AI into DevSecOps.

Some of the new areas where AI is proving to be beneficial are:

Automation of Routine Tasks: It is also possible for AI to automate mundane activities such as deployment, testing and incident response in DevOps and SecOps. This allows teams to avoid wasting their time to focus on more strategic activities, ultimately accelerating processes and reducing inaccuracies.

Predictive Analytics: AI/ML can extend predictive analysis for data and help know if there is something likely to go wrong. In the context of DevOps, this could mean predicting performance bottlenecks based on trends and past data whereas in SecOps, AI can anticipate security threats or breaches by analyzing patterns.

Improved Monitoring and Alerting: AI can augment monitoring systems, where more intelligent alert filtering and anomaly detection are in option. This gives more precision in detecting problems and helps businesses respond faster, whether it is a performance regression in some deployment or a security incident.

Detection and Response: SecOps powered by AI can automate incident response workflows to respond faster to threats Intelligence. Machine learning algorithms analyse incidents of the past, enhancing response strategies etc enabling faster resolution time frame for security anomalies

Code analysis for bug detection and coding standards enforcement: There are various tools that use AI to help check code for bugs and vulnerabilities at the stage of development. Integrating AI in CI/CD pipelines will help organizations put security first at the start to make production less vulnerable.

Continuous learning and growth: AI systems can learn more and more from additional data, adjusting to new patterns or dangers that are discovered. That continual learning factor is what powers both DevOps and SecOps to improve by adjusting processes based on real-world use cases and evidence.

NLP (Natural Language Processing): AI driven NLP can assist to parse and analyse the documentation, the communication logs, and incident reports enabling teams to gather intelligent insights which will help in enhancing DevOps with SecOps align better for collaboration.

Smart Resource Allocation: By managing the allocation of assets in cloud surroundings by deallocating resources appropriately, applications can run efficiently and safely through AI. This could be adjusting the resources per demand, and spotting assets that are not being utilized much to cut costs.

Use of AI in DevOps and SecOps aids improved operational efficiency along with robust security measures. In increasingly sophisticated IT environments, AI will play a central role in driving greater collaboration and automation, as well as enhanced performance across all facets.

To make sure that generative AI in DevSecOps works well and is reliable, standard security tests and code reviews must be used to confirm the AI's findings. AI can help find mistakes and weak spots, but it should be used along with regular methods, not instead of them.

Recently, the advancement of artificial intelligence (AI) has revolutionized automation in various software domains, including software security. AI-driven security approaches, particularly those leveraging machine learning or deep learning, hold promise in automating security workflows. By leveraging AI/ML algorithms, organizations can empower their DevSecOps teams to proactively identify and address security threats, thereby reducing the risk of breaches and downtime while accelerating time-to-market. Furthermore, AI/ML-driven insights enable organizations to make data-driven decisions, optimize resource allocation, and continuously improve their security posture.AI is a key part of cloud security because it helps protect data, apps, and systems in environments that are always changing and getting more complicated. AI-powered algorithms are great at analyzing big datasets in real time, which makes it easier to spot new and complex security risks. This makes it faster for companies to spot and react to possible security events, which weakens threats. Modern businesses can protect their most important data assets, improve performance, and keep getting better throughout the data lifecycle by using a unified system for data protection and management that is powered by AI.

3.6 Challenges and considerations

There are many benefits of using AI & ML in combination with DevSecOps on cloud infrastructure. However, the benefits do come with challenges in terms of privacy, security & compliances. Businesses need to focus on the areas of concerns to have a consistent development life cycle.

Adding AI to DevSecOps has a lot of benefits, but it also has some problems and issues. To protect data privacy and security, businesses need to put in place strong defenses and create AI models that think about privacy. There are ways to check for and handle security alerts because false positives and negatives can happen. To close the AI and security skills gap, teams need to work together and get training. Concerns about compatibility can make integration more difficult, so thorough tests and teamwork are needed to make the move go smoothly. AI systems need to be checked for social problems like fairness and openness on a regular basis. When AI techniques are used, cost and resource distribution methods should be used with an eye toward the long-term benefits. Following the rules and norms that are specific to the business and industry are very important, and regular audits may help show that. To get past resistance and make sure the switch to AI-powered DevSecOps goes smoothly, it is important to have good change management that includes training and communication. Showing how AI can help improve security might help get backing from the team. Organizations must carefully discuss these problems and worries to use AI in DevSecOps while upholding security, privacy, and moral standards.

4. ETHICAL CONSIDERATIONS IN AI-DRIVEN DevSecOps

While AI in DevSecOps provides an augmented security capability, an increased level of automation, and enhanced operational resilience within cloud infrastructures, the accompanying transformation bears significant ethical challenges that organizations must proactively address to ensure equitable transparency and accountability. The foremost ethical issues involve biases in AI, opacity, data privacy issues, regulatory compliance, and human oversight. These challenges must be met for responsible legitimacy in the deployment of AI-driven security systems.

4.1 Algorithmic Bias in AI Systems

One of the most critical challenges facing AI-driven DevSecOps is algorithmic bias. Artificial intelligence tools depend on large amounts of data for training and decision-making. If the data is skewed, incomplete, or lacks diversity, then the AI models developed will likely be biased or inequitable in their outcomes.

False Positives and Negatives: A biased artificial intelligence system can create a false positive by identifying a benign activity as malicious, thus imposing unnecessary operational burdens. On the other hand, the real threat that is missed is a false negative and poses great security risk.

Bias Addressment: To reduce these issues, it is required that organizations take the necessary steps to see that training sets are varied, representative and are constantly being revised. The implementation of fairness checks and AI models auditing could be a step further in bias mitigation and accuracy enhancement.

4.2 Lack of Transparency and Explainability

Artificial intelligence security tools often function as "black boxes," hiding their decision-making process from the end user. Such opaqueness only serves to erode trust and accountability, particularly in high-stakes security situations.

XAI: Frameworks of Explainable AI ask how the decision-making process of an AI system is explained. Such information allows the stakeholders to verify and validate what an AI output is producing, thus gaining trust over it. By providing interpretable results, XAI guarantees that security teams can understand and justify the conclusions made by the AI.

Impact on Accountability: Transparency is especially crucial in heavily regulated industries such as finance and healthcare, where compliance and accountability are certainly not up for negotiation.

4.3 Data Privacy Risks

AI tools in DevSecOps require access to vast amounts of sensitive information to detect and monitor threats. This is crucial for the system's performance but poses substantial privacy issues.

Risks: In cases of unmanned access, data abuse, or breaches during AI operations, confidential information may be revealed.

Privacy Solutions: Data anonymization, encryption, and federated learning are techniques that enable AI systems to function optimally while safeguarding sensitive information.

Regulatory Standards: Compliance with privacy regulations, such as the General Data Protection Regulation (GDPR), safeguards users' rights to confidentiality.

4.4 Regulatory Compliance

Due to the rapid proliferation of AI, governments along with industry regulators have begun to impose stricter controls aimed at ensuring its ethical and responsible usage.

Challenges: Organizations using AI-driven security tools must comply with legal frameworks like GDPR, HIPAA, and new AI-specific regulations that are still evolving.

Solutions: AI governance frameworks ensure compliance with regulations. There is a need for continuous monitoring, auditing, and reporting to avoid the penalties of non-compliance and harm to reputation.

4.5 Human Oversight and Trust

While AI can take on much of the routine and paperwork in security operations and increase effectiveness, it can never replace human decision-making.

Importance of Human-in-the-Loop: Security analysts need to validate the output from AI, investigate any anomalies, and ensure that ethical standards are upheld. With human oversight in the loop, AI-driven systems are prevented from making unchecked or inappropriate decisions.

Balancing AI and Expertise: Blending of AI capabilities with human expertise strikes a perfect balance where AI comes to play in making decisions rather than replacing people entirely.

4.6 Accountability and Ethical Governance

Organizations need to put in place clear accountability frameworks so that the AI systems they deploy will be in accord with ethical principles throughout their life cycle.

Regular Audits: Regular audits help identify risks, biases, and ethical concerns in AI systems.

Shared Responsibility: All contributors to an AI system, including the developers, the executors, and leadership, are responsible for ensuring that whatever is built upholds fairness, transparency, and accountability in the deployment.

5. CONCLUSION

The integration of DevOps, SecOps, and AI has fundamentally transformed cloud infrastructure management. By embedding security into the development lifecycle, organizations can mitigate vulnerabilities early, enhance operational resilience, and maintain agility. Automation, predictive analytics, and continuous monitoring further bolster these frameworks, enabling proactive threat detection, streamlined compliance, and efficient resource allocation.

AI's role in this convergence extends beyond automation, offering advanced capabilities such as anomaly detection, predictive insights, and real-time response to emerging threats. However, ethical considerations, including algorithmic bias, transparency, and data privacy, must be addressed to ensure responsible and effective implementation. By adopting Explainable AI (XAI) frameworks and robust governance, organizations can maintain trust and accountability while leveraging AI-driven solutions.

Looking ahead, innovations such as zero-trust architectures, edge computing, and advanced predictive analytics will drive the evolution of AI-enabled DevSecOps frameworks. These advancements will empower organizations to navigate complex, dynamic cloud environments with confidence, fostering scalable, secure, and adaptive infrastructures capable of meeting future challenges and opportunities.

6. REFERENCES

Adams, D., & Bellucci, M. (2023). Embedding Security into Continuous Integration and Continuous Deployment (CI/CD) Pipelines. *IEEE Transactions on Secure Software Engineering*, 2(3), 56–71.

Al-Rashid, M., & Yahya, M. (2022). Multi-cloud Security: Challenges and Solutions. *International Journal of Cloud Computing*, 11(3), 237–251. DOI: 10.1504/IJCC.2022.121465

Battina, D. S. (2021). AI and DevOps in Information Technology and Its Future in the United States. [IJCRT]. *International Journal of Creative Research Thoughts*, 8(1), 108–112. DOI: 10.1234/ijcrt.108112

Chen, L., & Babar, M. A. (2014). Towards an evidence-based understanding of electronic data security and privacy risks. *Journal of Software (Malden, MA)*, 26(11), 974–990. DOI: 10.1002/smr.1666

Colliander, C. (2022). Challenges of DevSecOps. Master's thesis, University of Helsinki. Retrieved from http://hdl.handle.net/10138/342887

Coppola, P., & Verma, R. (2021). AI and Machine Learning in SecOps: Enhancing Resilience and Operational Efficiency. *Journal of Cybersecurity*, 10(2), 145–160. DOI: 10.1093/cybsec/123456

Davis, J., & Daniels, R. (2016). *Effective DevOps: Building a Culture of Collaboration, Affinity, and Tooling at Scale*. O'Reilly Media.

Ebert, C., Gallardo, G., Hernantes, J., & Serrano, N. (2016). DevOps. *IEEE Software*, 33(3), 94–100. DOI: 10.1109/MS.2016.68

Hoffman, C. M. (2021). *Securing DevOps: Security in the Cloud*. O'Reilly Media.

Jones, P., & Smith, R. (2023). Automating Cloud Security: The Role of AI in DevSecOps Pipelines. *Journal of Cloud Engineering*, 13(1), 33–52.

Kim, G., Humble, J., Debois, P., & Willis, J. (2016). *The DevOps Handbook: How to Create World-Class Agility, Reliability, and Security in Technology Organizations*. IT Revolution Press.

Li, Y., & Gong, X. (2020). Artificial intelligence in IT operations: Applications and ethical considerations. *Journal of Cloud Computing (Heidelberg, Germany)*, 9(1), 18. DOI: 10.1186/s13677-020-00195-y

Mann, A., Stahnke, M., Brow, A., & Kersten, N. (2019). State of DevOps Report. Puppet. Retrieved from https://puppet.com/resources/report/state-of-devops-report/

Mitra, S. (2021). Advanced Monitoring and Automation: Leveraging AI for Operational Excellence. *Cloud Operations Journal*, 8(2), 45–62. DOI: 10.1007/s13677-021-00456-9

Nelson, D., & Carter, T. (2021). Securing Multi-Cloud Environments: Strategies and Tools for Modern Enterprises. *Enterprise Cloud Journal*, 14(1), 44-58. https://doi.org/DOI: 10.5678/ecj.2021.58

Rahman, A. A. U., Helms, E., Williams, L., & Parnin, C. (2015). Synthesizing continuous deployment practices used in software development. *Agile Conference*, 1-10. DOI: 10.1109/Agile.2015.12

Sharma, R., & Gupta, P. (2023). Predictive Analytics in DevOps: Enhancing Security with Machine Learning. *International Journal of Security Systems*, 15(2), 102–115. DOI: 10.1002/ijss.2023.102

Taylor, K., & Finn, J. (2022). Ethics in Artificial Intelligence: Implications for DevSecOps in Cloud Computing. *AI & Society*, 37(4), 611–626. DOI: 10.1007/s00146-022-01456-x

Walker, L., & Morgan, J. (2020). DevSecOps: Breaking Down Silos to Build Security into Development. *Proceedings of the International Security Symposium*, 2020, 74-89.

Williams, B. (2019). *Continuous Security: Building Secure Systems in DevOps and Beyond*. TechBooks Press.

Wright, A., & Harris, T. (2018). Cloud Security Best Practices: A Comprehensive Guide for IT Professionals. *Cloud Journal*, 5(3), 201–224.

Zhao, X., Clear, T., & Lal, R. (2024). Identifying the primary dimensions of DevSecOps: A multi-vocal literature review. *Journal of Systems and Software*, 214, 112063. DOI: 10.1016/j.jss.2024.112063

Chapter 13
Building Resilient Systems: The Role of Containers and Kubernetes

Arun Pandiyan Perumal
https://orcid.org/0009-0000-7783-5784
Illinois Institute of Technology, USA

ABSTRACT

Cloud-native technologies have transformed the landscape of system design and deployment, establishing innovative frameworks for creating robust and resilient systems. This chapter explores the critical role of containers and Kubernetes in developing robust cloud-native systems that can withstand failures, scale dynamically, and recover seamlessly. Containers, with their portability, lightweight architecture, and modularity, enhance operational resilience by ensuring consistency across diverse environments, enabling isolation, and supporting rapid recovery and scaling. Kubernetes amplifies this resilience with features like automated deployment, self-healing capabilities, dynamic scaling, and multi-zone deployments. Additionally, the chapter highlights the challenges of managing stateful applications in a containerized ecosystem and proposes mitigation strategies, including Kubernetes StatefulSets and dynamic volume provisioning. Advanced topics such as Chaos Engineering, GitOps, and service meshes are explored to underline their role in fostering operational resilience.

INTRODUCTION TO CLOUD-NATIVE RESILIENCE

Cloud-native technologies introduce revolutionary avenues for understanding design, deployment, and management systems. The technologies assist in enhancing the functionality of modern infrastructure, addressing the constantly growing demand to deal with the digital landscape well. The use of these technologies increases the demand for resilience in addressing any actions. With the rapid innovation in the digital landscape and evolving user expectations, business entities have to deliver reliable and well-modeled systems helping to achieve the desired outcome (Wang et al., 2024). The element of resilience highlights the importance of designing cloud-native systems effectively to accomplish desired outcomes. Notably, this chapter tackles resilience and its redefinition using cloud-native approaches. This entire approach works to achieve fault tolerance, seamless recovery, and scalability measures.

DOI: 10.4018/979-8-3373-0365-9.ch013

REDEFINING RESILIENT SYSTEMS IN THE CLOUD ERA

Traditional measures of resilience focused on recovery from failures during times of network outages and hardware crashes. Traditional systems used failover mechanisms and redundant hardware aimed at ensuring critical management of the software at all levels. Cloud-native technology has enhanced the level of addressing resilience in systems, ensuring that they can adapt to and improve the management of unexpected changes and activities on the system. The cloud-native approach uses various technologies such as containerization, distributed systems, and even microservices to ensure resilience is achieved (Harika et al., 2023). Developing each of these components assists in tackling resilience to address not only recovery but also adapt to, withstand, and evolve within the dynamic nature of challenges as they occur. Cloud-native technologies enable the design of systems that can gracefully degrade their functionality instead of failing immediately. This ensures that, even under adverse conditions, the system remains operational and strives for optimal results. To address cloud-native resilience, these features have to be mastered to address every component as desired.

- **Automated Recovery:** Systems must be equipped with the proper framework to allow automated restarts, self-healing capacity, and rollbacks, allowing the system to have an aspect that does not depend on human intervention to achieve its results.
- **Real-Time Observability:** Resilience must be based on the ability to achieve advanced monitoring, which provides insights into system health and enables logging to assist with troubleshooting whenever issues arise.
- **Dynamic Adaptability:** Systems must ensure the capacity to adapt to either high or low workloads. This aspect helps address traffic dips and spikes at any moment while working with the system.
- **Distributed Redundancy:** The system needs to deploy applications across various regions and multiple zones to minimize the risk of failure at any point. This approach ensures that the entire system remains operational, even if an issue arises in one specific area.

Figure 1. Features of Cloud-native Resilience

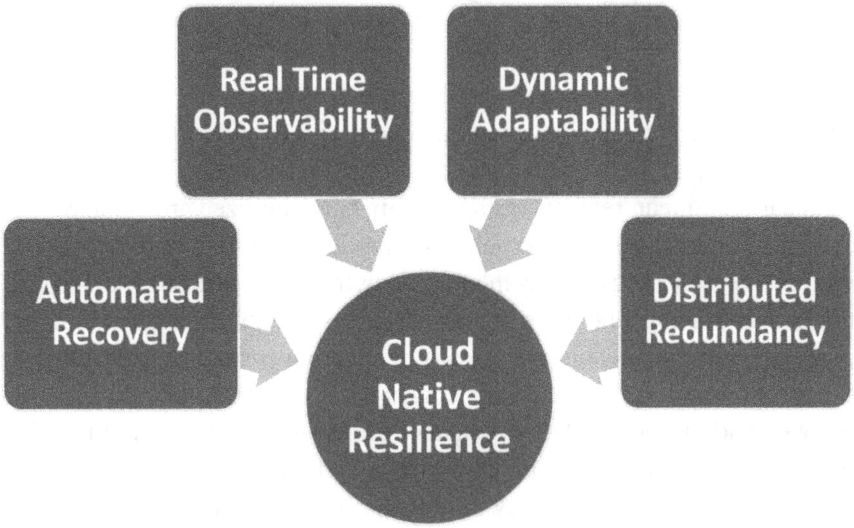

Fig.1 indicates the features of cloud-native resilience, such as real-time observability, automated recovery, distributed redundancy, and dynamic adaptability.

IMPORTANCE OF SCALABILITY, FAULT TOLERANCE, AND SEAMLESS RECOVERY

Scalability, seamless recovery, and fault tolerance are pillars of cloud-native resilience, leading to a remarkable point of addressing modern systems and their design frameworks. The use of the model ensures the achievement of uninterrupted activities and a good user experience even with fluctuations in the demands of the system.

1. Scalability

Scalability is the capacity of a system to manage workloads through adjustment to traffic adjustments or dips. Notably, scalability achieves the right level of marking system development and responsiveness to assist in addressing significant demands. Primarily, scalability helps with elastic resource allocation, which ensures that applications can scale either horizontally or vertically to assist in detailing predefined metrics that push them to achieve a required outcome. Scalability also leads to a high level of user management from various geographical locations, ensuring that the system is highly available and has low latency. When several users can deal with the system, it becomes an instructional capacity to achieve the most meaningful outcome as defined by any instance (Ghandour et al., 2023). Scalability leads to high scope and capacity to achieve cost optimization when companies do not have to spend more or less on performance, as scaling automatically sets the correct order and maintains the nature of providing value for the system across all points of use. An example of scalability is when a film streaming website automatically utilizes multiple containerized streaming servers during peak hours when there are many users and reduces them when user activity decreases. Thus, this enables all users, regardless of their number, to have a seamless experience, marking their capacity to have an interactive session with the site.

2. **Fault Tolerance**

Fault tolerance denotes a potential in the system, enabling it to operate correctly even when there are failures. Partial failures within the system must be handled well, ensuring that there is a way to assist in managing the standards and requirements of the system. Containerized architectures have the potential to handle various frameworks and steps to help with hardware malfunction, network issues, and software bugs. Cloud-native technology assists in addressing this by having relevant steps to assist with the proper functional needs. Having fault tolerance assists in ensuring health checks within the Kubernetes. Kubernetes handles liveness and readiness to assist in handling corrective action when an issue comes along. This creates the opportunity for load balancing, whereby the traffic can be managed with a healthy mechanism and level of administering the performance even with any failure. Additionally, fault tolerance assists in ensuring the functional management of distributed architecture, enabling multiple nodes and regions, which can considerably mitigate any failures whenever they arise.

3. **Seamless Recovery**

Seamless recovery assists in handling downtime, leading to the system having as minimal a stay within the downtime as possible. The seamless recovery leads to a swift return to normalcy even after failures. The element of seamless recovery is supported by automated rollbacks, which ensure that Kubernetes can revert to a stable version, ensuring that there is a minimal impact on the users within any platform of their action. This assists in handling and marking the growth of a beneficial scope in addressing activities. Therefore, instances of service outage are minimized through this approach, leading to a high level of configured use for every party. Seamless recovery also works with backup and restore to ensure that data integrity is always upheld. The maintenance of data integrity leads to consistent results, making seamless recovery essential for managing applications effectively to meet user needs at all times.

4. **Ensuring Resilience in the Cloud Technology Era**

Achieving synergy of fault tolerance, seamless recovery, and scalability assists in stamping fault tolerance across every entity and addressing their functionality at all levels. Notably, the nature of the modern world ensures that the level of resilience is well appreciated, achieving high performance and user-experience results. Notably, the availability of service gives business entities a high level of trust and loyalty, which is a mechanism that consistently achieves the best outcome. The element of resilience also calls for steps to adapt to future challenges that might be key in addressing the major challenges and needs in affirming the position of the organization. Redefining resilience to work within cloud technology systems marks the step to assist in handling automated recovery, proactive design, and intelligent scaling models, which ensure that cloud-native technologies achieve their highest level of performance and functionality (Welsh et al., 2020).

THE ROLE OF CONTAINERS IN OPERATIONAL RESILIENCE

Containers have led the transformation of application development and deployment. Using containers as a key resource can assist in handling operational resilience for cloud-native systems, leading to an even greater potential in addressing and handling every required need. Containers have the key benefits of being portable, lightweight, and efficient, enabling them to have functionality in various environments and assisting in achieving the right outcome in all aspects.

1. Use of Containers as Building Blocks

Containers have a unique architecture, ensuring that they can bundle all components that are needed within a single unit. The use of containers can work with microservices architecture and ensure each service operates independently. Using containers as building blocks for applications leads to a high level of efficiency as there is a shared operating system kernel, which leads to lower consumption of resources and assists in handling functionality by using comparable isolation and performance as needed (Adhikari et al., 2024). The use of containers also helps in handling modularity, where developers can have the capacity to build, test, and release every component independently, leading to a remarkable level of updating, debugging, and scaling in meaningful mechanisms that can ensure overall system resilience to achieve a reliable appeal at all levels of the system management. Containers provide high portability, enabling systems to function in different environments. This supports hybrid and multi-cloud strategies, helping organizations enhance their functionality effectively.

2. Enabling Consistency across Diverse Environments

Inconsistency of the software across various environments is a significant challenge that needs to be addressed to help advance, mark, and ensure that containers can work within meaningful levels. The use of containers will help in catering to the dependencies within a single unit, where they can have a high level of consistency. Through dependency isolation, containers can handle conflicts that come from mismatched dependencies. This implies that the various development and production environments are well addressed, marking a beneficial scope for managing their requirements. Containers work within the level of addressing immutable infrastructure, where they can work within the point of deployment, which does not affect the functionality and level of addressing infrastructure functionality. The scope of addressing immutability applies across various environments, leading to a highly remarkable point and level of advancing valuable functionality for applications. Containers also register their versions, ensuring that there is a capacity to track changes and investigate stable versions in case of any failures while administering any system requirements.

3. Using Isolation, Recovery, and Scaling to enhance Resilience

Containerization aids the development of resilience when working with each of these critical aspects. Containerization helps with isolation to ensure an appropriate level of functionality. The containerization process works with isolation to ensure there is a way to assist in addressing independent functionality and separation of entities that can lead to a cascaded effect when there is a failure. Isolation in containers helps to ensure that there is a limited level of fault management since a fault only occurs within a container, leaving out every other service that can continue operating without leading to downtimes for users. Isolation helps ensure that there is a limit for the CPU and Memory utilization, ensuring that the containers can function without any necessary deprivation of resources to the other categories that demand and need continued management of their requirements at all levels. Containerization leads to a security hardening, where the container minimizes the attack surface as the environment is secure, and any chances of attack will only be contained within the specific container and not spread onto other categories where they can continue with their functionalities well. Isolation, an element of containerization, is, therefore, key to managing system stability, compounding a highly flexible and stable system.

Scaling within containers effectively addresses demand without negative consequences. The scalability of containers is appealing due to their lightweight nature and quick startup times, allowing them to be managed efficiently. Containers use various scaling approaches to help them instruct and manage their requirements to a desired level. The horizontal scaling occurs when the containers can be added or subtracted depending on the amount of traffic. This ensures an increasingly beneficial way to understand and deal with the containers, leading to a remarkable scope of managing functional requirements at any instance. The cluster-orchestrated scaling is a mechanism where various tools can automate the scaling decision. Kubernetes can work towards adjusting containers and marking the level of use for metrics such as CPU Usage and request rates that satisfy the needed levels of managing their outcome in a desired manner. Containers can also be used to handle cost requirements and assist in gainful efficiency. The cost efficiency of the containers ensures that they can handle precise resource allocation and reduce wastages in meaningful ways to reduce the capacity of using virtual machines. Containers are exceptional for their ability to scale quickly and efficiently, creating a significant advantage for system development in a model that promotes continuous growth.

Containers can handle recovery, leading to expedited recovery times and managing the very core of supporting and dealing with their requirements at all levels. The rapid restarts when using containers assist in ensuring that they can work instantaneously, minimizing any downtime that might occur as required. Containers can also ensure immutable deployments, where a new version can be replaced within the container, enhancing their recovery without having to deal with configuration issues and managing the consistency of service for any program that is needed. Thus, the immutable deployments make containers stand out in recovery, as they minimize reaction time and lead to a higher functionality point of the applications. Aspects such as automatic restarts and rescheduling of failed containers assist in ensuring that the system can work in the provided state and address every step of handling the required value needs.

4. Real World Applications of Container Resilience

Containers are used across various sectors, each appealing to the creation and management of functional areas that assist in delivering the best results. Consequently, the implementation of container resilience offers multiple sectors the opportunity to operate without compromising their high level of functionality. Financial service industries like banks use containerized microservices to keep transaction processing systems operational even when there are failures or high traffic within the systems. Additionally, the healthcare system uses containerized applications to ensure they are always available, and they can isolate individual services and have a high rate of recovery for the systems when they need to be applied. Thus, elements such as patient record systems in healthcare assist in advancing solutions even when there are failures within the system (Prins et al., 2022). Containers are also used in E-commerce, which works to ensure users can handle the system during peak hours and downtime. This implies that conditions like flash sales do not interrupt the nature of work for systems, prompting them to have a higher level of constantly advancing and handling individual requirements for the system.

5. Impact of Containerization

Containers have different influences on business outcomes. They can effectively promote business development by providing unique benefits tailored to containers and Kubernetes. The potential to minimize downtimes and lead to performance management, leading to a seamless experience for users at any point that they use the containers. Containers also increase agility, measuring up the deployment and handling of recoveries at a meaningful level. This enables the organization to respond to market demands and disruptions in meaningful ways that enhance assisted development for the containers at any level. Consequently, containers provide organizations the opportunity to reduce costs associated with recoveries, resource allocation, and sales lost due to downtimes. These benefits are spread across various industries that continually use containers to address their requirements and achieve the right outcome in any engagement needed.

Figure 2. Impact of Containerization

Fig.2 indicates the various influences of containerization, such as customer satisfaction, increased agility to respond to market demands, reduced costs due to resource allocation and recovery budget, and seamless user experiences.

KUBERNETES: AMPLIFYING RESILIENCE IN CLOUD-NATIVE SYSTEMS

Kubernetes has been increasingly used to assist with cloud-native computing needs. It can manage containerized applications, as it is designed to handle distributed systems, and can enhance operational resilience using its automation potential and robust features to attain high results.

1. Kubernetes Features used in Operational Resilience

Kubernetes have a variety of features that attend to different functional areas. The need for Kubernetes ensures a resilience-enabling environment where these features continue addressing individual requirements and attend to every core definition in marking progressive resilience. Therefore, using Kubernetes to maintain containerized applications will help address and manage the core creations in marking system development and achieving fault-tolerant functionality.

- **ReplicaSet:** This feature helps set an automated number of pod replicas that are always running. Whenever a pod fails, it is replaced with a new one, enabling reliability and considerable points of running Kubernetes to achieve desired results. Thus, these replica sets assist in addressing functionality and marking downtime recovery for the containers.
- **Pod Management:** This feature organizes containers into individual pods where they can work and run efficiently. The pods can be built to address particular needs, additionally assisting in workload distribution and handling redundancy of any aspect of pod handling requirements. Pod Management is thus a key step to enabling the containers to continue working and addressing requirements as designed in any instance.
- **Node Management:** The approach to managing nodes will ensure that health is monitored and addressed to achieve the right frame of functionality. The step to ensure cluster nodes can have the same health status works within the maintenance approach, always leading to the system's availability and modeling to achieve stability. Any failure will ensure that the pods must be rescheduled to healthy levels, which administer valuable results at all times.
- **ConfigMaps and Secrets:** Kubernetes runs on the capacity to externalize configuration and sensitive data. This approach ensures that application codes can function in a secure environment that increasingly leads to operational parameters that engage their services to a desired level. These frameworks mark the growth of Kubernetes to address and achieve a modest outcome in any application framework.

These features of Kubernetes are highly relevant in addressing resilience and system management to achieve the desired results. Within the containers, these features enhance resilience and security and automate the scaling approach to handle the development of efficient functionality.

2. Automated Deployment, Self-Healing Capabilities and Scaling

Kubernetes primarily focuses on automation, which enhances operational resilience. Its ability to manage resilience simplifies the process of addressing, modeling, and implementing the essential functionalities of Kubernetes. Therefore, automated deployment, self-healing, and scaling are key to managing Kubernetes use within containerized applications.

- **Automated Deployment:** The deployment of applications in traditional mechanisms involved the use of error-prone processes and complex systems. The introduction of Kubernetes assists in addressing this challenge by ensuring that there is a way to have declarative configurations that continually appeal to every required need. The use of rolling updates ensures that new applications can be incrementally and appropriately deployed to enable uninterrupted service, where they can consistently work to prevent disruptions and even further the deployment of every scope of managing the applications. Moreover, canary deployments offer a way to handle new versions, where traffic is provided from a small percentage and can consistently be deployed to have testing activities. The management of the network system provides an opportunity to enhance administration and ensure proper role execution across all levels for optimal functionality.
- **Automated Scaling:** Kubernetes can offer automated scaling operations, which enable and achieve the variable workload management approach. The scaling can be conducted either through cluster autoscaling or horizontal pod autoscaling. The use of horizontal pod autoscaling works by adjusting several pods based on aspects such as request rates and CPU utilization metrics (Thurgood et al., 2019). A spike in traffic can lead to more pods to assist in managing the increased loads. The use of cluster autoscaling is applicable in situations where the nodes can be increased or reduced to assist in addressing resource use. The development of this approach ensures pods can run at an optimized cost and resources are well utilized to achieve an increasingly beneficial way to attract and attend to major requirements within the entities. Autoscaling using both horizontal pod and cluster models can ensure applications adapt to fluctuating demands and will achieve the proper levels of responsiveness and resilience in managing any demanded values.
- **Self-Healing:** Distributed systems have instances of failures that have to be addressed to ensure quick recovery and management of every demand at a required instance. Minimal manual intervention during failures is a key factor in ensuring the functionality of systems and the achievement of the correct result in all aspects. Self-healing can occur in different mechanisms and ways, each enabling the development and provision of steps to achieve remarkable results. Pod monitoring is a step that can be used to help address the Kubernetes and check pod health so they can investigate readiness levels and liveness levels, too. With any failure, Kubernetes can restart a pod or replace it where necessary. Additionally, Kubernetes can help reschedule and mark the nodes to ensure that pods always have healthy nodes. The process establishes a level of affirming and working with nodes to achieve their optimal functionality levels across all desired points of management. More to the point, rollback mechanisms used within the Kubernetes can help to revert to stable versions whenever there are failures with new systems. This method ensures that all aspects of Kubernetes are covered and meet essential needs and functional requirements.

Figure 3. Features of Kubernetes

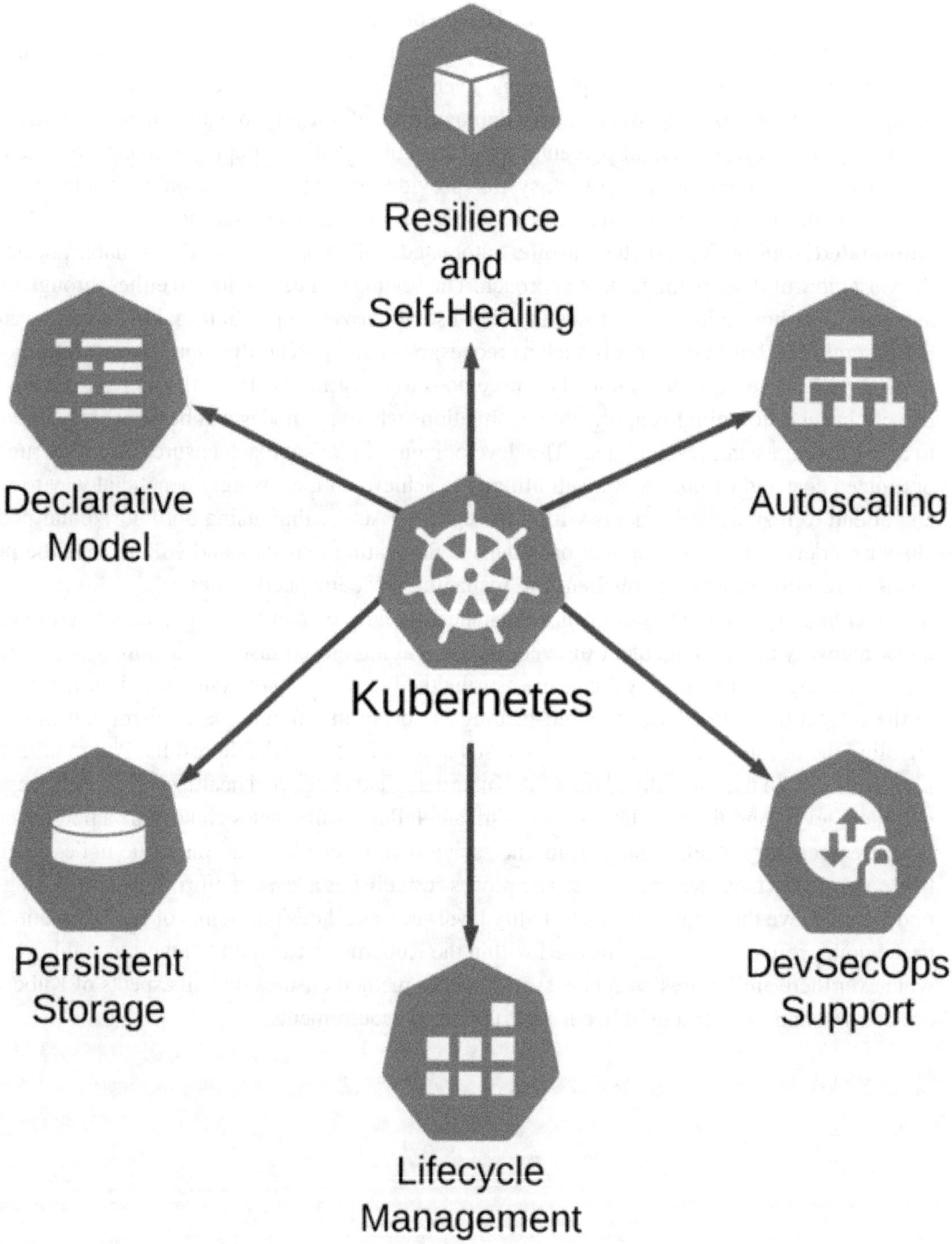

Fig.3 indicates the various features of Kubernetes, such as resilience and self-healing, persistent storage, autoscaling, lifecycle management, DevSecOps support, and Declarative models.

3. Service Discovery and Automated Rollbacks

Operational resilience demands efficient service management; Kubernetes ensures service management through service discovery and rollback mechanisms that enable complete service handling and management appeal. These elements ensure that Kubernetes can assist in addressing services, leading to high outcomes of their activities and managing the required outcomes at all points of engagement.

- **Service Discovery:** Seamless communication for the services in distributed systems ensures an increasingly dynamic functionality environment. Addressing the functionality will ensure an increasingly beneficial way to handle containerized applications and ensure their very needs are accomplished. The DNS-based service discovery works by ensuring that Kubernetes can work with services after assigning DNS names to them, ensuring that the pods can locate one another, communicate, and ensure they can handle the human-readable addresses to achieve every level of functionality demanded to address every level of outcome. Therefore, DNS-based service discovery works within the pods to ensure that they have seamless communication. Load Balancing can be conducted by Kubernetes when they ensure the even distribution of traffic within healthy pods and that none is overloaded, creating an optimal utilization for the pods. Endpoint management is achieved when Kubernetes tracks the pod IP addresses to ensure they can scale and restart when they cannot work in a meaningful manner.
- **Load Balancing:** Kubernetes works with traffic distribution to investigate whether healthy pods are free and when they can be configured to achieve a remarkable result. This approach ensures overloads are avoided, and no adverse outcomes are recorded.
- **Endpoint Management:** Kubernetes can track IP addresses and ensure that they can look into endpoints, offering an automated update for pods. The pods can then be scaled or restarted to ensure that their activities are appropriately organized to achieve a desired level of addressing their needs.

Kubernetes can provide automated rollbacks, which ensure the entire process can be conducted to ensure teams can get back to stable applications. The rollback process ensures that stable versions can be used to engage and mitigate valuable results, each instance leading to a reliable scope of functionality. The rollback can be conducted in various cases in which the system is threatened with a failure of service (Chinamanagonda et al., 2023). The deployment errors can lead to a rollback when there is an issue with the health criteria, ensuring that Kubernetes can roll back to a version where the containers can continue functioning with ease. In other instances, rollbacks can be executed when there are configuration issues within the systems. The misconfigured settings will lead to disruption of services, making sure that the use of quick restoration for functional configurations assists in catering a version that will help users meet their needs as every other aspect is being sorted and administered to achieve a good experience.

4. Real World Applications of Kubernetes Resilience

Kubernetes resilience is applied across various industries, enabling operational resilience to advance mission-critical applications that will have an exemplary meaning for all users. Multiple industries use Kubernetes resilience to achieve the proper backing and implementation at all levels of grounding and management. The healthcare industry uses Kubernetes resilience to ensure they have a constantly available patient management system. The use of Kubernetes ensures there is uninterrupted access to critical data that the patient management system can use in case of any infrastructure upgrades and failures. More to the point, the finance sector uses Kubernetes to help in looking at automated transaction observability. This assists in creating the best way to handle the spikes in transactions and managing fraud management and regulation, relating to the best step in marking and managing every step of dealing with occurring fraudulent transactions in real-time. The media streaming industry also uses Kubernetes to ensure seamless distribution of content. The seamless interaction with media across platforms enhances the user experience and drives improved outcomes.

Table 1. Kubernetes vs. Containers Resilience Features

Features	Containers	Kubernetes
Portability	Consistent deployment for applications and their dependencies on different environments	Manages containerized applications that are already portable across different infrastructures.
Scaling	Requires a manual scaling activity.	It has automated horizontal scaling.
Isolation	Applications have lightweight isolation	Resource-based allocation
Automated Rollbacks	Not supported	Supported
Self-Healing	Demands the use of external tools	Internal tools can be automatically configured

DESIGNING RESILIENT SYSTEMS WITH KUBERNETES

Cloud-native systems depend on resilience to establish their success, enabling instructional management of challenges and requirements in computer systems. The use of Kubernetes helps to provide patterns that enhance resilience, addressing functionality and challenges simultaneously.

1. **Multi-Zone Deployments for High Availability**

Resilient systems require handling through high availability (HA), which enables them to continue with operations in the face of failures. Kubernetes can enhance high availability by supporting multi-zone deployments, allowing the workload to be conducted across various zones in the region.

2. **Importance of Multi-Zone Deployments**
   - **Fault Tolerance:** It is the process of deploying pods in multiple zones, ensuring that there is no interruption even when a single pod fails. Failures can result from network problems, hardware issues, and power outages. Using multiple deployments allows for comprehensive management of each service element.

- **Load Distribution:** It is the process of ensuring traffic is distributed in various zones, achieving the proper utilization of resources, and ensuring overload risk is not experienced within any zone (Fogli et al., 2021).
- **Regulatory Compliance:** Ensuring deployments are conducted on multiple zones ensures that various disaster recovery approaches must be addressed, assuring users of the best scope and channel of detailing and managing their requirements.

3. **Implementation in Kubernetes**
   - **Multi-Zone Load Balancers:** Kubernetes can enable complete management of the cloud provider load balancers by enacting the distribution of traffic on various zones, assisting them to achieve consistent service delivery on multiple platforms.
   - **Topology Spread Constraints:** The use of Kubernetes assists in handling even distribution across various zones, ensuring that an instance of failure in a specific zone does not disrupt or cause an adverse outcome in whatever approach is taken.
   - **Node Affinity and Anti-Affinity Rules:** These rules on the nodes ensure that there are pods on nodes in different zones, ensuring that there is no single point of failure or redundancy of action on the pods.
4. **Readiness and Liveness Probes: Ensuring Application Health**

The health of applications is imperative to ensure resilience. Integrating Kubernetes assists in ensuring liveness probe and readiness in a bid to monitor application states. The process addresses an integral step to achieve sustainable results in attending to liveness approaches as needed by any category of managing their needs. Readiness problems have the potential to indicate the possibility of any container accepting the provided traffic. The integration of Kubernetes assists in appealing to readiness probes to ensure they can either remove or add pods from the service load balancer after checking the status of their health. More to the point, the element of liveness probe is conducted to assist by indicating whether the container can function well. The liveness probe can fail, but Kubernetes will work by automatically restarting the container to restore functionality in key areas. A liveness probe can be used to detect issues within pods, such as unresponsive states and deadlocks within the system. Probes work in enabling configuration and assisting within the TCP sockets and command executions to assist in returning outputs and status codes to a level that will support their needs (Dong et al., 2020). They enable administrators to define timeouts, thresholds, and intervals to monitor any actions taken. Using probes helps reduce downtime by detecting and recovering failing container states, ensuring the integrity of pods.

5. **Optimizing Resource Allocation for Stability**

The element of resource management through allocation ensures that systems are designed and built to have the utmost needed resilience. Using Kubernetes provides a determined set of tools that can prevent any form of instability affecting systems and marking their progressive modeling to assess and mark resource handling. Resource management is a critical aspect of designing resilient systems. Kubernetes provides tools to allocate resources effectively, preventing instability caused by over-commitment or underutilization.

6. **Resource Requests and Limits**

Resource requests work by specifying the minimum amount of space the CPU and memory have to work with to enhance their capacity to function efficiently. Kubernetes can use resource requests to ensure the correct scheduling of pods within the nodes and enable them to have access to sufficient resources. Moreover, the resource limits define the maximum space in memory and CPU that the container has to consume. They work to ensure that no single container uses more CPU space than every other requirement dealing with the workload.

7. **Configuring Resources**

Resources can be configured in various approaches. The use of a balanced allocation enables the provision of an overly restrictive limit that can contribute to throttling and even cases of high requests that can cause inefficiencies within the system. The role of Kubernetes administrators is to monitor application behavior, helping to identify and address underlying requirements for optimal performance. More to the point, the use of QoS classes, available within Kubernetes, ensures that classes are given to pods based on their workloads and resource requirements.

8. **Resource Optimization**

The process of optimization effectively addresses operational efficiency and cost management. Cost management improvements, such as leveraging Kubernetes to configure resources, represent a significant cost-saving step as waste is minimized. The performance is also enhanced by enabling pods and nodes to have the resources that they need to achieve optimal functionality (Rahman et al., 2023). Kubernetes deployment can be conducted using multiple codes, ensuring that they can appropriately handle the resources and achieve considerable handling of the entire approach to handle Kubernetes functionalities. A sample code that can be used is:

```
apiVersion: apps/v1

kind: Deployment

metadata:

  name: resilient-app

  namespace: default

spec:
```

```
replicas: 3

selector:

  matchLabels:

    app: resilient-app

template:

  metadata:

    labels:

      app: resilient-app

  spec:

    containers:

    - name: resilient-app

      image: my-app:latest

      imagePullPolicy: IfNotPresent

      ports:

      - containerPort: 8080
```

```
readinessProbe:
  httpGet:
    path: /health
    port: 8080
  initialDelaySeconds: 5
  periodSeconds: 10
livenessProbe:
  httpGet:
    path: /health
    port: 8080
  initialDelaySeconds: 10
  periodSeconds: 15
resources:
  requests:
    memory: "128Mi"
```

```
    cpu: "250m"

  limits:

    memory: "256Mi"

    cpu: "500m"
```

ADVANCED PRACTICES FOR BUILDING RESILIENT SYSTEMS

Organizations seek to constantly assess their systems and ensure they remain resistant to growing challenges. Resilient systems must be managed to secure the sustainable operation of the pods, utilizing service meshes, Chaos Engineering, and GitOps to enhance their operational capacities.

1. **Chaos Engineering for Resilience Testing**

Chaos Engineering is a step that uses proactive measures to ascertain resilience within the system. The mechanism works towards inducing controlled failures into the system, with each attempt indicating a scenario that must be addressed. The approach allows for consistent simulation of conditions, evaluation of behavior, and anticipation of improvements that will aid in managing the system effectively.

a) **Principles of Chaos Engineering:**

- **Simulation of Real-World Failures:** Scenarios from the real world, such as network disruptions, server crashes, and resource exhaustion, help ensure an excellent understanding of vulnerabilities that can affect normal operations.
- **Controlled Environment:** The process must be controlled with key installations to prevent any unintended harm to the system (Zhang et al., 2021).
- **Measuring Impact:** Impact must be addressed through various elements such as latency, throughput, and error rates, which must be assessed to ensure the performance before and after it is ascertained.

Figure 4. Principles of Chaos Engineering

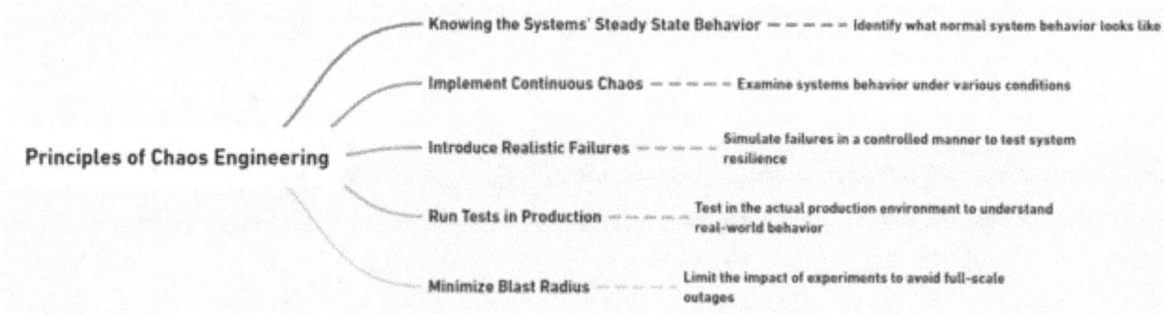

Fig.4 indicates the principles of Chaos Engineering, including understanding the steady state, using real failures, testing in production, limiting the blast radius, and continuous chaos implementation.

b) **Chaos Engineering tools and techniques:**

Various tools and techniques can be used to ensure that Chaos Engineering achieves the desired goal. The standard tools and methods that can be used include:

- **LitmusChaos:** This is a Kubernetes tool that works within chaos experiments because they have seamless integration with containerized environments.
- **Chaos Monkey:** This tool works by terminating the elements in a production environment to help in addressing system resilience. Netflix developed the system to assist them in targeting and managing their streaming service.
- **Gremlin:** This can be handled by ensuring an intuitive workflow and reporting mechanism that caters to the system's advanced and required development.

c) **Benefits of Chaos Engineering:**

Chaos Engineering has several benefits to the system. The process encourages and works within the proper framework of achieving relevant results in whatever classification is provided. The benefits include:

- **Enhanced Reliability:** The use of Chaos Engineering provides new confidence in the system's capacity to handle failures appropriately.
- **Cultural Shift:** The management of Chaos Engineering prepares an organization to be capable of continually improving, handling events, and ensuring that its engineering teams can consistently address its needs in a desired manner.
- **Proactive Resilience:** Proactive resilience leads to identifying, mitigating, and shaping system weaknesses before they impact the system.

2. **Traffic Resilience with Service Meshes**

Traffic plays a crucial role in microservices architecture. Service meshes provide a dedicated layer for service-to-service communication, enhancing observability, security, and traffic control without requiring changes to the original code. Service meshes can handle communication between microservices. They work with the data planes, which handle communication and work within the sidecar proxies of the unit, and the control plane ensures the configuration of policies within the data plane that achieve consistency in behavior across the systems (Saleh Sedghpour et al., 2022). Resilience within the system must be handled through the development of fault injection, traffic management, and load balancing. Each of these aspects must be managed to ensure that there are critical elements addressing functionality even during any downtime and service interruptions.

a) **Benefits of using Service Meshes:**

Service meshes have several benefits, enabling continued protection and management of valuable appeal to the system integrity. The core benefits include:

- **Enhanced Security:** The application of service meshes ensures additional features like mutual TLS that enable service-to-service communication.
- **Improved Observability:** The inclusion of service meshes enables the development of detailed insights into various aspects, such as service interactions. The interactions assist in debugging and optimization needs.
- **Decoupled Resilience:** The service meshes can ensure traffic resilience is enabled without any modifications to the application code.

Traffic mapping using service meshes can be conducted using various codes. A primary code that can be used in the instance is as follows:

```
apiVersion: networking.istio.io/v1beta1

kind: VirtualService

metadata:

  name: resilient-service

  namespace: default

spec:
```

```yaml
hosts:

- resilient-service.default.svc.cluster.local

http:

- route:

  - destination:

      host: resilient-service.default.svc.cluster.local

      subset: v1

    weight: 80

  - destination:

      host: resilient-service.default.svc.cluster.local

      subset: v2

    weight: 20
```

3. GitOps: Declarative Infrastructure for Enhanced Control

The use of GitOps has widely been accepted and implemented by various organizations. Notably, GitOps has the functionality of ensuring that it advances infrastructure and application management, which mainly uses Git repositories to help it source truth. In leveraging these configurations and automated workflows, GitOps ensures control, resilience, and consistency when working on cloud-native environments. GitOps functions on various principles, all aimed at providing a successful outcome in whatever activity is conducted. These principles include:

- **Declarative Infrastructure:** This provides that application states and infrastructure are defined in version-controlled files. The Helm charts, Kubernetes manifests, and configuration formats are commonly used to build the Kubernetes infrastructures.
- **Version Control:** Repositories are the source of all configurations. Changes to infrastructure and applications can be made using pull requests. They also enable audit trails and peer reviews, which help to understand the changes.
- **Automated Synchronization:** The development of tools like Flux and ArgoCD can monitor GIT repositories and also help with the synchronization of cluster states to help in matching declared configurations. The principle dictates that any drift between actual and desired states is detected, and an automatic correction is proffered.

a) **Benefits of GitOps:**

GitOps can be used to enable resilience and achieve the proper framework for addressing any provided variables in the state of engaging service needs. The use of the GitOps offers various benefits, such as:

- **Enhanced Collaboration:** Using GitOps helps provide stellar collaboration in an approach that allows mark transparency among team members.
- **Improved Consistency:** Configurations eliminate inconsistencies occasioned by manual changes, each affecting the level of consistency and resulting in much better results.
- **Faster Recovery:** Git history enables the capacity to restore application states and infrastructure in case of any disaster and data loss (Nordström, 2024).

b) **GitOps Use Cases:**

The development of Git for resilience can be applied in various situations. GitOps presents an opportunity for diverse applications, ensuring that all stakeholders can reap benefits and achieve outstanding results in every possible provision. Some of the use cases include:

- **Change Management:** Git Ops can be used in various instances where the proposed change can be reviewed and evaluated. After the testing, changes can be applied, reducing the risk of introducing instability in attending to every desired variable.
- **Environment Replication:** The development of GitOps enables an easy replication in a production-like environment, where they can conduct testing and staging activities. The process ensures an accurate consistency and deployment within secure frameworks and activities as needed.
- **Disaster Recovery:** GitOps can assist in case of failures or emergencies that occur at any given instance. The Git History can restore systems and data to the last known good state that appeals to every variable needed in selecting and appealing to every demanded element of the service system.

CHALLENGES IN CONTAINERIZED ECOSYSTEMS

Docker and Kubernetes changed the deployment and management process. These containerized ecosystems face various issues in ensuring consistent and appropriate results as needed at all levels. Two key challenges for these containerized ecosystems include addressing security concerns to enable safe containerized environments and managing stateful applications in a paradigm favoring statelessness.

1. **Managing Stateful Applications in a Stateless Paradigm**

Statelessness is a key principle of containerization. This implies the ability to handle containers by spinning up, tearing down, and marking their development to achieve application functionality. The management of the stateless functionality appeals to an even greater capacity and channel of ensuring suitable advancement to any level of marking their advancement needs. The model is, therefore, key in addressing applications, handling workloads, and ensuring stability in identity and storage, which favors the growth of the beneficial scope of needs for the containers. Applications exist either in a stateless or stateful state. Each of these states has unique features acting as identifiers, assisting in achieving the correct category of managing their advancement (Bentaleb et al., 2021). Primarily, the stateless applications store no data between sessions and can be scaled horizontally with the use of minimal complexity approaches. Stateful applications work by ensuring there is a framework to help in addressing data across sessions since they have persistent storage. They require consistent access to data at all times, particularly during the restart and migration processes of database systems. This consistency is essential to ensure seamless operations and minimize disruptions to service.

2. **Challenges of Managing Stateful Applications**
    - **Persistent Storage:** These containers need storage solutions where they can conduct their activities. Notably, ensuring consistency in storage during failures, migration, and scaling provides a significant challenge in targeting and achieving their desired results.
    - **Backup and Recovery:** Stateful workloads must be backed up and restored accurately within the containerized environment. This process is often complicated and does not always yield valuable results.
    - **Limitations in Scaling:** Stateful applications face a challenge in scaling as they require additional configuration and a series of manual interventions compared to stateless applications.
    - **Container Orchestration:** Stateful applications always need precision during orchestration to ensure dependencies are managed and that they are highly available in whatever actions they partake in. They must ensure that scheduling promotes data locality so every node has access to the data.
3. **Approaches to overcome these challenges**
    - **Kubernetes StatefulSet:** These are resources designed to help manage stateful applications. They offer benefits such as persistent storage volumes, network identities, and an ordered deployment approach for pods.
    - **Persistent Volumes (PVs) and Persistent Volume Claims (PVCs):** Kubernetes can decouple storage from containers, leading to data persistence when containers are replaced.
    - **Dynamic Volume Provisioning:** Automatic provisions for storage resources during the creation of the PVCs help in reducing any manual effort needed to address their needs.

- **Data Replication and Clustering:** Various databases such as Cassandra and Redis provide replication and native clustering to help address data availability and ensure distributed environments also have the desired consistency.

4. **Security Concerns and Mitigation Strategies**

Containerization and its widespread acceptance across industries have led to several security risks. These risks have to be addressed to ensure that containerized ecosystems achieve the desired needs. The security concerns demand a series of strategic applications that can help throughout the container lifecycle from the step of development to runtime, which assist in addressing valuable results in all aspects of containerization. Some common challenges encountered include:

- **Misconfigured Resources:** Container orchestrators might expose data and even enable unauthorized access. Unrestricted API access can also expose data and even access from various parties.
- **Image Vulnerabilities:** In most cases, containers are developed from images that might have been made from unsecured and vulnerable software. The public repositories that host these images might not be secured and evaluated, leading to higher chances of compromise.
- **Runtime Threats:** Containers can be compromised and share host operating system kernels, which increases the impact of kernel vulnerabilities and the likelihood of being affected by various threats.
- **Supply Chain Attacks:** During the build process, malicious code can be embedded into images, raising the likelihood that the completed container will be compromised.
- **Secrets Management:** Containers contain sensitive information like credentials, API keys, and tokens that must be guarded; weak secret management exposes them to several issues that can affect security provision.

Different approaches can be used to help in handling emerging security challenges and concerns. These mitigation approaches include steps such as:

- **Runtime Security:** This approach can help limit container privileges, run containers as non-root users, and ensure they do not have unnecessary capabilities. The use of Linux features such as AppArmor and seccomp can restrict container behavior, leading to further challenges within the entire unit.
- **Image Security:** Images must be used from reputed sources or private repositories or scanned to ensure that they meet the proper security needs. Policies to help manage these images offer a key step to advancing and ensuring that they mark their advances to a better state of security (Maenhaut et al., 2019).
- **Secrets Management:** Standard tools like Kubernetes Secretes and HashiCorp Vault support storing and managing sensitive data, each aimed at ensuring successful outcomes in whatever considerations are provided.
- **Network Security:** Network policies can be implemented to address communication between containers and prevent external access. Microservices also need to experience authentication and encryption to help ensure their actions are not unsecured.

- **Continuous Monitoring and Compliance:** Ensuring regular audits and management of access controls in compliance with security standards will improve the way of addressing underlying requirements in sustaining the systems.

Table 2. Containerized Ecosystems Challenges and Solutions

Challenge	Impact	Solution
Policy Enforcement	Difficulty in ensuring compliance with regulatory provisions	Using OPA to enable a centralized handling of policies.
Security Concerns	Potential vulnerabilities within images and runtime threats.	Using image scanning tools and runtime security tools
Managing Stateful Applications	The challenge in preserving state across pod restarts and instances of failures	Apply tools that ensure data persistence and consistency, such as Persistent Volumes and StatefulSets.
Observability	Limited insights and visibility into containerized applications	Implement the use of tools such as Prometheus and ELK Stack

ENHANCING RESILIENCE THROUGH OBSERVABILITY AND POLICY-DRIVEN PRACTICES

Systems demand constant observability and strict policy administration to enable better governance. They must also be advanced in keen models that can continually address emerging challenges and present complexities.

1. Robust Monitoring and Logging for Incident Detection

Cloud-native environments function based on distributed systems, where they have to detect, evaluate, and monitor incidents as they respond to them. The process of monitoring ensures that organizations can consistently advance their needs to achieve suitable results across all desired levels. Observability looks into metrics that can evaluate the system's performance and level of adjusting to significant channels of instructing better management of the system (Mayar et al., 2022). Metrics such as CPU usage, request latency, and memory consumption contribute to achieving valuable results across all aspects. Traces of requests as they traverse different microservices offer insight into the overall health of the system. Logs provide detailed insight and understanding of events as they occur within the system, which ensures that details are captured.

2. Importance of Monitoring and Logging

Monitoring and logging have a key influence on the functionality and performance of the system in any service. Key benefits include:

- **Root Cause Analysis:** Logs serve as a comprehensive record of system activities and transactions, enabling the identification of issues by tracing their origin and determining the underlying causes.
- **Proactive Issue Protection:** Observability ensures historical data trends when infused with tools that enable the identification of potential challenges before they occur.
- **Real-Time Incident Detection:** Solutions like Prometheus and Datadog ensure real-time alerts that enable a response to anomalies in ways that can achieve suitable results.
- **Performance Optimization:** Continuous monitoring analyzes resource utilization and identifies inefficiencies within the system, enabling the implementation of strategic measures to address and resolve these challenges.

3. **Steps to ensure effective Monitoring and Logging**

Key strategies used for the process of monitoring and logging include:

- **Granular Tracing:** Tools like Zipkin can help identify bottlenecks and challenges when handling microservice architectures.
- **Centralized Logging:** Tools such as EFK Stack and Graylog can help enable centralized logging systems, which aggregate logs from different sources to a single platform for analysis (Russo et al., 2021).
- **Retention Policies:** Storage costs and the need for historical data must be balanced. Clear retention policies for the logs and metrics will enable a successful outcome in handling system metrics and log demands.
- **Alerting and Visualization:** Business-critical metrics within the system must be addressed, ensuring that they can have thresholds, encouraging their performance, and handling them in a way that helps create the dashboard and has actionable insights to achieve a sustainable response to every key insight being provided.

Monitoring can be conducted through Prometheus using codes as shown below:

```
apiVersion: monitoring.coreos.com/v1

kind: ServiceMonitor

metadata:

  name: resilient-app-monitor

  namespace: monitoring
```

```
spec:
  selector:
    matchLabels:
      app: resilient-app
  endpoints:
  - port: http-metrics
    path: /metrics
    interval: 30s
  namespaceSelector:
    matchNames:
    - default
```

4. **Policy Driven Approaches for Compliance and Stability**

Policies enable the use of approaches that empower, establish critical values, and ensure an increasingly beneficial engagement with the cloud-native systems. Policies serve multiple functions, promoting compliance, providing stability, and creating opportunities to achieve desired outcomes.

- **Resource Management Policies:** These policies help set limits on resources such as storage, memory, and CPU, ensuring suitable results in addressing the use of these resources by the microservices.
- **Security Policies:** These policies define access controls, enable runtime restrictions, and ensure encryption requirements to achieve each user's desired outcome.

- **Deployment Policies:** These rules affect application deployment requirements, including change approvals and evaluating canary deployment methods for new versions.
- **Compliance Policies:** These advancements focus on registering and meeting regulatory requirements such as GDPR, PCI DSS, and HIPAA, which define and identify the necessary models to address these needs.

5. **Implementation of Policy Driven Practices**

- **Automated Enforcement:** The development of CI/CD pipelines will ensure increased policy enforcement, with the primary intention of achieving suitable production results.
- **Policy Definition:** The development of tools such as OPA can help define policies to handle system needs actively.
- **Monitoring and Auditing:** Monitoring and observability platforms assist in crafting the best result to achieve relevant outcomes by adjusting to the system's needs.
- **Regular Updates:** Continuous monitoring provides crucial insights into necessary changes. Enforcing regular updates allows for the management of policies that address evolving needs and emerging security threats within the system.

ENHANCING DATA GOVERNANCE WITH CONTAINERS AND KUBERNETES

Containers and Kubernetes have the capabilities to assist in addressing data integrity in various approaches. The use of data governance in this specific context helps to achieve security, data integrity, compliance, and availability of data. Therefore, the use of containers and Kubernetes will ensure an increasingly beneficial step in addressing valued management of data requirements. Data governance plays an integral role in organizational systems, each activity ensuring they can support their activities with great ease. Benefits of data governance include:

- **Data Integrity:** Data governance ensures that every piece of data remains accurate and consistent throughout its life cycle.
- **Data Availability:** Data governance assures the accessibility of data on request, making sure that disruptions and failures do not hinder the development of the approach to capture its advancement (Sandu et al., 2021).
- **Data Security:** Appropriate governance guarantees that unauthorized parties cannot access data. Governance also helps address breaches and data corruption.
- **Data Compliance:** Data governance ensures compliance and adherence to regulations such as PCI DSS, HIPAA, and GDPR.

Figure 5. Benefits of Data Governance

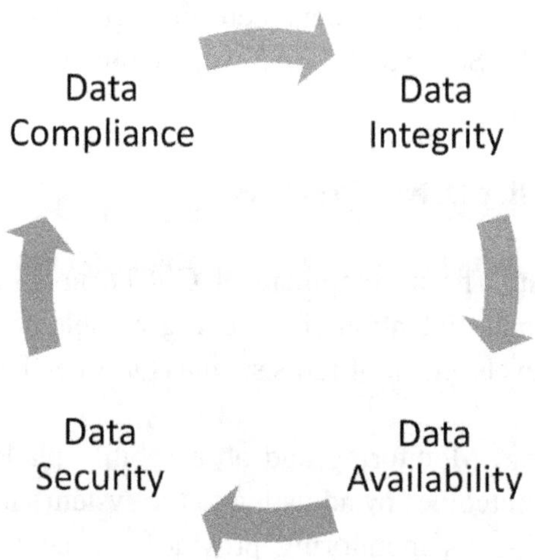

Fig.5 indicates the various benefits of data governance approaches, such as data availability, data security, data compliance, and data integrity.

1. **Using Containers to Manage Governance**

Governance using containers is an instrumental step since it provides a consistent environment, ensuring a more straightforward approach to governance.

- **Data Isolation:** This process ensures that the containers are used to enable process-level isolation where each microservice can work independently and execute its tasks. Furthermore, the isolation protects sensitive information from unauthorized access.
- **Consistent Environments:** Applications within the containers are bundled with their dependencies, ensuring that they can handle policies and are well executed through the lifecycle of development, testing, and production (Akbar et al., 2022).
- **Data Backup and Recovery:** Data management using Kubernetes allows reliable backups in persistent volumes, ensuring data availability and integrity during disruptions.

2. **Using Kubernetes for Data Governance**

In data governance, Kubernetes helps by bringing in more functionality that allows them to set about better needs and address their requirements. The Kubernetes offer an excellent platform for executing data handling.

- **Role-Based Access Control:** This enables access to people with only particular privileges.
- **Secrets Management:** Kubernetes ensures the management of API keys and credentials by encrypting them at rest and in transit (Pakalapati et al., 2023).

- **Compliance Automation:** Kubernetes can be used through OPA to help enforce compliance regulations automatically.

3. **Security in Dynamic Cloud Environments**

Dynamic cloud environments register rapid changes, ephemeral workloads, and distributed architectures. These features help secure the environment with a layered, proactive approach to managing risks throughout the life cycle. Key challenges include:

- **Distributed Systems:** Offers an increased attack surface for various malware and malicious activities.
- **Shared Infrastructure:** These are multi-tenant environments that require strict isolation policies.
- **Ephemeral Workloads:** Traditional security measures, such as Static IP, allow listing but do not work with containers and pods because they are short-lived.

4. **Strategies for Cloud Security**

Various security approaches can be applied to help in advancing the right amount of marking security to the cloud platform across all systems. The security strategies include:

- **Runtime Security:** This establishes a system that monitors containers and workloads. They evaluate functionality to ascertain suspicious behavior.
- **Service Mesh for Zero Trust:** Service meshes, primarily in models such as Istio, help ensure zero-trust security.
- **Infrastructure as Code (IaC) Security:** This enables the automation of infrastructure to ensure that every configuration is established, further advancing the nature of security within the platform.
- **Shift Left Security:** Strategies encompassing the development lifecycle will enable the management of vulnerabilities throughout the entire production process. Notably, tools such as Checkmarx and Snyk will ensure incremental value in addressing security needs.

REAL-WORLD APPLICATIONS AND CASE STUDY

Different companies have designed their systems based on resilient designs stemming from Kubernetes and containerization to help them achieve their intended goals. These companies use these advances to secure, manage, and ensure their actions can be conducted appropriately.

1. **Netflix Case Study**

Netflix is a global streaming platform with several millions of users. The company has to ensure that every user experiences an unparalleled service, which pushes them to engage and work within the best scope of advancing their needs in all desired categories (Torkura et al., 2020). The company has to ensure they can provide service despite any challenges like increasing demand, server failures, and network outages. Thus, they have built a resilient system. Considerably, Netflix began the use of Chaos Engineering to ensure they tested and evaluated the resilience of their system before deployment. Chaos Engineering ensured that Netflix engineers injected failures within the production environment, looking into their reactions and learning what could be conducted to avoid such shortcomings for the clients. Some failures that were injected in the development stage include random service interruptions, network latency, and server crashes, each working to ensure an enabled mechanism of looking into key advances in the system (Fossati, 2024). Using tools like Simian Army and Chaos Monkey, the company uncovered their weaknesses within the production environment. It ensured that the available architecture could handle and address every core issue to be tackled within their required instance. The approach ensured that Netflix could handle real-world disruptions without leading to latency when users are watching or crashing whenever they are carrying out their selection activities.

CONCLUSION

Resilient systems in the cloud-native era ensure the transformation of organizational activities. The inclusion of containers and Kubernetes ensures an increased capacity for organizations to achieve stellar results in whatever actions they undertake. Notably, the evolution includes emerging trends that will continue affecting resilient systems. Elements such as serverless architecture and Kubernetes ensure that there are more agile units in resilience, leading to a high level of proficiency in actions being conducted to address the desired outcomes. AI also seeks to advance the nature of resilience, ensuring that both AI and ML can be used to ensure the prediction of failures through predictive analytics. The inclusion of Kubernetes in this aspect would ensure an increased step to detect anomalies and ensure autoscaling to a new category in the systems. More developments in edge computing, through tools like KubeEdge, will ensure edge deployments and that they can manage containerized applications, which will ensure the constant availability of their systems. With the growing attention to resilience, challenges in containers and Kubernetes use for the same must be addressed, and solutions must be worked towards improving the marking and proficient handling of the activities. Significant steps to handle the challenges include policy-driven principles to ensure compliance and security for Kubernetes. Organizations should also focus on factors that are crucial for the future of resilient systems, such as developing multi-cloud deployment strategies and incorporating sustainability practices to engage stakeholders and reach their desired results.

REFERENCES

Adhikari, S., & Baidya, S. (2024). Cyber Security in Containerization Platforms: A Comparative Study of Security Challenges, Measures and Best Practices. *ArXiv (Cornell University)*. https://doi.org//arxiv .2404.18082DOI: 10.48550

Akbar, M., Rafi, S., Alsanad, A., Qadri, S., Alsanad, A., & Alothaim, A. (2022). Toward Successful DevOps: A Decision-Making Framework. *IEEE Access : Practical Innovations, Open Solutions*, 10, 51343–51362. DOI: 10.1109/ACCESS.2022.3174094

Bentaleb, O., Belloum, A. S. Z., Sebaa, A., & El-Maouhab, A. (2021). Containerization technologies: Taxonomies, applications and challenges. *The Journal of Supercomputing*. Advance online publication. DOI: 10.1007/s11227-021-03914-1

Chinamanagonda, S. (2023). Focus on resilience engineering in cloud services. *Academia Nexus Journal, 2*(1). https://academianexusjournal.com/index.php/anj/article/view/4

Dong, L., Yujia, L., Can, C., Huang Yunhao, & Di Fangchun. (2020). Research on safety protection technology of containerization applications based on probe detection. *2022 IEEE 10th Joint International Information Technology and Artificial Intelligence Conference (ITAIC)*, 386–389. DOI: 10.1109/ITAIC49862.2020.9339142

Fogli, M., Kudla, T., Musters, B., Pingen, G., Van Den Broek, C., Bastiaansen, H., Suri, N., & Webb, S. (2021). Performance Evaluation of Kubernetes Distributions (K8s, K3s, KubeEdge) in an Adaptive and Federated Cloud Infrastructure for Disadvantaged Tactical Networks. *2021 International Conference on Military Communication and Information Systems (ICMCIS)*, 1-7. DOI: 10.1109/ICMCIS52405.2021.9486396

Fossati, S. (2024). Leveraging Chaos Engineering to enhance data collection infrastructures' resilience: an industrial proof-of-concept study. *Handle.net*. https://hdl.handle.net/10589/222695

Ghandour, O., El Kafhali, S., & Hanini, M. (2023). Computing Resources Scalability Performance Analysis in Cloud Computing Data Center. *Journal of Grid Computing*, 21(4), 61. Advance online publication. DOI: 10.1007/s10723-023-09696-5

Harika, A., Tajuddin, S., Bhavani, P., Harsha, D., & Sriteja, P. (2023). Optimizing Scalability and Resilience: Strategies for Aligning DevOps and Cloud-Native Approaches. *2023 3rd International Conference on Innovative Mechanisms for Industry Applications (ICIMIA)*. DOI: 10.1109/ICIMIA60377.2023.10426288

Maenhaut, P., Volckaert, B., Ongenae, V., & De Turck, F. (2019). Resource Management in a Containerized Cloud: Status and Challenges. *Journal of Network and Systems Management*, 28(2), 197–246. DOI: 10.1007/s10922-019-09504-0

Mayar, K., Carmichael, D. G., & Shen, X. (2022). Resilience and Systems - A Review. *Sustainability (Basel)*, 14(14), 8327. DOI: 10.3390/su14148327

Nordström, A. (2024). Exploring GitOps for Smaller-Scale Applications. *Urn.fi*. https://www.doria.fi/handle/10024/188668

Pakalapati, N., Jeyaraman, J., & Sistla, S. (2023). Building Resilient Systems: Leveraging AI/ML within DevSecOps Frameworks. *Journal of Knowledge Learning and Science Technology ISSN: 2959-6386 (online)*. DOI: 10.60087/jklst.vol2.n2.p230

Prins, T., VanVossen, R., Barnett, T., & Elliott, L. (2022). Containerization in Embedded Trusted Computing. *SAE Technical Papers on CD-ROM/SAE Technical Paper Series, 1*. DOI: 10.4271/2024-01-3982

Rahman, A., Shamim, S. I., Bose, D. B., & Pandita, R. (2023). Security Misconfigurations in Open Source Kubernetes Manifests: An Empirical Study. *ACM Transactions on Software Engineering and Methodology*, 32(4), 1–36. Advance online publication. DOI: 10.1145/3579639

Russo, A., & Alexandre Proutiere. (2021). Towards Optimal Attacks on Reinforcement Learning Policies. *2021 American Control Conference (ACC)*, 4561–4567. DOI: 10.23919/ACC50511.2021.9483025

Saleh Sedghpour, M. R., Klein, C., & Tordsson, J. (2022). An Empirical Study of Service Mesh Traffic Management Policies for Microservices. *Proceedings of the 2022 ACM/SPEC on International Conference on Performance Engineering*. DOI: 10.1145/3489525.3511686

Sandu, A. K. (2021). DevSecOps: Integrating Security into the DevOps Lifecycle for Enhanced Resilience. *Technology & Management Review, 6*, 1–19. https://upright.pub/index.php/tmr/article/view/131

Thurgood, B., & Lennon, R. G. (2019). Cloud Computing with Kubernetes Cluster Elastic Scaling. *Proceedings of the 3rd International Conference on Future Networks and Distributed Systems*. DOI: 10.1145/3341325.3341995

Torkura, K., Sukmana, M., Cheng, F., & Meinel, C. (2020). CloudStrike: Chaos Engineering for Security and Resiliency in Cloud Infrastructure. *IEEE Access : Practical Innovations, Open Solutions*, 8, 123044–123060. DOI: 10.1109/ACCESS.2020.3007338

Wang, H., Liu, L., Yue, C., Wang, L., Li, B., Chang, J., & Pang, B. (2024). Cloud-native systems resilience assessments based on Kubernetes architecture graph. *Service Oriented Computing and Applications*. Advance online publication. DOI: 10.1007/s11761-024-00406-x

Welsh, T., & Benkhelifa, E. (2020). On Resilience in Cloud Computing: A survey of techniques across the cloud domain. *ACM Computing Surveys*, 53(3), 1–36. DOI: 10.1145/3388922

Zhang, L., Morin, B., Haller, P., Baudry, B., & Monperrus, M. (2021). A Chaos Engineering System for Live Analysis and Falsification of Exception-Handling in the JVM. *IEEE Transactions on Software Engineering*, 47(11), 2534–2548. Advance online publication. DOI: 10.1109/TSE.2019.2954871

Chapter 14
The Security Implications of Microservices in Modern Software Development

Areesha Fatima
https://orcid.org/0009-0001-7602-6691
Stanley College of Engineering and Technology for Women, India

C. Kishor Kumar
Stanley College of Engineering and Technology for Women, India

Syed Unais Panjathan
Muffakham Jah College of Engineering and Technology, India

Srinath Doss
Botho University, Botswana

ABSTRACT

Microservices architecture has revolutionized software development by enabling scalability, resilience, and agility. However, its distributed and decentralized nature introduces unique security challenges. This paper explores the implications of adopting microservices, emphasizing the expanded attack surface, inter-service communication vulnerabilities, and distributed data management risks. Key areas covered include robust authentication mechanisms (OAuth 2.0, JWT), secure inter-service communication via mutual TLS, and the role of service meshes like Istio in enhancing security. Emerging trends, such as the integration of AI/ML for anomaly detection and blockchain for transaction integrity, are discussed alongside future developments in API security standards. By addressing vulnerabilities and implementing proactive security measures, this paper aims to guide organizations in achieving a secure and efficient microservices environment.

DOI: 10.4018/979-8-3373-0365-9.ch014

1. INTRODUCTION

Microservices architecture is a software design where applications are designed as a collection of small, autonomous services communicating with each other (Bakshi, 2017). Every service is designed to perform one specific business function, which operates independently of its database and codebase. This modular design allows developers to build, deploy, and scale parts of an application without affecting others, making microservices a popular choice for modern, large-scale applications. Key principles of this architecture include autonomy, where each service functions independently; single responsibility, focusing on one task or business capability; loose coupling to minimize dependencies between services; decentralized data management to enable scalability; and lightweight communication using protocols like HTTP/REST, gRPC, or message queues.

Their significant advantages have driven the adoption of microservices. Such examples include scalability as different team services may be scaled independently based on their required demand, and flexibility, which ensures changes to or replacement of services could be done without stopping an entire application. Also, microservices help diversify technology, whereby several programs or frameworks could be chosen for different services of different teams, while promoting isolated faults, making a total system failure with just a single service impossible. These benefits have been particularly influential in the domains of e-commerce, finance, and cloud computing because agility and fast deployment become very crucial there. Companies like Netflix, Amazon, and Spotify have adapted well to such architecture and managed complex systems with very high demand (Blinowski, Ojdowska, & Przybyłek, 2022).

This architecture is compared with monolithic architectures where the application is built as a single, unified codebase. Although monolithic architectures are easier to develop and deploy initially, they get really tough to scale and maintain when applications become large in complexity. Even a small update in a monolithic system requires redeployment of the entire application which causes downtime and risks failure (Oyeniran, Adewusi, Adeleke, Akwawa, & Azubuko, 2024). On the other hand, microservices break up the application into independent services, allowing for faster development, easier scaling of individual components, and greater agility in deploying updates. But with this flexibility comes a cost. The distributed nature of microservices introduces significant operational complexity, requiring robust systems for service discovery, load balancing, and communication. It also increases the attack surface, making security a critical consideration.

Security is a prime factor in microservices environments with their decentralized and distributed architectures. In monolithic applications, security can be centralized at a single entry point, but in microservices, multiple independent services operate across networks, which also brings challenges such as implementing secure inter-service communication, ensuring consistent authentication and authorization mechanisms, and protecting sensitive data across multiple boundaries of services. Microservices applications are also exposed to the risk of injection attacks and data leaks because the application uses APIs, another aspect of microservices applications. All these complexities, in turn, require more proactive security, where best practices such as encryption and the use of API gateway with zero trust principles are being integrated into all layers of the development lifecycle with great precision.

2. UNDERSTANDING THE MICROSERVICES ATTACK SURFACE

Decentralization in microservices architecture poses unique security challenges from the very outset, primarily in the form of the number of independent components that have increased. In contrast to monolithic systems, which have a single cohesive structure that limits external interactions, microservices rely on a large number of small services working together. Every service is a potential entry point for attackers, significantly expanding the attack surface. Such decentralization calls for strong security measures at every level to protect individual services and their interactions. Effective implementation of microservice architecture security requires specific technological references to steer clear of identified dangers (Abdelfattah & Cerny, 2022).

Another important concern in microservices is inter-service communication. Services commonly communicate over networks using HTTP/REST, gRPC, or message queues and can be vulnerable to being intercepted, spoofed, or the subject of man-in-the-middle attacks (Mateus-Coelho, Cruz-Cunha, & Ferreira, 2021). Secure communication has to be ensured through encryption protocols like TLS, authentication like mutual TLS, and vigilant monitoring for anomalies in traffic patterns. Without this, an attacker could gain entry into the system or access sensitive data through those communication channels.

Distributed data management further complicates security in microservices. A monolithic architecture usually tends to centralize data within a single database, while microservices often maintain distributed databases, where each service controls its data store. This pattern, though beneficial for scalability and fault isolation, increases the risk of data breaches, as sensitive information may spread across multiple services, with difficulty in implementing consistent encryption, access controls, and compliance measures. Organizations must embrace a holistic data protection strategy, including strong encryption, secure key management, and regular audits, to mitigate the risks associated with distributed data. Figure 1 illustrates the microservices architecture, showcasing independent services communicating via APIs. It highlights decentralized data management, lightweight communication protocols, and the modularity that enables scalability and fault tolerance.

Figure 1. Overview of Monolithic and Miccroservice Application

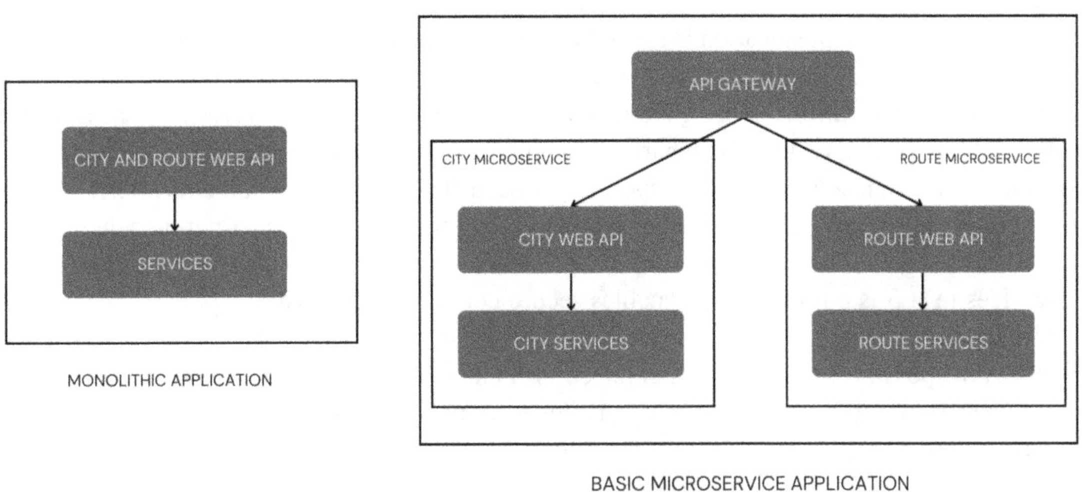

3. AUTHENTICATION AND AUTHORIZATION IN MICROSERVICES

This assurance that only valid users and services are accessing a particular resource is the major concern of security in microservices. Since the very nature of microservices is decentralized, authentication and authorization have to be done such that scalability, and resiliency with no latency occur and they stay secure as well.

Authentication is the act of validating the identity of any users or services that intend to access the system (Mateus-Coelho, Cruz-Cunha, & Ferreira, 2021). Most is true for microservices in employing access delegation protocols such as OAuth 2.0 and OpenID Connect which support secure delegation. In this case, users shall authorize access without having the secret credentials out of an abuser's hands. OpenID Connect provides for an identity layer atop OAuth 2.0 mainly by the use of JSON Web Tokens for the secured transfer of authentication data (de Almeida & Canedo, 2022). Equally relevant is service-to-service authentication where mutual TLS or API key can ensure that only the authorized service can interact.

Authorization explains what an authenticated user or service can do. In general, microservices make use of either Role-Based Access Control or Attribute-Based Access Control. RBAC is when permission is predefined in the manner of admin, user, or guest. Role-based access control significantly boosts the system's flexibility by configuring the user's authority through the role (ShuLin & JiePing, 2020). On the other hand, in ABAC, attributes may include the location of a user, the time of access, device type, etc., evaluated for access. ABAC is more flexible and especially fits dynamic situations. Most organizations make use of APIs or a service mesh architecture as a means to rationalize and centralize all such processes. API gateways provide for a single entry for authentication, rate limiting, and access control, while applying service meshes, such as Istio, enforce security policies at every point where there is interaction about service-to-service. Applying such mechanisms integrated into these microservices environments can very well maintain a high-security posture while remaining agile as well as scalable.

3.1 Service-to-Service Authentication

Service-to-service authentication is a critical component of securing communication between microservices, ensuring that only authorized services can interact with each other. As microservices gain popularity, this feature authentication is crucial for two communicating parties to verify and authorize their identities. Typically, mutual TLS and API keys are employed to achieve this.

One way to implement this is using Mutual Transport Layer Security (mTLS), which is an extension of TLS protocol that requires both parties, the client, and the server to be authenticated during the TLS handshaking sequence. Mutual Transport Layer Security (mTLS) is an authentication method that ensures the confidentiality and integrity of the data being transmitted by facilitating safe connection between microservices in a distributed system (Jack, Teck, Ming, & Hong, 2023). When we talk about microservices mTLS is a protocol that enables secure communication within applications by proving the identities of both communicating services through digital certificates. This mutual authentication mechanism is responsible for stopping the connection of unauthorized services, data encryption in transit, and digital certificates to prevent forwarding or altering of packets. mTLS plays a crucial role in service mesh architecture like Istio and Linkerd that automatically enforce the encrypted and authenticated communication between microservices.

As for the API keys, they reduce the complex procedure by creating a simpler authentication model. Simply put, an API key is a token that is assigned to a service and is then included in the request for the service to access another. The receiving service checks the API key for validity before granting access, which limits the access just to the authorized services. Having this easy to implement technology to transfer data it does not mean that it is not under risk, it is still the responsibility of the end-user organization to practice good security practices. API keys are usually preferred because they are straightforward, reliable, and easy to utilize when paired with powerful techniques (Matias, Ferreira, Mateus-Coelho, & Ferreira, 2024). Some of these practices would be, changing the API key frequently, and or making the keys available for only particular resources, additionally encrypting the transmission data using HTTPS.

Mutual TLS and API keys are both used to manage the issue of secure communication between different services in a microservices environment. On the one hand, mTLS ensures stronger security due to encryption and mutual verification, while API keys are used with simple use cases. Service-to-service authentication is the security guarantee of combining these with proper monitoring and access controls. As a result, the service-to-service authentication operates in a way that is strong, scalable, and is resistant to any kind of attacks.

3.2 User Authentication

Industry-standard protocols, such as OAuth 2.0, OpenID Connect, and JSON Web Tokens, are used to make access in the microservices environment secure and scalable. All these together authenticate a user and provide a seamless experience while being highly secured.

OAuth 2.0 is a very popular authorization protocol that helps ensure secure access. Rather than sharing a sensitive credential, OAuth 2.0 allows a user to give permission to third-party applications to access specific resources on behalf of the user (Kotenko, Moskalyk, Kovach, & Osadchyi, 2024). The protocol works on getting access tokens issued by the authorization server after successful authentication, which is further used by the clients to request secure access to the resource servers without revealing the user credentials. OpenID Connect (OIDC) is an extension to OAuth 2.0 and provides an identity layer over OAuth 2.0. Hence, it is also a full-fledged solution for authentication. OIDC allows clients to authenticate the user's identity by making use of the authentication that has been performed by an authorization server (Saravanan & Gogineni, 2024). It introduces the ID token, which serves as a verifiable, secure representation of the user identity information in the JWTs. In other words, services can rely on the identity of the user without having to manage any authentication processes themselves.

JSON Web Tokens, or JWTs are small, compact tokens often used in microservices for safe information transfer among parties. JWT has three parts: the header, payload, and signature. The payload may carry claims about the user or the entity being authenticated, including a user ID or roles; the signature assures that this token hasn't been tampered with. JWTs are particularly fit for microservices. Every microservice leverages the information given within the web token to fulfill its permission requirements (Matias, Ferreira, Mateus-Coelho, Ribeiro, & Ferreira, 2024). As JWTs are stateless, there is no need to store it on the server side, thus, it can be validated independently by each service with a shared secret or public key instead of dependency on some centralized session store. Microservices environments can easily implement strong user authentication by combining OAuth 2.0, OpenID Connect, and JWTs. These technologies support modern application needs: scalable and flexible authentication mechanisms protect user data and system resources.

3.3 Access Control Models

Access control models are essential when managing permissions in microservices in order to ensure that authenticated users or services have access to only authorized resources or operations. Two of the most implemented models are Role-Based Access Control (RBAC) and Attribute-Based Access Control (ABAC), each carrying different characteristics, strengths, and use cases.

3.3.1 Role-Based Access Control (RBAC)

Role-Based Access Control, in general, grants access permissions to the users or entities based on their roles in a system. The role-based access control (RBAC) approach is a centralized authorization method for microservices architecture (Venčkauskas, Kukta, Grigaliūnas, & Brūzgienė, 2023). A role represents a set of permissions associated with specific tasks or responsibilities. For example, the "user" role could have read permission, whereas the "admin" role could modify or delete. The most notable features of RBAC include simplicity, scalability, and granularity. It is easy to manage and understand the model since roles are predefined. It achieves scalability through the addition of new users assigned to existing roles in order to allow them quick access permissions, and it allows for role fine-tuning in the provision of varied levels of access. RBAC is best suited for applications that have a well-defined hierarchy of roles, such as "admin," "editor," and "viewer," and systems with stable permission requirements that do not frequently change. However, it is too cumbersome in complex systems that have many roles and overlapping responsibilities. It does not provide flexibility in making dynamic access decisions based on the context.

3.3.2 Attribute-Based Access Control (ABAC)

Attribute-Based Access Control (ABAC), on the other hand, uses attributes (or characteristics) to determine access permissions. Attributes can pertain to the user (e.g., job title, department), the resource (e.g., type, sensitivity), or the context (e.g., time, location). For instance, a policy might allow users in the "sales" department to access resources during business hours using a company device. ABAC's strengths include flexibility, granularity, and scalability. It enables dynamic and context-aware policies, allowing real-time adjustments to access permissions (Mohamed, Mostafa, Assaly, & Shalabi, 2024). By combining multiple attributes, ABAC supports highly specific access decisions, offering fine-grained control. Additionally, broad policies eliminate the need to manage numerous individual roles. ABAC is suitable for systems with dynamic access needs, such as geographically distributed teams or time-sensitive operations, and organizations requiring strict control over sensitive data. However, ABAC's complexity can pose challenges during implementation. It requires careful planning and robust systems to manage attributes and enforce policies, as misconfigurations may result in unintended access or restrictions. Table 1 explores some differences between the two access control systems.

Table 1. Differences between Role-Based Access Control and Attribute-Based Access Control

Aspect	RBAC	ABAC
Simplicity	Easier to implement and manage.	More complex due to dynamic attribute evaluation.
Flexibility	Limited; tied to predefined roles.	Highly flexible; supports dynamic policies.
Granularity	Role-based permissions; moderate granularity.	Attribute-based permissions; fine-grained.
Scalability	Works well in static, hierarchical systems.	Scales effectively in dynamic environments.

4. SECURING APIS AND INTER-SERVICE COMMUNICATION

The architecture of microservices needs to be designed to secure APIs and inter-service communications because most microservices systems heavily rely on APIs for communication. Among such measures of securing these aspects of communication are the use of HTTPS as an encryption protocol, plus mutual TLS-mTLS in authentication. Of course, API gateways feature prominently in this sense with access control, rate limiting, and authentication. It depends on OAuth 2.0 or OpenID Connect for secure token-based access. Rotation of the API keys or tokens, whitelist of IP, validation payload prevents unauthorized access and injecting attacks. Monitoring traffic, pattern analysis, intrusion detectors help identify anomalies much beforehand, mitigating real time threats.

4.1 API Gateway Role

An API gateway is an entry point to manage and secure API interactions within a microservices architecture (Jack, Teck, Ming, & Hong, 2023). It acts as a bridge between the clients and services, facilitating communication while enforcing critical security and operational policies. It has a primary role in managing authentication and authorization through integration with protocols such as OAuth 2.0 or OpenID Connect for verifying user and service credentials. It gives the client a simplified image of a microservice-based application by hiding its internal organization from them (Haindl, Kochberger, & Sveggen, 2024). Besides rate limiting for protection against abuse by limiting requests of a client within an explicit timeframe to prevent the overwhelming of services or even denial-of-service attacks, this gateway verifies incoming requests that conform to predefined conditions. Such conditions may involve compliance with the schema for certain types of data or, conversely, token validation in other types of scenarios to reduce the risk of injection attacks and malformed data. By centralizing these functions, an API gateway simplifies the management of microservices, enhances security, and improves system reliability. Figure 2 explains the role of an API gateway in securing microservices. It demonstrates processes like authentication, logging, Cashing, and permission granting to ensure secure API interactions.

Figure 2. API Gateway Authentication Process

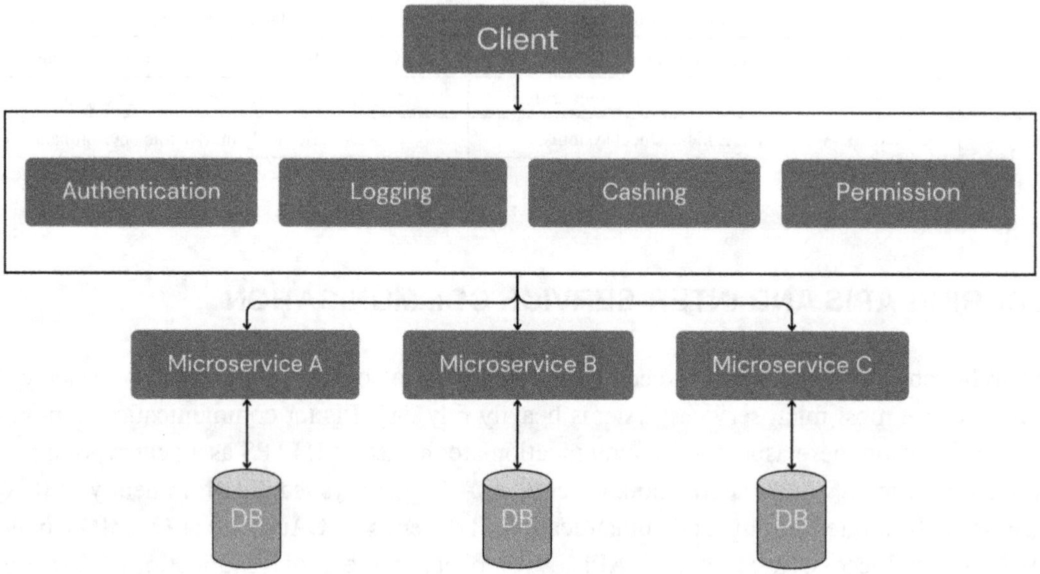

4.2 Common API Vulnerabilities

APIs are an essential part of microservices but also a favorite target for vulnerabilities. Injection attacks occur when bad input, such as SQL, NoSQL, or command injections, is sent to an API and then exploits poorly sanitized input fields to execute unauthorized commands or access data (Kamruzzaman, Thakur, & Ali, 2024). Broken authentication is another very common issue, often due to weak or poorly implemented authentication mechanisms, allowing attackers to impersonate users or services. This risk is more pronounced in APIs that do not validate tokens or enforce secure session handling. Excessive data exposure occurs when APIs return more information than needed, which inadvertently leaks sensitive data. This often happens because responses are not sufficiently filtered and data queries are too broad. The key to these vulnerabilities is enforcing strict input validation and well-designed authentication protocols such as OAuth 2.0, with careful design to API that would minimize the exposure of data and follow the principle of least privilege. Table 2 lists and categorizes common security vulnerabilities specific to microservices architectures, such as injection attacks, broken authentication, and excessive data exposure, along with examples and mitigation strategies (Kamruzzaman, Thakur, & Ali, 2024).

Table 2. Common Security Vulnerabilities in Microservices

Vulnerability Type	Description	Example Mitigation Techniques
Injection Attacks	Malicious input to exploit vulnerabilities	Input validation, parameterized queries
Broken Authentication	Flaws in identity verification mechanisms	OAuth 2.0, OpenID Connect, MFA
Excessive Data Exposure	Leaking more data than necessary in responses	Data filtering, enforcing least privilege

4.3 Encryption Protocols

Microservices require encryption protocols, mainly Transport Layer Security (TLS), to ensure secure communication. TLS encrypts the data in transit so that attackers cannot intercept or view the data during communication between clients and services or microservices. Digital certificates by TLS authenticate both parties within a connection, thus providing protection against man-in-the-middle attacks (Nookala, 2024). In addition, TLS ensures the integrity of data. Information transmitted cannot be changed while in transit. This is important in microservices architectures where services frequently communicate over networks. Therefore, confidentiality and trust in a system are ensured, which safeguards sensitive data such as credentials, tokens, and user information. As a result, TLS is an important part of modern applications and is widely adopted with its robust security features. Table 3 gives a comparison of encryption techniques for securing data both in transit and at rest within a microservices environment.

Table 3. Types of Encryption for Microservices

Encryption Type	Description	Use Case	Strengths
TLS	Encryption for secure communication over networks	Securing service-to-service communication	End-to-end encryption, widely adopted
AES	Symmetric encryption for data at rest	Encrypting sensitive data on disk or databases	Fast and secure
RSA	Asymmetric encryption for key exchange	Securing communications in distributed systems	Secure key exchange and authentication

5. DATA SECURITY IN A DISTRIBUTED ENVIRONMENT

Data security in a distributed environment, such as microservices architecture, is different in the sense that data is distributed and managed in a decentralized manner. In this system, unlike the centralized database in monolithic systems, each service stores its data independently. This offers good scalability and fault isolation but introduces complexity in terms of protecting sensitive information. The best data security should focus on addressing risks at different levels, including data transmission, storage, and access.

Securing communication channels while transferring data between services is pretty important. The most widely-used protocol to encrypt the data while it is in transfer is Transport Layer Security, or TLS (Jack, Teck, Ming, & Hong, 2023). It bars any unauthorized access or interceptions of data, which ensures that, during communication, both the client and server will be able to verify their identity. This protocol secures tokens, credentials, and even user information to exchange between services.

For data at rest, mechanisms for encrypting should be strong in the prevention of unauthorized access. Every microservice will be asked to make use of the same encryption standards such as AES-256 in order to protect the same data stores (Li et al., 2025). Best key management is also imperative that involves storing and rotating encryption keys with Hardware Security Modules or dedicated key management services (Salin & Fokin, 2022). However, as regards the handling of user data by these organizations, the main requirement is compliance with regulations like GDPR or CCPA and using strong encryption to protect information.

Thus, in a distributed system, one should implement access control at such a level that makes users or services see certain data (Venčkauskas, Kukta, Grigaliūnas, & Brūzgienė, 2023). RBAC as well as ABAC enable the right level of fine-grained permission enforcing when either roles or attribute contextual ones are used. Then, on top of the above, one will need to analyze or monitor the access log of all accesses for particular patterns, especially maliciously pointing out to the possible attack or security breach. This helps ensure scalability and flexibility offered by the microservices architecture while addressing specific data security challenges of distributed environments to secure sensitive information.

5.1 Data Encryption

Encryption of data forms the core of microservices security, which protects the sensitive information at rest as well as in transit. Each step of encryption is for an end: safeguarding information from unauthorized access, its integrity, and compliance with security standards. Encrypting data at rest safeguards information stored in databases, file systems, or backups from unauthorized access. This could be done using encryption algorithms like AES-256 which gives robust protection through symmetric key encryption (Mateus-Coelho, Cruz-Cunha, & Ferreira, 2021; Li et al., 2025). Good ways of securing data at rest are through encrypting a whole disk volume, database tables, or specific fields containing sensitive data. Proper key management is a fundamental process because encryption keys must be securely stored within HSMs or through cloud key management services (Salin & Fokin, 2022).

Data in transit refers to the movement of information between clients and servers or between microservices. Encryption during transmission prevents attackers from intercepting or tampering with the data. The most commonly used protocol for encrypting data in transit is Transport Layer Security (TLS). It ensures confidentiality and integrity. Mutual TLS (mTLS) extends this to authenticate both ends of the communication channel, thereby improving trust in service-to-service interactions (Jack, Teck, Ming, & Hong, 2023). All API endpoints should use HTTPS for data in motion, implement secure WebSocket protocols for real-time communication, and use VPNs or private networks for sensitive internal traffic (Thumburu, 2021). Protect sensitive information, maintain user trust, and ensure regulatory compliance by using robust encryption strategies for data both at rest and in transit. Encryption is very effective if combined with other security measures, like access control and monitoring, for adequate comprehensive data security.

5.2 Data Consistency vs. Security

Data consistency, security, and integrity in distributed databases are perhaps the biggest challenges in microservices architectures. Usually, for better availability and performance, distributed systems prioritize these aspects over data confidentiality and integrity. Data Consistency among replicas in distributed databases refers to the fact that these replicas should reflect the same data, even though this is spread across many geographical locations. Strong consistency models, like those offered by SQL systems, guarantee immediate synchronicity among nodes but bring some latency. Eventual consistency models, which are primarily used in NoSQL, focus on performance and availability by allowing temporary inconsistencies but ensuring that they get settled over time. Such performance optimizations can make security tough, especially when dealing with sensitive data (Soni & Jyotinagar, 2023).

Data security primarily addresses the protection of data against unauthorized access, tampering, or breach, typically involving encryption, access controls, and other mechanisms to ensure robust auditing. Still, these practices will inevitably influence performance and consistency. For example, encrypting data in rest and during transfer adds overhead to computations and hence affects the speed of reading and writing. Also, applying strong access controls or secure communication protocols such as TLS could cause a latency in transactions that could sometimes interfere with the requirements for real-time consistency.

To balance performance with security, organizations must implement policies that are tailored to the needs of their organization. Employing hybrid consistency models, where sensitive information uses strong consistency for precision and security, while less mission-critical data uses eventual consistency for performance, is possible. Data encryption should be optimized for efficient algorithms, and hardware-based encryption accelerators can reduce computation overhead. It minimizes the performance impact and maintains confidentiality by selectively encrypting or tokenizing only the most sensitive fields. Achieving a balance between data consistency and security in distributed databases requires a nuanced approach, leveraging tailored consistency models, optimized encryption techniques, and strategic system design. These factors can be aligned with the application's requirements to ensure high performance and robust data protection.

6. DevSecOps: INTEGRATING SECURITY INTO THE DEVELOPMENT LIFECYCLE

DevSecOps is an evolutionary version of DevOps and involves integrating security into every stage of the SDLC in order to identify vulnerabilities early and continuously (Zhang & Zhang, 2024). This means that security practice will be embedded into all development, testing, deployment, and operations, so that the responsibility of security is shared across teams and not treated as something afterthought. This starts from the planning phase, as threat modeling and risk assessments can determine possible vulnerabilities that may occur within the design of the system. Through development, best practices such as secure coding practices and static application security testing tools, help detect flaws in the codebase. Developers are nudged towards security best practices like input validation and using secure APIs, reducing vulnerability injection. Figure 3 visualizes the integration of security in the SDLC, highlighting stages like static and dynamic code analysis, automated vulnerability scanning in CI/CD pipelines, and continuous monitoring for real-time threat detection and mitigation.

Figure 3. Secure Software Development Life Cycle (SDLC)

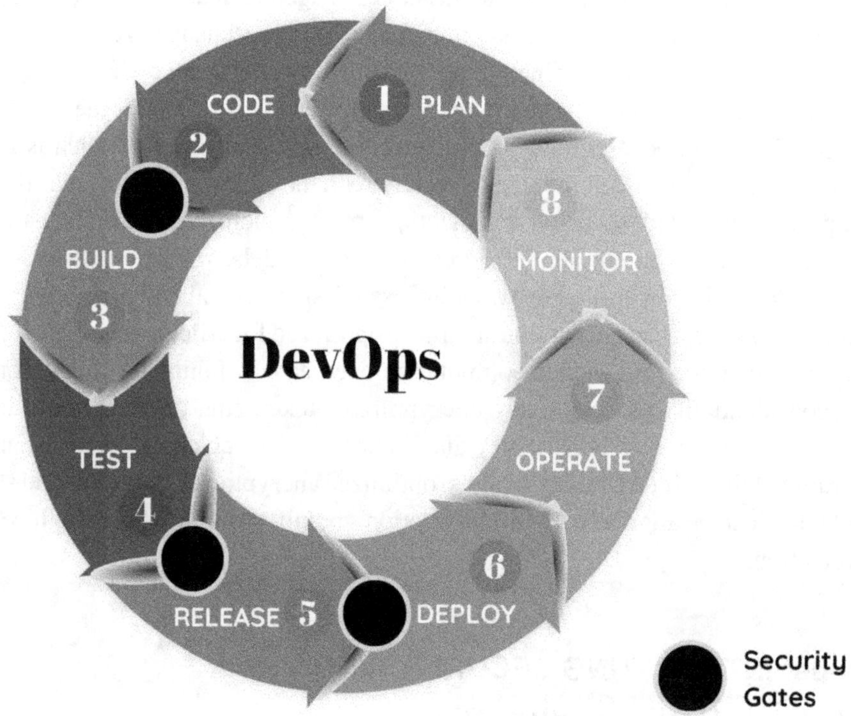

Dynamic application security testing (DAST) and penetration testing in the testing phase simulate real-world attacks to find weaknesses in running applications (Chandramouli, 2022). Security scanning is also automated as part of CI/CD pipelines, providing fast feedback and remediation. Another area of monitoring third-party libraries for known vulnerabilities through dependency analysis tools is important, given the wide usage of open-source components.

DevSecOps emphasizes continuous monitoring of applications and infrastructure to identify and respond to emerging threats in real time post-deployment. Operations workflow is integrated with tools such as log analysis, intrusion detection, and anomaly detection. Automated patch management helps maintain updates on vulnerabilities without impeding the development pace. By bringing development, operations, and security teams together, DevSecOps bridges the traditional silos of those groups and creates a culture of shared accountability. This proactive approach not only strengthens application security but also reduces the costs and delays associated with late-stage fixes, enabling organizations to deliver secure software at speed.

6.1 Shift-Left Security

Left-shift security is a proactive approach that incorporates security testing at the earliest possible stages in the software development lifecycle, especially in the CI/CD pipeline (Zareinia, 2023). The reduction of risks and remediation costs and ensuring secure software delivery are achieved through addressing vulnerabilities during the development phase. With the shift-left approach, security testing comes earlier in the development cycle. Security checks are included at the earliest stage of development, and security becomes integral to the development process. Developers will use static application security testing tools, such as source code scanning, to find vulnerabilities before it progresses any further into writing code. This helps eliminate problems such as SQL injection or insecure input handling early in the development process.

In the CI/CD pipeline, automated security testing ensures that every code commit is checked for compliance with security policies. DAST tools simulate runtime environments to identify issues that may not be apparent in static code analysis (Zareinia, 2023; Shekhar, 2023). Moreover, SCA scans for vulnerabilities in third-party dependencies, which are increasingly used in modern applications. Beyond tooling, shift-left security emphasizes a security-first mindset in developers. Training programs, security guidelines, and feedback loops in the development environment help teams write secure code from the very beginning. The integration of security in CI/CD pipelines further supports seamless collaboration between the development, operations, and security teams; this reduces friction and ensures their goals are aligned.

Table 4. Tools for Integrating Security into CI/CD Pipelines

Tool	Functionality	Integration Points	Example Tool
SAST	Static analysis of code for vulnerabilities	Pre-commit, build, or test stages	SonarQube, Checkmarx
Dependency Checker	Scanning dependencies for known vulnerabilities	Dependency management and build stages	Snyk, OWASP Dependency-Check
Secret Scanning	Identifying secrets or credentials in code	During code push or commit phases	TruffleHog, Git-secrets

Table 4 identifies automated security tools integrated into the CI/CD pipeline to support shift-left security, including tools for scanning code and dependencies. Shifting security leftward helps catch vulnerabilities early and often, which improves the overall security posture while not slowing down modern development practices. It makes sure that security is no longer a bottleneck but an integral part of the development process, and therefore, software delivery will be faster and safer.

6.2 Automated Security Tools

Automated security tools alleviate a majority of risks from microservices, and modern distributed systems, addressing fundamental flaws in Embedded Security Architecture as devsecops seeks to provide firsthand security management. Such tools are embedded into development life cycles as deploying seamlessly which aids early threat identification and provides perpetual cover (Theodoropoulos et al., 2023).

6.2.1 Vulnerability Scanners

Vulnerability scannners bring efficiency as well serve as the first line of defence against potential security breaches within applications, networks, or systems. SAST tools review the codes for major vulnerabilities like injection attacks, insecure setups, or secrets that are hard-coded while DAST studies the attack scenarios and its runtime effects like logic flaws or logics bypassing. Thus, once be it DAST or SAST, Vulnerability scanners can provide comprehensive reports that can enable developers and security agencies to mitigate the risks from all the weakpoints before an Attack (Chandramouli, 2022).

6.2.2 Dependency Checkers

Dependency checkers help identify known vulnerabilities in third-party components. As the use of open-source libraries is spreading, the need for dependency checkers arises to identify potential vulnerabilities. Tools like OWASP Dependency-Check and Snyk scan your project's dependencies against public databases like CVEs and flag your insecure versions. These tools also offer patched versions and mitigations that teams can secure their supply chain without sacrificing their development speed (Adhikari, 2024). Automated checks of dependency in CI/CD pipelines ensure only secure components reach production.

6.2.3 Runtime Protection Tools

Runtime application self-protection (RASP) and web application firewalls (WAF) are forms of active monitoring and protection for applications in production environments (Wang, Guo, Liu, & Zhu, 2022). RASP tools embed security directly into the application, detecting and blocking threats such as injection attacks or unauthorized access attempts as they occur (Edmundson & Hartman, 2022). WAFs act as a protective barrier between users and the application, filtering malicious traffic based on predefined rules or machine learning models. These runtime tools are critical to protecting against real-time attacks that bypass earlier testing stages.

Organizations can achieve comprehensive security coverage across their development and operational processes by leveraging these automated tools. When combined with manual testing and a security-first culture, these tools help maintain a robust security posture while enabling the rapid iteration demanded by modern software development.

6.3 Security as Code

The concept is security as code, how a security policy and its associated controls are addressed in some form of programmatic construct, hence directly embedded within the software development lifecycle, infrastructures, therefore managed in a version-controlled fashion just as code does. Security, once programmatically defined, automates itself and becomes version-controlled but consistently applied just as it has when application code is created and defined (Haverinen et al., 2024).

In Security as Code, security policies are defined using code, often through IaC tools such as Terraform, Ansible, or CloudFormation. Those tools define security settings for cloud resources, networks, access controls, and many other things (Alghawli & Radivilova, 2024). For example, the policy could be that certain VMs must have specific firewall rules or that storage buckets have to be encrypted. The enforcement of such policies happens through automated pipelines in which both code and infrastructure undergo verifications ensuring conformance with security specifications at deployment.

The first major benefit of Security as Code is to enable the automation of security, so the scope of human error will be significantly reduced; besides that, the same policies are deployed on all environments. Due to application code versioning, so security policies are versioned just like the code and consequently can be audited or tracked side by side with how it changes for the applications or infrastructures. This further increases visibility and traceability because security configurations are also integrated into the CI/CD pipeline and managed within version-controlled repositories, which then allows for easier review and modification if necessary.

Security as Code is closely coupled with CI/CD pipelines, which means security checks are run at each point in the development cycle (Reddy, Alluri, Thota, Ravi, & Bonam, 2021). As an example, one could include security linting tools in the pipeline, which scan for common security misconfigurations or policy violations in infrastructure code. This would mean that if checks fail, the deployments would automatically stop before insecure configurations are allowed into production.

Security policies articulated through code can be modified in real-time according to various factors, including evolving regulatory mandates, emerging security risks, or alterations in system configurations. For example, when a vulnerability is identified in a particular version of an application, it becomes possible to revise the security policy to implement a patch or alleviate the associated risk across all operational environments without the need for manual adjustments.

With the possibility of programmatically defining Identity and Access Management (IAM) rules, least-privilege access at all levels can be enforced with automated role assignment and permission enforcement (Kumar & Goyal, 2020). Employing infrastructure-as-code methodologies to delineate firewalls, subnets, and security group regulations to guarantee secure network configurations. Overall, Security as Code redefines security from being a collection of manual and reactive activities to becoming an integrated and automated procedure that is embedded within the application lifecycle. Through the codification of security policies, organizations can guarantee the ongoing and uniform maintenance of security, thereby diminishing the likelihood of breaches and facilitating accelerated and more secure development.

7. NETWORK SECURITY IN MICROSERVICES

Security in microservices networks is a critical component to maintaining the integrity, confidentiality, and availability of services within a distributed framework. In a microservices architecture, where various services interact over networks, it is imperative to implement stringent network security protocols to mitigate the risks of unauthorized access, data breaches, and service interruptions.

7.1 Zero Trust Architecture

Zero Trust Architecture (ZTA) is a security model that operates on the principle of no implicit trust, regardless of whether a request comes from inside or outside the network perimeter. In this framework, every interaction, be it between users, devices, or services—is considered untrusted until it is verified (Syed et al., 2022). This represents a departure from traditional security models that emphasize perimeter defenses, where anything within the network is often presumed to be safe. Instead, Zero Trust mandates continuous authentication, authorization, and validation before allowing access to any resources, thereby enhancing security in modern, distributed environments such as microservices architectures.

Zero Trust requires each user, device, and service to verify their identity before they are granted access to any resource, through multi-factor authentication (MFA), digital certificates, or some other identity-verifying mechanism. In addition, the request's context (e.g., time of access, location, device security posture) are also scrutinized to determine the authenticity of the request for access. Zero Trust operates on the principle of least privilege, whereby access is granted only to the resources and/or services strictly necessary for a user/device/service to function. All permissions are under continuous evaluation and modification based on the role of users, risk assessment, as well as the context of the request.

Zero Trust specifications require that access be continuously monitored and reported. It involves tracking what resources or services were accessed by whom and under what conditions. Suspicious activity raises a flag as real-time alerts can facilitate instant investigations. This constant watch guarantees that security threats are detected and remedied instantly. Zero Trust is the micro-segmentation that partitions the networks into smaller isolated zones (Syed et al., 2022). This step restricts lateral movement after the attacker has succeeded in breaching one segment since he will not have any direct access to other parts of the network. Each microservice or resource is treated as its own independent unit, with its security policies enforced individually. Figure 4 illustrates the Zero Trust principles in a microservices environment.

Figure 4. Zero Trust Model

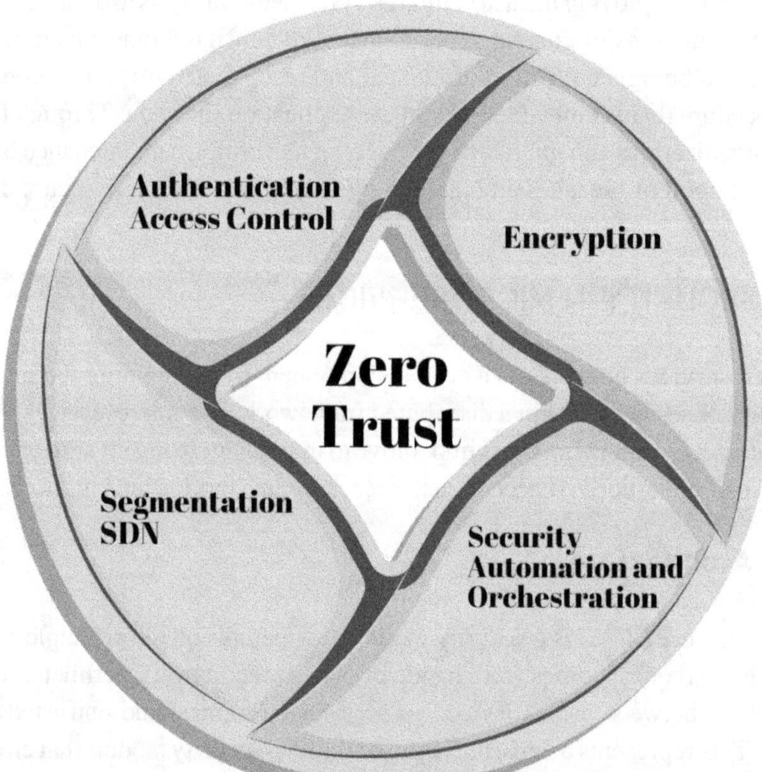

In a Zero Trust model, access decisions are not fixed. They are continuously reassessed based on real-time information regarding the user's context, device behavior, and other relevant factors. If the risk level rises (for instance, if a user logs in from an unfamiliar location), access permissions can be modified accordingly. Zero Trust guarantees that all data is encrypted both in transit and at rest, safeguarding against unauthorized access or interception during communication. Whether the data is exchanged between services or between users and servers, encryption ensures that even if the network is compromised, the data remains secure.

7.1.1 Advantages of Zero Trust Architecture

By validating every demand and holding in check trust where possible, Zero Trust shrinks the attack surface substantially. Even if an attacker gets inside one part of the ecosystem, it is quite difficult for him to gain seamless accretion or movement into other parts of the network. Thus, Zero Trust is continuously authenticated, with all access attempts logged to allow very detailed visibility into those accessing the network. Such visibility leads to proactive monitoring, early alerts, and faster time to detection. As organizations opt for hybrid, cloud-based, and distributed architectures like microservices, Zero Trust responds quickly and admirably well to this environment. The focus is not on the traditional network boundary, since it moves beyond securing data and securing the user and device independent of location.

7.1.2 Challenges of Implementing Zero Trust Architecture

Adopting a Zero Trust approach necessitates a thorough strategy and the right tools to effectively manage identities, policies, and ongoing monitoring. This can pose a significant challenge for organizations that rely on outdated systems or lack the necessary infrastructure for real-time oversight. Zero Trust typically requires several layers of authentication, encryption, and authorization checks, which can lead to delays in communication (Teerakanok, Uehara, & Inomata, 2021). If not optimized correctly, this can impact performance, particularly in real-time systems where speed is essential.

Transitioning to a Zero Trust framework involves a fundamental change in how security is viewed within an organization. It requires collaboration among security, IT, and operations teams, along with a shift in mindset where trust is built through ongoing verification instead of being taken for granted. In a microservice architecture, the Zero Trust concept becomes more elucidated; this is due to the disorganized nature of the system. Services interact over the network, and each service could be a potential entry point for an attacker. Zero Trust principles provide organizations with secure inter-service communication, service-level access controls, and so, each service interacts only with the necessary components.

7.2 Service Mesh Implementation

A service mesh is an infrastructure layer designed to manage and secure communication between microservices in a distributed architecture (Chandramouli & Butcher, 2020). In environments with microservices, services frequently need to interact over the network, which brings about various challenges related to security, reliability, and observability. A service mesh offers a dedicated solution for addressing these challenges, ensuring that communication between services is secure, resilient, and efficient. Popular service mesh solutions like Istio and Linkerd provide these essential capabilities.

Istio stands out as one of the most widely adopted service mesh frameworks. It includes a variety of features that enhance the security and management of communications among microservices. Istio works by deploying a lightweight proxy known as an Envoy proxy alongside each microservice (Lim, Kim, & Sun, 2021). These proxies intercept the traffic between services and offer functionalities such as mutual TLS (mTLS) for secure service-to-service communication, traffic routing and load balancing, and policy enforcement. By managing communication through the service mesh, Istio guarantees that the data exchanged between services is encrypted, authenticated, and authorized, safeguarding it from unauthorized access or interception. Furthermore, Istio supports advanced traffic management techniques like traffic shifting, circuit breaking, and fault injection, which bolster the resilience and fault tolerance of microservices by allowing for more precise control over traffic flow within the system.

Linkerd is another well-known service mesh that prioritizes simplicity and performance. Similar to Istio, it employs proxies that are deployed alongside microservices to manage traffic between them. However, Linkerd is built to be more lightweight, requiring minimal configuration, which makes it an attractive option for organizations that value simplicity and ease of use (Farkiani & Jain, 2024). Its core features include secure communication via mTLS, automatic load balancing, and observability tools for tracking service interactions. While Istio provides a broader range of features, such as advanced policy management and Kubernetes integration, Linkerd excels in scenarios where ease of deployment and low overhead are key concerns. Both Istio and Linkerd offer essential security features, ensuring that communication between services is encrypted, and they assist in managing the complexities of network failures and retries in a microservices architecture.

With a more advanced communicational strategy, service meshes such as Istio and Linkerd can also make communication between microservices more observable by providing metrics and tracing capabilities. These allow developer and operations teams to find insights about the behavior of services as well as their performance on an out-of-the-box basis. For instance, service communication monitoring and visualization are done via integrating Istio into Prometheus and Grafana (Sharma, 2022). On the other hand, Linkerd provides a very simple dashboard to view health and performance metrics of services. Such monitoring gives teams latency and down time figures for their services as they happen, allowing for quick turnaround on service downtimes, high latencies, and communication errors.

In as much as it is overly said that a service mesh would take a lot of work off service management-to-service management communication in the context of microservices, in real sense, it serves many security and operational purposes that otherwise would have to be created on the application level. It lays down a single toolchain to work with for enforcing security policies, traffic management, and resilience. With these, implementing a service mesh like Istio or Linkerd in an organization encourages and gives rise to a much-improved security environment in microservices, swifter operation of the entire system, and more resilience. It makes use of mutual TLS, automated traffic management, and deep observability to make a service mesh an important component of a security-scaled and robust architecture to develop for large and distributed environments (Sharma, 2022).

7.3 Firewall and Gateway Configuration

In a microservices architecture, effectively managing c between services and external entities is essential for maintaining both security and performance. Configuring firewalls and gateways to protect ingress (incoming) and egress (outgoing) traffic is a key step in shielding microservices from unauthorized access, data breaches, and various network-based attacks (Alsaqour, Motmi, & Abdelhaq, 2021). By securing both ingress and egress points, organizations can control access to their systems, safeguard sensitive information, and reduce threats across their distributed environment.

7.3.1 Ingress Traffic Security

Ingress traffic refers to the data that enters the microservices network, usually from external clients or other services. Properly configuring firewalls and gateways to secure ingress traffic is crucial for protecting the network perimeter and ensuring that only legitimate requests can reach the services (Kim, Yoon, Narantuya, & Lim, 2020). A widely used method for managing ingress traffic is the API Gateway, which functions as a reverse proxy that directs requests to the appropriate microservices while enforcing security policies. The API Gateway can carry out important tasks such as authentication (using protocols like OAuth 2.0 or JWT), rate limiting, and input validation, ensuring that only authorized and correctly formatted requests are permitted into the network.

Firewalls also play a significant role in ingress security by blocking unauthorized access attempts at the network level. They can be set up to allow or deny traffic based on IP address, protocol, port, or even specific application behaviors. By implementing network segmentation with firewalls, traffic can be managed and isolated within different segments of the network. For instance, a firewall can prevent external access to internal microservices, allowing only certain services that need to communicate with external clients to be exposed to the internet. This approach minimizes the attack surface and helps reduce the risks of data breaches.

7.3.2 Egress Traffic Security

Egress traffic refers to the data that exits the microservices network, whether it's directed towards external systems or exchanged between services within the architecture. While managing ingress traffic is about blocking unauthorized access to the network, managing egress traffic is crucial for preventing sensitive data from leaking out or being sent to unapproved destinations. It's essential to configure firewalls and gateways to monitor egress traffic to prevent data exfiltration and maintain control over information flow.

A practical approach to securing egress traffic is implementing a network egress firewall, which filters outbound requests according to established policies (Tudosi, Balan, & Potorac, 2022). These policies help ensure that only authorized services can interact with external systems or data stores. For instance, an egress firewall can block microservices from making HTTP requests to unauthorized IP addresses or domains, thus regulating the flow of sensitive information and reducing the risk of data exfiltration. Furthermore, egress traffic security can involve DNS filtering to block queries to potentially harmful domains and TLS inspection to decrypt encrypted egress traffic, ensuring that no malicious content is being transmitted.

8. MONITORING, LOGGING, AND INCIDENT RESPONSE

In a microservices architecture, maintaining the security, reliability, and performance of the system demands ongoing monitoring, comprehensive logging, and a clear incident response plan. These practices allow organizations to identify and tackle potential security threats, performance issues, and other operational challenges proactively. Effective monitoring, logging, and incident response are crucial elements of a strong security framework, empowering teams to keep the system healthy and react swiftly to any incidents that occur.

Monitoring is the process of keeping track of microservices and ensuring they perform optimally in terms of performance, availability, and health (Chinamanagonda, 2022). Because each microservice in a distributed microservices environment can generate its own kinds of metrics and logs, getting a view of the entire system becomes a huge challenge, requiring the use of monitoring tools that take feedback from all services and collate them into one full perspective of the health of the system. Here is where common monitoring, recording, and visualization tools like Prometheus, Grafana, and Datadog play their part in making performance metrics like response times, error rates, and resource usages visualizable in real-time across teams. Measurement is a very critical activity in monitoring (Waseem et al., 2021). Metrics such as - CPU usage, memory utilization, count of requests, error rates, latency, and other statistics that matter are crucial in determining trends or patterns, detecting anomalies, or pinpointing problems before they become full-blown incidents. For example, one can tell that a particular service or network has bottlenecks if increased response times or error rates are observed.

Another important aspect of monitoring is found in distributed tracing. Since most requests in a microservices environment travel through many services before they can yield their ultimate results, it can be difficult pinpointing where failures or delays occurred. Distributed tracing tools, for example, Jaeger or Zipkin, are both tracking requests throughout the system flow and tracking them through movement across various systems, assisting the team in indicating the exact service or step where delays or failures happened (Chinamanagonda, 2022). This greatly improves debugging and performance optimization, providing a complete picture for all request lifecycle stages.

Logging involves recording events, errors, and system activities to help teams analyze and troubleshoot issues effectively (Chinamanagonda, 2022). In a microservices architecture, each service usually produces its own logs, which may include details about the service's internal state, any errors or warnings encountered, and other important events. Centralized logging solutions like the ELK stack (Elasticsearch, Logstash, and Kibana) or Fluentd collect logs from all services into one central location, simplifying the process of searching, analyzing, and correlating logs from various sources (Chinamanagonda, 2022). To implement effective logging strategies, it's important to capture structured logs that include useful metadata such as timestamps, service names, request IDs, and error codes. This structured information makes it easier to filter and query logs when troubleshooting issues. For instance, if a user reports an error, logs can be searched using the request ID to track the request's path through the services and pinpoint where it failed.

8.1 Centralized Logging

Centralized logging comes under an important requirement in microservices architecture due to distributed services. Each service, in general, logs its own messages in a microservices environment. Without aggregation, however, logs become difficult to manage and analyze. Centralized logging tools like ELK Stack (Elasticsearch, Logstash, and Kibana) aggregate and store log data from all services at one place and thus provide a unified view on the health and performance of the system (Zong, 2023).

There are some widely used solutions to collect, analyze, and visualize logs with the help of an instrumentation library, ELK Stack comes to be one among them. Elasticsearch functions as a search engine to store the log data, Logstash manages collecting and processing logs from different sources, and Kibana then visualizes the data with a user-friendly dashboard to search, analyze and view logs in real-time. ELK Stack helps developers and security teams, monitoring activities in different microservices, identifying errors, and fault elimination easy (Zong, 2023).

8.2 Real-Time Monitoring

Such type of real-time monitoring is necessary because microservices architectures demand the need of constant visibility into system performance and health states. Such models, including Prometheus and Grafana, usually package tools for gathering, storing, and visualizing metrics in continuous processes to make it easy for teams to spot anomalies and respond quickly to possible issues before they impact users.

Prometheus is an open-source monitoring system that can ingest data using service collection metrics on time (Adinegoro et al., 2022). It pulls time series data based on application performance metrics, health stats of the system, and resource usage of those resources. Multi-dimensional data collection from Prometheus, having metric aggregation and real-time analysis, works well in microservices spaces where every service can manage its own metrics in Prometheus exporters. These exporters will contribute data to monitor the individual service health like CPU usage, memory consumption, Application Request Rate, and Application Error Rate related to each service.

Grafana is one of the best visualization and analysis tools for the data collected from Prometheus. It links to Prometheus and makes configurable dashboards displaying system metrics in real time. Grafana enables a team to represent metrics like service response time, throughput, and failure rate in visualizations (Adinegoro et al., 2022). Such types of dashboards will help arrange detection anomalies such as inquiry spikes in error rates or any possible performance degradation.

9. CONCLUSION

The adoption of microservices architecture has transformed the face of software development, bringing forth unprecedented flexibility, scalability, and fault tolerance. But with that comes unique security challenges due to the decentralized and distributed nature of microservices. Their security requires vulnerabilities in inter-service communication, data management, and user authentication. The security measures required to be in place for interactions should include mutual TLS (mTLS), API gateways, and role-based access control (RBAC). This will provide protection against interactions and block unauthorized access. Encryption protocols like TLS ensure confidentiality and integrity of data while in transit. Security frameworks such as OAuth 2.0 and OpenID Connect can enable secure user and service authentication.

The implementation of DevSecOps practices is essential to make sure that security is integrated through the lifecycle of software development. Security in CI/CD pipelines can be better achieved with automated vulnerability scanning tools, the adoption of Security as Code, which reduces risks and enhances compliance for organizations. Zero-trust architecture enhances the security posture of microservices by assuming every interaction as untrusted till verified, hence reducing the attack surface and the possibility of lateral movement during a breach.

Though microservices can be quickly innovated and operated at high performance, maintaining a strong security posture is the foundation for the success of such architecture. Organizations must, therefore adopt layered security, a combination of best practices, modern tools, and continuous monitoring of the evolving threat landscape. Microservices balance performance, scalability, and security for transformative benefits in safeguarding critical data and applications.

REFERENCES

Abdelfattah, A. S., & Cerny, T. (2022). Microservices Security Challenges and Approaches.

Adhikari, N. B. (2024). EVALUATING SECURITY TOOLS IN THE CONTEXT OF DEVSECOPS.

Adinegoro, F., Rahmania, C., Zaini, I. N., Negara, R. M., & Hertiana, S. N. (2022, December). Latency and RAM usage comparison of advanced and lightweight service mesh. In 2022 5th International Seminar on Research of Information Technology and Intelligent Systems (ISRITI) (pp. 369-372). IEEE. DOI: 10.1109/ISRITI56927.2022.10052905

Alghawli, A. S. A., & Radivilova, T. (2024). Resilient cloud cluster with DevSecOps security model, automates a data analysis, vulnerability search and risk calculation. *Alexandria Engineering Journal*, 107, 136–149. DOI: 10.1016/j.aej.2024.07.036

Alsaqour, R., Motmi, A., & Abdelhaq, M. (2021). A systematic study of network firewall and its implementation. *International Journal of Computer Science & Network Security*, 21(4), 199–208.

Bakshi, K. (2017, March). Microservices-based software architecture and approaches. In 2017 IEEE aerospace conference (pp. 1-8). IEEE.

Blinowski, G., Ojdowska, A., & Przybyłek, A. (2022). Monolithic vs. microservice architecture: A performance and scalability evaluation. *IEEE Access : Practical Innovations, Open Solutions*, 10, 20357–20374. DOI: 10.1109/ACCESS.2022.3152803

Chandramouli, R. (2022). Implementation of devsecops for a microservices-based application with service mesh. *NIST Special Publication*, 800, 204C. DOI: 10.6028/NIST.SP.800-204C

Chandramouli, R., & Butcher, Z. (2020). Building secure microservices-based applications using service-mesh architecture. *NIST Special Publication*, 800, 204A. DOI: 10.6028/NIST.SP.800-204a

Chinamanagonda, S. (2022). Observability in Microservices Architectures-Advanced observability tools for microservices environments. MZ Computing Journal, 3(1).

de Almeida, M. G., & Canedo, E. D. (2022). Authentication and authorization in microservices architecture: A systematic literature review. *Applied Sciences (Basel, Switzerland)*, 12(6), 3023. DOI: 10.3390/app12063023

Edmundson, C., & Hartman, K. G. (2022). SANS 2022 DevSecOps Survey: Creating a Culture to Significantly Improve Your Organization's Security Posture. URL https://www.sans.org/white-papers/sans-2022-devsecops-survey-creating-cultureimprove-organization-security

Farkiani, B., & Jain, R. (2024). Service Mesh: Architectures, Applications, and Implementations. arXiv preprint arXiv:2405.13333.

Haindl, P., Kochberger, P., & Sveggen, M. (2024). A Systematic Literature Review of Inter-Service Security Threats and Mitigation Strategies in Microservice Architectures. *IEEE Access : Practical Innovations, Open Solutions*, 12, 90252–90286. DOI: 10.1109/ACCESS.2024.3406500

Haverinen, H., Janhunen, T., Päivärinta, T., Lempinen, S., Kaartinen, S., & Merilä, S. (2024, October). Automating Cybersecurity Compliance in DevSecOps with Open Information Model for Security as Code. In Proceedings of the 4th Eclipse Security, AI, Architecture and Modelling Conference on Data Space (pp. 93-102). DOI: 10.1145/3685651.3686700

Jack, C. H., Teck, S. K., Ming, L. T., & Hong, D. Y. (2023, August). An Overview Analysis of Authentication Mechanism in Microservices-Based Software Architecture: A Discussion Paper. In 2023 IEEE 8th International Conference On Software Engineering and Computer Systems (ICSECS) (pp. 1-6). IEEE.

Kamruzzaman, A., Thakur, K., & Ali, M. L. (2024, July). Cybersecurity Threats using Application Programming Interface (API). In *2024 International Conference on Computing, Internet of Things and Microwave Systems (ICCIMS)* (pp. 1-6). IEEE. DOI: 10.1109/ICCIMS61672.2024.10690413

Kim, S., Yoon, S., Narantuya, J., & Lim, H. (2020). Secure collecting, optimizing, and deploying of firewall rules in software-defined networks. *IEEE Access : Practical Innovations, Open Solutions*, 8, 15166–15177. DOI: 10.1109/ACCESS.2020.2967503

Kotenko, M., Moskalyk, D., Kovach, V., & Osadchyi, V. (2024). Navigating the challenges and best practices in securing microservices architecture.

Kumar, R., & Goyal, R. (2020). Modeling continuous security: A conceptual model for automated DevSecOps using open-source software over cloud (ADOC). *Computers & Security*, 97, 101967. DOI: 10.1016/j.cose.2020.101967

Li, W., Li, Z., Yan, Z., Liu, Y., Zeng, D., Yu, H., Chen, W., & Wu, F. (2025). A data encryption and file sharing framework among microservices-based edge nodes with blockchain. *Peer-to-Peer Networking and Applications*, 18(1), 1–16. DOI: 10.1007/s12083-024-01856-y

Lim, H., Kim, Y., & Sun, K. (2021, January). Service management in virtual machine and container mixed environment using service mesh. In *2021 International Conference on Information Networking (ICOIN)* (pp. 528-530). IEEE. DOI: 10.1109/ICOIN50884.2021.9333888

Mateus-Coelho, N., Cruz-Cunha, M., & Ferreira, L. G. (2021). Security in microservices architectures. *Procedia Computer Science*, 181, 1225–1236. DOI: 10.1016/j.procs.2021.01.320

Matias, M., Ferreira, E., Mateus-Coelho, N., & Ferreira, L. (2024). Enhancing Effectiveness and Security in Microservices Architecture. *Procedia Computer Science*, 239, 2260–2269. DOI: 10.1016/j.procs.2024.06.417

Matias, M., Ferreira, E., Mateus-Coelho, N., Ribeiro, O., & Ferreira, L. (2024). Evaluating Effectiveness and Security in Microservices Architecture. *Procedia Computer Science*, 237, 626–636. DOI: 10.1016/j.procs.2024.05.148

Mohamed, S. I., Mostafa, M., Assaly, J., & Shalabi, A. S. (2024). ABACS: Attribute-Based Access Control System using digital keys.

Nookala, G. (2024). The Role of SSL/TLS in Securing API Communications: Strategies for Effective Implementation. *CIT. Journal of Computing and Information Technology*, 4(1).

Oyeniran, C. O., Adewusi, A. O., Adeleke, A. G., Akwawa, L. A., & Azubuko, C. F. (2024). Microservices architecture in cloud-native applications: Design patterns and scalability. *Computer Science & IT Research Journal*, 5(9), 2107–2124. DOI: 10.51594/csitrj.v5i9.1554

Reddy, A. K., Alluri, V. R. R., Thota, S., Ravi, C. S., & Bonam, V. S. M. (2021). DevSecOps: Integrating Security into the DevOps Pipeline for Cloud-Native Applications. *Journal of Artificial Intelligence Research and Applications*, 1(2), 89–114.

Salin, H., & Fokin, D. (2022). An Authenticated Accumulator Scheme for Secure Master Key Access in Microservice Architectures. In IoTBDS (pp. 119-126). DOI: 10.5220/0010989400003194

Saravanan, M. S., & Gogineni, N. (2024, March). A New Framework for Microservices with Single Sign-On, Security Assertion Markup Language and OpenID Connect. In 2024 3rd International Conference on Sentiment Analysis and Deep Learning (ICSADL) (pp. 539-543). IEEE.

Sharma, V. (2022, March). Managing multi-cloud deployments on kubernetes with istio, prometheus and grafana. In 2022 8th International Conference on Advanced Computing and Communication Systems (ICACCS) (Vol. 1, pp. 525-529). IEEE. DOI: 10.1109/ICACCS54159.2022.9785124

Shekhar, S. (2023). Proactive Security in the Cloud: How DevSecOps Shifts Left and Secures Right.

ShuLin. Y., & JiePing, H. (2020, October). Research on unified authentication and authorization in microservice architecture. In 2020 IEEE 20th international conference on communication technology (ICCT) (pp. 1169-1173). IEEE.

Soni, M., & Jyotinagar, V. (2023, July). SQL vs NoSQL Databases for the Microservices: A Comparative Survey. In 2023 2nd International Conference on Edge Computing and Applications (ICECAA) (pp. 17-22). IEEE. DOI: 10.1109/ICECAA58104.2023.10212190

Syed, N. F., Shah, S. W., Shaghaghi, A., Anwar, A., Baig, Z., & Doss, R. (2022). Zero trust architecture (zta): A comprehensive survey. *IEEE Access : Practical Innovations, Open Solutions*, 10, 57143–57179. DOI: 10.1109/ACCESS.2022.3174679

Teerakanok, S., Uehara, T., & Inomata, A. (2021). Migrating to zero trust architecture: Reviews and challenges. *Security and Communication Networks*, 2021(1), 9947347. DOI: 10.1155/2021/9947347

Theodoropoulos, T., Rosa, L., Benzaid, C., Gray, P., Marin, E., Makris, A., Cordeiro, L., Diego, F., Sorokin, P., Girolamo, M. D., Barone, P., Taleb, T., & Tserpes, K. (2023). Security in Cloud-Native Services: A Survey. *Journal of Cybersecurity and Privacy*, 3(4), 758–793. DOI: 10.3390/jcp3040034

Thumburu, S. K. R. (2021). Performance Analysis of Data Exchange Protocols in Cloud Environments. MZ Computing Journal, 2(2).

Tudosi, A. D., Balan, D. G., & Potorac, A. D. (2022, May). Secure network architecture based on distributed firewalls. In *2022 International Conference on Development and Application Systems (DAS)* (pp. 85-90). IEEE. DOI: 10.1109/DAS54948.2022.9786092

Venčkauskas, A., Kukta, D., Grigaliūnas, Š., & Brūzgienė, R. (2023). Enhancing microservices security with token-based access control method. *Sensors (Basel)*, 23(6), 3363. DOI: 10.3390/s23063363 PMID: 36992074

Wang, Z., Guo, G., Liu, C., & Zhu, W. (2022, November). Research on Railway DevSecOps System Construction Based on "People-Process-Technology". In 2022 2nd International Signal Processing, Communications and Engineering Management Conference (ISPCEM) (pp. 19-23). IEEE. DOI: 10.1109/ISPCEM57418.2022.00010

Waseem, M., Liang, P., Shahin, M., Di Salle, A., & Márquez, G. (2021). Design, monitoring, and testing of microservices systems: The practitioners' perspective. *Journal of Systems and Software*, 182, 111061. DOI: 10.1016/j.jss.2021.111061

Zareinia, K. (2023). From Shift Left to Secure Right: DevSecOps Strategies for Cloud-Native Cybersecurity.

Zhang, J. Y., & Zhang, Y. (2024). Quantitative DevSecOps Metrics for Cloud-Based Web Microservices. *IEEE Access : Practical Innovations, Open Solutions*, 12, 160317–160342. DOI: 10.1109/ACCESS.2024.3486314

Zong, Y. (2023, February). Distributed log collection for business processes based on ELK architecture. In 2023 IEEE 2nd International Conference on Electrical Engineering, Big Data and Algorithms (EEBDA) (pp. 1523-1529). IEEE. DOI: 10.1109/EEBDA56825.2023.10090786

Chapter 15
Adaptive Security at the Edge With Real-Time Access Control and Monitoring Beyond Zero Trust

Sanjay Poddar
https://orcid.org/0009-0000-8365-404X
Independent Researcher, USA

ABSTRACT

While edge computing has revolutionized where we process data, a shift away from the traditional cloud-based model results in an entirely new set of security challenges. Constant verification is a key feature of Zero Trust, but this approach is not optimal in decentralized edge settings, especially given the high latency demands of edge environments. In this chapter, we introduce real-time access control and monitoring as a solution for edge-embedded applications as it is quite dynamic. In comparison to static models, the real-time access control identifies and dynamically adapt according to user behaviour, location of the device and status of networks, thereby enabling edge devices to take actions independently to the threats. We examine innovations—low-latency detection, behavioral analytics, and dynamic policies—that drive edge security, through examples in IoT, healthcare, and smart cities. New developments like predictive access models and quantum-safe encryption are raising the bar for adaptive, resilient edge protection.

INTRODUCTION

As enterprises go faster in adopting edge computing, traditional paradigms of network security are being turned on their head. By processing data near its source, edge computing enables real-time operations and lower latency, transforming sectors such as healthcare, manufacturing and telecommunications. However, in its wake, this shift has also created higher security risks, as more decentralized nodes that need strong, flexible protections. The idea of centralized control of the orthodox model of Zero Trust

DOI: 10.4018/979-8-3373-0365-9.ch015

with an idea of validation and limited facilitation does not cater to the urgent requirement of the needful decision and localized security in edge computing eco-system.

This paper reviews the trends of access control from perimeter based access control models to role based access to Zero Trust architectures. This review illustrates how those frameworks must evolve again to address the unique features and issues of edge networks. With Adaptive, real-time access control and monitoring ecosystem (s) can run securely and effectively without the need to court their agility and performance.

Additionally, the distributed nature of edge computing and the dynamic nature of the data that it captures require that more traditional security models touted for their central processing and static policies do not apply. Dynamic Security: Edge environments require dynamic security solutions that can respond to changes in network conditions and threat landscape, providing real-time decision-making at the edge. This requires lightweight algorithms and local decision-making that provide security without sacrificing the performance of the resource-constrained edge devices.

All of this can be handled with the principles of adaptive security in an edge ecosystem, where challenges like transient connectivity, restricted resources, or low latency requirements come into play With many sectors, including IoT, healthcare, and manufacturing, poised to seize the adoption of safe and scalable edge infrastructures, these remedies offer an essential path to doing so. Adaptive security is a powerful enabler for greater use of edge computing in multiple industries.

SUMMARY

The chapter briefly discusses why traditional, static and Zero Trust security models are unfit in edge computing and that adaptive, dynamic real-time access control and monitoring is the solution. Focusing on the specific challenges presented by edge environments, including decentralization, latency sensitivity, resource constraints, and the need for more localized dynamic security mechanisms. Practical benefits and uses of this approach are illustrated through case studies in IoT, healthcare, and smart city. Adaptive security itself is supported by AI and lightweight algorithms, adding to the effectiveness of adaptive security and solid compliance in edge environments. Adaptive security, therefore, becomes a crucial prerequisite for the widespread implementation of edge computing in the 21st century.

Figure 1. Real-Time Adaptive Security Flow illustrating the steps involved in edge data generation, monitoring, policy updates, and secure access outcomes

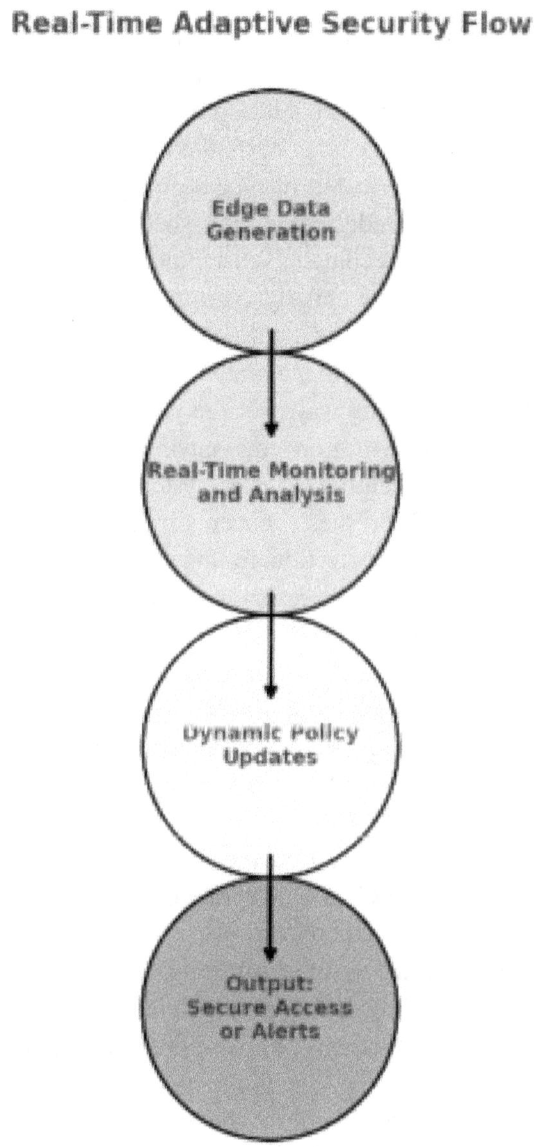

The Real-Time Adaptive Security Flow (Figure 1) demonstrates the sequential process of securing edge environments, starting from data generation to dynamic policy enforcement and secure access outcomes.

RELATED WORKS

Previous work in this area have focused on data access control mechanisms and monitoring criteria on edge computing and Zero Trust principles. Li et al. The potential of IoTs in edge computing, a game-changing paradigm that decentralizes data processing and enables real-time decision making (the future of IoT), was addressed by Huang et al. (2022). This work thus demonstrates substantial room for improvement and bodes strength of this domain, but it also futher emphasizes the limitations of centralized models that cannot satisfy the requirements of current edge systems in latency-sensitive settings.

Zero Trust principles have ushered in a new era of cybersecurity. Bicer et al. (2023) introduced a Zero Trust architecture designed specifically for edge computing, shedding light on the potential of decentralization in this context. However, their work contains substantial limitations, especially for networks with sporadic connectivity or power limitations. Similarly, Nguyen et al. (2021) analysed the challenges of mobile edge computing and multi-access edge computing (MEC) security while calling for lightweight and scalable solutions, but not providing full and integrated frameworks targeting dynamic ecosystems.

Identity & access control has come a long way over the years; Kaliya and Pawar (2023) also did a relook at Role-Based Access Control (RBAC) on edge environments. They pointed out its ongoing limitations dealing with dynamic and decentralized edge systems, especially ones that need real-time responses. Ali et al. (2023) further built on these concepts by applying adaptive policies to security models taking advantage of real-time threat detection, for fog and edge computing security frameworks; however, their design encountered challenges in resource-constrained environments.

Interest in the use of artificial intelligence (AI) for securing edge environments has emerged (Lin et al. (2023) and Liu et al. (2020) showing how machine learning and predictive analytics optimize the anomaly detection and access control. Zhang et al. (2021) delved deeper into federated learning is a privacy-preserving solution for decentralized systems with real-time decision-making capabilities without risking sensitive data exposure. While those advancements are substantial, they are narrow and do not address the full array of edge-specific challenges.

While research in individual aspects has advanced, the absence of such frameworks encompassing all approaches makes a significant gap remains in the new research opportunities contributing to adaptive security framework. Most of the existing methods, however, do not scale well, nor do they account for the complex interactions in decentralized systems. Promising, privacy-preserving methods remain yet to be fully compatible with practical needs of real-world implementations. Adaptive policies that enable rapid and flexible responses to changing contexts have yet to dispel challenges of resource constraints and features of connectivity.

This chapter expands on these foundational aspect studies by developing a cohesive integrated real-time adaptive security architecture uniquely suitable for edge environments. Privacy-preserving approaches including federated learning are incorporated for protecting the sensitive data while facilitating in-time rollout. To this end, dynamic access control mechanisms are integrated to adapt to changing network environments and user contexts, enabling agility and robustness.

EDGE SECURITY AND ACCESS CONTROL: THE ABCS

This section sets the stage by highlighting the security challenges introduced by edge computing and why traditional approaches struggle in such environments. With the evolution of digital, the fast-paced transition to edge computing has brought forth security challenges. In contrast, edge computing processes data at the proximity to the data origin, allowing real-time processing and latency reduction that have enabled transformation of some of the industries including healthcare, manufacturing, and telecommunications (Li et al., 2022). In conventional forms of centralized networks, data passes through a single point of access, which is easy to manage. But edge environments have multiple decentralized nodes processing data, which need access controls to be customized to ensure security for each node.

The traditional framework of Zero Trust security has completely changed the paradigm of how organizations view cybersecurity, most significantly by presuming that any user or device connecting to the network may be a potential threat. In turn, Zero Trust necessitates continuous validation, enforced access restrictions, and extensive supervision even for devices within the network boundary. Despite that, the Zero Trust model faces challenges in the edge computing era by the organizations adopting edge computing. Edge environments require fast, decentralized decision-making so that centralized access control and verification becomes difficult.

The increasing need for localized, in-the-moment, and adaptive security solutions has resulted in real-time access control right at the network edge. In contrary to traditional models, which tend to work on predefined authorizations and policies, with some delays in processing them, real-time access control and monitoring dynamically adapt to varying parameters, including the immediate context of users, devices and network status. This change in the function of security is a remedy for Zero Trust in this eye of the storm, making sure that edge-level systems can use a agile, efficient, and responsive protective method.

THE DEVELOPMENT OVER TIME OF ACCESS CONTROL MODELS

To grasp how far we've come and how much we have yet to do with modern frameworks like Zero Trust, however, we need to understand the history of access control models. Early examples of access control were heavily influenced by perimeter-based security, which understood that internal users are to be trusted and most of the threats came from the outside world. This mitigation strategy involved creating robust perimeters at the network edges, allowing only trusted users or devices to filter through known gateways. This approach worked well in smaller or insular networks but began to stumble as networks grew, became decentralized, and were targeted by increasingly sophisticated cyber attacks. Static rules and rigid policies could be applied to these environment to identify whether a certain device or connection is secure, but the reality is that threats evolve, as do insider risks, and critical vulnerabilities could be left unaddressed in dynamic situations. The modernized gradual approach to these challenges redefined into frameworks like Zero Trust to plug up the gaps created in traditional security policies, continually focusing on continuous authentication and limiting the extent of access to sensitive data where essential. This progress illustrates the importance of updating security paradigms to align with the needs of intricate and distributed architectures, especially during the age of edge computing and IoT.

Access control in cybersecurity has been an evolution rooted in the antiquated notion of at the perimeter security models of yesteryear, which characterized early means of protecting network environments. These models assumed that internal users could be trusted and that threats largely came from external actors, so access was controlled at the borders of a network. Although this method is efficient in isolated environments, when networks grew and developed, it became a problem to preserve a safe border as the separation became difficult.

As distributed networks and a mobile workforce emerged, the perimeter-based model began its demise, and Role-Based Access Control (RBAC) was born. Then RBAC came along and it provided a more granular level by implementing permissions based on users roles within an organization. This provided a more granular level of access, exposing only what was necessary according to job function and further minimizing the risk of unauthorized access. Nevertheless, RBAC struggled in more dynamic contexts, where user roles and access requirements are subject to constant change.

Zero Trust Or a New Approach to Access Control Zero Trust asked the user not to trust each and every entity—internal and external—by default and stressed upon constant verification for everyone no matter where they were located. This model mitigated many of the problems associated with traditional perimeter security, yet it was made with the idea for centralized networks where users and devices may regularly authenticate with a central authority. Zero Trust is limited without edge computing where the whole decentralization process along with demand for low latency has been increased. As a result, there is an increasing need to develop adaptive access control models that provide real-time security tailored to distributed edge-based networks that use local processing along with contextual information.

WHY EDGE ENVIRONMENTS AREN'T A GREAT FIT FOR ZERO TRUST

While Zero Trust has been a significant step forward, it reveals limitations when applied to decentralized, latency-sensitive edge networks, as discussed in the next section. While Zero Trust architectures excel in classic, centralized networks, they struggle in edge environments where decentralization and instantaneous response are paramount. Zero Trust models rely on a central server for continuous monitoring and authorization and require significant end device and end user level verification (Bicer et al., 2023). But edge devices are usually power constrained, connected to central servers in an intermittent fashion, causing a lag in real-time verification and update and thus, creating security holes.

Take for instance the example of an industrial use-case where different edge devices like robotic arms, sensors, and autonomous machines function on a factory floor. In these cases, there is no room for delay in access verification — as they could hinder productivity, and can at times be even a matter of life and death. Time Lag: Centralized Zero Trust processes, which require every single device to authenticate through a remote server, create time-lags that can hinder critical real-time functionality.

Moreover, most Zero Trust protocols are static policy-based, which is a challenge in an edge environment where devices, users, and network conditions are constantly changing — making adaptive policy implementations a necessity. An edge device in a healthcare context, for example, may need to quickly change access controls because of new personnel or even changes in patient status. In contrast, static policies lack the agility required for such environments, establishing the requirement for an access control model that is adaptive, low-latency, and more suited to deliver on the needs of the edge.

RISE OF REAL-TIME ACCESS CONTROL AT EDGE

Figure 2. Adaptive Security Workflow for Edge Environments

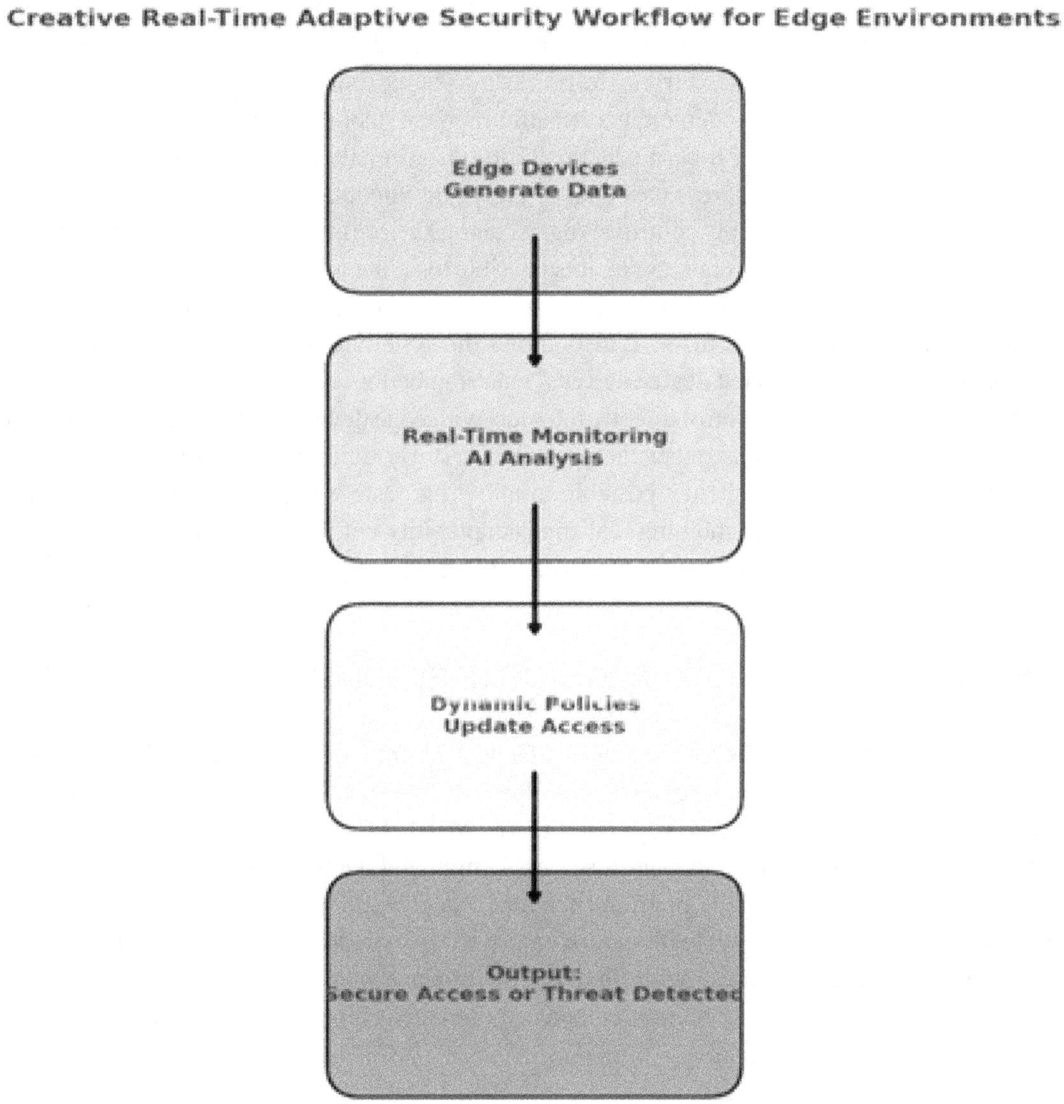

We present a real-time adaptive security workflow for the edge environments in Fig. 2. This model shows exactly how data generation, policy updates and threat detection walk hand-in-hand to secure access and respond to changing risks at the edge. The adaptive workflow continuously adapts security controls in real time according to context factors (like device location, user behavior, real-time threat intelligence) rather than following a static approach. Through decentralized decision-making and active monitoring, this framework guarantees that security policies are dynamically adjusted to new vulnerabilities, allowing or blocking access in real-time depending on the state of affairs

To overcome the challenges of static models and centralized decision-making, real-time access control emerges as a promising approach for edge environments. Edge application access control works on the Zero Trust principle but adds an adaptive layer to it, based on adaptability to changing conditions in real-time. Real-time access control, on the other hand, continually adapts based on circumstances like the device's location, the user who is trying to access a resource, and even the latest threat intelligence feeds, so that access is granted or denied in a specific moment, using dynamic data, rather than simply rules that were rote learned over time. Such flexibility is especially helpful when access permissions need to be adjusted quickly to address new data or emerging threats.

A key benefit of real-time access control is that it can make access decisions based on context before, during and after authentication. For example, it is possible to create access policies that take the physical location into account. For example, if a device pops up in an unusual location there can be blocks on access until further verification is made. It also allows the system to respond to abnormal events, such as login behaviors and unexpected device activity, ensuring better security.

Generally, real-time access control directly interacts with edge devices, where lightweight processing algorithms enable local decisions rather than server-based. By doing processing in local devices, the access decision takes the least latency possible to allow the fastest response to both common access requests and zero-day threats. Combining real-time adaptability with the vigilance of Zero Trust makes this approach a monumental leap for decentralized network security.

THE HIGH-SPEED AND HIGH-PRECISION NEED: EDGE DATA MONITORING

Beyond access control, edge networks demand efficient data monitoring solutions that prioritize speed and accuracy while remaining resource-efficient. This is because, unlike traditional sensors where data is processed in a central hub, edge devices tend to be spread out across multiple locations and do not have the processing capabilities of a central server. Centralized networks allow monitoring data to be aggregated and analyzed at a single point in time and space, while edge networks need decentralized, lightweight solutions that are capable of localizing the process of information. It is required to respond at a high rate to mitigate the effects with time on system performance. Accuracy is just as important, so that necessary mitigations can be implemented by reducing false positives and avoiding business disruptions to legitimate operation.

The edge devices do not usually compose a powerful infrastructure so they lack in storage or processing capabilities to support a centralized monitoring system (or monitoring system choice) with service-oriented architecture, like IPFIX / RTCP). In contrast, outside of edge monitoring with optimized algorithms with high importance on critical data points continue to process the data with low importance but do not burden themselves with processing too much data, real-time attack alerts should come, and without processing on the device. For example, an edge video surveillance deployed system can use object recognition to analyze and determine if there is an intruder, and only process footage locally where it is relevant instead of sending all raw footage interpretation to a central server.

Real-time filtering and prioritization distinguishes routine edge activities from those that may be considered suspicious, which is another aspect of edge monitoring. With this prioritization on high value events, edge monitoring systems detect and respond to most threats much faster, maximizing security at minimal processing cost. This method can ensures rapid detection of threats while maintaining accuracy, even for resource-constrained environments.

DYNAMIC EDGE ACCESS-CONTROL: REAL-TIME ACCESS-CONTROL ON EDGE DEVICES

The application of real-time access control at the edge is further enhanced through dynamic policies and behavioral analysis. Then a series of novel learn ware techniques have been developed to make access control in real time at the edge effectively as follows:

Behavioral Analysis: Edge systems can also analyze user and device behavior in real-time to identify anomalies and potential security risks. If, for instance, an IoT device in an industrial setting suddenly starts to send vast amounts of data outside to an unknown location, the system can automatically send an alert or even lock down until the behavior is verified.

Dynamic Access Policies: In contrast to static policies, dynamic access policies change in real-time according to contextual information, such as time of day, device status, or user location. Such policies permit security implementations to be more flexible, by allowing temporary access where appropriate with the ability to take it away instantly if the risk profile changes. The use of technology to control access in near real-time.

Low-Latency Threat Detection: Access control implementations leverage low-latency detection techniques that enable edge devices to detect and respond to threats in real-time. This is the reason why there are technologies such as lightweight encryption protocols and quick-response firewalls that are designed to avoid delays however there is a need to keep the security of the fog data intact.

This allows a stricter access control and persistent surveillance but without the latency of centralized processing, thus, enhancing security and responsiveness at the edge.

DEMONSTRATING REAL-TIME EDGE ACCESS CONTROL: CASE STUDIES

Real-world applications across industries demonstrate the viability and effectiveness of adaptive, real-time access control solutions.

Industrial IoT: Real-time access control and monitoring ensure that sensitive machinery only has access to authorized personnel in a manufacturing plant. For example, a maintenance technician requires temporary access to a robotic arm; real-time access control could grant access privileges based on the technician's verified credentials, while also monitoring the device behavior for any anomalies.

Healthcare: Healthcare facilities possess many devices that require immediate access while the equipment demands that access be restricted to protect patient information, thus it is vital. In such remote healthcare, new sensitive data could be made accessible only to local people, with permissions dynamically changing as a doctor or a nurse takes a shift.

Smart Cities– Smart city infrastructure with real-time access control and monitoring helps public data systems security. Surveillance cameras and traffic sensors monitoring public safety, for instance, need data to be protected from unauthorized access while still being able to provide real-time information to authorized personnel.

OBSTACLES TO IMPLEMENTING IN-THE-MOMENT ACCESS CONTROL

Despite its benefits, implementing real-time access control at the edge presents several challenges that must be addressed. There are several technical and operational challenges in the implementation of the real-time access control in the edge environments. Edge environments, in contrast to quite a few centralized networks do not usually benefit from redundant, abundant bandwidth, reliable connectivity, and robust processing capacity. Specifically, bandwidth bottlenecks can hinder the rapid transmission of security information between edge devices and central servers, adding latency and reducing the effectiveness of real-time control.

These challenges are more severe in industries, such as manufacturing and healthcare, that require edge computing for time-sensitive operations. For example, if we have a factory full of IoT devices that are monitoring production lines, the ability to control access to the devices in real-time is critical to ensuring that only authorized personnel can change settings on the machines. But if the network is unable to withstand regular lapses in information between decentralized servers, this can lead to delays on the ability to update permissions, which means downtime of the system and perhaps even safety Hazards.

This comes with further complications due to latency and intermittent connectivity, which make it challenging to reliably monitor a streaming system in real-time. Edge devices are often located in faraway places, where the network quality can be somewhat old or low and affect how quickly data can be transmitted. Take healthcare, for instance, where patients can be monitored by devices in remote facilities that need to run continuously and often have no reliable connection to a main server. This limitation calls for the on-device mechanism to manage the real-time controls, operating independently at the edge, without ever losing access or visibility into the system, even when the network is impaired. To overcome such challenges, the solutions should be simple, self-sustainable, and deployable on a resource-constrained edge environment.

ARTIFICIAL INTELLIGENCE AND REAL-TIME ACCESS CONTROL

AI plays a critical role in enhancing real-time decision-making and adaptive security, overcoming many of the limitations of traditional approaches. AI is the key to improve the speed at which access is being allowed in real-time as it learns behavioral patterns and detects anomalies with higher accuracy than scaling human resources. AI-based models learn from data flows, patterns of device use, and user behavior in edge environments, spotting changes against normal activity that may signal the presence of a security threat. In contrast to conventional methods with static access policies, AI can implement predictive and context-aware access control that changes in real-time based on alterations in the environment.

One type of AI, machine learning, can leverage historical data to improve the predictions of access control of these entities. For instance, a predictive ML model can learn users' modes of access and predict upcoming access demands based on prior activity to dynamically tune permissions. Predictive access control in a smart city infrastructure where 100s of sensors and surveillance cameras constantly monitor public areas ensures that only authorized personnel can reach sensitive footage such as video from the public camera and is able to act on abnormal access across the city.

Deploying AI in edge environments poses new challenges, especially high computation at the edge and privacy. Given the resource-constrained nature of most edge devices, it becomes difficult to centrally access networks of edge devices to deploy complex AI models. Local processing of sensitive data such as patient or financial information is an important consideration for privacy of privacy focused industries. As such, AI models must respect privacy and still be able to analyze real-time data, and so we witness the rise of federated learning that allows edge devices to exchange insights while avoiding sending raw data. It is geared towards privacy preservation and lower bandwidth usage, enabling near real-time AI inference at the edge.

REAL-TIME VS TRADITIONAL ACCESS CONTROL

A comparison between traditional and real-time access control highlights the necessity of adopting dynamic, context-aware models for edge environments. This brings on a clear divide of on-grade access control towards edge in real-time from traditional access control mechanism, both having its own unique pros & cons. In traditional access control models, like role-based and attribute-based access control, policies are guided by static permissions that specify which users do what based on predefined categories. These types of models perform well in centralized settings that are static or do not change often in regard to access requirements. Nevertheless, static access controls remain inadequate for the dynamic edge environment, since they are not capable of flexibly responding to the dynamic and sometimes even unmanageable nature of interactions involving users and devices.

In contrast, access control in real time provides high responsiveness because it instantly responds to changes in the context. Such flexibility is crucial for edge environments, where devices are frequently in life- or-death situations, like health care best monitoring or commercial automation. In industrial scenarios, say a machine suddenly transitions to an important operating state, a real-time access control would rapidly restrict the user access to omit unauthorized changes made by the model which is impossible by the speed that the access control model works at

Additionally, the element of real-time access control systems with continuous monitoring and anomaly detection opens a way to a proactive security approach. With the continuous evaluation of access requests based on real-time behavior information, these systems can identify and thwart actions that could result in harm, providing a safeguard that traditional models cannot offer. This comparison points out the requirement of moving from static, rule-based controls to dynamic, real-time controls as organizations continue to adopt more edge computing.

EVALUATING SCALABILITY OF REAL-TIME ACCESS CONTROL SYSTEMS

The scalability and future potential of real-time access control systems ensure they are well-suited for the evolving needs of edge computing. New horizons Edge computing and security are constantly evolving and opening new horizons for real-time access control at the network edge. Adding quantum-resistant cryptography could revolutionize data protection by defending edge devices from eventual quantum threats — and, at decentralized nodes, providing improved security guarantees. Decentralized identity verification methods are expected to improve device authentication while lowering dependence on centralized identity management and providing more robustness against identity spoofing and credential-based attacks.

Such use cases are a promising ground for predictive access models where the need for access is predicted by machine learning to fulfill the expressive requirements ahead even without the requests been made. Based on historical access patterns, these predictive models could adapt permissions proactively, enabling an even more seamless and secure experience in the edge environment. Moreover, edge computing involves the utilization of self-healing networks, where self-healing networks are also gaining substantial interest—these networks can detect vulnerabilities in the system by themselves and fix them as well, which is mostly required in edge environments where the key focus is reducing downtime and security risk as much as possible.

In summary, adaptive security is an emerging area and its role at real-time access control at the edge is integrating rapidly with the latest technologies to accommodate the challenges of decentralized networks. With the continued enterprise adoption of edge computing, those innovations will now serve the vital role of enabling secure, low-latency, and operationally driven edge ecosystems.

CONCLUSION

Hence, adaptive and real-time access control offers solutions that are best suited to address the challenges posed by these systems for secure operations as well as agreement among collaborating systems. Here we decode how edge computing influences network security by its major impact on decentralized and latency-sensitive environments. Traditional identity and access frameworks, including but not limited to Zero Trust, have failed to accommodate the near-real-time needs of edge ecosystems. This chapter discussed those adaptive access control and monitoring mechanisms to deal with the challenges outlined in the previous sections, relying on lightweight, local, and contextual decision making processes. These methods allow edge systems to address changing security risks in real-time without sacrificing performance, by using Augmented Intelligence artificial technology, dynamic policies, and real-time anomaly detection.

As we look towards the future, adaptive security frameworks should also be continuously developing as new challenges arise. As quantum computing poses a risk to current encryption methods, the need for quantum-safe cryptographic techniques replacement becomes paramount. Furthermore, innovations in federated learning and edge-based AI will further support privacy-preserving decision-making policies and relies less on centralized data processing. Lastly, emphasis on energy efficiency in future frameworks can further support sustainable security solutions in resource-constrained edge environments. With the proliferation of 5G networks and the Internet of Things (IoT), adaptive security systems will have to continuously scale up to connect ever-increasing number of devices on the internet. These innovations will hold great significance in maintaining safe, resilient, and efficient functioning in the changing edge computing landscape.

REFERENCES

Abou-Nassar, E. M., & Osama, H. A. (2022). Quantum-safe cryptography for IoT devices: A new horizon for edge computing security. *Journal of Information Security and Applications*, 65, 103155. DOI: 10.1016/j.jisa.2022.103155

Ali, R., Khan, A., & Ahmed, A. (2023). AI-enabled predictive analytics in edge computing: A comprehensive survey. *Journal of Big Data*, 10(1), 1–27. DOI: 10.1186/s40537-023-00651-9 PMID: 36618886

Bicer, C., Murturi, I., Donta, P. K., & Dustdar, S. (2023). Blockchain-based zero trust on the edge. arXiv preprint arXiv:2311.16744. /arXiv.2311.16744DOI: 10.1109/CSCI62032.2023.00167

Cesarano, C. (2023). Security assessment and hardening of fog computing systems. arXiv preprint arXiv:2308.12707. /arXiv.2308.12707DOI: 10.1109/ISSREW60843.2023.00037

Feng, C., & Sun, H. (2022). Quantum computing and its impact on encryption protocols for IoT. *Computers & Security*, 118, 102740. DOI: 10.1016/j.cose.2022.102740

França, R. P., Monteiro, A. C. B., Arthur, R., & Iano, Y. (2020). An overview of the edge computing in the modern digital age. In Fog/Edge Computing For Security, Privacy, and Applications (pp. 33–52). Springer. DOI: 10.1007/978-3-030-57328-7

Kaliya, N., & Pawar, D. (2023). Unboxing fog security: A review of fog security and authentication mechanisms. *Computing*, 105(12), 2793–2819. DOI: 10.1007/s00607-023-01208-3

Kar, D., & Zhang, W. (2023). A survey on federated learning frameworks and applications in IoT. *Journal of Ambient Intelligence and Humanized Computing*, 14, 151–167. DOI: 10.1007/s12652-023-04121-x

Khan, L. U., Yaqoob, I., Tran, N. H., Dang, T. N., & Hong, C. S. (2020). Edge-computing-enabled smart cities: A comprehensive survey. *IEEE Internet of Things Journal*, 7(10), 10200–10232. DOI: 10.1109/JIOT.2020.2987070

Khan, L. U., Yaqoob, I., Tran, N. H., Dang, T. N., & Hong, C. S. (2020). Edge-computing-enabled smart cities: A comprehensive survey. *IEEE Internet of Things Journal*, 7(10), 10200–10232. DOI: 10.1109/JIOT.2020.2987070

Li, D., Zhang, E., Lei, M., & Song, C. (2022). Zero trust in edge computing environment: A blockchain-based practical approach. *Mathematical Biosciences and Engineering*, 19(4), 3687–3705. DOI: 10.3934/mbe.2022194 PMID: 35341294

Li, P., Wang, X., Huang, K., Huang, Y., Li, S., & Iqbal, M. (2022). Multi-Model Running Latency Optimization in an Edge Computing Paradigm. *Sensors (Basel)*, 22(16), 6097. DOI: 10.3390/s22166097 PMID: 36015856

Li, X., & Chen, H. (2018). Design of a lightweight authentication and key agreement protocol for multi-server architecture in 5G-enabled IoT environment. *IEEE Access : Practical Innovations, Open Solutions*, 6, 15900–15910.

Lin, Z., Xiong, H., He, W., & Zhou, W. (2023). Edge AI for adaptive security in IoT: Threat detection and prevention. *Future Generation Computer Systems*, 142, 112–127. DOI: 10.1016/j.future.2023.04.017

Liu, Y., Liu, C., & Zhang, J. (2020). Self-healing networks: Autonomous resilience strategies for edge computing. *Computer Networks*, 173, 107217. DOI: 10.1016/j.comnet.2020.107217

Nguyen, D. C., Pathirana, P. N., Ding, M., & Seneviratne, A. (2021). Blockchain for 5G and beyond networks: A state-of-the-art survey. *Journal of Network and Computer Applications*, 166, 102693. DOI: 10.1016/j.jnca.2020.102693

Ometov, A., Molua, O. L., Komarov, M. M., & Nurmi, J. (2022). A survey of security in cloud, edge, and fog computing. *Sensors (Basel)*, 22(3), 927. DOI: 10.3390/s22030927 PMID: 35161675

Patwary, A. A. N., Fu, A., Naha, R. K., Battula, S. K., Garg, S., Patwary, M. A. K., & Aghasian, E. (2020). Authentication, access control, privacy, threats, and trust management towards securing fog computing environments: A review. arXiv preprint arXiv:2003.00395. https://doi.org//arXiv.2003.00395DOI: 10.48550

Sun, Z., Han, Z., & Yu, H. (2020). Privacy-preserving machine learning for edge computing: A federated learning approach. *IEEE Transactions on Industrial Informatics*, 16(8), 5236–5244. DOI: 10.1109/TII.2019.2959955

Zhang, X., Wang, Q., Hu, S., Yu, J., & Zhou, H. (2021). Blockchain-based lightweight data access control for IoT in edge computing. *Journal of Parallel and Distributed Computing*, 148, 22–32. DOI: 10.1016/j.jpdc.2020.10.011

Zou, W., Tan, X., & Du, J. (2021). Anomaly detection in IoT networks with AI-based adaptive security. *IEEE Internet of Things Journal*, 8(10), 8210–8225. DOI: 10.1109/JIOT.2020.3023219

Chapter 16
Enhancing Cypher for OLAP:
Extending Syntax and Optimizing Queries Execution

Khalil abdelhak
https://orcid.org/0000-0002-7810-1683
ENCG Eljadida, Morocco

Mustapha Belaiassaoui
https://orcid.org/0000-0003-3877-9235
ENCG Settat, Morocco

ABSTRACT

The Cypher query language, widely used in Neo4j for graph data management, is optimized for Online Transaction Processing (OLTP) but lacks robust support for Online Analytical Processing (OLAP) operations. This limitation arises due to its high-level abstractions, which are not designed to handle complex analytical workloads efficiently. This chapter explores an approach to extend the Cypher syntax and implement query rewriting using Neo4j's low-level API to facilitate seamless OLAP operations. By enabling direct interaction with the underlying graph engine, the proposed extensions empower developers to define and execute sophisticated analytical tasks while maintaining the expressive simplicity of Cypher. The paper outlines the architectural modifications, illustrates query rewriting techniques, and demonstrates the benefits of this hybrid approach through practical use cases.

1. INTRODUCTION

In recent years, graph databases have gained significant traction as robust tools for managing and analyzing complex relationships between data entities(Bhattacharyya & Chakravarty, 2020; Kamphuis, 2020), especially in domains where traditional relational databases struggle to represent and query interconnected information. Among these, Neo4j has emerged as a prominent choice, thanks to its flexible

DOI: 10.4018/979-8-3373-0365-9.ch016

property graph model and its expressive declarative query language, Cypher. Cypher simplifies the process of navigating and manipulating graph data, making it accessible to both developers and data scientists.

However, while Cypher is well-suited for Online Transaction Processing (OLTP) tasks such as querying real-time data and handling frequent, small-scale transactions, it falls short in addressing the requirements of large-scale analytical processing, commonly referred to as Online Analytical Processing (OLAP). OLAP workloads often involve aggregating, summarizing, and analyzing vast amounts of data to uncover patterns, trends, or insights that are crucial for decision-making in fields like business intelligence, social network analysis, and recommendation systems.

To bridge the gap between Cypher's current capabilities and the demands of OLAP workloads, this chapter presents a conceptual model for extending Cypher to natively support analytical functionalities. The proposed model investigates innovative approaches to integrating OLAP features into the Neo4j engine, enabling high-performance computation across extensive datasets while retaining the graph-centric paradigm. By expanding Cypher's scope to include multidimensional analysis, hierarchical operations, and advanced aggregation, this work empowers Neo4j users to perform complex analytics with ease, preserving the simplicity and expressiveness that make Cypher a powerful and intuitive query language.

The remainder of this chapter is structured to provide a comprehensive exploration of extending Cypher for OLAP functionalities. Section 2 presents a thorough review of the state-of-the-art advancements in integrating OLAP capabilities into the Cypher query language. Then, we detail the proposed approaches. Finally, we conclude the chapter and outline potential directions for future work.

2. STATE OF THE ART

In what follows we present the state of the art, which comprises two key sections: the background and related works. The background provides an overview of fundamental concepts, including graph modeling, the formalization of graph databases, and their structural components such as nodes, edges, and properties. This section lays the groundwork for understanding the integration of analytical capabilities within graph databases. The related works section explores existing research on the application of OLAP in NoSQL databases, focusing on graph OLAP frameworks, extensions of Cypher, and approaches to implementing analytical systems within property graph databases.

2.1. Background

Our work is closely connected to NoSQL graph databases and graph modeling. Accordingly, we provide an overview of the fundamentals of these two topics. The formalization of the graph-oriented model involves defining the following three components: nodes, edges, and properties.

Graph databases can be formalized using graph theory, where data is represented as a graph $G = (N^G, E^G, P^G)$, comprising:

- $N^G = \{n_1, \ldots, n_p\}$ is a set of nodes (or vertices) that represent entities or objects in the data.
- $E^G \subseteq N^G \times N^G$, where an edge $E_k = (n_i, n_j)$ connects nodes n_i and n_j.
- P^G a set of properties representing a key-value pair assigned to each component of the graph, providing additional descriptive information.

Nodes and edges in a graph may belong to specific categories, identified by labels. For vertices, $L_N(n)$ is a labeling function that assigns one or more labels to a node n. Similarly, for edges, $L_E(e)$ is a labeling function that assigns labels to an edge e.

2.2. Related works

In recent years, the adoption of NoSQL technologies has grown rapidly within the field of big data analytics. Significant efforts have been made to model OLAP cubes using this technology. Various research studies have focused on implementing OLAP systems with columnar databases (Dehdouh et al., 2020; Khalil & Belaissaoui, 2023b) while others have explored the use of document-oriented databases (Bouaziz et al., 2019; Chevalier et al., 2015; Khalil & Belaissaoui, 2023a).

Although graph databases are extensively utilized in OLTP systems, particularly for scenarios requiring the modeling of complex relationships, there appears to be no existing OLAP solution on the market that leverages graph databases at the physical level. Nevertheless, the concept of graph OLAP has existed for years. Several notable studies have explored the implementation of OLAP systems using graph technology. Chen et al. (Chen et al., 2008, 2009) investigated the feasibility of conducting multi-dimensional analysis on graph data. They introduced a graph OLAP framework comprising two main subcategories: Informational OLAP and Typological OLAP and proposed basic definitions for OLAP operations within this framework. In (Castelltort & Laurent, 2014) the authors propose an extension of the Cypher language to support OLAP queries, where operators such as slice and dice are expressed in Cypher. However, no experimental evaluation was conducted to validate the proposal, as the focus was primarily on demonstrating its feasibility.

Several recent research studies have focused on implementing OLAP engines within property graph databases. In (Zhao et al., 2011), the authors introduce a novel data warehousing concept called *Graph Cube*, which provides an OLAP infrastructure designed to support analytical queries over multidimensional networks. Meanwhile, (Chou et al., 2018) presents the concept of *GOLAP*, an extension of Online Analytical Processing (OLAP) for graph databases, highlighting features such as semantic queries and structural analytics. In addressing GOLAP-related challenges, such as speed and storage limitations, the authors propose solutions like graph data reduction and query result approximation to manage extended execution times. However, their work remains focused on formalizing these ideas, as no implementation of the proposed framework is provided.

In a similar context. In (Gómez et al., 2017) and (Gómez et al., 2020), the authors introduced a formal multidimensional data model for graph analysis, referred to as graphoids, which are based on node and edge labeling. They also presented a proof-of-concept implementation using the Neo4j graph database.

In the context of instantiating data warehouses with property graph databases, in (Sellami et al., 2020) the authors proposed a set of transformation rules to map the multidimensional conceptual model to a NoSQL graph model.

All the referenced works collectively contribute a valuable foundation for advancing graph-based online analytical processing (OLAP). These studies have explored various approaches to integrating OLAP principles within graph structures, recognizing the unique potential of graph databases for handling complex, interconnected data.

Most of the research efforts have been centered on adapting graph structures to align with OLAP requirements. This includes modeling multidimensional data directly within graph representations, leveraging nodes and edges to represent facts, dimensions, hierarchies, and their relationships.

3. APPROACH OVERVIEW

The proposed approach for integrating OLAP extensions into the Neo4j graph engine involves four interconnected components. First, a Cypher OLAP syntax is introduced to provide a high-level query interface tailored for analytical tasks, incorporating new constructs and keywords for operations like rollups, cubes, and advanced aggregations. These queries are then processed through a query translation layer, which transforms Cypher OLAP queries into either well-formatted standard Cypher queries or direct low-level API calls, ensuring compatibility with Neo4j's existing infrastructure. The low-level API integration enables optimized execution of these queries by directly interacting with Neo4j's engine, bypassing certain abstractions for enhanced performance. Additionally, developer API extensions enhance the Neo4j SDK by introducing new methods and procedures for advanced OLAP functionalities, such as custom aggregations and reusable stored procedures. Together, these components create a robust hybrid model that simplifies query formulation, optimizes execution, and provides flexibility for developers, seamlessly extending Neo4j's capabilities for both transactional and analytical graph processing.

Figure 1. Approach overview

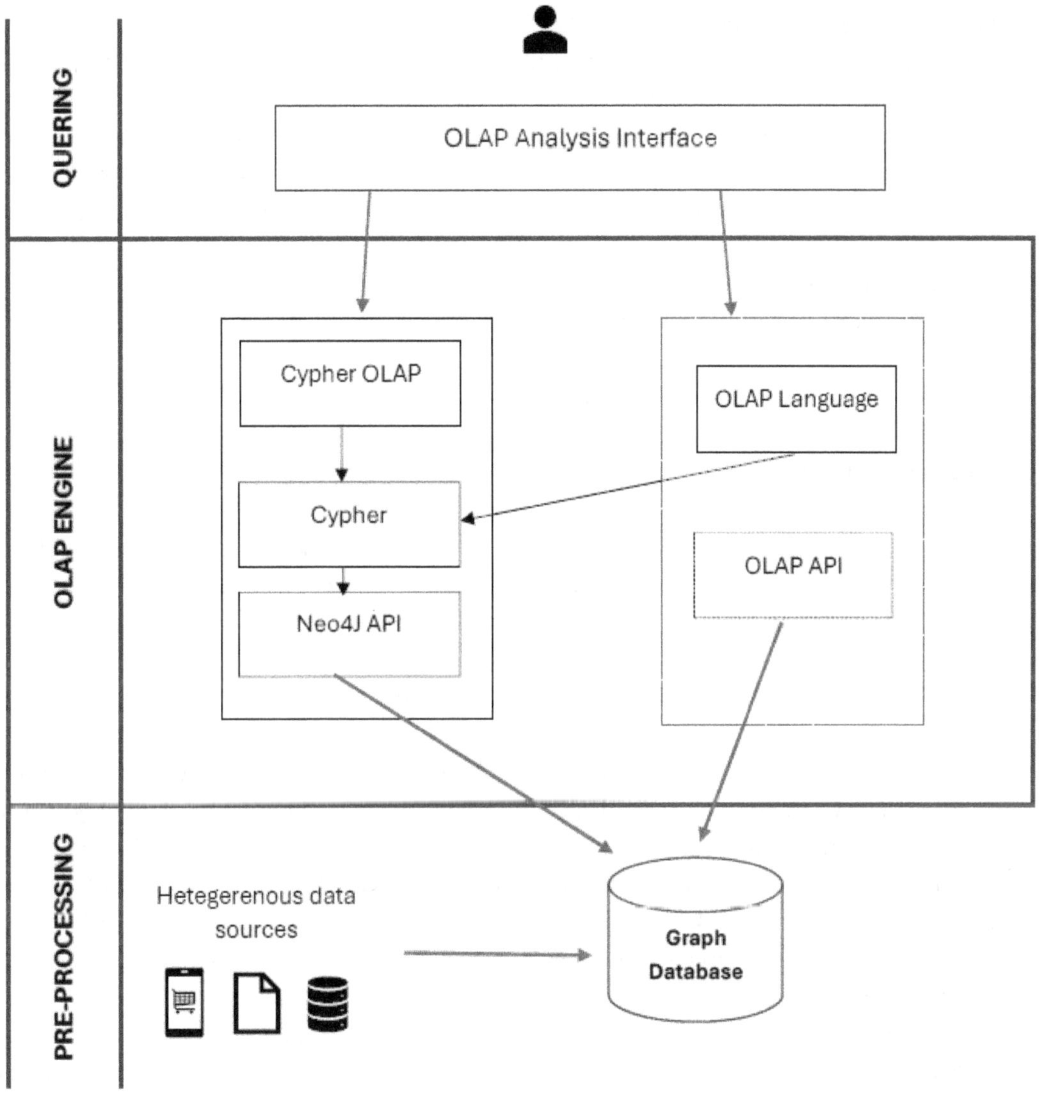

4. CYPHER OLAP: A DOMAIN-SPECIFIC LANGUAGE EXTENSION

One straightforward approach to integrating OLAP functionalities into Neo4j is the creation of a domain-specific language (DSL) called *Cypher OLAP*. This language builds on the existing Cypher syntax, extending its capabilities to meet the demands of analytical workloads. By retaining Cypher's declarative nature while introducing specialized constructs, Cypher OLAP can provide an intuitive and powerful interface for analysts and developers working with large-scale graph data. The process involves:

4.1. Syntax Extension

To support OLAP-specific operations, Cypher OLAP would introduce new keywords and constructs designed for advanced data aggregation and multidimensional analysis. These extensions could include enhanced support for complex aggregations, such as rolling averages, cumulative sums, and percentile calculations, as well as syntax for hierarchical or multidimensional aggregations across various dimensions of graph data, often referred to as rollups and cube operations. Additionally, it would incorporate constructs for defining analytic windows, enabling operations like ranking, moving averages, and lead/lag analysis within a dataset.

For example, Cypher OLAP might allow queries like:

```
MATCH (n:Product)-[:SOLD]->(s:Sale)
ROLLUP (n.category, s.year)
RETURN n.category, s.year, SUM(s.amount)
```

4.2. Query Rewriting

Translating Cypher OLAP queries into standard Cypher or intermediate representations for execution on the Neo4j engine requires several stages: parsing, translation, and optimization. Here is a more detailed breakdown of the process:

- Parsing: The first step is to parse the Cypher OLAP query and identify the analytical constructs, operations, and data structures involved. OLAP queries are typically designed to handle multidimensional analysis, such as rollups, slicing, and dicing of data across different hierarchical levels.
- Translation: The OLAP-specific constructs and operations must be translated into Cypher queries or a series of Cypher steps that perform the same analytical operations. Neo4j doesn't have native support for OLAP queries, so this process involves reworking OLAP-specific functionalities into standard Cypher that fits Neo4j's graph processing model. For instance, OLAP ROLLUP typically involves aggregating data along a hierarchical dimension. In Neo4j, this could be translated into multiple queries that perform incremental aggregation at each level of the hierarchy.
- Optimization: Once the query is translated, it is crucial to optimize it to ensure that the translated Cypher queries take full advantage of Neo4j's query planner and execution capabilities. This might include indexing and minimizing unnecessary traversals.

5. LOW-LEVEL API INTEGRATION FOR CYPHER EXTENSIONS

To achieve greater flexibility and performance, extending the Cypher query language to include OLAP-specific functionalities and integrating it with Neo4j's low-level API presents a robust approach. This extension would enable developers to execute complex analytical queries with enhanced precision, incorporating features tailored for multidimensional aggregations, hierarchy traversals, and other OLAP-specific operations directly within Cypher. By leveraging Neo4j's low-level API, developers gain granular control over query execution, enabling them to optimize performance by bypassing the higher-level abstractions typically associated with Cypher. This approach is particularly advantageous for handling complex OLAP workloads that demand custom optimizations, such as queries involving large-scale data aggregations or intricate graph traversals. It ensures that performance-critical analytical tasks can be executed with efficiency while maintaining the expressive power of the Cypher language, ultimately making Neo4j a more versatile platform for advanced data analytics. This approach involves:

- Query Parsing: Extend Cypher's parser to recognize new OLAP-specific clauses, such as GROUP BY, ROLLUP, or CUBE. This ensures that the query syntax aligns with the needs of analytical workflows while maintaining compatibility with existing Cypher queries.
- Query Translation: U se Neo4j's low-level API to translate the parsed OLAP queries into highly optimized execution plans. This involves mapping OLAP operations like aggregations and rollups directly to graph operations, bypassing the higher-level abstractions that might introduce overhead.
- Direct Execution: Execute the optimized queries through Neo4j's internal query processor. By directly interacting with the underlying storage and computation layers, this approach minimizes intermediate processing and delivers results with higher efficiency.

Figure 2. Low-Level API Integration workflow

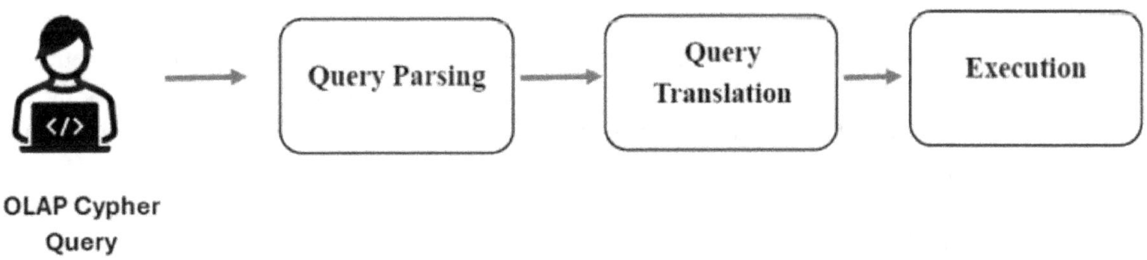

6. API EXTENSION FOR ADVANCED QUERYING FEATURES

Extending Neo4j's API to incorporate advanced OLAP querying capabilities can significantly enhance the platform's utility, providing developers with powerful and versatile tools for complex data analysis. This approach prioritizes a developer-centric methodology by embedding OLAP functionalities directly within the Neo4j Software Development Kit (SDK), ensuring seamless integration and ease of use across diverse programming environments. By doing so, developers can access a unified interface for both transactional and analytical operations, enabling them to construct multidimensional queries, analyze large-scale interconnected data, and derive insights without relying on external systems. This integration supports key features such as dimension hierarchy navigation, aggregate computations, and custom OLAP query extensions, empowering developers to design and implement tailored analytical solutions efficiently. Consequently, this initiative not only streamlines the development process but also opens new possibilities for leveraging Neo4j in advanced analytical applications across industries. This includes:

- Predefined OLAP Functions: Introducing predefined OLAP functions into Neo4j's API can significantly enhance analytical workflows by providing ready-to-use operations for common tasks such as rollup, cube, and slice-and-dice. These functions are designed to facilitate multidimensional data aggregation and exploration, enabling developers to quickly analyze large datasets without the overhead of crafting complex custom queries. The rollup function would allow users to summarize data across hierarchical dimensions, while the cube function could generate comprehensive aggregations across multiple dimensions, offering a holistic view of the data. Similarly, the slice-and-dice functionality would support flexible filtering and drilling into specific data subsets, empowering developers to uncover insights dynamically. By streamlining these operations, predefined OLAP functions not only improve efficiency but also reduce the learning curve for developers, making it easier to implement advanced analytics within graph-based systems and fostering innovation in data-driven applications.
- Custom Procedures: Enabling the definition and registration of custom stored procedures within Neo4j's API can greatly enhance its flexibility and utility for complex OLAP scenarios. These procedures would empower developers to encapsulate intricate business logic directly within the database, addressing advanced analytical needs such as hierarchical aggregations, multi-level filtering, and specialized calculations. By embedding these capabilities at the database level, custom procedures ensure optimized performance by reducing data transfer overhead and enabling computations to occur closer to the data source. Furthermore, this feature promotes reusability, as developers can create modular and shareable procedures tailored to specific analytical requirements. Whether it's implementing dynamic dimension rollups, calculating domain-specific metrics, or performing advanced transformations, custom procedures provide a powerful toolset for tackling sophisticated OLAP tasks, fostering greater efficiency and scalability in graph-based analytical applications.

An example of API method is depicted below:

```
GraphDatabaseService graphDb = new GraphDatabaseFactory().newEmbeddedData-
base();


Result result = graphDb.execute("CALL olap.aggregate('MATCH (p:Product)-
[:SOLD]->(s:Sale)', 'SUM(s.amount)')");
```

7. CONCLUSION

This paper presented a comprehensive approach to extending OLAP capabilities within the Neo4j graph engine, addressing the increasing demand for combining transactional and analytical processing in graph-based systems. We explored foundational concepts of graph databases, reviewed related works in graph OLAP. Our contribution aims at extending the Cypher language to support OLAP, for this, we proposed a multifaceted methodology, including the extension of Cypher for OLAP functionalities, query translation mechanisms, low-level API integrations, and developer-friendly tools for advanced analytics.

Our approach demonstrates the feasibility of integrating OLAP features into a graph database environment, enabling efficient analytical operations while maintaining Neo4j's inherent strengths in managing complex relationships and dynamic datasets.

As future work, there is significant potential to explore the combination of graph OLAP operations with machine learning frameworks. This integration could open new avenues for predictive analytics and graph embeddings. Achieving this would involve extending Neo4j's APIs to enable seamless connectivity with machine learning models and libraries.

REFERENCES

Bhattacharyya, A., & Chakravarty, D. (2020). (Graph Database: A Survey). *2020 International Conference on Computer, Electrical & Communication Engineering (ICCECE)*, 1–8. DOI: 10.1109/ICCECE48148.2020.9223105

Bouaziz, S., Nabli, A., & Gargouri, F. (2019). Design a Data Warehouse Schema from Document-Oriented database. *Procedia Computer Science*, 159, 221–230. DOI: 10.1016/j.procs.2019.09.177

Castelltort, A., & Laurent, A. (2014). NoSQL Graph-based OLAP Analysis: *Proceedings of the International Conference on Knowledge Discovery and Information Retrieval*, 217–224. DOI: 10.5220/0005072902170224

Chen, C., Yan, X., Zhu, F., Han, J., & Yu, P. S. (2008). Graph OLAP: Towards Online Analytical Processing on Graphs. *2008 Eighth IEEE International Conference on Data Mining*, 103–112. DOI: 10.1109/ICDM.2008.30

Chen, C., Yan, X., Zhu, F., Han, J., & Yu, P. S. (2009). Graph OLAP: A multi-dimensional framework for graph data analysis. *Knowledge and Information Systems*, 21(1), 41–63. DOI: 10.1007/s10115-009-0228-9

Chevalier, M., El Malki, M., Kopliku, A., Teste, O., & Tournier, R. (2015). Implementation of Multidimensional Databases with Document-Oriented NoSQL. In Madria, S., & Hara, T. (Eds.), *Big Data Analytics and Knowledge Discovery* (pp. 379–390). Springer International Publishing. DOI: 10.1007/978-3-319-22729-0_29

Chou, C.-H., Hayakawa, M., Kitazawa, A., & Sheu, P. (2018). GOLAP: Graph-Based Online Analytical Processing. *International Journal of Semantic Computing*, 12(04), 595–608. DOI: 10.1142/S1793351X18500071

Dehdouh, K., Boussaid, O., & Bentayeb, F. (2020). Big Data warehouse: Building columnar NoSQL OLAP cubes. In *International Journal of Decision Support System Technology* (Vol. 12, Issue 1, pp. 1–24). DOI: 10.4018/IJDSST.2020010101

Gómez, L., Kuijpers, B., & Vaisman, A. (2017). Performing OLAP over Graph Data: Query Language, Implementation, and a Case Study. *Proceedings of the International Workshop on Real-Time Business Intelligence and Analytics*. DOI: 10.1145/3129292.3129293

Gómez, L., Kuijpers, B., & Vaisman, A. (2020). Online analytical processsing on graph data. *Intelligent Data Analysis*, 24(3), 515–541. DOI: 10.3233/IDA-194576

Kamphuis, C. (2020). Graph Databases for Information Retrieval. In Jose, J. M., Yilmaz, E., Magalhães, J., Castells, P., Ferro, N., Silva, M. J., & Martins, F. (Eds.), *Advances in Information Retrieval* (pp. 608–612). Springer International Publishing. DOI: 10.1007/978-3-030-45442-5_79

Khalil, A., & Belaissaoui, M. (2023a). A Data Placement Strategy for Distributed Document-oriented Data Warehouse. *IAENG International Journal of Computer Science*, 50(4), 1541–1549.

Khalil, A., & Belaissaoui, M. (2023b). An Approach for Implementing Online Analytical Processing Systems under Column-Family Databases. In *IAENG International Journal of Applied Mathematics* (Vol. 53, Issue 1). https://www.scopus.com/inward/record.uri?eid=2-s2.0-85149634233&partnerID=40&md5=1e0e4fbb81c9f2f969dfffd87b08daa1

Sellami, A., Nabli, A., & Gargouri, F. (2020). Transformation of Data Warehouse Schema to NoSQL Graph Data Base. In Abraham, A., Cherukuri, A. K., Melin, P., & Gandhi, N. (Eds.), *Intelligent Systems Design and Applications* (Vol. 941, pp. 410–420). Springer International Publishing., DOI: 10.1007/978-3-030-16660-1_41

Zhao, P., Li, X., Xin, D., & Han, J. (2011). Graph cube: On warehousing and OLAP multidimensional networks. *Proceedings of the 2011 ACM SIGMOD International Conference on Management of Data*, 853–864. DOI: 10.1145/1989323.1989413

Chapter 17

Exploring the Internet of Behaviors Capabilities: A Comprehensive Survey

Imane Moustati
https://orcid.org/0009-0002-3159-5038
ENSA Khouribga, LaSTI Laboratory, Sultan Moulay Slimane University, Morocco

Noreddine Gherabi
ENSA Khouribga, LaSTI Laboratory, Sultan Moulay Slimane University, Morocco

ABSTRACT

IoT systems have provided humans with incredible benefits. However, its features related to analyzing collected data and automatically executing established guidelines restrict them from comprehending the intent of these data, retrieving human intention, or understanding behaviors. The Internet of Behaviors (IoB) could be considered an ecosystem that combines technology, advanced data analysis, edge analytics, and behavioral science to aggregate, analyze, and comprehend human data gathered from IoT devices or online utilizing human psychology. Then, this understanding can be applied to change or affect human behavior. In this work, we present an in-depth review of the latest research in the IoB field and comprehensively describe the IoB, its fundamental features, and its relationship with IoT and the DKIW pyramid. Then, we examine key distinctions between IoB and IoT and delve into the IoB architecture and core enabling technologies. Furthermore, we comprehensively identify the major challenges to be addressed by the IoB framework, notably in terms of ethics, security, and privacy.

I. INTRODUCTION

After being originally suggested by Professor Kevin Ashton of the Massachusetts Institute of Technology (MIT) in 1999, the Internet of Things (IoT) has been around for more than 20 years. Since then, this field of study has drawn attention from the scientific community and made significant strides in a number of application areas. It was mostly concerned with connecting gadgets and sharing their data. Its main idea was to link common digital devices—like every day electronic appliances or devices—with each other so that users could keep an eye on their status and obtain precise data from the devices' network

DOI: 10.4018/979-8-3373-0365-9.ch017

without actually having to be close to any of these devices. As of this moment, the IoT is widely used in many different contexts, and IoT gadgets are becoming more and more common. International Data Corporation estimates that in the year 2025 there will be 55.7 billion connected IoT gadgets globally, and that the volume of data gathered will reach 73.1 Zettabytes (Moustati et al., 2023). These large amounts of data include a great lot of useful information for every aspect of our everyday lives. These massive IoT devices are continuously collecting our private and environmental data. Consequently, a number of ingenious Artificial Intelligence (AI) technologies, including data mining and Machine Learning (ML) algorithms, have been created to reveal such information. However, IoT systems, including the AI algorithms they have adopted, are limited to interpreting the data we pre-collect and automatically following our defined rules. They are unable to comprehend the purpose of the data collection or its application. The ability of IoT systems to serve people is limited by their very nature. When seen from the DIKW pyramid's standpoint, IoT systems usually only interact with data and information levels. As a result, the knowledge layer and information layer are very different from one another. A relatively new idea related to the Internet of Things has emerged in recent years. In his blog in 2012, the professor of psychology at the University of Helsinki, Dr. Gote Nyman initially introduced the concept of the Internet of Behaviors (IoB) (Moghaddam et al., 2022) to fill the information-to-wisdom gap in the DIKW pyramid. However, related research has only begun after Gartner raised the IoB in 2019, and ranked it in the first place of his strategic predictions in 2020 (Gartner, 2020; Panetta, 2019). The IoB, according to Dr. Nyman, is a specialized component of IoT architectures, and the distinction between IoT and IoB is that the former addresses devices and maintains device data and their behavior in accordance with those devices, while the latter targets human behaviors and handles data related to those behaviors. He stated that the same technical framework could be used by both (Nyman, 2022). In his view, the IoB offers methods for creating, encoding, addressing, and handling behavioral data for the good of individuals, companies, services, and the entire human race. Recently, on 5 September 2023, a study by Emergen Research predicted that the size of the worldwide IoB market will rise to USD 3000 billion by 2032 (Emergen Research, 2023). The IoB can be considered as the fusion of the IoT and Artificial Intelligence of Things (AIoT), utilized to analyze behavioral patterns to determine people's requirements, interests, and preferences (Mezair et al., 2023), after which users' actions are modified or influenced. AI and 6G are two infrastructural components that will help make the IoB successfully deployed. Data from various IoT environmental sensor sources, commercial data on consumers, citizen-driven data, social media data, data processed by government agencies and public departments, and geographic information science data can all be combined in an IoB system. Data mining and ML are able to assess people's behavior based on such data sets. This allows IoB to facilitate the better interpretation of human behavior by many stakeholders, including corporations, authorities, and citizens. The IoB has come a long way, but numerous aspects continue to be in the conceptual stage, and there are still few practical studies on the topic. This paper provides a comprehensive survey of recent advancements in the IoB realm, provides a thorough literature review including state-of-the-art research applying IoB to different sectors, along with discussing potential IoB architecture, key differentiators of the IoB and the IoT, and key enabler technologies of the IoB can leverage. Furthermore, we extensively discussed the main security threats and challenges the IoB still needs to address.

II. RELATED WORK

Researchers in various fields have recently shown an increasing interest in the IoB (Moustati et al., 2023, 2024a, 2024b). As a result, the number of studies available on the topic continues to grow, which we will discuss in this section. In their tutorial (Zhao et al., 2023), Quinglin Zhao, et al., presented a five-layer architecture for the IoB that includes behavior perception, networking, computing, service provision, and security/privacy. In return to Dr. Nyman's behavior-identity-separation notion, they offered a decentralized privacy-protection approach. They also explored intention inference, behavior derivation, behavior programming, and behavior chain optimization, which they considered to be the four major implications of behavior computing, and looked into the functional specifications and potential domains of an IoB address to designate human behavior. There have also been attempts to apply the IoB in the insurance sector by managing drivers' scores based on their driving behaviors. The statistical and managerial value of telematics in insurance pricing was shown by research (Henckaerts & Antonio, 2022). The authors revealed that, under various assumptions about the price elasticity of the clientele, telematics promotes profitability and retention rates, improves the process of classifying risks, and leads to a more accurate evaluation of claim risk through the utilization of usage-based insurance premiums. Additionally, different research (Abri et al., 2023) suggested extending the examination of driving behaviors to include driving habits. Its goal was to examine abnormal actions that have the potential to develop into abnormal driving habits and stop them from doing so. To manage a driver's driving behaviors and their mutual intra-and/or inter-impacts, the authors proposed modeling the behaviors as a network of interacting and cooperating entities inside the Internet of Driving Behaviors (IoDB). In energy sector, authors in (Moustati et al., 2024a) proposed an IoB ecosystem that aims to continually influence energy consumption behavior, in order to avoid electricity waste and reduce costs. They used an LSTM-based DL model for accurately predicting future energy consumption. The LSTM has proven its ability to efficiently predict time-series energy consumption data in comparison with other models (Moustati et al., 2024c). Zhang Guangyuan et al. (Zhang et al., 2021) employed an IoB model to gain a deeper understanding of the connection between incidents of air pollution and the daily activities of the locals. In fact, they conducted a quantitative investigation to determine whether and how variations in air pollution affect people's specific daily activities. Authors of this survey (Sun et al., 2022) sought to give an IoT-focused research status of the IoB, and examined some of the traits, uses, and trends associated with IoB. Other scholars also made an effort to examine the IoB from the perspective of other disciplines. For instance, Imane Moustati, et al., (Moustati et al., 2024b) studied the implementation of an IoB ecosystem in the financial realm. Others (Amiri et al., 2023; Javaid et al., 2022) discussed the IoB in healthcare sector and examined some of the difficulties facing its growth. This research (Shatkin & Orlov, 2023) also presented an overview and conception of the IoB from the standpoint of social science and identified three models of the Internet of Behaviors.

III. THE INTERNET OF BEHAVIORS

1. IoB architecture

Since the IoB is still in its early stages, no official architecture has yet been established. Nevertheless, researchers in their tutorial (Zhao et al., 2023), suggested a five-layer design as an architecture for the IoB (Fig.1). They modeled the IoB network with a directed graph of behavior nodes, in which behaviors are represented by vertexes and a behavior transition is represented by an edge connecting two vertexes. The optimal probability is responsible for selecting the subsequent conduct. The behavior perception layer gathers data about behavior from the Internet and IoT devices in various forms (e.g., text, image, video, voice). Subsequently, the behavior is paired to IoB in the behavior network layer, and the intention is deduced in the behavior computing layer. Following the completion of the intention inference, the service provision layer will achieve a process of decision-making, service delivery, or user behavior alteration.

Figure 1. Five-layers architecture of an IoB system

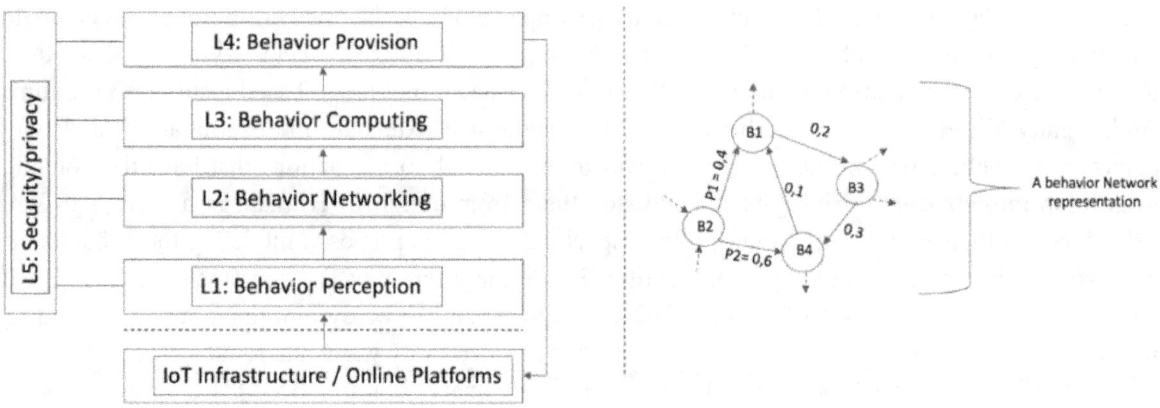

2. From IoT to IoB: the IoB's added value

As seen in the previous section, the IoB can be applied to various activity sectors (healthcare, energy consumption, insurance, etc.), and can bring unprecedented capabilities to these domains. Contrary to the IoT, the IoB takes into account human psychology factors when analyzing data (Fig2.) (Moustati et al., 2024b), and has a primary focus on human behaviors and interactions. IoB expands on IoT by addressing the gathering, processing, and interpreting of human behavioral data in both digital and physical contexts. On the other hand, the IoT deals with sensor-generated data and is mainly concerned with connectivity and data sharing between devices and systems. Taking this further, the IoB creates comprehensive profiles of each person's tastes and habits by combining information from various sources, such as location-based data, online transactions, social media interactions, and biometric signals. The IoB places a strong focus on using data created by connected gadgets or obtained from online platforms to study, analyze, and influence human behavior. Exploring people's motives, preferences, and decision-making processes goes beyond the technical aspects of the IoB and opens the door to a deeper comprehension of user demands, enabling more individualized and context-aware interventions. A summary of the key differences between IoB and IoT is presented in Table 1.

Table 1. Comparing IoB and IoT

	IoT	IoB
Core mission	**The connectivity and data exchange between devices and systems**	**The collection, analysis, and interpretation of human behavioral data within digital and physical environments, to predict and influence human behaviors.**
Development stage	Mature	Immature
DIKW pyramid level	The two first levels (Data and Information)	Takes in charge the transition from Information level to Knowledge and Wisdom layers
Data nature	Non-behavior data	Human-behavior-centered data
Design principle	Information-centered	Intent-centered
AI Model	ML or DL	Preferably DL
Quality of Service (QoS)	Moderate	Enhanced
Quality of Experience (QoE)	Average	Improved
Computing requirements	Moderate	High
Service provision	Mainly based on static rules	Dynamic, based on human intentions
Application sectors	Energy, customer services, smart transportations, marketing, smart homes, healthcare, education, etc.	

3. The IoB workflow

The workflow of the IoB includes the IoT one; however, it also adds additional layers, as described in Fig. 2 (Moustati et al., 2024b). It first tracks users' behaviors and gathers behavioral data through various channels, including smart devices, IoT sensors, and online and social media platforms, to assess users' behavioral patterns and characteristics, preferences, opinions, etc. Data can be of all forms and a mix of structured, semi-structured, and unstructured data, depending on the sources and nature of the information being collected and analyzed. It also includes heterogeneous data (image, text, voice, video, graphs, etc.), meaning it necessitates special technical requirements to be considered when processing and handling it. These data must then go through an advanced phase of data analysis and machine learning treatment to sort and analyze the processed data to extract useful information. This obtained information, which represents the information layer in the Data-Information-Knowledge-Wisdom (DIKW) pyramid (Moustati et al., 2023; Wikipedia, 2021), must be mined with behavioral science mechanisms combined with mainly deep learning algorithms to have an exact knowledge of the effects these patterns have on human behavior. Deep learning (DL) is preferable in most IoB cases due to its ability to work with large volumes of data and its superior accuracy to ML in such scenarios (Moustati et al., 2024c). Depending on the available data, DL algorithms such as LSTM with time-series data, CNN with visual data, and GCNN with graph data have been used in IoB applications and confirmed their utility [connected vehicles]. In this phase, after the analysis of behavioral data, the system has the necessary knowledge needed to approach individuals for optimum results, thus reaching the wisdom layer in the DIKW pyramid. An IoB system would use the corresponding knowledge acquired to achieve the wisdom level, in which it can automatically make autonomous appropriate decisions, develop informed strategies, predict users' behaviors, and then influence or alter their behaviors accordingly. An IoB system has a continuous mission of learning human behaviors, analyzing them, acting accordingly (changing actuators), observing the new behaviors, and reacting to them respectively (Moustati et al., 2024b). Thus, an IoB system has and offers a unique value through this continuous loop, allowing a dynamic real-time reaction to human behaviors. The IoB surpasses conventional analytics by leveraging feedback loops, IoB data, and technology, thus optimally impacting human behavior within specific circumstances.

Figure 2. The IoB workflow

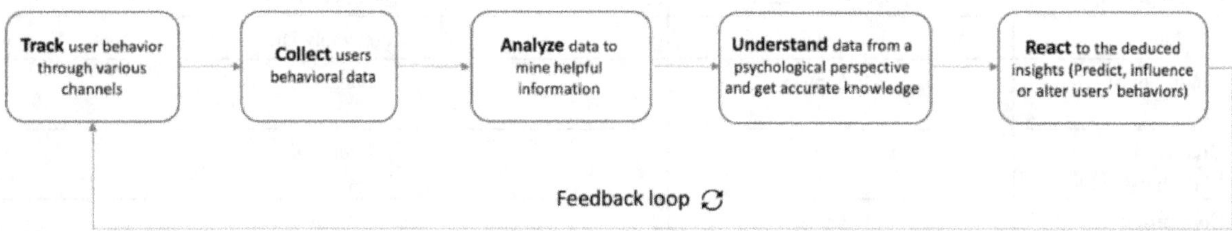

4. IoB characteristics

The IoB has several unique features that set it apart from traditional data-driven paradigms, and to fully realize its potential, modern technologies must be employed. The IoB is mainly distinguished by its emphasis on gathering, analyzing, and interpreting human behavioral data in both digital and physical realms. This implies calling for a comprehensive strategy for data processing and acquisition. Moreover, managing structured, semi-structured, and unstructured data formats, as well as integrating various data sources including social media interactions, online transactions, biometric signals, and location-based data, are some of the key characteristics of the IoB. To effectively address these challenges, an IoB system needs to fulfill some technical requirements (Malek et al., 2017). It should guarantee minimal latency, ensure real-time processing of behavioral data, and maintain high throughput and accuracy in its prediction models (Malek et al., 2017). The IoB framework should ensure a continuous and reliable feedback loop for users, provide personalized real-time reminders to them, and ensure a high quality of experience and service. The system users are indifferent to its technical features; therefore, it should be hidden from them. For instance, UI should be unified within all components of the IoB ecosystem so that users wouldn't feel the change in processes. Users should not feel latency when data are transmitted from edge computing devices to the cloud or when data is synchronized, processed, or qualified, even with workload variations. The IoB system must guarantee writing data reliably and constantly in every component of the ecosystem and leverage technologies such as edge computing and distributed processing frameworks to handle the scalability and real-time processing requirements of large-scale behavioral data streams. Analysis dimensions in the IoB settings are determined based on changing needs according to the analysis process and data nature. Therefore, an IoB system should support a flexible multidimensional analysis of data to intelligently process the heterogenous data. An IoB system must attain an autonomous decision-making level based on the computational analysis it performs, accurately predict the future possible user' behaviors from a certain scenario, adapt itself on the scenario that has the highest probability, feedback, and personalize it actions accordingly. An IoB system is required to be extremely reliable in itself and ensure the reliability of its constituent components (network, systems, devices, computation outputs, etc.) (Chaudhry et al., 2020; Mavrogiorgou et al., 2018), in addition to offer tailored approaches for specific data conditions depending on data requirements (larger retention periods, multiple copies, rapid/frequent access, etc.), and integrating privacy-preserving technologies such as differential privacy and homomorphic encryption to ensure the ethical and secure handling of sensitive behavioral data, thus safeguarding individuals' privacy rights.

5. Key technologies enablers

Various cutting-edge technologies exist and which an IoB system can leverage. An IoB system can be designed on a blockchain-like architecture (Zhao et al., 2023) to ensure decentralization, reliability of the ecosystem, and security, confidentiality, immutability, privacy and transparency of the behavioral data in IoB platforms. Biometric technologies like facial and voice recognition mechanisms, fingerprint scanners, and other behavioral or psychological biometrics can be used to gather behavioral data and have thorough insights into human emotions and interactions. HCI based technologies, such as virtual reality, augmented reality, and natural user interfaces can aid in IoB mission by implementing engaging and immersive user experiences.

ML algorithms, and specifically deep learning, can be used to analyze and interpret the vast amount of data gathered from various channels. It can uncover behavioral patterns and useful insights that will aid in understanding and then approaching users in an informed manner. DL models are also being used to predict the future behaviors of IoB system users (Moustati et al., 2024a). Different DL models can be used, depending on the nature of the data and the use case. However, Recurrent Neural Networks (RNNs) and Convolutional Neural Networks (CNNs) are at present the most used models when dealing with IoB scenarios (Amiri et al., 2023; Elayan et al., 2023; Mezair et al., 2023). Integrating human judgment into the AI process when determining the final answer by Human In The Loop (HITL) also aids in improving the model and solving problems that were classified as human-solvable only.

There is a symbiotic relationship between the IoB, big data, and cloud computing, where each component plays a critical role in enabling the collection, processing, and analysis of behavioral data at scale, driving innovation, and creating value in the digital era. The IoB can rely on big data tools and concepts to collect, aggregate, and integrate diverse data sets from multiple sources, enabling organizations to gain a comprehensive understanding of individuals' behaviors and preferences. Cloud computing will provide the necessary infrastructure and computational resources to process and analyze the gathered behavioral data at scale, facilitating the extraction of actionable insights and the delivery of personalized experiences in real time. Furthermore, cloud-based platforms and services will aid in deploying and scaling IoB applications rapidly, leveraging advanced analytics capabilities to derive value from behavioral data and drive innovation across various domains. Large-scale connectivity, lightning-fast wireless communication, and dependability and security are all anticipated benefits of the IoB, and the deployment of 5G would boost real-time analytical capability, decrease decision-making times, and improve transmission efficiency. While there are currently many issues with the centralized management of IoT devices, the decentralized architecture of 6G can solve them. The IoB can also leverage Natural Language Processing (NLP) and XAI technologies. Practically, NLP will aid in analyzing textual data from social media posts, emails, customer reviews, online forums, etc., to extract accurate sentiment, identify topics or reviews, and categorize content, providing valuable insights into individuals' opinions, preferences, and behaviors. At the same time, XAI will ensure the transparency and interpretability of AI models and AI-driven decisions, in addition to their understandability for humans. Thus, overcoming models' black-box issues and providing a robust and acceptable system to its users.

IV. IoB CHALLENGES AND OPEN ISSUES

While the IoB holds promise for various applications, there are also several challenges and concerns that need to be addressed. The most essential component of the IoB ecosystem is people's behavioral data, it is its' driving force. This data reveals all aspects of a person's living habits, and the privacy leakage issue is highly implicated. Therefore, several issues need to be considered regarding how to protect peoples' private behavioral data. For IoB data, security is mainly concerned with the unwanted actions of unauthorized users, while privacy is mainly concerned with hiding or removing the identities of owners of IoB data. Promoting security and privacy in IoB includes data encryption, laws, and technology regulations and standards, by specifying responsibilities in protecting and controlling access to data for every participant in the IoB ecosystem. Within an IoB framework, people's behavior is recorded through various channels, i.e., mobile applications, smart devices, sensors, locators, etc. Therefore, the type, extent, and scope of the collected data must be defined. Moreover, using behavioral data also necessitates creating relevant laws and regulations to protect users' legitimate rights and interests, such as privacy rights, and setting clear rules on the ethical use of personal information. The behavioral data is collected from various sources, implying multiple data structures, standards, formats and protocols. Ensuring the accuracy and reliability of collected data can be challenging. Data may be incomplete, inconsistent, or subject to biases, leading to inaccurate or misleading insights. For example, the IoT device undetectable issue known as "fail-dirty" that designs the circumstances in which the gadget malfunctions and sends misleading information (Lan et al., 2021). Integrating and interoperating diverse data sources can be complex and challenging, requiring robust data integration frameworks and data harmonization efforts. Also, the scalability of IoB systems and handling the complexity of data analytics, DL-based models, and behavioral modeling pose significant challenges (Shi-Nash & Hardoon, 2017). With the utilization of these behavioral data here, multiple risks appear. Particularly, the risk of data breaches, unauthorized access, and misuse of personal information. Users' private data (e.g., IP address, residential address, contact information) are closely linked, meaning that if only one information is exposed, other ones can be also accessed by hackers, resulting in problems with privacy disclosure. Consequently, to protect data privacy, for example, behavioral data should be encrypted, biometrics should be erased when required, and data storage must be trustworthy.

The security of an IoB system implies the security of each of its components. Therefore, an IoB system should ensure that the equipments' hardware and software are reliable and can be efficiently updated in time, protect the identity of the IoT devices and the behaviors nodes within the IoB network, ensure high availability and delivery of service, and solve issues such as service degradation due to lossy network, and network latency (Kundu et al., 2021). The IoB system should also protect the identity of the IoT devices and the behaviors nodes within the IoB network and enable dynamic trust in IoT network, since IoT devices can join and leave the network when required. It is necessary to implement lightweight encryption algorithms on the IoT devices, knowing that they are small with limited power, processing, and memory capabilities, to reduce the possibility of eavesdropping, but must not compromise the security level. Issues like battery failure of devices, lack of access to the mobile power supply can interrupt the service at a critical time and decrease the quality of service and the quality of experience to the systems' users. Also, there is a threat that if the wide adoption and intelligence of the environment increases, the destructive effects of their malfunctions and the impact of biases become more severe.

V. CONCLUSION

The Internet of Behaviors is relatively a new research area, that is gaining increasing interest among academics and the research community. It is a concept that focuses on the collection, analysis, and utilization of data related to human behaviors and interactions in both digital and physical environments, to predict and alter or influence human behaviors. It can be seen as the extension of IoT that primarily seeks to find patterns and comprehend data via the lens of behavioral psychology, and encompasses the integration of various sources of behavioral data, including online activities, social media interactions, mobile device usage, biometric data, location tracking, and more. The IoB ecosystem is still in its early stages, but it is projected to play an expanding role in intelligently addressing human needs and fostering desired, human behaviors. It holds promise for various applications and benefits, even though there are also several concerns, technical and non-technical challenges that need to be addressed. The aim of this paper is to provide a comprehensive survey of recent advancements in the IoB realm, provide a thorough literature review including state-of-the-art research applying IoB to different sectors, along with discussing potential IoB architecture, key differentiators of the IoB and the IoT, and key enabler technologies the IoB can leverage. Furthermore, we extensively discussed the main security threats and challenges the IoB still need to address. Through this survey we not only highlight the achievements made but also urges action towards exploring uncharted territories to light the route forward at this captivating intersection of technology and human behavior.

REFERENCES

Al Abri, K. A. S., Mastouri, M., Bouyahia, Z., Haddad, H., Yasar, A.-U.-H., & Shakshuki, E. (2023). On the Interest of Extending Internet of Behaviors to Internet of Habits: A Preliminary Exploration. *Procedia Computer Science*, 224, 122–130. DOI: 10.1016/j.procs.2023.09.019

Amiri, Z., Heidari, A., Darbandi, M., Yazdani, Y., Jafari Navimipour, N., Esmaeilpour, M., Sheykhi, F., & Unal, M. (2023). The Personal Health Applications of Machine Learning Techniques in the Internet of Behaviors. *Sustainability (Basel)*, 15(16), 12406. DOI: 10.3390/su151612406

Chaudhry, S. A., Yahya, K., Al-Turjman, F., & Yang, M. H. (2020). A Secure and Reliable Device Access Control Scheme for IoT Based Sensor Cloud Systems. *IEEE Access : Practical Innovations, Open Solutions*, 8, 139244–139254. DOI: 10.1109/ACCESS.2020.3012121

Elayan, H., Aloqaily, M., Karray, F., & Guizani, M. (2023). Internet of Behavior and Explainable AI Systems for Influencing IoT Behavior. *IEEE Network*, 37(1), 62–68. DOI: 10.1109/MNET.009.2100500

Emergen Research. (2023). *Global Internet of Behaviors (IoB) Market Size to Reach USD 3,087.86 Billion in 2032*. https://finance.yahoo.com/news/global-internet-behaviors-iob-market-150000141.html

Gartner. (2020). *Gartner top strategic technology trends for 2021*. https://www.gartner.com/smarterwithgartner/gartner-top-strategic- technology-trends-for-2021/

Henckaerts, R., & Antonio, K. (2022). The added value of dynamically updating motor insurance prices with telematics collected driving behavior data. *Insurance, Mathematics & Economics*, 105, 79–95. DOI: 10.1016/j.insmatheco.2022.03.011

Javaid, M., Haleem, A., Singh, R. P., Khan, S., & Suman, R. (2022). An extensive study on Internet of Behavior (IoB) enabled Healthcare-Systems: Features, facilitators, and challenges. *BenchCouncil Transactions on Benchmarks. Standards and Evaluations*, 2(4), 100085. DOI: 10.1016/j.tbench.2023.100085

Kundu, S. S., Sarkar, D., Jana, P., & Kole, D. K. (2021). *Personalization in Education Using Recommendation System: An Overview* (pp. 85–111). DOI: 10.1007/978-981-15-8744-3_5

Lan, F., Huang, Q., Zeng, L., Guan, X., Xing, D., & Cheng, Z. (2021). Tourism Experience and Construction of Personalized Smart Tourism Program Under Tourist Psychology. *Frontiers in Psychology*, 12, 691183. Advance online publication. DOI: 10.3389/fpsyg.2021.691183 PMID: 34367015

Malek, Y. N., Kharbouch, A., El Khoukhi, H., Bakhouya, M., De Florio, V., El Ouadghiri, D., Latre, S., & Blondia, C. (2017). On the use of IoT and Big Data Technologies for Real-time Monitoring and Data Processing. *Procedia Computer Science*, 113, 429–434. DOI: 10.1016/j.procs.2017.08.281

Mavrogiorgou, A., Kiourtis, A., Symvoulidis, C., & Kyriazis, D. (2018). Capturing the Reliability of Unknown Devices in the IoT World. *2018 Fifth International Conference on Internet of Things: Systems, Management and Security*, 62–69. DOI: 10.1109/IoTSMS.2018.8554720

Mezair, T., Djenouri, Y., Belhadi, A., Srivastava, G., & Lin, J. C.-W. (2023). Towards an Advanced Deep Learning for the Internet of Behaviors: Application to Connected Vehicles. *ACM Transactions on Sensor Networks*, 19(2), 1–18. DOI: 10.1145/3526192

Moghaddam, M. T., Muccini, H., Dugdale, J., & Kjagaard, M. B. (2022). Designing Internet of Behaviors Systems. *2022 IEEE 19th International Conference on Software Architecture (ICSA)*, 124–134. DOI: 10.1109/ICSA53651.2022.00020

Moustati, I., Gherabi, N., El Massari, H., & Saadi, M. (2023). From The Internet of Things (IoT) to The Internet of Behaviors (IoB) for Data Analysis. *2023 7th IEEE Congress on Information Science and Technology (CiSt)*, 634–639. DOI: 10.1109/CiSt56084.2023.10409989

Moustati, I., Gherabi, N., & Saadi, M. (2024a). Building an IoB ecosystem for influencing energy consumption in smart cities. *Data and Metadata*, 3. Advance online publication. DOI: 10.56294/dm2024.441

Moustati, I., Gherabi, N., & Saadi, M. (2024b). Leveraging the internet of behaviours and digital nudges for enhancing customers financial decision-making. *International Journal of Computer Applications in Technology*, 1(1), 10065772. Advance online publication. DOI: 10.1504/IJCAT.2024.10065772

Moustati, I., Gherabi, N., & Saadi, M. (2024c). Time-Series Forecasting Models for Smart Meters Data: An Empirical Comparison and Analysis. *Journal Européen des Systèmes Automatisés*, 57(05), 1419–1427. DOI: 10.18280/jesa.570517

Nyman, G. (2022). *Internet of Behaviors (IoB): With a human touch* .

Panetta, P. (2019). *Gartner top strategic predictions for 2020 and beyond*. https://www.gartner.com/smarterwithgartner/gartner-top-strategic- predictions-for-2020-and-beyond/

Shatkin, M. A., & Orlov, M. O. (2023). Internet of Behavior: Types, models, principles. *Vestnik of Saint Petersburg University.Philosophy and Conflict Studies*, 39(2), 368–380. DOI: 10.21638/spbu17.2023.212

Shi-Nash, A., & Hardoon, D. R. (2017). DATA ANALYTICS AND PREDICTIVE ANALYTICS IN THE ERA OF BIG DATA. In *Internet of Things and Data Analytics Handbook* (pp. 329–345). Wiley., DOI: 10.1002/9781119173601.ch19

Sun, J., Gan, W., Chao, H.-C., Yu, P. S., & Ding, W. (2022). *Internet of Behaviors: A Survey*. http://arxiv.org/abs/2211.15588

Wikipedia. (2021). *DIKW pyramid*. https://en.wikipedia.org/wiki/DIKW

Zhang, G., Poslad, S., Rui, X., Yu, G., Fan, Y., Song, X., & Li, R. (2021). Using an Internet of Behaviours to Study How Air Pollution Can Affect People's Activities of Daily Living: A Case Study of Beijing, China. *Sensors (Basel)*, 21(16), 5569. DOI: 10.3390/s21165569 PMID: 34451012

Zhao, Q., Li, G., Cai, J., Zhou, M. C., & Feng, L. (2023). A Tutorial on Internet of Behaviors: Concept, Architecture, Technology, Applications, and Challenges. *IEEE Communications Surveys and Tutorials*, 25(2), 1227–1260. Advance online publication. DOI: 10.1109/COMST.2023.3246993

Chapter 18
Navigating the Internet of Behaviors (IoB) Potential Across Domains

Imane Moustati
https://orcid.org/0009-0002-3159-5038
ENSA Khouribga, LaSTI Laboratory, Sultan Moulay Slimane University, Morocco

Noreddine Gherabi
ENSA Khouribga, LaSTI Laboratory, Sultan Moulay Slimane University, Morocco

ABSTRACT

The Internet of Behaviors (IoB) emerged as the next frontier in data-driven innovation, leveraging the vast amount of behavioral data collected through Internet of Things (IoT) devices and online to understand, predict, and influence human behavior. It holds enormous advantages in shaping individuals' daily lives. The IoB has the potential to optimize processes, personalize experiences, and fundamentally reshape people's interactions with technology; however, the widespread adoption of the IoB also faces challenges. This paper offers a thorough state-of-the-art snapshot of the IoB research area, examines multiple potential use-case application scenarios of the IoB across various industries and disciplines, and presents critical ethical and technical challenges that should be addressed.

I. INTRODUCTION

The introduction of the IoT has increased the amount of data available for collection and analysis; the more data available, the more user behavior can be understood. To create efficient IoB applications, we can generally adhere to a workflow model that comprises five key elements, primarily focused on user behavior and behavioral psychology background knowledge: user behavior monitoring, gathering data, analyzing it, extracting knowledge, and wisdom (Moustati et al., 2023). However, security and privacy features have to be present in every system that handles personal data. Dr. Nyman dreamed and envisioned the IoB concept to enable the useful utilization of behavioral data without identifying the individual engaging in the action. Unless the individuals in question choose to disclose their names, their identities would remain undisclosed. According to him, we need to build technologies that enable

DOI: 10.4018/979-8-3373-0365-9.ch018

people to easily provide data on their ongoing behavior, either manually or partially automatically, and that incorporate what he refers to as confirmational artificial intelligence (CoAI). In CoAI, a system or service gets confirmation from the relevant person, who can offer feedback or clarify if the AI's calculations, recommendations, and interpretations are accurate or pertinent. The emergence of IoB will open up new avenues for organizations to gain deeper insights into consumer behaviors, optimize operations, and drive innovation. An IoB system empowered by its built-in technologies can potentially be deployed to provide value to almost any activity area. The IoB can benefit from cutting-edge technologies (Moustati et al., 2023) such as DL, XAI, Big data, edge computing, advanced data analysis, 5G/6G etc. In this paper, we first provide a state-of-the-art snapshot of the IoB research area, then we give an in-depth exploration of IoB applications across diverse sectors and domains. Through a series of use-case scenarios, we will analyze how IoB can revolutionize industries like healthcare, finance, marketing, and supply chain management, among others. We will highlight the potential for IoB to optimize processes, personalize experiences, and ultimately, reshape the way we interact with technology in various aspects of our lives. Finally, we will examine the challenges that currently hinder the widespread adoption of IoB systems. Issues such as data privacy concerns, interoperability limitations, and the ethical considerations surrounding potential manipulation will be discussed.

II. LITERATURE REVIEW

Within the travel and tourism industry, Antonio Salis (Salis, 2021) investigated the concept of creating better real-time travel support tools on smartphones with the use of cloud-based ML and fog computing, which stands between the IoT and the cloud. By making use of the proximity marketing idea, he covered the critical route from the least crowded security line to the gates, gate changes, and other distractions that passengers face in airports. Utilizing a machine learning-based recommender system that may provide coupons and make recommendations based on a user's tastes or similarities to other visitors, the application allows tourists to explore the airport's amenities. In finance, authors in this study (Moustati et al., 2024b) proposed an IoB ecosystem to influence customers' decision-making process and improve it. In another research (Moghaddam et al., 2022), a conceptual model to monitor crowds and manage queues at the Uffizi Galleries in Florence, was proposed. The primary goal of the system was to record and model human behavior to create a mechanism that can adjust to changes in real-time and continually learns from visitors' recurrent activities. In healthcare, an IoB technique utilizing low-resolution, continuous thermal photography, and advanced image processing techniques was offered (Lai et al., 2023). In their research, they trained a deep neural network (DNN) to choose the most suitable region of interest for accurately monitoring respiration rate by combining data from a piezoelectric respiratory belt and insights from the IoB. Along with discussing some healthcare use cases where the IoB may be very helpful in empowering and enhancing this field, Mohd Javaid, et al., (Javaid et al., 2022) also touched on some of the difficulties facing its growth. There was also tentative to survey the applications of ML in the healthcare sector within the context of IoB (Amiri et al., 2023). In the connected vehicles sector, in their study (Mezair et al., 2023), the authors created an algorithm that can take in charge three different forms of data as input: graph, pictures, and time-series data. As a result, we may use this extra data to obtain information that is more precise. They validated their framework using four datasets of connected cars, and they discovered that their framework performs better than the conventional solutions in terms of runtime and accuracy. Both cognitive performance analysis and smart education systems may benefit substantially from the IoB. In their work (Srimaharaj & Chaisricharoen, 2022), authors suggested a machine learning model based on the ideas and characteristics of the Internet of Behaviors and human brainwaves which is significantly more precise than traditional data analysis for evaluating cognitive function. The suggested approach can classify students based on their actual brain function levels using decision trees and Internet of Behavior analytics. These techniques directly improve classroom management and expand the capacity to regulate and modify learning styles. Other academics also applied the IoB concept to design an ecosystem to continually influence citizens' energy consumption behavior and avoid electricity waste and reduce costs (Moustati et al., 2024a). Their framework utilizes and LSTM-based DL model to accurately infer future energy consumption. The proposed model showed promising results and confirmed the LSTM performance on time-series data (Moustati et al., 2024c). In another research (Zhang et al., 2021), the authors used an IoB model to better analyze the relationship between air pollution and residents' everyday activities. The researchers conducted a quantitative study to see if and how differences in air pollution influence locals' everyday behaviors. Other initiatives in applying IoB in the insurance industry also exist. In this study (Henckaerts & Antonio, 2022), authors attempted to control drivers' ratings depending on their behaviors and habits while driving and demonstrated the statistical and managerial usefulness of telematics in price determination for insurance. The authors discovered that telematics by utilizing usage-based insurance premiums improves the assessment of claim risk and risk classification process, retention rates, and profitability, under various assumptions about the clientele's price elasticity. Furthermore, a different study (Abri et al., 2023) proposed broadening the evaluation of driving behaviors to encompass driving habits. Its purpose was to investigate strange activities that might lead to improper driving habits and prevent them from happening. Authors suggested representing drivers' behaviors as a network of interacting and cooperating entities inside the Internet of Driving Behaviors (IoDB) to handle them and their mutual intra- and/or inter-impacts.

III. IoB IN ACTION: APPLICATIONS ACROSS SECTORS

This section explores the IoB and its applications in diverse sectors and domains. By examining use-case scenarios, we will analyze how the IoB can optimize processes, personalize experiences, and ultimately transform how individuals interact with technology in various aspects of their lives.

1. Marketing

In Table 1 below, we examine and categorize key IoB application scenarios within the marketing domain, highlighting their underlying mechanisms, potential impacts, and technological enablers.

Table 1. IoB use-case applications scenarios in Marketing

Marketing	**A/B Testing and Optimization**	IoB enables companies to conduct A/B testing (Fedorchenko & Ponomarenko, 2019; Hynninen & Kauppinen, 2014) and optimization at a scale. By analyzing consumer responses to different marketing strategies, an IoB system can fine-tune marketers' campaigns and identify the most effective tactics.
	Customer Journey Mapping	An IoB system gathers data from different sources (online platforms, social media, IoT devices, etc.) and then can create detailed customer behavioral journey maps (Rosenbaum et al., 2017), helping marketers understand how consumers interact with their brand across various channels (Verhoef et al., 2015) and touchpoints, while identifying potential pain points. This knowledge allows identifying opportunities for improvement and streamlining the customer experience at each stage of the journey.
	Customer Segmentation	Surpassing the classical demographic and geolocational segmentation, IoB data can help create more accurate and refined customer segments based on behavior patterns. This level of segmentation will allow marketers to tailor their marketing strategies to specific customer groups, leading to more relevant and engaging campaigns.
	Sentiment Analysis and Behavioral Retargeting	IoB will efficiently analyze and mine customers' sentiments through behavioral data gathered from social media, online platforms, or IoT devices and understand how customers perceive business products and services. The deduced insights aid in discovering the customer's intent, preferences, affinities, price sensitivity, etc. And help craft appropriate responses and engagement strategies. IoB data can be used for retargeting customers based on their previous behavior and interactions with the brand. This helps in optimizing ad spending and increasing the effectiveness of marketing campaigns.
	360° view of the customer	IoB will enable businesses to closely and humanly know their clients and their personality traits so that marketers can build a thorough relationship with them. Moreover, an IoB-embedded CRM system can act as an assistant to the customer care team, thus enhancing customer relationship management within the company.

2. Supply chain

The IoB can provide several significant benefits to the supply chain sector, revolutionizing how companies operate and interact with their customers. Table 2 presents some ways in which IoB can benefit this industry.

Table 2. IoB use-case applications scenarios in Suply chain

Supply chain	**Enhanced Supply Chain Visibility**	IoB will enable real-time tracking and monitoring of assets, products, and inventory throughout the supply chain. This visibility allows sensing changes in demand patterns, identifying bottlenecks, tracking shipments, and gaining insights into the movement of goods, thus leading to better coordination and improved response times.
	Improved Efficiency and Productivity	An IoB system can facilitate automation and process optimization, streamlining supply chain operations. IoB can leverage the behavioral data generated by IoT devices and sensors to identify inefficiencies, optimize maintenance schedules, minimize disruptions, and implement targeted improvements, leading to cost reductions and increased productivity (Sharma Sivadevuni & Ravichandran, 2023; Sivadevuni & Kumar Ravichandran, 2023).
	Enhanced Supplier Relationships	By analyzing supplier behavior and performance data, an IoB system can help identify reliable suppliers, assess their responsiveness and reliability, and help in negotiating favorable terms and contracts. This fosters stronger partnerships and collaboration throughout the supply chain, leading to improved efficiency and resilience.
	Risk Management and Compliance	IoB systems can help identify potential risks and compliance issues throughout the supply chain, such as labor violations, security breaches, or regulatory non-compliance. By monitoring employee behavior, supplier practices, and environmental factors, supply chain managers can mitigate risks, ensure compliance with regulations, and uphold corporate social responsibility standards.
	Supply Chain Optimization	By integrating IoB data with other sources such as weather forecasts, traffic patterns, and market trends, supply chain managers can optimize logistics, transportation, and distribution processes. This enables more efficient route planning, load balancing, and resource allocation, reducing costs and improving overall supply chain performance.

3. Healthcare

In the healthcare sector, the IoB would be extremely beneficial by helping in personalizing treatments, aiding in the medical research and more. Table 3 below discusses different scenarios in which the IoB can aid the healthcare sector.

Table 3. IoB use-case applications scenarios in healthcare

Healthcare	**Predictive Analytics and Preventing Diseases** (Minvielle et al., 2014)	IoB may be used for predictive analytics, detecting behavioral patterns and factors of risk linked to certain diseases. This proactive strategy enables healthcare practitioners to conduct preventative measures and early interventions, therefore lowering the burden of chronic illnesses. Moreover, an IoB system is able to forecast and assess the number of patients who are visiting a hospital at the same time, and notify them, for instance, via a mobile application, whether the hospital's current available medical resources are sufficient to accept more patients, or it will recommend the nearest one with available resources. The IoB can monitor persons' behaviors in specific places in real time to evaluate whether they are following regulations and determining patients' intents, allowing emergency situations to be detected before they occur.
	Personalizing Treatment	The customization process is in great demand in the healthcare industry, as it is in all other industries (Minvielle et al., 2014). IoB allows for the gathering, treatment, and analysis of individual patient data, such as lifestyle and medical history. This data-driven approach enables healthcare practitioners to give tailored therapies and interventions based on each patient's specific requirements (Vatian et al., 2019).
	Tracking Users' Behavioral Health and Intervening	Devices in the IoB ecosystem will track patients' health practices such as physical activity, sleep patterns, and medication adherence. Furthermore, IoB built-in technologies (Deep Learning, Computer Vision, Behavioral Analytics, etc.) (*IoT-Based Data Analytics for the Healthcare Industry*, 2021) can recognize aberrant behavioral patterns, forecast patients' goals, and respond appropriately to ensure patients' safety, achieving wisdom level. Healthcare professionals may use the disclosed health behavioral insights and the system's suggestions to build tailored treatments to encourage healthy habits and enhance patient outcomes.
	Medical Research and Clinical Experiments	IoB data can help in medical studies and clinical trials by providing insights gained from analyzing real-time behavioral data on patients' reactions to treatments and interventions. Using these insights, the IoB system may provide data-driven recommendations and speed the development of novel medical remedies.

4. Transportation

Also in the transportation sector, implementing an IoB system would help companies optimize traffic, implement intelligent parking approaches, etc. In Table 4 we explore some of these key use case scenarios.

Table 4. IoB use-case applications scenarios in the transportation sector

Transportation	**Predicting and Optimizing Traffic**	Predictive analytics may be utilized to predict the patterns of traffic and enhance the flow of traffic by means of dynamic route planning and signal management, enabling proactive efforts to reduce congestion and increase the effectiveness of transportation. Real-time behavioral data, gathered from sensors, automobiles, infrastructures, and people's online behaviors can also provide relevant insights.
	Environmental Effects	The IoB facilitates the adoption of environmentally friendly transportation choices by tracking and warning drivers about their emissions, supplying relevant educational materials about carbon dioxide emissions, and offering real-time data on emissions and pollutants related to traffic. This will raise people's awareness and sense of responsibility while encouraging them to select environmentally friendly forms of transportation.
	Intelligent Parking Approaches	Real-time details about available parking spots may be obtained using the available IoB data collected by sensors (Alsafery et al., 2018). This can save time and fuel while looking for a place to park. In addition, it has the ability to forecast and control future traffic movements to the parking area, which helps to lessen pollution and traffic in cities.
	Improving road safety	By highlighting dangerous driving habits, accident-prone areas, and unsafe behaviors, The IoB helps increase road safety. When the IoB system recognizes that a driver's physical or emotional signals are abnormal or when it detects unsafe or inadequate driving, it can use this information to trigger tailored safety measures, provide driving performance-based feedback, suggest improvements, send timely tailored alerts and messages, and present drivers with educational content when they are feeling relaxed and likely to receive it. Even while driving, the IoB can help, warn, and emit sounds or noises to make the driver stop when the system senses that he is tired. The IoB system could even take over the control on the vehicle if it notices that he has fallen asleep and parks at the closest rest place.

5. Education

The IoB can offer transformative benefits to the education sector, reshaping how institutions deliver learning and engage with students. Table 5 outlines various ways in which IoB can enhance this domain, from enabling personalized education experiences to improving administrative efficiency and student outcomes.

Table 5. IoB use-case applications scenarios in the education sector

Sector	Application	Description
Education	**Assistance and Early Intervention**	We can identify behavioral patterns and insights about the mental and physical well-being of pupils, predict their intentions, and ascertain whether they have a tendency to harm themselves or experience depression by analyzing their available data (physiological information and behaviors) collected through smart devices, IoT gadgets, and online platforms. An IoB system will then respond appropriately. It can progressively provide instructional materials about certain behaviors that may be detrimental to their mental health and provide relevant, individualized content to support them in succeeding and overcoming their current challenges. Additionally, the IoB system will notify parents and instructors in case it's an urgent matter and ensure they take action quickly.
	Adaptive Learning Systems and Tailored Learning	An IoB system can use technologies such as sensors and computer vision to collect relevant data about students' activities during class, tests, pauses, and their learning habits. It can then analyze this data using a human psychology lens to draw conclusions about students' behavior and recommend a suitable lesson plan for each student or set of students who share similar characteristics (Kundu et al., 2021). Instructors can then modify future course designs and pedagogical approaches accordingly.
	Educators' Professional Grow	The IoB behavioral data would be utilized to give behavioral insights into instructors' teaching styles and areas where they require professional development and training. An IoB system may recommend relevant material and provide focused training programs to improve instructor effectiveness by assessing behavioral data on teacher-student interactions and learning outcomes (Crompton & Sykora, 2021), which is advantageous for educational institutions.

6. Smart cities and environments

The IoB can bring substantial advantages to the development of smart cities, revolutionizing urban living through data-driven decision-making and interconnected services, and holds significant potential for addressing environmental challenges by enabling smarter resource management and promoting sustainable practices. Table 6 highlights several ways in which IoB contributes to this sector.

Table 6. IoB use-case applications scenarios in smart cities and environments

Sector	Application	Description
Smart cities and environments	**Sustainable Resource Governance and Environmental Conservation**	IoB technological advancements can enable real-time data gathering and correlation from a variety of environmental sensors, assisting in the monitoring of air and water quality, biodiversity, and the health of ecosystems. By utilizing real-time data on the consumption of resources and waste, an IoB system may assist in identifying inefficiencies and promoting the adoption of sustainable practices. It may assist optimize resource management in a variety of industries, including agriculture and energy, by altering behavior and automatically limiting resource usage based on previous behaviors and data (Elayan et al., 2021, 2023), as well as providing relevant warnings and instructive information to optimize resource use.
	Circular Economy	IoB can help implement circular economy concepts by facilitating effective garbage collection, reuse, and recycling procedures. Real-time data on waste creation and disposal may assist optimize waste management methods and send targeted educational information to the appropriate person at the right time, increasing awareness and influencing societal behaviors.
	Energy Efficiency in Smart Cities	IoB helps develop smart cities by improving energy efficiency by identifying, for example, excessive energy consumption and ineffective habits in homes or office buildings, raising awareness about them, and persuading citizens to embrace more sustainable behaviors. Furthermore, IoB-enabled equipment, such as refrigerators, may learn about food habits by surveying and analyzing inventory. Before the stock runs out, the IoB system can indicate what to add or even start a purchase based on the individual preferences of the owner.
	Managing and Resilience to Disaster	IoB would improve individual and community disaster preparedness and response by giving real-time insights into the conditions of the environment, early warning, and safety guidelines. An IoB system, for instance, via a mobile application, would display separate high and low danger zones, shelter occupancy rates, and so on. This helps to mitigate the effects of natural catastrophes and improve the resilience of communities.

7. Smart tourism

The IoB has the potential to revolutionize the smart tourism sector by enhancing visitor experiences, optimizing resource management, and supporting sustainable tourism practices. Table 7 outlines various ways in which IoB applications can transform this industry, from personalized travel recommendations to real-time monitoring of tourist activities and efficient destination management.

Table 7. Examples of IoB use-case applications scenarios in tourism sector

Smart tourism	**Personalized Visitor Experiences**	IoB can provide the large amount of tourism behavioral data required for behavioral analysis and mining since it can gather behavioral data from many channels, like online platforms and IoT devices worn by tourists or present in hotels and scenic spots. These data contain information about tourists' behaviors, preferences, and destination interactions. They can be psychologically analyzed to detect patterns and extract insights to create personalized travel recommendations, tailored itineraries, and targeted promotions, thus enhancing the overall visitor experience by designing and developing it according to tourists' intents and travel psychology (Lan et al., 2021).
	Real-Time Destination Management	Behavioral data gathered by the IoB ecosystem can be used to monitor visitor flows, crowd densities, and resource utilization in real time. Then, IoB systems can utilize these insights to predict future mass destinations, optimize crowd management, allocate resources efficiently, and ensure a seamless visitor experience (Kwok, 2023).
	Data-Driven Marketing Strategies	Leveraging the large behavioral datasets and the IoB built-in technologies such as DL algorithms and advanced Big Data analysis combined with behavior psychology techniques would comprehensively analyze tourists' experiences in terms of traveling, shopping, entertainment, etc. Giving governments and institutions practical insights which can be used to understand tourists' preferences, behaviors, and intentions, find new growth points, enhance proposed services and products, strengthen interactions and communications with tourists, and detects which areas they still need to invest in, and which ones have a little return on investment. These discovered behavioral insights would be used to create targeted marketing campaigns, optimize advertising efforts, and attract specific customer segments.

8. Finance

An IoB system would offer transformative opportunities for the finance sector, enabling more personalized services, enhanced risk management, and improved fraud detection (Moustati et al., 2024b). Table 8 highlights various ways in which IoB applications are reshaping this industry, from leveraging behavioral data for tailored financial solutions to optimizing decision-making processes in real time.

Table 8. Examples of IoB use-case applications scenarios in finance

Finance	**Fraud Discovery and Risk Management**	By evaluating the large volume of behavioral data, such as transaction histories, device interactions, and browsing habits, and mining behavioral patterns, biases, and anomalies, an IoB system may help with risk management and identifying fraudulent activity. Smart fraud detection techniques that can recognize suspicious activity and adjust to changing fraud schemes will be possible thanks to built-in IoB technologies like ML and particularly DL algorithms (Choi & Lee, 2018).
	Tailored Financial Experience	Through a variety of channels, IoB enables the collection of massive quantities of behavioral data on individuals' financial necessities, preferences, activities and habits. This behavioral data may be utilized to provide suggestions, individually priced and tailored customer-centric products and services, and customized financial services based on each client's specific needs, goals and aspirations. Financial institutions would improve their consumers' experience and loyalty by offering tailored suggestions and guidance, recommendations for improved financial budgeting and planning, simpler procedures, and proactive assistance (Wang et al., 2017).
	Financial Literacy	By tracking and psychologically analyzing customers' financial goals, obstacles, and spending patterns, financial institutions and banks can utilize an IoB system to provide relevant educational materials, like customized savings plans, money management techniques, or investment advice, at the exact time when the customer is most open to receiving it (Hasan et al., 2020). Through a mobile application, the system may send the client real-time warnings and reminders to help him stick to his budget and set long-term investment goals. This will increase his financial literacy and dedication to his goals.

9. Business

The IoB can deliver significant advantages to the business sector by enhancing operational efficiency, improving customer engagement, and enabling data-driven decision-making. Table 9 highlights various ways in which IoB applications are transforming businesses, from data-informed decision making to real-time analytics and streamlined workflows.

Table 9. Examples of IoB use-case applications scenarios in business

Business	**Data-Informed Decision-Making**	IoB will give organizations actionable insights generated from behavioral data on consumer behaviors, employee habits, trends in the market, and operational procedures. Following this data-driven strategy, an IoB system could recommend ameliorations as well as improve strategic planning, developing products, and the entire efficiency of the company.
	Activity Assignment and Cooperation	Analyzing IoB behavioral data allows businesses to assign tasks to employees' abilities and attitudes. This encourages teamwork and ensures that people work on assignments that match their skills. Whenever the IoB system recognizes that an employee is having difficulty with particular activities, it may prompt relevant personalized educational information, guide tailored development and training initiatives to improve his abilities and advancement in his career and notify his manager in order to help and support him.
	Monitoring Employees	An IoB system would track employees' work routines, organizational skills, adherence, wellness, and productivity patterns. This will contribute to identifying regions in which employees require additional training while preventing serious problems, especially turnover among workers. The collected data on how employees interact in their workplaces, make use of their personal computers or workstations, and engage with others could be studied in order to identify patterns regarding collaboration, efficiency, as well as additional factors that could affect how businesses perform. Following that, the IoB system may recommend and propose for every particular scenario what steps should be taken for mitigation and prevention and monitor to what degree it is obeyed.

IV. DISCUSSION

Implementing an Internet of Behaviors (IoB) system across various domains and sectors presents a multitude of advantages. However, there are also several challenges that must be carefully addressed to ensure successful deployment and adoption. The IoB raises ethical questions related to consent, transparency, and fairness. The collection and use of behavioral data may raise concerns about consent, as users may not always be fully aware of the data being collected or how it is being used. There are also concerns about fairness in the analysis and use of behavioral data, as it could potentially result in discrimination or bias. Therefore, ensuring compliance with relevant laws and regulations, and navigating legal challenges is an ongoing challenge for IoB implementations, particularly knowing that the IoB can be used to manipulate user behavior through targeted advertising or other forms of persuasion. This can be a concern if the manipulation is not transparent or if it crosses ethical boundaries. In the domain of marketing, for instance, the collection and analysis of consumer behavioral data raise significant privacy concerns and ethical considerations, as highlighted by this research (Hemker et al., 2021). Similarly, in the finance sector, IoB systems face challenges related to data security and regulatory compliance, as financial institutions must adhere to stringent regulations to protect sensitive customer information (Arner Y. et al., 2017). In case of missing regulations, the IoB framework should push toward creating relevant laws and regulations to protect users' legitimate rights and interests. Furthermore, understanding human behavior and incorporating human factors into IoB implementations can be challenging. Human behavior is complex and dynamic, and incorporating psychological, social, and cultural factors into IoB models and systems requires careful consideration.

V. CONCLUSION

The IoB's applications across various sectors and domains hold immense potential for driving innovation, enhancing efficiency, and improving outcomes. From personalized marketing campaigns, financial risk assessment, and cross-sectors tailored services to supply chain optimization and healthcare services delivery, IoB technologies can revolutionize how organizations understand and interact with individuals. However, adoping the IoB also presents significant challenges, including privacy concerns, data security risks, and ethical considerations, which must be carefully addressed to ensure responsible deployment and adoption. There are remarkable opportunities within this field. Therefore, we urge interested researchers to begin exploring potential implementation areas and scenarios, as they appear to be highly promising and ripe for new investigations. In this paper, we gave thorough state-of-the-art snapshot of the IoB research area, examined multiple potential use-case application scenarios of the IoB across various industries and domains, and presented critical challenges that should be addressed. A potential future direction would be to apply the IoB in untouched sectors (e.g., supply chain, finance) and further develop the security and privacy areas in the IoB ecosystem to ensure high deployment of the IoB frameworks.

REFERENCES

Al Abri, K. A. S., Mastouri, M., Bouyahia, Z., Haddad, H., Yasar, A.-U.-H., & Shakshuki, E. (2023). On the Interest of Extending Internet of Behaviors to Internet of Habits: A Preliminary Exploration. *Procedia Computer Science*, 224, 122–130. DOI: 10.1016/j.procs.2023.09.019

Alsafery, W., Alturki, B., Reiff-Marganiec, S., & Jambi, K. (2018). Smart Car Parking System Solution for the Internet of Things in Smart Cities. *2018 1st International Conference on Computer Applications & Information Security (ICCAIS)*, 1–5. DOI: 10.1109/CAIS.2018.8442004

Amiri, Z., Heidari, A., Darbandi, M., Yazdani, Y., Jafari Navimipour, N., Esmaeilpour, M., Sheykhi, F., & Unal, M. (2023). The Personal Health Applications of Machine Learning Techniques in the Internet of Behaviors. *Sustainability (Basel)*, 15(16), 12406. DOI: 10.3390/su151612406

Arner, Y., & Douglas, W.. (2017). *FinTech and RegTech: Enabling Innovation While Preserving Financial Stability*. Georgetown Journal of International Affairs.

Choi, D., & Lee, K. (2018). An Artificial Intelligence Approach to Financial Fraud Detection under IoT Environment: A Survey and Implementation. *Security and Communication Networks*, 2018, 1–15. DOI: 10.1155/2018/5483472

Crompton, H., & Sykora, C. (2021). Developing instructional technology standards for educators: A design-based research study. *Computers and Education Open*, 2, 100044. DOI: 10.1016/j.caeo.2021.100044

Elayan, H., Aloqaily, M., Karray, F., & Guizani, M. (2021). *Internet of Behavior (IoB) and Explainable AI Systems for Influencing IoT Behavior*. http://arxiv.org/abs/2109.07239

Elayan, H., Aloqaily, M., Karray, F., & Guizani, M. (2023). Internet of Behavior and Explainable AI Systems for Influencing IoT Behavior. *IEEE Network*, 37(1), 62–68. DOI: 10.1109/MNET.009.2100500

Fedorchenko, A., & Ponomarenko, I. (2019). A/B-testing as an efficient tools for digital marketing. *Problems of Innovation and Investment Development*, 19(19), 36–42. DOI: 10.33813/2224-1213.19.2019.4

Hasan, M., Popp, J., & Oláh, J. (2020). Current landscape and influence of big data on finance. *Journal of Big Data*, 7(1), 21. DOI: 10.1186/s40537-020-00291-z

Hemker, S., Herrando, C., & Constantinides, E. (2021). The Transformation of Data Marketing: How an Ethical Lens on Consumer Data Collection Shapes the Future of Marketing. *Sustainability (Basel)*, 13(20), 11208. DOI: 10.3390/su132011208

Henckaerts, R., & Antonio, K. (2022). The added value of dynamically updating motor insurance prices with telematics collected driving behavior data. *Insurance, Mathematics & Economics*, 105, 79–95. DOI: 10.1016/j.insmatheco.2022.03.011

Hynninen, P., & Kauppinen, M. (2014). A/B testing: A promising tool for customer value evaluation. *2014 IEEE 1st International Workshop on Requirements Engineering and Testing (RET)*, 16–17. DOI: 10.1109/RET.2014.6908673

IoT-Based Data Analytics for the Healthcare Industry. (2021). Elsevier. DOI: 10.1016/C2019-0-03210-4

Javaid, M., Haleem, A., Singh, R. P., Khan, S., & Suman, R. (2022). An extensive study on Internet of Behavior (IoB) enabled Healthcare-Systems: Features, facilitators, and challenges. *BenchCouncil Transactions on Benchmarks. Standards and Evaluations*, 2(4), 100085. DOI: 10.1016/j.tbench.2023.100085

Kundu, S. S., Sarkar, D., Jana, P., & Kole, D. K. (2021). *Personalization in Education Using Recommendation System: An Overview* (pp. 85–111). DOI: 10.1007/978-981-15-8744-3_5

Kwok, A. O. J. (2023). The next frontier of the Internet of Behaviors: data-driven nudging in smart tourism. *Journal of Tourism Futures*. DOI: 10.1108/JTF-11-2022-0288

Lai, C.-F., Chen, S.-Y., Wei, Y.-F., Chen, M.-Y., & Lai, S.-Y. (2023). IoB-Enhanced Deep Learning for Non-specific Thermal Respiratory Rate Monitoring. *2023 IEEE International Conference on Networking, Sensing and Control (ICNSC)*, 1–6. DOI: 10.1109/ICNSC58704.2023.10319043

Lan, F., Huang, Q., Zeng, L., Guan, X., Xing, D., & Cheng, Z. (2021). Tourism Experience and Construction of Personalized Smart Tourism Program Under Tourist Psychology. *Frontiers in Psychology*, 12, 691183. Advance online publication. DOI: 10.3389/fpsyg.2021.691183 PMID: 34367015

Mezair, T., Djenouri, Y., Belhadi, A., Srivastava, G., & Lin, J. C.-W. (2023). Towards an Advanced Deep Learning for the Internet of Behaviors: Application to Connected Vehicles. *ACM Transactions on Sensor Networks*, 19(2), 1–18. DOI: 10.1145/3526192

Minvielle, E., Waelli, M., Sicotte, C., & Kimberly, J. R. (2014). Managing customization in health care: A framework derived from the services sector literature. *Health Policy (Amsterdam)*, 117(2), 216–227. DOI: 10.1016/j.healthpol.2014.04.005 PMID: 24837516

Moghaddam, M. T., Muccini, H., Dugdale, J., & Kjagaard, M. B. (2022). Designing Internet of Behaviors Systems. *2022 IEEE 19th International Conference on Software Architecture (ICSA)*, 124–134. DOI: 10.1109/ICSA53651.2022.00020

Moustati, I., Gherabi, N., El Massari, H., & Saadi, M. (2023). From The Internet of Things (IoT) to The Internet of Behaviors (IoB) for Data Analysis. *2023 7th IEEE Congress on Information Science and Technology (CiSt)*, 634–639. DOI: 10.1109/CiSt56084.2023.10409989

Moustati, I., Gherabi, N., & Saadi, M. (2024a). Building an IoB ecosystem for influencing energy consumption in smart cities. *Data and Metadata*, 3. Advance online publication. DOI: 10.56294/dm2024.441

Moustati, I., Gherabi, N., & Saadi, M. (2024b). Leveraging the internet of behaviours and digital nudges for enhancing customers financial decision-making. *International Journal of Computer Applications in Technology*, 1(1), 10065772. Advance online publication. DOI: 10.1504/IJCAT.2024.10065772

Moustati, I., Gherabi, N., & Saadi, M. (2024c). Time-Series Forecasting Models for Smart Meters Data: An Empirical Comparison and Analysis. *Journal Européen des Systèmes Automatisés*, 57(05), 1419–1427. DOI: 10.18280/jesa.570517

Rosenbaum, M. S., Otalora, M. L., & Ramírez, G. C. (2017). How to create a realistic customer journey map. *Business Horizons*, 60(1), 143–150. DOI: 10.1016/j.bushor.2016.09.010

Salis, A. (2021). Towards the Internet of Behaviors in Smart Cities through a Fog-To-Cloud Approach. *HighTech and Innovation Journal*, 2(4), 273–284. DOI: 10.28991/HIJ-2021-02-04-01

Sharma Sivadevuni, S., & Ravichandran, S. K. (2023). Tracking and Localization of Devices - An IoT Review. *2023 International Conference on Inventive Computation Technologies (ICICT)*, 1321–1325. DOI: 10.1109/ICICT57646.2023.10134278

Sivadevuni, S. S., & Kumar Ravichandran, S. (2023). *Systematic Literature Review—IoT-Based Supply Chain Management in Industry 4.0* (pp. 291–302). DOI: 10.1007/978-3-031-18497-0_22

Srimaharaj, W., & Chaisricharoen, R. (2022). Internet of Behavior and Brain Response Identification for Cognitive Performance Analysis. *2022 Asia-Pacific Signal and Information Processing Association Annual Summit and Conference (APSIPA ASC)*, 1308–1311. DOI: 10.23919/APSIPAASC55919.2022.9980191

Vatian, A., Dudorov, S., Ivchenko, A., Smirnov, K., Chikshova, E., Lobantsev, A., Parfenov, V., Shalyto, A., & Gusarova, N. (2019). Design Patterns for Personalization of Healthcare Process. *Proceedings of the 2019 2nd International Conference on Geoinformatics and Data Analysis*, 83–88. DOI: 10.1145/3318236.3318249

Verhoef, P. C., Kannan, P. K., & Inman, J. J. (2015). From Multi-Channel Retailing to Omni-Channel Retailing. *Journal of Retailing*, 91(2), 174–181. DOI: 10.1016/j.jretai.2015.02.005

Wang, M., Cho, S., & Denton, T. (2017). The impact of personalization and compatibility with past experience on e-banking usage. *International Journal of Bank Marketing*, 35(1), 45–55. DOI: 10.1108/IJBM-04-2015-0046

Zhang, G., Poslad, S., Rui, X., Yu, G., Fan, Y., Song, X., & Li, R. (2021). Using an Internet of Behaviours to Study How Air Pollution Can Affect People's Activities of Daily Living: A Case Study of Beijing, China. *Sensors (Basel)*, 21(16), 5569. DOI: 10.3390/s21165569 PMID: 34451012

Chapter 19
Generative AI Ethical Dimensions:
Data Privacy Challenges and Future Prospects

Oussama El Mahboubi
https://orcid.org/0009-0008-5537-6810
Faculty of Sciences, Ibn Tofail University, Kenitra, Morocco

Mohamed Amnai
Faculty of Sciences, Ibn Tofail University, Kenitra, Morocco

ABSTRACT

Generative Artificial Intelligence (AI) has rapidly become a powerful influence in modern technology, allowing machines to produce novel content that closely resembles human creativity. This chapter explores the ethical, privacy, and future implications of Generative AI and Large Language Models (LLMs). It outlines how biases emerge from training data, why transparency and accountability are essential, and how regulations strive to protect personal information. The text considers the social and cultural impacts of AI-generated content, examines workforce transformations due to automation and augmentation, and addresses the environmental costs of running large-scale models. It also highlights human-AI collaboration, the evolution of tools and policies for responsible AI, and the importance of integrating ethics at every step of technological development. Ultimately, it calls for thoughtful guidance and compassionate stewardship as Generative AI shapes the future of human creativity, knowledge, and interaction.

1. INTRODUCTION

Generative Artificial Intelligence (AI) stands out as one of the most transformative developments in modern technology (Clinton, 2023; Bommasani et al., 2021). Its impact spans numerous fields—from healthcare and automated content creation to educational innovation and cutting-edge scientific research (Clinton, 2023; Bommasani et al., 2021). By harnessing advanced neural network frameworks such as Generative Adversarial Networks (GANs) and transformer-based architectures like GPT, generative AI empowers machines to produce original text, images, video, and music that closely mirror human cre-

DOI: 10.4018/979-8-3373-0365-9.ch019

ativity (Bommasani et al., 2021; Floridi & Chiriatti, 2020). This capability has become a powerful driver of efficiency and innovative problem-solving in sectors where imagination and adaptability are critical.

However, these impressive capabilities come with significant ethical and practical considerations. The rapid surge in generative AI adoption raises concerns about data misuse, privacy breaches, misinformation, and the amplification of existing biases (Hagendorff, 2024; Bender et al., 2021). These challenges are especially visible in Large Language Models (LLMs) like ChatGPT, which—despite their remarkable functionality—sometimes generate outputs reflecting societal inequities or disseminate disinformation (Weidinger et al., 2021). Illicit industries exploiting generative AI for deepfakes and counterfeit imagery add another layer of ethical complexity, while educational spheres must address emerging questions around fairness, authenticity, and academic integrity (Pournaras, 2023; Zhang et al., 2023). Such issues highlight the pressing need to responsibly integrate generative AI into society.

This chapter, "Generative AI: Ethical Dimensions, Data Privacy Challenges and Future Prospects," probes the evolving landscape of generative AI with a focus on its moral implications, data privacy vulnerabilities, and avenues for responsible progress. It provides a thorough analysis of how generative AI is reshaping diverse industries while scrutinizing the interconnected legal and societal dilemmas it poses. By synthesizing contemporary research and industry strategies, this chapter offers a comprehensive guide for understanding both the opportunities and pitfalls that define generative AI's future.

2. FOUNDATIONS OF GENERATIVE AI

2.1. The Evolution and Foundations of Modern Generative AI

The evolution of modern Generative AI is inextricably linked to advancements in hardware, computational methodologies, and foundational AI research (Clinton, 2023). Early efforts in the 1970s, 1980s, and early 2000s were hampered by costly, low-capacity computers with limited memory and storage. The environment began to shift significantly with the emergence of GPUs, TPUs, and cloud-based platforms that made large-scale AI training far more accessible. Simultaneously, the proliferation of massive datasets and the application of parallel processing and distributed computing further accelerated AI progress. Steady improvements in transistor density also followed Moore's Law, opening the door to the deep learning revolution that saw Recurrent Neural Networks (RNNs) and Long Short-Term Memory (LSTM) networks adeptly model long-range language dependencies.

A defining milestone arrived in 2017 with the introduction of the Transformer architecture, which dramatically enhanced text generation and laid the groundwork for advanced generative systems like GPT (Bommasani et al., 2021). Powered by extensive parameter counts, robust training corpora, and architectures that capitalize on parallelizable processing, these Transformer-based models exhibit capabilities ranging from basic reasoning and code writing to conversational understanding (Floridi & Chiriatti, 2020). This marked a realization of earlier visions that were previously thwarted by technological constraints. Today, generative models continue to evolve, reshaping creative processes and enabling breakthroughs across varied sectors—from automated content creation to cutting-edge scientific simulations.

2.2. Core Architectures and Model Types

Early generative models predominantly utilized statistical techniques and comparatively simple neural networks (Clinton, 2023; Bommasani et al., 2021). Recent breakthroughs, however, have unveiled architectures capable of generating highly realistic content in text, visual, and auditory domains:

- **Generative Adversarial Networks (GANs):** These systems incorporate a generator and a discriminator, with the generator striving to produce outputs indistinguishable from authentic data. This adversarial approach often creates highly convincing images, audio, or text (Clinton, 2023).
- **Transformer-Based Models (e.g., GPT):** Transformers leverage attention mechanisms for both sequence processing and generation, making them especially effective in language and other structured data tasks. Models like GPT excel in producing human-like text and can adapt seamlessly to diverse writing styles, topics, and formats (Bommasani et al., 2021; Floridi & Chiriatti, 2020).
- **Variational Autoencoders (VAEs):** VAEs adopt an encoder-decoder setup to capture latent data representations. While VAEs typically yield outputs slightly less refined than GAN-generated content, they provide enhanced interpretability and granular control over the generative process (Bommasani et al., 2021).

2.3. Domains of Application (Text, Images, Music, Video)

Generative AI technology offers extensive applicability across a spectrum of media, reshaping creative processes and expanding innovative opportunities (Clinton, 2023; Bommasani et al., 2021):

- **Text:** Advanced language models generate coherent paragraphs, draft articles, summarize documents, and participate in meaningful dialogues (Clinton, 2023). These abilities benefit content creation, customer support, and language learning.
- **Images:** By training on large image datasets, models can produce aesthetically appealing visuals, assist artists and designers in rapid prototyping, craft illustrations from textual prompts, and even refine or restore photographs (Bommasani et al., 2021).
- **Music:** Trained on diverse musical compositions, generative models can compose novel pieces or guide composers in creating fresh themes. They also allow exploration of varied musical styles, genres, and structural elements (Clinton, 2023; Bommasani et al., 2021).
- **Video:** Emerging advancements enable generative AI to develop short video segments, animations, and special effects, facilitating entertainment production and providing creators with cutting-edge tools for storytelling (Bommasani et al., 2021; Floridi & Chiriatti, 2020).

Taken together, these domains emphasize both the extensive promise of generative AI and the intricate challenges associated with integrating it responsibly into society.

2.4. Comparative Analysis of Prominent LLM Architectures

The table below provides a succinct comparison of several prominent Large Language Models (LLMs), focusing on their training data size, core strengths, and potential drawbacks. Key considerations include ethical guidelines, versatility, efficiency, and integration within specific platforms or ecosystems

(Bommasani et al., 2021). By evaluating these attributes, readers can better discern which LLM aligns most effectively with their particular requirements and objectives.

Table 1. Comparative Analysis of Prominent LLM Architectures

LLM Architecture	Training Data Size	Strengths	Weaknesses
Claude	Diverse internet data curated for safety and alignment	Strong emphasis on ethical AI, safety-focused design, reliable contextual understanding	Output constraints to ensure safety may limit flexibility, less extensive knowledge than GPT-4
GPT-4	Trillions of tokens from varied sources (multi-modal)	Highly versatile, strong multi-modal performance, emergent reasoning capabilities	Requires significant computational resources and may replicate biases found in training data (Bender et al., 2021; Weidinger et al., 2021).
LLAMA 3	Optimized for efficiency, sourced from diverse internet data	Efficient resource usage, scalable for multiple tasks, potentially cost-effective	Limited public information, might demand fine-tuning for specialized applications
Gemini	Vast data from Google services, the web, and multi-modal inputs	Advanced multi-modal processing, strong integration in Google's ecosystem, cutting-edge AI	Specific limitations remain undisclosed, platform exclusivity could constrain broader deployment

This overview underscores the varying degrees of ethical considerations, resource demands, and technical constraints each model brings to the table. Practitioners and researchers alike can utilize these distinctions to select a model that not only meets task-specific needs but also aligns with broader values of accountability and responsible AI adoption.

3. TRANSFORMATIONAL IMPACT ON INDUSTRIES

3.1. Healthcare and Life Sciences

Generative AI is catalyzing significant advances in healthcare and life sciences by speeding up drug discovery, refining diagnostic accuracy, and enabling personalized treatment regimens (Clinton, 2023; Bommasani et al., 2021). For instance, AI-driven simulations of molecular behavior can pinpoint viable drug candidates more quickly, reducing both research expenses and time-to-market. Additionally, synthetic medical images and patient data produced by generative models bolster the training of diagnostic systems, thereby enhancing the detection and treatment of life-threatening illnesses like cancer and cardiovascular diseases (Clinton, 2023). Personalized medicine further benefits from AI-generated patient profiles that guide clinicians in tailoring therapies to individual biological markers, often leading to improved outcomes and a more targeted approach to patient care.

3.2. Content Creation and Media

In content creation and media, generative AI significantly decreases the time and resources required to produce top-quality text, images, videos, and music (Bommasani et al., 2021). By automating narrative generation and streamlining editorial workflows, it paves the way for inventive storytelling techniques. Artists can also leverage AI for exploratory design, venturing into aesthetic concepts that were previously difficult to realize. Media organizations profit from expedited production pipelines and greater adaptability in evolving market conditions, while rapid prototyping and iterative experimentation foster more engaging, tailored content for diverse audiences (Bender et al., 2021).

3.3. Education and Learning

Generative AI has the potential to revolutionize educational strategies by enabling adaptive and individualized learning resources (Pournaras, 2023). Language-learning applications, for example, can offer personalized exercises, real-time feedback, and immersive practice scenarios. Teachers additionally gain from automated summaries of extensive reading materials and AI-generated teaching aids, all of which help address varied learning needs. Such innovations promote inclusion, boost student engagement, and ultimately support enduring skill retention and comprehension (Zhang et al., 2023).

3.4. Scientific Research and Innovation

In scientific inquiry, generative AI creates opportunities for novel hypothesis formulation, data generation, and experimentation (Bommasani et al., 2021; Floridi & Chiriatti, 2020). Researchers can leverage AI to simulate multiple scenarios before embarking on costly lab work, thereby refining research designs and expediting the discovery process. These models also enhance analysis of extensive datasets, enabling scientists to gain insights and identify patterns that might be missed with traditional approaches. From climate science and genetics to materials engineering, generative AI lays the groundwork for transformative breakthroughs by broadening research scopes and reducing barriers to rigorous experimentation.

3.5. Job Displacement and Emerging Skill Demands

Generative AI is changing the way we work, especially in industries like content creation, media, and healthcare. Tools that generate articles, edit videos, or perform diagnostic imaging have made tasks faster and more efficient, but they've also taken over jobs that were once done by people. For example, some media companies now use AI to write news articles, which means fewer opportunities for entry-level journalists (Bommasani et al., 2021).

Still, these changes aren't all negative. They're also opening doors to new skills and careers. Content creators are now focusing on guiding and refining AI-generated work to ensure it's accurate and high-quality (Bender et al., 2021). In healthcare, professionals are learning to combine their expertise with AI tools, interpreting data and making decisions in ways that improve patient care (Clinton, 2023). By investing in retraining programs, we can help people adapt to these changes, keeping human expertise at the center of innovation while taking advantage of what AI has to offer (Brundage et al., 2020).

4. ETHICAL DIMENSIONS OF GENERATIVE AI

4.1. Core Ethical Challenges

Generative AI's expanding capabilities reveal that these systems do more than simply process data; they often embed and propagate inherent cultural norms, hierarchies, and biases (Hagendorff, 2024; Bender et al., 2021). For instance, a Large Language Model trained primarily on Western, English-language data may inadvertently minimize non-Western perspectives or reinforce stereotypes. Likewise, an image generation tool that has seen an overrepresentation of men in scientific roles and women in domestic contexts could subtly perpetuate such outdated perceptions. These unintentional biases highlight the need for proactive data curation, diverse representation in training corpora, and regular audits to mitigate potential harm to marginalized voices.

4.2. Responsibility and Accountability in Content Creation

As generative AI increasingly takes on creative tasks, issues of responsibility and accountability become more pronounced (Pournaras, 2023; Zhang et al., 2023). Traditional definitions of authorship clash with the emergence of AI-generated content, complicating the determination of who holds legal and ethical ownership. Questions concerning credit and potential compensation must be addressed when content is produced without direct human intervention. Additionally, stakeholders must assess the social and economic implications of automating creative roles, including the displacement of certain professions. Adopting transparent guidelines and clearly labeling AI-generated work helps consumers identify the source of the material, ensuring that both AI and human creators are held to appropriate standards of accountability and ethics.

4.3. Bias and Fairness

Generative AI models often inherit biases from their training data, reflecting historical and cultural inequities (Hagendorff, 2024; Bommasani et al., 2021). If left unchecked, these biases can exacerbate social injustices and marginalize certain groups (Bender et al., 2021). Ensuring fairness in AI-generated outputs requires careful selection and curation of training data, as well as the development of evaluation metrics that explicitly measure and mitigate biased outcomes (Hagendorff, 2024; Bommasani et al., 2021). Ongoing audits, stakeholder consultations, and improvements in data representativeness are crucial steps in building more equitable generative AI systems (Bender et al., 2021; Luccioni et al., 2022). By actively addressing bias, developers and organizations can work toward models that promote fairness, inclusivity, and respect for diversity (Bommasani et al., 2021; Brundage et al., 2020).

4.4. Integrity and Authenticity of Information

The capacity of generative AI to produce highly realistic yet synthetic content poses significant challenges to the integrity of information (Bender et al., 2021). Deepfakes, manipulated images, fabricated text, and other AI-generated media can be exploited to spread misinformation, erode public trust, and undermine democratic processes (Weidinger et al., 2021; Whittaker et al., 2018). Safeguarding authenticity involves a combination of strategies: technical solutions like digital watermarks and detection algorithms, educational initiatives to improve media literacy, and regulatory measures to hold bad actors accountable (Ghosh & Lakshmi, 2023). Recognizing the potential harm of disinformation, governments, industry leaders, and civil society must collaborate to ensure that generative AI is harnessed in ways that uphold truthfulness, credibility, and societal well-being (Brundage et al., 2020).

5. DATA PRIVACY AND SECURITY CHALLENGES

5.1. Data Sourcing, Handling, and Protection

Generative AI relies heavily on large volumes of data, raising critical questions about the origins, legality, and quality of this information (Novelli et al., 2024; Zhang et al., 2023). Ethically sourcing data involves adhering to existing privacy regulations and ensuring that personal information is obtained and utilized responsibly (Li et al., 2024). Implementing robust data handling and protection measures, such as encryption and secure storage, is essential to prevent unauthorized access and misuse (Novelli et al., 2024). As regulatory frameworks continue to evolve, organizations must remain vigilant by regularly updating their data governance policies to maintain compliance and uphold the confidentiality of sensitive information (Brundage et al., 2020). These practices are vital in fostering trust and ensuring that generative AI technologies are developed and deployed in a manner that respects individual privacy and societal norms.

5.2. Risks of Data Leakage and Model Inversion

The complexity of models employed in generative AI makes them susceptible to data leaks and model inversion attacks aimed at extracting sensitive information (Novelli et al., 2024). Such vulnerabilities present significant risks to individuals and organizations, potentially exposing personal data or trade secrets (Zhang et al., 2023). To mitigate these threats, developers and security experts must implement robust defense techniques, conduct regular audits, and establish contingency plans for swift response in the event of breaches (Ghosh & Lakshmi, 2023). Securing models against malicious actors requires ongoing efforts, including adaptability and continuous improvement in cybersecurity strategies (Li et al., 2024).

5.3. Transparency and Explainability

As generative AI systems become increasingly integrated into decision-making processes, there is a growing demand for transparency and explainability (Hagendorff, 2024; Bommasani et al., 2021). Stakeholders, including users, regulators, and the general public, need to comprehend how these models function and the rationale behind their outputs (Jobin et al., 2019). Achieving explainability often involves simplifying model architectures, thoroughly documenting development processes, and incorporating interpretability tools (Mittelstadt et al., 2016; Brundage et al., 2020). By promoting openness regarding data usage, model training, and algorithmic logic, developers can enhance trust in generative AI solutions (Bender et al., 2021). Ultimately, transparency empowers users, supports informed consent, and fosters a more accountable environment for AI-driven innovation (Weidinger et al., 2021).

6. SOCIETAL AND LEGAL CONSIDERATIONS

6.1. Regulatory Frameworks and Policy Development

As generative AI technologies advance, both Europe and the United States are actively developing comprehensive legal and regulatory frameworks to address the unique challenges they present (Novelli et al., 2024; Jobin et al., 2019). These efforts are crucial in balancing the promotion of innovation with the mitigation of potential harms, ensuring that generative AI does not compromise human rights, security, or the public interest (Ghosh & Lakshmi, 2023).

6.1.1. European Union Approach

In Europe, the European Union has taken a proactive stance with the proposed Artificial Intelligence Act, which aims to establish extensive regulations for AI systems, including generative models (Novelli et al., 2024). This legislation categorizes AI applications based on their risk levels, imposing strict requirements on high-risk systems to ensure transparency, accountability, and the protection of fundamental rights. Additionally, the EU's emphasis on data privacy, embodied in the General Data Protection Regulation (GDPR), plays a critical role in governing how generative AI systems handle personal data, ensuring that user consent and data minimization principles are upheld (Jobin et al., 2019). The EU also focuses on ethical guidelines that mandate the inclusion of human oversight and the prevention of biases in AI outputs, thereby fostering trust and reliability in AI technologies.

6.1.2. United States Approach

In contrast, the United States has adopted a more sectoral approach to AI regulation, focusing on specific areas such as data privacy, intellectual property, and consumer protection (Ghosh & Lakshmi, 2023). While there is no overarching federal AI legislation akin to the EU's Artificial Intelligence Act, various initiatives and guidelines are being developed by agencies like the Federal Trade Commission (FTC) and the National Institute of Standards and Technology (NIST). These efforts aim to promote ethical AI development, mitigate biases, and enhance transparency in AI applications. The US also emphasizes innovation and competitiveness, encouraging the growth of AI technologies through funding and support for research and development while addressing regulatory gaps as they emerge (Brundage et al., 2020). This approach allows for flexibility and adaptability, enabling the US to respond swiftly to technological advancements and market dynamics.

6.1.3. Balancing Innovation and Regulation

Both regions recognize the importance of international collaboration in shaping AI governance. Europe and the United States are engaging in dialogues to harmonize their regulatory approaches, aiming to balance the promotion of technological innovation with the safeguarding of ethical standards and societal values (Novelli et al., 2024; Ghosh & Lakshmi, 2023; Brundage et al., 2020). This bilateral cooperation is essential for addressing the global nature of AI technologies and ensuring that generative AI systems are developed and deployed responsibly across borders. Continuous dialogue between legislators, industry leaders, and civil society is essential for creating adaptive policies that evolve alongside technological advancements and address emerging ethical, economic, and social challenges (Brundage et al., 2020).

6.1.4. Addressing Jurisdictional Complexities

Policymakers must also navigate jurisdictional complexities, as AI-generated content easily transcends national borders (Novelli et al., 2024). Developing international standards and agreements can help manage these challenges, ensuring consistent regulatory practices and facilitating cross-border cooperation. By establishing common frameworks, both Europe and the United States can better regulate generative AI technologies, promote interoperability, and prevent regulatory arbitrage where companies might relocate to jurisdictions with more lenient regulations.

6.1.5. Future Legislative Efforts

As generative AI continues to evolve, ongoing legislative efforts in Europe and the United States will be pivotal in defining the legal landscape, fostering trust, and ensuring that AI advancements contribute positively to society (Novelli et al., 2024; Ghosh & Lakshmi, 2023; Brundage et al., 2020). Future policies are expected to increasingly address issues such as accountability in AI decision-making, ethical use of AI in sensitive sectors, and the protection of intellectual property rights related to AI-generated content. These efforts will also likely focus on enhancing public understanding of AI technologies, promoting transparency in AI operations, and ensuring that the benefits of generative AI are distributed equitably across different segments of society.

6.2. Intellectual Property Rights

Generative AI raises complex questions about the ownership of the content it produces (Novelli et al., 2024). Existing intellectual property laws, designed with human creators in mind, may not adequately cover works generated by machines (Bommasani et al., 2021). Determining the rightful owners, beneficiaries, and licensors of AI-generated material requires legal clarity and potentially new categories of rights (Novelli et al., 2024). Organizations must address how to attribute credit, manage licensing agreements, and fairly distribute profits associated with AI-generated creations (Zhang et al., 2023). Clear guidelines will help reduce legal uncertainties, protect both creators and consumers, and foster a stable environment for innovation (Brundage et al., 2020). As generative AI continues to produce increasingly sophisticated and original content, evolving intellectual property laws will be essential to accommodate the unique nature of AI-generated works and ensure fair compensation and recognition for all stakeholders involved.

6.3. Public Perception and Trust

Public acceptance of generative AI depends on transparency, reliability, and clear benefits (Whittaker et al., 2018; Jobin et al., 2019). However, concerns about misinformation, such as deepfake videos eroding trust in democratic institutions, and rapid dissemination on social media, pose significant challenges. To address these, organizations must prioritize transparency, ethical standards, and clear labeling of AI-generated content. Tools like watermarking and digital literacy campaigns can help the public identify genuine material, fostering trust and resilience. By involving diverse stakeholders and promoting education, generative AI can build public confidence and preserve societal cohesion (Weidinger et al., 2021; Brundage et al., 2020).

7. RESPONSIBLE DEVELOPMENT AND GOVERNANCE

7.1. Ethical Design Principles and Best Practices

Achieving responsible development of generative AI begins with embedding ethics into every stage of the design process (Hagendorff, 2024). This involves establishing clear guidelines that prioritize user welfare, protect privacy, and respect intellectual property (Jobin et al., 2019). Developers should strive for inclusivity by considering the needs and perspectives of diverse communities, mitigating biases, and aligning technological capabilities with broader social values (Mittelstadt et al., 2016). By integrating human oversight, transparent algorithms, and mechanisms for accountability, organizations can ensure that ethical principles guide both the creation and deployment of generative AI systems (Brundage et al., 2020).

7.2. Cross-Sector Collaborations

No single entity can address all the challenges posed by generative AI. Collaboration among businesses, academic institutions, governments, and civil society is essential for establishing shared standards, identifying best practices, and promoting knowledge exchange (Bommasani et al., 2021). Joint efforts can lead to the creation of industry-wide ethical frameworks, international regulatory guidelines, and targeted training programs for developers and users (Ghosh & Lakshmi, 2023). By pooling resources and expertise, stakeholders can work together to shape a more responsible and beneficial AI ecosystem that balances innovation with societal well-being (Brundage et al., 2020).

7.3. Technology Audits and Monitoring

As generative AI evolves, continuous oversight is necessary to assess compliance, effectiveness, and unintended consequences (Novelli et al., 2024). Technology audits involve evaluating models for bias, security vulnerabilities, and potential misuse, as well as verifying adherence to privacy regulations and intellectual property rules (Zhang et al., 2023). Regular monitoring can help identify emerging issues before they escalate, providing opportunities to fine-tune policies, retrain models, or improve data management practices (Ghosh & Lakshmi, 2023). Through ongoing evaluation and responsive governance, organizations and regulators can uphold high standards of safety, ethics, and accountability while maintaining the forward momentum of AI-driven innovation (Li et al., 2024).

8. CONCLUSION AND FUTURE PROSPECTS

Generative Artificial Intelligence (AI) is revolutionizing industries such as healthcare, education, media, and scientific research by creating original content—from text and images to music and video. In healthcare, it accelerates drug discovery, enhances diagnostics, and enables personalized treatments, leading to improved patient outcomes and reduced costs. In creative fields, AI empowers artists and designers to explore new aesthetics, streamline workflows, and deliver personalized content to diverse audiences.

However, generative AI also presents significant ethical, privacy, and regulatory challenges. Issues like bias, misinformation, and data security highlight the need for transparency, fairness, and robust safeguards. Embedding ethical principles into every stage of AI development is crucial to prioritize user welfare, protect privacy, and ensure inclusivity. Clear guidelines for responsibility and accountability in content creation are essential to address concerns about authorship and the fair distribution of benefits.

Looking ahead, the future of generative AI is promising and multifaceted. Technological advancements will lead to more sophisticated and contextually aware AI systems, enhancing applications in multiple industries. Innovations such as advanced transformer models and hybrid neural networks will drive the next wave of AI capabilities, enabling more nuanced and accurate content generation. Additionally, integrating generative AI with emerging technologies like the Internet of Things (IoT) and blockchain will enhance data security and interoperability, transforming sectors like healthcare and research.

A responsible approach to generative AI involves proactive stewardship, including thorough auditing, continuous dialogue among diverse stakeholders, and adherence to ethical principles that prioritize human well-being. By embracing balanced policies and fostering collaborations, society can mitigate risks while maximizing the benefits of generative AI, ensuring it remains a catalyst for positive change and upholds essential moral and societal values.

REFERENCES

Bai, Y., Jones, A., Ndousse, K., Askell, A., Chen, A., DasSarma, N., . . . Kaplan, J. (2022). Training a helpful and harmless assistant with reinforcement learning from human feedback. arXiv preprint arXiv:2204.05862.

Bender, E. M., Gebru, T., McMillan-Major, A., & Shmitchell, S. (2021, March). On the dangers of stochastic parrots: Can language models be too big? In *Proceedings of the 2021 ACM conference on fairness, accountability, and transparency* (pp. 610-623). DOI: 10.1145/3442188.3445922

Bommasani, R., Hudson, D. A., Adeli, E., Altman, R., Arora, S., von Arx, S., . . . Liang, P. (2021). On the opportunities and risks of foundation models. arXiv preprint arXiv:2108.07258.

Brundage, M., Avin, S., Wang, J., Belfield, H., Krueger, G., Hadfield, G., . . . Anderljung, M. (2020). Toward trustworthy AI development: mechanisms for supporting verifiable claims. *arXiv preprint arXiv:2004.07213.*

Clinton, D. (2023). *The complete obsolete guide to generative AI.* Independently Published.

Crawford, K., & Paglen, T. (2021). Excavating AI: The politics of images in machine learning training sets. *AI & Society*, 36(4), 1105–1116. DOI: 10.1007/s00146-021-01301-1

Floridi, L., & Chiriatti, M. (2020). GPT-3: Its nature, scope, limits, and consequences. *Minds and Machines*, 30(4), 681–694. DOI: 10.1007/s11023-020-09548-1

Ghosh, A., & Lakshmi, D. (2023). Dual Governance: The intersection of centralized regulation and crowdsourced safety mechanisms for Generative AI. arXiv preprint arXiv:2308.04448.

Hagendorff, T. (2024). Mapping the ethics of generative ai: A comprehensive scoping review. *arXiv preprint arXiv:2402.08323.*

Jobin, A., Ienca, M., & Vayena, E. (2019). The global landscape of AI ethics guidelines. *Nature Machine Intelligence*, 1(9), 389–399. DOI: 10.1038/s42256-019-0088-2

Li, Q., Hong, J., Xie, C., Tan, J., Xin, R., Hou, J., . . . Song, D. (2024). Llm-pbe: Assessing data privacy in large language models. *arXiv preprint arXiv:2408.12787.*

Luccioni, A. S., Corry, F., Sridharan, H., Ananny, M., Schultz, J., & Crawford, K. (2022, June). A framework for deprecating datasets: Standardizing documentation, identification, and communication. In *Proceedings of the 2022 ACM Conference on Fairness, Accountability, and Transparency* (pp. 199-212). DOI: 10.1145/3531146.3533086

Mittelstadt, B. D., Allo, P., Taddeo, M., Wachter, S., & Floridi, L. (2016). The ethics of algorithms: Mapping the debate. *Big Data & Society*, 3(2), 2053951716679679. DOI: 10.1177/2053951716679679

Novelli, C., Casolari, F., Hacker, P., Spedicato, G., & Floridi, L. (2024). Generative AI in EU law: liability, privacy, intellectual property, and cybersecurity. *arXiv preprint arXiv:2401.07348.*

Pournaras, E. (2023). Science in the Era of ChatGPT, Large Language Models and Generative AI: Challenges for Research Ethics and How to Respond. *Beyond Quantity. Research with Subsymbolic AI*, 6, 275–290. DOI: 10.14361/9783839467664-015

Raji, I. D., & Buolamwini, J. (2019, January). Actionable auditing: Investigating the impact of publicly naming biased performance results of commercial ai products. In *Proceedings of the 2019 AAAI/ACM Conference on AI, Ethics, and Society* (pp. 429-435). DOI: 10.1145/3306618.3314244

Weidinger, L., Mellor, J., Rauh, M., Griffin, C., Uesato, J., Huang, P. S., . . . Gabriel, I. (2021). Ethical and social risks of harm from language models. *arXiv preprint arXiv:2112.04359.*

Whittaker, M., Crawford, K., Dobbe, R., Fried, G., Kaziunas, E., Mathur, V., & Schwartz, O. (2018). *AI now report 2018.* AI Now Institute at New York University.

Zhang, D., Xia, B., Liu, Y., Xu, X., Hoang, T., Xing, Z., . . . Zhu, L. (2023). Navigating privacy and copyright challenges across the data lifecycle of generative ai. arXiv preprint arXiv:2311.18252.

Zhang, D., Xia, B., Liu, Y., Xu, X., Hoang, T., Xing, Z., . . . Zhu, L. (2023). Navigating privacy and copyright challenges across the data lifecycle of generative ai. *arXiv preprint arXiv:2311.18252.*

Compilation of References

Abdelfattah, A. S., & Cerny, T. (2022). Microservices Security Challenges and Approaches.

Abou-Nassar, E. M., & Osama, H. A. (2022). Quantum-safe cryptography for IoT devices: A new horizon for edge computing security. *Journal of Information Security and Applications*, 65, 103155. DOI: 10.1016/j.jisa.2022.103155

Abraham, R., Schneider, J., & Vom Brocke, J. (2019). Data governance: A conceptual framework, structured review, and research agenda. *International Journal of Information Management*, 49, 424–438. DOI: 10.1016/j.ijinfomgt.2019.07.008

Adams, D., & Bellucci, M. (2023). Embedding Security into Continuous Integration and Continuous Deployment (CI/CD) Pipelines. *IEEE Transactions on Secure Software Engineering*, 2(3), 56–71.

Adhikari, N. B. (2024). EVALUATING SECURITY TOOLS IN THE CONTEXT OF DEVSECOPS.

Adhikari, S., & Baidya, S. (2024). Cyber Security in Containerization Platforms: A Comparative Study of Security Challenges, Measures and Best Practices. *ArXiv (Cornell University)*. https://doi.org//arxiv .2401.18082DOI: 10.48550

Adinegoro, F., Rahmania, C., Zaini, I. N., Negara, R. M., & Hertiana, S. N. (2022, December). Latency and RAM usage comparison of advanced and lightweight service mesh. In 2022 5th International Seminar on Research of Information Technology and Intelligent Systems (ISRITI) (pp. 369-372). IEEE. DOI: 10.1109/ISRITI56927.2022.10052905

Agasisti, T., & Bowers, A. J. (2017). Data analytics and decision making in education: towards the educational data scientist as a key actor in schools and higher education institutions. In *Handbook of contemporary education economics* (pp. 184–210). Edward Elgar Publishing. DOI: 10.4337/9781785369070.00014

Agrawal, R. (2024). The Role of Infrastructure as Code in Disaster Recovery and Business Continuity. *Journal*, 14(11). http://www. ijmra. us

Ahmad, K., Maabreh, M., Ghaly, M., Khan, K., Qadir, J., & Al-Fuqaha, A. (2022). Developing future human-centered smart cities: Critical analysis of smart city security, Data management, and Ethical challenges. *Computer Science Review*, 43, 100452. DOI: 10.1016/j.cosrev.2021.100452

Akbar, M. A., Smolander, K., Mahmood, S., & Alsanad, A. (2022). Toward successful DevSecOps in software development organizations: A decision-making framework. *Information and Software Technology*, 147, 106894. DOI: 10.1016/j.infsof.2022.106894

Akbar, M., Rafi, S., Alsanad, A., Qadri, S., Alsanad, A., & Alothaim, A. (2022). Toward Successful DevOps: A Decision-Making Framework. *IEEE Access : Practical Innovations, Open Solutions*, 10, 51343–51362. DOI: 10.1109/ACCESS.2022.3174094

Akto. (2023). *Cloud Native Security | Cloud Native Application Protection - Akto*. Akto.io. https://www.akto.io/devsecops/securing-cloud-native-applications-in-devsecops

Al Abri, K. A. S., Mastouri, M., Bouyahia, Z., Haddad, H., Yasar, A.-U.-H., & Shakshuki, E. (2023). On the Interest of Extending Internet of Behaviors to Internet of Habits: A Preliminary Exploration. *Procedia Computer Science*, 224, 122–130. DOI: 10.1016/j.procs.2023.09.019

Al-Badi, A., Tarhini, A., & Khan, A. I. (2018). Exploring big data governance frameworks. *Procedia Computer Science*, 141, 271–277. DOI: 10.1016/j.procs.2018.10.181

Algarni, S. (2021). *"Cybersecurity attacks: Analysis of "wannacry" attack and proposing methods for reducing or preventing such attacks in future." ICT Systems and Sustainability: Proceedings of ICT4SD 2020* (Vol. 1). Springer Singapore.

Alghawli, A. S. A., & Radivilova, T. (2024). Resilient cloud cluster with DevSecOps security model, automates a data analysis, vulnerability search and risk calculation. *Alexandria Engineering Journal*, 107, 136–149. DOI: 10.1016/j.aej.2024.07.036

Ali, R., Khan, A., & Ahmed, A. (2023). AI-enabled predictive analytics in edge computing: A comprehensive survey. *Journal of Big Data*, 10(1), 1–27. DOI: 10.1186/s40537-023-00651-9 PMID: 36618886

Alkhard, A. (2024). Enhancing asset management through integrated facilities data, digital asset management, and metadata strategies. *Construction Economics and Building, 24*(3), 76-94. https://search.informit.org/doi/10.3316/informit.T2024081300001000356599362

Alkhatib, R., & Gaede, K. I. (2024). Data management in biobanking: Strategies, challenges, and future directions. *Biotech*, 13(3), 34. DOI: 10.3390/biotech13030034 PMID: 39311336

Almeida, H. (2024). *IaC Security and Compliance Tools*. BoldLink. https://boldlink.io/2022/06/07/iac-security-and-compliance-tools/

Alquwayzani, A., Aldossri, R., & Frikha, M. (2024). Prominent Security Vulnerabilities in Cloud Computing. *International Journal of Advanced Computer Science and Applications*, 15(2). Advance online publication. DOI: 10.14569/IJACSA.2024.0150281

Al-Rashid, M., & Yahya, M. (2022). Multi-cloud Security: Challenges and Solutions. *International Journal of Cloud Computing*, 11(3), 237–251. DOI: 10.1504/IJCC.2022.121465

Alsafery, W., Alturki, B., Reiff-Marganiec, S., & Jambi, K. (2018). Smart Car Parking System Solution for the Internet of Things in Smart Cities. *2018 1st International Conference on Computer Applications & Information Security (ICCAIS)*, 1–5. DOI: 10.1109/CAIS.2018.8442004

Alsaqour, R., Motmi, A., & Abdelhaq, M. (2021). A systematic study of network firewall and its implementation. *International Journal of Computer Science & Network Security*, 21(4), 199–208.

Al-Saqqa, S., Sawalha, S., & AbdelNabi, H. (2020). Agile software development: Methodologies and trends. *International Journal of Interactive Mobile Technologies*, 14(11).

Alzaabi, F. R., & Mehmood, A. (2024). A review of recent advances, challenges, and opportunities in malicious insider threat detection using machine learning methods. *IEEE Access : Practical Innovations, Open Solutions*, 12, 30907–30927. DOI: 10.1109/ACCESS.2024.3369906

Amazon Web Services. (2023, July 24). *Building better container images | Amazon Web Services*. Amazon Web Services. https://aws.amazon.com/blogs/containers/building-better-container-images/

Ametepe, W., Dukeman, J., & Walker, S. (2021). Data provenance collection and security in a distributed environment: A survey. *International Journal of Computers and Applications*, 43(1), 11–25. DOI: 10.1080/1206212X.2018.1501937

Amiri, Z., Heidari, A., Darbandi, M., Yazdani, Y., Jafari Navimipour, N., Esmaeilpour, M., Sheykhi, F., & Unal, M. (2023). The Personal Health Applications of Machine Learning Techniques in the Internet of Behaviors. *Sustainability (Basel)*, 15(16), 12406. DOI: 10.3390/su151612406

Anand, P., & Honeycutt, T. C. (2020). Long-term outcomes for transition-age youth with mental health conditions who receive postsecondary education support. *Journal of Disability Policy Studies*, 30(4), 223–232. DOI: 10.1177/1044207319848069

Anjaria, D., & Kulkarni, M. (2022). Effective DevSecOps Implementation: A Systematic Literature Review. *Cardiometry*, (24), 410–417.

Aqua. (n.d.). *Aqua Cloud Native Security, Container Security & Serverless Security*. Aqua. https://www.aquasec.com/

Arner, Y., & Douglas, W.. (2017). *FinTech and RegTech: Enabling Innovation While Preserving Financial Stability*. Georgetown Journal of International Affairs.

Ashwani, K. (2023, September 15). *What is OWASP ZAP and use cases of OWASP ZAP?* DevOpsSchool.com. https://www.devopsschool.com/blog/what-is-owasp-zap-and-use-cases-of-owasp-zap/

Astuti, H. M., Wibowo, R. P., & Herdiyanti, A. (2024). Towards the National Higher Education Database in Indonesia: Challenges to Data Governance Implementation from The Perspective of a Public University. *Procedia Computer Science*, 234, 1322–1331. DOI: 10.1016/j.procs.2024.03.130

Atlassian. (2024). *Bitbucket Snyk Integration to Enable DevSecOps | Atlassian*. Atlassian. https://www.atlassian.com/devops/security-tutorials/jira-snyk-devsecops

Atlassian. (2024). DevSecOps tools. Retrieved from https://www.atlassian.com/devops/devops-tools/devsecops-tools

Atwal, H., & Atwal, H. (2020). DevOps for DataOps. In Practical DataOps: Delivering Agile Data Science at Scale (pp. 161-189). DOI: 10.1007/978-1-4842-5104-1_7

Auhl, Z., Chilamkurti, N., Alhadad, R., & Heyne, W. (2022). A Comparative study of consensus mechanisms in blockchain for IoT networks. *Electronics (Basel)*, 11(17), 2694. DOI: 10.3390/electronics11172694

Awotunde, J. B., Ogundokun, R. O., & Misra, S. (2021). Cloud and IoMT-based big data analytics system during COVID-19 pandemic. In *Efficient Data Handling for Massive Internet of Medical Things: Healthcare Data Analytics* (pp. 181–201). Springer International Publishing. DOI: 10.1007/978-3-030-66633-0_8

AWS. (n.d.). *What is Data Masking? - Static and Dynamic Data Masking Explained - AWS*. Amazon Web Services, Inc. https://aws.amazon.com/what-is/data-masking/

Aziz, W. A., Eleraky, M. W., & Soliman, J. N. (2023). Using Cloud Infrastructure as a Code IaC to Set Up Web Applications. *International Journal of Simulation--Systems, Science & Technology, 24*(3).

Babu, R. G., Srinivasan, P., Kumar, N., & Reddy, S. (2021). Multimedia security and privacy on real-time behavioral monitoring in machine learning IoT application using big data analytics. In Multimedia Technologies in the Internet of Things Environment (pp. 137–156).

Bagja, A., Amri, Z., Imtihan, K., Rodi, M., & Rusniatun, S. Y. (2024). Enhancing Public Sector IT Governance through COBIT 2019: A Case Study on Service Continuity and Data Management in the Central Lombok. *Journal of Information Systems and Informatics*, 6(4), 2761–2776.

Bahaa, S., Ghalwash, A. Z., & Harb, H. (2023). DataOps lifecycle with a case study in healthcare. *International Journal of Advanced Computer Science and Applications*, 14(1), 15–29. DOI: 10.14569/IJACSA.2023.0140115

Bai, Y., Jones, A., Ndousse, K., Askell, A., Chen, A., DasSarma, N., . . . Kaplan, J. (2022). Training a helpful and harmless assistant with reinforcement learning from human feedback. arXiv preprint arXiv:2204.05862.

Bakare, S. S., Adeniyi, A. O., Akpuokwe, C. U., & Eneh, N. E.,. (2024). Data privacy laws and compliance: A comparative review of the EU GDPR and USA regulations. *Computer Science & IT Research Journal*, 5(3), 528–543. DOI: 10.51594/csitrj.v5i3.859

Bakshi, K. (2017, March). Microservices-based software architecture and approaches. In 2017 IEEE aerospace conference (pp. 1-8). IEEE.

Balan, A., Alboaie, S., Kourtit, K., & Nijkamp, P. (2023). Blockchain systems for smart cities and regions: an illustration of self-sovereign data governance. Knowledge Management for Regional Policymaking, 163-190

Balan, A., Alboaie, S., Kourtit, K., & Nijkamp, P. (2023). Blockchain systems for smart cities and regions: an illustration of self-sovereign data governance. Knowledge Management for Regional Policymaking, 163-190.

Bammidi, T. R., Gutta, L. M., Kotagiri, A., & Samayamantri, L. S., & krishna Vaddy, R. (2024). The Crucial Role of Data Quality in Automated Decision-Making Systems. *International Journal of Management Education for Sustainable Development*, 7(7), 1–22.

Battina, D. S. (2021). The Challenges and Mitigation Strategies of Using DevOps during Software Development. International Journal of Creative Research Thoughts (IJCRT), ISSN, 2320-2882.

Battina, D. S. (2021). AI and DevOps in Information Technology and Its Future in the United States. [IJCRT]. *International Journal of Creative Research Thoughts*, 8(1), 108–112. DOI: 10.1234/ijcrt.108112

Bell, L., Arnold, J., & Evans, T. (2017). *Agile application security: Enabling security in a continuous delivery pipeline*. O'Reilly Media, Inc.

Bender, B. J., Gahbauer, S., Luttens, A., Lyu, J., Webb, C. M., Stein, R. M., Fink, E. A., Balius, T. E., Carlsson, J., Irwin, J. J., & Shoichet, B. K. (2021). A practical guide to large-scale docking. *Nature Protocols*, 16(10), 4799–4832. DOI: 10.1038/s41596-021-00597-z PMID: 34561691

Bender, E. M., Gebru, T., McMillan-Major, A., & Shmitchell, S. (2021, March). On the dangers of stochastic parrots: Can language models be too big? . In *Proceedings of the 2021 ACM conference on fairness, accountability, and transparency* (pp. 610-623). DOI: 10.1145/3442188.3445922

Benfeldt, O., Persson, J. S., & Madsen, S. (2020). Data governance as a collective action problem. *Information Systems Frontiers*, 22(2), 299–313. DOI: 10.1007/s10796-019-09923-z

Bentaleb, O., Belloum, A. S. Z., Sebaa, A., & El-Maouhab, A. (2021). Containerization technologies: Taxonomies, applications and challenges. *The Journal of Supercomputing*. Advance online publication. DOI: 10.1007/s11227-021-03914-1

Bernardino, N. A., Sequeira, B., Piza, E., Henriques, F., Neves, F., & Reis, C. I. (2024, June). Enhancing DevSecOps: Three Custom Tools for Continuous Security. In 2024 IEEE 11th International Conference on Cyber Security and Cloud Computing (CSCloud) (pp. 53-58). IEEE.

Berndtsson, M., Ericsson, A., & Svahn, T. (2020). Scaling up data-driven pilot projects. *AI Magazine*, 41(3), 94–102. DOI: 10.1609/aimag.v41i3.5307

Bhaskaran, S. V. (2020). Integrating Data Quality Services (DQS) in Big Data Ecosystems: Challenges, Best Practices, and Opportunities for Decision-Making. *Journal of Applied Big Data Analytics, Decision-Making, and Predictive Modelling Systems*, 4(11), 1–12. http://polarpublications.com/index.php/JABADP/article/view/4

Bhat, A. K. (2021). Improve real-time fraud detection with DataOps on resilient elastic platforms. *Journal of Resilient Data Platforms*, 5(2), 210–222.

Bhattacharyya, A., & Chakravarty, D. (2020). (Graph Database: A Survey). *2020 International Conference on Computer, Electrical & Communication Engineering (ICCECE)*, 1–8. DOI: 10.1109/ICCECE48148.2020.9223105

Bicer, C., Murturi, I., Donta, P. K., & Dustdar, S. (2023). Blockchain-based zero trust on the edge. arXiv preprint arXiv:2311.16744. /arXiv.2311.16744DOI: 10.1109/CSCI62032.2023.00167

Bigelow, S. J. (2021, May 13). *CI/CD pipelines explained: Everything you need to know*. SearchSoftwareQuality. https://www.techtarget.com/searchsoftwarequality/CI-CD-pipelines-explained-Everything-you-need-to-know

Blau, I., & Presser, O. (2013). e-L eadership of school principals: Increasing school effectiveness by a school data management system. *British Journal of Educational Technology*, 44(6), 1000–1011. DOI: 10.1111/bjet.12088

Blinowski, G., Ojdowska, A., & Przybyłek, A. (2022). Monolithic vs. microservice architecture: A performance and scalability evaluation. *IEEE Access : Practical Innovations, Open Solutions*, 10, 20357–20374. DOI: 10.1109/ACCESS.2022.3152803

Block, S. (2023). How to Adapt and Implement a Large-Scale Agile Framework in Your Organization. In *Large-Scale Agile Frameworks: Agile Frameworks, Agile Infrastructure and Pragmatic Solutions for Digital Transformation* (pp. 65–168). Springer Berlin Heidelberg. DOI: 10.1007/978-3-662-67782-7_4

Bommasani, R., Hudson, D. A., Adeli, E., Altman, R., Arora, S., von Arx, S., . . . Liang, P. (2021). On the opportunities and risks of foundation models. arXiv preprint arXiv:2108.07258.

Bonta, R. (2022). California consumer privacy act (CCPA). *Retrieved from State of California Department of Justice:*https://oag. ca. *gov/privacy/ccpa*. Accessed January 22, 2025.

Boppiniti, S. T. (2021). Real-time data analytics with ai: Leveraging stream processing for dynamic decision support. *International Journal of Management Education for Sustainable Development*, 4(4).

Borgogno, O., & Colangelo, G. (2019). Data sharing and interoperability: Fostering innovation and competition through APIs. *Computer Law & Security Report*, 35(5), 105314. DOI: 10.1016/j.clsr.2019.03.008

Bouaziz, S., Nabli, A., & Gargouri, F. (2019). Design a Data Warehouse Schema from Document-Oriented database. *Procedia Computer Science*, 159, 221–230. DOI: 10.1016/j.procs.2019.09.177

Bratanic, T. (2024). *Graph Algorithms for Data Science: With Examples in Neo4j*. Simon and Schuster.

Brous, P., Herder, P., & Janssen, M. (2016). Governing asset management data infrastructures. *Procedia Computer Science*, 95, 303–310. DOI: 10.1016/j.procs.2016.09.339

Brous, P., Janssen, M., & Vilminko-Heikkinen, R. (2016). Coordinating decision-making in data management activities: a systematic review of data governance principles. In Electronic Government: 15th IFIP WG 8.5 International Conference, EGOV 2016, Guimarães, Portugal, September 5-8, 2016 [Springer International Publishing.]. *Proceedings*, 15, 115–125.

Brundage, M., Avin, S., Wang, J., Belfield, H., Krueger, G., Hadfield, G., . . . Anderljung, M. (2020). Toward trustworthy AI development: mechanisms for supporting verifiable claims. *arXiv preprint arXiv:2004.07213.*

Cadet, E., Ndiaye, T., Parker, S., & Leclerc, A. (2024). AI-powered threat detection in surveillance systems: A real-time data processing framework. *ResearchGate*, 21(10), 125–138.

Caliskan, A., Dangwal, S., & Dandekar, T. (2023). Metadata integrity in bioinformatics: Bridging the gap between data and knowledge. *Computational and Structural Biotechnology Journal*, 21, 4895–4913. Advance online publication. DOI: 10.1016/j.csbj.2023.10.006 PMID: 37860229

Castelltort, A., & Laurent, A. (2014). NoSQL Graph-based OLAP Analysis: *Proceedings of the International Conference on Knowledge Discovery and Information Retrieval*, 217–224. DOI: 10.5220/0005072902170224

Castro, H. (2024, December 9). *Integrating Infrastructure as Code (IaC) and Security into AWS DevSecOps Pipelines*. https://www.researchgate.net/publication/387270734_Integrating_Infrastructure_as_Code_IaC_and_Security_into_AWS_DevSecOps_Pipelines

Cesarano, C. (2023). Security assessment and hardening of fog computing systems. arXiv preprint arXiv:2308.12707. /arXiv.2308.12707DOI: 10.1109/ISSREW60843.2023.00037

Chakravorty, R. (2020). Common challenges of data governance. *Journal of Securities Operations & Custody*, 13(1), 23–43. DOI: 10.69554/GAKU4007

Chandramouli, R. (2022). Implementation of devsecops for a microservices-based application with service mesh. *NIST Special Publication*, 800, 204C. DOI: 10.6028/NIST.SP.800-204C

Chandramouli, R., & Butcher, Z. (2020). Building secure microservices-based applications using service-mesh architecture. *NIST Special Publication*, 800, 204A. DOI: 10.6028/NIST.SP.800-204a

Chaudhry, S. A., Yahya, K., Al-Turjman, F., & Yang, M. H. (2020). A Secure and Reliable Device Access Control Scheme for IoT Based Sensor Cloud Systems. *IEEE Access : Practical Innovations, Open Solutions*, 8, 139244–139254. DOI: 10.1109/ACCESS.2020.3012121

Chauhan, M., & Shiaeles, S. (2023). An Analysis of Cloud Security Frameworks, Problems and Proposed Solutions. *Network (Bristol, England)*, 3(3), 422–450. https://www.mdpi.com/2673-8732/3/3/18

Chavan, M. (2020). Integrating DataOps practices in signature verification systems for seamless data orchestration. *Journal of DataOps Practices*, 45(2), 102–114.

Chen, M. (2024, May 2). *What Is Data Sovereignty?* Oracle.com; Oracle. https://www.oracle.com/ke/cloud/sovereign-cloud/data-sovereignty/

Chen, C., Yan, X., Zhu, F., Han, J., & Yu, P. S. (2008). Graph OLAP: Towards Online Analytical Processing on Graphs. *2008 Eighth IEEE International Conference on Data Mining*, 103–112. DOI: 10.1109/ICDM.2008.30

Chen, C., Yan, X., Zhu, F., Han, J., & Yu, P. S. (2009). Graph OLAP: A multi-dimensional framework for graph data analysis. *Knowledge and Information Systems*, 21(1), 41–63. DOI: 10.1007/s10115-009-0228-9

Chen, J., Ramanathan, L., & Alazab, M. (2021). Holistic big data integrated artificial intelligent modeling to improve privacy and security in data management of smart cities. *Microprocessors and Microsystems*, 81, 103722. DOI: 10.1016/j.micpro.2020.103722

Chen, L., & Babar, M. A. (2014). Towards an evidence-based understanding of electronic data security and privacy risks. *Journal of Software (Malden, MA)*, 26(11), 974–990. DOI: 10.1002/smr.1666

Cheong, B. C. (2024). Transparency and accountability in AI systems: Safeguarding wellbeing in the age of algorithmic decision-making. *Frontiers in Human Dynamics*, 6, 1421273. DOI: 10.3389/fhumd.2024.1421273

Chevalier, M., El Malki, M., Kopliku, A., Teste, O., & Tournier, R. (2015). Implementation of Multidimensional Databases with Document-Oriented NoSQL. In Madria, S., & Hara, T. (Eds.), *Big Data Analytics and Knowledge Discovery* (pp. 379–390). Springer International Publishing. DOI: 10.1007/978-3-319-22729-0_29

Chinamanagonda, S. (2021). DevSecOps: Integrating Security in DevOps Pipelines-Security becoming an integral part of DevOps practices. Innovative Computer Sciences Journal, 7(1).

Chinamanagonda, S. (2022). Observability in Microservices Architectures-Advanced observability tools for microservices environments. MZ Computing Journal, 3(1).

Chinamanagonda, S. (2023). Focus on resilience engineering in cloud services. *Academia Nexus Journal, 2*(1). https://academianexusjournal.com/index.php/anj/article/view/4

Chinamanagonda, S. (2021). DevSecOps: Integrating Security in DevOps Pipelines-Security becoming an integral part of DevOps practices. *Innovative Computer Sciences Journal*, 7, 1.

Chintale, P. (2023). *DevOps Design Pattern: Implementing DevOps best practices for secure and reliable CI/CD pipeline (English Edition)*. Bpb Publications.

Chittala, S. (2024). Securing DevOps Pipelines: Automating Security in DevSecOps Frameworks. [JRTCSE]. *Journal of Recent Trends in Computer Science and Engineering*, 12(5), 31–44. DOI: 10.70589/JRTCSE.2024.5.5

Choi, D., & Lee, K. (2018). An Artificial Intelligence Approach to Financial Fraud Detection under IoT Environment: A Survey and Implementation. *Security and Communication Networks*, 2018, 1–15. DOI: 10.1155/2018/5483472

Choi, Y. B., & Williams, C. E. (2022). A HIPAA security and privacy compliance audit and risk assessment mitigation approach. In *Research Anthology on Securing Medical Systems and Records* (pp. 706–725). IGI Global. DOI: 10.4018/978-1-6684-6311-6.ch032

Chou, C.-H., Hayakawa, M., Kitazawa, A., & Sheu, P. (2018). GOLAP: Graph-Based Online Analytical Processing. *International Journal of Semantic Computing*, 12(04), 595–608. DOI: 10.1142/S1793351X18500071

Chui, M., Issler, M., Roberts, R., & Yee, L. (2023). Technology trends outlook 2023.

Clinton, D. (2023). *The complete obsolete guide to generative AI*. Independently Published.

Colliander, C. (2022). Challenges of DevSecOps. Master's thesis, University of Helsinki. Retrieved from http://hdl.handle.net/10138/342887

Confluent. (2025). Use role-based access control (RBAC) for authorization in Confluent Platform | Confluent Documentation. Confluent.io. https://docs.confluent.io/platform/current/security/authorization/rbac/overview.html

Coppola, P., & Verma, R. (2021). AI and Machine Learning in SecOps: Enhancing Resilience and Operational Efficiency. *Journal of Cybersecurity*, 10(2), 145–160. DOI: 10.1093/cybsec/123456

Côté, P. O., Nikanjam, A., Bouchoucha, R., Basta, I., Abidi, M., & Khomh, F. (2024). Quality issues in machine learning software systems. *Empirical Software Engineering*, 29(6), 149. DOI: 10.1007/s10664-024-10536-7

Crawford, K., & Paglen, T. (2021). Excavating AI: The politics of images in machine learning training sets. *AI & Society*, 36(4), 1105–1116. DOI: 10.1007/s00146-021-01301-1

Crompton, H., & Sykora, C. (2021). Developing instructional technology standards for educators: A design-based research study. *Computers and Education Open*, 2, 100044. DOI: 10.1016/j.caeo.2021.100044

Dal Maso, A. (2019). The evolution of Data Governance: a tool for an improved and enhanced decision-making process.

DAMA International. (2017). *DAMA-DMBOK: Data management body of knowledge*. Technics Publications, LLC.

Davis, J., & Daniels, R. (2016). *Effective DevOps: Building a Culture of Collaboration, Affinity, and Tooling at Scale*. O'Reilly Media.

Davoudian, A., & Liu, M. (2020). Big data systems: A software engineering perspective. *ACM Computing Surveys*, 53(5), 1–39. DOI: 10.1145/3408314

de Almeida, M. G., & Canedo, E. D. (2022). Authentication and authorization in microservices architecture: A systematic literature review. *Applied Sciences (Basel, Switzerland)*, 12(6), 3023. DOI: 10.3390/app12063023

de Vicente Mohino, J., Bermejo Higuera, J., Bermejo Higuera, J. R., & Sicilia Montalvo, J. A. (2019). The application of a new secure software development life cycle (S-SDLC) with agile methodologies. *Electronics (Basel)*, 8(11), 1218.

Deekshith, A. (2021). Data engineering for AI: Optimizing data quality and accessibility for machine learning models. *International Journal of Management Education for Sustainable Development*, 4(4), 1–33.

Deepfactor. (2023, March 22). *Use Case: Cloud Native Application Security*. Deepfactor. https://www.deepfactor.io/cloud-native-application-security/

Dehdouh, K., Boussaid, O., & Bentayeb, F. (2020). Big Data warehouse: Building columnar NoSQL OLAP cubes. In *International Journal of Decision Support System Technology* (Vol. 12, Issue 1, pp. 1–24). DOI: 10.4018/IJDSST.2020010101

Demchenko, Y. (2020). From DevOps to DataOps: Cloud based software development and deployment. In *The International Conference on High Performance Computing and Simulation (HPCS 2020)* (pp. 321-330).

Demichev, A., Kryukov, A., & Prikhod'ko, N. (2021). Business process engineering for data storing and processing in a collaborative distributed environment based on provenance metadata, smart contracts and blockchain technology. *Journal of Grid Computing*, 19(1), 3. DOI: 10.1007/s10723-021-09544-4

Dhaduk, H. (2022). How Netflix Became A Master of DevOps? An Exclusive Case Study. Retrieved from https://www.simform.com/blog/netflix-devops-case-study/

Dhaduk, H. (2022, February 23). *Capital One DevOps Case Study: A Bank with the Heart of Tech Company*. Insights on Latest Technologies - Simform Blog. https://www.simform.com/blog/capital-one-devops-case-study/

Dibouliya, A., & Jotwani, D. V. (2023). Review on Data Mesh Architecture and its Impact. *Journal of Harbin Engineering University*, 44(7), 2353–2363.

Djenna, A., Harous, S., & Saidouni, D. E. (2021). Internet of things meet internet of threats: New concern cyber security issues of critical cyber infrastructure. *Applied Sciences (Basel, Switzerland)*, 11(10), 4580. DOI: 10.3390/app11104580

Doidge, F. (2024). *Best practices to beat container misconfiguration*. ComputerWeekly.com. https://www.computerweekly.com/feature/Best-practices-to-beat-container-misconfiguration

Domoney, C. (2024). *7 DevSecOps tools to secure each step of the SDLC*. Search Security; TechTarget. https://www.techtarget.com/searchsecurity/tip/DevSecOps-tools-to-secure-each-step-of-the-SDLC

Dong, L., Yujia, L., Can, C., Huang Yunhao, & Di Fangchun. (2020). Research on safety protection technology of containerization applications based on probe detection. *2022 IEEE 10th Joint International Information Technology and Artificial Intelligence Conference (ITAIC)*, 386–389. DOI: 10.1109/ITAIC49862.2020.9339142

Duggineni, S. (2023). Impact of controls on data integrity and information systems. *Science and Technology*, 13(2), 29–35.

Dulam, N., Gade, K. R., & Gosukonda, V. (2022). Data Mesh and Data Governance: Finding the Balance. *Journal of AI-Assisted Scientific Discovery*, 2(2), 226–250.

Durango, I., Gallud, J. A., & Penichet, V. M. (2024). Human-Data Interaction Framework: A Comprehensive Model for a Future Driven by Data and Humans. *arXiv preprint arXiv:2407.21010.*

Dutta, P., Choi, T. M., Somani, S., & Butala, R. (2020). Blockchain technology in supply chain operations: Applications, challenges and research opportunities. *Transportation research part e: Logistics and transportation review, 142*, 102067.

Duzha, A., Alexakis, E., Kyriazis, D., Sahi, L. F., & Kandi, M. A. (2023, August). From Data Governance by design to Data Governance as a Service: A transformative human-centric data governance framework. In *Proceedings of the 2023 7th International Conference on Cloud and Big Data Computing*(pp. 10-20). DOI: 10.1145/3616131.3616145

Ebert, C., Gallardo, G., Hernantes, J., & Serrano, N. (2016). DevOps. *IEEE Software*, 33(3), 94–100. DOI: 10.1109/MS.2016.68

Edmundson, C., & Hartman, K. G. (2022). SANS 2022 DevSecOps Survey: Creating a Culture to Significantly Improve Your Organization's Security Posture. URL https://www.sans.org/white-papers/sans-2022-devsecops-survey-creating-cultureimprove-organization-security

Eghbal, N. (2020). *Working in public: the making and maintenance of open source software*. Stripe Press.

Ejjami, R., & Boussalham, K. (2024). Industry 5.0 in Manufacturing: Enhancing Resilience and Responsibility through AI-Driven Predictive Maintenance, Quality Control, and Supply Chain Optimization. *International Journal For Multidisciplinary Research, 6*(4).

Ekle, O. A., & Eberle, W. (2024). Anomaly Detection in Dynamic Graphs: A Comprehensive Survey. *ACM Transactions on Knowledge Discovery from Data*, 18(8), 1–44. DOI: 10.1145/3669906

Elayan, H., Aloqaily, M., Karray, F., & Guizani, M. (2021). *Internet of Behavior (IoB) and Explainable AI Systems for Influencing IoT Behavior*. http://arxiv.org/abs/2109.07239

Elayan, H., Aloqaily, M., Karray, F., & Guizani, M. (2023). Internet of Behavior and Explainable AI Systems for Influencing IoT Behavior. *IEEE Network*, 37(1), 62–68. DOI: 10.1109/MNET.009.2100500

Elugbaju, W. K., Okeke, N. I., & Alabi, O. A. (2024). Conceptual framework for enhancing decision-making in higher education through data-driven governance. Global Journal of Advanced Research and Reviews, 2(02), 016-030.

Emergen Research. (2023). *Global Internet of Behaviors (IoB) Market Size to Reach USD 3,087.86 Billion in 2032*. https://finance.yahoo.com/news/global-internet-behaviors-iob-market-150000141.html

Eryurek, E., Gilad, U., Lakshmanan, V., Kibunguchy-Grant, A., & Ashdown, J. (2021). *Data governance: The definitive guide*. O'Reilly Media, Inc.

Fan, W., Geerts, F., & Jia, X. (2007). Improving data quality: Consistency and accuracy. ACM.0

Faraj, O., Megias, D., & Garcia-Alfaro, J. (2024). Security Approaches for Data Provenance in the Internet of Things: A Systematic Literature Review. *arXiv preprint arXiv:2407.03466*.

Farhad, M. A. (2024). Consumer data protection laws and their impact on business models in the tech industry. *Telecommunications Policy*, 48(9), 102836. DOI: 10.1016/j.telpol.2024.102836

Farkiani, B., & Jain, R. (2024). Service Mesh: Architectures, Applications, and Implementations. arXiv preprint arXiv:2405.13333.

Fastercapital. (2024). *Pipeline Auditing: How to Check and Assess the Compliance and Conformance of Your Pipeline - FasterCapital*. FasterCapital. https://fastercapital.com/content/Pipeline-Auditing--How-to-Check-and-Assess-the-Compliance-and-Conformance-of-Your-Pipeline.html

Fawzy, A., Tahir, A., Galster, M., & Liang, P. (2024). Data Management Challenges in Agile Software Projects: A Systematic Literature Review. *arXiv preprint arXiv:2402.00462*.

Fedorchenko, A., & Ponomarenko, I. (2019). A/B-testing as an efficient tools for digital marketing. *Problems of Innovation and Investment Development*, 19(19), 36–42. DOI: 10.33813/2224-1213.19.2019.4

Feng, C., & Sun, H. (2022). Quantum computing and its impact on encryption protocols for IoT. *Computers & Security*, 118, 102740. DOI: 10.1016/j.cose.2022.102740

Finch, H. (2024, February 15). *Managing Secrets in Your CI/CD Pipeline: Best Practices and Strategies*. Medium. https://medium.com/@haroldfinch01/managing-secrets-in-your-ci-cd-pipeline-best-practices-and-strategies-aef0d10e5395

Floridi, L., & Chiriatti, M. (2020). GPT-3: Its nature, scope, limits, and consequences. *Minds and Machines*, 30(4), 681–694. DOI: 10.1007/s11023-020-09548-1

Fogli, M., Kudla, T., Musters, B., Pingen, G., Van Den Broek, C., Bastiaansen, H., Suri, N., & Webb, S. (2021). Performance Evaluation of Kubernetes Distributions (K8s, K3s, KubeEdge) in an Adaptive and Federated Cloud Infrastructure for Disadvantaged Tactical Networks. *2021 International Conference on Military Communication and Information Systems (ICMCIS)*, 1-7. DOI: 10.1109/ICMCIS52405.2021.9486396

Fossati, S. (2024). Leveraging Chaos Engineering to enhance data collection infrastructures' resilience: an industrial proof-of-concept study. *Handle.net*. https://hdl.handle.net/10589/222695

França, R. P., Monteiro, A. C. B., Arthur, R., & Iano, Y. (2020). An overview of the edge computing in the modern digital age. In Fog/Edge Computing For Security, Privacy, and Applications (pp. 33–52). Springer. DOI: 10.1007/978-3-030-57328-7

Fu, M., Pasuksmit, J., & Tantithamthavorn, C. "AI for DevSecOps: A Landscape and Future Opportunities." *arXiv preprint arXiv:2404.04839* (2024).

Fu, Y., & Soman, C. (2021, June). Real-time data infrastructure at uber. In *Proceedings of the 2021 International Conference on Management of Data* (pp. 2503-2516). DOI: 10.1145/3448016.3457552

Gadde, H. (2020). AI-Enhanced Data Warehousing: Optimizing ETL Processes for Real-Time Analytics. *Revista de Inteligencia Artificial en Medicina*, 11(1), 300–327.

Gade, K. R. (2023). Data Governance in the Cloud: Challenges and Opportunities. MZ Computing Journal, 4(1).

Gajbhiye, B., Goel, O., & Pandian, G. (2024). Managing Vulnerabilities in Containerized and Kubernetes Environments. *Journal of Quantum Science and Technology.*, 1(2), 59–71. DOI: 10.36676/jqst.v1.i2.16

Garey, L. (2024, October 3). *What Is Zero Trust Security?* Oracle.com; Oracle. https://www.oracle.com/ke/security/what-is-zero-trust/

Gartner. (2020). *Gartner top strategic technology trends for 2021*. https://www.gartner.com/smarterwithgartner/gartner-top-strategic- technology-trends-for-2021/

George, A. S., George, A. H., & Baskar, T. (2023). Digitally immune systems: Building robust defences in the age of cyber threats. *Partners Universal International Innovation Journal*, 1(4), 155–172.

Ghandour, O., El Kafhali, S., & Hanini, M. (2023). Computing Resources Scalability Performance Analysis in Cloud Computing Data Center. *Journal of Grid Computing*, 21(4), 61. Advance online publication. DOI: 10.1007/s10723-023-09696-5

Ghosh, A., & Lakshmi, D. (2023). Dual Governance: The intersection of centralized regulation and crowdsourced safety mechanisms for Generative AI. arXiv preprint arXiv:2308.04448.

Gittlen, S. (2021, August). *What Is Identity and Access Management? Guide to IAM*. SearchSecurity. https://www.techtarget.com/searchsecurity/definition/identity-access-management-IAM-system

Goedegebuure, A., Kumara, I., Driessen, S., Van Den Heuvel, W. J., Monsieur, G., Tamburri, D. A., & Nucci, D. D. (2024). Data mesh: A systematic gray literature review. *ACM Computing Surveys*, 57(1), 1–36. DOI: 10.1145/3687301

Gómez, L., Kuijpers, B., & Vaisman, A. (2017). Performing OLAP over Graph Data: Query Language, Implementation, and a Case Study. *Proceedings of the International Workshop on Real-Time Business Intelligence and Analytics*. DOI: 10.1145/3129292.3129293

Gómez, L., Kuijpers, B., & Vaisman, A. (2020). Online analytical processsing on graph data. *Intelligent Data Analysis*, 24(3), 515–541. DOI: 10.3233/IDA-194576

González-Granadillo, G., González-Zarzosa, S., & Diaz, R. (2021). Security information and event management (SIEM): Analysis, trends, and usage in critical infrastructures. *Sensors (Basel)*, 21(14), 4759. DOI: 10.3390/s21144759 PMID: 34300500

Goshisht, M. K. (2024). Machine learning and deep learning in synthetic biology: Key architectures, applications, and challenges. *ACS Omega*, 9(9), 9921–9945. DOI: 10.1021/acsomega.3c05913 PMID: 38463314

Gregorczuk, H. (2022). Retail analytics: Smart-stores saving bricks-and-mortar retail or a privacy problem? *Law. Technology and Humans*, 4(1), 63–78. DOI: 10.5204/lthj.2088

Grover, V., Chiang, R. H., Liang, T. P., & Zhang, D. (2018). Creating strategic business value from big data analytics: A research framework. *Journal of Management Information Systems*, 35(2), 388–423. DOI: 10.1080/07421222.2018.1451951

Guitton, F., Oehmichen, A., Bossé, É., & Guo, Y. (2024). Honest Computing: Achieving demonstrable data lineage and provenance for driving data and process-sensitive policies. *Data & Policy*, 6, e84. DOI: 10.1017/dap.2024.68

Gunnam, V., Cheemakurthi, S. K. M., & Kilaru, N. B. (2023). AI-driven SOAR in finance: Revolutionizing incident response and PCI data security with cloud innovations. *Journal of Financial Security*, 12(4), 130–142.

Gupta, A. (2022). An Integrated Framework for DevSecOps Adoption. arXiv preprint arXiv:2207.04093.

Gupta, R., & Soni, S. (2020). Developing Effective Big Data Strategies and Governance Frameworks: Principles, Tools, Challenges and Best Practices. *International Journal of Responsible Artificial Intelligence*, 10(8), 10–19.

Guyer, N. (2024, January 18). *Critical Considerations for Sensitive Information in a Data Breach*. Complete Discovery Source. https://cdslegal.com/insights/advisory-services/critical-considerations-for-sensitive-information-in-a-data-breach/

Habib, G., Sharma, S., Ibrahim, S., Ahmad, I., Qureshi, S., & Ishfaq, M. (2022). Blockchain technology: Benefits, challenges, applications, and integration of blockchain technology with cloud computing. *Future Internet*, 14(11), 341. DOI: 10.3390/fi14110341

Hagen, H. (2023, March 17). *Open Policy Agent for AWS and Terraform*. Tecracer.com. https://www.tecracer.com/blog/2023/03/open-policy-agent-for-aws-and-terraform.html

Hagendorff, T. (2024). Mapping the ethics of generative ai: A comprehensive scoping review. *arXiv preprint arXiv:2402.08323*.

Hahn, R. W., & Layne-Farrar, A. (2006). The law and economics of software security. *SSRN*, 30, 283. DOI: 10.2139/ssrn.897725

Haidabrus, B., Grabis, J., Psarov, O., & Druzhinin, E. (2023). Agile Framework as a Key to Information Management Systems Delivery. In *Design, Simulation, Manufacturing: The Innovation Exchange* (pp. 113–120). Springer Nature Switzerland. DOI: 10.1007/978-3-031-32767-4_11

Haindl, P., Kochberger, P., & Sveggen, M. (2024). A Systematic Literature Review of Inter-Service Security Threats and Mitigation Strategies in Microservice Architectures. *IEEE Access : Practical Innovations, Open Solutions*, 12, 90252–90286. DOI: 10.1109/ACCESS.2024.3406500

Harika, A., Tajuddin, S., Bhavani, P., Harsha, D., & Sriteja, P. (2023). Optimizing Scalability and Resilience: Strategies for Aligning DevOps and Cloud-Native Approaches. *2023 3rd International Conference on Innovative Mechanisms for Industry Applications (ICIMIA)*. DOI: 10.1109/ICIMIA60377.2023.10426288

Harvard Business Review. (2024, January 16). *How SolarWinds Responded to the 2020 SUNBURST Cyberattack*. Harvard Business Review. https://hbr.org/podcast/2024/01/how-solarwinds-responded-to-the-2020-sunburst-cyberattack

Hasan, M., Popp, J., & Oláh, J. (2020). Current landscape and influence of big data on finance. *Journal of Big Data*, 7(1), 21. DOI: 10.1186/s40537-020-00291-z

HashiCorp. (2024). *Dynamic secrets | HashiCorp Cloud Platform | HashiCorp Developer*. Dynamic Secrets | HashiCorp Cloud Platform | HashiCorp Developer; HashiCorp. https://developer.hashicorp.com/hcp/docs/vault-secrets/dynamic-secrets

Hassani, H., & MacFeely, S. (2023). Driving excellence in official statistics: Unleashing the potential of comprehensive digital data Governance. *Big Data and Cognitive Computing*, 7(3), 134. DOI: 10.3390/bdcc7030134

Hastig, G. M., & Sodhi, M. S. (2020). Blockchain for supply chain traceability: Business requirements and critical success factors. *Production and Operations Management*, 29(4), 935–954. DOI: 10.1111/poms.13147

Haverinen, H., Janhunen, T., Päivärinta, T., Lempinen, S., Kaartinen, S., & Merilä, S. (2024, October). Automating Cybersecurity Compliance in DevSecOps with Open Information Model for Security as Code. In Proceedings of the 4th Eclipse Security, AI, Architecture and Modelling Conference on Data Space (pp. 93-102). DOI: 10.1145/3685651.3686700

Haynes, D. (2018). *Metadata for Information Management and Retrieval: Understanding metadata and its use*. Facet Publishing. DOI: 10.29085/9781783302161

Heijstek, A. (2023). Bridging Theory and Practice: Insights into Practical Implementations of Security Practices in Secure DevOps and CI/CD Environments (Doctoral dissertation, Ph. D. thesis, Universiteit van Amsterdam).

Hemker, S., Herrando, C., & Constantinides, E. (2021). The Transformation of Data Marketing: How an Ethical Lens on Consumer Data Collection Shapes the Future of Marketing. *Sustainability (Basel)*, 13(20), 11208. DOI: 10.3390/su132011208

Henckaerts, R., & Antonio, K. (2022). The added value of dynamically updating motor insurance prices with telematics collected driving behavior data. *Insurance, Mathematics & Economics*, 105, 79–95. DOI: 10.1016/j.insmatheco.2022.03.011

Herridge, C. (2024). The Patterns and Structures of Information Technology Departments in Higher Education.

Heusser, M. (2024). *CI/CD pipeline security: Know the risks and best practices.* IT Operations; TechTarget. https://www.techtarget.com/searchitoperations/tip/9-ways-to-infuse-security-in-your-CI-CD-pipeline

He, Z., & Fang, W. (2024). Research data management in institutional repositories: An architectural approach using data lakehouses. *Digital Library Perspectives.*

Hikmawati, S., Santosa, P. I., & Hidayah, I. (2021). Improving Data Quality and Data Governance Using Master Data Management: A Review. [International Journal of Information Technology and Electrical Engineering]. *IJITEE*, 5(3), 90–95. DOI: 10.22146/ijitee.66307

Hilliman, C. A. (2013). Data Privacy, Security, and Compliane through Data Governance. N. Bhansali, Data Governance: Creating Value from Information Assets, 125-148.

Hillman, V. (2023). Bringing in the technological, ethical, educational and social-structural for a new education data governance. *Learning, Media and Technology*, 48(1), 122–137. DOI: 10.1080/17439884.2022.2052313

Himeur, Y., Ghanem, K., Alsalemi, A., Bensaali, F., & Amira, A. (2021). Artificial intelligence based anomaly detection of energy consumption in buildings: A review, current trends and new perspectives. *Applied Energy*, 287, 116601. DOI: 10.1016/j.apenergy.2021.116601

Ho, T. K. K., Karami, A., & Armanfard, N. (2023). Graph-based time-series anomaly detection: A survey. *arXiv preprint arXiv:2302.00058.* IBM (nd.). IBM Manta Data Lineage. Retrieved from https://www.ibm.com/products/manta-data-lineage Accessed January 15, 2025.

Hoffman, C. M. (2021). *Securing DevOps: Security in the Cloud.* O'Reilly Media.

Hong, J. H. (2023). Harnessing AI-Driven Data Cataloging Techniques for Enhanced Discoverability and Usability in Big Data Ecosystems. *Journal of Computational Innovation*, 3(1).

Honig, J. (n.d.). *What is Version Control & Why Is It Important?* Start.docuware.com. https://start.docuware.com/blog/document-management/what-is-version-control-why-is-it-important

Hosen, M. S., Islam, R., Naeem, Z., Folorunso, E. O., Chu, T. S., Al Mamun, M. A., & Orunbon, N. O. (2024). Data-driven decision making: Advanced database systems for business intelligence. *Nanotechnology Perceptions*, 20(3), 687–704.

Hossain, M. I., Gonzalez, A. R., & Kar, N. (2024). Enhancing data integrity and traceability in industry cyber physical systems (ICPS) through blockchain technology: A comprehensive approach. arXiv Preprint, arXiv:2405.04837.

Hossain, M. I., Steigner, T., Hussain, M. I., & Akther, A. (2024). Enhancing data integrity and traceability in industry cyber physical systems (ICPS) through Blockchain technology: A comprehensive approach. *arXiv preprint arXiv:2405.04837*.

Hynninen, P., & Kauppinen, M. (2014). A/B testing: A promising tool for customer value evaluation. *2014 IEEE 1st International Workshop on Requirements Engineering and Testing (RET)*, 16–17. DOI: 10.1109/RET.2014.6908673

IBM. (n.d.). *The power of AI: Security*. IBM. https://www.ibm.com/thought-leadership/institute-business-value/en-us/report/ai-security-automation

Ige, A. B., Chukwurah, N., Idemudia, C., & Adebayo, V. I. (2024). Managing Data Lifecycle Effectively: Best Practices for Data Retention and Archival Processes. International Journal of Engineering Research and Development e-ISSN, 453-461.

Inau, E. T., Sack, J., Waltemath, D., & Zeleke, A. A. (2023). Initiatives, concepts, and implementation practices of the findable, accessible, interoperable, and reusable data principles in health data stewardship: Scoping review. *Journal of Medical Internet Research*, 25, e45013. DOI: 10.2196/45013 PMID: 37639292

Indu, I., Anand, P. M. R., & Bhaskar, V. (2018). Identity and access management in cloud environment: Mechanisms and challenges. *Engineering Science and Technology, an International Journal*, 21(4), 574–588. DOI: 10.1016/j.jestch.2018.05.010

IoT-Based Data Analytics for the Healthcare Industry. (2021). Elsevier. DOI: 10.1016/C2019-0-03210-4

Jack, C. H., Teck, S. K., Ming, L. T., & Hong, D. Y. (2023, August). An Overview Analysis of Authentication Mechanism in Microservices-Based Software Architecture: A Discussion Paper. In 2023 IEEE 8th International Conference On Software Engineering and Computer Systems (ICSECS) (pp. 1-6). IEEE.

Jacobsen, A., de Miranda Azevedo, R., Juty, N., Batista, D., Coles, S., Cornet, R., Courtot, M., Crosas, M., Dumontier, M., Evelo, C. T., Goble, C., Guizzardi, G., Hansen, K. K., Hasnain, A., Hettne, K., Heringa, J., Hooft, R. W. W., Imming, M., Jeffery, K. G., & Schultes, E. (2020). FAIR principles: Interpretations and implementation considerations. *Data Intelligence*, 2(1-2), 10–29. DOI: 10.1162/dint_r_00024

Jacobs, P. G., Herrero, P., Facchinetti, A., Vehi, J., Kovatchev, B., Breton, M. D., Cinar, A., Nikita, K. S., Doyle, F. J., Bondia, J., Battelino, T., Castle, J. R., Zarkogianni, K., Narayan, R., & Mosquera-Lopez, C. (2023). Artificial intelligence and machine learning for improving glycemic control in diabetes: Best practices, pitfalls, and opportunities. *IEEE Reviews in Biomedical Engineering*, 17, 19–41. DOI: 10.1109/RBME.2023.3331297 PMID: 37943654

Jahnke, N., & Otto, B. (2023). Data catalogs in the enterprise: Applications and integration. *Datenbank-Spektrum: Zeitschrift fur Datenbanktechnologie: Organ der Fachgruppe Datenbanken der Gesellschaft fur Informatik e.V*, 23(2), 89–96. DOI: 10.1007/s13222-023-00445-2

James, E., & Rabbi, F. (2023). Fortifying the IoT landscape: Strategies to counter security risks in connected systems. *Tensorgate Journal of Sustainable Technology and Infrastructure for Developing Countries*, 6(1), 32–46.

Janssen, M., Brous, P., Estevez, E., Barbosa, L. S., & Janowski, T. (2020). Data governance: Organizing data for trustworthy Artificial Intelligence. *Government Information Quarterly*, 37(3), 101493. DOI: 10.1016/j.giq.2020.101493

Javaid, M., Haleem, A., Singh, R. P., Khan, S., & Suman, R. (2022). An extensive study on Internet of Behavior (IoB) enabled Healthcare-Systems: Features, facilitators, and challenges. *BenchCouncil Transactions on Benchmarks. Standards and Evaluations*, 2(4), 100085. DOI: 10.1016/j.tbench.2023.100085

Jobin, A., Ienca, M., & Vayena, E. (2019). The global landscape of AI ethics guidelines. *Nature Machine Intelligence*, 1(9), 389–399. DOI: 10.1038/s42256-019-0088-2

Jones, P., & Smith, R. (2023). Automating Cloud Security: The Role of AI in DevSecOps Pipelines. *Journal of Cloud Engineering*, 13(1), 33–52.

Joseph, A. (2023). A Holistic Framework for Unifying Data Security and Management in Modern Enterprises. *International Journal of Social and Business Sciences*, 17(10), 602–609.

Kaledio, P., & Lucas, D. (2024). Agile DevOps Practices: Implement agile and DevOps methodologies to streamline development, testing, and deployment processes.

Kaliya, N., & Pawar, D. (2023). Unboxing fog security: A review of fog security and authentication mechanisms. *Computing*, 105(12), 2793–2819. DOI: 10.1007/s00607-023-01208-3

Kamphuis, C. (2020). Graph Databases for Information Retrieval. In Jose, J. M., Yilmaz, E., Magalhães, J., Castells, P., Ferro, N., Silva, M. J., & Martins, F. (Eds.), *Advances in Information Retrieval* (pp. 608–612). Springer International Publishing. DOI: 10.1007/978-3-030-45442-5_79

Kamruzzaman, A., Thakur, K., & Ali, M. L. (2024, July). Cybersecurity Threats using Application Programming Interface (API). In *2024 International Conference on Computing, Internet of Things and Microwave Systems (ICCIMS)* (pp. 1-6). IEEE. DOI: 10.1109/ICCIMS61672.2024.10690413

Kanchepu, N. (2023). Cloud-Native Architectures: Design Principles and Best Practices for Scalable Applications. *International Journal of Sustainable Development Through AI. ML and IoT*, 2(2), 1–21.

Kar, D., & Zhang, W. (2023). A survey on federated learning frameworks and applications in IoT. *Journal of Ambient Intelligence and Humanized Computing*, 14, 151–167. DOI: 10.1007/s12652-023-04121-x

Karo, M. B., Miller, B. P., & Al-Kamari, O. A. (2024). Leveraging data utilization and predictive analytics: Driving innovation and enhancing decision making through ethical governance. [ITEE]. *International Transactions on Education Technology*, 2(2), 152–162.

Katari, A., & Ankam, M. (2022). Data Governance in Multi-Cloud Environments for Financial Services: Challenges and Solutions. [IJMCER]. *Educational Research*, 4(1), 339–353.

Kayyali, M. (2024). Quality Enhancement Frameworks in Higher Education. In *Quality Assurance and Accreditation in Higher Education: Issues, Models, and Best Practices* (pp. 61–141). Springer Nature Switzerland. DOI: 10.1007/978-3-031-66623-0_2

Kenyon, G. N., Goldsmith, M., Neureuther, B. D., & Zhou, D. (2018). Improving the return on investment in ports: Opportunities in data management. *Maritime Economics & Logistics*, 20(4), 514–530. DOI: 10.1057/s41278-017-0078-4

Keployio. (2024, October 11). *Mock Data: A Developer's Essential Tool for Testing and Development*. Medium. https://medium.com/@keployio/in-the-world-of-software-development-and-testing-mock-data-plays-a-crucial-role-in-simulating-e66b7b0182ca

Khair, M. A. (2018). Security-Centric Software Development: Integrating Secure Coding Practices into the Software Development Lifecycle. *Technology & Management Review*, 3(1), 12–26.

Khalid, M., & Hidayatullah, R. (2024). THE ROLE OF EDUCATIONAL ADMINISTRATION IN ENHANCING LEARNING QUALITY: A LITERATURE REVIEW. *Sindoro: Cendikia Pendidikan*, 7(4), 21–30.

Khalid, N., Qayyum, A., Bilal, M., Al-Fuqaha, A., & Qadir, J. (2023). Privacy-preserving artificial intelligence in healthcare: Techniques and applications. *Computers in Biology and Medicine*, 158(1), 106848. DOI: 10.1016/j.compbiomed.2023.106848 PMID: 37044052

Khalil, A., & Belaissaoui, M. (2023b). An Approach for Implementing Online Analytical Processing Systems under Column-Family Databases. In *IAENG International Journal of Applied Mathematics* (Vol. 53, Issue 1). https://www.scopus.com/inward/record.uri?eid=2-s2.0-85149634233&partnerID=40&md5=1e0e4fbb81c9f2f969dfffd87b08daa1

Khalil, A., & Belaissaoui, M. (2023a). A Data Placement Strategy for Distributed Document-oriented Data Warehouse. *IAENG International Journal of Computer Science*, 50(4), 1541–1549.

Khan, M. (2024, August 30). *The Importance of Enforcing Proper Role-Based Access Control (RBAC) in Web Security*. Medium. https://medium.com/@mustafa_kamal/the-importance-of-enforcing-proper-role-based-access-control-rbac-in-web-security-7375415f0503

Khan, H. U., Ali, F., & Nazir, S. (2024). Systematic analysis of software development in cloud computing perceptions. *Journal of Software (Malden, MA)*, 36(2), e2485. DOI: 10.1002/smr.2485

Khan, L. U., Yaqoob, I., Tran, N. H., Dang, T. N., & Hong, C. S. (2020). Edge-computing-enabled smart cities: A comprehensive survey. *IEEE Internet of Things Journal*, 7(10), 10200–10232. DOI: 10.1109/JIOT.2020.2987070

Khan, M. S., Khan, A. W., Khan, F., Khan, M. A., & Whangbo, T. K. (2022). Critical challenges to adopt DevOps culture in software organizations: A systematic review. *IEEE Access : Practical Innovations, Open Solutions*, 10, 14339–14349. DOI: 10.1109/ACCESS.2022.3145970

Khan, S., Kabanov, I., Hua, Y., & Madnick, S. (2022). A Systematic Analysis of the Capital One Data Breach: Critical Lessons Learned. *ACM Transactions on Privacy and Security*, 26(1), 1–29. Advance online publication. DOI: 10.1145/3546068

Khanyi, M. B., Xaba, S. N., Mlotshwa, N. A., Thango, B., & Matshaka, L. (2024). A Roadmap to Systematic Review: Evaluating the Role of Data Networks and Application Programming Interfaces in Enhancing Operational Efficiency in Small and Medium Enterprises. *Sustainability (Basel)*, 16(23), 10192. DOI: 10.3390/su162310192

Khatri, V., & Brown, C. V. (2010). Designing data governance. *Communications of the ACM*, 53(1), 148–152. DOI: 10.1145/1629175.1629210

Khodijah Kadarsah, D. R. A., Govindaraju, R., & Prihartono, B. (2023). Leveraging Data Management Capabilities for Innovation Capabilities: The Moderating Role of Cross-Functional Integration. *Journal of ICT Research & Applications*, 17(3), 385–411. DOI: 10.5614/itbj.ict.res.appl.2023.17.3.7

Kim, G., Humble, J., Debois, P., & Willis, J. (2016). *The DevOps Handbook: How to Create World-Class Agility, Reliability, and Security in Technology Organizations*. IT Revolution Press.

Kim, S., Yoon, S., Narantuya, J., & Lim, H. (2020). Secure collecting, optimizing, and deploying of firewall rules in software-defined networks. *IEEE Access : Practical Innovations, Open Solutions*, 8, 15166–15177. DOI: 10.1109/ACCESS.2020.2967503

Kirvan, P. (2024, October 16). *5 critical steps to creating an effective incident response plan*. SearchSecurity. https://www.techtarget.com/searchsecurity/feature/5-critical-steps-to-creating-an-effective-incident-response-plan

Kodekloud. (2023, May 16). *What Are Docker Image Layers and How Do They Work?* DevOps Blog. https://kodekloud.com/blog/docker-image-layers/

Koltay, T. (2016). Data governance, data literacy and the management of data quality. *IFLA Journal*, 42(4), 303–312. DOI: 10.1177/0340035216672238

Kompaniiets, F. (2024, February 15). *Role-Based Access Control (RBAC) in Your CI/CD Pipeline: Best Practices for DevSecOps*. Gart. https://gartsolutions.com/role-based-access-control-rbac-in-your-ci-cd-pipeline-best-practices-for-devsecops/

Kong, L., Tan, J., Huang, J., Chen, G., Wang, S., Jin, X., Zeng, P., Khan, M., & Das, S. K. (2022). Edge-computing-driven internet of things: A survey. *ACM Computing Surveys*, 55(8), 1–41. DOI: 10.1145/3555308

Kotenko, M., Moskalyk, D., Kovach, V., & Osadchyi, V. (2024). Navigating the challenges and best practices in securing microservices architecture.

Kranz, G. (2022, July). *What is Data Classification and Why is it Important?* SearchDataManagement. https://www.techtarget.com/searchdatamanagement/definition/data-classification

Kraus, S., Jones, P., Kailer, N., Weinmann, A., Chaparro-Banegas, N., & Roig-Tierno, N. (2021). Digital transformation: An overview of the current state of the art of research. *SAGE Open*, 11(3), 21582440211047576. DOI: 10.1177/21582440211047576

Kumar, V. (2024, June 9). *The Critical Role of Incident Response in DevSecOps - Practical DevSecOps*. Practical DevSecOps. https://www.practical-devsecops.com/the-critical-role-of-incident-response-in-devsecops/

Kumar, A., Mishra, A., & Kumar, S. (2023). Data Democratization, Governance, and Security. In *Architecting a Modern Data Warehouse for Large Enterprises: Build Multi-cloud Modern Distributed Data Warehouses with Azure and AWS* (pp. 255–305). Apress.

Kumara, I., Kayes, A. S. M., Mundt, P., & Schneider, R. (2023). Data governance. In *Data Science for Entrepreneurship: Principles and Methods for Data Engineering, Analytics, Entrepreneurship, and the Society* (pp. 37–62). Springer International Publishing. DOI: 10.1007/978-3-031-19554-9_3

Kumar, R., & Goyal, R. (2020). Modeling continuous security: A conceptual model for automated DevSecOps using open-source software over cloud (ADOC). *Computers & Security*, 97, 101967. DOI: 10.1016/j.cose.2020.101967

Kumar, Y., Marchena, J., Awlla, A. H., Li, J. J., & Abdalla, H. B. (2024). The AI-Powered Evolution of Big Data. *Applied Sciences (Basel, Switzerland)*, 14(22), 10176. DOI: 10.3390/app142210176

Kundu, S. S., Sarkar, D., Jana, P., & Kole, D. K. (2021). *Personalization in Education Using Recommendation System: An Overview* (pp. 85–111). DOI: 10.1007/978-981-15-8744-3_5

Kwok, A. O. J. (2023). The next frontier of the Internet of Behaviors: data-driven nudging in smart tourism. *Journal of Tourism Futures*. DOI: 10.1108/JTF-11-2022-0288

Labadie, C., & Legner, C. (2023). Building data management capabilities to address data protection regulations: Learnings from EU-GDPR. *Journal of Information Technology*, 38(1), 16–44. DOI: 10.1177/02683962221141456

Lai, C.-F., Chen, S.-Y., Wei, Y.-F., Chen, M.-Y., & Lai, S.-Y. (2023). IoB-Enhanced Deep Learning for Non-specific Thermal Respiratory Rate Monitoring. *2023 IEEE International Conference on Networking, Sensing and Control (ICNSC)*, 1–6. DOI: 10.1109/ICNSC58704.2023.10319043

Lan, F., Huang, Q., Zeng, L., Guan, X., Xing, D., & Cheng, Z. (2021). Tourism Experience and Construction of Personalized Smart Tourism Program Under Tourist Psychology. *Frontiers in Psychology*, 12, 691183. Advance online publication. DOI: 10.3389/fpsyg.2021.691183 PMID: 34367015

Laszewski, T., Arora, K., Farr, E., & Zonooz, P. (2018). *Cloud Native Architectures: Design high-availability and cost-effective applications for the cloud*. Packt Publishing Ltd.

Lekkala, C. (2024). Implementing Efficient Data Versioning and Lineage Tracking in Data Lakes. *Available atSSRN* 4907973.

Leshchenko, B., Snisar, B., Stupak, A., & Osadchyi, V. (2024). Integrating DevSecOps into the software development lifecycle: A comprehensive model for securing containerized and cloud-native environments. *CPITS II 2024-Cybersecurity Providing in Information and Telecommunication Systems*, (3826), 153-161.

Li, Q., Hong, J., Xie, C., Tan, J., Xin, R., Hou, J., . . . Song, D. (2024). Llm-pbe: Assessing data privacy in large language models. *arXiv preprint arXiv:2408.12787*.

Li, D., Zhang, E., Lei, M., & Song, C. (2022). Zero trust in edge computing environment: A blockchain-based practical approach. *Mathematical Biosciences and Engineering*, 19(4), 3687–3705. DOI: 10.3934/mbe.2022194 PMID: 35341294

Lim, H., Kim, Y., & Sun, K. (2021, January). Service management in virtual machine and container mixed environment using service mesh. In *2021 International Conference on Information Networking (ICOIN)* (pp. 528-530). IEEE. DOI: 10.1109/ICOIN50884.2021.9333888

Lindkvist, L., & Llewellyn, S. (2003). Accountability, responsibility and organization. *Scandinavian Journal of Management*, 19(2), 251–273. DOI: 10.1016/S0956-5221(02)00027-1

Lin, Z., Xiong, H., He, W., & Zhou, W. (2023). Edge AI for adaptive security in IoT: Threat detection and prevention. *Future Generation Computer Systems*, 142, 112–127. DOI: 10.1016/j.future.2023.04.017

Li, P., Wang, X., Huang, K., Huang, Y., Li, S., & Iqbal, M. (2022). Multi-Model Running Latency Optimization in an Edge Computing Paradigm. *Sensors (Basel)*, 22(16), 6097. DOI: 10.3390/s22166097 PMID: 36015856

Liu, C. W., Huang, P., & Lucas, H. C.Jr. (2020). Centralized IT decision making and cybersecurity breaches: Evidence from US higher education institutions. *Journal of Management Information Systems*, 37(3), 758–787. DOI: 10.1080/07421222.2020.1790190

Liu, Y., Liu, C., & Zhang, J. (2020). Self-healing networks: Autonomous resilience strategies for edge computing. *Computer Networks*, 173, 107217. DOI: 10.1016/j.comnet.2020.107217

Li, W., Li, Z., Yan, Z., Liu, Y., Zeng, D., Yu, H., Chen, W., & Wu, F. (2025). A data encryption and file sharing framework among microservices-based edge nodes with blockchain. *Peer-to-Peer Networking and Applications*, 18(1), 1–16. DOI: 10.1007/s12083-024-01856-y

Li, X., & Chen, H. (2018). Design of a lightweight authentication and key agreement protocol for multi-server architecture in 5G-enabled IoT environment. *IEEE Access : Practical Innovations, Open Solutions*, 6, 15900–15910.

Li, Y., & Gong, X. (2020). Artificial intelligence in IT operations: Applications and ethical considerations. *Journal of Cloud Computing (Heidelberg, Germany)*, 9(1), 18. DOI: 10.1186/s13677-020-00195-y

Li, Z., Kant, H., Hai, R., Katsifodimos, A., Brambilla, M., & Bozzon, A. (2023). Metadata representations for queryable repositories of machine learning models. *IEEE Access : Practical Innovations, Open Solutions*, 11, 125616–125630. DOI: 10.1109/ACCESS.2023.3330647

Lloyd, W., Ramesh, S., Chinthalapati, S., Ly, L., & Pallickara, S. (2018). Serverless Computing: An Investigation of Factors Influencing Microservice Performance. *2018 IEEE International Conference on Cloud Engineering (IC2E)*. DOI: 10.1109/IC2E.2018.00039

Luccioni, A. S., Corry, F., Sridharan, H., Ananny, M., Schultz, J., & Crawford, K. (2022, June). A framework for deprecating datasets: Standardizing documentation, identification, and communication. In *Proceedings of the 2022 ACM Conference on Fairness, Accountability, and Transparency* (pp. 199-212). DOI: 10.1145/3531146.3533086

Lutkevich, B. (2023, February). *What is Tokenization?* SearchSecurity. https://www.techtarget.com/searchsecurity/definition/tokenization

Maayan, G. D. (2022, November 28). *Why Microsegmentation is Critical for Securing CI/CD.* Security Boulevard. https://securityboulevard.com/2022/11/why-microsegmentation-is-critical-for-securing-ci-cd/

Machado, I. A., Costa, C., & Santos, M. Y. (2022). Data mesh: Concepts and principles of a paradigm shift in data architectures. *Procedia Computer Science*, 196, 263–271. DOI: 10.1016/j.procs.2021.12.013

MachOne Digital. (2024). DevSecOps tools and techniques: A guide to optimizing your development pipeline. Retrieved from https://www.machonedigital.com/blog/devsecops-tools-and-techniques-a-guide-to-optimizing-your-development-pipeline

Maenhaut, P., Volckaert, B., Ongenae, V., & De Turck, F. (2019). Resource Management in a Containerized Cloud: Status and Challenges. *Journal of Network and Systems Management*, 28(2), 197–246. DOI: 10.1007/s10922-019-09504-0

Magowan, K. (2020, November 30). *Shift Left Testing: What, Why & How To Shift Left.* BMC Blogs. https://www.bmc.com/blogs/what-is-shift-left-shift-left-testing-explained/

Mahanti, R., & Mahanti, R. (2021). Introduction to Data, Data Governance, and Data Management. Data Governance and Data Management: Contextualizing Data Governance Drivers, Technologies, and Tools, 1-3

Mahanti, R., & Mahanti, R. (2021). Introduction to Data, Data Governance, and Data Management. Data Governance and Data Management: Contextualizing Data Governance Drivers, Technologies, and Tools, 1-3.

Mahanti, R., & Mahanti, R. (2021). Strategy and Data Governance. *Data Governance Success: Growing and Sustaining Data Governance*, 67-98.

Mahanti, R. (2019). *Data quality: dimensions, measurement, strategy, management, and governance.* Quality Press.

Mahmudnia, D., Arashpour, M., & Yang, R. (2022). Blockchain in construction management: Applications, advantages and limitations. *Automation in Construction*, 140, 104379. DOI: 10.1016/j.autcon.2022.104379

Makitalo, K. (2023). Using custom data quality maturity tool for improving data quality in an organization.

Malek, Y. N., Kharbouch, A., El Khoukhi, H., Bakhouya, M., De Florio, V., El Ouadghiri, D., Latre, S., & Blondia, C. (2017). On the use of IoT and Big Data Technologies for Real-time Monitoring and Data Processing. *Procedia Computer Science*, 113, 429–434. DOI: 10.1016/j.procs.2017.08.281

Manchana, R. (2024). *DataOps: Bridging the Gap Between Legacy and Modern Systems for Seamless Data Orchestration* (Vol. 3, No. 2, pp. 2-10). SRC/JAICC-137. DOI: doi. org/ (3) E137 J Arti Inte & Cloud Comp.DOI: 10.47363/JAICC/2024

Mann, A., Stahnke, M., Brow, A., & Kersten, N. (2019). State of DevOps Report. Puppet. Retrieved from https://puppet.com/resources/report/state-of-devops-report/

Manoharan, G. (2024). Data governance frameworks for AI implementation in banking: Ensuring compliance and trust. [IJARET]. *INTERNATIONAL JOURNAL OF ADVANCED RESEARCH IN ENGINEERING AND TECHNOLOGY*, 15(3), 101–109.

Mao, Z., Wu, J., Qiao, Y., & Yao, H. (2022). Government data governance framework based on a data middle platform. *Aslib Journal of Information Management*, 74(2), 289–310. DOI: 10.1108/AJIM-03-2021-0068

Martinez, I., Viles, E., & Olaizola, I. G. (2021). Data science methodologies: Current challenges and future approaches. *Big Data Research*, 24, 100183. DOI: 10.1016/j.bdr.2020.100183

Martínez, J., & Durán, J. M. (2021). Software Supply Chain Attacks, a Threat to Global Cybersecurity: SolarWinds' Case Study. *International Journal of Safety and Security Engineering*, 11(5), 537–545. DOI: 10.18280/ijsse.110505

Mateus-Coelho, N., Cruz-Cunha, M., & Ferreira, L. G. (2021). Security in microservices architectures. *Procedia Computer Science*, 181, 1225–1236. DOI: 10.1016/j.procs.2021.01.320

Matias, M., Ferreira, E., Mateus-Coelho, N., & Ferreira, L. (2024). Enhancing Effectiveness and Security in Microservices Architecture. *Procedia Computer Science*, 239, 2260–2269. DOI: 10.1016/j.procs.2024.06.417

Matias, M., Ferreira, E., Mateus-Coelho, N., Ribeiro, O., & Ferreira, L. (2024). Evaluating Effectiveness and Security in Microservices Architecture. *Procedia Computer Science*, 237, 626–636. DOI: 10.1016/j.procs.2024.05.148

Mavrogiorgou, A., Kiourtis, A., Symvoulidis, C., & Kyriazis, D. (2018). Capturing the Reliability of Unknown Devices in the IoT World. *2018 Fifth International Conference on Internet of Things: Systems, Management and Security*, 62–69. DOI: 10.1109/IoTSMS.2018.8554720

Maxwell, R. (2024). Automation in the Era of ML and AI. In *Azure Arc Systems Management: Governance and Administration of Multi-cloud and Hybrid IT Estates* (pp. 217–250). Apress. DOI: 10.1007/978-1-4842-9480-2_9

Mayar, K., Carmichael, D. G., & Shen, X. (2022). Resilience and Systems - A Review. *Sustainability (Basel)*, 14(14), 8327. DOI: 10.3390/su14148327

McCarvill, A. (2023, August 11). *An Introduction to the Importance of Input Validation in Preventing Security Vulnerabilities*. Bright Security. https://brightsec.com/blog/an-introduction-to-the-importance-of-input-validation-in-preventing-security-vulnerabilities/

McNamara, R. (2021, August 31). *Implementing Shift Left Security Effectively*. Snyk. https://snyk.io/articles/shift-left-security/

Mehmood, M., Amin, R., Muslam, M. M. A., Xie, J., & Aldabbas, H. (2023). Privilege Escalation Attack Detection and Mitigation in Cloud using Machine Learning. *IEEE Access : Practical Innovations, Open Solutions*, 11, 1–1. DOI: 10.1109/ACCESS.2023.3273895

Mezair, T., Djenouri, Y., Belhadi, A., Srivastava, G., & Lin, J. C.-W. (2023). Towards an Advanced Deep Learning for the Internet of Behaviors: Application to Connected Vehicles. *ACM Transactions on Sensor Networks*, 19(2), 1–18. DOI: 10.1145/3526192

Micheli, M., Ponti, M., Craglia, M., & Berti Suman, A. (2020). Emerging models of data governance in the age of datafication. *Big Data & Society*, 7(2), 2053951720948087. DOI: 10.1177/2053951720948087

Migeon, J. H., & Bobbert, Y. (2022, July). Leveraging zero trust security strategy to facilitate compliance to data protection regulations. In *Science and Information Conference* (pp. 847-863). Cham: Springer International Publishing. DOI: 10.1007/978-3-031-10467-1_52

Miglani, R. (2023). DevSecOps at Netflix: Digital Security. Retrieved from https://blog.nashtechglobal.com/netflix/

Miller, S. J. (2022). *Metadata for digital collections*. American Library Association.

Minvielle, E., Waelli, M., Sicotte, C., & Kimberly, J. R. (2014). Managing customization in health care: A framework derived from the services sector literature. *Health Policy (Amsterdam)*, 117(2), 216–227. DOI: 10.1016/j.healthpol.2014.04.005 PMID: 24837516

Mishra, A., & Otaiwi, Z. (2020). DevOps and software quality: A systematic mapping. *Computer Science Review*, 38, 100308. DOI: 10.1016/j.cosrev.2020.100308

Mitchell, S. N., Lahiff, A., Cummings, N., Hollocombe, J., Boskamp, B., Field, R., Reddyhoff, D., Zarebski, K., Wilson, A., Viola, B., Burke, M., Archibald, B., Bessell, P., Blackwell, R., Boden, L. A., Brett, A., Brett, S., Dundas, R., Enright, J., & Reeve, R. (2022). FAIR data pipeline: Provenance-driven data management for traceable scientific workflows. *Philosophical Transactions. Series A, Mathematical, Physical, and Engineering Sciences*, 380(2233), 20210300. DOI: 10.1098/rsta.2021.0300 PMID: 35965468

Mitra, S. (2021). Advanced Monitoring and Automation: Leveraging AI for Operational Excellence. *Cloud Operations Journal*, 8(2), 45–62. DOI: 10.1007/s13677-021-00456-9

Mittelstadt, B. D., Allo, P., Taddeo, M., Wachter, S., & Floridi, L. (2016). The ethics of algorithms: Mapping the debate. *Big Data & Society*, 3(2), 2053951716679679. DOI: 10.1177/2053951716679679

Moghaddam, M. T., Muccini, H., Dugdale, J., & Kjagaard, M. B. (2022). Designing Internet of Behaviors Systems. *2022 IEEE 19th International Conference on Software Architecture (ICSA)*, 124–134. DOI: 10.1109/ICSA53651.2022.00020

Mohamed, S. I., Mostafa, M., Assaly, J., & Shalabi, A. S. (2024). ABACS: Attribute-Based Access Control System using digital keys.

Mohanan, R. (2023, April 11). *Aqua Security vs. XebiaLabs: What Tool Is Right For You?* Spiceworks Inc; Spiceworks. https://www.spiceworks.com/tech/devops/articles/aquasecurity-vs-xebialabs/

Morgan, G., Yanckello, R., Thayer, T. L., Sheehan, T., Farrell, G., Mahmood, S., ... & MacDonald, N. (2022). Top technology trends in higher education for 2022.

Moses, B., Gavish, L., & Vorwerck, M. (2022). *Data quality fundamentals*. O'Reilly Media, Inc.

Moustati, I., Gherabi, N., El Massari, H., & Saadi, M. (2023). From The Internet of Things (IoT) to The Internet of Behaviors (IoB) for Data Analysis. *2023 7th IEEE Congress on Information Science and Technology (CiSt)*, 634–639. DOI: 10.1109/CiSt56084.2023.10409989

Moustati, I., Gherabi, N., & Saadi, M. (2024a). Building an IoB ecosystem for influencing energy consumption in smart cities. *Data and Metadata*, 3. Advance online publication. DOI: 10.56294/dm2024.441

Moustati, I., Gherabi, N., & Saadi, M. (2024b). Leveraging the internet of behaviours and digital nudges for enhancing customers financial decision-making. *International Journal of Computer Applications in Technology*, 1(1), 10065772. Advance online publication. DOI: 10.1504/IJCAT.2024.10065772

Moustati, I., Gherabi, N., & Saadi, M. (2024c). Time-Series Forecasting Models for Smart Meters Data: An Empirical Comparison and Analysis. *Journal Européen des Systèmes Automatisés*, 57(05), 1419–1427. DOI: 10.18280/jesa.570517

Mpamugo, E., & Ansa, G. (2024). Enhancing Network Security in Mobile Applications with Role-Based Access Control. *Journal of Information Systems and Informatics*, 6(3), 1872–1899. DOI: 10.51519/journalisi.v6i3.863

Mulgund, P., Mulgund, B. P., Sharman, R., & Singh, R. (2021). The implications of the California Consumer Privacy Act (CCPA) on healthcare organizations: Lessons learned from early compliance experiences. *Health Policy and Technology*, 10(3), 100543. DOI: 10.1016/j.hlpt.2021.100543

Munagandla, V. B., Dandyala, S. S. V., & Vadde, B. C. (2024). Improving Educational Outcomes Through Data-Driven Decision-Making. *International Journal of Advanced Engineering Technologies and Innovations*, 1(3), 698–718.

Munappy, A. R. (2021). *Data management and Data Pipelines: An empirical investigation in the embedded systems domain*. Chalmers Tekniska Hogskola.

Munappy, A., Raj, A., Bosch, J., & Homström Olsson, H. (2020). Data pipeline management in practice: Challenges and opportunities. In Product-Focused Software Process Improvement: 21st International Conference, PROFES 2020, Turin, Italy, November 25–27, 2020 [Springer International Publishing.]. *Proceedings*, 21, 123–135.

Mushtaq, M. S., Mushtaq, M. Y., Iqbal, M. W., & Hussain, S. A. (2022). Security, integrity, and privacy of cloud computing and big data. In *Security and privacy trends in cloud computing and big data* (pp. 19–51). CRC Press. DOI: 10.1201/9781003107286-2

Nai, S., Rifai, A., Sadiq, A., & Bakrim, M. H. (2022, May). Preliminary Study Of A Smart Computer System For Scholar Support. In 2022 IEEE 9th International Conference on Sciences of Electronics, Technologies of Information and Telecommunications (SETIT) (pp. 249-253). IEEE. DOI: 10.1109/SETIT54465.2022.9875526

Nelson, D., & Carter, T. (2021). Securing Multi-Cloud Environments: Strategies and Tools for Modern Enterprises. *Enterprise Cloud Journal*, 14(1), 44-58. https://doi.org/DOI: 10.5678/ecj.2021.58

Nguyen, D. C., Pathirana, P. N., Ding, M., & Seneviratne, A. (2021). Blockchain for 5G and beyond networks: A state-of-the-art survey. *Journal of Network and Computer Applications*, 166, 102693. DOI: 10.1016/j.jnca.2020.102693

Nishat, A., & Azmat, H. (2021). Enhancing Data Governance through AI-Driven Data Lineage Tracking and Impact Analysis in Complex Data Ecosystems. *Artificial Intelligence Horizons*, 1(1), 1–9.

Nofer, M., Bauer, K., Hinz, O., van der Aalst, W., & Weinhardt, C. (2023). Quantum Computing. *Business & Information Systems Engineering*, 65(4), 361–367. DOI: 10.1007/s12599-023-00823-w

Noman, A. H. M., Mustaquim, S. M., Molla, S., & Siddique, I. M. (2024). Enhancing Operations Quality Improvement through Advanced Data Analytics. *Journal of Computer Science Engineering and Software Testing*, 10(1), 1–14. DOI: 10.46610/JOCSES.2024.v10i01.001

Nookala, G. (2022). Metadata-Driven Data Models for Self-Service BI Platforms. *Journal of Big Data and Smart Systems*, 3(1).

Nookala, G. (2024). Adaptive Data Governance Frameworks for Data-Driven Digital Transformations. *Journal of Computational Innovation*, 4(1).

Nookala, G. (2024). The Role of SSL/TLS in Securing API Communications: Strategies for Effective Implementation. *CIT. Journal of Computing and Information Technology*, 4(1).

Nordström, A. (2024). Exploring GitOps for Smaller-Scale Applications. *Urn.fi*. https://www.doria.fi/handle/10024/188668

Novelli, C., Casolari, F., Hacker, P., Spedicato, G., & Floridi, L. (2024). Generative AI in EU law: liability, privacy, intellectual property, and cybersecurity. *arXiv preprint arXiv:2401.07348*.

Nyame, G., & Qin, Z. (2020). Precursors of Role-Based Access Control Design in KMS: A Conceptual Framework. *Information (Basel)*, 11(6), 334. DOI: 10.3390/info11060334

Nyman, G. (2022). *Internet of Behaviors (IoB): With a human touch* .

Obaloluwa Ogundairo, & broklyn, peter. (2024). Natural Language Processing for Cybersecurity Incident Analysis. *Journal of Cyber Security*. https://www.researchgate.net/publication/382917950_Natural_Language_Processing_for_Cybersecurity_Incident_Analysis

Ohrimenco, S., Borta, G., & Cernei, V. (2024). The digital world has a long shadow. In *The Elgar Companion to Information Economics* (pp. 481–504). Edward Elgar Publishing. DOI: 10.4337/9781802203967.00035

Olaniyi, O. O., Olaoye, O. O., & Okunleye, O. J. (2023). Effects of Information Governance (IG) on profitability in the Nigerian banking sector. Asian Journal of Economics. *Business and Accounting*, 23(18), 22–35.

Ometov, A., Molua, O. L., Komarov, M. M., & Nurmi, J. (2022). A survey of security in cloud, edge, and fog computing. *Sensors (Basel)*, 22(3), 927. DOI: 10.3390/s22030927 PMID: 35161675

OneTrust. (2022, September 12). *ISO 27001 vs. NIST Cybersecurity Framework*. OneTrust. https://www.onetrust.com/blog/iso-27001-vs-nist-cybersecurity-framework/

Orban, S. (2018, April 6). *Capital One's Cloud Journey Through the Stages of Adoption.* AWS Enterprise Collection. https://medium.com/aws-enterprise-collection/capital-ones-cloud-journey-through-the-stages-of-adoption-bb0895d7772c

Oteemo. (2024, October 23). *ScienceLogic's Transformation into a Cloud Native and DevOps organization | Oteemo.* Oteemo. https://oteemo.com/case-study/sciencelogic-cloud-native-and-devsecops-transformation/

Othman, M., Chan, T., Foo, E., & Timbrell, G. (2011). Barriers to information technology governance adoption: a preliminary empirical investigation. In Knowledge Management and Innovation-A Business Competitive Edge Perspective: Proceedings of the 15th International Business Information Management Association Conference (pp. 1771-1787). International Business Information Management Association.

Oyeniran, O., Okechukwu, A., Adams, N., Anthony, L., & Azubuko, F. (2024). Microservices architecture in cloud-native applications: Design patterns and scalability. *Computer Science & IT Research Journal,* 5(9), 2107–2124. DOI: 10.51594/csitrj.v5i9.1554

Özcan, F., Lei, C., Quamar, A., & Efthymiou, V. (2021, June). Semantic enrichment of data for AI applications. In *Proceedings of the Fifth Workshop on Data Management for End-To-End Machine Learning* (pp. 1-7).

Ozdenizci Kose, B. (2024). Mobilizing DevOps: Exploration of DevOps adoption in mobile software development. *Kybernetes.* Advance online publication. DOI: 10.1108/K-04-2024-0989

Pachouly, J., Ahirrao, S., Kotecha, K., Selvachandran, G., & Abraham, A. (2022). A systematic literature review on software defect prediction using artificial intelligence: Datasets, Data Validation Methods, Approaches, and Tools. *Engineering Applications of Artificial Intelligence,* 111, 104773. DOI: 10.1016/j.engappai.2022.104773

Pahuja, A. (2022, January 4). *15 Best Dynamic Application Security Testing (DAST) Software.* Astra Security. https://www.getastra.com/blog/security-audit/top-dast-tools/

Paik, H. Y., Xu, X., Bandara, H. D., Lee, S. U., & Lo, S. K. (2019). Analysis of data management in blockchain-based systems: From architecture to governance. *IEEE Access : Practical Innovations, Open Solutions,* 7, 186091–186107. DOI: 10.1109/ACCESS.2019.2961404

Pakalapati, N., Jeyaraman, J., & Sistla, S. (2023). Building Resilient Systems: Leveraging AI/ML within DevSecOps Frameworks. *Journal of Knowledge Learning and Science Technology ISSN: 2959-6386 (online).* DOI: 10.60087/jklst.vol2.n2.p230

Palo Alto Networks. (2024). *What Is Sensitive Data?* Palo Alto Networks. https://www.paloaltonetworks.com/cyberpedia/sensitive-data

Palo Alto Networks. (n.d.). *What Is Insufficient Logging and Visibility?* Palo Alto Networks. https://www.paloaltonetworks.com/cyberpedia/insufficient-logging-visibility-cicd-sec10

Palo Alto. (n.d.). *Cloud Security Posture Management | CSPM.* Palo Alto Networks. https://www.paloaltonetworks.com/prisma/cloud/cloud-security-posture-management

Panetta, P. (2019). *Gartner top strategic predictions for 2020 and beyond.* https://www.gartner.com/smarterwithgartner/gartner-top-strategic- predictions-for-2020-and-beyond/

Pansara, R. (2023). Unraveling the Complexities of Data Governance with Strategies, Challenges, and Future Directions. *Transactions on Latest Trends in IoT*, 6(6), 46–56.

Pansara, R. R. (2022). Cybersecurity Measures in Master Data Management: Safeguarding Sensitive Information. *International Numeric Journal of Machine Learning and Robots*, 6(6), 1–12.

Parciak, M., Suhr, M., Schmidt, C., Bönisch, C., Löhnhardt, B., Kesztyüs, D., & Kesztyüs, T. (2023). FAIRness through automation: Development of an automated medical data integration infrastructure for FAIR health data in a maximum care university hospital. *BMC Medical Informatics and Decision Making*, 23(1), 94. DOI: 10.1186/s12911-023-02195-3 PMID: 37189148

Parker, A., Spoonhower, D., Mace, J., Sigelman, B., & Isaacs, R. (2020). *Distributed tracing in practice: Instrumenting, analyzing, and debugging microservices*. O'Reilly Media.

Pasquier, T., Singh, J., Powles, J., Eyers, D., Seltzer, M., & Bacon, J. (2018). Data provenance to audit compliance with privacy policy in the Internet of Things. *Personal and Ubiquitous Computing*, 22(2), 333–344. DOI: 10.1007/s00779-017-1067-4

Patel, J. (2019). Bridging data silos using big data integration. International Journal of Database Management Systems, 11(3), 01-06.

Patni, A. (2023, January 23). *What is DevSecOps Automation and its 5 Benefits*. Practical DevSecOps. https://www.practical-devsecops.com/devsecops-automation/

Paul, D., Soundarapandiyan, R., & Krishnamoorthy, G. (2021). Security-First Approaches to CI/CD in Cloud-Computing Platforms: Enhancing DevSecOps Practices. *Australian Journal of Machine Learning Research & Applications*, 1(1), 184–225.

Payne, B. D. (2017, June 20). *Netflix Culture Meets Product Security*. Medium. https://medium.com/@bdpsecurity/netflix-culture-meets-product-security-599ceecd615d

Pazho, A. D., Noghre, G. A., Purkayastha, A. A., Vempati, J., Martin, O., & Tabkhi, H. (2023). A survey of graph-based deep learning for anomaly detection in distributed systems. *IEEE Transactions on Knowledge and Data Engineering*, 36(1), 1–20. DOI: 10.1109/TKDE.2023.3282898 PMID: 36506788

Piasecki, J., & Cheah, P. Y. (2022). Ownership of individual-level health data, data sharing, and data governance. *BMC Medical Ethics*, 23(1), 104. DOI: 10.1186/s12910-022-00848-y PMID: 36309719

Pinnepu, H. (2023, March 11). *How Netflix embraced Chaos*. Medium. https://medium.com/@haasitapinnepu/how-netflix-embraced-chaos-b1f054ab9892

Pinoli, P., Ceri, S., Martinenghi, D., & Nanni, L. (2019). Metadata management for scientific databases. *Information Systems*, 81, 1–20. DOI: 10.1016/j.is.2018.10.002

Piskachev, G., Becker, M., & Bodden, E. (2023). Can the configuration of static analyses make resolving security vulnerabilities more effective? - A user study. *Empirical Software Engineering*, 28(5), 10–20. DOI: 10.1007/s10664-023-10354-3

Polimeno, A., Conte, G., Lamina, D., & Pellizzi, F. (2024). Balancing protection and quality in big data analytics pipelines. *Big Data*, 18(1), 124–137. DOI: 10.1089/big.2023.0065 PMID: 38603580

Ponta, S. E., Plate, H., & Sabetta, A. (2020). Detection, assessment and mitigation of vulnerabilities in open source dependencies. *Empirical Software Engineering*, 25(5), 3175–3215. DOI: 10.1007/s10664-020-09830-x

Popoola, O. A., Adama, H. E., Okeke, C. D., & Akinoso, A. E. (2024). Conceptualizing agile development in digital transformations: Theoretical foundations and practical applications. *Engineering Science & Technology Journal*, 5(4), 1524–1541. DOI: 10.51594/estj.v5i4.1080

Pournader, B. (2024, July 17). *Kubernetes and Container Security - Ben Pournader - Medium*. Medium. https://benpournader.medium.com/kubernetes-and-container-security-146b4dc7c742

Pournaras, E. (2023). Science in the Era of ChatGPT, Large Language Models and Generative AI: Challenges for Research Ethics and How to Respond. *Beyond Quantity. Research with Subsymbolic AI*, 6, 275–290. DOI: 10.14361/9783839467664-015

Prasad, A. N. (2024). Establishing a Data Governance Framework. In *Introduction to Data Governance for Machine Learning Systems: Fundamental Principles, Critical Practices, and Future Trends* (pp. 49–108). Apress. DOI: 10.1007/979-8-8688-1023-7_2

Prates, L., & Pereira, R. (2025). DevSecOps practices and tools. *International Journal of Information Security*, 24(1), 1–25. DOI: 10.1007/s10207-024-00914-z

Praveen, R. V. S. (2024). *Data Engineering Concepts: From Basics To Advance Techniques*. Addition Publishing House.

Praveen, R. V. S. (2024). *Data Engineering for Modern Applications*. Addition Publishing House.

Precedence Research. (2024). Cloud infrastructure market size and forecast 2024 to 2034. Retrieved from https://www.precedenceresearch.com/cloud-infrastructure-market

Prins, T., VanVossen, R., Barnett, T., & Elliott, L. (2022). Containerization in Embedded Trusted Computing. *SAE Technical Papers on CD-ROM/SAE Technical Paper Series, 1*. DOI: 10.4271/2024-01-3982

Purcarea, I. M. (2023). The importance of disruptive technologies in e-commerce for higher education. *Journal of Information Systems & Operations Management*, 17(1), 186–199.

Pushkin, E. (2020). Theoretical Model and Practical Considerations for Data Lineage Reconstruction. *arXiv preprint arXiv:2001.11506*.

Qualys (2024). Capital One: Building security into DevOps. Retrieved from https://www.qualys.com/customers/success-stories/capital-one-building-security-devops/

Quazi, S., Saha, R. P., & Singh, M. K. (2022). Applications of artificial intelligence in healthcare. *Journal of Experimental Biology and Agricultural Sciences*, 10(1), 211–226. DOI: 10.18006/2022.10(1).211.226

Radoslav, L. (2024). Enhancing Data Governance through AI-Driven Data Lineage Tracking and Impact Analysis in Complex Data Ecosystems. *Journal of Big Data and Smart Systems*, 5(1).

Rahman, A. A. U., Helms, E., Williams, L., & Parnin, C. (2015). Synthesizing continuous deployment practices used in software development. *Agile Conference*, 1-10. DOI: 10.1109/Agile.2015.12

Rahman, A., Shamim, S. I., Bose, D. B., & Pandita, R. (2023). Security Misconfigurations in Open Source Kubernetes Manifests: An Empirical Study. *ACM Transactions on Software Engineering and Methodology*, 32(4), 1–36. Advance online publication. DOI: 10.1145/3579639

Rajapakse, R. N., Zahedi, M., Babar, M. A., & Shen, H. (2022). Challenges and solutions when adopting DevSecOps: A systematic review. *Information and Software Technology*, 141, 106700. DOI: 10.1016/j.infsof.2021.106700

Raji, I. D., & Buolamwini, J. (2019, January). Actionable auditing: Investigating the impact of publicly naming biased performance results of commercial ai products. In *Proceedings of the 2019 AAAI/ACM Conference on AI, Ethics, and Society* (pp. 429-435). DOI: 10.1145/3306618.3314244

Rane, N., Choudhary, S., & Rane, J. (2023). Hyper-personalization for enhancing customer loyalty and satisfaction in Customer Relationship Management (CRM) systems. *Available atSSRN* 4641044. DOI: 10.2139/ssrn.4641044

Ranga, D., Rana, A., Prajapat, S., Kumar, P., Kumar, K., & Vasilakos, A. V. (2024). Quantum Machine Learning: Exploring the Role of Data Encoding Techniques, Challenges, and Future Directions. *Mathematics*, 12(21), 3318. DOI: 10.3390/math12213318

Rao, B. T. (2016). A study on data storage security issues in cloud computing. *Procedia Computer Science*, 92, 128–135. DOI: 10.1016/j.procs.2016.07.335

Reddy, A. K., Alluri, V. R. R., Thota, S., Ravi, C. S., & Bonam, V. S. M. (2021). DevSecOps: Integrating Security into the DevOps Pipeline for Cloud-Native Applications. *Journal of Artificial Intelligence Research and Applications*, 1(2), 89–114.

Reddy, A. K., Kumar, S., & Mishra, V. (2021). DevSecOps: Integrating security into the DevOps pipeline for cloud-native applications. *Journal of Artificial Intelligence Research and Applications*, 1(2), 89–114.

Revesai, Z. (2024). Ethical Implications of AI-Driven Education Systems on Digital Rights: A Comparative Analysis. The Fountain. *Journal of Interdisciplinary Studies*, 8(1), 126–152.

Rodriguez, W. (2021). *API Security Best Practices | Blog | Fluid Attacks*. Fluidattacks.com. https://fluidattacks.com/blog/api-security-best-practices/

Rosenbaum, M. S., Otalora, M. L., & Ramírez, G. C. (2017). How to create a realistic customer journey map. *Business Horizons*, 60(1), 143–150. DOI: 10.1016/j.bushor.2016.09.010

Russo, A., & Alexandre Proutiere. (2021). Towards Optimal Attacks on Reinforcement Learning Policies. *2021 American Control Conference (ACC)*, 4561–4567. DOI: 10.23919/ACC50511.2021.9483025

Sadovykh, A., & Ivanov, V. (2024). Enhancing DevSecOps with continuous security requirements analysis and testing. *Computer*, 16(7), 1687–1702.

Saffady, W. (2020). *Managing information risks: threats, vulnerabilities, and responses*. Rowman & Littlefield Publishers.

Saleh Sedghpour, M. R., Klein, C., & Tordsson, J. (2022). An Empirical Study of Service Mesh Traffic Management Policies for Microservices. *Proceedings of the 2022 ACM/SPEC on International Conference on Performance Engineering*. DOI: 10.1145/3489525.3511686

Salin, H., & Fokin, D. (2022). An Authenticated Accumulator Scheme for Secure Master Key Access in Microservice Architectures. In IoTBDS (pp. 119-126). DOI: 10.5220/0010989400003194

Salis, A. (2021). Towards the Internet of Behaviors in Smart Cities through a Fog-To-Cloud Approach. *HighTech and Innovation Journal*, 2(4), 273–284. DOI: 10.28991/HIJ-2021-02-04-01

Sánchez-Gordón, M., & Colomo-Palacios, R. (2020, June). Security as culture: a systematic literature review of DevSecOps. In *Proceedings of the IEEE/ACM 42nd international conference on software engineering workshops* (pp. 266-269). DOI: 10.1145/3387940.3392233

Sandhu, A. K. (2021a). Big data with cloud computing: Discussions and challenges. *Big Data Mining and Analytics*, 5(1), 32–40. DOI: 10.26599/BDMA.2021.9020016

Sandobalin, J., Insfran, E., & Abrahão, S. (2017). *An Infrastructure Modelling Tool for Cloud Provisioning*. DOI: 10.1109/SCC.2017.52

Sandu, A. K. (2021). *DevSecOps: Integrating Security into the DevOps Lifecycle for Enhanced Resilience*. 6(1), 1–19. https://www.researchgate.net/publication/380629263_DevSecOps_Integrating_Security_into_the_DevOps_Lifecycle_for_Enhanced_Resilience

Sandu, A. K. (2021). DevSecOps: Integrating Security into the DevOps Lifecycle for Enhanced Resilience. *Technology & Management Review, 6*, 1–19. https://upright.pub/index.php/tmr/article/view/131

Sandu, A. K. (2021). DevSecOps: Integrating Security into the DevOps Lifecycle for Enhanced Resilience. *Technology & Management Review*, 6, 1–19.

Saravanan, M. S., & Gogineni, N. (2024, March). A New Framework for Microservices with Single Sign-On, Security Assertion Markup Language and OpenID Connect. In 2024 3rd International Conference on Sentiment Analysis and Deep Learning (ICSADL) (pp. 539-543). IEEE.

Sargiotis, D. (2024). Data Governance Policies and Standards: Development and Implementation. In *Data Governance: A Guide* (pp. 247–277). Springer Nature Switzerland. DOI: 10.1007/978-3-031-67268-2_7

Sarker, I. H., Kayes, A. S. M., Badsha, S., Alqahtani, H., Watters, P., & Ng, A. (2020). Cybersecurity data science: An overview from machine learning perspective. *Journal of Big Data*, 7(1), 1–29. DOI: 10.1186/s40537-020-00318-5

Sayles, J. (2024). Aligning AI Governance, AI Development Lifecycle, and Systems Development Lifecycle Processes. In *Principles of AI Governance and Model Risk Management: Master the Techniques for Ethical and Transparent AI Systems* (pp. 383–408). Apress. DOI: 10.1007/979-8-8688-0983-5_21

Schildkamp, K., Lai, M. K., & Earl, L. (Eds.). (2012). Data-based decision making in education: Challenges and opportunities.

Schmitt, J. (2022, April 15). *SAST vs DAST: what they are and when to use them*. CircleCI. https://circleci.com/blog/sast-vs-dast-when-to-use-them/

Schroeder, P. (2020, August 6). *Capital One to pay $80 million fine after data breach*. Reuters. https://www.reuters.com/article/business/capital-one-to-pay-80-million-fine-after-data-breach-idUSKCN2522D8/

Security Compass. (2024, February 16). *Speed and Security: Recent Innovations in Secure Design and Development*. Security Compass. https://www.securitycompass.com/whitepapers/delivering-both-speed-and-security-through-secure-design-and-development-practices/

Seiner, R. S. (2014). *Non-invasive data governance: The path of least resistance and greatest success*. Technics Publications.

Sellami, A., Nabli, A., & Gargouri, F. (2020). Transformation of Data Warehouse Schema to NoSQL Graph Data Base. In Abraham, A., Cherukuri, A. K., Melin, P., & Gandhi, N. (Eds.), *Intelligent Systems Design and Applications* (Vol. 941, pp. 410–420). Springer International Publishing., DOI: 10.1007/978-3-030-16660-1_41

Sermpezis, E., Karapiperis, D., & Tjortjis, C. (2024, July). Integration of Security in the DevOps Methodology. In 2024 15th International Conference on Information, Intelligence, Systems & Applications (IISA) (pp. 1-6). IEEE.

Serrano, J. Y., & Zorrilla, M. (2021). A data governance framework for industry 4.0. *Revista IEEE América Latina*, 19(12), 2130–2138. DOI: 10.1109/TLA.2021.9480156

Shahin, M., Ali Babar, M., & Zhu, L. (2017). Continuous Integration, Delivery and Deployment: A Systematic Review on Approaches, Tools, Challenges and Practices. *IEEE Access : Practical Innovations, Open Solutions*, 5, 3909–3943. DOI: 10.1109/ACCESS.2017.2685629

Sharma Sivadevuni, S., & Ravichandran, S. K. (2023). Tracking and Localization of Devices - An IoT Review. *2023 International Conference on Inventive Computation Technologies (ICICT)*, 1321–1325. DOI: 10.1109/ICICT57646.2023.10134278

Sharma, V. (2022, March). Managing multi-cloud deployments on kubernetes with istio, prometheus and grafana. In 2022 8th International Conference on Advanced Computing and Communication Systems (ICACCS) (Vol. 1, pp. 525-529). IEEE. DOI: 10.1109/ICACCS54159.2022.9785124

Sharma, P. (2024). DevSecOps integration-security in the software delivery pipeline: Exploring the integration of security practices into the software delivery pipeline to ensure secure software development practices. *Australian Journal of Machine Learning Research & Applications*, 4(1), 46–54.

Sharma, P. (2024). DevSecOps Integration-Security in the Software Delivery Pipeline: Exploring the integration of security practices into the software delivery pipeline to ensure secure software development practices. *Australian Journal of Machine Learning Research & Applications*, 4(1), 46–54.

Sharma, P., Johari, R., & Sarma, S. S. (2012). Integrated approach to prevent SQL injection attack and reflected cross site scripting attack. *International Journal of System Assurance Engineering and Management*, 3(4), 343–351. DOI: 10.1007/s13198-012-0125-6

Sharma, R., & Gupta, P. (2023). Predictive Analytics in DevOps: Enhancing Security with Machine Learning. *International Journal of Security Systems*, 15(2), 102–115. DOI: 10.1002/ijss.2023.102

Sharp, D., Anwar, M., Goodwin, S., Raven, R., Bartram, L., & Kamruzzaman, L. (2022). A participatory approach for empowering community engagement in data governance: The Monash Net Zero Precinct. *Data & Policy*, 4, e5. DOI: 10.1017/dap.2021.33

Shatkin, M. A., & Orlov, M. O. (2023). Internet of Behavior: Types, models, principles. *Vestnik of Saint Petersburg University.Philosophy and Conflict Studies*, 39(2), 368–380. DOI: 10.21638/spbu17.2023.212

Shekhar, S. (2023). Proactive Security in the Cloud: How DevSecOps Shifts Left and Secures Right.

Shenoy, S. (2024, February 2). *Authentication of Data Pipelines: Key Strategies to Secure and Control Your Workflow*. Learn | Hevo; Hevo Data. https://hevodata.com/learn/authentication-of-data-pipelines/

Shi-Nash, A., & Hardoon, D. R. (2017). DATA ANALYTICS AND PREDICTIVE ANALYTICS IN THE ERA OF BIG DATA. In *Internet of Things and Data Analytics Handbook* (pp. 329–345). Wiley., DOI: 10.1002/9781119173601.ch19

Shi, Y., Peng, F., & Sun, F. (2022). A blended learning model based on smart learning environment to improve college students' information literacy. *IEEE Access : Practical Innovations, Open Solutions*, 10, 89485–89498. DOI: 10.1109/ACCESS.2022.3201105

Shiyal, B. (2021). Modern data warehouses and data lakehouses. In *Beginning Azure Synapse Analytics: Transition from Data Warehouse to Data Lakehouse* (pp. 21–48). Apress. DOI: 10.1007/978-1-4842-7061-5_2

Shrivastava, S., & Agrawal, Y. (2024). Multi-cloud deployments and hybrid cloud architecture. *International Journal of Cloud Systems*, 18(3), 4754–4760.

ShuLin. Y., & JiePing, H. (2020, October). Research on unified authentication and authorization in microservice architecture. In 2020 IEEE 20th international conference on communication technology (ICCT) (pp. 1169-1173). IEEE.

Shu, R., Gu, X., & Enck, W. (2017). A Study of Security Vulnerabilities on Docker Hub. *Proceedings of the Seventh ACM on Conference on Data and Application Security and Privacy*, 15–25. DOI: 10.1145/3029806.3029832

Singh, J., Cobbe, J., & Norval, C. (2018). Decision provenance: Harnessing data flow for accountable systems. *IEEE Access : Practical Innovations, Open Solutions*, 7, 6562–6574. DOI: 10.1109/ACCESS.2018.2887201

Singh, V., & Peddoju, S. K. (2017). Container-based microservice architecture for cloud applications. *2017 International Conference on Computing, Communication and Automation (ICCCA)*. DOI: 10.1109/CCAA.2017.8229914

Singu, S. K. (2021). Real-time data integration: Tools, techniques, and best practices. *ESP Journal of Engineering & Technology Advancements*, 1(1), 158–172.

Sivadevuni, S. S., & Kumar Ravichandran, S. (2023). *Systematic Literature Review—IoT-Based Supply Chain Management in Industry 4.0* (pp. 291–302). DOI: 10.1007/978-3-031-18497-0_22

Smith, J. (2020, March 19). *DevSecOps Culture*. Snyk. https://snyk.io/articles/devsecops/culture/

Smith, J. (2020, October 19). Infrastructure as Code in a DevSecOps World. Snyk. https://snyk.io/articles/infrastructure-as-code-iac/

Smith, J. (2022, May 19). *Code security auditing 101*. Snyk. https://snyk.io/articles/code-security-audit/

Son, S. J., & Kwon, Y. (2017, November 1). *Performance of ELK stack and commercial system in security log analysis*. IEEE Xplore. DOI: 10.1109/MICC.2017.8311756

Soni, M., & Jyotinagar, V. (2023, July). SQL vs NoSQL Databases for the Microservices: A Comparative Survey. In 2023 2nd International Conference on Edge Computing and Applications (ICECAA) (pp. 17-22). IEEE. DOI: 10.1109/ICECAA58104.2023.10212190

SparkFabrik . (2022). Container Security: what it is and how to implement it. Sparkfabrik.com. https://doi.org/DOI: 1031595/1712911637336/module_29821031595_gallery-masonry

Srimaharaj, W., & Chaisricharoen, R. (2022). Internet of Behavior and Brain Response Identification for Cognitive Performance Analysis. *2022 Asia-Pacific Signal and Information Processing Association Annual Summit and Conference (APSIPA ASC)*, 1308–1311. DOI: 10.23919/APSIPAASC55919.2022.9980191

Srivastav, S., Allam, K., & Mustyala, A. (2023). Software Automation Enhancement through the Implementation of DevOps. *International Journal of Research Publication and Reviews*, 4(6), 2050–2054. DOI: 10.55248/gengpi.4.623.45947

Starr, K. (2011). Principals and the politics of resistance to change. *Educational Management Administration & Leadership*, 39(6), 646–660. DOI: 10.1177/1741143211416390

Stier, S. P., Kreisbeck, C., Ihssen, H., Popp, M. A., Hauch, J., Malek, K., Reynaud, M., Goumans, T. P. M., Carlsson, J., Todorov, I., Gold, L., Räder, A., Wenzel, W., Bandesha, S. T., Jacques, P., Garcia-Moreno, F., Arcelus, O., Friederich, P., Clark, S., & Kozdras, M. (2024). Materials Acceleration Platforms (MAPs): Accelerating Materials Research and Development to Meet Urgent Societal Challenges. *Advanced Materials*, 36(45), 2407791. DOI: 10.1002/adma.202407791 PMID: 39239995

Subramaniam, P., Ma, Y., Li, C., Mohanty, I., & Fernandez, R. C. (2021). Comprehensive and comprehensible data catalogs: The what, who, where, when, why, and how of metadata management. *arXiv preprint arXiv:2103.07532*.

Sun, J., Gan, W., Chao, H.-C., Yu, P. S., & Ding, W. (2022). *Internet of Behaviors: A Survey*. http://arxiv.org/abs/2211.15588

Sun, Z., Han, Z., & Yu, H. (2020). Privacy-preserving machine learning for edge computing: A federated learning approach. *IEEE Transactions on Industrial Informatics*, 16(8), 5236–5244. DOI: 10.1109/TII.2019.2959955

Su, X., Chen, M., Yur-Austin, J., & Liu, Y. (2020). Restructuring degree roadmaps to improve timely graduation in higher education. *International Journal of Educational Management*, 34(2), 432–449. DOI: 10.1108/IJEM-07-2019-0257

Sweeney, T. J. (2021). Leadership for the counseling profession. In *Professional counseling excellence through leadership and advocacy* (pp. 3–21). Routledge. DOI: 10.4324/9781003049050-2

Syed, S. (2020). Data Lineage Strategies-A Modernized View. *Educational Administration: Theory and Practice*.

Syed, N. F., Shah, S. W., Shaghaghi, A., Anwar, A., Baig, Z., & Doss, R. (2022). Zero trust architecture (zta): A comprehensive survey. *IEEE Access : Practical Innovations, Open Solutions*, 10, 57143–57179. DOI: 10.1109/ACCESS.2022.3174679

Synk. (2024). *Fix your vulnerabilities | Snyk User Docs*. Snyk.io. https://docs.snyk.io/scan-with-snyk/snyk-open-source/manage-vulnerabilities/fix-your-vulnerabilities

Tadi, V. (2020). Optimizing Data Governance: Enhancing Quality through AI-Integrated Master Data Management Across Industries. *North American Journal of Engineering Research*, 1(3).

Tahir. (2024, December 15). *Encrypt Data with AWS Key Management Service KMS - Tahir - Medium*. Medium. https://medium.com/@tahirbalarabe2/encrypt-data-with-aws-key-management-service-kms-ccdddeb46b59

Tall, A. M., & Zou, C. C. (2023). A framework for attribute-based access control in processing big data with multiple sensitivities. *Applied Sciences (Basel, Switzerland)*, 13(2), 1183. DOI: 10.3390/app13021183

Tariq, U., Ahmed, I., Bashir, A. K., & Shaukat, K. (2023). A critical cybersecurity analysis and future research directions for the internet of things: A comprehensive review. *Sensors, 23*(8). MDPI. DOI: 10.3390/s23084117

Tatineni, S. (2024a). Applying DevOps Practices for Quality and Reliability Improvement in Cloud-Based Systems. *DevOps-An Open Access Journal*, 3(1), 25–31.

Tatineni, S. (2024b). Compliance and Audit Challenges in DevOps: A Security Perspective. *DevOps-An Open Access Journal*, 3(2), 53–60.

Taylor, K., & Finn, J. (2022). Ethics in Artificial Intelligence: Implications for DevSecOps in Cloud Computing. *AI & Society*, 37(4), 611–626. DOI: 10.1007/s00146-022-01456-x

Team, C. I. (2024, September 16). *A DevSecOps transformation story*. Www.cognizant.com. https://www.cognizant.com/us/en/insights/insights-blog/devsecops-digital-transformation

Teerakanok, S., Uehara, T., & Inomata, A. (2021). Migrating to zero trust architecture: Reviews and challenges. *Security and Communication Networks*, 2021(1), 9947347. DOI: 10.1155/2021/9947347

Telo. (2024, June 24). *Telos Announces Latest Version of its Next-Generation Cyber Risk Management Platform - Telos Corporation*. Telos Corporation. https://www.telos.com/press-release/telos-announces-latest-version-of-its-next-generation-cyber-risk-management-platform/

Temple-Raston, D. (2021, April 16). *A "worst nightmare" cyberattack: the untold story of the SolarWinds hack*. NPR. https://www.npr.org/2021/04/16/985439655/a-worst-nightmare-cyberattack-the-untold-story-of-the-solarwinds-hack

The Turing Way Community. (2024). *Types of Sensitive Data - overview — The Turing Way*. The-Turing-Way.org. https://book.the-turing-way.org/project-design/sdp/types.html

Theodoropoulos, T., Rosa, L., Benzaid, C., Gray, P., Marin, E., Makris, A., Cordeiro, L., Diego, F., Sorokin, P., Girolamo, M. D., Barone, P., Taleb, T., & Tserpes, K. (2023). Security in Cloud-Native Services: A Survey. *Journal of Cybersecurity and Privacy*, 3(4), 758–793. DOI: 10.3390/jcp3040034

Thomas, K., & Praseetha, N. (2020). Data Lake: A Centralized Repository. *Int. Res. J. Eng. Technol*, 7, 2978–2981.

Thumburu, S. K. R. (2021). Performance Analysis of Data Exchange Protocols in Cloud Environments. MZ Computing Journal, 2(2).

Thurgood, B., & Lennon, R. G. (2019). Cloud Computing with Kubernetes Cluster Elastic Scaling. *Proceedings of the 3rd International Conference on Future Networks and Distributed Systems*. DOI: 10.1145/3341325.3341995

Thusoo, A., & Sarma, J. (2017). *Creating a data-driven enterprise with DataOps*. O'Reilly Media, Inc.

Torkura, K., Sukmana, M., Cheng, F., & Meinel, C. (2020). CloudStrike: Chaos Engineering for Security and Resiliency in Cloud Infrastructure. *IEEE Access : Practical Innovations, Open Solutions*, 8, 123044–123060. DOI: 10.1109/ACCESS.2020.3007338

Tovino, S. A. (2022). Health Privacy, Security, and Information Management. In *Laws of Medicine: Core Legal Aspects for the Healthcare Professional* (pp. 223–238). Springer International Publishing. DOI: 10.1007/978-3-031-08162-0_13

Truong, T., George, R., & Davidson, J. (2017). Establishing an effective data governance system. *Pharmaceutical Technology*, 41(11), 42–45.

Tudosi, A. D., Balan, D. G., & Potorac, A. D. (2022, May). Secure network architecture based on distributed firewalls. In *2022 International Conference on Development and Application Systems (DAS)* (pp. 85-90). IEEE. DOI: 10.1109/DAS54948.2022.9786092

Ugwueze, V. U., & Chukwunweike, J. N. (2024). Continuous integration and deployment strategies for streamlined DevOps in software engineering and application delivery. *Int J Comput Appl Technol Res*, 14(1), 1–24.

University of Edinburgh. (2022, October 27). *Definition of sensitive data*. The University of Edinburgh. https://infosec.ed.ac.uk/how-to-protect/encrypting/use-cases/short-definition-of-sensitive-data

Upadhyay, D., & Sampalli, S. (2020). SCADA (Supervisory Control and Data Acquisition) systems: Vulnerability assessment and security recommendations. *Computers & Security*, 89, 101666. DOI: 10.1016/j.cose.2019.101666

Vagadia, B., & Vagadia, B. (2020). Data integrity, control and tokenization. *Digital Disruption: Implications and opportunities for Economies, Society, Policy Makers and Business Leaders*, 107-176.

Valleru, V., & Alapati, N. K. K. (2022). Breaking Down Data Silos: Innovations in Cloud Data Integration. Advances in Computer Sciences, 5(1).

van Ooijen, C., Ubaldi, B., & Welby, B. (2019). A data-driven public sector: Enabling the strategic use of data for productive, inclusive and trustworthy governance.

Vaño, R., Lacalle, I., Sowiński, P., S-Julián, R., & Palau, C. E. (2023). Cloud-native workload orchestration at the edge: A deployment review and future directions. *Sensors (Basel)*, 23(4), 2215. DOI: 10.3390/s23042215 PMID: 36850813

Vatian, A., Dudorov, S., Ivchenko, A., Smirnov, K., Chikshova, E., Lobantsev, A., Parfenov, V., Shalyto, A., & Gusarova, N. (2019). Design Patterns for Personalization of Healthcare Process. *Proceedings of the 2019 2nd International Conference on Geoinformatics and Data Analysis*, 83–88. DOI: 10.1145/3318236.3318249

Vemula, S. R. (2024). Automating Security Testing: Strategies for Vulnerability Scanning, Penetration Testing, and Compliance Checks. *International Research Journal of Engineering Science Technology and Innovation, 11*(7), 560–568. https://www.researchgate.net/publication/382737843_Automating_Security_Testing_Strategies_for_Vulnerability_Scanning_Penetration_Testing_and_Compliance_Checks

Vemulapalli, G. (2023). Optimizing Analytics: Integrating Data Warehouses and Lakes for Accelerated Workflows. *International Scientific Journal for Research*, 5(5), 1–27.

Venčkauskas, A., Kukta, D., Grigaliūnas, Š., & Brūzgienė, R. (2023). Enhancing microservices security with token-based access control method. *Sensors (Basel)*, 23(6), 3363. DOI: 10.3390/s23063363 PMID: 36992074

Venkatraman, A. (2014). *Netflix releases its AWS monitoring tool Security Monkey into the wild.* ComputerWeekly.com. https://www.computerweekly.com/news/2240223908/Netflix-releases-its-AWS-monitoring-tool-Security-Monkey-into-the-wild

Verhoef, P. C., Kannan, P. K., & Inman, J. J. (2015). From Multi-Channel Retailing to Omni-Channel Retailing. *Journal of Retailing*, 91(2), 174–181. DOI: 10.1016/j.jretai.2015.02.005

Verma, P., Kumar, V., Mittal, A., Rathore, B., Jha, A., & Rahman, M. S. (2023). The role of 3S in big data quality: A perspective on operational performance indicators using an integrated approach. *The TQM Journal*, 35(1), 153–182. DOI: 10.1108/TQM-02-2021-0062

Vijayalakshmi, A., & Jayasudha, M. (2024). *Artificial Intelligence And Data Analytics.* Academic Guru Publishing House.

Virmani, M. (2015, May). Understanding DevOps & bridging the gap from continuous integration to continuous delivery. In Fifth international conference on the innovative computing technology (intech 2015) (pp. 78-82). IEEE.

Voss, W. G. (2019). Cross-border data flows, the GDPR, and data governance. Wash. Int'l LJ, 29, 485. Ayereby, M. P. M. (2018). Overcoming data breaches and human factors in minimizing threats to cybersecurity ecosystems (Doctoral dissertation, Walden University).

Voss, W. G. (2019). Cross-border data flows, the GDPR, and data governance. *Wash. Int'l LJ*, 29, 485.

Wagner, D. E., & Klein, A. M. (2020). Lineage tracing meets single-cell omics: Opportunities and challenges. *Nature Reviews. Genetics*, 21(7), 410–427. DOI: 10.1038/s41576-020-0223-2 PMID: 32235876

Walker, L., & Morgan, J. (2020). DevSecOps: Breaking Down Silos to Build Security into Development. *Proceedings of the International Security Symposium*, 2020, 74-89.

Wang, Z., Guo, G., Liu, C., & Zhu, W. (2022, November). Research on Railway DevSecOps System Construction Based on "People-Process-Technology". In 2022 2nd International Signal Processing, Communications and Engineering Management Conference (ISPCEM) (pp. 19-23). IEEE. DOI: 10.1109/ISPCEM57418.2022.00010

Wang, H., Liu, L., Yue, C., Wang, L., Li, B., Chang, J., & Pang, B. (2024). Cloud-native systems resilience assessments based on Kubernetes architecture graph. *Service Oriented Computing and Applications*. Advance online publication. DOI: 10.1007/s11761-024-00406-x

Wang, J., Liu, Y., Li, P., Lin, Z., Sindakis, S., & Aggarwal, S. (2024). Overview ofdata quality: Examining the dimensions, antecedents, and impacts of data quality. *Journal of the Knowledge Economy*, 15(1), 1159–1178. DOI: 10.1007/s13132-022-01096-6

Wang, M., Cho, S., & Denton, T. (2017). The impact of personalization and compatibility with past experience on e-banking usage. *International Journal of Bank Marketing*, 35(1), 45–55. DOI: 10.1108/IJBM-04-2015-0046

Waseem, M., Liang, P., Shahin, M., Di Salle, A., & Márquez, G. (2021). Design, monitoring, and testing of microservices systems: The practitioners' perspective. *Journal of Systems and Software*, 182, 111061. DOI: 10.1016/j.jss.2021.111061

Weidinger, L., Mellor, J., Rauh, M., Griffin, C., Uesato, J., Huang, P. S., . . . Gabriel, I. (2021). Ethical and social risks of harm from language models. *arXiv preprint arXiv:2112.04359.*

Welsh, T., & Benkhelifa, E. (2020). On Resilience in Cloud Computing: A survey of techniques across the cloud domain. *ACM Computing Surveys*, 53(3), 1–36. DOI: 10.1145/3388922

Whittaker, M., Crawford, K., Dobbe, R., Fried, G., Kaziunas, E., Mathur, V., & Schwartz, O. (2018). *AI now report 2018.* AI Now Institute at New York University.

Wibisono, N., Soetomo, M. A., Ipung, H. P., Bawono, M. W. A., & Budiarto, E. (2021, October). Data Integration Readiness Analysis in Merged Telecommunication Company. In *2021 International Conference on Informatics, Multimedia, Cyber and Information System (ICIMCIS* (pp. 317-322). IEEE. DOI: 10.1109/ICIMCIS53775.2021.9699131

Wikipedia. (2021). *DIKW pyramid.* https://en.wikipedia.org/wiki/DIKW

Williams, B. (2019). *Continuous Security: Building Secure Systems in DevOps and Beyond.* TechBooks Press.

Wilson, E., Roche, T., Goode, E., & McKenzie, J. W. (2024). Creating the conditions for student success through curriculum reform: The impact of an active learning, immersive block model. *Higher Education*, •••, 1–21. DOI: 10.1007/s10734-024-01283-1

Wright, A., & Harris, T. (2018). Cloud Security Best Practices: A Comprehensive Guide for IT Professionals. *Cloud Journal*, 5(3), 201–224.

Xiao, Y., Zheng, S., & Li, H. (2019). Edge computing security: State of the art and challenges. *Proceedings of the IEEE*, 107(8), 1608–1631. DOI: 10.1109/JPROC.2019.2918437

Yadav, B., Choudhary, G., Shandilya, S. K., & Dragoni, N. (2021). AI Empowered DevSecOps Security for Next Generation Development. In *Frontiers in Software Engineering:First International Conference, ICFSE 2021,Innopolis, Russia,June 17–18, 2021, Revised Selected Papers 1* (pp. 32-46). Springer International Publishing. DOI: 10.1007/978-3-030-93135-3_3

Yang, W., Fu, R., Amin, M. B., & Kang, B. (2024). Impact and influence of modern AI in metadata management. *arXiv preprint arXiv:2501.16605.*

Yebenes, J., & Zorrilla, M. (2019). Towards a data governance framework for third generation platforms. *Procedia Computer Science*, 151, 614–621. DOI: 10.1016/j.procs.2019.04.082

Yudatama, U., Nazief, B. A., & Hidayanto, A. N. (2017, September). Benefits and barriers as a critical success factor in the implementation of IT governance: Literature review. In 2017 International Conference on ICT For Smart Society (ICISS) (pp. 1-6). IEEE.

Zahid, R., Altaf, A., Ahmad, T., Iqbal, F., Vera, Y. A. M., Flores, M. A. L., & Ashraf, I. (2023). Secure data management life cycle for government big-data ecosystem: Design and development perspective. *Systems*, 11(8), 380. DOI: 10.3390/systems11080380

Zareinia, K. (2023). From Shift Left to Secure Right: DevSecOps Strategies for Cloud-Native Cybersecurity.

Zaydi, M., & Nassereddine, B. (2020). DevSecOps practices for an agile and secure it service management. *Journal of Management Information and Decision Sciences*, 23(2), 1–16.

Zeydan, E., & Mangues-Bafalluy, J. (2022). Recent advances in data engineering for networking. *IEEE Access : Practical Innovations, Open Solutions*, 10, 34449–34496. DOI: 10.1109/ACCESS.2022.3162863

Zhang, D., Xia, B., Liu, Y., Xu, X., Hoang, T., Xing, Z., . . . Zhu, L. (2023). Navigating privacy and copyright challenges across the data lifecycle of generative ai. arXiv preprint arXiv:2311.18252.

Zhang, W., & Chen, L. (2024). Real-Time Transaction Monitoring Using AI: Detecting Suspicious Activities and Money Laundering in Banking. *Asian American Research Letters Journal, 1*(3).

Zhang, G., Poslad, S., Rui, X., Yu, G., Fan, Y., Song, X., & Li, R. (2021). Using an Internet of Behaviours to Study How Air Pollution Can Affect People's Activities of Daily Living: A Case Study of Beijing, China. *Sensors (Basel)*, 21(16), 5569. DOI: 10.3390/s21165569 PMID: 34451012

Zhang, J. Y., & Zhang, Y. (2024). Quantitative DevSecOps Metrics for Cloud-Based Web Microservices. *IEEE Access : Practical Innovations, Open Solutions*, 12, 160317–160342. DOI: 10.1109/ACCESS.2024.3486314

Zhang, L., Jeong, D., & Lee, S. (2021). Data quality management in the internet of things. *Sensors (Basel)*, 21(17), 5834. DOI: 10.3390/s21175834 PMID: 34502723

Zhang, L., Morin, B., Haller, P., Baudry, B., & Monperrus, M. (2021). A Chaos Engineering System for Live Analysis and Falsification of Exception-Handling in the JVM. *IEEE Transactions on Software Engineering*, 47(11), 2534–2548. Advance online publication. DOI: 10.1109/TSE.2019.2954871

Zhang, Q., Sun, X., & Zhang, M. (2022). Data matters: A strategic action framework for data governance. *Information & Management*, 59(4), 103642. DOI: 10.1016/j.im.2022.103642

Zhang, X., Wang, Q., Hu, S., Yu, J., & Zhou, H. (2021). Blockchain-based lightweight data access control for IoT in edge computing. *Journal of Parallel and Distributed Computing*, 148, 22–32. DOI: 10.1016/j.jpdc.2020.10.011

Zhao, P., Li, X., Xin, D., & Han, J. (2011). Graph cube: On warehousing and OLAP multidimensional networks. *Proceedings of the 2011 ACM SIGMOD International Conference on Management of Data*, 853–864. DOI: 10.1145/1989323.1989413

Zhao, Q., Li, G., Cai, J., Zhou, M. C., & Feng, L. (2023). A Tutorial on Internet of Behaviors: Concept, Architecture, Technology, Applications, and Challenges. *IEEE Communications Surveys and Tutorials*, 25(2), 1227–1260. Advance online publication. DOI: 10.1109/COMST.2023.3246993

Zhao, X., Clear, T., & Lal, R. (2024). Identifying the primary dimensions of DevSecOps: A multi-vocal literature review. *Journal of Systems and Software*, 214, 112063. DOI: 10.1016/j.jss.2024.112063

Zhou, S., Liu, C., Ye, D., Zhu, T., Zhou, W., & Yu, P. S. (2022). Adversarial Attacks and Defenses in Deep Learning: From a Perspective of Cybersecurity. *ACM Computing Surveys*, 55(8), 1–39. Advance online publication. DOI: 10.1145/3547330

Zong, Y. (2023, February). Distributed log collection for business processes based on ELK architecture. In 2023 IEEE 2nd International Conference on Electrical Engineering, Big Data and Algorithms (EEBDA) (pp. 1523-1529). IEEE. DOI: 10.1109/EEBDA56825.2023.10090786

Zou, W., Tan, X., & Du, J. (2021). Anomaly detection in IoT networks with AI-based adaptive security. *IEEE Internet of Things Journal*, 8(10), 8210–8225. DOI: 10.1109/JIOT.2020.3023219

About the Contributors

Bahaa Eddine Elbaghazaoui is a professor at ENSA Beni Mellal and a PhD holder in Computer Science and Artificial Intelligence. With extensive experience in software engineering, he specializes in full-stack development, microservices, AI integration, and cloud computing. As a project manager and trainer, he has led and contributed to innovative solutions in telecommunications, insurance, and government sectors. His research focuses on data profiling and predictive analytics, with numerous publications in high-impact journals. Passionate about technology and education, he actively mentors, reviews scientific work, and advances cutting-edge software solutions. He can be reached at elbaghazaoui.bahaa@gmail.com and b.elbaghazaoui@usms.as.ma.

Mohamed Amnai is a Full Professor at the Faculty of Sciences, Ibn Tofail University, specializing in Computer Science and Telecommunications. With a Ph.D. in Quality of Service Management and Mobility Control in Ad Hoc Networks, his expertise spans big data, AI-driven decision support systems, machine learning, and network security. Dr. Amnai has contributed extensively to academia as a researcher, supervisor, and journal reviewer, with numerous publications in high-impact journals and conferences. His work focuses on advancing AI applications in data profiling, recommendation systems, and network optimization. He can be reached at mohamed.amnai@uit.ac.ma.

Noreddine Gherabi is an Full Professor of Computer Science at ENSA Khouribga, Sultan Moulay Slimane University. With a Ph.D. in Database Migration and Semantic Web, he specializes in data science, artificial intelligence, semantic technologies, and cybersecurity. He has led significant research on machine learning, recommendation systems, and big data integration, contributing to high-impact publications, books, and conferences. Dr. Gherabi is actively involved in academic leadership, Ph.D. supervision, and scientific committees worldwide. He can be reached at n.gherabi@usms.ma and gherabi@gmail.com.

***

Areesha Fatima is pursuing Bachelors of Engineering in Computer Science and Engineering from Stanley College of Engineering and Technology for Women, Hyderabad, India. Her research interest spans across the various fields of technology applications. She is keenly active in the area of medicine and Astrophysics.

Abdelhak Khalil is a professor of computer science at the National School of Business and Management in El Jadida, Morocco. He also serves as an engineer at the Ministry of Interior of Morocco. He holds an engineering degree from the National School of Applied Sciences in Marrakech. His research interests include the evolution of business intelligence in the big data era, big data analytics, value creation from big data, and cluster computing.

Belaissaoui Mustapha is a Professor of Computer Science at Hassan 1st University of Settat, Morocco. He was deputy director during the period 2018-2020 of the National School of Business and Management of Settat, Morocco. He was the Head of the Management Department and Head of the Master Management Information System and Communication at the National School of Business and Management. He obtained his Ph.D. in Artificial Intelligence from Mohammed V University in Rabat. His research interests are Combinatorial Optimization, Artificial Intelligence, and Information Systems. He is the author and co-author of more than 100 papers, including 8 books, 20 book chapters, 33 peer-reviewed journal articles, and 35 peer-reviewed conference manuscripts. He has served on Program Committees of more than 40 conferences and events and has organized many Symposiums/Workshops.

Soukaina Nai, IT Engineer and a research student at Department of Computer Science, Faculty of Sciences, Ibn Tofail University (Kenitra Morocco). Her research interests include machine learning, integrated management systems, decision-making systems, evolutionary algorithms and education systems. She has published numerous articles in several journals. She can be contacted at the following e-mail address: soukaina.nai@gmail.com

Busra Ozdenizci Kose is an Associate Professor of Management Information Systems at Gebze Technical University. She teaches a wide range of topics, including Management Information Systems, Business Analysis, Software Design and Development, Agile methodologies, Business Process Management, Mobile and Wireless Technologies, Near Field Communication (NFC), Blockchain and Machine Learning. She co-authored "Near Field Communication: From Theory to Practice" (2012) and "Professional NFC Application Development for Android" (2013). She places great importance on the relationship between academia and industry, serving as a project manager, researcher, and consultant for national and international companies.

Pravin Pandey is a highly experienced Cloud Solution Architect with over two decades in IT, specializing in data center transformation, data storage, backup and disaster recovery, multi-cloud strategy, DevOps, automation, security, risk compliance, FinOps, data analytics, artificial intelligence, integration, and middleware solutions. Pravin is adept at delivering hybrid cloud solutions, leveraging On-Prem (Private Cloud) alongside Public Cloud platforms such as AWS, Azure, GCP, and Alibaba Cloud, to drive secure, scalable, and cost-effective digital transformations across industries, including retail, insurance, education, real estate, media, banking, and government. Pravin is known for fostering collaboration between IT and business teams, promoting Infrastructure as Code (IaC), advanced automation, and AI-driven analytics to optimize cloud operations and enhance decision-making. His deep expertise in data storage, disaster recovery, FinOps, middleware, and multi-cloud environments ensures seamless system integration, cost optimization, and operational resilience. As a trusted advisor in security and compliance, Pravin bridges technical and business goals, consistently delivering impactful and innovative solutions tailored to client needs.

Advait Patel is a highly accomplished Senior Site Reliability Engineer with over 8 years of experience in cloud computing, site reliability engineering, and cloud security domains. Holding a Master's degree in Computer Science with a specialization in Software Engineering and cloud computing from DePaul University, Advait has consistently demonstrated expertise in building scalable, secure, and cost-efficient systems on major cloud platforms such as AWS and Google Cloud Platform. Currently at Broadcom, Advait spearheads the development and maintenance of a globally distributed SaaS-based metrics monitoring and analytics platform. He leverages cutting-edge technologies such as Kubernetes, Terraform, Ansible, and Python. Advait has led initiatives to improve vulnerability management, compliance frameworks, and disaster recovery, significantly reducing security risks and operational costs. Beyond his professional role, Advait actively contributes to the tech community. He serves as a technical reviewer for leading technical publications and academic conferences, such as IEEE Transactions on Cloud Computing, the ACM Symposium on Applied Computing, Manning, and Packt book publications. An advocate for knowledge sharing, he has authored thought-provoking articles on securing AI workloads and multicloud optimization for platforms like HackerNoon and The New Stack.

Arun Pandiyan Perumal, an accomplished Technology Infrastructure Specialist working as a Site Reliability Engineer at Adobe, boasts over eleven years of experience in Cloud Infrastructure Management, DevOps, Site Reliability Engineering, and Cloud Security. His career at top organizations has been marked by leading teams and projects in building secure cloud infrastructures, designing highly scalable systems, integrating DevOps tools for automation, enforcing cloud security practices, and managing globally distributed multi-cloud infrastructures for hosting several critical business applications. A distinguished alumnus of the Illinois Institute of Technology, Chicago, United States, he excelled academically, earning a Master's degree in Information Technology and Management. He was recognized with "The Outstanding Student Award" for his exceptional academic performance. Beyond his professional responsibilities, Arun has been deeply involved in the research and technical communities, sharing his knowledge and collaborating with experts on various research initiatives. His academic contributions include authoring and publishing research and review articles at IEEE and Springer conferences and peer-reviewed journals within his area of specialization. He has also served on the technical program committees for conferences such as the IEEE Cloud Summit, AICTC, and IEEE CLOUD 2024 to peer-review research papers. He received the "Titan Business Platinum Winner 2024", "Bronze Globee Business Winner 2024", "Claro Awards Silver Winner 2024", and "Global Recognition Award 2024" awards for his dedication and contributions to Technology Infrastructure and Cloud Computing.

Sanjay Poddar is a seasoned IT professional with expertise in Networks, Network Security, account management, and technology solutions. With a robust academic foundation in Information Technology, he drives innovation and delivers impactful results across diverse industries. Excelled in News & Media, Telecom, and Cybersecurity, Sanjay specializes in strategic partnerships and client relationships. His adept project management ensures seamless execution, exceeding client expectations. Sanjay's tech experience spans multiple vendor technologies, reflecting his passion for evolving landscapes. Thriving in collaboration, his communication and leadership contribute to team success. Forward-thinking, Sanjay remains committed to learning, abreast of emerging tech and trends. Dedicated to excellence, he's a valuable asset in any organization.

Karthik Venkatesh Ratnam is a skilled Network, Cloud, and Security Engineer with over seven years of experience in cloud computing, cybersecurity, and automation. Currently a Public Cloud Engineer at Workday, he specializes in AWS, Terraform, Python, DevOps, SecOps and security frameworks like FedRAMP, SOC 2, and ISO 27001. He has worked at Amazon AWS, Sana Biotechnology, and Caterpillar, managing cloud security, network infrastructure, and compliance. With expertise in AWS GuardDuty, IAM policies, and networking protocols like BGP and OSPF, he holds certifications including AWS Solutions Architect – Professional, CCNP Security, and CISA Certification. He earned an M.S. in Telecommunications from Southern Methodist University and a B.E. in Electronics and Telecommunication from Xavier Institute of Engineering. Passionate about cloud security and automation, he integrates security best practices with infrastructure management, ensuring optimized and secure cloud environments. His expertise in DevOps, monitoring tools, and CI/CD pipelines helps businesses enhance security, streamline operations, and achieve digital transformation.

Amal Rifai, Professor of Computer Science at the Regional Center for the Professions of Education and Training (RCPET), Rabat, Morocco. She is also head of the research team in Computer Environment Engineering for Human Learning. His research interests include Artificial Intelligence, machine learning, digital systems and technology, evolutionary algorithms and educational systems. He has published extensively in numerous journals. She can be contacted by e-mail: rifaiamal10@gmail.com.

Abdelalim Sadiq, Professor of Higher Education of Computer Science, at Ibn Tofail University in Kinetra, and head of the Computer Science Research Laboratory, his research interests are Artificial Intelligence, Machine Learning, Digital Systems and Technology, Evolutionary Algorithms. He has published numerous articles in a wide range of journals and he can be contacted by e-mail: a.sadiq@uit.ac.ma.

Khalil Soussane is a PhD student at the Faculty of Sciences, Ibn Tofail University, Morocco, specializing in computer science and data engineering. He holds an engineering degree from the National School of Applied Sciences (ENSA) Khouribga and is an Oracle Java SE 17 Developer certified professional. As a software engineer, he has expertise in Java, Spring, full-stack development, DevOps, and cloud computing. Khalil working on large-scale software solutions. His research focuses on data management, software architecture, and distributed systems. Passionate about technology and innovation, he actively contributes to both academia and industry.

Rajesh Vayyala is a highly skilled Principal Data Architect with 10 years of experience in designing, optimizing, and implementing scalable data solutions in both cloud and enterprise platforms. With a sophisticated knowledge of data governance, data strategy, and architecture, he has helped various companies unlock their potential using their data to fuel innovations, informed decisions, and streamline business processes. He has led large-scale data transformations that enable companies to move from legacy systems to contemporary, cloud-native architectures. He published research and technical contributions in data architecture and cloud-based enterprise solutions reflecting commitment to innovation and continuous learning. His fellow memberships in two professional organizations further underscore his active involvement in advancing best practices in data management. He can be reached at vayyalarajesh@gmail.com.

Index

A

C

D

E

G

H

I

K

L

M

N

O

P

R

S

T

Z

www.ingramcontent.com/pod-product-compliance
Lightning Source LLC
LaVergne TN
LVHW060358300926
849162LV00006B/1297